THE DECLINE OF THE ARAB-ISRAELI CONFLICT

MIDDLE EAST POLITICS
AND THE QUEST FOR REGIONAL ORDER

AVRAHAM SELA

STATE UNIVERSITY OF NEW YORK PRESS

Published by
State University of New York Press, Albany

© 1998 State University of New York

For information, address State University of New York Press,
State University Plaza, Albany, N.Y. 12246

Production by M. R. Mulholland
Marketing by Nancy Farrell

Library of Congress Cataloging-in-Publication Data

Sela, Avraham.
    The decline of the Arab-Israeli conflict : Middle East politics
and the quest for regional order / Avraham Sela.
        p.   cm.
    Includes bibliographical references (p.   ) and index.
    ISBN 0-7914-3537-7 (alk. paper). — ISBN 0-7914-3538-5 (pbk. :
alk. paper)
    1. Arab countries—Politics and government—1945–   2. Israel-Arab
conflicts. I. Title.
DS63.1.S432   1997
956.04—dc21   96-51943
                                                                    CIP

10 9 8 7 6 5 4 3 2 1

THE DECLINE OF THE ARAB-ISRAELI CONFLICT

TO MY PARENTS

CONTENTS

VI. The Dialectic of Force and Diplomacy
Between the Palestinian and Gulf Crises

PREFACE

On September 13, 1993, in a ceremony on the White House lawn, the State of Israel and the Palestine Liberation Organization signed an agreement, establishing mutual recognition and the principles for ending the century-long conflict in the Holy Land. This agreement was followed by the advent of the Israel-Jordanian peace treaty, the eclipse of the Arab boycott of Israel, and the opening of a diplomatic dialogue between Israel and several Arab countries. Such events would have been unthinkable in previous periods, and not only because of the Cold War. Peace, rather, was precluded as long as the struggle against Israel remained pivotal to Arab politics.

The peace process signified the culmination of an arduous process of state formation in the Arab world. The political history of the post-Ottoman Middle East had been marked by a quest for new regional order, an order characterized by sovereign and mutually-recognized states. This quest, however, was challenged by indigenous movements—and occasionally by ruling elites—which, by conveying symbolically charged messages of radical political and social reforms, succeeded in mobilizing Arab public opinion, blurring the boundaries between state and nation.

The Palestine conflict was integral to this message. Palestine embodied the values fundamental to Arab-Islamic identity: solidarity, anti-imperialism, and collective dignity. It became a crucial issue in domestic as well as in inter-Arab politics, the *sine qua non* for establishing a leader's political legitimacy, and for impugning that of his rivals. The Palestine conflict was caught in the contradiction between the ruling elites' interest in exclusive state authority and the popular vision of supra-national unity.

Mutual recognition between Israel and the PLO effectively removed the Palestine conflict—the touchstone of modern Arab-Islamic identity—from the jaws of this contradiction. Henceforth, neither Arab elites nor opposition movements could employ the Palestine issue as an instrument of political power at the same magnitude as in past decades.

This book presents a historical analysis of the interplay between inter-Arab politics and the Arab-Israeli conflict. The conflict was central to the formation of an Arab regional system in the period between the World Wars, just as, later, it would play a paramount role in reshaping that system in favor of individual Arab states. Beginning in the 1960s, the Arab-Israeli conflict served as a catalyst for redefining the rules of inter-Arab politics on the basis of mutual recognition and sovereignty and, conversely, for the weakening of collective Arab commitments. The study will address a number of compelling issues, among them:

- The dynamics governing the relationship between inter-Arab and Arab-Israeli politics.
- The impact of international diplomacy on this relationship.
- The mechanisms regulating inter-Arab relations and sanctioning change in Arab policies toward Israel.

Underlying these issues are two basic premises:

- Arab policy toward the conflict was a dependent variable determined by domestic and regional conditions, exacerbated by non-regional powers.
- Arab attitudes toward Israel assumed a systemic pattern which deserves to be studied as a unit of analysis, involving qualitative and quantitative factors. The systemic approach is necessary to gauge the changing balance between supra-national commitments and the interests of individual states.

A central theme of this study is the efforts of leading Arab states to refashion inter-Arab relations through summit conferences. Convened ostensibly to shore up Arab solidarity on Palestine, the conferences in fact legitimated deviations from traditional policies. They evoked the ideal of Arab-Islamic consensus as a means of legitimating the avoidance of war with Israel, and of redefining commitments to the Palestinians. The proceedings, moreover, provided a forum for constructive discussion on the nature of inter-Arab relations. By their very nature, the summit conferences were instrumental in the related processes of state formation and the weakening of rallying Arab-Islamic ideals.

This study seeks to fill a gap in the existing literature on the history of regional Arab politics. Compared to the large body of literature on contemporary Middle East affairs, only a few have focused on the relationship between inter-Arab politics and the Arab-Israeli conflict. Fewer still have dealt empirically with this dialectic over a significant historical period. Some of the studies have addressed only the formal activities of institutions such as the Arab League, while overlooking the complexities of inter-Arab group dynamics.

The book contains six parts. Part I addresses the regional Arab system, its political dynamics and its effect on Arab policy making. This introductory section also examines the evolution of the regional Arab system in conjunction with the Palestine question, from the formative inter-war years to the dawn of summitry.

Parts II through VI present an analysis of the major historical events that laid the bases for new assumptions and initiated new processes, culminating in the Gulf crisis and its consequences—the Madrid Conference and the subsequent peace process, inaugurating a new era in Middle East politics.

I wish to express my gratitude to all the people and institutions that helped me in the long process of bringing this project to completion. The Harry S Truman Institute for the Advancement of Peace provided me with financial and administrative support. Norma Schneider, Ralph Mandale, Chaya Beckerman, and Steve Mazie took care, at different stages, of editing parts of the manuscript. The library staff—Cecile Panzer, Avi Greenhause, and Amnon Ben-Arieh—were of great assistance to me. I am also thankful to my research assistants, Gia Lavern, Avi Simon, and Amir Weissbrode. I am very grateful to L. Carl Brown, Barry Rubin, Bruce Maddy-Weitzman, Michael Oren, Byron Gold, and Sasson Sofer for reading parts of the manuscript and offering useful comments, as well as to Michael Barnett, Joel Migdal, and Benjamin Miller for their observations. I am especially indebted to Shaul Mishal, whose friendship, encouragement, and advice helped me in finalizing this book.

ABBREVIATIONS

ACC	Arab Cooperation Council
ACSP	Arab Collective Security Pact
ADC	Arab Defence Council
ADF	Arab Deterrence Forces (in Lebanon)
AHC	Arab Higher Committee
AL	Arab League (The League of Arab States)
ALC	Arab League Council
ALSG	Arab League Secretary General
AMU	Arab Maghreb Union
AOI	Arab Organization for Industrialization
AP	Associated Press
ASF	Arab Security Forces (in Lebanon)
ASQ	Arab Studies Quarterly
CoS	Chief of Staff
DPM	Deputy Prime Minister
DM	Defense Minister
FBIS/DR	Foreign Broadcasting Information Service/Daily Report, Near East and North Africa
EC	Eastern Command
EEC	European Economic Community
FAR	Federation of Arab Republics
FoF	Facts on File
FRG	Federal Republic of Germany
FM	Foreign Minister
FSC	Front of Steadfastness and Confrontation
GNA (or WAKH)	Gulf News Agency
GCC	Gulf Cooperation Council
GODE	Gulf Organization for the Development of Egypt
IAQ	International Arab Quarterly
ICO	Islamic Conference Organization
IDF	Israel Defense Forces
IHT	International Herald Tribune
IJMES	International Journal of Middle East Studies
ISQ	International Studies Quarterly
ILO	International Labor Organization

IMF	International Monetary Fund
INA	Iraqi News Agency
INWC	Israel's National Water Carrier
IPC	Iraqi Petroleum Company
JAA	Journal of Arab Affairs
JAC	Joint Arab Command
JNA	Jamahiriyya News Agency (Libya)
JSS	Journal of Strategic Studies
JPS	Journal of Palestine Studies
KNA	Kuwaiti News Agency
LAT	The Los Angeles Times
LF	The Lebanese Forces
MENA	Middle East News Agency (Egypt)
MER	Middle East Record
MECS	Middle East Contemporary Survey
MEI	Middle East International
MEJ	The Middle East Journal
NPT	Non-Proliferation Treaty
NYT	The New York Times
OAU	Organization of African Unity
ONAS	Organization of Non-Aligned States
OPEC	Organization of Petroleum Exporting Countries
PDRY	People's Democratic Republic of Yemen
(P)DFLP	(Popular) Democratic Front for the Liberation of Palestine
PFLP	Popular Front for the Liberation of Palestine
PFLP-GC	Popular Front for the Liberation of Palestine -General Command
PLA	Palestine Liberation Army
PLO	Palestine Liberation Organization
PM	Prime Minister
PNA	Palestinian News Agency
PNC	Palestine National Council
PNSF	Palestinian National Salvation Front
PR	Palestinian Resistance
QNA	Qatari News Agency
SANA/SPA	Saudi News Agency/Saudi Press Agency
SANA	Syrian Arab News Agency
SoS	Secretary of State
SWB	Summary of World Broadcastings (BBC)
UAE	United Arab Emirates
UAR	United Arab Republic

UNCTAD	United Nations Conference on Trade and Development
UNDOF	United Nations Disengagement Observer Force
UNEF	United Nations Emergency Force
UNIFIL	United Nations Interim Force in Lebanon
UNGA	United Nations General Assembly
UNL	United National Leadership (of the Intifada)
UNSC	United Nations Security Council
UPI	United Press International

I

NATION, STATE, AND REGIONAL CONFLICT

"We are Arabs but the idea of Arab nationalism is meaningless . . . other than in its religious context, because Islam and Arabism are like a hand to glove."

—King Husain, June 14, 1966 (Quoted in Ahmad al-Shuqairi, *'Ala Tariq al-Hazima Ma'a al-Muluk wal-Ru'asa'*, Beirut, 1972, p. 174).

"I don't believe in merger [of Arab states] but in consultation and mutual understanding. . . . I don't believe in unity of merger, not now, not tomorrow. . . . [We] ought to build the pillars and the walls before we build the roofs. This [mission] may last decades because various kinds of nationalism have emerged even before the Caliphate that are not easy to abolish. Tunisia is Tunisia, and Algeria is Algeria . . ."

—President Habib Bourguiba, *al-Usbu' al-'Arabi,* September 23, 1974.

"[The Arabs'] divisions, no matter how serious, need to be seen in the context of one nation in search of its identity."

—Mohamed H. Heikal, *Illusions of Triumph* (London: Harper Collins, 1993), p. 8.

1

INTRODUCTION: EXPLAINING REGIONAL ARAB POLITICS

The Conceptual Approach

This book is about regional Arab politics and the conflict with Israel. It examines the interplay between Arab multilateral, collective politics and the individual Arab state through the prism of the Arab-Israeli conflict as the ultimate sphere of interaction between state interests and all-Arab commitments. My main concern is with the impact of this interplay on shaping international rules and institutions prescribed to realize common goals and enhance regional order, i.e., regularized pattern of state behavior.

More specifically, the study is interested in answering the following questions: What was the role of the Arab states system and its collective institutions in regulating inter-state relations and managing the conflict with Israel? How did the Arab-Israeli conflict affect the tension between *raison d'état* and *raison de la nation,* that is, between individual state interests and collective Arab obligations? And finally, what were the strategies and means used by the individual Arab actors, states and non-states, to enhance their autonomous capabilities and authority in conjunction with, and at the expense of, other actors and the Arab regional system as a whole?

These questions are validated by the inconsistency between the expected roles and practical behaviors of each of these political institutions.[1] Imbued by the ideal of Arab unity, Arab collective institutions have been expected to enhance Arab regional solidarity and conformity, particularly on issues of common Arab concern, of which the Palestine conflict[2] is most prominent. Practically, however, these institutions were predominantly concerned with procedures protecting the regional multi-sovereign Arab states. On the other hand, collectivism along strictly Arab considerations collides with a central attribute of the state as a distinct political actor in international relations, namely, its claim for exclusive authority over its national decision making. Yet being a member of the regional Arab system also entails opportunities for the state to enlist external moral, political, and economic resources, ultimately contributing to state formation. Indeed, inter-Arab politics often seem fraught with ambivalent, sometimes contradictory, political behavior. The interchangeably restrictive-distributive role of the regional Arab system, and the individual states' inherent quest for further capabilities and autonomous decision making constitute a guiding theme in this study.

Unlike the European state, the Arab state was, by and large, a juridical rather than empirical phenomenon, whose emergence expressed foreign will rather than a process of state formation from within. Many Arab states thus reached independence while lacking effective institutions, socio-political cohesion, and popular legitimacy. Furthermore, the Arab modern state inherited an extremely complicated social and economic structure marked by nomadic pastoralism, long distance trade, and semi-autonomous primordial groups—tribes, ethnic or religious minorities—concentrated in mountainous or arid areas where the premodern central administration was irregular.[3] These social structures have remained a major obstacle in the process of state formation in the Middle East as a whole, especially with regard to building centralized state capabilities. Moreover, like most of the new states, the political borders of many Arab states were in varying degrees incongruent with their social structure and political or economic orientations. In addition, however, state formation in the Arab world confronted an incomparable problem among Third World states, namely the blurred boundaries between state and collective, supra-state[4] identity inspired by common Arab-Islamic culture, history, and vision. Hence, post-colonial ruling elites in the Arab world had to confront, in addition to Third World conventional agonies of state building and social change, constant ideological challenges to their institutional legitimacy from both domestic and regional actors.

State formation in the Arab world was indeed inherently linked to inter-Arab, regional power politics, the origins of which were rooted in the colonial and early independence period. The phenomenon of Arab regional politics represented interrelated processes of state formation, quest for regional hegemony, rapid socio-political changes, and the emergence of Pan-Arab nationalism as a dominant regional discourse. Hence, internal as well as regional competition for power have been increasingly conducted in the name of all-embracing ideals—primarily Pan-Arab nationalism—in disregard of borders and state sovereignty. Pan-Arabism thus became both a curse and an asset for ruling elites, serving their quest for legitimacy and claims for regional power or solidarity and yet entangling them in a costly game of eroding each other's legitimacy and intensifying domestic and regional instability. Indeed, every actor could *speak* in the name of the Arab nation though none could claim to *be* the nation itself,[5] that is, to enforce his hegemony on the Arab region as a whole. Arab regional politics were further intensified by the elasticity and self-interested interpretation that marked Pan-Arabism as well as the role of institutions established to fulfill its goals.

Although the confusion of nation and state has been the watermark of Arab regional politics, it fluctuated along time and space in close interaction with decolonization, socio-political changes and domestic stability. Under the revolutionary regimes, assertive Arab nationalism, and anti-Western outcry, was elevated to a state religion, reflecting its central role in building their new authority and legitimacy. The result was inter-Arab turbulence and regional disorder through the 1950s and 1960s, typically marking the novelty of these states and their social incoherence. This was particularly evident in the Fertile Crescent, reflecting the weakness of state capabilities, socio-political turbulence, and direct involvement in the Palestine conflict. Indeed, nowhere else in the Arab world was the outcry for supra-state conformity as compelling as in the Fertile Crescent countries which, combined with Egypt's bold interference and efforts to coerce its all-Arab hegemony, constituted the core of the regional Arab system.

Despite strong centripetal forces advocating Arab collectivism, however, modern inter-Arab relations have been marked by a quest for stable regional order based on equality and mutual recognition among its member states. As the leading agent of social modernization and secularization, the Arab state was bound to contain, if not defeat, supra-state concepts of identity and establish its own space and status. Notwithstanding the absence of a hegemonic power, vast discrepancies among Arab states' capabilities and social structures, Arab regional politics have undergone a slow transition from one dominated by culture, identity, and symbols, to state-based formal institutions and negotiated order. This transformation was a result of interrelated intra- and extra-state processes: The Arab state's grown capability to enforce its authority over the society and defy external intrusion, and the Arab regional system's stipulation of mechanisms—such as balance of power, diplomacy, and interdependence—and formal institutions legitimizing individual states' power and enhancing inter-Arab coexistence. Struck by growing limits of power and resources as well as by domestic and mutual regional threats, Arab regimes manifested growing willingness to work together within a regional states system based on commonly accepted norms and institutions prescribed to protect actors' sovereignties, prevent hegemony, and reduce inter-Arab conflicts.[6]

Hence, the gulf between Arab nationalist vision and political reality has become increasingly a character trait of state-society relations in the Arab world, underlaid by traditional political cleavages and frustrated hopes for social and economic progress so typical among developing societies.[7] Still, the viability of the Arab state vis-à-vis Pan-Arab nationalism has remained debated, with survey analyses pointing to a gap between elite groups identifying with the state, and the masses, among whom Pan-Arab identity appeared to be strong.[8] This underlines the need for a historical study examining the developing relationships between the Arab state and the supra-state centripetal symbols and ideas.

The comparative literature on Middle East politics[9] has been marked by a dichotomy between regionalist, focusing on the Arab states system, and state-centric, identifying the Arab state as an independent actor. Both approaches refer to the dialectic between Arab collectivism and state particularism as a conflict, disrupting domestic and regional stability.[10] By and large, this conflict has been tackled in the context of state formation, explaining the constraints confronting the legitimation of this process in terms of both state-society relations and external claims for Pan-Arab conformity. The discussion of Arab state formation focused on state-based strategies employed by ruling elites to insulate their societies and defy external ideological challenges to state sovereignty. However, little attention was given to the role of the Arab regional system as an institutional actor shaping inter-state relations and, in fact, playing a role in state formation.[11]

Concluding the European experience of state building, the main attributes of the state have been identified as control over a well-defined territory, centralized government, differentiation from other organizations, and claim for monopoly of the physical means of coercion within its territory. Yet in addition to these Weberian, state-centric attributes, theorists of state building and international relations also emphasize the international dimensions of state building, namely, the emergence and evolution of an international system of states, acknowledging, and to some extent guaranteeing, each other's existence as distinct and sovereign within recognized territorial boundaries.[12]

International recognition may depend on the state's capability to enforce its authority within a given territory and defend it against external challenges. Yet capability is neither a prerequisite for international recognition nor necessarily state-centered. Since most developing states do not possess the ability to defend themselves, the significance of international legitimacy for their sovereignty and territorial integrity is essential. This has been manifested in Africa, where states have "adopted institutional armor" to protect their independence and sovereignty, undertaking self-restrictions on state action externally.[13]

The dimension of international legitimacy is especially complex in the case of Arab states where legitimacy of authority draws on both local constituency and regional collective acquiescence. If sovereignty means "an ultimate and exclusive political authority within a given territory" to "decide for itself how it will cope with its internal and external problems,"[14] the Arab state suffers from an inherent weakness. Indeed, nowhere else was sovereign policymaking of states challenged by external actors as strongly as in the case of Arab states, facing delegitimation, military threats, and diplomatic sanctions that demonstrated the weakness of the state (*dawla*) and claim for its deference to the all-Arab nation (*umma*). Hence, Arab states' foreign policy on issues of common Arab concern had been inherently restricted by interactive forces both regional and within society.

Furthermore, one's assertion of Pan-Arab nationalism could, by virtue of its threat to other actors' sovereignty, serve as a source of state capability. Still, state power was a significant factor in determining sovereignty in inter-Arab dynamics. Military capability, especially when combined with determination to employ it against adversaries, including Arabs, enabled governments to monopolize violence and enforce control over society. In addition, it could serve as a coercive means to extract economic resources and obtain political influence on the regional level in the name of collective Arab interest. In time, however, given the price of turbulent inter-Arab relations, Arab ruling elites were obliged to seek ways of mutual accommodation.

Just as the European modern nation-state was a product of prolonged violent intra- and inter-state struggles, so was it a product of routinized relationships between states in peacetime, allied by common institutions. Such cooperation was essential for generating stability and mutuality in inter-Arab relations, representing common interests such as stable regional order—hence, control of societal and non-state actors—and advancement of common goals.[15] Precisely because Arab ruling elites shared both a quest for bolstering their sovereignty and defying threats of non-state actors and supra-state symbolism, it was necessary to create a normative regional order.

Charles Tilly's "War made the state, and the state made war," is especially appropriate in the case of those Arab states immediately concerned with the Palestine conflict. The state of war with Israel legitimized claims for sharing or redistribution of "collective Arab resources," namely oil—crucial, given the poor taxation in most of the Arab states—as well as claims for regional leadership. Prolonged involvement in external military threats such as the state of war with Israel or the Gulf war justified a considerable growth of the armed forces as well as the expenditures for their maintenance and armament. Conditions of war also justified sustaining the military in power, enabling the state to deepen its penetration into society and to repress dissidents and rebels.[16] Yet the Palestine conflict, by virtue of its symbolic significance, was also bound to enhance inter-Arab competition, disrupting regional order and mutual recognition. It was in this context that the Arab states sought to regularize their multilateral relations through regional institutions whose all-Arab status lent legitimacy to incremental departure from Arab common obligations toward the Palestine conflict through recurrent redefinition of Arab collective strategy in the conflict with Israel. Indeed, if state sovereignty is ultimately measured by its capacity to make war and peace, the shifting relationships between Arab states and Israel from war to contractual peace during the period under discussion manifests a triumph of the state over supra-state commitments.

This book presents a systemic scrutiny of more than three decades of Middle East international history, demonstrating the changing patterns of state behavior, primarily on the regional level. My approach is both comparative—discussing real inter-state relations—and region-centered, in terms of the Arab world's specific commonality of history and culture. The study considers the regional Arab system as an independent causal factor explaining state behavior in international relations. Apart from inter-state relations, this study focuses on collective institutions as the common ground where Arab states' interests and shared obligations converge to produce collective policies and disagreements on core issues. It is the arena where supra-state allegiances and commitments, reflecting the region's common Arab-Muslim history, culture, and vision, play an important role in generating both opportunities and constraints for state building. This leads to the assumption that the relation between the regional system and the individual state is complementary, not merely antagonistic, with routinizing impact on state formation and regional order. Focusing on the Arab-Israeli conflict enables me to examine the degree to which Arab states grew stronger in terms of their ability to withstand external supra-state symbolic pressures, to keep their societies at bay from such influences and conduct autonomous foreign policy, particularly on Arab core issues.

2

THE REGIONAL ARAB SYSTEM

The Systemic Attributes

A study into the international relations of the Arab states requires considering not only their behavior as independent actors but also their continuous, group dynamics and multilateral interactions shaped by both their common Arab-Islamic identity and their distinct interests. Thus, approaching inter-Arab politics as a system is essential for explaining the international behavior of Arab states both as a group and as separate actors, requiring a review of qualitative as well as quantitative themes.

Beginning in the late 1950s, the study of regional systems indicated a widening conviction that the bipolar system approach was inadequate for explaining the whole scope of small states' international behavior in terms of subordination to global power and resources. Hence the growing attention to regional and domestic—rather than global—causes shaping the postcolonial politics of Third World states.[1] This trend has been reaffirmed by the renewed interest in the complex relationship between state and society in the process of state formation and the primacy of domestic politics in shaping the foreign policies of developing states. Thus, whereas developed Western states' national security usually relates to the protection of their independence or political values from external threats, national security in new states is bound up with domestic threats to the regime's stability, emanating from problems of legitimacy, political integration, and identity.[2] In the Arab case, the artificiality of the colonial entity that distinguished most Arab states, contrasted with the sense of cultural and political unity particularly prevalent among the Fertile Crescent elites. As such, inter-Arab politics have been affected predominantly by domestic and regional causes, limiting manipulation by outside powers of their respective "clients."[3]

Comparative regional studies have identified basic variables defining a regional system: common cultural, social, and historical bonds, interdependence, geographic proximity, a high level of interaction among the units constituting the system, and a sense of regional identity which tends to increase in response to non-regional actors' intrusive actions.[4] Whereas the Middle East delineation as well as the applicability of the regional system concept to this region have remained debatable—preference is given to Arab or Islamic definitions[5]—the systemic approach is highly applicable to the group of Arab states.

The main attribute defining the Arab system is culture. Not only do the Arab states excel in an incomparable intensity of interactions and, except for the Horn of Africa, are geographically contiguous, they are distinguished by relatively comprehensive linguistic and religious homogeneity and a shared sense of common history, identity, and vision. Furthermore, all Arab states incorporated into an exclusively Arab regional organization, the League of Arab States, indicating that Arab identity (*'uruba*) is a prerequisite for a state to be included in the organization. In macro-social terms, the Arab world constitutes a "trans-national political community"—imagined and abstract as that may be—or a "pan-national regional system" (*nizam iqlimi qawmi*), marked by a strong inclination toward collectivism and conformity, especially when confronting an alien or extra-regional power.[6]

The Arab collective identity is evident in Arab political thought, which tackles the nation as the unit of discourse. As such, it has been identified as "panacean" and non-instrumental, saturated with ideology and cultural symbols. Be it Pan-Arab nationalism, Arab socialism, anti-imperialism, or radical Islamism, a common "canon" of discontented and defiant Arab political language has become prevalent among the urban, educated middle class, underlaid by the socio-political and cultural tensions of a rapidly changing society. This political culture of symbols and ideas, once portrayed as knowing "no half-tones," has made inter-Arab politics often seem as a "zero-sum game."[7]

The salience of culture as the mainstay of the regional Arab system is unique especially when compared to the Latin American countries, which also share a sense of common culture and regional identity. Even though the idea of regional unity has been pervasive among Latin American countries, deriving from common colonial history, language, and (Catholic) church, it has never been a trait defining individuals' identity, as Arabism has been for Arabs. Moreover, while the Arabs inherited from Western colonialism the structure of the state and the idea of ethnic nationalism, with the latter challenging the former's legitimacy, most postcolonial Latin American communities developed from the beginning as independent nation-states.[8]

The ethnocentric identity of the Arab peoples is also indicated by the nature of inter-Arab—conflictual as well as cooperative—"transactions," which assume predominantly expressive, rather than practical, form. With the exception of labor migration and official monetary flow from the oil states to non-oil states, trade and capital investment among Arab states have remained strictly limited compared to the scope of their interactions with the international economic system. While this phenomenon prevails among developing countries, inter-Arab economic integration has been much lower than among Latin American countries.[9]

The blurred boundaries between nation and state in the Arab world have obstructed the emergence of the state as an all-embracing authority able to impose exclusive sovereignty, articulate common cultural values for its constituents, and claim their loyalty and obedience.[10] From a Pan-Arab viewpoint, prevalent among the masses, Arab states' boundaries constitute an artificial and temporary partition of the territorial and ethnic contiguity of the Arab homeland.[11] Hence, while ruling elites must defy competitive supra-state Arab and Islamic challenges, they themselves frequently resort to extensive use of Arab and Islamic ideologies to legitimize their authority. Given the close interplay between domestic and regional politics, Arab regimes are obliged to seek legitimacy from other Arab regimes, as well as from their own constituencies.[12]

The degree of intensity to which supra-state ideologies are employed is a function of the regional and domestic needs of a given regime. It reflects an interrelation between the level of state capability and the regional systemic order. Hence, the ability of an Arab state to exercise full sovereignty in domestic or foreign affairs depends on its ability to enforce an exclusive authority over its constituency and contain external Arab-Islamic pressures applied in the name of collective Arab interest. Yet strong states may just as well resort to extensive use of supra-state symbols and values as a means to claim regional leadership or delegitimize rivals. The Arab masses have responded to and rallied around such symbols largely due to the power of protest implied by them, reflecting a collective sense of predicament and wounded Arab national pride.[13]

Arab regimes vary in their ideological strategies and means of attaining legitimacy in accordance with their particular social conditions and political capabilities. Monarchs tend to establish their legitimacy through patrimonial tradition, building tribal or group loyalty, as well as through Islamic legitimacy, claiming descendence of the ruler-patron from the Prophet's House. In the oil-rich Arab monarchies wealth constitutes an important source of legitimacy which compensates for a relatively low level of state power and penetration into society. Revolutionary regimes, besieged by myriad socio-economic difficulties and threats to their authority, have adopted popular, modernist discourse compatible with their campaigns against the removed traditional elites and postcolonial foreign influence. These ideologies—Pan-Arabism, anti-imperialism, socialism, and Islamic reformism—assume a messianic and symbolic nature, providing the regime with an instrumental legitimacy for authoritarian and repressive policies.[14]

Inter-Arab politics have assumed a high level of "negative" interdependence, indicating mutual sensitivity and vulnerability to both domestic and foreign policies that might alter the Arab balance of power. The manipulation of militant ideologies in the region's politics has served as a bargaining card or a means of coercion toward rival actors in the name of Arab collectivism. The systemic pattern of Arab commonality and interdependence has often been analogized to an extended family in conflict with an external actor. The familial character of inter-Arab relations has also been manifested in the prevalence of voluntary diplomatic conciliation and mediation efforts by Arab leaders as a mechanism of conflict resolution in inter-state conflicts.[15]

The AL's foundation in 1945 introduced a "Westphalian order" in the Arab Middle East based on the principle of a decentralized system of equal sovereign states.[16] Like the Latin American and African systems, the advent of the regional Arab system was marked by a strong call for political unity. Yet the foundation of the AL, like the OAU eighteen years later, indicated a triumph of the approach that favored a regional framework for political and economic cooperation between independent states. This approach drew on the UN Charter's concept of regionalism and was reinforced by the regional organization's commitment to the liberation of other territories still under colonial rule. In both Arab and African cases, the regional organization served a diplomatic need of the member states: to guarantee their sovereignty and territorial integrity from mutual interference in their internal affairs, to resolve conflicts and enhance collective action on common interests.[17]

The Arab states system epitomized by the AL crumbled in the 1950s, primarily because of domestic instability and struggles for power, representing the weakness of the Arab states, rapid social change, and economic difficulties. The permeability of most Arab states was vehemently demonstrated by Nasir's effective appeals to the masses in the Fertile Crescent in defiance of their governments. Inter-Arab struggles for power assumed a "state of war of all against all" in the name of Pan-Arab nationalism, whose magnitude in Arab political life in the 1950s and 1960s indicated a profound longing for regional unity under a hegemonic political center traditionally anchored in Islam as a "religion and state" (*din wa-dawla*). Over time, however, these efforts have shown an ever-diminishing ability to seriously endanger the regional status quo.[18]

The region-based destabilizing conditions were aggravated by the European and American Powers' long-standing penetration and competition over geostrategic influence and oil resources. Yet the leading powers, whether in conflict or agreement, were by no means exclusive or dominant in shaping the region's politics. Nor were Cold War considerations exclusive in determining their Middle East policies, as demonstrated by the U.S. intervention against Iraq's invasion of Kuwait. Arab ruling elites themselves frequently "imported" Powers' involvement in attempting to counterbalance regional threats. This, in

turn, aggravated inter-Arab jealousy, agitation of public anti-Western sentiments, and ideological controversies. Islam's history of confrontation with
European civilization, the recent decolonization of Arab states, and Israel's
special relations with Western allies—all left an unmistakable imprint on the
region's troubled politics, nourishing anti-Western sentiments and claims for
Arab conformity, and undermining state and regional security.[19]

Notwithstanding the obstacles facing Arab state building, in the course
of the 1970s Arab ruling elites proved more durable and coherent. Political
borders and sovereignty became progressively recognized by both domestic
and external actors, shaping the regional Arab system as an increasingly "ordered" one. In the absence of real political participation, institutional legitimacy remained limited and stability was secured by coercive means. And yet,
the enormous growth of state machinery since the 1960s—reflected in the
development of the bureaucracy, armed forces and security agencies, as well as
the state's control of economic life—has enhanced the Arab regimes' survivability, governing capability, and political penetration into society. State
authority and symbols of power have been internalized through widespread
coercion and socialization.[20]

The decline of Pan-Arabism as a dominant discourse following the 1967
war, coupled with the degradation and internal failures of the radical national
Arab regimes, gave way to growing sense of local-national identity and rise of
Islamism as a political ideology. Both trends benefited the process of state- and
nation-building. Thus, even the Syrian and Iraqi Ba'th regimes, while adhering
to their sworn Pan-Arab nationalist rhetoric and institutions, began construct-
ing since the late 1970s particular territorial identities linked to the pre-Islamic
era. On the other hand, the territorial state as a legitimate political unit won the
overt support of radical Islamic leaders who confine their political and social
goals within, rather than out, of the state's boundaries. Although leading Islamists do envision an Islamic commonwealth of sovereign states based on economic and cultural unity, the phenomenon of radical Islam assumes a highly
fragmented form along local and personal leadership lines with no common
supra-state institutional or spiritual authority.[21]

Actors, Core and Periphery

The Arab world "from the Ocean to the Gulf" covers a huge area with
relatively small islands of cultivation and settlement separated by vast barren
spaces, which have shaped its political division from time immemorial. The
Arab world is divided into five sub-regional systems: The Maghreb (Morocco,
Mauritania, Algeria, Tunisia, and Libya), the Nile Valley (Egypt and Sudan),
the Fertile Crescent (Iraq, Syria, Lebanon, Jordan, and Palestine), the Arabian
Peninsula (Saudi Arabia, Yemen, Kuwait, Qatar, Bahrain, Oman, and the

UAE) and the Horn of Africa (Somalia, Djibouti, and Eritrea). Indeed, the political disunity of the Arab world, arising from the geographical, historical, socio-economic, and political differences among its member states, is no less evident than its cultural unity (see appendix A).

The modern Arab states emerged mainly in response to and out of inter-action with European imperial power and actual rule, and achieved indepen-dence with varying degrees of "stateness,"[22] i.e., socio-political integration and state capabilities. The emergence of modern states in the Maghreb and Egypt reflected a history of distinctive communal identity and centralized administration that had already existed or been developed under Ottoman suzerainty. These attributes were a result of relative geographic isolation, early penetration of, and rule by, the European powers, and continuity of the central administration.

In the Fertile Crescent the emergence of modern states was far more complicated due to the markedly varying geography, history, and social struc-tures prevalent in this region. It is characterized by relative contiguity of inhabited areas but with society and territory divided by different religious and ethnic identities; a history of regional economic unity but lack of centralized administration. The division of the region into Mandate territories by the European powers matched none of the earlier Ottoman administrative divi-sions, and imperial policies further intensified inter-communal tensions and obstructed the emergence of central administration. With the added factor of external threats posed by proximate non-Arab powers (Turkey, Iran, and Is-rael), Fertile Crescent politics was marked by intensive interplay between domestic and regional politics, a high degree of permeability of the state, and the salience of supra-state revisionist movements.[23]

In the Arabian peninsula, apart from populated Yemen, states emerged around family power centers and West-protected interests. The aridity, scarcity of population, and tribal tradition that characterize this area determined the weakness of their state capabilities and central administrations, as well as the absence of active political life. State capabilities have thus developed in con-junction with oil wealth and the involvement of Western powers. Underpopu-lated, enormously oil-rich, and yet extremely vulnerable to domestic as well as external threats to their national security, the Gulf monarchies have also suf-fered from a negative image among other Arab societies of traditionalism and longstanding economic and political alignment with the West.

Historically, the regional Arab system has evolved around two main conflictual foci—inter-Arab competition for regional hegemony and the Pal-estine problem. The interplay between them since the interwar period has shaped a concentric regional system, revolving around core actors' struggle for power as well as cultural issues rooted in the meta-ideological level of shared symbols and beliefs in Arab-Islamic societies. The emergence of a Jewish state in the heart of the Arab homeland and House of Islam (*dar al-islam*), in conjunction with other regional processes, played a central role in the formation of Pan-Arab nationalism and the crystallization of the Arab regional system. The reference to Israel's territory as *Palestine* represents a powerful Arab-Islamic claim for its liberation, underlying the perception that Israel is "in but not of the region."[24] The idea of liberating Palestine has remained pivotal in all Arab political discourses—Arab nationalism, social revolution, and Muslim fundamentalism—as the essence of the ethos of struggle against the foreign invader. This ethos has been primarily manifested in continuous warfare against Israel, passing from the Palestinian revolution to Lebanon's Shi'i militias, to the Intifada and finally to the Islamic resistance movements. A typical example was Iraq and Iran's argument during their long war that this war would lead to the liberation of Jerusalem.[25]

As observed by others, the Palestine conflict played an essential role in the emergence of the Arab regional system.[26] This role, however, fluctuated in form and intensity, along with intra-state and regional processes, as well as the Powers' politics. Thus, except for the Suez war of 1956, the Palestine conflict during the 1950s and early 1960s assumed primarily a rhetorical form in Arab politics due to inter-Arab disputes and thrusts for power. In view of the central role of rhetoric in Arab politics during those years, however, the intensive employment of the Palestine issue in Arab political discourse reflected its high place on the Arab public agenda, hence its cumulative causal effect on the escalation to the 1967 war.

The core Arab area included the two main claimants for hegemony over the Fertile Crescent—Egypt and Iraq—as well as Saudi Arabia, Syria, Transjordan, Lebanon, and Palestine. The definition of this area as a "core" has remained principally unchanged although the regional Arab system has, since then, tripled its number of members. Three interconnected core issues have prevailed in regional Arab politics since the mid-1930s, representing the essence of the Arab collective agenda: national liberation and the quest for Arab unity, the Palestine conflict, and rejection of foreign domination and interference.[28]

The concentric structure of the Arab regional system reflected a formula that combined power and cultural identity: strong states capable of exercising influence on collective political processes pertaining to all-Arab core issues. The Arab states system, however, has been structurally pluralized, lacking a durable hierarchy or a single hegemonic center despite striking disparities in natural and human resources among its members. The absence of hierarchical structure has underlaid systemic instability, occasioned by rivalries and competition among Arab actors for regional influence and leadership.[29]

The regional stature of Arab actors was determined mainly by political resources such as a regime's capabilities, population, economic strength, military power, and geostrategic location.[30] Inter-Arab balance could only partly fluctuate to follow changes in leadership, economy, international support, and domestic stability. Thus, Egypt remained the pivotal actor in the Arab regional system, effectively with no single competitor—though intermittently out-weighed by adversary inter-Arab coalitions. Iraq, Saudi Arabia, and Syria, each with specific political attributes and links to Arab core issues, have also played leading roles in the regional Arab system, mainly by forming alliances with each other, or with lesser regional powers.

Adversely, geographical distance from the core area of regional Arab politics and involvement in other regional and sub-regional conflict systems—such as the Maghreb, the Gulf, or the Horn of Africa—has often underlaid the peripheral role of some Arab actors in the regional Arab system. The centripetal force of the Arab core area explains attempts by peripheral actors to en-hance their own prestige by demonstrating active involvement in the Palestine conflict or in conciliation and mediation efforts between disputing core actors. Hence, for example, Morocco's consistent efforts to host Arab summit meetings, Libya's hyper-nationalist policies against Israel and the West, and the Gulf monarchies' official financial aid to the confrontation states and the PLO.

Issues and actors related to the Arab regional core have thus topped the agenda of collective Arab institutions, primarily Arab summit conferences. With rare exceptions, the Palestine conflict has officially rationalized the con-vening of Arab summit conferences, even when they were triggered by inter-Arab disputes. Indeed, collective Arab policies have often represented a ma-nipulation of the periphery by strong core actors, employing power and ideo-logical pressures to impose their own priorities and needs on the regional system as a whole. Thus, while all-Arab core issues have prevailed in summit conferences, issues concerning peripheral states had been given superficial treatment and rarely brought up in the collective decision-making process. An effective regional core capable of shaping collective Arab policies and norms, however, depends on alignment between leading actors whose combined weight can direct the system's decisions.

The relative weight of Arab actors in the system has also been affected by qualitative attributes, namely their prestige as dedicated Arab nationalists and practitioners of hostility to Israel and its Western allies. Such prestige has been instrumental in legitimizing collective deviation from established Arab norms related to Arab regional order and security as well as relations with Israel. Hence, the significance of Syria's participation in the international coalition against Iraq during the Gulf War derived not from its token—and inactive—force. Rather, it was Syria's image as a militant nationalist power *par excellence* and a bitter enemy of Israel that made Syria's involvement in the war a valuable source of legitimacy for Saudi Arabia and other Gulf monarchies seeking Western protection from Iraq.

The Dynamics of Inter-Arab Relations

Pan-Arabism and State Formation

In the dialectic relationship between Pan-Arab nationalism (*qawmiyya*) and the Arab multi-state system, the former has virtually been turned against itself. The umbrella of Pan-Arab nationalism has been mobilized by Arab state builders as a source of legitimacy to bolster their political authority and autonomy.[31] Especially among the revolutionary regimes, this "Arab double-standard game" has been pervasive. Political leaders establish their credentials as unswerving Arab nationalists only to obtain freedom to exercise statehood (*wataniyya*). "Qawmiyya thus furnished the rhetoric; Wataniyya, the reality. Not infrequently, however, the rhetoric became a reality . . . aspiration treated as achievement, tended to immobilize the policymaker and frustrate action."[32]

The magnitude of Pan-Arabism was embedded in its mythical nature and ethos of struggle against the foreign invader, which rendered it a useful instrument of state building on both domestic and regional levels. Pan-Arab rhetoric was used to solicit popular support at home and to discredit Arab rivals as unfaithful to the Arab national cause. This manipulation has been a temporary necessity in the process of state building, when new, often weak and artificial states struggle to acquire internal stability and regional recognition.[33] Even the Palestinian people, self-defined as "the most pan-nationalist (*qawmi*) of all [Arab] peoples," were inseparable from this phenomenon. Compelled by regional as well as intra-Palestinian realities, the PLO developed, as of the late 1960s, a dual personality of Pan-Arab revolution and state-like entity.[34]

The inter-Arab game has clearly been one of mixed motives, with both conflicting and harmonious interests underlining situations of interdependence.[35] Competition for power and access to resources has been the predominant feature of modern inter-Arab relations. The quest for regional Arab leadership is designed to enhance position and prestige in the international arena and thereby, given the region's significance in world politics, maximize chances to obtain foreign material and political support. In this competition, Arab regimes have often utilized political subversion, propaganda, bribe money, violence by surrogate agents, economic pressures, and direct military action—accompanied by ideological justifications related to the Palestine conflict, Western imperialism, and Arab nationalism.

The volatile nature of inter-Arab relations, especially in the 1950s and 1960s, was manifested in the frequent emergence of ad hoc alignments seeking to balance domestic and regional threats. States susceptible to pressure by claimants for regional leadership sought alignment with the latter's rivals, evoking counter-alignments that kept the regional system off balance. This explains the inconsistency of inter-Arab rivalries and alignments, particularly in the Fertile Crescent where states' permeability in the face of Nasir's symbolically loaded appeals to their masses blurred the boundaries between domestic and external pressures. A state's attempt to align with another Arab state may constitute a threat to the object state but, at the same time, appeal to the latter's domestic opposition, thus adding a domestic dimension to the external threat.[36] Extreme sensitivity of Arab actors to any change in the regional balance leads them to perceive newly established inter-Arab alliances as directed against others rather than as implementating the idea of Arab unity. Hence, the inclination of Arab leaders involved in a new inter-Arab alliance is to assure their counterparts that it is not directed against anyone.[37]

The initial pattern of inter-Arab alignment at the AL's foundation clearly indicated the primacy of external threats, reflecting the Hashemite rulers' thrust for regional Arab unity of the Fertile Crescent under their crown. Hence the object states' alignment with Egypt and Saudi Arabia to counterbalance the Hashemite pressures. With the growing political instability of Arab regimes following the 1948 war, coalitions became increasingly motivated by domestic causes, representing new regimes' quest for external recognition and legitimacy.[38]

The post-1967 Arab alignments became more externally oriented, motivated by the growing impact of the conflict with Israel on the region's politics. The priority of retrieving the Arab occupied territories, either through force or diplomacy, became a guiding consideration in the Arab states' alignment behavior, emphasizing the primacy of material resources over ideology. This was even more evident in the essential change of Arab strategy in the conflict with Israel, assuming practical, rather than visionary goals.[39] From the late 1970s through the 1980s, other conflicts—the Western Sahara, the Lebanon and Iraq-Iran wars—as well as growing Soviet threats, accounted for most inter-Arab coalitions. The prevalence of regional conflicts underlaid the emergence of coalitions between geographically proximate neighbors regardless of the regime's ideology, in defiance of third-party threats and anticipation of taping financial aid.[40]

If any one state has been central to the regional system, it is Egypt. Indeed, the main theme of inter-Arab politics since 1945 has been Egypt's aspiration for regional leadership and other states' efforts to limit its influence and power. Even when Egypt was officially out of the "Arab fold" (1979–1989), its salience in regional politics was not diminished, given the system's disarray. Egypt assumed this role by virtue of its cultural weight as a center of Islamic and secular higher education, huge human resources, strong statehood, and strategic location. Ambitious states saw Egypt as a competitor; weaker ones feared it might threaten their political independence. Yet, in the case of threat by a non-Arab power to any Arab state, Egypt's strategic weight could hardly be ignored. Nonetheless, the distribution of power and resources in the Arab world gave no single state a decisive advantage or the ability to knock out all its rivals. Even at the apex of Nasir's prestige Egypt failed to assume effective regional hegemony.[41]

Under Nasir's charismatic leadership, however, the margins of interpretation of Arab cultural symbols and beliefs diminished, making compromises and half-solutions impossible and illegitimate. Personifying Egypt's quest for regional hegemony, Nasir played the role of the rebuking prophet, a standard bearer whose choices and interpretations were beyond debate. Nasir's claim for legitimate interference in the internal affairs of other Arab states in the name of Pan-Arab national revolution was tantamount to a state's classic claim on the monopoly of power. Nasir's inter-Arab policy was marked by a sense of national insecurity and frustration arising from Egypt's own limits and those put on it by other Arab states contesting its search for hegemony.

Whatever rhetoric was deployed in the sphere of inter-Arab relations or the conflict with Israel, its mainstay was the consolidation of individual state sovereignty and capabilities available to the ruling elite. The thrust by the strong Arab states for regional power in the name of Pan-Arabism forced the others to develop counter-alliances and economic relations, sometimes with non-regional powers, as a means to deter regional Arab threats and enhance national security. It is indeed ironic that Nasirism, often conceived as the epitome of Pan-Arabism, was a powerful catalyst in accelerating the process of state building in the Arab world, contrary to its proclaimed ideology.

Except for short intervals, Nasir himself was halfhearted in his self-aggrandizement. He was more interested in Egyptian hegemony in the Arab regional system than in merging with the other Arab states. Pan-Arab ideology was a useful myth in Nasir's Arab policy rather than an operating principle. Paradoxically, he was willing to cooperate with monarchist, Western-oriented Arab regimes that were less of an ideological challenge to him, against revolutionaries, when it suited him.[42] Conversely, Nasir's inter-Arab policy became marked by revolutionary Pan-Arab ideology when Egypt's hegemonic position in the region or his own political leadership at home were challenged. The fluctuations in Nasir's inter-Arab policy can best be explained by the ups and downs in his domestic and regional stature. Indeed, Fouad Ajami's description of Nasir's Pan-Arabism as a fusion of idea and policy is hardly supported by historic evidence.[43]

Nasir's inter-Arab policy was marked by a contradiction between his quest for regional hegemony in the name of Pan-Arab nationalist revolution—which, apparently, was more appealing to the masses in the Fertile Crescent than in Egypt itself—and his responsibility as a head of state. Nasir's ambivalence toward Pan-Arab unity was evident in his initial reluctance regarding Syria's urge for a merger with Egypt and his recognizing Kuwait's independence and right to be a member of the AL in the summer of 1961, a few months before Syria's secession from the UAR. Whether or not Nasir was motivated by the need to contain Iraq's irredentist claim on Kuwait, he effectively supported the creation of another Arab state by British imperialism. When the UAR broke up a few months later, Nasir did not object to the resumption of secessionist Syria's membership in the AL, though he symbolically preserved the UAR as Egypt's name. Nasir also accounted for Arab recognition of an institutionalized "Palestinian entity," in the form of the PLO.[44]

Nasir's revolutionary inter-Arab policy was above all geared to secure regional Arab conformity under Egyptian hegemony, rather than to radically alter the regional order itself. Thus, in late 1963, when his inter-Arab aggressive policy reached a deadlock, with Syria threatening to entangle Egypt in an undesirable war against Israel, Nasir opted to return to a "Westphalian" Arab regional order. To support the shift, besides bringing the AL back in, Nasir revived the forum of all Arab heads of state as an overall authority entrusted with supervising the new Arab regional order. Yet a shift from collectivism to state sovereignty necessitated a parallel process of "normalization" of the conflict with Israel, which had become subject to collective Arab strategy for a joint action on the Palestinian issue. That Egypt led this trend is explained by both its high military stake in the conflict and its national capabilities, strategic weight, and self-image as the leading Arab power.

Arab Summit Conferences: Roles and Processes

Beginning in January 1964, Arab summitry heralded a new era in regional Arab politics. Nasir's messianic and revolutionary Pan-Arabism, inciting the Arab masses against their governments, was replaced by a growing inter-Arab dialogue conducted on a state-to-state level. The shifting nature of inter-Arab relations, from the politics of symbols and beliefs to a "negotiated order," reflected recognition of the detrimental gulf between revisionist visions and political realities, and the need to control this contradiction. The transformation—albeit fragile and reversible at its start—was determined by the state system's obligation to face its limited resources and capabilities.

The prestigious forum of all heads of Arab states inherited the AL's primary role as an institutional expression of the regional states system in which every member was equal regardless of its capabilities or political philosophy. The single most important factor that led to the institutionalization of summitry after 1964 was the steady pressure from the core Arab states— primarily Egypt—to support their policies in the conflict with Israel. The impact of the new Arab regional order had been apparent in Arab intellectuals' interpretation of Pan-Arab nationalism in terms of solidarity and cooperation rather than of political unity.[45]

The summit conference served as a mechanism of collective moral authority assigned the task of bridging the contradictions between Pan-Arab nationalism and realpolitik through reinterpretation of *raison de la nation* and adjustment to *raison d'état*. In the absence of an overall Arab authority, policy making on all-Arab core issues that deviated from Islamic and Pan-Arab national commitments needed legitimation by a supra-state forum representing the whole Arab national community, that is, of all Arab states. Unanimity of opinion in this forum served as a modern secular version of medieval Islam's principle of consensus (*ijma'*), one of the four bases (*usul*) of Islamic religious legislation by virtue of collective acceptance of norms and regulations by the Muslim community (*umma*).[46] Arab summits followed the AL's rule that only unanimous decisions committed the member states. With one exception (Cairo 1990) and two summit breakdowns (Rabat 1969; Fez 1981), all Arab summits closed with statements emphasizing a united position.

By virtue of representing the collective Arab will, the summit could legitimize deviation from hitherto sacrosanct core Arab norms and values and diminish their potential use by militant state and non-state actors for claiming all-Arab conformity. Whereas no Arab summit was needed to confirm the ethos of war against Israel, this forum was repeatedly called to legitimize the post-1967 efforts of the confrontation states to retrieve their occupied territories through diplomatic means. Arab summits thus played an essential role in the process of state building by legitimizing the gradual departure of individual Arab regimes from supra-state commitments. That the Arab summit conducted this process while handling the Palestine conflict, the core issue of Arab-Muslim collectivism, lent it credibility and moral legitimacy. The longevity of the Arab summit institution through more than three decades underlines its significant role in shaping a "normal" regional system of sovereign states (see appendix B).

The quest for inter-Arab unanimity was often criticized as both an artificial attempt to satisfy Pan-Arab ideological imperatives and a major obstacle to collective Arab action. Yet attempts to replace unanimity by a majority vote were rebuffed by either assertive states, primarily Syria, or oil monarchies adamant about preventing imposition of external limitations on their national policies.[47] Even unanimous decisions, however, did not prevent member states from ignoring them if they so chose. In the absence of collective procedural coercion of decisions, summit resolutions were only as powerful as the core states' interest in their implementation and the perceived material and political losses consequent to their violation.

To be sure, Arab regimes differed in their practical commitments to collective Arab regional procedures and decisions. For weak states such as the Gulf monarchies and Jordan, Arab collective institutions constituted a shield against strong militant regimes threatening their sovereignty. Conversely, militant regimes tended to capitalize on their reputed militancy and Pan-Arab nationalist rhetoric to exhort conformity or disregard collective decisions incompatible with their individual interests. The dichotomy between the two groups is shown by the consistent high-ranking representation and attendance of the Gulf monarchies, Jordan, and Morocco at Arab summits, as opposed to the frequency with which radical regimes such as Syria, Libya, Algeria, and Iraq have boycotted the Arab summits (see appendix C). Similarly, whereas summits' decisions on financial aid to the confrontation states and the PLO were widely acted on by the Gulf monarchies, militant oil producers—Libya, Algeria, and, except in 1979–80, Iraq—for the most part reneged on their financial commitments.

The decision to convene Arab summits was largely determined by core actors' needs, defined in the context of the Palestine conflict. Various Arab regimes tended to use inter-Arab tension or events related to the Palestine conflict as a pretext to call for a summit meeting, yet its actual convening depended on the consent of the core Arab states. Arab summits attracted regional and international attention, hence the competition to host them and the prestige bestowed on the regimes actively involved in their procedures. Many summit conferences could convene only after "purifying the Arab atmosphere" or following lengthy negotiations over the agenda, which sometimes involved power struggles, threats, and boycotts by militant regimes. Discontented actors boycotted the summit or delegated lesser figures than their heads of state. What determined the summit's effectiveness, however, was the level of agreement among core actors representing military and economic capabilities in the context of the Palestine conflict.

Much of any summit's outcome was the product of behind-the-scenes meetings in which disputing leaders were conciliated and financial bargaining was conducted. Indeed, summits involved financial opportunities as well as political stakes such as unfavorable collective proclamations—not insignificant, given the highly expressive nature of inter-Arab relations. In order to close with a demonstration of consensus, financial incentives would sometimes be offered by Gulf monarchies to bring reluctant regimes into line.

As in the case of Western summitry, Arab leaders attended summits in order to gain wider legitimacy for their current policies, not to discuss changing those policies. Yet Arab summits were concerned with images more than with the practical, result-oriented diplomacy that has characterized Western summitry. The Arab meetings represented "heroic" diplomacy, focusing on Pan-Arab attitudes and principles of foreign policy rather than on practical economic or social matters. This emphasis on issues over policy may explain the relatively poor record of the AL as well as the summit conferences in playing an effective role in resolving inter-state conflicts and unifying Arab capabilities toward effective collective action.[48]

Arab summits lacked bureaucratic attributes, but were effectively facilitated by the AL's apparatus, whose prestige and practical role diminished as summits became the ultimate inter-Arab forum. The AL's offices were needed mainly for convening the heads of state; inter-Arab diplomatic discourse was left to the individual sovereign regimes. The absence of bureaucratization of the summit suited the Arab regimes' authoritarian natures and their corresponding objections to an inter-Arab central authority that might erode their own individual sovereignty. It has also been consistent with the perception of foreign policy as the exclusive privilege of heads of state.[49]

Inter-Arab Financial Aid

Although economic interdependence is fundamental for economic progress, a low level of economic interrelationship prevails among developing countries, as opposed to their high level of dependence on the world economy for imported technologies and monetary flow. This phenomenon may derive from structurally similar economies and a lack of economic diversity within the developing countries, but more often it reflects an economic policy motivated by paramount considerations of national sovereignty.[50] In the Arab case, in addition to similar structural economic bases, politics plays a primary inhibiting role in inter-Arab economic relations, in conjunction with regional inter-Arab dynamics.[51] Paradoxically, it appears that Pan-Arab nationalism impeded the numerous official efforts to establish economic integration among Arab states, because it threatened the exclusive control, particularly of oil states, over their economic resources.

The extreme disparity of oil wealth and economic constraints among Arab states has been a constant source of inter-Arab tension because, from a Pan-Arab viewpoint, oil is an all-Arab resource.[52] At the same time, major oil pipelines from Iraq and the Gulf to the Mediterranean and the Red Sea created a high level of economic interdependence between oil-producing and transit states, exposing the former to the latter's blackmail and punishment in instances of conflict.[53] In modern Arab history, needy actors have suggested that oil-rich states allocate a permanent percentage of their oil revenues to collective economic development or military buildup. Radical confrontation actors (Syria and the PLO), as well as radical oil producers (Libya and Iraq), repeatedly called for the use of oil as a political weapon in the conflict with Israel, mostly by applying an oil embargo against its Western allies. Yet these calls for economic warfare have been largely a subterfuge for inducing direct aid from Gulf oil monarchies, which have often been blackmailed into contributing their capital. Although these wealthy monarchies have been loath to place their own resources at the disposal of collective Arab strategies or economic development projects, they have often exchanged wealth for security.[54]

Although inter-Arab aid was presented as an expression of Pan-Arab solidarity, the patterns of financial flow and foreign aid illustrate that the assistance was equally inspired by realpolitik considerations.[55] Confrontation states and the PLO have typically received financial aid mainly from the Gulf

monarchies—whose high surplus capital has diametrically opposed their vulnerable security and incapability to protect themselves—rather than from militant oil states (Iraq, Libya, and Algeria). Radical oil states have been less
susceptible to blackmailing pressures from the confrontation states, and not
just because their surplus funds were limited. Given their assertive natures and
militant attitudes toward Israel and the West, these regimes have been more
immune from external threats to their legitimacy or national security. Hence,
they have often justified their reluctance to extend financial aid by alleging that
the Arab confrontation states have not been militant enough toward Israel.

A conspicuous example of the oil producers' behavior on inter-Arab
financial aid was the 1978 Baghdad summit's decision to grant $100 million a
year for ten years to the Palestinians in the occupied territories. Saudi Arabia,
Kuwait, Qatar, and UAE were to contribute 62 percent of the total aid, with the
rest divided among Iraq, Libya, and Algeria. In practice, the monarchies' share
in the total aid of $378.3 million for the years 1979–84 was 91.7 percent, due to
the failure of the radicals to implement their full commitments. As of 1981,
only the Gulf monarchies, Saudi Arabia in particular, continued to
contribute.[55]

For the Gulf oil "rentier" monarchies, regional and national security
were primary concerns which they endeavored to promote through massive use
of the one resource they had in abundance: capital. Financial aid thus became a
major instrument of foreign policy, extended to Arab and non-Arab developing
states to mitigate poor-rich tensions, and contributed to international financial
institutions. The Gulf monarchies used their financial wealth to promote regional stability, curtail political radicalism, and resolve inter-Arab conflicts.
Hence, their official financial undertakings toward the Arab confrontation
states and the PLO, made at Arab summit conferences, were aimed not to
finance the conflict with Israel but to bolster the donors' legitimacy and national security vis-à-vis jealous neighbors.[56]

The dynamics and scope of inter-Arab foreign aid had a direct impact on
Arab strategic capabilities in the conflict with Israel. Yet oil wealth also played
an important role in the growth of state machinery and capabilities, as well as
in the development of a normative Arab states system. Especially for oil-poor
states, oil has been a significant source of state revenue through direct foreign
aid funds or labor migrants' remittances, substantiating their behavior as
"semi-rentier" states. Following the 1967 war, the growing economic needs of
the confrontation states converged with the Gulf oil monarchies' rising wealth
and international influence, laying the bases for a new normative order in the
Arab regional system based on shared interests and collaboration between
needy and wealthy Arab states.

The centrality of the Gulf monarchies' official aid was overwhelming in
the Arab arena as well as on the world-wide level, especially following the

1973 war. From 1973 to 1981, Arab oil producers accounted for more than 95 percent of OPEC's total foreign aid to developing countries, of which the Gulf monarchies' share was 82.6 percent. More than 85 percent of this Arab foreign aid was channelled bilaterally, from one government to another, a pattern that continued through the 1980s. The rest was channelled primarily through Arab state funds and multilateral financial institutions. A third channel of assistance was through international institutions, such as the World Bank, the IMF, and the UN's Development Fund. These channels served the donors' interest in demonstrating support for Third World countries and attaining influence with international monetary institutions.[57]

In the first half of the 1980s, OPEC's total oil export earnings fell by 50 percent, from $261.2 billion in 1981 to $131.5 billion in 1985. As a result, the Gulf countries' earnings declined by 66 percent during this period, exacerbating their account deficits. Confronted with a widening imbalance-of-payments, OPEC donors progressively reduced their aid programs through the first half of the 1980s by more than 50 percent, from $9.7 billion to $3.9 billion. The trend was especially conspicuous in the small oil states, resulting in a relative increase of Saudi Arabia's and Kuwait's share of total OPEC members' foreign aid from 79 percent in 1980 to 91 percent in 1985. Qatar for example, ceased assistance to previous recipients, such as Morocco, Syria, Sudan, and Jordan. At the same time, the UAE's foreign aid declined by 1985 to one-fifth of its $1 billion volume in 1980. Even then, foreign aid by the Gulf monarchies was still higher compared to the developed countries in terms of aid/oil revenues ratio, comprising an average of 7.2 percent in 1984–85.[58]

Arab foreign aid reached its zenith in 1975–1978, representing the large balance-of-payments surpluses of the Gulf monarchies. Between 1973 and 1981, the rate of OPEC members' foreign aid amounted to more than 17 percent of their total surplus. 53 percent of the aid was given in grants, and 80 percent was in the form of budget and balance-of-payments support, with only a minuscule proportion in the form of project finance. Arab oil states' investment in the Arab world was, until the mid-1980s, less than 5 percent of their total foreign investments. The major part of the oil-rich surplus was invested in Western banks.[59]

Until the early 1980s, most Arab foreign aid had been given to the confrontation states—Egypt, Syria, and Jordan—and the PLO. Other Arab states, including Morocco and those with low per capita income levels— Yemen, Sudan, Somalia and Mauritania—also received bilateral financial aid. The third group of beneficiaries were non-Arab Muslim states, foremost of which was Pakistan. African states comprised another group of recipients. In the years 1974–78, Egypt was the main recipient of Arab aid, with 30 percent, Syria received 15 percent, and Jordan 7 percent. The confrontation actors' total share of Arab foreign aid remained relatively unchanged after Egypt ceased to receive official aid following its peace agreement with Israel in 1979. This meant a substantial increase in aid to Syria (30 percent), Jordan (21 percent), and the Palestinians (11.4 percent). But beginning in the early 1980s, Iraq, bogged down in a war with Iran, became the recipient of an unprecedented scope of Saudi and Kuwaiti aid.[60]

For more than two decades, Arab financial aid related to the conflict with Israel was a cornerstone of the Arab states system. Collective commitments of Arab oil producers for multi-annual aid to the confrontation states and the PLO were pivotal in Arab summit conferences from the advent of the forum in 1964, highlighting the growing role of the Gulf monarchies' capital in regulating regional inter-Arab relations. The collective form of financial aid came to an end in 1987, indicating the declining priority of the conflict with Israel on the Arab agenda against the backdrop of a lengthy war in the Gulf and disputed inter-Arab relations, which overburdened the oil economies. Even during its zenith, however, Arab financial aid for the confrontation with Israel was far below the recipients' needs and was divided into installments so as to ensure the contributors' effective control over funds. As a result, it became a constant source of bitterness in inter-Arab relations.[61]

The donors preferred setting the scope and terms of aid to the confrontation states on a collective basis, sanctioned by summit resolutions and demonstrating their share in the common Arab effort for Palestine. Had the aid been given on a bilateral basis, it might have cost the contributors more, though the Gulf monarchies also responded to the requests of needy Arab governments for economic aid, particularly Egypt before it concluded its peace treaty with Israel. Besides direct financial aid assigned for military purposes, the Gulf monarchies also contributed to Egypt through various channels (loans, deposits, investments) for civil economic development. And yet, between 1967 and 1978 the total financial aid from these states to Egypt was only $17 billion.[62]

An important non-governmental aspect of inter-Arab economic links was labor migration from poor to oil-rich countries. With the explosion of oil prices in the 1970s, oil states embarked on ambitious development projects, boosting the demand for imported labor, especially to the underpopulated Gulf states and Libya. Arab labor migration was estimated at 1.3 million workers for the mid-1970s, increasing markedly in the early 1980s following the doubling of oil prices in 1979. In the mid-1980s, Arab labor migration was estimated at 4 million, placing the overall number of Arab workers who had ever worked abroad at 12–21 million—mostly Egyptians, Yemenites, Jordanians, and Palestinians.[63]

The magnitude of the Arab labor migration introduced social and political tension into the host countries that did not exist in the case of non-Arab workers. The tension originated from the receiving states' fears that Arab migrants would seek to establish residence and subsequently claim citizenship and an equal share of the oil states' wealth. Thus, in addition to being prevented from conducting independent private business and obtaining citizenship or permanent residential rights, Arab migrant workers were also subjected to threats of mass expulsion at times of political conflict between the exporting and receiving states.[64]

Migrant workers' remittances became a primary source of foreign exchange for the sending countries, by far larger than the oil states' official aid. Yet the large-scale labor migration to the oil states exacerbated shortages of professional workers in the labor-exporting countries. Given the already poor social and economic conditions in the countries of origin, the bulk of migrant workers' wages from abroad were spent on private consumption rather than production-oriented investment. This led to increased inflation, higher external debt, and intensified socio-economic tensions.[65]

The Dialectic of the Palestine Conflict

The Palestine conflict was an essential instrument of Arab systemic processes epitomized by its primary role in Arab summit conferences. Its intensive employment by Arab regimes served as a stopgap, legitimacy-rich mechanism to compensate for their poor legitimacy at home, inter-state divisions, and failure to materialize the masses' social and economic expectations. The common Arab commitment to the cause of Palestine represented both a substitute for the unattained vision of Pan-Arab unity and a continuation of the Arab struggle for national liberation from Western domination.[66]

This, however, was of primarily ideological significance, linked to state-society relations and representing an essential component of Arab nationalist rhetoric. Practically, the Arab commitment to Palestine meant a head-on collision with Israel, for which most Arab states were both reluctant and unprepared prior to the 1967 war. Articulating total hostility to Israel was a useful pretext to justify the compulsive style of Pan-Arab conformity, often defined as a prerequisite for the liberation of Palestine. It was precisely this empty formula that the Palestinian Resistance (PR) came to alter, by suggesting armed struggle against Israel as a means to realize Arab unity.

With the loss of Arab territories to Israel in 1967, Israel could no more be tackled as a nonentity—"the so-called" (al-maz'uma). In fact, the war results turned Israel into a tacitly recognized actor in regional politics with growing influence over inter-Arab alignment.[67] Clearly, the 1967 war marked the beginning of a shift in the conflict's essence: from the issue of Israel's legitimacy to the question of its boundaries. In other words, the conflict began to turn away from "paradigmatic," that is, cultural, religious, and ideological, to a "normal" political—and thus more manageable—dispute. This became possible when Arab states could relate to the conflict with Israel as states rather than as representatives of a supra-state nation or religion.[68]

The 1970s witnessed the fruition of historical processes of state formation, dialectically linked to structural and normative changes in the regional Arab system. Accounting for this change were, mainly, the post–1973 war oil boom and U.S.-mediated Arab-Israeli diplomacy. Earlier, the "Arab Cold War" was necessary to bury the idea of Arab political unity and internalize the notion of separate Arab states. After the 1967 war, the thrust to retrieve particular occupied Arab territories from Israel brought the Arab states into a growing clash with Arab conformity on the Palestine conflict. The diplomatic process and state-owned oil wealth provided core Arab states with varying degrees of opportunities and constraints regarding collective vs. individual action in the conflict with Israel, enhancing their sense of *raison d'état*. The oil boom also indicated the emergence of a new regional center of Arab power comprised of Saudi Arabia and other Gulf monarchies, eroding the centrality of the Palestine conflict and its immediately involved Arab actors.[69]

The 1980s witnessed increasing disintegration of the regional Arab system, indicating further decline of the Arab-Israeli conflict as a core issue. Whereas Egypt's peace treaty with Israel practically eliminated the Arab military option, the Iraq-Iran war and Shi'i revolution in Iran shifted the Gulf Arab states' concern as well as a substantial segment of their financial resources away from the Palestine conflict arena. Furthermore, growing threats to states' security by regional disputes and socio-economic constraints underlaid the Arab world's return to geographic sub-regions. This was manifested by the emergence of separate cooperation councils to meet the needs of specific states, marking further growth of Arab states' autonomy and departure from obligatory Pan-Arab conformity.[70]

Israel's peace treaty with Egypt and Syria's alliance with Iran against Iraq attested more than anything to the erosion of the "[Pan-]Arab national security" (*al-amn qawmi al-'arabi*) concept, an outcry for Arab conformity against the foreigner.[71] This concept finally went bankrupt in the Kuwait crisis when major Arab actors participated in the international coalition against Iraq. The October 1991 Madrid conference and consequent peace process witnessed the further decline of previously core attributes of regional Arab politics, indicated by the PLO's and Jordan's autonomous diplomatic efforts, which led to the Oslo agreement and peace agreement, respectively, with Israel, despite Syrian discontent.

A commonly accepted observation is that inter-Arab disputes in which the Palestine issue was used as a whip against rivals helped boost the Palestine issue, whereas intervals of accord led to its marginalization.[72] Inter-Arab competition indeed underlaid the PLO's foundation in 1964. It sometimes has benefitted the PLO, but has also accounted for some of its worst disasters—as indicated by the Kuwait crisis—just as short periods of accord among core Arab actors have resulted in Palestinian gains. On the whole, Arab regimes— with varying degrees of cynicism—treated the PLO and its cause as pawns in their persistent struggle for legitimacy and power, summit resolutions and Arab nationalist principles notwithstanding. Palestinians term their problem in the context of Arab politics as "'Uthman's Tunic" (*qamis 'uthman*), pointing to the employment of the blood-soiled tunic of the assassinated 'Uthman Ibn 'Afan, the third Caliph, by his relative Mu'awiya, ostensibly to vindicate the murder but in fact to serve his own ambitions for succession.[73]

The Arab states' attitude toward the PLO and its national cause during the period under discussion reflects the historical development of regional Arab order. State fragility and regional struggle for power underlaid the emergence of militant Palestinian nationalism, whose revolutionary approach and social bases in the Arab states soon became a threat to the Arab social and political order. This, in turn, obliged the Arab states to undertake separate and collective measures—tacitly cooperating with Israel—to contain the PLO's revolutionary threat or eliminate its autonomous violent capabilities. Following the 1967 war the Arab states system's main impact on the Palestinian issue was the persistent effort to tame the PR's revolutionary activity and reshape its strategy toward statehood over part of Palestine. By encouraging its institutionalization and acknowledging it as the sole legitimate representative of the Palestinian people, the Arab states virtually associated the PLO with international procedures and constraints, as well as with the Arabs' limited capabilities.

The process was motivated both by the PLO's growing prestige and political capabilities, and by the Arab states' jealousy for their own sovereignty and regime security. As a national structure, controlling resources, political institutions, military power, media, and international relations, the PLO became a full—albeit non-territorial—actor in the Arab region's political web. In an attempt to impose its own needs and political agenda on Arab regimes the PLO often appealed directly to popular sentiments and opposition groups, further alienating Arab regimes.[74] The PR's military presence and vehement interference in Jordan's and Lebanon's domestic affairs were viewed with ambivalence by most Arab regimes, which explains the eruption of armed conflicts between the state and the revolution.

The PLO's relationship with the Arab states from its foundation to the Oslo accord was marked by increasing antagonism. The PLO strove for full Arab political backing for its national struggle, yet insisting on the principle of "independence of the Palestinian decisionmaking" (*istiqlaliyyat al-qarar al-filastini*), which tended to exacerbate under pressure by assertive Arab regimes—Syria in particular—to subordinate it to their own individual interests.[75] The PLO's self-proclaimed standing as the Arab world's standard bearer by virtue of the identity between its national cause and Arab nationalism was exorbitantly frustrated by the Arab states' individual priorities and strict protection of their individual sovereignty. Hence, the PLO's lament that Arab regimes betrayed its cause: "the territorial [state] (*iqlimi*) defeated the pannational (*qawmi*)" and "regime security superseded Pan-Arab national security."[76]

The depth of the schism between the PLO and Arab regimes has been indicated by the former's shrinking opportunities in the Arab countries since the early 1970s. The result was a growing thrust for self-reliance and territorialization—increasingly focusing on the occupied West Bank and Gaza Strip—culminating in the eruption of the Intifada in December 1987.[77] The prolonged Intifada—and the Arab states' passivity—underlined the return of the Arab-Israeli conflict to its initial pattern as a local inter-communal strife within historic Palestine. In retrospect, the "Palestinization of the Arab-Israeli conflict" culminated a continuous disengagement of the Arab states from the Palestinian cause, beginning in the mid-1960s.[78] It is primarily against this backdrop that the PLO concluded its agreement with Israel—independently and in disregard of other Arab parties concerned—on mutual recognition and the beginning of a PLO-led interim self-government in the West Bank and Gaza Strip.

3

THE EMERGENCE OF A REGIONAL CONFLICT SYSTEM

The Origins of the Arab Regional System

The Arab regional system emerged during the inter-war period, based on common identity and competition among ruling elites, revolving on revisionism and the status quo. It was shaped by a wide array of processes: colonial rule, modernization and social change, state formation and power politics. This era witnessed the creation of new Arab political entities by British and French imperialism on the wreckage of the Ottoman Empire. At the same time a Pan-Arab nationalist ideology arose, gained acceptance from a growing body of opinion among these new entities, and evolved to a dominant force in domestic as well as regional politics.

Nationalism among Arab societies emerged mainly in response to a sense of crisis caused by the West's overwhelming military, technological, and political power, which seemed a menace to traditional social and cultural values. Nationalism was especially attractive to the educated classes because it appeared to be associated with the West, which represented power and efficacy. Borrowing its philosophical concepts, its views of history, and its vision of society from European sources, Arab nationalism essentially reflected a personal, class, or communal sense of disorientation concerning the existing social and political structures. For modern elites located on the front line of social change and Western culture, this disorientation motivated an intensive search for a new theoretical framework with which they could respond to political problems.[1]

The concept of nationalism also represented a general trend of cultural and Islamic renaissance (*nahda*) across the Arab world, which assumed different forms and contents as well as varying degrees of localism. Arab nationalist theorists described the confrontation with European imperialism in absolute terms: as one between civilizations and as a struggle of destinies. The painful reality of inferiority and wounded pride drove Arab intellectuals to call on the Arab-Muslim empire's glorious past as proof that the Arabs' current decline was not essential and that they could regain their lost political and cultural grandeur. While secular Arab nationalism adopted the cultural-linguistic model of Italian and German types of nationalism, Islamic revival-ism (*salafiyya*)—calling for a return to ancestral moral values, social justice, and unity of the community of believers (*umma*)—was directed toward the solidification of a civil society in the face of corrupting foreign influence.[2]

Between the two world wars, the Arabs struggled for national liberation from British and French colonial rule, and in Palestine against a Zionist move-ment which Arab nationalists perceived as an extension of European imperial-ism. Those years also witnessed rapid social changes as a result of moderniza-tion, which, increasingly affecting the political realm and reshaping collective identities, culminated in the ascendancy of Arab nationalism. Based on ethnicity—the people's common linguistic, cultural, and historical bonds—rather than on a defined territory, Arab nationalism was primarily concerned with politics of independence and power, culminating in the ideal of Pan-Arab unity. Under colonial rule, it developed into a romantic, populist, and compul-sive ideology, strongly upheld by the emerging middle class.

The idea of Pan-Arab unity was rooted in the perceptions of social elites in the Fertile Crescent, who shared a common Ottoman legacy and for whom the region's political, economic and cultural unity was a vivid experience. Yet what turned local proto-nationalist movements into a driving politico-cultural force in Arab societies was the dialectic of struggle for national liberation, a growing need of newly established rulers for legitimacy, and a quest for re-gional hegemony. Foremost in this respect were Iraq's Hashemite nationalists, whose desire for independence from foreign domination coalesced with their aspiration for leadership of a regional unity. The Iraqi monarchy adopted an official policy of forging Arab nationalist doctrine and spreading it among the literate younger generation through the state school system. Syrian and Pales-tinian teachers, recruited and employed in key positions, contributed to spread-ing these ideas in Iraq and in neighboring Arab countries as well.[3]

Notwithstanding their secular-liberal background, Arab national ideolo-gists embarked on an intensive effort to coopt Islamic terminology, symbols, and history as a component of Arab national identity (*'uruba*) and discourse. The marketing value of such a combination in a predominantly Muslim so-ciety, whose political notions had been hitherto governed solely by religious terms, was obvious. Arab nationalism's overriding concern with defying for-eign domination was compatible with Islamic doctrine and part and parcel of Islam's modern resurgence. The cooptation of Islam into Arab nationalism proved to be a powerful rallying theme among the newly urbanized masses, whose migration into the cities contributed to the process of modernization and state-building. For these masses, the notions of political identity were primarily rooted in Islamic symbols and beliefs, and they shared a strong emotional alienation with regard to foreign influence. Indeed, the nationalization of the masses brought about the Islamization of nationalism, which explains the relative ease of the later shifting of the dominant discourse to Islamism.[4]

Spreading education, media, and communication helped bringing the masses into the political process, eroding the Westernized ruling elite's position and questioning the relevance of its liberal approach. Soon enough, radical Arab nationalists began to identify the ruling elite with the dominating foreign powers, thereby merging national liberation with a reshaping of society on a just basis explained in both Islamic and socialist terms. By the mid-1930s, Arab nationalism had become a radicalizing force in the Fertile Crescent and Egypt's domestic politics, effectively employed by opposition groups to mobilize political support and challenge the ruling elites.[5]

The twin processes of politicization and nationalization of the masses turned politics into the art of stirring public sentiment through Arab-Islamic rallying myths and symbols as means to mobilize political power and motivate action. The concept of Pan-Arab nationalism thus became part of an obligatory political ideology in urban Arab societies—a focus of collective political identity interwoven with the struggle against Western domination. Indeed, whereas in its earlier stages Arab nationalism, especially in Egypt, had been a reflection of cultural flourishing and European liberal nationalism, it turned, under the impact of Syrian and Iraqi nationalists, into a reflection of European totalitarian nationalism in the inter-war period.[6]

The arbitrary shaping of the post-Ottoman Middle East by the European powers notwithstanding, the new political entities were, by and large, based on long-lived political centers and social elites. Differences in systems of foreign rule and progress toward representative institutions and independence all reinforced and formalized the colonial-based division of the Arab Middle East. Once independence was achieved, political elites confronted a myriad of socio-economic and political problems and came under growing domestic pressures from opposition movements. This resulted in the official adoption of Arab nationalism as an instrumental rhetoric for domestic and regional political purposes regardless of rulers' practices aimed to reinforce their sovereignty. Typically, for actors aspiring after regional hegemony, narrowly based nationalism was rejected as harmful provincialism (*iqlimiyya*). The continued struggle for the national liberation of European-dominated Arab territories was to be a necessary process in pursuit of realization of yearned-for Arab unity.[7]

Pan-Arabism was thus a constant challenge to the state, serving regional actors' thrusts for hegemony as well as domestic opposition groups' claims for redistribution of power. Particularly in the Fertile Crescent, the new Arab entities suffered from a lack of the basic requirements of statehood: institutional inadequacy; lack of distinctive political and territorial identity, and of a well-trained bureaucracy; a highly fragmented population along ethno-religious as well as socio-economic lines; and scarcity of economic resources. In addition, their newly established boundaries cried out for adjustment.[8]

The foundations of the regional Arab system were laid by the Powers' division of the Fertile Crescent, the varied processes of state formation conducted in each of the new entities under foreign domination, and a growing sense of common Arab identity among the educated elites. Already in the late-1930s, relations among the Arab rulers in the Fertile Crescent and Egypt were marked by conflicts emanating from dynastic rivalries and competition for regional hegemony. Indeed, the regional Arab system was shaped primarily by conflicting interests between revisionist and status quo powers.

Even before independence, the Hashemite rulers in Iraq and Transjordan competed for control of Syria, which they both viewed as the core of a unified Arab kingdom they sought to lead. Whereas the Iraqi Hashemite aspirations were defined in terms of a "Fertile Crescent Unity," Amir ʿAbdallah of Transjordan advocated the idea of "Greater Syria" (*suria al-kubra*)—loosely defined by the historic term *bilad al-sham,* including Lebanon, Palestine, Transjordan, Syria, and Hijaz.[9] The Hashemite aspirations were viewed as a threat by their old enemy Ibn Saʿud who, in 1925, had captured Hijaz from the Hashemite King Husain Ibn ʿAli (father of King Faisal of Iraq and Amir ʿAbdallah) and, later, founded the Kingdom of Saudi Arabia. For the next three decades, relations between Ibn Saʿud and his northern Hashemite neighbors were marked by inactive hostility evolving around border disputes and competition for regional leadership. Concerned about Hashemite dreams to restore their reign over Hijaz, Ibn Saʿud's regional policy aimed to block any change in the regional status quo that favored the Hashemite rulers. The Saudi throne thus became a natural ally of the nationalist movements in Syria, Lebanon, and Palestine, which largely rejected the Hashemites' ambitions, preferring independence over any unity plan.

The intensifying Arab-Zionist conflict in Palestine also became an indivisible part of the competition for regional unity and the efforts to mobilize British support to this effect. Recognizing the growing constraints faced by Britain's policy in Palestine, both Hashemite rulers offered British and Zionist policymakers package deal programs of regional unity that would rid the Mandate power of its Palestine burden, partially meet Zionist needs by offering them widened autonomy, and alleviate the Arab-Palestinians' fear of Jewish domination. Although the Hashemites' programs were unacceptable to either the Zionists or the Arab Palestinians, they remained on the regional agenda through the early 1950s, feeding inter-Arab suspicions and tensions. The common interest of the House of Saʿud and the political elites of Damascus, Beirut, and Jerusalem was the mainstay of an anti-Hashemite coalition which Egypt actively joined in the mid-1940s.[10] This pattern of inter-Arab relations remained basically unchanged through the fall of Iraq's Hashemite regime in 1958.

The formation of modern Lebanon as a French mandate in 1921 entailed the annexation of predominantly Muslim territories and the city of Beirut to the autonomous, overwhelmingly Maronite Christian, area of Mount Lebanon. Under the rule of its French protector, the Maronite Christian community enhanced its position as the dominant social group in Lebanon, with the factional system later institutionalized as the main determining factor of the division of power. However, the fine demographic balance between Christians and Muslims within "Greater Lebanon" planted the seeds of the civil war that broke out in 1975. The establishment of modern Lebanon placed a significant imprint upon the future relationship between Syria and Lebanon.[11]

From a Syrian nationalist viewpoint, the Muslim-inhabited territories annexed to Lebanon were an integral part of Syria, traditionally linked to Damascus administratively, socially, and economically. They also provided the shortest and most convenient route to the Mediterranean. Regardless of who held power in Damascus, the loss of these territories has never been fully accepted and even though Lebanon's independence was recognized by Damascus, it remained conditional on the former's response to Syrian needs. Their proximity and the common commercial, financial, and transit interests developed under French rule made it all the more natural for independent Syria to perceive Lebanon as its vital sphere of influence. Particularly difficult for Syria was to sustain the Maronite community's independent economic policies and Western-oriented political and cultural separatism from Arab nationalism. Practically, the relations between the two states took the form of Syrian patronage often expressed in the use of coercive interference in Lebanon's domestic and foreign affairs, and collaboration with Lebanese opposition groups. A salient expression of this relationship has been the fact that Syria and Lebanon have never maintained diplomatic relations.[12]

Egypt's involvement in the sphere of regional Arab politics began relatively late, motivated by political and strategic, rather than ideological considerations. In spite of its Arabic-speaking population, it was not until the late 1930s that it became recognized by Fertile Crescent ruling elites as an Arab country. The political distance of Egypt from other Arab countries stemmed from its unique national attributes: a long history of territorial identity and a strong political center. These characteristics formed the foundations of a distinctive national secular identity which prevailed in the Turco-Egyptian elite until the late 1930s. The evolution of Egypt's role in contemporary regional Arab politics stemmed from domestic social developments, resulting in a shift of symbols and values of collective identity as well as of elite political interests. Unlike the Fertile Crescent—where Arab nationalism emerged as a secular anti-Ottoman sentiment—nationalism in Egypt assumed a strong Islamic character as a result of early British domination beginning in 1882. As of the late 1920s, the emergence and spread of Islamic revivalist movements became an ever-increasing social force in Egypt, which boosted the sense of Islamic identity in its political community at the expense of a distinctive Egyptian nationalism.[13]

Egypt's political involvement in the Fertile Crescent affairs toward the late 1930s was a result of the royal court's aspiration to assume the Islamic Caliphate and the adoption of the intensifying Palestine conflict during the 1936–39 Arab revolt by the Muslim Brotherhood movement and Pan-Arab proponents. With the growing power struggle between King Faruq and the leading Wafd party after nominal independence was achieved, the Palestine cause became an official Egyptian concern. On the eve of World War II, Egypt already presided over the Arab states' collective involvement in the Palestine question. Egypt's leading role in the Arab world gained momentum through growing cultural and economic influence, soon to be recognized by spokesmen of Arab nationalism in the Fertile Crescent. At the same time, Egyptian Pan-Arab figures emphasized their society's need for the Arab world as a natural hinterland.[14] Egypt's role as Britain's military and administrative center in the Middle East during World War II contributed to its leading stature in the region. Its leading inter-Arab role was institutionalized when its government, headed by Nahhas Pasha, led the deliberations over Arab unity that resulted in the foundation of the League of Arab States in March 1945.

Inter-Arab Politics and the Palestine Question

From the late 1930s on, the intensifying Arab-Zionist conflict in Palestine became a focal Arab issue on both domestic and regional agendas, culminating in the invasion of Palestine by the Arab states' regular armies in mid-May 1948. The process represented a convergence of interests, though not of identical political goals, of the Arab-Palestinian community and the neighboring Arab countries. From the early 1920s on, Arab-Palestinians strove to mobilize Arab and Muslim support for their struggle against the Zionist movement and the British Mandate. The Palestinians focused their efforts on the Zionist threat to the country's Muslim-Arab character and particularly to the Muslim shrines in Jerusalem. The defense of Palestine was thus presented as an Islamic and Pan-Arab national duty.[15]

The Arab states' involvement in the Palestine conflict represented aspirations for regional leadership as well as a response to domestic pressures stemming from strong religious and national sentiment for the Arab-Palestinans' cause. This involvement had undergone a major shift during the 1936–1939 Arab revolt in Palestine, when the issue developed from a domestic public matter to a central regional concern involving official policies of Arab governments. The result was an unprecedented series of inter-Arab conferences and inter-governmental consultations held in Damascus and Cairo, which established instruments for collective Arab action on the Palestine issue. The contribution of the Palestine question was indeed unique in enhancing common Arab action and crystallizing the regional system's nucleus, comprising Palestine, Transjordan, Iraq, Syria, Lebanon, Egypt, Saudi Arabia, and Yemen.[16]

An essential factor in this shift was Britain's encouragement of Arab rulers to become involved in the Palestine question, in hopes of mitigating Arab-Palestinian positions and, ultimately, Anglo-Arab tension regionwide. This strategy underlaid the "round table" conference convened in London early in 1939 to discuss Palestine's future. In addition to Arab-Palestinian and Zionist delegates, official representatives of Egypt, Iraq, Saudi Arabia, Yemen, and Transjordan also participated. The growing domestic difficulties and anti-government agitation after independence was achieved induced Arab ruling elites in the neighboring countries to espouse this issue to legitimize their authority. Encapsulating Islamic, Arab nationalist, and anti-Western sentiments, the Palestine cause became a core political and moral theme in Arab public life. As such, it turned into an indispensable source of legitimacy intensely and continually exploited by politicians both domestically and regionally. Rhetorical support of, and manifestations of solidarity with, the Palestine cause became the character trait of Arab regional politics, and a core of intellectual Pan-Arab nationalist discourse. Palestine thus came to serve as a focus of regional Arab politics, stirred by supra-state Pan-Arab and Islamic networks and movements as well as by rulers' schemes and ambitions for power.[17]

The fragmented Arab-Palestinian community itself became a microcosm of regional Arab politics. Rival Arab regimes aligned with rival Palestinian factions, offering support for the struggle against Zionism and the British Mandate but also against each other. Arab regimes were too divided by rivalry, mistrust, and jealousy to present a united front, and their cross-alliances with the Palestinian leadership further deepened their division. This pattern was repeated in the post-1948 war when Arab governments recruited, armed, and financed armed Palestinian activist refugee groups to establish influence over the Palestine issue.

By the 1940s, the Palestine Question (*qadiyyat filastin*) had become a central component of the emerging doctrine of Pan-Arab nationalism. Palestine's symbolic significance, on the one hand, and its territorial implications on the regional status quo on the other, made the issue both divisive and a rallying force in inter-Arab politics. Ideologically, there was an all-Arab consensus on the need to defeat Zionist ambitions. Practically, however, Arab states' policies on the issue were shaped by realistic and self-interested considerations. Typically for a balance-of-power system, the Arab actors' behavior was marked by a constant quest to increase their own individual political gains while seeking to undermine other actors' efforts to do the same at their expense.[18]

The foundation of the AL in March 1945 was a paradoxical result of the Arab rulers' intense competition to lead a regional unity. The thrust was instigated by the approaching end of the war, and was perceived as a historic opportunity to reshape the Arab region. Yet Arab rulers were reluctant to cede their newly achieved independence (Transjordan was still under British Mandate) and to shift "loyalties, expectations and political activities toward a new center whose institutions possess or demand jurisdiction over the pre-existing national state." Having struggled for their national liberation, Arab elites insisted on no less than total independence and sovereignty. Contrary to the common perception of the AL as an instrument for promoting Pan-Arab unity, it was initially shaped as a loose regional organization of independent Arab states whose *raison d'être* was to reinforce and protect the status quo and balance of power among its member states.

Concern over the Hashemites' aspirations for regional hegemony spurred Egypt, together with Syria, Lebanon, Saudi Arabia, and Yemen, to compose a Charter that would preserve each member state's political sovereignty and territorial integrity. The Charter focused on the principle of non-intervention in other members' domestic affairs, giving it priority even over the objective of mutual protection from external aggression. The Charter stipulated that only unanimous decisions would be binding. Majority decisions would commit only those who voted for them except in cases of arbitration and mediation, where majority decisions would suffice. Although the Charter emphasized the AL's role in resolving inter-Arab conflicts, it was not granted authority over the states involved. The Charter does not discuss unity even as an ultimate goal. In fact, the word "unity" never appears in the Charter's text. The AL was indeed a far cry from the unity of merger envisioned by Arab national ideologists or even the federative union advocated by Hashemite Iraq. In retrospect, it certainly was not "something more than the sum of its parts."[19]

The AL Charter included a "Special Appendix on Palestine," in which the signatories recognized Palestine's independence and undertook to allow representation of its Arab people in the League's work. The exceptional concern with Palestine in the AL Charter, though it was not the only Arab country still under colonial rule, attested to its unique stature in Arab regional politics and essential role in the AL foundation. That the AL coopted the Palestine question, turning it into a collective Arab matter *par excellence* which dominated most of its meetings, reflected a majority interest in preventing the possible threat to the regional balance of power that would result if it were employed to benefit individual states.[20]

Given the structural weakness of the Arab-Palestinian national movement, the AL in fact appropriated the former's sovereignty over its cause, undertaking actual responsibility for shaping and implementing the collective Arab policy on the issue. This included diplomacy and propaganda, as well as an economic boycott against the Jewish community in Palestine, ostensibly on behalf of the Palestinian Arabs. But the AL members were divided between an Iraq-Jordan Hashemite alignment and an Egyptian-led majority coalition. Besides Egypt's own political weight and capacity to counterbalance the Hashemites' regional ambitions, Egypt's success rested on its quest for regional leadership and commitment to maintaining the regional status quo. Moreover, Egypt's long struggle for a full withdrawal of British forces from Egypt's soil coincided with the Arab ideal of national liberation. By contrast, the Hashemites had been stigmatized by their collaboration with Britain—in suppressing the brief Iraqi nationalist revolt in 1941—and were portrayed as stooges of British imperialism whose very survival depended on their alliance with Britain.[21]

The Egypt-Iraq rivalry had an indirect impact on collective Arab policy concerning Palestine. Iraq's frustrated ambition for regional leadership generated separatist ultra-extremist positions concerning Palestine with the aim of persuading the rest of the Arab rulers to accept Baghdad's lead in this respect. Regardless of the intentions of the AL's founders and the limits put on its action, the organization's bi-annual meetings—often attended by PMs—aroused high expectations among the politically conscious Arab masses. Such hopes were promoted by the Arab leaders themselves, who presented an unrealistic image of the organization as a manifestation of Arab unity, solidarity, and joint action, primarily on Palestine.[22]

In effect, the AL did not improve the Arab states' ability to cooperate or deal more effectively with the issues in conflict. It became an arena of constant tension and rivalry as the Arab member states made it an instrument for advancing their own interests, impeding their adversaries' policies, and passing resolutions they did not mean to implement. Such an example was King Faruq's initiative of convening the first Arab summit conference at Inshas in May 1946. Ostensibly it was meant to forge a collective Arab response to the recommendations made by the Anglo-American Committee of Inquiry on Palestine. In fact, Faruq sought to promote his own quest for regional Arab leadership and to serve Egypt's particular cause in its conflict with Britain.[23] The early expectations at the AL soon gave way to frustration and contempt for its failure to supervise the Arab collective diplomatic and military effort during the 1947–49 Palestine war, which was aimed at preventing the partition of this land and the establishment of a Jewish state.

The Arab fiasco in handling the Palestine conflict—the one theme on which an all-Arab consensus was theoretically guaranteed—was a reflection of serious inter-state rivalries and conflicting interests even in the face of a common enemy. Efforts to forge collective Arab action in the war notwithstanding, Arab governments sought to serve their individual interests. Hence, the Arab collective thrust in the war proved always too late and too little to tip the scales in the Arabs' favor. The divided Arab military front allowed Israel to wage separate successful offensives against each Arab army consecutively and to conclude separate armistice agreements with each of its contiguous neighboring states. The end of the war indicated not only Israel's military eminence but also the primacy of particular state interests over the fate of Palestine.

The Arab military defeat and the Palestinians' tragedy led to fierce disputes and mutual recriminations among Arab governments over responsibility for the loss of Palestine. Arab societies were thrown into turmoil, political assassinations of Arab leaders, and military coups. Militant Arab nationalists called for revenge and a "second round" of war to wipe out the shame, perceiving it to be the Arab nation's fateful test. The defeat fomented political radicalization and revolutionary trends in which Palestinian refugees from an urban, educated, middle-class background played an important role. Pan-Arab nationalism came to be perceived as a prerequisite for the national resurgence and liberation of Palestine and the removal of the Arab stooges of imperialism blamed for the disaster. Faced with domestic and regional turmoil, Arab ruling elites tended to ideologize their rejection of Israel's existence, using this as a major source of legitimacy. The failure in Palestine also diminished the AL's prestige, resulting in lower-ranking representation of Arab states at its main forums. It also put an end to the potent ALSG 'Abd al-Rahman 'Azzam's effort to turn the AL into a supra-state representative officially recognized by the great powers. The scope of the AL's activities thus shrunk mainly to supervising the Arab boycott against Israel.[24]

The traumatic results of the war, phrased in terms of a catastrophe (*nakba*), disaster (*karitha*), and ordeal (*mihna*), and the ongoing conflict with Israel became the focus of collective Arab political cognition and a touchstone of Arab dignity and self-esteem. The unresolved conflict turned into a black hole that sapped the Arab energies and served as a center of gravity of Arab regional politics. Israel's existence in the heart of the Arab homeland became a painful reminder of Arab weakness and division. The Jewish state epitomized everything the Arabs hated about the West and its historical influence and power; an intolerable monument on which Arab incompetence and ineptitude was inscripted.[25]

For the Arab-Palestinians, the 1948 war ended with a disaster the scope of which reached beyond the loss of lives and land, the uprooting of more than half of them from their homes, social disintegration, and economic devastation. Politically, the war results amounted to a total loss for the Arab-Palestinian people, manifested by the disintegration of its national leadership and the blurring of the fragile collective identity that had crystallized during the Mandate years. The annexation of the West Bank to Jordan following the war underlined the tragedy and loss of the Palestinians, although they were granted full Jordanian citizenship. The Palestinian identity, however, was administratively and politically repressed by the Hashemite regime, which sought to appropriate Arab Palestine and consolidate a Jordanian identity. The incorporation of the Palestinians into the kingdom—now composing two-thirds of the total population—was represented by the euphemistic slogan, "Unity of the Two Banks" (*wahdat al-daffatain*). In the Gaza Strip, the Egyptian government adopted a different policy, the thrust of which was the highlighting of the Palestinian identity and of the temporary nature of the Egyptian military government in this area. In contrast to Jordan's policy, no citizenship was granted to the Palestinians of Gaza, who were subjected to strict limitations on movement across the Egyptian border as well as on political activity.[26]

The 1948 war resulted in a structural shift of the Palestine conflict from an inter-communal dispute to a regional conflict between sovereign states bound by international rules and constraints. Due to domestic and regional inter-Arab turbulent politics during the first decade after the war, the Palestine issue was held on a low burner, which proved to be only temporary.

Regional Politics and the Wave of Nasirism

The first fifteen years of Israel's existence were the most tumultuous in the modern history of the Arab world in terms of both domestic and inter-Arab politics. The prolonged turbulence of Arab politics reflected rapid social and political change, as well as state-building efforts combined with a power struggle over the essence of inter-Arab relations and their global orientation in the postcolonial era. So intense was this struggle for power that the Palestinian issue was effectively shunted aside, except for propaganda purposes. A major phenomenon of this period was the tide of supra-state ideological movements, whose militant outcry against foreign influence and challenge to the very existence of separate Arab states attested to the weakness of the state and the strength of society.

The turbulence marking Syria's domestic politics during 1949 prompted new Iraqi efforts to advance the idea of unity with Syria. Although this unity was officially meant to enhance Syria's defense against Israeli threats, these efforts failed as a result of both domestic politics in Syria and Iraq and Egyptian-Saudi antagonism. Confronted with the threat of a Syrian-Iraqi union, Egypt initiated an Arab Collective Security Pact as an alternative way to offset Israel's threat to Syria.[27] The Egyptian démarche was also a nationalist response to Anglo-American efforts to conclude a regional defense pact that would have left the British in the Suez area and diminished Cairo's leading position in the Arab world. The new Arab pact might have drawn on the Western example of NATO, founded in April 1949, which included provisions for both military and economic cooperation. The Pact of Joint Defense and Economic Cooperation, known as the Arab Collective Security Pact (ACSP), included the AL's same seven member states. The controversial nature of the new treaty was evident in its delayed acceptance by the Hashemites. Although the treaty was concluded in June 1950, almost three years passed until each individual Arab state ratified it.[28]

The ACSP stipulated that all member states would support any state that faced external aggression, following collective consultations and coordination among their armed forces. The Pact also stipulated the establishment of a Permanent Military Committee to function within the AL subject to a joint Arab Defense Council (ADC) composed of Foreign and Defense Ministers and Chiefs of Staff. In two main respects the ACSP went beyond the AL Charter. First, it was agreed that decisions of the ADC made by a two-thirds' majority would bind all the signatories. Second, signatory states pledged not to sign any international agreement or take any political line that might conflict with the Pact's provisions. The pact, however, remained a mere scrap of paper: no joint command was formed and no coordination was maintained. Egypt intended mainly to use this pact to ensure the regional status quo, by preventing Iraqi-Syrian unification, and to defy the Anglo-American project of a regional defense system.

Iraq sought to enhance its regional status by serving as a link between the Arab states, Turkey, and the Western powers, and by weakening Egypt's re-gional Arab leadership and use of the AL to undercut their hopes for unity with Syria. For Britain, a system of defense treaties with Middle East states was to preserve its political influence and military presence in the eastern Mediterra-nean, especially in view of the prospective total evacuation of British forces from the Canal zone in 1956 and the expiration, a year later, of the Anglo-Iraqi treaty of 1930. True, the Soviet threat was by far more real to Iraq than to any other Arab state due to its territorial proximity. Yet the Western scheme col-lided head-on with the growing sense of Arab nationalism in Arab societies, the obsessive drive for no less than total independence, and the deep alienation toward Britain following the 1948 war. The Tripartite Declaration of May 1950 by the United States, Britain, and France, which guaranteed the territorial status quo in the region and restricted arms supplies to states involved in the Middle East conflict, was tantamount to an imposition of Western patronage over the region. Furthermore, the Western endeavor was combined with a proposal to resolve the Arab-Israeli conflict on the basis of Arab recognition of Israel—in return for the latter's concession of the Negev, which would mini-mize Israel's threat to the Arabs and enable contiguity between Egypt and Jordan—at a time when Arab nationalist movements sought to develop a military option for the recovery of Palestine.[29]

Public opposition to the West's prolonged presence or even indirect influence in the Arab countries was already irreversible in the late 1940s when radical leftist and nationalist groups joined forces to defeat the efforts of their governments to revise the existing Anglo-Egyptian and Anglo-Iraqi treaties, in 1946 and 1948 respectively. Later on, it was forcefully expressed in the strong Egyptian opposition to the 1951 Anglo-American proposal to establish the Middle East Defense Organization as part of their strategy of containment in the Cold War. But a major gap separated the Hashemite rulers from their Egyptian counterparts on this matter even before the 1952 revolution. The former considered their political survival and prosperity contingent on continued alliance with Britain, hence their support for its effort to sustain strategic primacy in the Middle East. In contrast, Egypt sought to ensure its own regional posture by eliminating the British presence and weakening the Hashemites' primacy in the Fertile Crescent.

The advent of Nasirism in the mid-1950s as a movement of protest and defiance of Western influence renewed the traditional Egypt-Iraq competition for regional hegemony, which now assumed an unprecedented ideological context. The conflict sprang from Iraq's intention in the fall of 1954 to sign a British-backed defense pact with Turkey, which other Arab states could join. These efforts, however, triggered an inter-Arab struggle of wills, represented by Iraq and Egypt, over reshaping the region's political orientation in the postcolonial era.[30]

The new Egyptian regime perceived the intended pact as an intolerable threat to its regional Arab leadership and national security. The pact was to consolidate Iraq's leadership in the Fertile Crescent—with Syria and Jordan joining—leaving Egypt isolated in the face of Israel's military threat, deprived of substantive sources of arms. In October 1954, an Anglo-Egyptian agreement on British withdrawal from the Suez Zone was concluded. It brought the new Egyptian regime under heavy domestic and regional criticism, from the Muslim Brothers on the right to the Communists on the left. Thus, Iraq's plan to sign the pact with Turkey and Britain provided the Egyptian military junta a golden opportunity to adopt an assertive Arab nationalist foreign policy and a stance of non-alignment in the Cold War, to enhance their patriotic, independent image.

In a last-ditch effort to dissuade Iraq from joining the proposed treaty, Nasir gathered the Arab PMs in a conference in Cairo in January 1955, at which he proposed conformity of Arab states' policies toward non-Arab actors. Nasir insisted that the AL and the ACSP were the only bases for Arab states' foreign and security policies and that no Arab state was allowed to join another defense pact without the previous consent of other ACSP signatories. Nonetheless, a month later Iraq and Turkey signed the treaty—which came to be known as the "Baghdad Pact"—later joined by Iran, Pakistan, and Britain. Indeed, for "Nuri Said's political school," Arab neutralism was a revolutionary thought. Yet the main cause for the conference's failure was the Iraqi-Egyptian competition for regional leadership and their determined quest for narrow individual state interests.[31]

The Baghdad Pact was a watershed in the historical course of Arab regional politics. It indicated a growing drift toward power struggles saturated with ideological rhetoric and tightly linked to domestic affairs. Nasir isolated Iraq and kept other Arab states from joining the Pact despite Jordan's declared interest in doing so. The campaign against the Baghdad Pact was taken to the public throughout the Arab world by the mass media, particularly the Voice of the Arabs (*sawt al-'arab*) radio, broadcasting from Cairo. The Egyptian propaganda, combined with indigenous political agitation, succeeded in moving the Arab masses in the Fertile Crescent countries to defy their respective governments. Nasir's success in challenging the sovereignty and authority of other Arab regimes evidently attested to the latter's weakness and permeable borders. His campaign against Britain's efforts to induce Jordan and Syria to join the new alliance elevated him to the status of an Arab national hero, reflecting the masses' yearning for a daring leader whose challenge to the West instilled a sense of national pride. Nasir's appeal to the masses to reject Western domination proved a potent source of legitimacy in the inter-Arab struggle for power. Typically, those identifying with the West were portrayed as taking the reverse flow of history and denounced as unpatriotic.[32]

The fortunes of Arab nationalism, led by Nasir, seemed on the upswing throughout the 1950s. Nasir's success against the Baghdad Pact was followed by an ever-increasing campaign against British and American influence in the Middle East, which could have well reflected his sense of insecurity. His prestige soared following his role in the April 1955 Bandung conference of nonaligned states; the Czech-Egyptian arms deal in September, which was hailed by the Arab world as a courageous assertion of Arab independent will and an elimination of the Western arms monopoly; nationalization of the Suez Canal in June 1956, and the joint Anglo-French-Israeli offensive against Egypt in October of that year, from which Nasir emerged as a victor.[33]

The growing force of Arab nationalism across the region reflected the worldwide withdrawal and collapse of European colonialism, including in the Middle East. The process of de-colonization and the expanding phenomenon of national liberation in Asian and African countries boosted hopes for a new era of renaissance and resurgence for the newly independent Arab states. From 1955 on, Cairo became the Mecca of national liberation movements in Africa. Egypt's primacy forced other Arab rulers to take a clear position concerning Nasir's policies. More than ever before, the Arab regional status quo became politically threatened by militant Pan-Arab alliances of cross-national movements and official regimes.

Nowhere was Nasir's influence on the Arab masses' behavior more visible than in Jordan, especially among its Palestinian residents. In March

1956, under pressure from the Jordanian-Palestinian nationalist-leftist opposition and Egypt's propaganda campaign, King Husain was forced to expel the Arab Legion's British command and join a military pact with Syria, Egypt, Saudi Arabia, and Yemen. Ostensibly it was to serve as a common Arab defense shield for Jordan. In effect it was a ploy to force an abrogation of the Anglo-Jordanian treaty of alliance of 1946, offering to replace the British subsidy to Jordan by Arab aid. The treaty proved to be a broken reed when, six months later, the signatories remained idle in the face of the joint British-French-Israeli offensive against Egypt. The summit conference convened in Beirut (two weeks after the Suez campaign had begun) to discuss a collective Arab response expressed support for the UN decision on the matter and denounced the tripartite aggression against Egypt. Palestine was not mentioned.[34]

The Egypt-Iraq struggle over the Baghdad Pact and the results of Suez also intensified the struggle for power in Syria among ideological parties, especially the Pan-Arab Ba'th Party, the Communists, and the Muslim Brothers, amid growing involvement of the military in politics. Syria's domestic turbulence underpinned the Ba'thi civilian and military leaders' sudden appeal to Nasir for unity with Egypt, which came into effect with the announcement of the United Arab Republic in February 1958. The Hashemite monarchs' response—a hasty declaration of a federal unity of their own—was meant to preempt expected pressures to join the UAR, attesting to their domestic and regional vulnerability in the face of Nasirism. The merger of Syria and Egypt into the UAR at first appeared to be the apex of Nasir's Arab national achievements despite his initial reluctance to undertake such a union. In September 1961, however, a new military coup in Damascus declared secession and put an end to the union with Egypt. The UAR was the first attempt—and the only one until the 1989 merger of the republics of North and South Yemen—at fusing two Arab sovereignties into one. Retrospectively, the union's breakdown served to consolidate still more the political forces within Arab states that were determined to preserve their independence.[35]

The roots of the UAR's failure lay in the circumstances under which it took place. It was a hasty action that purportedly drew on a shared political vision of Pan-Arab unity, but practically was intended to serve different goals of the two partners. The union was not a result of experienced practice or genuine conviction regarding the advantages of unity. Rather, it stemmed from Syria's domestic chaos and threats to Ba'thi political and military leaders, who perceived unity with Egypt as the only feasible strategy for securing their political future. Hence the acceptance of Nasir's humiliating terms—actual surrender of Syrian sovereignty—which was tantamount to a Syrian political suicide. Paradoxically, what made the union possible was probably the lack of territorial contiguity between Egypt and Syria, so that the merger with Egypt could under no circumstances alter Syria's national boundaries or stop Syria from secession.[36]

The demise of the Iraqi Hashemite regime in July 1958 as the result of a military coup led by Colonel Qasim radically changed the inter-Arab balance of power and the region's traditional alignment. The coup, which was initially interpreted as part of the Nasirist wave, accelerated Arab nationalist sentiments in Jordan as well as in Lebanon—where the regime had been confronted with a rebellion led by Sunni Muslim Nasirists. The perceived crisis of Western posture in the region led Britain and the United States to send token military forces to Jordan and Lebanon, respectively, to prevent the collapse of their regimes and their fall into the radical nationalist orbit. Another reaction was a Saudi-Jordanian rapprochement which led to a coalition of conservative regimes to protect themselves from the Nasirist trend. In the new inter-Arab alignment, Saudi Arabia was to replace Iraq as the main power countering Egypt.

The expectations for Iraq-UAR unity were soon frustrated by the new Iraqi regime due to their fear of Nasir's hegemony and domestic Kurdish and communist opposition. Within a few months, relations with the UAR came under a heavy strain of mistrust and tension, expressed by an ever-intensifying mutual propaganda war. Several plots by adherents of unity with the UAR against the new Iraqi regime, perceived as inspired by Nasir, deepened the hostility between the two regimes, which came to a peak in March 1959 with diplomatic relations between the two states cut off until Qasim's demise in 1963. The Baghdad-Cairo feud became a total war of propaganda and mutual subversion, reaching unprecedented levels of hostility. The battle of rhetoric assumed an ideological character of mutual de-legitimation, employing the Palestine cause in the service of the rhetoric of national liberation and anti-Western domination.[37]

Iraq's revolutionary regime posed a serious challenge to Nasir's hegemonic and unionist concept because it too had turned against the West and become a recipient of Soviet arms. The Iraqi challenge threatened the fragile unity with Syria, which experienced growing discontent among the Syrian Ba'thi leaders, who, by the summer of 1959, began undermining the union when they realized they would be given no real power in it. The UAR's breakup in September 1961 marked a new escalation of inter-Arab conflicts, reflecting Nasir's efforts to recover his injured prestige, as well as his political isolation in the Arab world. Nasir could deny the new Syrian regime's legitimacy but could not prevent other Arab rulers from extending their hands to Damascus and overtly rejoicing at his frustration.

Nasir perceived Syria's secession as a response to the radical nationalization policy he had undertaken in the summer of 1961 against the "bourgeoisie and feudalism," which indeed reinforced the conservatives' objection to Nasir. Blaming the "reaction" for Syria's secession from the UAR, Nasir embarked on a more radical concept of social revolution, which he undertook to implement both domestically and regionally, to secure his power. His National Charter of May 1962, which focused on Egypt's domestic affairs, stipulated a series of radical social, political, and economic reforms geared to suppress political opponents, reduce private enterprise, and enhance the state-run economy. Nasir's response to Syria's secession was tantamount to a declaration of indiscriminate war against his Arab rivals—"reactionaries" and "revolutionaries" alike—expressing his wounded pride and threatened regional leadership.[38]

Nasir defined his new ideological approach with the slogan "Unity of Purpose" (*wahdat al-hadaf*), said to represent the Arab nation's overriding desire for unity through social revolution. He openly took the liberty—in the name of this goal—to interfere in other Arab states' domestic affairs. The previous slogan, "Unity of Rank" (*wahdat al-saff*), denoting inter-Arab coexistence regardless of ideological differences—would bring disaster on the Arab nation, Nasir declared. The new guiding principle was to reflect Egypt's solidarity with Arab peoples, not their rulers. Implicit here was Nasir's true purpose: to besiege his Arab rivals by bringing internal pressures to bear on them.

Nasir's entrenchment in his ultra-radical Pan-Arab ideology aggravated his isolation in the Arab arena and rendered compromise with his rivals inconceivable. The Egyptian political elite showed its readiness to accept the logical consequences of Nasir's Arab policy, such as severing diplomatic relations with Jordan for having recognized the secessionist Syrian regime. Yet Nasir's intrusive Arab policy endangered the fragile improvement discerned in U.S.-Egypt relations under the Kennedy administration, the main result of which was a significant American food aid to Egypt. In 1962, this food aid accounted for 99 percent of Egypt's wheat imports and 53 percent of its net supply of wheat. The repercussions of Nasir's revolutionary policy on his relations with Washington did not linger for long. Just as the Cairo-Washington rapprochement culminated in October 1962 in an agreement to supply food aid to Egypt for three years, Nasir's intervention in Yemen that month aroused new difficulties between Washington and Cairo.[39]

The military coup in Yemen and the new rulers' appeal to Nasir for support against the Imam's loyalists provided Nasir with an opportunity to restore his prestige and implement his new revolutionary ideology. Whatever the motives and calculations that drove Nasir to entangle Egyptian forces in Yemen, the decision coincided with his new self-declared war against the Arab monarchies. A foothold in Yemen would enable Nasir to outflank and threaten the Saudi regime, which he perceived as the bastion of Arab Reaction, and establish a potential foothold near the British-dominated Arab territories of Aden and the Gulf emirates, where the UAR could fulfill its commitment to

Arab national liberation from Western imperialism. But the intervention in Yemen risked provoking American concern for their oil interests in Saudi Arabia, a scenario Nasir could hardly overlook.[40]

For the next five years, Yemen was the battleground of a violent inter-Arab conflict that drained Egypt's scant economic resources, served as the focus of regional Arab politics, and, indirectly, shaped Egypt's relations with the United States and the Soviet Union. The Yemen war obliged Egypt to increase its arms procurement from the Soviet Union; this arms trade helped improve relations between the two countries, which had been strained since the late 1950s. At the same time, the Egyptian military buildup, accompanied by growing animosity toward conservative regimes and air raids of Saudi towns, intensified the tension with the United States.

The Yemen war assumed an ideological character, with the UAR fighting for the new republican regime while Saudi Arabia and Jordan supported the Royalists, led by the deposed Imam. The employment of massive Egyptian forces in Yemen, in turn, pulled Riyad and Amman closer, leading to an accord on military, economic, and political cooperation in November 1962. Furthermore, with U.S. backing, the Saudis formed the Muslim League to heighten Islamic consciousness and combat radical secular ideologies—a blatant challenge to Nasir's militant Pan-Arab nationalism.[41]

In February and March 1963, Ba'thi regimes came to power following military coups in Baghdad and Damascus, respectively. The fall of Qasim and Syria's secessionist regime seemed to vindicate Nasir's Arab policy and hold the possibility of restoring unity with Syria, to be joined by Iraq. The instant initiation of tripartite unity deliberations was a typical example of political manipulation of Pan-Arab nationalism by these regimes. What appeared as an earnest action toward unity was in part a response to public expectations and in part a political maneuver to influence rivals in both domestic and regional spheres. The unity deliberations in Cairo were marked by deep mistrust and suspicion, mainly on the part of Nasir; his bitter experience with the Syrian Ba'thi leaders constituted a significant part of the talks. On April 17, 1963, the three parties proclaimed an agreement on a two-year transition period of loose unity and close cooperation, at the end of which a federal constitution would be promulgated and elections held. Yet the parties undertook no firm commitment to promote their unity during the interim period, indicating the unbridgeable gap between Nasir and the two Ba'th regimes on issues of ruling institutions and political leadership. The stance adopted by the Iraqi and Syrian delegates showed unmistakably that their governments were not interested in a union but wished to use Nasir's prestige to gain domestic and regional legitimacy.[42]

Within two weeks of the signing ceremony, the propaganda machineries of the three countries were engaged in a fierce war, combined with political subversion by Nasir's adherents, which led to an abyss of hostility, especially between Cairo and Damascus. The ruthlessness marking the inter-Arab struggle—especially the July bloodbath in Damascus following an abortive Nasirist coup—epitomized the contrast between the high hopes aroused in the Arab world by the prospect of a tripartite unity and the deadly struggle of the new Ba'th regime for political survival, for which control of the domestic arena was paramount. The Egypt-Syria crisis spurred a rapprochement between the Ba'th regimes in Damascus and Baghdad, resulting, in October 1963, in a treaty of military union that was to be followed by a federal union. Yet this honeymoon between the ideological twins soon came to an end following a bloodless coup in Baghdad in November, which removed the Ba'th Party from power and brought on a renewed propaganda war with Damascus.[43]

By the end of 1963, large sections of the entire Arab world, from the Indian Ocean to the Atlantic, were in ferment. In addition to the exhausting Yemen war, entangling Egypt, Saudi Arabia, and Jordan, the advent of newly independent states in the Maghreb involved serious inter-Arab conflicts deriving from Moroccan irredentist claims for the "Greater Moroccan Homeland." The September border clashes between Morocco and Algeria over the Tinduf area dragged Nasir into yet another violent inter-Arab conflict, albeit on a smaller scale than Yemen's war. At Algeria's request, Nasir sent arms and advisors to the infant independent state, whose leadership he had supported during its long struggle for national liberation. This resulted in Morocco's joining the anti-Nasir camp portraying the AL an "Egyptian puppet." Morocco found itself also at loggerheads with Tunisia after the latter, together with Algeria, recognized the independence of Mauritania, on which Morocco had a claim as an integral part of its historic homeland.[44]

The prolongation and proliferation of inter-Arab disputes rendered futile Nasir's distinction between "progressives" and "reactionaries," in the name of which he had justified his "Unity of Purpose." The intensive employment of symbolically loaded language by Arab regimes in their mutual propaganda wars underlined the cheap instrumentality of hitherto sacrosanct values. The fierce inter-Arab struggle for power—although by far more violent than Malcolm Kerr's term "Arab Cold War" denotes—was crucial to state formation and the definition of state sovereignty and boundaries challenged by an abstract Pan-Arab national entity. This was particularly critical to the "revolutionary" regimes, where the breakdown of pre-independent socio-political and value systems necessitated the construction of new viable political institutions and sources of legitimacy. Nasir's compulsive concept of Pan-Arabism represented a new version of the power struggle between advocates of the regional status quo and claimants of regional hegemony. His revolutionary interpretation of Pan-Arabism was geared to serve his aspired regional hegemony—a pursuit motivated by political and strategic needs. Yet such hegemony was clearly beyond Egypt's political capabilities, and its failure only fortified the walls of suspicion and segregation among Arab regimes.

Egypt's primary role in the inter-state Arab disputes of the late 1950s and early 1960s further weakened the AL's capabilities and stature because it had been identified as an Egyptian political instrument. During this period, Arab governments refrained from approaching it on disputes with Egypt, preferring to complain directly to the UNSC, as attested by Lebanon's (1958) and Saudi Arabia's (1963) complaints against the UAR. Still, Nasir was powerful enough to rally the Arab states around a common cause that coincided with their interests as sovereign states, as revealed in the Kuwait crisis of June 1961, following Iraq's claim that Kuwait was "an indivisible part of Iraq." The threat of an Iraqi invasion of Kuwait was eventually rebuffed by British troops deployed on the emirate's soil, a presence later replaced by a joint Arab Security Force under the AL auspices comprising UAR, Saudi, and Jordanian troops. The awkward presence of British forces in Kuwait provided Nasir with an opportunity to lead the joint Arab venture, using the AL to isolate Iraq. Although the crisis remained a bone of contention in Iraq-Kuwait relations, the AL proved effective in serving a coalition of core members.[45]

The AL survived criticism of its ineptitude as well as years of intense inter-state Arab disputes. Whereas it helped to settle the Kuwaiti crisis, the AL was paralyzed by Egypt's direct involvement in the Yemen war. Although it never stopped being the stage for discussing core Arab issues, the AL's activity was kept at a low profile and its finances were limited. Disputes among members were reflected in the occasional boycotts of meetings by regimes subjected to attacks or interference in their domestic affairs by Egypt. Even Egypt boycotted the League's meetings for about six months following the AL's session in Shtura (August 1962) to protest Syria's accusation that Egypt had betrayed the Palestinian cause.

Regional Politics and the Conflict with Israel

Until 1964, Arab strategy in the conflict with Israel was marked by uncertainty, lack of a defined political or military plan, and a vast discrepancy between vision and reality. Israel's existence in the heart of the Arab homeland was essentially rejected as an injustice to the Palestinian people, an obstacle to the realization of Pan-Arab goals, and a permanent cultural, economic, and political threat to the neighboring Arab countries. Considering Israel an illegitimate entity, the Arabs' objective in the conflict was defined in terms of elimination of the state of Israel. Practically, however, no clear Arab program of action—whether political or military—had been worked out to accomplish this objective. Arab strategic and political thought focused on justifying the objective and explaining its feasibility regardless of practical constraints, pos-tulating that the disappearance of Israel was historically inevitable. Indeed, the Arab objective in the conflict with Israel was a utopian goal that fitted well into the messianic doctrine of Arab nationalism.[46]

The absence of a specific program of action reflected the Arab states' awareness of the impracticability of their objective—vague and undefined as it was—in view of their limited military capabilities, political weakness and division, and the wide international support for Israel's right of existence. The lack of a clear Arab program of action before 1964 might have reflected the absence of domestic pressure on the Arab regimes; the Palestinians were in disarray and it was only **their** national territory that came under Israeli occupa-tion; and Jordan's annexation of the West Bank was obviously an obstacle to the advancement of the liberation of Palestine. The Palestinian problem was not a priority for the Arab states, whose policy remained confined until 1964 to diplomatic activity in the UN and repetition of resolutions pertaining to the right of the Palestinian refugees to return to their homes. Thus, Nasir's impor-tant manifest The National Charter (*al-Mithaq al-Watani*) of 1962 made no reference to Palestine at all.

Arab governments were incapable of either liberating Palestine or admit-ting their powerlessness and, hence, adopting a peaceful strategy. Their divi-sions and jealousies made secret and separate diplomacy the only practical option for an Arab-Israeli dialogue. It is noteworthy that Jordan, Egypt, Lebanon, and Syria were each involved in separate secret diplomacy with Israel in the aftermath of the 1948 war. Diplomatic contacts between Israel and Egypt's revolutionary regime continued even through the mid-1950s. How-ever, all these efforts ended in failure before they were exposed to the public or reached a substantial level. The futility of these efforts was demonstrated by the Israel-Jordan five-year non-belligerency agreement initialled in February 1950. Deferring to the combined pressures of Arab governments and his own political elite, King 'Abdallah suspended the agreement and virtually ceased further peace talks with Israel.[47]

Early Israeli-Arab diplomacy revealed the unbridgeable gap between the conflicting parties. Israel wanted peace based on the status quo, whereas the Arab parties insisted on Israeli territorial concessions and repatriation of the Palestinian refugees—demands that Israel perceived as detrimental to its very existence. The Arab rulers' opposition to direct and official negotiations with Israel reflected both their shaky domestic positions and the Arab public con-sensus that any political agreement with Israel was illegitimate. Especially because of their responsibility for the 1948 defeat, Arab ruling elites needed a substantive Israeli concession—Egypt insisted on the Negev, which would give it territorial contiguity to the Mashreq—the Arab world's East—to justify a settlement. The pitfalls of this phase of Arab-Israeli diplomacy reflected the sense of insecurity in Israel, the weakness of the Arab states vis-à-vis powerful Arab popular opposition movements and the depth of their hostility toward Israel, and growing calls for a "second round."[48]

In the absence of a real capability to destroy Israel, Arab states adopted a policy of hostility short of war, accompanied by measures of containment. These measures included: economic boycott, strategic blockade, sporadic guerrilla warfare—carried out by Palestinians, mainly under Egyptian supervision—political and diplomatic warfare in the international arena, and continued pressure to bring Israel to implement UN resolution 194 concerning the return of the Palestinian refugees to their homes. Yet the more distant the goal seemed, the louder Arab leaders tended to voice their hostility against Israel and reinforce their commitment to the objective of eliminating it. The inclination to define the objective in such terms nevertheless stemmed from the domestic and regional political radicalization and social turmoil that swept the Arab states, threatening the ruling elites' legitimacy and survivability. This, in addition to inter-Arab disputes, subjected any Arab ruler who sought accommodation with Israel to immense opposition, delegitimation, and even threats to his life.[49]

Under Nasir's leadership, the absence of clear Arab strategy in the conflict with Israel was officially admitted. Nasir was increasingly pressured by radical Arab opponents who aimed to embarrass him into launching the Arab war against Israel even before unity was achieved, claiming that such a strategy would hasten the achievement of Arab unity. But with his prestige tarnished after Syria's secession from the UAR, confronted by Arab opponents and entangled in a deadlocked war in Yemen, Nasir was least of all able to lead an Arab war against Israel. Until May 1967, Nasir repeatedly argued that there was no Arab option for war against Israel, giving priority instead to his thrust for establishing regional hegemony in the name of Arab unity. He advocated an indefinite postponement of war against Israel to give the Arabs time to prepare for the decisive, all-out showdown, preparation that he portrayed as a comprehensive Arab effort—military, economic, and industrial—to build an immense Arab capability, not only to fight Israel but also to deter "those behind Israel." The total war envisioned by Nasir turned into an instrument to enhance and legitimize his regional policies.[50]

At the peak of his strife with Qasim, at the ALC's session in March 1959, Nasir brought up the idea of establishing a "Palestinian entity," namely an institutional representation of the Palestinian national identity and political cause. The timing of Nasir's initiative might have been determined by other, international initiatives regarding the resolution of the Palestinian refugee problem and growing discontent among the Palestinians in the Gaza Strip. But the decisive reason for his proposal was apparently the intensive criticism of his inaction on behalf of the Palestine cause by Arab adversaries, primarily Qasim. The initiative indicated Nasir's interest in demonstrating political action for this cause at a time when the military option in the conflict with Israel was missing. The Palestinian entity idea was meant to shift the form of the conflict with Israel from an international one between the Arab world and Israel—in which he was expected to assume a leading role—to a Palestinian struggle for national liberation spearheaded by the Palestinians themselves and only supported by the Arab world.[51]

Advocating a Palestinian entity was another manifestation of Nasir's inconsistent quest for Pan-Arab unity; a pragmatic decision underlined by international and regional constraints that prevented an all-out war against Israel. Shifting the Arab-Israeli conflict to a struggle of national liberation indeed constituted a radical change in the Arab concept of war against Israel, which had been hitherto unspecified. Yet Nasir's policy concerning the Palestinian entity before 1967 clearly manifested an intention to confine the struggle for Palestinian national liberation to the political sphere, at least as long as the Arabs had no military option against Israel. Nasir's new concept gathered momentum in the coming years. It corresponded with the rapid process of decolonization in Asia and Africa, Moscow's official endorsement of national liberation movements in early 1961, and Nasir's efforts to establish himself as a primary leader of the Third World. In hindsight, the Palestinian entity idea was Nasir's first step toward limiting his role in the liberation of Palestine.[52]

The Palestinian entity idea aggravated the competition between Nasir and Qasim who embarked each on a propaganda race to champion the project. With no common border with Israel and eager to embarrass Nasir, Baghdad called for turning the West Bank and Gaza Strip into a "Palestinian Republic" to serve as a basis for an armed struggle against Israel. Inter-Arab conflicts and competition for legitimacy rendered the Palestinian entity mainly an instrument in the vicious inter-Arab propaganda campaign. However, Egypt (1957) and Iraq (1960) also made symbolic gestures to substantiate their positions and further propagate their arguments by establishing units of the "Palestinian Liberation Army" under the command of their respective General Staffs. These units were comprised of Palestinian refugees, whose voluntary recruitment might have diverted some of their bitterness and drive for action. Additionally, Nasir took measures toward the political organization of the Palestinians within the UAR. In addition to the popular-military component, Nasir initiated the establishment of representative Palestinian National institutions in the Gaza Strip and Syria as an organic part of a political realignment within the UAR. In 1962, a temporary constitution was given to the Palestinians in Gaza, to function until "the promulgation of the permanent constitution of the Palestinian State." The public debate on the "Palestinian Entity" in Arab forums gathered further momentum because it was brought up in conjunction with Israel's beginning to construct its National Water Carrier (INWC) which was perceived as a strategic threat to the Palestine cause and the Arab countries.[53]

The intensifying debate on the Palestinian entity in the Arab world paralleled, and interacted with an authentic process of political awakening, revitalization of Palestinian nationalism, and social radicalization among the Palestinian refugees. Growing education and social mobilization; a strong sense of Palestinian identity brought into focus by humiliating social and economic conditions in the refugee camps; the restrictive and suspicious attitudes of the Arab "hosting" countries; and frustrated hopes for a rapid redemption by the Arab states—all these contributed to the development of a new generation of young professional Palestinian activists whose role was to become crucial in the Palestinian Resistance (PR) MOVEMENT from the mid-1960s onward. The newly emerging leadership in the Palestinian refugee society called for self-organization of the Palestinians and their assumption of an active role as a vanguard in the war of national liberation against Israel.[54]

II

꙰

THE POLITICS OF ESCALATION: FROM THE "ARAB COLD WAR" TO THE JUNE 1967 WAR

"It is about time to face realities . . . . Let me tell you, and forgive my candor, that what has been going on between us is demonstrative rather than a real action. We have announced the establishment of a unified political leadership, held meetings . . . and spoke of issues, all of which are general and superficial. I am afraid that we have not taken them seriously at all . . . . We meet [for] long hours and do nothing but examining positions, but we never unify wills capable of action. Thus, we uphold placards behind which there is nothing."

—Nasir to an Iraqi delegation headed by President 'Abd al-Rahman 'Arif, February 4, 1967, Heikal, *Al-Infijar, 1967,* p. 408.

"We actually have no plan for the liberation of Palestine now, and we do not have the means to realize that goal [even] if we have had a plan. I believe that the conflict between us and Israel is a matter of a hundred years."

—Nasir to King Faisal, August 1965, *ibid.,* p. 208.

"[Israel] hates to the extent of death everything we do in the cause of progress. Because [progress] for us, is the death for Israel."

—Nasir, *Al-Ahram,* March 10, 1965.

4

FOR THE SAKE OF PALESTINE: "UNITY OF ACTION"

The Undesirable War Against Israel

Arab politics in the early 1960s demonstrated the abyss between the vision and the reality of Pan-Arab nationalism and the costly price of political extremism shaped by intransigent interpretations of this doctrine. By late 1963, Nasir's aggressive Pan-Arabism, expressed in the slogan, "unity of purpose," had reached an impasse, forcing him to revise his regional Arab strategy, though not his quest for all-Arab leadership. The shift was heralded by Syria's pressures for war against Israel which threatened to entangle Nasir, hence his call for inter-Arab truce and dialogue through a summit meeting, which he explained by citing the need to effect a joint Arab response to Israel's threats—embodied by the INWC, which was due for completion in mid-1964.

Nasir's real goal was to avoid the risk of an untimely war and obtain acknowledgment of a collective Arab responsibility for an indefinite postponement of the war under the slogan, "Unity of Action." In return, he was willing to shelve his revolutionary Arab policy and mend fences with his conservative rivals on the basis of ad hoc cooperation. As it turned out, however, Nasir was unwilling to abandon his ideological commitment to fight Western imperialism and would treat his conservative rivals as equal partners only as long as they accepted his leadership. Nasir assigned the AL to implement his new inter-Arab policy, revitalizing the dormant regional Arab forum and demonstrating its usefulness as a mechanism for regulating inter-Arab relations. As such, the AL was to legitimize an indefinite postponement of the war against Israel and save Nasir's prestige.

The INWC—from Lake Tiberias to the northern Negev, using the Jordan River—had been a permanent item on the AL's agenda since its official announcement in 1959. In February 1960, The ALC decided that the Israeli project was "an act of aggression against the Arabs, which justifies Arab collective defence"; that it was "necessary to utilize the waters of the Jordan River for the benefit of the Arab States and the Arab refugees who have a legitimate right to it"; and that a special technical committee attached to the AL should coordinate work in this respect. Consequently, a plan was worked out by the AL for the diversion of the Jordan headwaters into Arab territories, which would deny them to Israel. The implied effects of such a plan on Israel's project and the prospects of an Israeli retaliation, however, could not be over-looked, hence the need to provide a military backup for the Arab project. By mid-1961, the ADC had approved the diversion plan to prevent Israel's completion of the project, "by force if necessary," and drafted a proposal to create a Joint Arab Command (JAC). This was followed by a series of meetings of Arab CoS's to discuss the appropriate military responses to possible Israeli moves and to give further consideration to the idea of a JAC.[1]

The AL diversion plan reflected the Arab perception of the conflict with Israel as a "zero sum" game and of Israel as an abstract and illegitimate entity. As such, Israel had no rights for water allocation as one of the riparian states of the Jordan River. In 1955, the AL rejected a regional plan for the utilization of water in the Jordan basin prepared by Special Ambassador Eric Johnston, an envoy of President Eisenhower. The plan was to be financially supported by the United States on condition that it would include the settlement of the Palestinian refugees. Though a later version of the plan was technically accepted by Israel and Jordan, other Arab states, led by Syria, remained officially hostile to Israel's sharing in the Jordan waters. Israel, for its part, would not agree to any further delay of its project pending Arab consent, arguing that its national water project was compatible with international law, and that it meant to use its legitimate share of water as a riparian state, recognized by the Johnston plan. Jordan, as well, continued its water project.[2]

Syria was active in agitating the issue in the AL forums, particularly following its secession from the UAR. Syria's turbulent domestic politics and its conflict with Nasir following the breakup with the UAR, rendered Damascus' ultra militant position in the conflict with Israel a primary source of legitimacy on both domestic and regional levels. Escalating the conflict with Israel became all the more significant for the Syrian Ba'th regime following its accession of power in March 1963, and took the form of intensive border incidents across the demilitarized zone along the Upper Jordan River. Syria's policy toward Israel was meant to exert pressure on Nasir—who denied recognition to the Ba'th regime—by exposing his inaction on the issue of Palestine and "Arab national waters." Already in mid-1962, Nasir was attacked by his Arab adversaries, Syria in particular, for acquiescing to a soft line on Israel in return for U.S. aid. In this context the INWC project and the border clashes with Israel served Damascus well, validating its call to adopt an active all-Arab military stand in the conflict over the Jordan waters. Syria's efforts to commit Nasir to the "liberation of Palestine" resembled Iraq's challenge to Egypt's regional leadership in 1945–48, when Iraq had advocated an ultra-militant policy on Palestine.[3]

For Nasir, however, the time for a military operation against Israel could hardly have been worse. Not only had there not been a joint Arab war plan but inter-Arab relations were at a deep crisis and Egypt's costly involvement in the Yemen war was deadlocked. Nasir could not overlook the possiblity that joining an action against a legitimate Israeli water project would aggravate his relations with the United States, already strained over the Yemen war, and endanger the flow of American economic aid to Egypt—which amounted to $264 million in 1962 and was to increase by 50 percent in 1963. Finally, in late 1963 Nasir was engaged in extensive diplomatic efforts aimed at enhancing his prestige and leading role in the Third World by hosting a summit conference of the nonaligned states in Cairo.[4]

The Syrian-Egyptian dispute culminated at the Arab CoS's meeting in Cairo on December 7, 1963, in which the Arab response to INWC was discussed. Syria's demand for immediate war was rebuffed by the UAR delegate, who opposed a military solution, at least for the present. This dispute was followed by an overt showdown in the media, triggering another Egyptian outburst of propaganda war that accused Saudi Arabia, Jordan, and Syria of "stabbing Egypt in the back" by trying to drag it into war. Egypt, it was stressed, would take no military action on the Jordan River issue until Arab unification had been achieved. Damascus responded by excoriating Egypt for evading its national responsibility vis-à-vis the Palestinian question, which encouraged Israel to proceed with its aggressive project. The Syrians dismissed the proposal to divert the Jordan headwaters as a gimmick designed to conceal a refusal to fight. They warned that, besides depleting the water sources of Lebanon, Syria, and Jordan, Israel's project would strengthen its economic, demographic, and military capabilities and lead to further expansion of the Jewish state at the Arabs' expense.[5]

The Syrian propaganda campaign—echoed by Egypt's other adversaries, notably Saudi Arabia—severely questioned Nasir's credibility and prestige in the Arab world. Nasir was on the horns of a dilemma, compelled to seek a respectable way out of the political impasse into which he had been driven by his own revolutionary Pan-Arabism and the new Syrian Ba'thi regime. Aware of Syria's inability to prevent the Israeli project alone, on December 23 Nasir called for the earliest possible meeting of Arab presidents and monarchs to discuss thoroughly a collective Arab military response to the Israeli water project. Nasir declared that "Palestine supersedes all differences of opinion. For the sake of Palestine, we are ready to meet with all those with whom we have disagreements." The quarrels and disputes of recent years should be relegated to history. Israel's water diversion of the Jordan waters must be resisted by force because the campaign over the Jordan was inseparably linked with the struggle for Palestine. Egypt was ready to do its duty in this regard, Nasir emphasized, but the time was not yet ripe for military action: "It is no shame to decide that we cannot employ force at this time. If I were to say that it is possible to go to war now, I would be bringing disaster on you."[6]

Nasir's new approach to regional Arab politics was designed to coopt the Ba'th regime into an all-Arab strategy under Egyptian control and at the same time preserve his position as the Arab champion of the Palestine cause. Nasir's effort to prevent war and defy Syria's militancy in the conflict with Israel underlined his need for an alignment with the conservative regimes, which was tantamount to an admission that his campaign against them had miscarried. Hence, Cairo's new message to the Arab world was marked by a conciliatory approach, emphasizing that inter-Arab wrangling must not be allowed to prevent cooperation in realizing the common goal of struggle for Palestine. Egypt pronounced itself ready to allow each Arab country to act as its interests and resources allowed.[7]

Nasir's call for a summit meeting drew an immediate affirmative response from all the AL members, enabling the ALSG 'Abd al-Khaliq Hassuna to issue invitations to the thirteen member states without delay. Only Saudi Arabia withheld its reply, reflecting the power struggle within the Saudi royal family and disagreement about who was to head the delegation: King Sa'ud or Crown Prince Faisal, the Saudi regime's "strong man." Finally, the king announced that he would serve as his country's official delegate to the meeting— a decision that may have bolstered the monarch's tenuous position in the Saudi court but that would have a deleterious effect on Egyptian-Saudi talks over Yemen.

Purely selfish considerations prompted Arab leaders to accede at once to Nasir's invitation. His powerful charisma among the masses and his moral stature as the Arab nation's hero meant that his extraordinary gesture could not be disregarded. The Saudis interpreted Nasir's invitation as an acknowledgment of his need to hold talks with them. His declared intention to postpone war with Israel and remove inter-Arab disputes was consistent with the interests of the conservative regimes, whose political vulnerability and interest in regional stability turned them into natural allies of Nasir's new inter-Arab policy. For the Syrian regime, whose legitimacy had been challenged by Nasir, participation in a conference with the Egyptian leader meant tacit recognition by Cairo, and boosted legitimacy at home. Syria's Ba'th leaders could utilize the occasion to promote their campaign to expose Nasir's indecisive policy on the question of Palestine. Above all, Arab leaders apparently wished to share— especially with Nasir—a collective responsibility for the decision on the Israeli water project, whatever line of action was to be adopted.[8]

Arrangements for the conference under Hassuna's direction included the preparation of working papers and agenda that virtually reflected Nasir's needs and priorities. The AL proved to be a useful Egyptian instrument of regional policy when used in accordance with *raison de status quo*. The agenda included the INWC and its ramifications, the "Palestinian Entity," and the need to "clear the atmosphere" in the Arab world and settle all outstanding differences. This last, catchall, item had been placed on the agenda, it was explained, so that practical discussions could be held on all issues not covered by the first three items. Thus, the most bitter inter-Arab disputes, such as the one between Nasir and the Syrian Ba'th regime, or the Yemen war, were not officially included in the agenda, a familiar practice in inter-Arab meetings. Inter-Arab disputes were to be veiled by ambiguous phrases: the issues to be underlined were those capable of consolidating consensus, namely those related to threats originating from non-Arab actors, especially Israel.[9]

The Arab Diversion Plan

Ways to scuttle the INWC, and the formation of a JAC to prepare for a consequent war with Israel, were the main Arab instruments to be pursued in the conflict with Israel. Since the summit conference's underlying rationale was to secure official sanction for postponing war against Israel, an alternative Arab response was required in the form of a counter-plan for diversion of the Jordan waters. This had already been fully studied by the AL's apparatus, namely the "Technical Committee on the Jordan River," and the Arab CoS's.

The Arab diversion plan was comprised of two stages. It called, in the short term, for the diversion of the Jordan headwaters in Syria and Lebanon to prevent Israel from using them; and, in the long term, for the construction of an inter-state system of dams, water reservoirs, and hydro-electric stations to let the Arabs utilize the available water. The Arab plan's maximum effect would have reduced the quantity of water available to Israel annually by 200–250 mcm. However, it would also have increased the salinity of Lake Tiberias, which would have reduced the quantity of water available to Israel by a much larger figure. It was estimated that completion of the plan's initial stage would require eighteen months to two years; and eight to ten years would pass before the project's second stage would be fully operable. At the summit conference, $17.5 million was allocated for the first stage of development, with each country contributing in proportion to its share in the AL budget. The actual diversion work was to get underway once approval was given by the mooted JAC.[10]

The diversion plan turned into a bone of inter-Arab contention over allocation of water and funds. Jordan objected to the original plan, which called for the Hasbani waters to be diverted into the Litani River, and urged instead that they be integrated into its Ghor project. On the other hand, the Lebanese wanted the prior construction of the Nabatiyya dam for collecting the Hasbani waters and requested funds to this end from the diversion project budget. The final diversion plan approved by the second summit conference, held in September 1964, indeed added Jordan's Mukhaiba dam to the Arab-funded project, whose estimated total cost was £10.25 million, in addition to the £6.25 million allocated at the first summit meeting. The diversion plan was portrayed as a legitimate self-defense action in the face of Israel's aggression against "the Arab waters." Hence, the summit's final communique apologetically emphasized adherence to international legitimacy in accordance with the UN charter. The effort to counter negative international reactions was even more salient in the final version of the diversion plan, presented as an economic development scheme, a large-scale irrigation project, rather than an anti-Israeli measure.[11]

Given Lebanon's military weakness and traditional reluctance to become entangled in hostilities with Israel, the diversion plan depended most heavily on Syria, which was charged with implementing its main part. This served well Nasir's intention to defy Syria's militancy and discourage Damascus from provoking Israeli military action. Against this backdrop, Syria raised objections to the procedures and duties of the JAC, which, as designed by Cairo, were meant to secure Egypt's control of the joint Arab military effort and thereby forestall an undesirable slide into war. Egypt would argue that coordination and cohesiveness among the Arab armies was not yet at a level that would make a war with Israel feasible. Syria, on the other hand, wished to use the JAC both to enhance Nasir's military commitment to her and to help underwrite its own military buildup.[12]

Ultimately it was agreed to subordinate the JAC to an Egyptian General, 'Ali 'Ali 'Amir, and to entrust it with several tasks: to coordinate among the Arab armies and bring about standardization of their weapons systems and military terminology; to examine the vulnerable defense points of Syria, Jordan and Lebanon and to determine their arms requirements. The bulk of the JAC's budget—which the summit participants were to pay by February 1964—was earmarked for aid to these three countries. Under the JAC's supervision, these states were to prepare a military force able to hold on its own against Israel if the latter resorted to armed action in response to the Arab diversion project. A ten-year budget of $345 million was allocated to the JAC, with Kuwait's share, for example, put at $11.5 million per year, Saudi Arabia's at $6.9 million, and Iraq's at $3.45 million. Egypt was not to receive Arab financial aid since "its military readiness was complete."[13]

In June 1964, the INWC became operational, entirely unhindered. "Unity of action" soon proved impractical because the Arab regimes remained mutually suspicious and fearful lest their independence and sovereignty be hampered by other Arab regimes in the name of action for the sake of Palestine. Nowhere was this suspicion more evident than in regard to military cooperation under a joint command, which touched on the precarious security of individual Arab regimes. From the outset, the JAC found itself confronting intractable problems. It had to study the confrontation states' armies and ways to strengthen them but without having any reliable information. The JAC lacked the authority to coordinate among the Arab armies, including the Egyptian one. Furthermore, a basic premise of the JAC was an early deployment of Iraqi forces in Jordan and Lebanon to help defend the Arab diversion works. Jordan and Lebanon, however, refused to permit foreign Arab forces on their soil and insisted on ironclad guarantees against Israeli reprisals before they would allow the diversion work to begin. Standardization of Arab armies' weapons was another obstacle. Jordan and Lebanon not only categorically rejected Egypt's proposal that they acquire Soviet-manufactured arms, to match Egypt's, Syria's, and Iraq's, but demanded that the JAC give them funds to purchase additional Western weaponry, leaving the JAC no choice but to partially meet their demand. Indeed, "The Arab command may have been united, but it lacked unified armies."[14]

The JAC report, as well as the diversion plan and its military ramifications, topped the agenda of the second summit conference, which convened in Alexandria in early September 1964. In his report, the JAC commander offered the assessment that Israel would react militarily to the Arab plan once it was put into effect. The report suggested that the Israelis had the capacity to rout any Arab state they attacked before other countries could come to its aid. Therefore, he argued, it was essential that he be vested with the authority to transfer Arab forces from one country to another in accordance with the JAC's overall plan, in war or peacetime. However, Syria, Jordan and Lebanon, the main states expected to host expeditionary forces, rejected this idea.

Syria's continued attacks on Nasir between the summits foreshadowed the fierce debate that errupted over these issues at the summit, which had to be extended by another two days beyond the original timetable in order to reach consensus. Nasir himself, increasingly pressured by Syria, escalated his threatening tone, declaring that the war with Israel was inevitable. Syria's president Amin al-Hafiz was eager to force Nasir to Syria's position of immediate all-Arab military showdown with Israel despite the JAC commander's view that Syria's forces needed more than any other Arab army to be beefed up. Hafiz insisted that it was necessary to make "the liberation of Palestine" the cardinal goal of collective Arab strategy, a statement that coincided with Syria's growing support of the "popular armed struggle" and of Palestinian guerrilla groups. Lebanon sought to avoid conflict with Israel over the water issue, insisting that their shaky political system precluded the entry of foreign Arab forces into their territory. Jordan contended that the stationing of Iraqi or Saudi troops on its soil would be conceived by Israel as a cause for war. Both Jordan and Lebanon objected to the proposed idea of military training for their Palestinian refugees. The discussion of the JAC's report led to a unanimously endorsed resolution, originally suggested by Nasir, that adopted the essence of Syria's position and reflected the advent of the PLO. It consisted of three main points:

1. A comprehensive Arab plan of action—political, economic, and military—would be drawn up to liberate Palestine and ensure "the elimination of the Israeli aggression."

2. The Arab states would report on their ability to assist the confrontation states with manpower and funding (no deadline was set).

3. The JAC was empowered to prepare an overall plan so that an estimate could be made of its needs in terms of budget, manpower, and weaponry.[15]

Nasir also directed the summit to adopt a clear resolution calling for immediate commencement of the Jordan River diversion project. In view of the expected Israeli reaction, the summit approved Nasir's proposal to entrust the JAC's commander with the authority to instruct Arab armies to move even before hostilities with Israel broke out. According to the terms, however, the movement of Arab forces was to take into consideration each individual country's constitutional makeup and customary modalities—a provision that effectively subordinated the JAC's authority to the policies of each Arab state concerned. The restriction on the JAC command stemmed from Lebanon's demand that no foreign Arab forces enter its territory except at the government's explicit request and with parliamentary approval. It was also resolved that expeditionary forces from Syria, Saudi Arabia, and Iraq would be massed near the confrontation lines in order to rapidly reinforce the Jordanian and Lebanese armed forces in an emergency. It was agreed that no additional funds would be allocated for military procurement and infrastructure installations.[16]

The Alexandria summit resolved to form a followup committee—headed by the ALSG and comprised of representatives of the heads of the Arab states—to monitor the resolutions' implementation and to report to the next summit conference. This revealed a fundamental problem of discrepancy between resolutions and actions, which necessitated additional inter-Arab meetings and the work of followup committees on major issues such as the diversion project and the JAC's powers. The summits of Cairo and Alexandria resolved to institutionalize the summit and provide for an annual session.[17]

From a "Palestinian Entity" to the PLO

Since the Arab-Israeli conflict had become the pivotal issue of the summit meeting, it was incumbent on the organizers to include the "Palestinian Entity" on the agenda as a separate item. As mentioned above, this issue had been on the ALC's agenda since March 1959, following Nasir's allusion to the matter in the course of inter-Arab feuding about commitment to the cause of Palestine. Notwithstanding the momentum this issue gathered in the Arab world in the early 1960s, no practical progress was made in the AL's forums, mainly due to Jordanian rejection, which foiled an Arab consensus on this issue. Nonetheless, the ongoing debate of the subject in the AL forums as well as among the Palestinians, had unmistakably eroded Jordan's objection. Nasir—and Qasim as well—consciously and publicly challenged Jordan's rule in the West Bank and its legitimacy as the heir of Mandatory Arab Palestine. The ongoing debate contributed to the concept and principles that shaped the ultimate Palestinian national organization.

Cairo was also active in advancing the establishment of a separate Palestinian representation in the AL as well as in various international forums. This, however, clashed head-on with Hashemite Jordan, which blocked all the efforts made at the AL's forums to adopt a resolution substantiating a Palestinian national representation. The "Palestinian Entity" concept threatened to split the West Bank from Jordan and further undermine the Hashemite dynasty's shaky existence. The threat to Jordan's integrity and political stability was very real for a state that had always been anathema to Arab nationalists and in which the Palestinians constituted a majority of the population. This threat was reflected in the government's oppressive measures against opposition groups, some of which had been backed by other Arab states.[18]

At the ALC session held in September 1963 at a FMs level, a combined Iraqi-Egyptian pressure was exerted on Jordan to accept the idea of a "Palestinian Entity" and national representation. The session decided to appoint Ahmad al-Shuqairi, a prominent Palestinian figure (originally from Acre), well known in inter-Arab and international diplomatic circles, as the new "representative of Palestine" at the AL. Shuqairi succeeded the late Ahmad Hilmi 'Abd al-Baqi, who had headed the "All-Palestine Government" (*hukumat 'umum Filastin*) at its foundation in September 1948 in Gaza. The ALC resolved to empower Shuqairi to form and head a Palestinian delegation to the UNGA, practically dismissing the historic Palestinian leadership embodied by al-Haj Amin al-Husaini's AHC and replacing it with the ensuing "Palestinian Entity." The ALC session reiterated the Palestinian people's national rights, and expressed support for Iraq's proposal to establish a Palestinian National Council (PNC) and government.[19]

Palestinian participation in the first Arab summit faced a procedural problem, since the Palestinian delegate was not a head of state. Shuqairi's participation was eventually approved—after he allegedly threatened to resign—but he was allotted a smaller chair than the heads of state, to indicate his inferior status. Discussing "the Palestinian personality" (*al-shakhsiyya al-filastiniyya*) and the organizational measures required to give it expression, the first summit resolved that Ahmad al-Shuqairi would continue his contacts with the member states of the AL and the Palestinian people "in order to establish the proper foundations for the organization of the Palestinian people, to enable it to fulfil its role in the liberation of its homeland and its self-determination."

The inconclusive wording of the final resolution indicated Nasir's decision to reach consensus on the principle of establishing a representative Palestinian institution. It was a compromise between supporters and opponents of the "Palestinian Entity" idea.[20]

Nasir led the move to recognize a Palestinian Entity and establish a political body of Palestinian refugees, and was seconded by other rulers, albeit with different purposes. Presidents Bourguiba of Tunisia and Ben-Bella of Algeria proposed the creation of a Palestinian liberation organization based on the model of the Algerian FLN. On the opposition side, only Jordan was adamant in rejecting recognition of any organization whose very existence implied contradiction of the Hashemite rule on both banks of the River Jordan. The Saudis were reserved, identifying the creation of a Palestinian political organization with Egypt's inter-Arab policy. They also had an unsettled account with Shuqairi who, as their recent UN ambassador, had disobeyed Riyad's order to submit a complaint against Egypt for violation of Saudi sovereignty in the Yemen war and had resigned.[21]

Shuqairi made repeated efforts to mitigate King Husain's fears, assuring him that the "Palestinian Entity" "is not a government and it lacks sovereignty," and that the envisaged organization would not try to separate the West Bank from Jordan. It would aim, explained Shuqairi, at mobilizing the Palestinian people's military and political potential, and at cooperating with all Arab countries. King Husain's strong objection to either incorporating the term "Palestinian Entity" into the resolution or stipulating its inclusion forced the summiteers to drop any reference to it. The final resolution thus carried a vague wording to be accepted by all participants, leaving this matter to further elaboration by the three leading figures concerned, namely Nasir, Husain, and Shuqairi. Officially, Shuqairi had not been empowered to take any practical action in establishing the Palestinian organization, but could only consult the Palestinians about it—as he himself, as well as his Arab rivals, later argued. However, the summit conference resulted in inter-Arab and intra-Palestinian political dynamics that were to facilitate Shuqairi's mission and generate sufficient conditions for the birth of the PLO less than five months later.[22]

The summit indeed set in motion the process of institutionalizing a Palestinian national movement, thereby opening a new era in the history of the Arab-Israeli conflict. The change was manifested by the use of new terms, which henceforth gained ever-growing Arab support, such as "liberation of Palestine" and "self-determination of the Palestinian people." These were soon to replace the phrase "implementation of UN resolutions," which had gained currency at high-level Arab gatherings. The emergence of the Palestinian cause as a matter of national liberation gathered momentum due to growing competition between Syria and Egypt over championing this issue following the first summit. Underlying the adoption of the phrase was also the desire to garner the support of Third World leaders by subsuming the Palestinian issue under the rubric of liberation from colonial rule and the right to self-determination, goals with which these leaders could readily identify. The final communique repeatedly appealed for the moral and political support of the Third World countries for "the legitimate Arab struggle against Zionist aspirations." This appeal was reinforced by expressions of support for the struggle against imperialism everywhere (particularly in South Yemen, Oman, Angola, and South Africa), pointing to "the dangers and aspirations of imperialism and Zionism, particularly in Africa."[23]

From the outset, Shuqairi made no secret of his intention to establish a political organization for the Palestinians, with Nasir's full endorsement. His efforts in this regard were no doubt facilitated by the Cairo-Amman rapprochement and the general atmosphere of detente in inter-Arab relations combined with the Arab governments' growing interest in the Palestinian question. Still, Shuqairi had his work cut out for him due to the deep suspicion and antagonism of some Arab regimes regarding everything identified with Nasir, and divided opinions about what the "Palestinian Entity" should be. Shuqairi sought to deal with this situation by allaying Jordan's apprehensions, reluctantly reiterating that the Palestinian organization would not be a government nor would it hold a referendum or elections before the liberation of Palestine itself. Shuqairi made clear his view of the correct distribution of tasks between his nascent organization and the Arab states. The Palestinian people, he asserted, would take responsibility for its own fate, and the Arab states' task would be to support the Palestinians until the establishment of their independent entity.[24]

Jordan remained hostile to the idea and took measures to scuttle Shuqairi's assignment, but could not overlook the strong emotional response of Palestinians to Shuqairi's visit to the West Bank. No less important for Husain was to reach conciliation with Nasir that would enhance his legitimacy both at home and in the Arab world. Nasir's patronage of the "Palestinian Entity" provided the Jordanian monarch with an opportunity to mend fences with him by taking a calculated risk and going along with Shuqairi's efforts in convening what would become the PLO's constituent assembly. Husain apparently hoped to gain control of the fledgling organization by forcing Shuqairi to accept a pro-Hashemite orientation at the conference.[25]

Shuqairi also encountered resistance from Syria and Saudi Arabia. The Ba'th regime in Damascus, which advocated armed struggle to liberate Palestine, contemptuously dismissed Shuqairi's plans as a mere tool in the hands of Nasir and Husain. The Saudis, for their part, threw their support behind al-Haj Amin al-Husaini, former Mufti of Jerusalem and veteran national leader of the Palestinian Arabs, who still retained his title as head of the AHC. So reluctant was Riyad to cooperate with Shuqairi that it barred him from entering the country. Other states were more forthcoming. Lebanon, although it objected to Shuqairi's intention to establish training bases for the Palestinians in their countries of residence, favored organizing the Palestinians politically. Both Iraq and Kuwait unreservedly welcomed Shuqairi.[26]

Shuqairi's activity ran into opposition also from Palestinian activist groups who, due to their links with some Arab regimes, came to represent the divided Arab arena over Shuqairi's mandate. Al-Haj Amin al-Husaini maintained that the AHC was the sole legitimate representative of the Palestinian people, and tried to garner support among the Arab states. Also opposing Shuqairi's program were the Palestinian sections of Pan-Arab bodies such as the Ba'th, the Arab Nationalist Movement (*al-qawmiyyun al-'arab*), and the Communists, as well as Palestinian underground groups affiliated with Syria, such as Fatah and the Palestine Liberation Front (PLF).[27]

After four months of incessant lobbying in Arab and Palestinian circles, however, Shuqairi was able to override and outmaneuver his critics, mainly due to Nasir's backing and King Husain's consent to holding the constituent Palestinian conference in Jerusalem. On May 28, 1964, the conference convened in the presence of King Husain and official representatives of Arab governments, providing the PLO's ceremonial proclamation a collective Arab imprint. After endorsing the Palestinian National Charter and the PLO's basic law, the conference elected Shuqairi as president of the organization and chairman of its Executive Committee, with power to appoint that body's members as he saw fit. Almost simultaneously, six Palestinian underground groups announced their unification within the framework of a different liberation organization that held that Palestine could be liberated only by force of arms.[28]

The *fait accompli* of the PLO's foundation exacerbated inter-Arab differences on this matter when it was discussed at the second summit conference. Saudi Crown Prince Faisal lashed out at the creation of the PLO as a violation of the summit's mandate to Shuqairi, while Ben-Bella, serving as Nasir's mouthpiece, sided with the PLO leader. Shuqairi himself submitted far-reaching requests, including the formation, training, and outfitting of a large Palestinian army for the liberation of Palestine. He also called for the creation of an Arab financial institution devoted to this purpose that would raise £45 million through tax levies, principally from oil production. Of this, £15 million would be allocated to the PLO, an amount that would also cover the military budget. Shuqairi's sweeping requests were opposed even by Egypt, as well as Jordan, Saudi Arabia, and Lebanon. The main dividing issue, however, concerned the PLO's objectives and structure.[29]

Ba'thi Syria wanted a revolutionary body, with sovereignty over the Palestinian territories held by the Arab states—namely, the West Bank, the Gaza Strip, and al-Hama.[30] The Palestine Liberation Army (PLA), Syria argued, must be subject to the authority of the Palestinian government to be formed by the organization, and Egypt must desist from exploiting the PLO against other Arab states for its own purposes. Both the Syrians and the Saudis insisted that the PNC be an elected body and not appointed by Shuqairi, obviously to limit Nasir's control of the PLO, only to be rebuffed by Shuqairi's comments about the lack of election procedures in those countries. King Husain, adamant to control the threat to his throne caused by the PLO's advent, refused to countenance even a hint of Palestinian sovereignty. Above all, Husain rejected the creation of independent Palestinian military units, arguing that a Palestinian army already effectively existed in the form of Jordan's army and National Guard. As for Nasir, although he was Shuqairi's bulwark of support, he could not permit the formation of an Arab independent force that might risk his own strategy of long-range preparations for the decisive war against Israel by creating the hazard of premature entanglement. Thus, while Nasir paid lip service to the idea of the liberation of Palestine—even declaring that the Gaza Strip and Sinai would be placed at the PLA's disposal as forward bases—he was in fact bent on full subordination of the PLO's military activity to the JAC.

Ultimately, the summit resolved to express support for the PLO as the Palestinians' representatives in the political arena. The PLA's creation was also approved in a decision-making process typical of Arab summit conferences: since the heads of state were loath to make the decision themselves, at Nasir's proposal, which won unanimous approval, Shuqairi himself was to do it, following which the summit approved "the organization's decision to create the PLA." Both the PLO and the PLA were to be funded, with the latter being allocated £5.5 million: £2 million from Iraq and Kuwait, £1 million from Saudi Arabia, and £0.5 million from Libya.[31]

In a series of talks held by Shuqairi and the JAC, it was concluded that PLA units would be formed in Syria, Iraq, and the Egyptian-held Gaza Strip, with the assistance of each country's army. Shuqairi reluctantly agreed to subordinate these units to the Arab armies, in coordination with the JAC as far as funding and training were concerned. Nevertheless, Shuqairi was given the nominal right to name the first titular commander of the PLA, Lt. Col. Wajih al-Madani, a Palestinian officer serving in the Syrian army.[32]

"Unity of Action" and Inter-Arab Relations

The summit meetings heralded a new era of inter-Arab accord and cooperation. Even though the main inter-Arab disputes remained unresolved, the new conciliatory atmosphere mitigated their gravity. The summit did, however, pave the way for further conciliatory efforts in some secondary conflicts, giving most of its participants a sense of accomplishment. Nasir's wish to avoid war with Israel was implicitly sanctioned by all Arab leaders in return for his conciliatory approach toward his adversaries and acceptance of their legitimacy. An attack on Israel was made contingent on an Israeli offensive against the Arab water-diversion project, which he might have hoped would never come. Nasir could count on Lebanon's unequivocal reluctance to become involved in such a project and its willingness to do all in its power to derail it. However, Syria's militant drive was only loosely and temporarily tamed, and Israel's response was out of Nasir's control.

Of all the inter-Arab feuds the one between Nasir and the Syrian Ba'th regime remained unchanged, with no renewal of their diplomatic relations after Syria's secession from the UAR. Nasir, while willing to overlook his ideological differences with conservative regimes for the sake of collective Arab action, remained hostile to Syria's revolutionary Ba'th regime. Throughout the conference, Nasir adamantly refused to meet with Syrian President Amin al-Hafiz. Obviously, Hafiz was more interested in rapprochement with Nasir than the other way around, and tried to prolong his stay in Cairo after the summit in the hope of meeting Nasir personally, but to no avail. Syria thus remained isolated politically, reluctantly accepting the conference resolutions while reserving the right to respond militarily to Israeli actions.

Between the Cairo and Alexandria summits, the enmity between Nasir and the Syria's Ba'th regime continued to cast a pall over the inter-Arab atmosphere of conciliation. Aggravating the situation was a renewed outbreak of vicious verbal sparring by Syria against Egypt and Iraq in April 1964, generated by mounting unrest in Syria, which quickly erupted into street riots. The Syrian outburst reflected a growing sense of isolation in the Arab arena following the Egypt-Iraq rapprochement during and after the first summit. President 'Arif gained Nasir's support presumably for having toppled the Ba'th Party in Iraq and his effort in reconciling Egypt-Saudi differences on Yemen. Rescued from its traditional isolation, the Iraqi regime became Nasir's main partner in his strategy toward Israel through the JAC and as a supervisor of the meeting's resolutions. In May, a new unity pact between Egypt and Iraq was furiously assailed by Damascus as being directed against itself and contradicting the conciliatory atmosphere of the January summit meeting. Relations between Cairo and Damascus deteriorated further following the former's disregard of Syria's request for aid after a series of armed clashes with Israeli forces in the demilitarized zone in early July. Only after repeated demands did Egypt send General 'Ali 'Amir to Damascus to allay a Syrian sense of isolation that threatened to push it into renewed military action against Israel.[33]

With the threat of untimely war against Israel seemingly under control, and his Arab leadership reaffirmed in the summit, Nasir turned to dealing with his entanglement in Yemen, by trying to reach an understanding with the Saudi royal family. Substantive negotiations were impossible both because of King Sa'ud's failing health and his eroded authority. Though Sa'ud refused to commit the Monarchists in Yemen to a compromise solution with Nasir, the summit did lay the ground for future dialogue and negotiation between Egypt and Saudi Arabia on the issue. King Husain was active in the mediation efforts between Cairo and Riyad, following his own reconciliation with Nasir. Egyptian-Saudi relations temporarily improved following a visit to Riyad by Egypt's Vice-President 'Abd al-Hakim 'Amir in March 1964, accompanied by Iraqi and Algerian ministers. The visit resulted in an agreement on resumption of diplomatic relations, a joint announcement endorsing Yemen's independence, and a commitment to seek peaceful resolution of all conflicts. But Egypt-Saudi relations remained in abeyance due to the Yemen war, where the rival factions' intransigence blocked any resolution. Nasir found himself increasingly trapped in his commitment to the corrupt, incompetent Republican regime whose leaders were engaged in constant political intrigues and power struggles. Riyad, where the power struggle within the royal family had been decided in March 1964 in Faisal's favor—though Sa'ud was to remain king until November—continued to refuse to make any concessions to Egypt. Meanwhile, tension between British authorities in South Yemen and the Republic of Yemen were aggravated, in the form of armed border clashes, as a result of British military support to the Royalists, which was matched by Egyptian financial assistance to the Free Liberation Organization of South Yemen (FLOSY).[34]

The Yemen war was not discussed at the summits' official sessions. At the second summit, however, differences arose between Egypt and Saudi Arabia over Egypt's request to consider the issues of Yemen and the "Arab South"—referring to British-dominated South Yemen and Aden. Egypt's demand obviously was meant to link its continued intervention in the Yemen war to the issue of national liberation from British colonialism in an attempt to exert pressure on the Saudis to expedite resolution of the former issue. In spite of vehement Saudi opposition, Egypt managed to impose the issue on the summit through the ALSG, who overrode objections by the conference chairman, Saudi Crown Prince Faisal, and raised the Yemen issue in his report to the plenum. He denounced the British for their continuing rule in South Yemen and their takeover of the Buraimi oasis, urging a joint action in order to expel the British from the Arabian Peninsula. Egypt may have scored a point in justifying its military presence in Yemen, but could hardly affect the Saudi position.[35]

Intensive behind-the-scenes mediation efforts took place at the second summit meeting, as various Arab leaders tried to reconcile Nasir and Faisal. Direct talks between the two leaders led to an agreement in which the two sides undertook to cooperate in stopping the fighting and mediating between the parties in Yemen. The agreement, published as a joint communique, was a considerable victory for Faisal, since Nasir implicitly recognized the Royalist side in the conflict. As a result of the Nasir-Faisal accord, delegates of the rival Yemeni factions met in Sudan at the end of October. They agreed that a cease-fire would take force within a week, to be followed by a national congress of Muslim scholars (*'ulama'*), tribal chieftains and public figures, within less than a month, to work out conditions for making peace. Although the cease-fire came into effect, the national congress never convened. Too many conflicting interests existed among the two Yemeni groups, which foiled their respective patrons' efforts to reach a settlement.[36]

The Hashemite regime obtained legitimacy after years of being subjected to Nasir's subversion and abusiveness; Jordan's Ghor Canal project was endorsed, and Husain's receipt of Western military aid legitimized. On January 15, 1964, even before the conference had ended, Egypt and Jordan officially resumed diplomatic relations. The rapprochement between Husain and Nasir was confirmed in a "private" visit to Cairo paid by King Husain in March, enhancing the latter's respectability and stature in the Arab world. This seemed to have entailed a *quid pro quo* on the king's part that involved his facilitating Shuqairi's efforts to establish the PLO in late May. Moreover, in July 1964 Husain recognized the Republican regime in Yemen, to Saudi Arabia's chagrin. Yet the price of warmer relations with Egypt was soon to become hardly tolerable for Husain. On July 2, Shuqairi declared that the whole territory of Jordan's kingdom "was part of Palestine," provoking criticism from Jordanians and Palestinians alike. Husain made a second visit to Cairo, evidently to get Nasir to tame the PLO's energetic chairman who had already become anathema to Amman.[37]

The new chapter of inter-Arab relations was supplemented by Nasir's successful mediation efforts in the Morocco-Algeria border dispute—enabling Egypt to recall its 3,000 troops from Algeiria—and resumption of diplomatic relations between Rabat and Algiers. Diplomatic relations between Morocco and Tunisia, which had been broken off by Morocco following Tunisia's recognition of Mauritania, were also resumed after the first summit conference.[38]

Nonetheless, the obstacles confronting Nasir's "Unity of Action" strategy, particularly his acrimonious relations with Damascus and the unresolved Yemen war, stood in contrast to his rising stature in the Third World. In July 1964, Cairo was the venue of the first summit conference of the OAU since its establishment. As the host and leading speaker, Nasir appeared as a recognized spokesman of the nonaligned countries, urging his guests to mobilize their political influence against Israel, which he defined as a hostile, imperialistic, and racist element whose threat to Africa was equal to that of South Africa. A series of articles published on the eve of the second summit by Nasir's mouthpiece and *al-Ahram*'s editor, Heikal, provided an illuminating look at Nasir's disenchantment with the response of the Arab states to his "Unity of Action" strategy. Heikal confirmed the conditional nature of Nasir's truce with his rivals, which would be the main character trait of Egypt's inter-Arab policy until 1967. He castigated other Arab governments for their stands, accusing

Saudi Arabia, Lebanon, Jordan, and Syria of hampering implementation of the resolutions adopted at the first summit conference. Heikal argued that Saudi Arabia was continuing the Yemen war; Lebanon and Jordan were not cooperating on military standardization; and Syria's domestic instability was debilitating the entire Arab front. Heikal charged that Arab states were intervening excessively in the Palestinian issue. He cautioned that if more cooperation was not forthcoming in the spirit of the summit resolutions, Egypt would be forced to revert to the revolutionary policy it had practiced previously.[39]

Heikal's vehement warning coincided with Nasir's escalating tone of threat toward Israel and commitment to the liberation of Palestine, reiterated in Nasir's opening speech to the second summit conference. Egypt, he declared, had upgraded its economic and military strength and was enjoying considerable success in the international arena. The unmistakable implication was that Egypt's adversaries in the Arab world should adopt Cairo's line with regard to war with Israel—otherwise Egypt would find it impossible to cooperate with them concerning the other urgent questions on the agenda.[40]

The summits set in motion a shift in the pattern of regional Arab politics, from a zero-sum game, marked by inter-Arab struggle for hegemony, to a mixed-motives game, of cooperation in the conflict with Israel. This shift might have helped Nasir to postpone a risky entanglement in war with Israel, but not to prevent it. Championing the all-Arab effort against Israel was indeed the lesser evil if it ensured Nasir adequate cooperation from his Arab partners. In effect, however, Nasir embarked on a tiger's back, which would eventually lead him exactly to the disaster he wanted to avoid. The Arab response to Israel's water project may have been defensive and preparations for war may have never gotten off the ground. Israel, however, perceived the diversion plan as a potential Arab threat to its national security and would respond accordingly.[41]

Given the disputed inter-Arab relations, the adoption of the Palestine issue as the focus of collective Arab action triggered an escalating Arab hostility toward Israel, driven by the quest for Palestinian legitimacy. Nasir seemingly succeeded in defusing the risk of being entangled in an undesirable war, but had to adopt Damascus' militant line, defining "the liberation of Palestine" as the all-Arab national goal and war with Israel as inevitable. The centrality of the conflict with Israel in the Arab states system was further underlined in the two summits' calls for all Arab states to "regulate their political and economic relations with other countries in accordance with the policy of those countries toward the legitimate Arab struggle against Zionist designs in the Arab world." Thus, the Palestine conflict, as the Pan-Arab national "core issue," was to supersede and constrain the individual Arab states' sovereignty in shaping their own foreign relations according to their best particular interests. The incongruence of this principle with any Arab state's inclination to preserve its independent decision-making was soon to surface and aggravate inter-state Arab tensions.[42]

The summits' final communiques clearly meant to serve as an instrument for rallying the Arab states around all-Arab core values, primarily the Palestine conflict and the continued struggle against British imperialism. Hence the decisions to welcome the PLO's establishment as the "vanguard of the joint Arab struggle for the liberation of Palestine"; to denounce British imperialist rule in the southern Arabian Peninsula and to undertake to support liberation movements in Oman and South Yemen; to declare support for liberation movements in black Africa, and welcome Afro-Arab cooperation in the anti-imperialist struggle.

5

COLLAPSE OF SUMMITRY AND THE ROAD TO WAR

In 1965, the enthusiasm for summitry in inter-Arab relations gradually faded because of Nasir's frustrated expectations for cooperation with his Arab rivals, primarily over the Yemen war. By mid-1966, Nasir's conditional "truce" with the Arab conservative regimes came to an end, giving way to fierce ideological conflict. This renewed inter-Arab dispute, combined with Israeli-Arab military escalation, eventually led to the crisis of May–June 1967.

"Unity of Action" in Practice

Nasir's frustration stemmed from differences with his Arab partners over the implementation of summit resolutions on the diversion plan, the JAC, and the PLO. The shift of regional Arab politics to collective action on the Palestine conflict was intensified by the commencement of guerrilla warfare against Israel by Palestinian activist factions, challenging Nasir's concept of long-delayed decisive war. "Unity of Action" was no less frustrating inasmuch as it provided the Saudis an opportunity to consolidate their regional position at Nasir's expense. Nasir's credibility came under serious attack by his Arab rivals, monarchist and revolutionary alike, who exploited his difficulties to promote their own individual goals. What had been meant to be an excuse for inaction against Israel turned into a trap for Nasir.[1]

Two meetings of the Arab PMs' followup committee—held in Cairo in January and May 1965—failed to reach an agreement on implementation of the summits' resolutions concerning the Palestine conflict. The disputed items were deferred until the summit due to convene in Casablanca in September 1965, which meant that no joint Arab defensive measures could be taken in the meantime. This, however, did not preclude Syria from implementing its own agenda. Though it had originally rejected the Jordan diversion project, Syria began, in March 1965, actually working on it, with the obvious intention of provoking a military crisis and forcing Nasir to align with her. Armed clashes with Israel indeed broke out in March, May, and August 1965, leading to Syrian demands for Arab action on other fronts and for the creation of a joint

Arab deterrent force, to include air defense. Egypt, however, dismissed Syria's demands, declaring that only in the event of a direct Israeli threat to Syrian territory would it provide such military support.[2]

Expectedly, the Saudis lost no time exploiting Nasir's stand, and called on him to cease military intervention in Yemen in order to enhance Egypt's ability to defend the diversion project. Egypt's position became even more tenuous when Syria expressed its readiness to let Iraqi troops deploy on its territory as a staging ground prior to a possible move into Lebanon and Jordan. Damascus now supported the JAC commander's request that he be vested with the authority to order the transfer of Arab forces from one country to another in peacetime, and not only in a war situation. Syria also pressed for the establishment of new Arab defense instruments to meet the challenge posed by Israel— in addition to, or instead of, the ACSP—and allocation of Arab oil revenues for the liberation of Palestine. Moreover, at the PMs' meeting in May, Syria demanded evacuation of the UN peacekeeping forces from Sinai and the Gaza Strip to give Egypt the freedom to maneuver against Israel, arguing that Cairo would then be free to dispatch commando squads (*fida'iyyun*) to sabotage the INWC. Syria's demand was utterly rejected by Egypt as an unnecessary act which might provoke an Israeli attack against the unprepared Arab armies. Cairo argued that the UN force could be asked to withdraw from Sinai anytime Egypt wanted and meanwhile, it did not lessen the deterrent effect of the division-size Egyptian force deployed in Sinai.[3]

Syria found itself virtually isolated, confronted by an unholy coalition of Nasir and the conservative regimes determined to prevent war with Israel. The JAC, representing Egypt's stand, maintained that it could take no action since it lacked Jordanian and Lebanese cooperation and, in any case, its military preparations were not yet complete and international intervention would stop any fighting between Israel and the Arabs. Iraq's refusal to place its aircraft at the JAC's disposal, as well as Jordan's and Lebanon's reluctance to permit the deployment of Arab forces on their soil, lent credence to the JAC report. Meanwhile, funding for the diversion project lagged as oil-producing states complained that they were being asked to pay too large a share of the costs.[4]

In Yemen, hostilities resumed in November 1964 after a month-long cease-fire hammered out by Nasir and Faisal in Alexandria. The financial burden imposed on Egypt by its military commitment to Yemen grew crippling, as domestic economic problems were aggravated following a cutback in U.S. aid in early 1965 as a result of Nasir's policies both in Yemen and in the conflict with Israel. Although the aid was renewed in mid-1965—only to complete the 1962 agreement on three-year food aid to Egypt—Cairo-Washington relations grew hostile. In contrast to Egypt's strained relations with the United States, the latter increased its coordination with, and arms supplies to, Israel.[5]

The Arabs' inability to defend the diversion project from Israeli attacks, and Saudi and Syrian propaganda disparaging Egypt for this failure, made Nasir publicly question the wisdom of continuing his conciliatory regional Arab policy. Yet despite Egyptian complaints that Saudi Arabia was exploiting the summit spirit to undermine Egypt's standing, Nasir's message clearly reflected a quest for a settlement in Yemen that would put an end to the conflict. In a speech to the second PNC session in Gaza in late May 1965, Nasir admitted that the Arabs were unprepared for war against Israel and unable to defend the Jordan River diversion works, and that Arab joint action was difficult given mutual suspicions and inter-Arab rivalries. For the first time he drew a direct linkage between the presence of 50,000 Egyptian troops in Yemen and the Arab military weakness in confronting Israel. Nasir remained adamant in his objection to deploying Egyptian air force units in Syria, as the latter had requested, explaining that this might lead to accusations that he was seeking to subvert that regime. Nasir was willing to send such a force only on condition that it be fully independent and enjoy Egyptian protection. In a gesture toward Syria and the Palestinian guerrilla groups, Nasir admitted that Palestine would be liberated by revolution, not by speeches and conferences, calling on the Palestinians themselves to be the vanguard, albeit under Egypt's aegis. Despite his skepticism, Nasir clearly indicated his adherence to the Arab summit as the instrument for joint Arab action.[6]

The efforts to organize the Palestinians militarily showed progress, with PLA units taking shape in Iraq, Syria, and the Gaza Strip. In December 1964, Nasir, eager to demonstrate his support for the Palestinian cause, provided that the PLO would become the official political framework for the Palestinian inhabitants of Gaza. On March 15, 1965, the Gaza Legislative Council introduced conscription for Palestinians living there. Nasir's demonstrative action notwithstanding, it was perceived as a threatening precedent by Hashemite Jordan and Lebanon, which had opposed the recruitment of Palestinians in their territory for the PLA units. In addition, PLO broadcasts from Cairo against Hashemite Jordan aggravated the mistrust and tension between Husain and Shuqairi.[7]

Nasir's praise for the guerrilla groups and Shuqairi's tireless efforts to highlight the fighting character of the PLO and its role in the "liberation of Palestine," indicated the PLO's deteriorating prestige among both Palestinians and Arab masses. The regional conditions that gave birth to the PLO, and Shuqairi's controversial personality, doomed the organization's image by casting it as a hollow vessel that epitomized Arab inaction regarding the Palestine cause. The advent of the PLO expedited the rise of activist Palestinian groups whose "armed struggle" platform posed a moral and political challenge to Shuqairi. The guerrilla activity was carried out by Syria-based Palestinian groups, primarily Fatah, whose first sabotage action on Israeli soil took place on January 1, 1965. Syria's isolation in the Arab arena at this juncture was reflected in the hostile attitude of other Arab regimes—notably Jordan, Egypt, and Lebanon—toward Fatah as a Syrian instrument that threatened to drag them into war with Israel.[8]

Fatah was founded in 1959 as an independent Palestinian group led by Yasir 'Arafat. Its main purpose was to revive the Palestinian national identity and assert the centrality of the Palestinian people in the Arabs' campaign for the liberation of Palestine. Disenchanted with the Arab states' reluctance to resume fighting against Israel, and aware of their individual military and political constraints, Fatah's founding fathers adopted the concept of the "popular armed struggle" in which the Palestinians would be serving as the revolutionary vanguard. The vanguard's purpose was to ignite the Arab peoples' capabilities and dedication for war against Israel, serving as a "detonator" for the main charge. Fatah challenged the Nasirist assertion that Arab unity would lead to the liberation of Palestine. Instead, Fatah maintained, the popular armed struggle against Israel was the road to Arab unity; an ever-escalating process of (Palestinian) action and (Israeli) retaliation that would eventually tighten inter-Arab commitment and participation in the comprehensive struggle. Underlying Fatah's theory was the assumption that the Palestinians must entangle Arab states in war with Israel, even against their will.[9]

In 1963, Syria's Ba'th regime adopted the strategy of "popular armed struggle" as a means to enhance its domestic and inter-Arab legitimacy. The upshot was to call into question Nasir's efforts to postpone the war against Israel. The differences between Fatah and the PLO thus constituted a miniature copy of Syria-Egypt cleavage. Fatah's doctrine and practices aroused Jordan's and Lebanon's fears of Israeli retaliation, resulting in efforts to suppress Fatah's activity on their soil. Hence, Fatah would cable the summit conference in Casablanca, urging war against Israel forthwith and demanding a halt to the persecution of its personnel by "various Arab states." Cooperation with the PLO would take place on the battlefield alone, Fatah asserted, and not in offices or at conferences. Above all, the Palestinian struggle must be divorced from inter-Arab disputes.[10]

In addition to low prestige, the PLO also suffered from financial difficulties as Arab governments shirked their commitments to the PLO. The PLO scored a diplomatic success when, following Shuqairi's visit to the People's Republic of China in March 1965, the latter recognized the PLO as the representative of the Palestinian people and made a pledge of military aid, including arms and guerrilla warfare training. But Nasir's cold response to Shuqairi's achievement in China reconfirmed his perception of the PLO as a subordinate political instrument of Egypt's regional policy with no attributes of independence or armed capability. More suited to Nasir's Palestinian policy were such gestures as allowing the PLO to use Egyptian facilities for its "Voice of Palestine" broadcastings and to operate offices in Arab and Muslim capitals, as well as in New York.[11]

The West Germany and Bourguiba Affairs

Inter-Arab differences were exacerbated by two occurrences that touched on individual states' sovereignty in matters such as articulating unconventional attitudes toward Israel or conducting their own foreign policy on issues related to the Palestine conflict. The first was triggered by the decision of the Federal Republic of Germany (FRG) in February 1965 to establish diplomatic relations with Israel. At Egypt's initiative, the issue was placed on the ALC's agenda in an effort to forge collective Arab diplomatic pressure to dissuade the FRG.

Cairo's reaction was part of a previous controversy between Egypt and the FRG that had arisen in the wake of the latter's decision to grant Israel a $100 million worth of arms—as part of their reparations agreement. The arms deal faced strong criticism in the German Bundestag, prompting Egyptian diplomatic pressure on Bonn to cancel the deal. The FRG-Israel arms deal was welcomed by U.S. President Lyndon Johnson, reflecting his sympathy to Israel's defense needs in view of the Arab summits' military plans against her and the growing arms race between Israel and Egypt. Besides calling for an emergency meeting of the ALC, Nasir attempted to counter the FRG's policy toward Israel by inviting East Germany's leader Walter Ulbricht to Cairo. Whether this invitation was meant to serve as a bargaining chip in Nasir's diplomacy with the FRG or had been on the Egyptian agenda anyway, it proved instrumental in pressuring Bonn to cancel the arms deal with Israel, albeit while sustaining its commitment to finance Israeli arms procurement from other sources. To mitigate the blow to Israel, however, the FRG government announced its decision to establish diplomatic relations with Israel, provoking another confrontation with Egypt and other Arab states.[12]

Ulbricht's visit to Egypt deepened the Bonn-Cairo crisis, leading to the FRG's decision to sever economic relations with Egypt. The declaration adopted by the first two summit meetings, by which Arab states would determine their attitudes toward other states according to the other states' approach to the Arab-Israeli conflict, was now tested. An AL meeting held on March 9 in Cairo unanimously adopted Shuqairi's proposal to recommend that Arab governments sever relations with the FRG once it formally established diplomatic relations with Israel. Meanwhile, Arab states should recall their ambassadors from Bonn as a warning, and oil-producing states should notify clients that their oil supply would be cut off if they continued to aid Israel. However, when the Arab FMs met in mid-March to approve these resolutions, snags arose. Libya, Tunisia, and Morocco were the most vocal in their objections. Disagreement erupted over Egypt's call for an economic boycott of West Germany, and recognition of East Germany. Saudi Arabia and Libya, the two major suppliers of oil to West Germany refused to participate in the boycott. Supporting Egypt were Syria, Iraq, Sudan, Algeria, Kuwait, and Yemen. In Lebanon, Iraq, and Yemen, mobs were incited to go on the rampage against West German property. In the end, ten Arab states broke off relations with Bonn, but Saudi Arabia, Libya, Tunisia, and Morocco did not follow suit. To prevent a widening the rift with the FRG and exacerbating inter-Arab differences, Egypt decided to defer recognition of East Germany, and those Arab states that did sever relations with Bonn confined their move largely to the diplomatic sphere, maintaining business as usual on economic matters.[13]

Another dividing issue on the public Arab agenda erupted following Tunisia's President's public calls—beginning in March 1965—for a phased solution of the Palestinian problem. Bourguiba suggested that the Arabs accept the UNGA resolutions on partition of Mandatory Palestine into Arab and Jewish states (181) and on the return of the Arab refugees to their homes (194), and recognize Israel within the 1947 partition-plan boundaries. If Israel assented to these resolutions, the Arabs would recognize Israel's existence and could then raise new demands. If Israel rejected them, it would lose international support whereas the Arabs would gain morally and their use of force against Israel would be legitimized.[14]

Bourguiba's proposals generated fierce attacks, forcing him to adopt an apologetic attitude. In a message to Nasir in April 1965, he maintained that there was absolutely no difference between them with respect to the strategic goal of the struggle against Israel. Since the Arabs were unable to restore Palestine to its rightful owners by force, his proposal meant to break the political impasse while not excluding any future options. Nasir, however, remained hostile to Bourguiba and to his ideas, denouncing them as treasonous and a dangerous deviation from Pan-Arab nationalism.[15]

Bourguiba's pronouncements were discussed at an AL meeting in Cairo at the end of April 1965. Shuqairi accused the Tunisian president of treason and demanded Tunisia's expulsion from the AL. Taking a more moderate line, Syria, Egypt, and Iraq called for Bourguiba to be condemned on a personal basis, although Saudi Arabia, Lebanon, Morocco, and Kuwait objected even to this. The May 1965 meeting of the PMs' followup committee played down the issue, disregarded Shuqairi's proposals and contented itself with rejecting the Tunisian president's approach. Uppermost in the PMs' minds was the maintenance of inter-Arab cooperation, which could collapse if an Arab leader was condemned—even if he had violated the Pan-Arab consensus on non-recognition of Israel. Shuqairi protested the inaction by walking out of the conference.[16]

Unmollified, Bourguiba boycotted the Casablanca summit conference and circulated a memorandum among its participants arguing that his position stemmed from the first summit's resolutions, Arab military weakness, and realpolitik. Bourguiba also launched a scathing attack on Nasir's emotional and fanatic Pan-Arab policy, blaming him for the deep divisions in the Arab world. The summit ignored the memorandum, which asserted that Tunisia would boycott Arab summit meetings as long as the AL remained an instrument in Cairo's efforts to gain hegemony in the Arab world.[17]

Bourguiba's suggestions, that the Palestine problem should be addressed pragmatically and that the Palestinians should establish their own government-in-exile, coincided with the rationale that guided Fatah's founders. Unlike Fatah, however, Bourguiba's estimate of Arab limited capabilities led him to resort to a diplomatic option rather than an armed struggle. Bourguiba's initiative meant to exploit the summitry atmosphere by suggesting an alternative to Nasir's doctrine of total confrontation with Israel, which Nasir himself considered unrealistic. Underlining the fierce ideological debate triggered by the Tunisian President was the conflict between Nasir's compulsive version of Pan-Arabism and Bourguiba's state particularism. Bourguiba's concept of a phased struggle against Israel would be officially adopted by the Arab summits following the 1973 war. But in 1965 the Arab world was not yet ready for it, least of all Nasir, who had already been on the defensive in the face of Arab adversaries. Pressured by Syria to commit himself to war against Israel, Nasir could not but fiercely attack Bourguiba's ideas and reconfirm the summit's plans in order to preserve his all-Arab leadership, credibility, and prestige. By ignoring Bourguiba's memorandum—though their own opinions might have been virtually identical to Bourguiba's—Arab leaders showed that they were united on removing all controversial issues from their collective agenda.[18]

The Jidda Agreement and "Arab Solidarity Charter"

In August 1965, prompted by a deteriorating economy, military defeats of the Yemeni Republicans, and American pressure on both Cairo and Riyad to reach a compromise, Nasir arrived in Jidda for talks with King Faisal. That Nasir was willing to meet with the Saudi monarch on the latter's home ground afforded further evidence of Nasir's difficulties. His visit to Jidda was unmistakably designed to prevent a discussion of the Yemen war at the summit conference scheduled to convene within less than a month, and to preserve the atmosphere of inter-Arab truce. On August 24, the two leaders signed an agreement, arranging a cease-fire and scheduling a plebiscite in Yemen no later than November 23, 1966, to determine that country's form of government.

Under the agreement's terms, Saudi Arabia would cease military aid to the Royalists and would not permit attacks on the Yemeni government to be launched from Saudi territory. Egypt, for its part, would begin withdrawing its forces from Yemen in September 1965 and complete their evacuation before the date set for the plebiscite. The two sides also agreed on a conference of fifty members, representing various sectors in Yemen, to convene at Harad on November 23, 1965, and decide how the country would be ruled during the interim period until the plebiscite was held. Saudis and Egyptians were to form a joint peace commission to supervise the process and oversee the cease-fire. Riyad got the better of the Jidda Agreement, as Egypt dropped its earlier prerequisite that the principle of a republican regime be accepted and the royal family be excluded. The agreement was welcomed by the two superpowers and most Arab states, although Damascus accused Nasir of "murdering the Yemeni revolution."[19]

The Jidda agreement eventually failed, mainly because the signatories were unable to deliver their warring Yemeni clients. It did, however, produce a spirit of accord in the Casablanca summit meeting that opened on September 14, even though it left the main disputed issues on the agenda unresolved. The standstill that marked Arab "Unity of Action" was manifested in the reports presented to the summit by the ALSG Hassuna, the JAC's Commander-in-Chief, and PLO chairman Shuqairi. General 'Amir reiterated his request to enable the entry of Saudi and Iraqi forces into Jordan and Lebanon, which still objected strenuously. As a result, Saudi and Iraqi expeditionary forces were obliged to deploy outside Jordan, increasing the distance they would have to travel and heightening the risk of coming under air attacks by Israel once they started moving. Shuqairi renewed his military and financial demands, stressing that Palestine could be liberated only by military force. He called for the establishment of PLA units in Jordan and Lebanon and a general conscription of Palestinians in the Arab states to form additional units.

The Arab leaders' willingness to attend a summit conference despite their disputes indicated that their priority was to preserve the inter-Arab truce rather than forge radical solutions to the problems besetting Arab "Unity of Action" for Palestine. Particularly for Nasir, the summit's rationale was to rid himself of the pressure to go to war and leave him free to concentrate on Egypt's domestic affairs. On the eve of the summit he warned his Arab counterparts not to turn the summit into an outbidding (*muzayada*) stage that would nullify its chances to produce practical decisions. Reflecting his dire domestic and inter-Arab straits, he warned that in such case the UAR would withdraw from the summit and carry on "its national historic responsibility alone." At a formal visit by King Faisal to Cairo on his way to Casablanca, Nasir reasserted his view that the option of war against Israel was absolutely unrealistic, and complained about those Arab regimes who had turned Palestine and the war against Israel into a matter of rhetorical competition.[20]

At the summit itself, Nasir established a compromising tone by expressing appreciation for the fact that the meeting had actually taken place as scheduled, adding, however, that efforts to implement the previous summits' resolutions were inadequate. Despite Nasir's conciliatory tone, a clash was touched off at the very outset by Shuqairi's military and financial demands and complaints about the Arab states' indifference to the Palestine problem. Since none of the thirteen AL states had contributed its full share for creating the PLA, and Jordan, Kuwait, Lebanon, Libya, and Morocco had entirely reneged on their financial commitments to the PLO, he recommended a tax on Arab oil-producing states. The Arab states ignored the Palestinians' needs for employment and housing, and prevented the PLA's freedom of operation. Hence, Shuqairi urged that the PLO be permitted to hold elections among the Palestinians in the Arab states for the PNC, which, in turn, would produce a leadership with authority over Palestinians throughout the Arab world. Both motions were rejected, and so was Shuqairi's request to establish another seven commando battalions. Spearheading the opposition was Saudi Arabia, which questioned the PLO's financial conduct. Criticism of the PLO was also sounded by the new Algerian leader, Houari Boumedienne, veering away from his predecessor Ben-Bella's constant backing of Egypt. Boumedienne downgraded the PLO and supported Fatah's guerrilla warfare against Israel.[21]

The summit's most acrimonious dispute, however, involved the Jordan waters diversion project and the means to defend it. Syria's President al-Hafiz lashed out at Nasir for doing nothing in this regard and charged the JAC with being Nasir's tool. He argued that the Arabs could defeat Israel with forty brigades and urged that they should lose no time in this respect. Nonetheless, he pointed to the high rate of military spending in his country's budget and demanded that the oil-producing states share this burden. General 'Amir informed the conference that the forces under the JAC command would require millions of dollars' worth of equipment, as well as four years of preparation, before they could be committed to war against Israel. 'Amir also acknowledged that Syria, Lebanon, and Jordan were unable to pursue the water diversion project because the JAC could not yet provide adequate protection against Israel.[22]

Lebanon and Jordan held fast to their refusal to allow Syrian and Iraqi troops, respectively, on their territory. In response, Iraqi President 'Arif announced unilaterally that his country's expeditionary force, deployed since 1964 close to Jordan's border, would withdraw to its bases. Despite their reluctance regarding the JAC requests, Jordan and Lebanon requested additional Arab undertakings for local irrigation projects outside the framework of the original water diversion plan. The deadlocked deliberations led to bitter bickering and mutual recriminations. Nasir accused both Syria and Jordan of encouraging the Muslim Brothers and of backing their attempts to undermine his regime. A fierce row also broke out between the Iraqi and Syrian leaders over their own propaganda war. Intensifying the friction, news arrived during the meeting of an abortive military coup in Iraq, led by Brigadier 'Arif 'Abd al-

Raziq, who fled to Cairo, resulting in a hasty return of Iraq's President to his country.[23]

After three days of protracted debate, the Arab heads of state managed to hammer out an "Arab Solidarity Charter" designed to put an end to the media warfare and demonstrate Arab unity, all in the name of the ensuing Arab battle for the liberation of Palestine. Drawn up by Sudan's PM Muhammad Mahjub, the document was the product of intensive behind-the-scenes mediatory efforts. Under the Charter's terms, the signatories undertook to respect the sovereignty and existing regimes of other Arab states, to refrain from interference in their domestic affairs, and to "preserve the rules and norms of political game according to the principles of international law and custom." Short-lived as it was, the Arab Solidarity Charter reasserted the core principles that had underpinned the AL foundation, formalizing the departure from Nasir's revolutionary "Unity of Purpose." Epitomizing the ascendancy of the Arab state over Pan-Arab commitments was the decision to restrict the PLO's freedom of action, making it contingent on the good will of the countries where the PLO operated. The Charter tacitly rejected enlarging the PLA or introducing conscription for Palestinians in Jordan and Lebanon.[24]

Underlying the charter was the oil-producing countries' commitment to finance arms procurement by Jordan and Syria as well as the building of military infrastructure in these countries. Jordan and Lebanon would receive financial aid for strictly local irrigation projects which had been acceptable to Israel as well. It was decided that three years was the minimum span of time needed to accomplish military parity with Israel, on condition that the latter's power would not increase by then. Yet despite Nasir's indication that the summit's results would enable the Arab armies to shift from defense to offense in the Palestine conflict, using the term "elimination of Israel," the main result was another postponement of war with Israel.[25]

Indeed, the summit was a success in terms of building consensus and realpolitik, using financial and political tradeoffs to bridge inter-Arab differences. The Charter prioritized the maintenance of an inter-state Arab conciliatory atmosphere at the expense of the Arabs' official goals: diversion of the Jordan waters and preparation for war against Israel. The Arab heads of state acknowledged that their hands were tied and confrontation with Israel was to be deferred, in theory, until the JAC could complete military preparations. Even the Syrian Ba'th Party's spokesman stated that his country viewed war with Israel as neither feasible nor desirable in the near future. The freedom of decision accorded to Arab states as to implementation of the diversion project was tantamount to a cessation of the work, at least in areas prone to a military retaliation. Consequently, the need to station Arab forces in Syria, Jordan, or Lebanon no longer existed. In a final analysis, then, the Arab leaders found themselves accepting the main point made by Bourguiba in his memorandum: that the Palestine problem was not at this time amenable to a military solution.[26]

The summit's main loser was the PLO. Shuqairi's request for additional funding was cynically responded to by applying a tax on the Palestinians themselves throughout the Arab world—between three and six percent of their income. Not only were all his requests to extend the PLO's freedom of action turned down, but prospects for joint Arab military action against Israel seemed more remote than ever. The new charter lessened the likelihood that a war against Israel could be induced by pitting one Arab state against the other in a competition for militancy. That the summit approved a joint action plan for dealing with Palestinian affairs at the UN was consistent with the general Arab tendency to lower the PLO's profile of activities while demonstrating moral commitment to its cause. Shuqairi's bitter lesson of the summit was that this forum was sinking into the same dangerous routine that had caused the demise of the AL in all but name and that the PLO must be liberated before the liberation of Palestine.[27]

The international realm—primarily regarding Afro-Asian affairs—was tackled by the conference communique on its own merits, not necessarily within the Arab or Arab-Israeli context. Strikingly absent from the resolutions was any mention of the principle that Arab relations with other countries would be based on the latter's attitudes on the Palestinian issue—a point that had been designed to discourage Western powers from aiding Israel. This omission might have indicated Nasir's recognition of his limited coercive power over Arab states' foreign policies in light of his experience with the FRG case. Perhaps Nasir also wished to show moderation toward the United States, hoping for a renewal of American economic aid to his country.[28]

Inter-Arab Polarization and the Road to War

The atmosphere of accord that marked the conclusion of the Casablanca summit was short-lived. Gradually, old rivalries and conflicts reasserted themselves and inter-Arab relations reverted to their troubled pre-summitry nature. The change was determined by Nasir's declining interest in a truce with the conservative regimes, giving way to the latent enmity between revolutionary and conservative regimes. In addition, Nasir's new approach represented a rapprochement with the leftist Ba'th regime that had taken power in Syria in February 1966, culminating in the signing of a joint Egyptian-Syrian defense pact that November.[29]

The renewal of Nasir-Faisal rift was caused by the collapse of the Jidda Agreement and Faisal's effort to enhance his regional stature through convening a conference of conservative-Islamic states. The realization of the Jidda agreement was impeded by the Yemeni clients, who had not been consulted on the assumption that they would accept whatever accord was concluded between their respective patrons. Neither of the disputed Yemeni parties was willing to consider deference to and acceptance of its rival's concept of political regime, rendering the gap between the Royalists and the Republicans unbridgeable. Thus, the Harad conference stipulated by the Jidda agreement was indeed held in December 1965, but soon reached a deadlock and never reconvened.[30]

Cairo and Riyad failed to bridge the gaps between their Yemeni proteges, entrenching instead in their clients' positions. The Saudis demanded an expeditious withdrawal of the Egyptian forces from Yemen. Nasir, while committed in principle to withdraw his forces from Yemen, was unwilling to implement it before a transitional government was formed, ensuring the republican regime's survival. Before the end of 1965 the Saudis had already ceased to participate in the joint "Peace Commission." In March 1966, Nasir effectively cancelled his agreement with Faisal by announcing that Egypt's army was ready to remain in Yemen "even for five years" and threatening to attack Saudi Arabia.[31]

Nasir's alleged readiness to remain in Yemen might have been influenced by Britain's announcement in February that it would evacuate the Aden military base by 1968. Yet what underlined Nasir's declaration was mainly opposition to the Saudi monarch's initiative to convene an Islamic summit conference in Mecca, for which he had toured several Middle Eastern Muslim states, including Jordan, Iran, and Turkey, as of December 1965. The participants in this conference were to be Western-oriented Arab regimes as well as Iran and Turkey—major non-Arab actors and America's allies, who maintained diplomatic relations with Israel. The undeclared purpose of Faisal's efforts was believed to be the consolidation of a regional conservative bloc based on Islamic identity, under his leadership and with American backing.[32]

Nasir viewed Faisal's move as an attempt to forge an anti-revolutionary and pro-Western alliance, in the guise of a Muslim-oriented organization, that meant to ruin his own Arab leadership and challenge his revolutionary ethos. Faisal's clarifications that his efforts were intended to include revolutionary regimes as well failed to convince Nasir, whose political perceptions at this juncture became increasingly shaped by fears of a well-designed American effort to besiege him. On February 22, Nasir compared Faisal's initiative to the Baghdad Pact. In the next month, Nasir warned that Egypt was on the verge of suspending its summitry policy and returning to "Unity of Purpose," advocating joint Arab action.[33]

Underlying Nasir's growing sense of an American-based political and strategic siege on Egypt was a series of developments in early 1966, all of which seemed detrimental to Egypt's national interests. Faisal's initiative of the Islamic conference was followed by the announcement of a British-American $400 million arms deal with Saudi Arabia in early 1966. The lingering American response to Egypt's request for a long-term commitment on surplus food supplies, which ultimately generated only a six-month agreement in early 1966; the IMF's refusal to Egypt's request for a $70 million loan; a growing Israeli-Iranian economic and strategic cooperation; and evident coordination between President Johnson's administration and Israel. Washington's growing alienation toward Cairo and support of Nasir's rivals were perceived in Cairo as a collusion designed to "unleash" Israel and other Middle East allies against Egypt and Syria. The fall of leading nonaligned leaders, such as Sukarno of Indonesia and Nkrumah of Ghana, is also said to have added to Nasir's sense of a Western collusion against him. Whether Nasir genuinely perceived this series of events as a hostile American-based master plan to defeat him, or merely used it to explain his inaction toward Israel and the new ideological warfare against the conservative regimes, is not clear. Conceivably, Nasir's attitude in this respect might also have been influenced by Soviet concern at the U.S. attempt to bolster its position in the region.[34]

A new test confronted Nasir with the rise to power in Damascus of the Syrian Ba'th party's leftist wing in February 1966, following a coup that deposed Amin al-Hafiz and ousted the party's historic leadership of 'Aflaq, Bitar, and Razzaz. The new Syrian regime demanded an immediate militant struggle against both Israel and the Arab "reactionary" regimes, posing a new challenge to Nasir's regional policy. On the other hand, Damascus also sought legitimacy from Nasir as well as protection from Israel, and indicated its desire to cooperate with the Egyptian leader provided he gave proof of his revolutionary attitude and desisted from cooperation with the conservative regimes. To force Nasir to radicalize his policy toward the Arab monarchies, the Syrians provoked frequent armed clashes on the border with Israel and actively assisted Palestinian sabotage operations against Israeli targets. Damascus vociferously encouraged the PLO and fiercely attacked the rulers of Jordan, Saudi Arabia, and Iraq.[35]

The growing enmity between Nasir and Faisal had a direct impact on Egypt-Jordan relations given the latter's support of Faisal and the counterrevolutionary forces in Yemen. Another source of animosity in Cairo-Amman relations was Jordan's continued reluctance to implement the JAC's plans while misusing the funds it provided. Thus, despite the financial aid Jordan had received from the JAC to purchase Soviet MIG aircraft, Amman announced on April 2, 1966, its intention to acquire more costly American planes, which in fact had been given Jordan for nothing. Jordan's intensifying rift with Shuqairi was another dividing cause between Nasir and King Husain. In February, Nasir expressed support for the Palestinian people's right to wage their own war of liberation without Arab interruption, though Egypt itself continued to block such activity from its own territory. Nasir's verbal attacks on Jordan aggravated the already uneasy relations between the Hashemite regime and the PLO.

In June 1966, Husain declared that he was breaking off cooperation with the PLO because of its interference in Jordan's internal affairs. Shuqairi responded with a barrage of verbal attacks, accusing the king of violating all the summit resolutions; seeking to erase the Palestinian identity and liquidate the Palestinian problem; and blaming the Hashemites for all the Arab nation's troubles, including the loss of Palestine.[36]

The confrontation between Husain and the PLO intensified following massive arrests of the latter's members in Jordan. Amman's efforts to repress Fatah's activity in the West Bank caused a growing tension with Damascus. In June, Syria and the PLO declared that toppling Husain was a precondition for the liberation of Palestine. Tension mounted in September 1966, when Jordan gave sanctuary to the Druze General Salim Hatum, following his abortive coup attempt against the Ba'th regime in Damascus. Nasir's deteriorating relations with Riyad and Amman culminated in his call on July 22, 1966, for the indefinite postponement of all future summit meetings, cancelling the one scheduled for September in Algiers. Instead of helping the cause of Palestine, Nasir explained, the meetings had let Arab reactionary regimes attack revolutionary ones. Cairo, he stated, would no longer cooperate with regimes antagonistic to his stance, insisting that the liberation of Palestine required a revolutionary solution to be carried out by revolutionary regimes. To demonstrate his readiness to renew the war in Yemen, Nasir allowed the Yemeni Republican leader, 'Abdallah al-Sallal, to return to San'a, after having been held in Cairo under house arrest for nearly a year. No sooner had al-Sallal arrived in San'a than he overthrew the government, which had conducted talks with the Royalists.[37]

Syria's vituperative attacks on Jordan were echoed by Nasir, although the Egyptian media refrained from denouncing Husain personally until early September. On December 23, Nasir himself took the lead, asserting that because Husain, Faisal, and Bourguiba were ready to sell out the Arab nation—as King 'Abdallah had done in 1948—they were untrustworthy and should be barred from taking part in any summit conference. Nasir's renewed hostility to the Saudi regime was now indicated also by the refuge he gave to the deposed king, Sa'ud. Nasir's excoriation of King Husain as "the Jordanian whore" (*al-'ahir al-urduni*) in February 1967 proved too much, and Jordan recalled its ambassador to Cairo.[38]

In late 1966 and early 1967, three high-ranking inter-Arab meetings were held, highlighting the renewed animosity between radicals and conservatives. The meetings drew a gloomy picture of the Arab states' joint action and preparations for war: Arab states had misused funds allocated for the diversion plan and the JAC and had failed to live up to their financial pledges for the joint projects, including the PLO, which had virtually ground to a halt.[39] Above all, the March 1967 JAC report to Nasir emphasized the poor defensive capability of the Arab states, warning that in case of an Israeli offensive, "Arab lands in the countries surrounding Israel will be in danger of loss." This was echoed by Nasir's own repeated warnings as late as May 15, 1967, against entering a "premature war."[40]

Ironically, the collapse of previous summit decisions and instruments seemed all the more discernible as tension on Israel's borders with Syria and Jordan rose. The tension stemmed mainly from Palestinian sabotage actions and Israeli retaliations, and Syrian-Israeli artillery and air battles. Thus, Israel's wide-scale punitive raid on the village of Samu', south of Hebron, in November, aggravated inter-Arab recriminations and revealed the absence of common Arab action. Jordan charged that the JAC had failed to come to its aid, while Egypt pressed at the ADC meeting in December for the admission of Iraqi and Saudi forces into Jordan. Amman, however, evaded the decision and linked its implementation to completion of the Arab defense plan, withdrawal of the UNEF from Sinai and of the Egyptian forces from Yemen, which would free Egypt's hands to defend Jordan, and reception of the financial aid pledged to it. In December, the Saudis announced that given the cancellation of the scheduled fourth summit conference, they were dropping their financial support for war preparations against Israel and for the AL's administrative machinery.[41]

The following ADC session in March 1967 decided in the absence of Jordan and Saudi Arabia, which boycotted the session, to freeze economic aid to Jordan. The decision was a severe blow to the JAC, which had been portrayed by its CoS 'Amir as a "dangerous illusion." The growing hostility between the Saudi and Jordanian monarchs and the radicals was expressed in the former's attacks against Shuqairi as Nasir's protege. Since the end of 1966, calls for Shuqairi's replacement had been voiced by King Faisal and President Bourguiba who charged that by his outrageous abuse of various Arab leaders, the PLO chief was seriously undermining Arab solidarity. The ALC's session in March 1967, however, resolved to express support for Shuqairi and to condemn Jordan.[42]

The escalating military tension between Israel and Syria following the coup of February 1966, amid a continued domestic military and party factional struggle for power in Damascus, was a source of concern to Cairo and Moscow. Syria's military weakness and Nasir's determination to refrain from being dragged into war with Israel led to Soviet-Egyptian consultations about a way to offset the dangers latent in Syria's policy. In a visit to Cairo in May 1966, Soviet PM Kosygin apparently convinced Nasir to meet the Syrians halfway. The consequent rapprochement between Cairo and Damascus culminated in resumption of their diplomatic relations and the signing of a mutual defense pact in November. Nasir's effort to incorporate Iraq into this pact failed due to the schism between Damascus and Baghdad. But if the Egypt-Syria defense pact was designed to mitigate the latter's militancy and fears and provide Nasir with some control over Damascus' military moves through the pact's instruments, the May–June 1967 crisis showed that it turned into a trap for Nasir. Damascus persisted in encouraging Palestinian guerrilla activity against Israel, rejecting Cairo's offer to deploy its air force units on Syrian soil, and demanding that Egypt end the UNEF presence in Sinai.[43]

The February 1966 coup in Syria aggravated the schism between Damascus and Baghdad, with Syria's neo-Ba'th regime assailing the Iraqi leadership for lacking sufficient revolutionary fervor. Relations between Baghdad and Damascus deteriorated further as a result of the rapprochement between Cairo and Damascus and the anti-Ba'th coup of 'Arif. In December, Syria sealed off the oil pipeline of the Iraq Petroleum Company (IPC), which ran from northern Iraq to the Mediterranean and on which the Iraqis depended for half their oil exports. The Syrian action was directed against the Western-owned IPC, seeking to force it to pay higher royalties for oil piped across Syrian territory. The three-month crisis demonstrated Syria's utter disregard of Iraqi interests, as Baghdad's loss of royalties was about ten times that sustained by Damascus.[44]

Just as the internecine strife among the Arab states seemed to have reached the crisis point, the Middle East political scene was dramatically altered by heightened military tension between Israel and Syria. This was sparked by a series of guerrilla sabotage raids by Syrian-backed Palestinian groups led by Fatah, and exacerbated by repeated artillery battles along the border, culminating on April 7, when six Syrian fighters were shot down in a wide-scale air battle that brought Israeli jets over Damascus. This, and Israeli loud threats to take a large-scale action against Syria because of its backing for the guerrilla operations, aggravated the latter's fears of war. Combined with Soviet reports that Israel had allegedly massed forces for a broad-based offensive against Syria, the escalation led Nasir to move, rather demonstratively, Egyptian troops into Sinai on May 14, 1967. Nasir's abrupt action set in motion a rapid escalation to the brink of war and beyond, culminating in a total Arab-Israeli confrontation.[45]

Nasir's moves ran counter to the position he had enunciated at every summit meeting: that war with Israel must be postponed until the Arabs attained strategic superiority. Moreover, the high Egyptian command had been informed by the CoS's eyewitness report that there were no Israeli troop concentrations, though it remains unclear whether this information reached Nasir or his deputy, 'Amir.[46] Evidently, Nasir's estimate as to Egypt's military readiness for war against Israel had remained unchanged even when Jordan and Iraq joined the military siege against Israel. Nasir had apparently adopted a defensive approach throughout the crisis, despite the order given to the forces in Sinai to start an offensive on May 27, which was postponed at Washington's and the Kremlin's urgent appeals to refrain from hostilities. Despite his deliberate escalation of the crisis, Nasir adhered to what he perceived as a defensive strategy, hoping to end the crisis without war, through the Powers' diplomatic involvement. Indeed, the Egyptian buildup in Sinai lacked a clear offensive plan and Nasir's defensive instructions explicitly assumed an Israeli first strike.[47]

It has been argued that Nasir's decisions in the crisis were at least partly motivated by his concern over Israel's nuclear program reflected in warnings—already proclaimed in December 1960—that the Arabs would go to war to prevent Israel from obtaining a nuclear weapon. This argument draws primarily on the Eyptians' two reconnaissance flights over the Dimona reactor in May 1967, following their massive deployment in Sinai.[48] Israel's nuclear capability was indeed discussed at the Arab PMs' meeting in March 1966, reflecting Arab—and American—estimates that Israel could produce a nuclear weapon within two to three years. Between February 1966 and February 1967, with Egypt's missile program halted due to economic constraints, Nasir repeatedly spoke of a "preemptive war" as an inevitable measure to prevent Israeli nuclear capability.[49] While Nasir's proclamations to this effect can be seen as an indivisible part of the growing inter-Arab schism and his wish to rally the Arab regimes around his leadership, it still remains unclear what was the role, if any, of the nuclear factor in the escalation to the June 1967 war. If the Dimona reactor played any role in the May–June crisis, why was it never mentioned by Nasir in his diplomatic contacts with the American administration during that period?[50]

Whatever prompted Nasir's decisions, they cannot be divorced from his declining leadership in the Arab world. This ongoing process was fraught with serious implications not only for his personal prestige but also for Egypt's tottering economic situation. His initial decisions to pour his forces into Sinai and request the removal of the UNEF may have assumed that by creating an apparent threat to Israel he could restore his prestige and profit politically without a bullet's being fired. But Nasir's decisions in May 1967 resembled a spiral series of self-compelled acts dictated by high expectations placed on his leadership by the Arab world. Indeed, contrary to the Israeli estimate that its accelerating pressure on Syria would not drag Egypt into the fray, Nasir was obliged to implement his defense commitment to Syria in order to preserve his prestige and credibility. Yet, once he made the first step of introducing forces into Sinai, he found himself obliged by inflamed popular Arab militancy and rising expectations for his leadership to commit the next step, ever-escalating the danger of war. Hence, to lend credibility to the influx of forces into Sinai he was compelled to remove the UNEF from the border, especially in view of his Arab adversaries' long-standing demand in this regard. Once Egyptian soldiers deployed in Sharm al-Shaikh, the strategic southeast tip of Sinai controlling the waterway to Eilat, Nasir found himself obliged to declare a blockade on Israeli navigation through the Straits of Tiran, which to Israel constituted a *casus belli*. Israel's initial response to the massing of Egyptian forces in Sinai might have been interpreted as hesitant, encouraging Nasir to raise the threshold of risk of confrontation, while in fact it reflected an estimate that Nasir meant only a demonstration of power as he had in 1960.[51]

Yet if Nasir believed that Israel's threats against Damascus were a reflection of an American-Israeli premeditated collusion ultimately aimed at him, as suggested by Heikal, his decisions turned his belief into a self-fulfilling prophecy. Nasir headed to the brink of war without having any specific political goal save deterring Israel from attacking Syria. Memoirs of Egyptian figures cast doubt on Nasir's control of the decision-making process that led to the May–June crisis. These sources indicate a hidden power struggle and a mistrust between Nasir and his deputy, 'Abd al-Hakim 'Amir, who is said to have been seeking a military confrontation with Israel, and whose uninterrupted authority as the Commander in-Chief of Egypt's armed forces limited Nasir's information and control of the military scene.[52]

Since late 1966, 'Amir had been the leading advocate of removing the UNEF from Sinai, as the UNEF presence had hampered Egypt's inter-Arab legitimacy, although Nasir too toyed with that option. Yet Egypt's request to the UN on 16 May to remove the UNEF from the border with Israel intended to leave its presence in Gaza and Sharm al-Shaikh intact, purposely to limit the risks of escalation that such a step entailed. However, the appeal to the UN was marked by miscommunication and misperception within the Egyptian innermost circle, which led to the total withdrawal of the UNEF from Egyptian soil. The Egyptian decisions between May 14 and 22 seem to have been designed to respond to a specific problem, though without being prepared for the worst-case scenario that those decisions, especially the blockade on the Straits of Tiran, invited.[53]

Nasir's moves from May 14 on had an immediate effect throughout the Arab world, generating militant enthusiasm that could not be easily contained. Never had Nasir's prestige been more overwhelming: a rapprochement between Iraq and Egypt on the one hand, and Iraq and Syria on the other, was followed—immediately after the closure of the Straits of Tiran—by declarations of support from Jordan and Tunisia, both urging that past disputes be forgotten, and Tunisia also rescinded its boycott of the AL. Even King Faisal asserted that inter-Arab quarrels would not prevent the formation of a united Arab stand against the Israeli threat.[54]

The crisis led Nasir to declare on May 28 that "the issue today is not the problem of 'Aqaba, or the Strait of Tiran, or UNEF. The problem is the rights of the Palestinian people. . . . We claim the rights of the Palestinian people in their entirety." On May 30, Nasir's soaring prestige led to King Husain's surprising visit to Cairo during which he signed a defense pact with Nasir, which Iraq joined a few days later. The king now gave his full consent to deployment of Iraqi forces in his country and, at Nasir's urging, a reconciliation was effected between him and Shuqairi. Husain requested that Nasir appoint an Egyptian general as commander of the Jordanian front. But none of this could induce Syria or Algeria to change their attitude toward Husain. The Syrians acquiesced reluctantly in the Nasir-Husain agreement under which Damascus became, without having been consulted, an indirect party. Husain's sudden crossing of all his "red lines" of the previous three years regarding entanglement in war with Israel stemmed from the growing domestic agitation and pressure on him, particularly from Palestinians. This pressure, and the growing prospect of war, left the king with no choice but to join Nasir and share responsibility with him for any future results of the crisis.[55]

The growing momentum of the Arab war coalition under a joint command and the arrival of expeditionary forces from Egypt and Iraq in Jordan tightened the all-Arab siege on Israel and, with a declared call for the "recovery of the plundered land of Palestine," posed a threat to Israel's very existence. The closure of the Strait of Tiran resulted in the full mobilization of Israeli reserve forces which, given its devastating effect on the economy, meant that unless the Arab siege was removed, an Israeli offensive would be inevitable. Fruitless international efforts to end the crisis, and a vague American message of understanding for an Israeli preemptive action, led up to Israel's surprising attack on June 5, 1967. Within six days, Israeli forces captured Sinai, the West Bank, Gaza Strip, and the Golan Hights.

The wave of Arab solidarity during the crisis led to an unprecedented resolution by the Arab oil ministers, on June 4–5, to impose an oil boycott on every country supporting Israel or adversely affecting Arab interests. Yet the resolution had no solid economic or political basis. As soon as its economic cost became apparent, the oil producers backtracked. Within less than a week, Saudi Arabia resumed oil exports—except to the United States and Britain—quickly followed by Kuwait, Iraq, and Libya. As of late June, Arab oil producers led by Saudi Arabia began to call for the revocation of the boycott.[56]

Interim Summary

Nasir's summitry initiative was a major, if temporary, shift in the form and substance of inter-Arab politics as they had been ever since the mid-1950s. Nasir's "Unity of Action" against Israel was a preemptive measure by escalation, reflecting his narrowing options for securing his regional stature. Bogged down in Yemen and challenged by the conservative regimes, Nasir was under Syrian threat to entangle him in a war with Israel for which he was not prepared, or sustain a serious blow to his all-Arab leadership. "Unity of Action" represented a conditional retreat from the revolutionary "Unity of Purpose." The joint Arab plan of action for the sake of Palestine was an alternative rallying theme to serve Nasir's thrust for regional hegemony and legitimacy, but also a device to save him from an untimely war against Israel.

Nasir's regional policy attested to the intolerable burden of being a champion and living symbol of Pan-Arabism and, at the same time, a head of state with limited capabilities. He had to brandish the sword against Israel and yet preach restraint; to collaborate with the Arab monarchs but keep threatening them with resumption of his revolutionary policy. This ambivalence enabled Syria to hoist the banner of war against Israel and question Nasir's legitimacy and claim for Pan-Arab leadership, which eventually forced him to adopt Syria's own regional policy. Nasir's failure to maintain strict control of the joint Arab plan through inter-Arab financial and political tradeoffs resulted from the turbulent nature of domestic and inter-Arab politics. His conditional truce with Saudi Arabia failed to produce a solution to the Yemen war and underpinned the Saudi effort to challenge his regional standing. The Yemen war overburdened Egypt's economy and strained relations with the United States while Syria—and after 1965, Algeria and other Arab radical states as well—attacked Nasir's vacillation about war against Israel and his alignment with the "reaction."

The net result of this dynamics, exacerbated by Israel's military response to the Arab diversion works and guerrilla activity, was Nasir's return to his "Unity of Purpose," indicating a tightening commitment to involve himself in the conflict with Israel. Despite improved relations with the Soviet Union and a growing arms supply, Nasir was obsessed with the need to redeem his declining leadership. In responding to the Soviet alarm concerning Syria in mid-May 1967, Nasir was apparently tempted to take a calculated risk of deterring Israel, which dragged him to further escalation and turned into a disastrous miscalculation.

The collapse of summitry notwithstanding, the summits proved instrumental in temporarily papering over problems threatening peaceful inter-Arab relations. The "Arab Solidarity Charter" highlighted the summit's role as a mechanism for regulating inter-Arab relations and establishing agreed norms, even if temporary. The summitry also revealed a correlation between Arab consensus and the low priority that accrued to the Palestinian issue. Nonetheless, since the Arab states' conflict with Israel was subject to changing domestic and inter-Arab affairs, it provided the Palestinian national movement the needed space to develop and gather momentum. The PLO was a product of Arab summitry but also expressed a growing authentic Palestinian nationalism, aspiring to ensure independence from Arab patronage.

III

THE POLITICS OF REAPPRAISAL AND ADAPTATION

". . . there is agreement between the United States and the Soviet Union to resolve the problem by political means. This . . . was based on two major points: an end to the state of war (with Israel) and withdrawal from the occupied Arab territories, . . . I hope that we all understand that when we talk of political action, it means not only taking, but giving as well. . . . Is it possible to regain the occupied land by military means at present? . . . . [T]he answer . . . is evident. . . . Thus we have before us only one way . . . : political action."

—Nasir at the Khartoum summit conference, August 31, 1967 (Mahmud Riyad, *The Struggle for Peace in the Middle East,* London: Quartet Books, 1981, p. 55).

". . . the pretence of a united Arab effort against Israel has disappeared, and on the military, political and international levels the only reality is the confrontation of two states, Egypt and Israel. The Arab world as a whole is absent from the scene except as spectators on the sidelines. . . . [W]e cannot be surprised or indignant if the Egyptian regime decides its policies in the light of its capacities and interests of Egypt alone."

—Cecil A. F. Hourani, "In Search of a Valid Myth," *Middle East Forum,* Vol. 47, (Spring 1971): p. 40.

"The fate of the Arab nation (*umma*), even the Arab existence itself, is dependent on the fate of the Palestinian cause."

—Article 14 of the PLO's National Charter.

6

A Turning Point in Khartoum

The Dialectic of Defeat

The swift and heavy defeat in the Six Day War was traumatic for the Arab world. Although named "setback" (*naksa*), denoting its indecisive and limited significance, it triggered a profound soul-searching for the underlying causes of the Arabs' weaknesses demonstrated in the June crisis, and the ways to cure them. The ensuing debate in the Arab world revealed a deep ideological crisis and quest for alternatives. The crisis that had befallen the Arabs was epitomized by Nasir's announcement of his resignation on June 9. His admission of responsibility for the debacle, however, was incomplete. He accused the United States and Britain of fighting alongside Israel, hence his decision to cut off diplomatic relations with them, which was followed by other Arab states. Yet it was anything but an admission of the failure of his vigorous concept of Pan-Arab nationalism, whose main weapon was militant ideology. Nasir survived his resignation, which was withdrawn under Egyptian mass pressure—genuine or orchestrated—but his philosophy did not. A new era in Arab political life began.[1]

The results of the Six Day War confronted the Arab collective with an urgent need to redefine its objectives in the conflict with Israel, as well as to rethink the concept of war and its role in the overall Arab strategy. Until 1967, the Arabs had been unable to set a clear program of action against Israel, which became evident in Nasir's efforts to legitimate an indefinite postponement of war. With the occupation by Israel of Arab national territories and symbolic assets such as East Jerusalem and the Suez Canal, such inaction was no longer a viable option. As before, Egypt's needs and constraints shaped the terms of the ensuing change. In addition to the loss by mass destruction of arms and combat units, the loss of the main sources of revenues in foreign currency—the Suez Canal, the Sinai oil, and tourism—was devastating for Egypt's economy, which would hardly grow in the years until the 1973 war.[2] Militarily defeated and besieged by new domestic pressures, Nasir adopted the concept of limited war which, combined with diplomatic efforts on the international level, was to gain time for military recovery, thus keeping all options open for reclaiming the lost territories.

Such a change, however, had to be made consistent with the Arab national premises and goals, from which Nasir could not have easily departed and without which he would have lost further legitimacy in the Arab world. In his resignation speech, Nasir stated that "what was taken by force will be returned by force," calling for a unified Arab effort and the use of Arab oil to realize this goal. Indeed, a political settlement with Israel was entirely rejected by Egypt and Syria, which insisted on unconditional Israeli withdrawal to the pre-war borders. Thus, they rejected Israel's official proposals—submitted through the United States less than two weeks after the war ended—for direct talks on permanent peace in return for its full withdrawal to the international borders—save only those modifications needed for security (Jerusalem and Gaza Strip were not included in the proposal). Indeed, Israel's earlier decision to annex East Jerusalem to its territory and its administrative actions in the West Bank and Gaza might have hardened the Arab line. In retrospect, however, it is doubtful whether such a radical turnabout from war to peace could have been made so shortly after the war, against the backdrop of a humiliating military defeat inflicted by Israel and the drive for a joint Arab effort to recover "the lost territory and Arab honor."[3]

Recovering the lost territories was given priority at the expense of the Palestine issue, although without spelling this out explicitly. This was defined by Nasir's phrase, "elimination of the traces of aggression and restoration of the rights of the Palestinian people." Nasir's phrase was ambiguous enough to permit a wide range of interpretations of the Arab objective, from an Israeli withdrawal from the territories it had captured in the Six Day War to a broader interpretation that entailed the elimination altogether of the State of Israel, which, by Arab standards, constituted an act of aggression by its very existence. Nasir's ambiguity was meant to placate Arab extremists while simultaneously demonstrating a pragmatic approach for the international community. Such a stance was also instrumental for gaining the three to four years required to prepare for another war.[4]

Egypt's new approach to the conflict with Israel was based on the premise that the international community would not look favorably on Israel's occupation of Arab territories, especially in view of the wide international advocacy of a political settlement for the Middle East crisis. By adopting a combination of power and diplomacy, Nasir sent a message of political realism as well as of perseverance and insistence to redeem his declining leadership. Nasir, however, perceived war as a prominent and necessary means in the thrust to recover Sinai from Israel, hence the priority he gave to rebuilding the Egyptian armed forces. It reflected a realistic conclusion that no matter what the prospects of recovering the lost territories by diplomatic means were, the minimal requirements would oblige a restoration of Egypt's military capability and continued armed pressure on Israel. Resumption of the military option would also strengthen his bargaining position toward Israel and promote his legitimacy on both domestic and regional levels. To realize this end Nasir was willing to turn fully toward the Soviet Union even at the expense of eroding the hitherto sacrosanct value of absolute Egyptian sovereignty, by offering Moscow military and naval facilities in Egypt. As of June 9, Egypt began an intensive process of absorbing Soviet arms and experts, amidst a gradual escalation of hostilities in the Canal area, which enabled Nasir to gain time and sustain international pressures to respond to diplomatic solutions of the crisis.

Nasir's ambiguous definition of the Arab objective in the conflict with Israel reflected a key lesson the Arabs had learned from their inability to drum up international support for their cause before the 1967 war, which was due to their crude slogans calling bluntly for Israel's annihilation. Yet the innovative terminology also generated Arab disagreement. Highly visible at Arab postwar meetings was a clash of views between Jordan and Egypt—both having lost territories and vital resources in the war—and Syria supported by Algeria and the PLO. For Nasir and Husain the paramount objective was to secure the return of the territories—if possible, by diplomatic means—with the liberation of Palestine taking second place. The PLO advocated the reverse order, fearing that Arab states would make political concessions to Israel in order to obtain their land, and in so doing would set back the Palestinian cause. Syria, Algeria, and Iraq renounced diplomatic efforts, adhering to a continued armed struggle against Israel and the liberation of all of Palestine—not just the return of the newly occupied territories.[5]

Ironically, Nasir—and King Husain—triggered a renewed debate around the concept originally raised by Bourguiba in 1965. Their antagonists, notably Syria and the Palestinians, reasonably argued that the combination of limited war and diplomacy would compromise the Arab strategic goal of eliminating Israel, hence they demanded continued military struggle. The incremental process would not be allowed to reach its final goal, they argued, since by adopting diplomacy the Arabs would have to acknowledge Israel and refrain from the use of force. The gap between these two concepts—a new phenomenon in the Arab attitude to Israel—was to reflect itself in the divided and volatile inter-Arab relations in the years to come. Yet Nasir's own approach was still marked by intrinsic inconsistency between the incremental process and the absoluteness of the objective.[6]

The priority given to Egypt's national interest over the Pan-Arab issue of Palestine was clearly defined in Egypt's strategic war goal, elaborated by its General Command and approved by the government in November 1967 on the basis of the Khartoum summit resolutions. It was phrased as the "liberation of the occupied land of Sinai . . . till the Egypt-Palestine border, and *political use* [*emphasis added*] of the success for restoration of the Palestinian people's rights."[7]

The Arab debacle, mainly the losses sustained by Egypt, led to a new inter-Arab alignment, both in structure and substance. Ideological disputes were shelved to facilitate a framework for cooperation between confrontation states, headed by Nasir's Egypt, and the conservative oil-producing countries whose chief spokesman was King Faisal. Nasir remained the key Arab actor, yet his eroded prestige and the heavy economic damage inflicted on Egypt as a result of the war forced him to accommodate his conservative adversaries. Nasir's need for urgent economic support could only be met by the conservative oil producers, and his willingness to accept a "political action" in the conflict with Israel caused a rupture with Damascus, substantially weakening the revolutionary camp. Nasir's new agenda brought him into close alignment with King Husain, who served as a convenient bridge to the oil-producing monarchies and the United States, but also served as an excuse for adopting a political process on the grounds of the need to redeem the Palestinians in the West Bank and East Jerusalem from Israel's domination.

Syria continued to head the line of militancy in the conflict with Israel and antagonism toward the conservative regimes, as well as to Egypt and Iraq. Syria's military, territorial, and economic losses in the war were relatively limited compared to Egypt's and Jordan's. However, its political leadership had been afflicted by severe internecine strife, which was aggravated considerably as a result of the war. More than ever before, Syria's militant attitude in the conflict with Israel served as powerful leverage for raising Syria's prestige and legitimacy on both domestic and regional levels. Yet Syria's intransigent militancy was also meant to serve its own national security goals in the conflict. By pressuring Nasir to preserve his commitment to the Palestine issue, Syria sought to prevent its own isolation in the face of Israel as well as undermine Nasir's new alignment with King Husain and other conservative regimes.[8]

That Egypt's regional policy was approaching a substantial change was evident from the debate conducted in its state-owned press regarding future foreign and domestic policies, obviously to test the Arab public opinion's response and prepare it for the change. The contending views urged a dialogue with the United States and greater democratization of Egypt's political life, as opposed to continued socialist revolution and reliance on the USSR.[9] Nasir himself adopted a pragmatic middle way, whose first evidence was to surface in the Khartoum summit.

In Search of a Collective Postwar Strategy

The Khartoum summit was preceded by laborious efforts to resolve entrenched inter-Arab disputes which not even the war had dislodged. The major obstacle lay in Syria's and Algeria's uncompromising revolutionary line and their refusal to take part in collective Arab endeavors of any kind unless they were based on struggle against the monarchies, the West, and Israel. This stance was a calculated affront to Nasir, who had no choice but to abandon his revolutionary orientation and agree to collaborate with regimes only recently anathema to him in order to tap financial aid for his tottering economy, as well as to secure their political support. Nasir was possibly encouraged to adopt this line due to the financial aid Egypt had received from Kuwait even before the war, and the grants given to it in the immediate aftermath of the war by Kuwait, Libya, and Algeria. By early July, these grants to Egypt alone reached at least $60 million. Yet the scope of aid was a far cry from Nasir's expectations from the oil-producing states, particularly from Saudi Arabia. Nasir intended to claim a price for his willingness to collaborate with the oil-producing monarchies. On July 23, he stated: "We should meet in a summit conference so that everyone will face his responsibility. . . . We do not ask anyone to give more than he can, but neither shall we accept less than what he can give."[10]

Thus, Nasir responded with alacrity to the call for a summit meeting issued just after the war by Sudan's President al-Azhari, declaring that the common struggle against Israel must override differences between the Arab states. Nasir was reluctant to meet his yesterday's adversaries so shortly after his defeat, while residues of the past still prevailed. Indeed, the Saudis seized the opportunity to stipulate that a summit conference be preceded by the total withdrawal of Egypt's forces from Yemen. Several Arab governments objected to the idea of a summit conference at this juncture, proposing instead a meeting of FMs in Kuwait in order to prepare the Arab case for the Soviet-initiated emergency session of the UNGA to debate the Middle East crisis.[11] Although a summit meeting was eventually held, a series of inter-Arab meetings was necessary to overcome deep antipathies and define a new order of collective Arab action.

Even at the FMs' meeting in Kuwait on June 17, it appeared that Egypt and Jordan were bent on employing diplomatic means to regain the territories captured by Israel. King Husain was the leading advocate of this approach, calling for a summit conference at which a joint Arab strategy would be worked out along these lines. Failing this, he said, he would consider unilateral action to solve Jordan's problems. Husain's diplomatic orientation won Egypt's support and was given concrete expression in the FMs' decision to take part in the UNGA debate, at which King Husain himself would be the senior Arab representative. Yet the UNGA proceedings underlined the disparity between Jordan and Egypt, on the one hand, and the radicals—Syria, Algeria, and the PLO—who urged the USSR to adopt an unbending line against Israel on the other.[12]

Nasir's new posture notwithstanding, a mini-summit of "revolutionary" states was held in Cairo on July 13–16, attended by the presidents of Egypt, Syria, Iraq, and Algeria. Nasir failed to convince Syria and Algeria to drop their opposition to a summit conference in return for further cooperation on his part. The two ultra-radical regimes remained adamant in their refusal to attend any inter-Arab meeting in which the "reactionary" states also participated. However, Iraq's and Algeria's stand was mitigated following their presidents' short visit to Moscow, which firmly opposed any idea of resuming the war and fully supported a diplomatic option under UN aegis. At this meeting, Nasir endorsed the resumption of Arab oil sales to the West in return for financial aid from the oil producers to the confrontation states.[13]

For the conservative regimes, while they were pleased with Moscow's response, the Cairo meeting was a warning signal that Nasir—his defeat notwithstanding—was liable under Syrian pressure to renew his ideological campaign against them. However, Saudi Arabia, Kuwait, and Libya were also seeking a legitimate way to rescind the oil embargo imposed on the United States and Britain for their alleged active participation in the Israeli attack at the outset of the war—an embargo that was costing them dearly in oil revenues. Such a step could only be taken if sanctioned by a collective Arab decision shared by the main confrontation states. These concerns were at the background of Nasir's call on July 23 for a summit conference in order "to share the burden of the battle." Nasir adopted a conciliatory tone toward the conservative regimes, declaring that the era of exporting the social revolution was over.[14]

Pursuant to the Cairo mini-summit and Nasir's call, all Arab FMs convened in Khartoum on August 1–5, with the ALSG Hassuna and PLO chief Shuqairi also participating, indicating a collective willingness to iron out major differences regarding the full summit. Although Sudan was the formal host of the meeting, Egypt played the leading role in establishing the principles for a common Arab action and backed Sudan's proposal to hold a summit meeting shortly. At the FMs' meeting, readiness was expressed to use diplomatic means in the conflict with Israel since the military option was infeasible. At the same time, it was stressed that no concessions had to be made to Israel—indeed, economic and political pressure needed to be brought against that country while an effort was being made to rehabilitate the Arab armies and build a viable military option.[15]

The tension between Egypt and Saudi Arabia was indicated by the indirect character of the discussions they conducted regarding the settlement of the main dividing issues: financial aid and the Yemen conflict. Tunisia undertook to put forth the positions of the conservative oil-producing states, taking care to avoid accusations of shirking responsibility in the all-Arab struggle against Israel. Similarly, Sudanese PM Mahjub apparently acted at Egypt's behest in suggesting the establishment of a tripartite committee to recommend to the summit how to resolve the Yemen crisis. The Saudis, seeking to capitalize on Egypt's enfeebled position, made their assent to such a committee contingent upon the prior definition of its role in overseeing the evacuation of Egyptian forces from Yemen. Although the Yemen issue was deferred to the summit meeting, the Egyptians made no secret of their urgent wish to settle the dispute, in order to render the summit's interference in this issue unnecessary.

The changing inter-Arab atmosphere was indicated by Shuqairi's isolation and marginality. His very presence at the conference irked Tunisia and Saudi Arabia, while the Egyptians were at pains to restrain him. In his memoirs, Shuqairi relates that Tunisia, Saudi Arabia, Morocco, and Libya tried to block his invitation to Khartoum because of his outspoken extremism and calls for a continued war until the complete liberation of Palestine. Shuqairi's proposal that the Arab states recognize East Germany and break off relations with Western countries did not even reach the floor.[16]

Iraq's traditional interest in using rhetorical extremism concerning the Palestine conflict to establish its Arab leadership came to the fore in its proposed plan to exert economic pressures on the Western powers. These were to include an oil embargo against the United States, Britain, and West Germany, withdrawal of Arab deposits from U.S. and British banks and nationalization of foreign monopolies in Arab countries. An Arab development fund was to be established to prop up Arab economies and assist the military effort. The Iraqi plan was forcefully seconded by Syria, while Saudi Arabia, Kuwait, and Libya objected. The plan failed to gain Egypt's support, however, significantly weakening the radicals' bargaining position. The disagreement concerning the use of Arab oil against Israel's Western allies remained unchanged in a conference of Arab oil, finance, and economic ministers held in Baghdad August 15–20 to consider the Iraqi plan.[17]

The differences between the radicals and the conservative regimes, especially on the use of oil against the West, remained unresolved in the FMs' meeting, held on the summit's eve to draw up the final agenda. Egypt adopted a noncommittal position toward either side, which turned out to be most beneficial. While it encouraged the oil monarchies to persist in their objection to the Iraqi plan, it maintained the radicals' pressure on the oil states to use their wealth for the benefit of the Arab collective, forcing the reference of this issue to the summit. The same treatment was accorded to far-reaching draft resolutions presented by Shuqairi to increase the PLO's military capability and freedom of action.[18]

Egypt set the tone of the meeting but failed to mitigate the radicals' alienation from its results. At the conclusion of the FMs' deliberations, Syria announced its boycott of the summit conference in protest against the Arab states' inaction on using the oil weapon against the United States and Britain. Algeria, which found itself isolated on this issue, took a noncommittal stance.

The official agenda approved for the summit hinged on the vaguely-worded goal of "elimination of the traces of Israeli aggression" by joint Arab economic and political effort, including the possibility of resuming the war.[19]

A settlement of the Yemen dispute was universally perceived as a precondition for the success of the entire summit. Yet it was not even on the agenda, presumably because it was seen as a bilateral issue falling under the exclusive purview of Faisal and Nasir. In fact, before the summit was convened, Nasir and Faisal achieved an agreement on the unconditional withdrawal of Egypt's forces from Yemen which may have been tacitly linked to an understanding on Saudi financial *quid pro quo*. Moreover, Nasir began to withdraw Egyptian forces from Yemen even before the summit began, although it was only on August 30 that he and Faisal concluded a formal agreement, following behind-the-scenes talks under Sudanese PM Mahjub's mediation. The agreement's main terms were: withdrawal of Egyptian forces from Yemen, phasing out Saudi aid to the Royalists, and assistance to realization of Yemen's right to full independence and sovereignty in line with its inhabitants' will. Implementation of these terms would be supervised by a three-member commission consisting of representatives from Egypt, Saudi Arabia, and Sudan's president whose work was to be completed within three months. The Nasir-Faisal accord was reached over the protests of Yemeni President al-Sallal. Unlike the Jidda Agreement, however, it avoided questions such as the form of the regime to be established in Yemen.[20]

The New Arab Agenda

The Khartoum summit conference focused on three main issues:

1. Shaping a realistic policy to gain international support for the Arabs' demand that Israel withdraw completely from the territories occupied in June 1967. At the same time, Arab national honor and principles in the conflict must be preserved, first and foremost vis-à-vis the Palestinian issue.
2. The extent of freedom of action to be accorded the confrontation states to solve their problems unilaterally as opposed to their obligation to act within the framework of the joint Arab effort.
3. The most effective way to utilize the oil weapon: whether to try to undermine the West's economy, or use oil revenues to increase aid to the confrontation states and support for the Arab struggle against Israel.[21]

The inferiority of the radical regimes at the summit was demonstrated by their minority and low representation. Although Iraqi President 'Arif attended, Algeria's delegation was led by FM Buteflika, while Syria boycotted the proceedings. This situation stemmed largely from Nasir's tactical shift toward the conservative oil producers and his ability to garner support for his new approach that while another war with Israel remained an option, it was not feasible at present and must be deferred until such time as the Arab armies "could stand on their own feet." Until then, Arab states had to use international diplomacy, and pressure by the superpowers and the UN, to bring about the return of the territories occupied by Israel. Peacemaking, or indeed any form of negotiation with Israel, was ruled out. In line with this gambit, calls for a renewal of hostilities should be played down and extreme language, liable to lose the Arabs support in the international arena, should be avoided.

Nasir explained the need for a more flexible Arab policy toward Israel as stemming from the United States–USSR talks and agreement on the principle that the Arabs should end their state of war with Israel in return for the latter's withdrawal from the occupied territories.[22] While Egypt could wait patiently until its military capability was rebuilt to wage another war against Israel, Nasir said, every possible political means should be explored and used to restore the West Bank and Jerusalem, even if it entailed Arab concessions. Thus, Nasir sanctioned King Husain's request to be granted the right to act independently to recover the West Bank through third-party intermediaries, including a tacit acceptance of Israel, if the possibility arose in practice.

Given Syria's absence and the low profile maintained by Iraq and Algeria, Shuqairi assumed the mantle of chief spokesman for the radical camp, advocating an unabated armed struggle against Israel. But he found himself isolated, running afoul not only of the conservative leaders, who were displeased at his very participation in the deliberations, but also Nasir. The PLO leader's militancy collided head-on with the position of Nasir and Husain, whose paramount goal was to retrieve their lost territories.

Shuqairi's primary concern was to prevent a possible separate settlement between Jordan and Israel in which the former regained the West Bank in return for ending the state of war against Israel, thus pushing the Palestinian issue aside. This concern was amplified by Nasir's apparent support for Husain's inclination to launch an independent diplomatic initiative to restore Jordan's sovereignty in the West Bank—though the king insisted that any agreement should be part of a comprehensive settlement. Shuqairi made a clear distinction between the Palestinians and the rest of the Arab world regarding the Palestine cause. It was, indeed, the problem of all Arabs and everyone was entitled to defend it and discuss its resolution, but only the Palestinians were entitled to make concessions on it, and even this would need the sanction of an all-Arab summit consensus. He warned Arab leaders not to make concessions at the Palestinians' expense, spelling out the principles for solving the Palestinian problem: No peace or negotiations with Israel or recognition of its conquests; no agreement on any settlement adversely affecting the Palestinian cause; no ceding of any territories or undertaking unilateral solution by any Arab state to the Palestinian problem; the Palestinian people possessed the supreme right to their homeland.[23]

Shuqairi also urged that Palestinians in the West Bank and Gaza Strip be instigated to rise up against the Israeli occupation, with PLA units to be infiltrated into the territories and resistance bases established. Husain, however, opposed the idea of an armed struggle, insisting that only a political solution would ensure the end of Israel's occupation. Two days after the summit meeting, Jordan's king voiced over Amman Radio his adamant opposition to resuming guerrilla activity. This, he said, had been the main cause of the 1967 War, and renewing such operations would give Israel a pretext to retain the occupied territories and oppress the inhabitants.[24]

Shuqairi's motion to the conference put equal emphasis on the liberation of Palestine, but the Arab leaders maintained that it should be left for the future and so concluded their talks after discussing the first three topics. The summit's core resolution pertaining to the conflict with Israel undertook to unite Arab efforts "in a political action on the international and diplomatic levels in order to eliminate the traces of aggression and ensure the withdrawal of Israel's forces from the Arab territories it occupied after June 5, subject to the fundamental principles adhered to by the Arab states: no peace with or recognition of Israel, no negotiation with it and adherence to the Palestinian people's right for their homeland." Although Shuqairi had every reason to feel personally humiliated and politically abandoned, he had had an obvious impact on the summit's resolutions, particularly the adoption of the three prohibitions regarding future Arab-Israeli relations. Shuqairi himself walked out of the conference and refused to sign the concluding communique, protesting the failure to formulate a plan for total confrontation with Israel, including diplomatic and economic sanctions against the West. In his memoirs Shuqairi takes credit for the three "nays" among the conference resolutions, maintaining that the conference had refused to approve a fourth "nay" he had proposed: No separate negotiations between an Arab state and Israel—a stipulation that would have accorded the PLO effective veto power over any settlement.[25]

Shuqairi's hard line at the summit must be seen as part of his desperate efforts to shore up his political position as the PLO's chairman, which had been in a constant decline since the beginning of Fatah's guerrilla activities in 1965 but suffered a serious blow in the wake of the war. Confronted with Nasir's alliance with King Husain, the soaring prestige of the Palestinian armed struggle, and strengthening calls by PLO's leading figures for his resignation, Shuqairi endeavored, in vain, to forge an alliance with the Palestinian armed groups, notably Fatah, which would preserve his overall leadership of the PLO.[26]

On the economic issue, Nasir had his way, with Sudan's Premier Mahjub serving as his tacit spokesman regarding the volume and modalities of financial support to the confrontation states. Faisal rejected the original, Egyptian proposal that oil producers be given a quota for providing aid based on their revenues but accepted the principle of extending financial aid to the confrontation states. Nasir's proposal—that the oil boycott against the United States, Britain, and West Germany be ended, with part of the ensuing revenues used to underwrite Arab military and political programs—gained majority support and was strongly endorsed by Saudi Arabia, Kuwait, and Libya. In Syria's absence, only Egypt and Jordan were pledged assistance, signalling that Syria would have to discuss financial support directly with the oil producers. In practice, the summit left the issue of maintaining diplomatic relations with Britain and the United States to the discretion of each participating country.[27]

The final communique stipulated that the Arabs would work as a united bloc to eliminate "the consequences of the aggression." To this end, all Arab resources would be mobilized and aid proffered "to the Arab countries whose revenues were directly affected by the war." The conference thus accorded legitimacy to resuming oil sales to the West in the name of the struggle against Israel. The amount of financial aid the oil producers would undertake to make available was to be shared—albeit not equally—by Saudi Arabia, Kuwait, and Libya. Thus, from the middle of October these three countries were to pay £50 million, £55 million, and £30 million, respectively, in quarterly installments until "all consequences of the aggression are eliminated." Of the total aid of £135 million, Jordan was allotted £40 million, most of which was meant to enhance the West Bank population's "steadfastness," and more specifically, to maintain the Hashemite king's posture there. Another noteworthy resolution linked to oil use approved a Kuwaiti plan to establish an Arab foundation for social and economic development.[28]

The amount of aid the Arab oil producers had been willing to grant Egypt reportedly exceeded Nasir's expectations. Following the summit, Egypt's official media justified the decision to lift the oil embargo on the grounds of its potential economic and social damage to Arab oil producers. Indeed, under the circumstances of Arab defeat and Nasir's declared determination to continue the military pressure on Israel, the oil monarchies could hardly refuse to help him financially, or withstand the temptation to acquire a leverage on him through such aid. Both Iraq and Algeria opposed the renewed supply of oil to the West and played to the end the rhetoric of purist Arab nationalism. Aware of being outnumbered by Egypt and the conservatives, Algeria and Iraq could afford to manifest such a position, which would be well accepted at home and at the same time justify their refusal to share the collective economic burden of support to the confrontation states. Baghdad urged that the Arabs break diplomatic and economic ties with the United States and Britain, a proposal that encountered stiff resistance, notably from Jordan, Tunisia, Lebanon, and Saudi Arabia. But Iraq itself—which, in contrast to Algeria, announced that it would maintain its embargo on the delivery of oil and natural gas to the United States and Britain even after the conference—proved less than credible in implementing this decision. Shortly after the summit conference concluded, Iraqi President 'Arif declared that his country was resuming oil shipments to both Western states (though diplomatic and trade relations remained frozen), ostensibly in order to utilize the revenue to beef up Arab armies.[29]

Isolated among the confrontation states, Syria stated that it intended to implement only the conference's "positive" resolutions. Thus, Damascus would participate unconditionally in the effort "to eliminate the traces of the aggression." In practice, the Syrians continued their support of Palestinian guerrilla activities and infiltration into Israel, though mainly through the Lebanese and Jordanian territories. In a blatantly anti-Nasirist stance, Syria called for the resumption of armed struggle, the severance of all political and economic relations with the United States and Britain, and the withdrawal of all Arab deposits from banks in those two countries.[30]

The Khartoum conference marked the beginning of a shift of Arab perception of the conflict with Israel from one revolving on Israel's legitimacy to one focusing on territories and boundaries. This was underlined by Egypt and Jordan's immediate acceptance of UNSC Resolution 242 (November 22, 1967), which was to become the cornerstone for future peacemaking efforts in the Arab-Israeli conflict. Yet the Khartoum recognition of the need to employ diplomacy and international pressure on Israel as the main instrument to retrieve the occupied territories, did not include the option of a settlement *with* Israel, even in return for the territories. The overriding goal of Nasir and Husain was to drum up international support from both the Eastern and Western blocs to force Israel to repeat the pattern of its 1957 withdrawal from occupied Sinai. Yet in spite of the strong support of the superpowers and Third World states for a political settlement that would at least end the state of war with Israel, the Arab leaders remained captives of their own ideological and domestic constraints. The new Arab strategy was underpinned by the false assumption that Israel's withdrawal from the occupied territories could be delivered by the United States, with little say from Israel itself. The three "nays" might have provided for the summit's successful end and consensual decisions, but by excluding Israel from the diplomatic thrust they effectively doomed their strategy to failure. Israel, having entertained hopes for direct negotiations with the Arab states, border rectifications, and peace, saw the "nays" of Khartoum as renewed evidence that not even the defeat and loss of territories had induced the Arabs to modify their long-standing hostility toward the Jewish state. Though the absence of decisions on renewal of the war was not overlooked, Israeli media and leaders perceived the Arabs' new approach as unrealistic tactics designed to gain time to prepare for a new round of violence, which made the occupied Arab territories all the more crucial for Israel's defense.[31]

The post-1967 years indeed witnessed a diplomatic stalemate, rapid military recovery and build-up of the Egyptian armed forces, and intensive effort by Nasir to promote inter-Arab military cooperation. These years also witnessed an unprecedented intensity, scope, and diversity of hostilities in between the all-out wars in the Arab-Israeli conflict. Yet this military escalation, combined with diplomacy, indicated a new Egyptian approach to the conflict with Israel. In hindsight, this intensified violence proved to be a crucial element in the process of adjustment to the limits of capabilities and departure from the lure of romantic visions.

The Khartoum summit also signalled a turning point in inter-Arab relations. Above all, the distinction which had been drawn between revolutionary and conservative regimes was seen to be outmoded, as Egypt dropped its ideological slogans, which had torn the Arab world apart. This was most dramatically shown by Egypt's turnabout on the Yemen issue. The entire remaining Egyptian expeditionary force was withdrawn and Cairo pointedly refrained from seeking to gain influence in the Arabian Peninsula—most notably in the Federation of South Arabia, which acquired independence in November 1967. 'Abdallah al-Sallal, who more than anyone symbolized the Egyptian involvement in Yemen, was deposed. However, two years elapsed before Riyad granted recognition to the Republican regime in Yemen.

Egypt's failure in the Yemen conflict, compounded by the fact that it was now receiving quarterly payments from the oil monarchies, attested to the decline of Nasirism and Egypt's standing in the Arab world, along with Saudi Arabia's growing political strength. The financial aid proffered by the oil-rich states on the periphery of the Arab world to the resource-poor core confrontation states rendered a central element in the post-1967 Arab regional order, even though it soon became a new bone of contention in inter-Arab relations.

7

THE BELEAGUERED NASIR

In Quest of Joint Arab Action

The Khartoum summit heralded the collapse of Arab consensus against the employment of diplomacy in the conflict with Israel, which then became the main dividing issue among Arab states. By late 1967, collective Arab activity had once again returned to the back burner, giving way to growing contention over the UNSC Resolution 242 and the mediation mission of Gunnar Jarring to the Middle East that it spawned. Nasir's official acquiescence to international mediation notwithstanding, he could not allow Egypt's military defeat and his own weakness to shape the conditions of a political settlement of the crisis. Besieged by growing domestic unrest that challenged his authoritarian regime, with his regional stature on the decline, Nasir had an urgent interest in resuming hostilities against Israel as a key to securing his own political survival and Egypt's regional primacy.[1] Thus, for the three-year period until his death, Nasir's strategy in the conflict with Israel was based on increasing military pressure while keeping the door open to international mediation.

The Nasir-Husain alliance, based on joint endorsement of Resolution 242, sustained Arab criticism. Yet it also limited the Hashemite king's freedom of action regarding a separate or directly negotiated peace settlement, whose prospects he had revealed to be meager through direct secret talks with Israeli top officials since September 1967.[2] Having accepted Resolution 242, both Egypt and Jordan advocated convening a summit conference as early as possible to obtain broad Arab backing for their position. A summit conference scheduled for January 1968 was deferred indefinitely due to inter-Arab disagreement.[3]

Two major obstacles stood in the way of a new summit meeting and joint Arab action. First, Syria and Algeria adhered to their refusal to maintain formal contact of any kind with the conservative states. Secondly, Syria and Saudi Arabia—representing two poles of the Arab world's political spectrum—objected to a summit meeting to discuss Resolution 242. Syria rejected the essence of Resolution 242 and called for the Arabs to desist from their efforts to regain the occupied territories by political means. It called for resuming the "war of liberation," assuming the stance of patron for the Palestinian armed struggle against Israel. The PLO and the armed Palestinian groups that mushroomed after the war dismissed the resolution out of hand for its implicit recognition of Israel's right to exist "within secure and recognized boundaries," and for overlooking their national rights, referring only to "a just settlement of the refugee problem." Riyad's motives were different: it sought to avoid Egyptian requests for added financial aid to meet its military needs. At the same time, however, it sought to prevent Nasir from using the summit to reassert his regional leadership by drumming up broad support for his strategy of regaining the occupied territories by political means.

The conservative oil producers appeared ready to adopt a militant posture toward Israel and to help the confrontation states financially up to a level sufficient to keep the radical regimes preoccupied with that effort rather than with inter-Arab conflicts. This tactic, however, was liable to increase Egypt's already heavy dependence on the USSR and the latter's regional influence, which would not be to the conservatives' benefit. From their standpoint, a situation of "no war and no peace" was thus the optimal one. Faisal cited the Khartoum resolutions to support his case, pointing out that as long as the Arabs persisted in efforts to resolve the Middle East crisis by political means, the Khartoum resolutions remained in effect. Since those resolutions placed responsibility for dealing with the conflict exclusively on those states who opted for this policy, inter-Arab deliberations at the summit level were not needed.[4]

Another source of discontent among Arab states concerned the funds oil producers were to give to Egypt and Jordan. The Khartoum resolutions had not specified the aid's longevity, manner of transfer, or precise purpose. This gave way to bitter differences over the recipients' request that the aid continue as long as the results of the war had not changed. Although the oil producers did finally agree to prolong their financial aid beyond the first year, they forced the confrontation states into a more subservient attitude by insisting that they submit an annual formal request for a renewal. Moreover, they required that the money be transferred directly to the foreign banks through which payments for military procurement were made, to ensure that the money was not siphoned off for other purposes.[5]

Reassured about Soviet strategic backing and massive support for rebuilding Egypt's armed forces, Nasir embarked on escalating military operations against Israel along the Canal. By mid-1968 it took the form of an ongoing limited operation that included mainly artillery fire and commando raids. At the same time, Nasir turned to the Arab world to enlist military and economic support for the battle against Israel. Nasir's strategy required enhanced military cooperation with the eastern-front states—Jordan, Syria, and Iraq—and among those countries themselves, in order to enhance military pressure on Israel and minimize the danger of a full-scale Israeli attack on Egypt. In September 1968, the "Eastern Command" (EC) was indeed established, with Iraq at the helm. Practically, however, this was a paralyzed body, as political and ideological antagonisms among its member states, considerably affected by domestic turmoil and the struggle for power, precluded effective military cooperation. Damascus-Baghdad relations went from bad to worse following the Ba'th ascendancy in Iraq in July 1968. Henceforth, the long-standing rivalry between them turned into a bitter political and ideological struggle in which each side claimed to be the authentic representative of the Ba'th's Pan-Arab nationalism, accompanied by mutual subversive efforts and vitriolic propaganda. Jordan's relations with Syria and Iraq were also at loggerheads due to the former's advocacy of a political solution and the latter's military and political support for the PR. Their growing military and political buildup on Jordanian soil was a threat to the Hashemite regime in which the king found himself bound to acquiesce, but it became another focus of inter-Arab contention.[6]

Friction between the three EC states was tempered somewhat following the seizure of most of the power in Syria by DM General Hafiz al-Asad, in March 1969, although a full takeover was accomplished only in late 1970. The army-party struggle for power in Syria had an indirect impact on Damascus' inter-Arab policy, as well as on its strategy in the conflict with Israel. Contrary to the party's revolutionary strategy of "popular armed struggle," the army, led by Asad, conceived the war against Israel as one to be fought by an alliance of the Arab regular armies. Guerrilla warfare was to be subordinated to Syria's military plans, to avoid the risk of provoking an untimely war with Israel. Unlike the antagonistic approach advocated by the neo-Ba'th leadership, Asad sought to promote military cooperation with other Arab states, allowing a token Iraqi force to enter southern Syria. In addition, an Iraqi division and a Saudi brigade were stationed in Jordan as part of the EC. Yet Egypt's efforts to convince the EC states to fight and thus pin down large numbers of Israeli troops came to naught due to the basic mistrust among them.[7]

Nasir's thrust to mobilize active Arab military and economic support took on greater urgency following the breakdown of the UN-sponsored diplomatic efforts based on Resolution 242 and his decision to open, in April 1969, a wide-scale "war of attrition" along the Suez Canal. Israel, in response, escalated the war and, as of July, began employing its air force against Egyptian targets west of the Suez Canal. Equipped with advanced American F-4 fighter-bomber aircraft, Israel adopted, from late 1969, a strategy of deep-penetrating bombing raids against Egypt aimed at forcing Nasir to cease hostilities. The intensity and damage of these bombings, demonstrating Israel's unchallenged superiority in the air, forced Nasir to appeal to Moscow for a strategic, all-inclusive, ground-to-air defense system, following which two fully equipped Soviet air force brigades and an air defense division became actively involved in the battlefield as of April 1970.[8]

The War of Attrition prompted a joint diplomatic effort by the four permanent SC members—the United States, the USSR, Britain, and France—while Washington began direct talks with Jordan and Egypt, which underlined the latter's readiness for a settlement even without Syria.[9] Nasir, however, continued his efforts to activate the EC, but to no avail. In August, a joint political command was established with Syria, reflecting Asad's growing influence on Damascus' decision-making, but also the hollowness of the EC. Egypt's standing alone in the battle against Israel provided Nasir with a strong claim for collective military and financial Arab support. A summit meeting was therefore required to unite the Arab world around Nasir's plan as a way to step up pressure on the West—and especially the United States—to force Israel to withdraw to the lines of June 4, 1967.

During the escalating War of Attrition, in Summer 1969, Nasir renewed his call for an Arab summit meeting, stating that the failure of international mediation efforts had created a new political situation that urged joint Arab action. To allay Riyad's apprehensions, Nasir emphasized that he was not necessarily seeking new undertakings for financial aid, nor asking any Arab country to act beyond its means and capabilities.[10] But despite intensive contacts with Arab leaders, only Jordan and Sudan backed Nasir's plea, while the Saudis remained unmoved in their opposition to a summit meeting.

The inter-Arab deadlock came to an end when, on August 21, a fire broke out in Jerusalem's al-Aqsa mosque, the third most sacred shrine for Muslims, and Egypt pounced on the opportunity to lead a regional and international outcry on the matter. The immense rallying power of Islamic sentiment was demonstrated in the general Arab response to Nasir's call. Within a few days, Arab FMs gathered in Cairo, with even a low-level Tunisian delegation participating, despite Bourguiba's official boycott of the AL. Faisal apparently gave his consent to the meeting in return for Nasir's assent to the convening of an Islamic summit meeting, which the Saudi leader had long been seeking as a political framework to counter the radical camp.[11]

At the meeting, Egypt and Jordan repeated their request that an Arab summit conference be convened at the earliest possible date. With Egypt's backing, the PLO filed a similar motion, calling for upgrading military and economic aid to the PR to let them step up operations against Israel. The Saudis countered by proposing an Islamic summit to consider the ramifications of the al-Aqsa blaze and discuss measures to be taken against Israel. Egypt's attempt to trade off support of the Saudi proposal in return for Riyad's approval of a separate Arab summit conference was met by a strict refusal. The Saudis adhered to their attitude that an Arab summit was not needed as long as the

Arab world was not ready for a substantive discussion of war against Israel. The debate offered further testimony to Nasir's waning leadership in the Arab world and the concomitant growing strength of Saudi Arabia. Finally, it was resolved that an Islamic summit would be convened by Saudi Arabia and Morocco. A decision on holding an Arab summit conference was deferred until November, when, at Egypt's insistence, the ADC was to meet for the first time since the 1967 War.

Cairo's lackluster performance at the FMs' meeting was partially offset by a mini-summit meeting of the confrontation states that opened in Cairo on September 1. Attending the meeting, the first of its kind since the Khartoum summit, were Nasir, King Husain, Syrian President al-Atasi, and Iraqi DPM Mahdi 'Ammash (Lebanon was not invited). Sudan's and Algeria's rulers also arrived in Cairo at the end of the meeting to confer with Nasir. Although the meeting's keynote was the enhancement of military cooperation between the confrontation states, it failed to resolve the difficulties blocking effective activation of the EC against Israel. Jordan maintained that it was already doing its part by assisting the PR; Syria cited "strategic difficulties" on the Golan Heights; and Iraq pointed to its lack of common border with Israel. Syria, Iraq, and Jordan, eager to avoid commitment to military operations against Israel, competed in playing up their help for the PR's activities. Strategically, it was agreed, the Lebanese border with Israel constituted the optimal sector for expanding the front against Israel by the PR. The emphasis placed on Palestinian military activity against Israel from southern Lebanon came against the backdrop of continued governmental crisis in this country, generated by the controversial presence of armed Palestinian groups on Lebanese soil and activity therefrom against Israel.

In the absence of Lebanon, this decision was practically worthless. Yet it demonstrated the conference's cynicism in projecting its failure to reach effective strategic resolutions on the weakest of all the Arab confrontation states, wrapping it in praise for the PR's activity. The resolutions adopted were declarative and with no practical meaning, such as the need to coordinate inter-Arab action in the event of Israeli reprisal raids for operations carried out by the PR. The meeting also reminded the oil producers of their obligation to step up aid to the confrontation states. According to the concluding statement, all Arab states must redouble their hitherto inadequate efforts to put all their resources at the campaign's disposal.[12]

The Islamic summit meeting that convened in Rabat on September 22, 1969, was far from a resounding success. Only twenty-five of the thirty-five invited countries sent delegations and no more than ten heads of state turned up. Syria and Iraq boycotted the conference altogether on ideological grounds. The conference indeed showed the disparity between the radical states—led by

Egypt, which sought to enlist material and moral support for the struggle against Israel—and the non-Arab Muslim states, which were quite content to demonstrate purely verbal and definitely non-binding solidarity in the wake of the al-Aqsa fire. Turkey, Iran, and other non-Arab Muslim states rejected the Arab states' attempt to embroil them in practical undertakings directed against Israel. They were also unmoved by the lobbying of the Arab states to obtain full status for the PLO in the meeting; the most they would allow the PLO was an observer status. In sum, the Islamic summit, at which some 300 million Muslims—half the world's total Muslim population—were represented, contributed little to the Arab cause. It did, however, help smooth the way for an Arab summit meeting.[13]

On November 10, Nasir opened the ADC meeting in Cairo with the declaration—aimed pointedly if tacitly, at Saudi Arabia—that war was unavoidable. The focal point was a comprehensive military report submitted by Egyptian DM General Fawzi, analyzing the need for a successful Arab war with Israel. The gist of the report was that all Arab states would have to contribute their share to the war effort and that it would take at least three years before such war could be launched.[14] The report was approved and referred to the forthcoming summit conference, to be held in Rabat on December 20, to determine each country's share in the war preparations. To that end, every country was requested to outline the commitments it could feasibly undertake.

The Saudis objected on the grounds that the meeting should not take place while UN envoy Gunnar Jarring and the Powers were trying to work out a Middle East settlement. However, after the ADC declared that attempts to solve the Middle East problem peacefully had failed irrevocably, and following Syria's assent to a summit meeting, Riyad also accepted Nasir's initiative. The ADC resolutions would serve as an agenda for the fifth summit, focusing on full Arab military and political mobilization against Israel; supporting the PR and the inhabitants of the occupied West Bank and Gaza Strip; and condemning the United States for supplying arms to Israel.[15]

The Saudi position at the ADC meeting indicated its deference not only to the powerful joint stance of Egypt and Syria. Coups in Sudan and Libya bringing to power pro-Nasirist regimes under Ja'far al-Numairi and Mu'ammar al-Qadhafi, respectively, and the PLO-Lebanon Cairo Agreement, concluded under Nasir's auspices in late November, had enhanced the Egyptian president's prestige, as had the escalation of fighting along the Suez Canal. Riyad had no desire to run afoul of Nasir, who seemed to be riding a new wave of popularity. Indeed, by its very agreement to hold a summit conference—however unenthusiastically given—Riyad tacitly recognized the reascendancy of Nasir and Egypt in the Arab world, while making it clear that no additional aid would be offered to the confrontation states.

Ambiguous Strategy, Deadlocked Action

The ADC's recommendation notwithstanding, vigorous diplomatic maneuvering by Egypt, Jordan, and Morocco was required to ensure participation
by most Arab leaders, foremost by King Faisal. To placate the Saudi king,
Egypt released previously frozen Saudi deposits in Egyptian banks and proposed expanded bilateral economic cooperation. Nasir also tried to mediate a
border dispute between Saudi Arabia and the PDRY to ensure that the latter
would not raise the matter at the summit conference. These conciliation gam-
bits were capped by Nasir's invitation to Faisal to meet him in Cairo prior to
the summit meeting for talks that could determine the conference's outcome.

Nasir wanted from Faisal a *carte blanche* for his policymaking in the
conflict with Israel: to accept Egypt's involvement in the international mediation efforts based on Resolution 242 without diminishing its eligibility for
Saudi financial aid for military purposes. Faisal, for his part, did not wish to be
pushed into using the oil weapon against the West or be obliged to increase
substantially his financial aid to the confrontation states. At their meeting,
however, it was apparent that residues of past mutual suspicion and animosity
still remained. The Saudi king reportedly complained about Nasir's continued
subversion against the Saudi regime, accusing him of abetting sabotage operations by Palestinians against the TAPLINE oil pipeline running from Saudi
Arabia to the Mediterranean in southern Lebanon. Nasir dwelt on the great
importance he attached to maintaining good relations with Riyad, assuring
Faisal that he was not in the habit of intervening in the internal affairs of any
Arab state, least of all Saudi Arabia. The two leaders failed to overcome their
differences and arrived in Rabat without mutual understanding.[16]

Syria and Iraq encountered the summit with their own problems. Syria's
continued party-army struggle for power resulted in a decision to participate in
the summit conference at a ministerial level only. Baghdad, which ever since
the July 1968 coup had been dominated by a coalition of the army and the Ba'th
civilian, anti-Syrian wing, could not seem to take a less militant position than
Syria and thus decided to follow the Syrian example and name its DM as head
of the delegation. Thus, although the ultra-revolutionary regimes backtracked
somewhat from their principle of rejecting collaboration with "reactionary"
regimes, inter-Arab differences reduced the prospects for forging a strong
coalition advocating effective resolutions concerning the military option
against Israel.[17]

Nasir's perspective and his expectations for the summit, as well as his
concept of war as a means to achieve a political settlement, were encouraged
by Heikal's editorials in *al-Ahram* suggesting that Israel and the Arabs were
inevitably heading toward a new war. Heikal argued that Israel had been unable

to impose its version of peace on its neighbors while the Arabs could renew the war due to their decisive edge over Israel in resources and strategic depth. The Arabs, he concluded, would be able to impose their will on Israel if they utilized their resources sensibly and formulated a war doctrine consistent with regional and international affairs.[18]

Cairo indicated its attitude by rejecting the American initiative for an Israeli-Egyptian peace settlement based on Resolution 242 and modelled on the 1949 Rhodes armistice talks—separate and indirect—with Jarring's mediation. The American initiative, named after SoS William Rogers, was triggered by the Arab decision to hold a summit and intended to soften its rhetoric and resolutions. However, even though the American proposal met the key Arab demands, Egypt rejected the Rhodes formula and insisted on applying the same principles also on the Jordanian and Syrian fronts, a stand tantamount to a demand for a comprehensive settlement. At the same time, Cairo's media continued to lobby for the idea of war while publicly excoriating Washington's Middle East policy and rejecting the American proposal to hold talks with Israel.[19]

Two days before the summit convened, a plan for an Israeli-Jordanian peace settlement was presented to the parties by Washington, based on the same principles and modalities as the one earlier offered to Egypt. The plan implied separate tracks of negotiations, proposing, *inter alia,* that Israel and Jordan share responsibility for a unified Jerusalem; that the refugee problem be resolved through repatriation or resettlement with compensation; and that the agreement come into force only after the attainment of peace between Israel and Egypt. Yet despite King Husain's unequivocal commitment to a political settlement and his discussion of the plan with the U.S. ambassador to Morocco, he found himself obliged to join the summit's conclusion asserting that peace efforts had failed. The vigorous rejection by both Egypt and Israel of the American proposals doomed it, at least for a time. The summit itself offered no official response to the American proposal, a silence Jordan chose to interpret as Arab consent to its exploring the subject further.[20]

Meanwhile, the ultra-radical camp, which had been advocating immediate war, was not sitting idly by. On the eve of the summit meeting, the leaders of Iraq, Libya, Sudan, and the PDRY met in Algeria, at Boumedienne's initiative. The meeting appeared to be an effort to press the Saudi king to comply with Nasir's wishes. But the Algerian president's stand at the summit was to show that the gathering in Algiers meant to enhance his political posture as a radical leader, even at the expense of Nasir's interests. Thus, Algeria expressed support for the PDRY's cause in its border dispute with Saudi Arabia and its discussion at the summit, despite the Saudi monarch's threat to walk out of the meeting if the case should be raised. Notwithstanding this rhetoric, however, the summit deliberations focused chiefly on Nasir's war intentions and consequent requests for generous financial aid to enable the Arabs to prepare for war. The debate indicated a clash of interests between the confrontation states, led by Nasir, and oil-producing Saudi Arabia and Kuwait. Nasir struck a pose of ambivalence on the war-or-peace question, which indicated his determination to keep all options open. Yet this ambivalence divided the confrontation states and exposed Nasir to vitriolic criticism from both radicals and conservatives. Above all, it enabled the prospective financiers to avoid an explicit refusal of his needs and focus instead on pressing for a clear strategy.

Nasir elaborated on the overwhelming economic burden of the struggle against Israel—which, he said, could be made to withdraw from the territories only by pressure and force. The summit was thus asked to approve General Fawzi's report, which sparked a fierce row among the heads of state due to the huge financial outlays entailed—500 million Egyptian pounds—and its recommendation to increase Egypt's and the EC's combat troop strength to 1.4 million altogether. Egypt's plan seemed like a thinly veiled ploy to extract funds from the oil producers. Skeptics argued that even if the plan's objectives were attained within the allotted three years, Israel's strength would remain an unknown factor.[21]

The Egyptian plan provoked another disagreement over the allocation of the joint financial and military effort among the Arab states, intended to be under Egyptian control. The participants rejected Egypt's proposal to cast all Arab undertakings in the form of contractual obligations with the AL supervising their implementation, arguing that the ACSP was sufficient. Inasmuch as this pact had not been implemented, they argued, it would be pointless to create other instruments that would meet the same fate. In any event, Nasir remained unwilling to give a definite undertaking that the funds he requested would be earmarked for waging war against Israel in the near future, speaking rather of comprehensive preparations to last about three years. Iraq and Syria also refused to commit themselves to joining in a war in the immediate future.

Boumedienne was the most outspoken critic of Nasir, taking advantage of his ambivalence to proclaim Algeria's readiness to rally behind Nasir's command if he were only specific about war aims and timetable. Syria—still not a beneficiary of the oil producers' aid—and Iraq played their own game of militancy with an eye on securing Arab funds on grounds of their active part in the joint military effort. Thus, while identifying with Egypt's main line of augmenting the financial aid to the confrontation states—which Iraq claimed it was—each of them capitalized on its own share of the EC military burden.

Nasir's far-reaching requests for financial aid deterred the Saudi and Kuwaiti monarchs, who were willing to adhere to their commitment made at Khartoum but refused to pay more. King Faisal and the Kuwaiti Amir maintained that their current financial aid to Egypt and Jordan had already become a heavy burden on their economies, claiming that it constituted 11 percent (£50 million) and 4.5 percent (£55 million) of their budgets, respectively. Faisal also reminded the summit of the Saudi brigade deployed in Jordan. He was willing to continue the financial support, yet repeated his humiliating demand that he be apprised of how the money was spent and for what purposes. Libya's Qadhafi, attending his first summit meeting, was also reluctant on further support for Egypt. The new Libyan leader offered to increase his share by only £10 million, although following further consultation with Nasir, he was willing to pay £20 million for special arms deals.[22]

The focal point of King Husain's remarks was the adverse effects to Jordan of the Palestinians' use of its territory as a base for raids against Israel. He also submitted a long list of arms and other equipment, including fighter aircraft, that Jordan needed. Lebanon echoed Jordan in complaining about the deleterious effect of the Palestinian presence on its territory and asked for financial aid.

Despite feverish consultations and mediating efforts played mainly by the hosting king, the gap between Nasir and the Arab financiers remained unbridgeable. Tension reached a crisis point when Nasir, frustrated and humiliated by the summit's rebuff of his requests, unleashed a furious tirade in the plenary session of the heads of state. The issue was not money, Nasir asserted, but that all Arabs—not just Egypt—must share the burden of war. With £120 million in revenues from the Suez Canal and another £10 million from the Sinai's oil, his country could forego Arab aid. On concluding his remarks, Nasir stalked out of the meeting, followed by the Iraqi and Syrian delegations, whose excuse was that the summit had ignored their concerns.[23]

Nasir was soon lured back to the discussion by King Hasan for a further attempt to resolve inter-Arab differences, only to have it end with a hopeless, irreconcilable split between two interest-driven parties. Five states—Algeria, Saudi Arabia, Kuwait, Tunisia, and Morocco—were unwilling either to approve the Egyptian plan or come up with a compromise formula acceptable to all sides. Nine states—Egypt, Syria, Iraq, Jordan, Libya, Lebanon, Sudan, the PDRY, and Yemen—supported a draft resolution under which each Arab state would spell out the troops and arms it could allot for the campaign. Since a joint statement was out of the question, a brief, festive final session was convened, from which the delegations of Syria, Iraq, the PDRY, and Yemen absented themselves. King Hasan, in a short, off-the-cuff statement, said the conference had opened the eyes of the Arab leaders, and expressed the hope that another summit meeting could take place soon. Hasan gave his blessing to the struggle of the Palestinian people and urged them to stand fast in the knowledge that the entire Arab world was behind them. Indeed, the PLO emerged highly prestigious at Rabat. The Arab states' inability to formulate an agreed strategy directly benefitted the PR, whose unequivocal, strongly enunciated position stood out in bold relief against the backdrop of confusion and vacillation in the Arab world. The "honorable goal," as King Hasan described the Palestinian cause in his concluding speech, was the only issue on which the Arab rulers could close ranks, at least declaratively, especially when dissent prevailed at their summit.[24]

Nasir concluded bluntly that the summit "achieved nothing, and we should have declared its failure instead of bemusing our people with false hopes." It did, however, result in augmenting Arab financial aid to the confrontation states and the PR. Hence, the amount set at the Khartoum conference would be increased by £35 million, with Libya paying £20 million of the extra sum, Saudi Arabia £10 million, and Kuwait £5 million. It was far less than Nasir had requested, especially in view of the staggering cost of the arms procured from the USSR, even though they were acquired at half-price. The amount of aid allotted to the PLO was £26 million, of which £11 million was designated for steadfastness (*sumud*) of the inhabitants of the occupied West Bank and Gaza Strip, to be funneled through the PLO.[25]

The Saudi-PDRY border dispute was not raised at the summit, thanks to Nasir's influence on the PDRY leaders. Another victim of the changing balance of power between Nasir and Faisal was North Yemen, whose delegate complained that Saudi Arabia was continuing to aid the Royalists. Faisal dismissed the charge as an internal Yemeni matter, and refused the mediation attempts of Iraq and Algeria. The conduct of the Yemeni-Saudi conflict illustrated the center-driven nature of the summit meetings and the primacy of the conflict with Israel. It equally showed the disdain and neglectfulness that peripheral Arab countries would face if they were embroiled in a conflict with one of the central Arab actors.

The refusal of the Gulf oil monarchies to meet Nasir's request for increased financial aid indicated their concern that he reinstate himself as an all-Arab leader. Indeed, the summit's impasse reflected chiefly Nasir's failure to rally the Arab leaders behind him and the subsequent leadership vacuum in the Arab states system. While Israel was engaged in intensive deep-penetration air raids against Egypt, with only King Husain supporting the diplomatic option and the eastern front states split and unwilling to pursue war against Israel, Nasir's isolation and weakness in the Arab world was more visible than ever. Nasir's analysis of Israel's invincibility—a view reinforced by the Soviet call for restraint in military activity against Israel and its hesitation to supply the arms requested by Cairo—underpinned his ambiguous strategy, in which both war and diplomacy appeared inconclusive.[26]

Nasir's ambivalent concept of action in the conflict with Israel not only failed to enlist adequate Arab support, but unified radicals and oil monarchs against it. A bizarre coalition of Boumedienne and Faisal, with Iraqi backing, was formed against Nasir, demanding that he either go to war or forfeit Saudi aid. Boumedienne's sudden animus was apparently the result of Egypt's coordination with Libya and Sudan, which Algeria viewed as liable to upset the power balance in North Africa. Faisal, in a gambit worthy of Machiavelli, was actually trying to prod Nasir into launching war and thereby be rid of him. Failing this, he wished to show that Nasir was insincere about the war option, hence that any increase in aid was unjustified. Nasir, however, called the Saudis' bluff by announcing that he would go to war if the Arab states undertook to provide the specified economic and military aid. Nasir was well aware that the rich Arab rulers would never agree to transfer the huge sums he needed and, in a Machiavellian ploy of his own, may have wished to exploit this certain refusal in order to justify his adherence to the political solution option he had been advocating ever since the Six Day War.[27]

Nasir's willingness to attend the closing session despite the rejection of his economic requests attested to his enfeebled standing and increased dependence on Saudi Arabia and Kuwait. Against this backdrop, Nasir visited Algeria en route home from the conference, where he met with Boumedienne, followed by a stopover in Tripoli where a tripartite agreement of cooperation, later to be known as the "Tripoli Charter," was concluded between Nasir, Qadhafi, and Numairi. This accord was pounced upon by the Egyptian press in its campaign to play up the conference as a forum for Egyptian achievements and to conceal Nasir's devastating failure at Rabat.[28]

Nasir's failure at the Rabat summit spurred his efforts to reactivate the EC, leading to a mini-summit meeting in Cairo on February 7, 1970, of the leaders of Egypt, Iraq, Jordan, Syria, and Sudan. However, since no substantial change had occurred on either domestic or inter-state tensions, each of the EC members remained locked into its previous positions and the talks bore no fruit. Jordan and Syria reiterated their refusal to let Egyptian and Iraqi air force units deploy on their soil, while Iraq said it could not commit additional forces to the EC due to rising tensions on its border with Iran. The primary reason for the Cairo summit's failure, however, lay in the disagreement among the EC member states regarding a political settlement. Syria and Iraq remained adamantly opposed, preempting Husain's desire to adopt the American peace plan, while Nasir, steering a middle course, endeavored to keep the door open for further U.S. diplomatic initiatives. Nasir's own non-committal stance was once again the main stumbling block to reaching an agreement on an Arab military plan. Under these circumstances—and given the continuing massive U.S. arms shipments to Israel—the participants concluded that the EC lacked the minimum forces needed to function effectively. Nonetheless, the meeting's decision to escalate military operations on the eastern front intensified armed clashes in the Syria-Israel border area and Israeli air strikes in retaliation. Yet these incidents resulted primarily from Palestinian guerrilla operations launched from the Golan Heights, indicating Syria's continued army-party struggle for power, while the EC remained essentially dormant.[29]

Another effort to mend fences between the confrontation states was made at a mini-summit meeting held in Tripoli on June 21, to mark the U.S. evacuation of Wheelus air force base. The meeting was attended by the heads of state of Egypt, Iraq, Jordan, Libya, and Syria, and ministers from Sudan and Algeria. Their discussions centered on a grandiose military plan, drawn up by Iraq and Libya, for the total mobilization of the Arab world's resources and the transfer of forces from the Egyptian sector to the eastern front. Although the plan was approved in principle, it was worthless in view of the lack of agreement on war objectives. Nasir, in his May 1 speech, made an implicit call to open a dialogue with the United States, and Husain emphasized the need to retrieve the occupied territories as the primary objective. In contrast, Iraq and Syria would not budge from their position that the war's purpose was "the liberation of all Palestine," adding that only through combat (*qital*) could the Arab-Israeli conflict be resolved.[30]

The Tripoli meeting, which bore a strong anti-American tenor, came two days after a new American initiative was officially submitted to Israel and Egypt, requesting the parties to agree to a three-month cease-fire and renewed talks under Ambassador Jarring's auspices on the basis of Resolution 242. The American initiative was a result of a renewed American diplomatic thrust toward a Middle East settlement, which had been prepared through direct contacts with Israel and Egypt. Washington's new effort was prompted by Israel's deep-penetrating bombings, which resulted in the direct involvement of Soviet military in the War of Attrition, and its modest goals reflected the lesson of the Rogers plan's failure. Nasir and Israel showed willingness to cooperate with Washington against the background of an increasingly costly and inefficacious war for both parties in the wake of the massive deployment of Soviet air defense units on Egyptian soil in April and the heavy losses they inflicted on Israel's air force. Nasir welcomed Washington's resumed efforts, and, according to the Soviets, was willing to end the state of war with Israel with the signing of an agreement.[31]

Practically, the American initiative applied only to the Egyptian front, since Jordan and Israel had been committed to a cease-fire between them, and Syria had never accepted Resolution 242. In view of the PR guerrilla warfare, however, it was essential that Jordan and Egypt be committed to halt Palestinian operations from their soil. On July 22, 1970, following a visit to Moscow where the cease-fire proposal was discussed, Nasir announced his acceptance of the American initiative, typically without having consulted with or notified any of his Arab partners, including King Husain, who soon followed suit. Nasir's acceptance of the American initiative was apparently meant to gain time for further preparations for war, and was combined with a decision to withdraw Egypt's air force from Syria and disconnect from the EC. The cease-fire was to enable Egypt to deploy anti-aircraft missiles along the Suez Canal, thus gaining further depth of air defense and preparing for a future crossing operation under its umbrella. Reportedly, he had little hope—"one chance in a thousand"—that the American initiative would bear fruits.

Israel's acceptance of the American initiative was harder to obtain. Aside from further American commitments for arms supplies, Israel received a presidential assurance that no pressure would be applied on it to accept the Egyptian views on borders and refugees, effectively giving Israel a veto power over any peace proposal. Soon after a cease-fire prevailed along the Suez Canal on August 7, however, it was verified that Egypt had moved missiles into the Canal Zone in violation of the standstill provision. One month after the cease-fire began, Israel, whose acceptance of the Rogers' Plan had occasioned a breakup of its national coalition government, announced its refusal to attend the Jarring talks unless the Egyptian violation was rectified. With Egypt's rejection of this demand, the American initiative was virtually doomed.[32]

Nonetheless, the acceptance by Nasir and Husain of the American initiative had far-reaching consequences on inter-Arab relations and the Arab world's approach to the conflict with Israel. Egypt and Jordan quickly came under verbal fire from Syria, Iraq, Algeria, and the PLO. In Jordan, tension between the Hashemite regime and the PR soared, bringing both sides to the brink of a violent showdown. As the inter-Arab rift intensified, Qadhafi reconvened the Tripoli conference on August 5, including a PLO delegation, to unsuccessfully discuss the EC. Iraq and Algeria absented themselves following Egypt's declaration that its decision to accept the American initiative was final. Algeria demonstrated its objection to Naisr's decision by recalling its brigade from the Suez Canal front. While rebuffing Arab criticism of his decision to accept Washington's June initiative as intervention in Egypt's internal affairs, Nasir was nevertheless careful not to aggravate his relations with the PLO or with Iraq. Thus, when King Husain met with him in Egypt on August 21, Nasir took an uncommittal position concerning the refusal of the PR and the Iraqi expeditionary force in Jordan to respect the cease-fire.[33]

To mitigate Palestinian criticism, Nasir summoned the PR's leadership and explained his policy. He strongly argued in favor of U.S. diplomacy based on Resolution 242 (while developing the military option) and urged the PLO leaders to be realistic and accept a mini-state solution in the West Bank and Gaza Strip rather than seeking the liberation of Palestine as a whole. Nasir also asserted to the PLO leaders that he had warned King Husain not to use force against them. Nasir's efforts, however, fell on deaf ears, as the PLO continued its attacks against Egypt. In reaction, Egypt shut down the Cairo-based PLO radio station and expelled Palestinian agitators from the country.[34]

Just as the American initiative came to its deadlock, the focus of regional and international attention turned to the ensuing Hashemite-Palestinian crisis in Jordan, which became the battleground for inter-Arab differences over the strategy in the conflict with Israel.

The Palestinian Resistance: Glory and Crisis

The 1967 war resulted in boosting Palestinian nationalism, reshaping its institutional frameworks, and enhancing its role in the Arab-Israeli conflict. Most discernible was the rapid growth of Palestinian "self-sacrificers" (*fida'iyyun*) guerrilla groups and expansion of their warfare against Israel. For these groups, the regular Arab armies' defeat provided a golden opportunity to put themselves at the forefront of the armed struggle and substantiate their claim that the Palestinians should be the vanguard in the Arabs' war against Israel. Furthermore, the occupation by Israel of the West Bank and Gaza Strip seemed to provide them with the opportunity to wage a popular liberation struggle along the lines of classical guerrilla warfare from within their indigenous social and territorial base.[35]

Palestinian guerrilla warfare captured the Arab world's imagination, boosting the Palestinians' prestige and material opportunities, which in turn had an immediate impact on their operational capability. Apart from its fresh popular nature, the PR's soaring prestige in the Arab world was underpinned by three major factors: First, the salience of Palestinian guerrilla activity on Israel's borders, against the background of reluctance of Jordan, Syria, and Iraq to use their armies on the eastern front. In effect, the Palestinian guerrilla warfare provided Syria and Jordan with an excuse to claim that they were implementing their share in the joint Arab effort against Israel by enabling the Palestinian armed groups to use their territories for attacks against Israel and sustaining Israel's military retaliations. This helped establish the PR's status as a confrontation force in the conflict with Israel with all the moral attributes that entailed in the Arab world.

Second, the implicit overlapping of the Arab claim for recovery of the Arab lands occupied in 1967—including the Palestinian-populated West Bank and Gaza Strip—and the claim for recognizing the Palestinian people's national rights for liberation and self-determination. Early in 1968, Heikal wrote that "The Palestinian question has become the principal focus of contemporary political, social and national Arab action."[36] Thus, the PR became the Arab regional "trump card" over which central Arab states sought to gain control, through patronage, media, financial and military support, to serve their own interests. The growing activity of Palestinian guerrilla groups and Israel's reprisals substantiated their claim for political representation of the Palestinian people, including in the occupied territories whose liberation seemed to be the PR's exclusive practical concern. This, in turn, had an immense influence on the development of the PLO from a symbol of an abstract Palestinian entity to a national liberation movement whose aims were defined in specific political and territorial terms.

Third, the structural and ideological changes undergone by the PLO after the war as a result of its bankruptcy under Shuqairi's leadership. These changes essentially turned the PLO from an AL-based political instrument into an authentic, all-Palestinian national umbrella organization for political, civilian, and armed Palestinian groups. The process was expedited by the war results, which highlighted the PLO's irrelevance and inept leadership while boosting the *fida'i* Palestinian groups that were still not incorporated in the organization. In December 1967, Shuqairi had been forced to resign amid growing pressure by Fatah on the PLO's new leader, Yahya Hammuda, to allocate wider representation to the armed Palestinian groups in the organization. The PLO was forced to acknowledge these groups due to their soaring popularity among Palestinians and Arabs alike, particularly after the large-scale Israeli raid on their bases at Karama in the Jordan Valley in March 1968, and their threat to establish a rival Palestinian national movement.[37]

In the PNC's fourth meeting, held in Cairo in July 1968, half of the members represented *fida'i* organizations, which had an essential bearing on the PLO's new strategy and role in the conflict with Israel. These changes were reflected in the revised Palestinian National Covenant which indicated a quest for sovereign Palestinian nationalism on an equal footing with other Arab states, as opposed to the Pan-Arab character of Shuqairi's PLO. The new Covenant also highlighted the Palestinian armed struggle as a strategy, indicating the PLO's commitment to resist any political compromise with the State of Israel. Within seven months, Fatah had gained control of the PLO, and its leader, Yasir 'Arafat, was elected chairman. At about the same time, 'Arafat accompanied Nasir on his visit to Moscow, where he was introduced to the Soviet leadership. Nasir's championing the PR was intended to serve an urgent need to recover his fallen legitimacy in the Arab world and rebuff his rivals' criticism. More specifically, Nasir sought to foster Fatah's prestige and political stature as the central power and Egypt's main agent of influence in the PR movement against the radical Ba'th-based and Marxist factions.[38]

Other Arab regimes competed for influence within the PR, turning it into a mirror of inter-Arab cleavages. Syria and Iraq, in particular, became directly involved in the PLO's internal affairs by establishing their own Ba'th-based Palestinian organizations—al-Sa'iqa (1968) and the Arab Liberation Front (1969), respectively. The PLO itself became a competing political power in the region due to its military and political presence, but mainly by assuming the role of a national authority for the Palestinians in the Arab countries. The PR came to play a greater role in the political and social affairs of its own cause, which was bound to threaten, if not to diminish, the Arab states' say on the matter, aggravating Arab-Palestinian frictions and mutual resentment.

The Rabat summit unmistakably reflected the remarkable metamorphosis of the Palestinian issue since 1967. The media's attention was focused at Yasir 'Arafat, who turned up in full military uniform, representing eight *fida'i* factions. While in previous summits the PLO was considered an AL institution—hence of an inferior status—this time it was accorded equal footing with the member states. 'Arafat was given a place in the front row, among the kings and presidents, and the Palestinian flag was displayed as prominently as all the others.[39]

Yet these gestures manifested just as well the tendency of politicians to demonstrate cheap declarative support for the PR as an indispensable source of legitimacy in Arab political life. In line with this posture, Sudan's new leader, Numairi, who delivered the opening keynote address, called for lifting all restrictions placed on the PR in the countries bordering Israel. Numairi was clearly referring to Lebanon, where the heads of the Christian-Maronite community, apprehensive of being dragged into conflict with Israel by the implications of the PR's activity, pleaded with the Arab leaders to show consideration for Lebanon's unique character and communal structure. Numairi asserted that it was the activity of the PR that would restore the Arab nation's honor, which had been trampled in June 1967. King Hasan, who as the leader of the host country served as conference chairman, also emphasized the overriding character of the Palestinian issue, declaring, "The fate of Palestine and the soil of Palestine are the first thing and the last thing."[40]

The PLO's main thrust at the summit was to enhance its status as a national representative of the Palestinians in the West Bank at King Husain's expense, primarily by obtaining control over allocating the "steadfastness funds." The PLO's euphoria was indicated by 'Arafat's far-reaching claims that it should be integrated into the overall Arab military strategy, giving it part of that operation's budget plus a say on inter-Arab decisions in the military sphere. In this context, he called on the summit to issue an official statement to the effect that efforts to settle the conflict politically would be abandoned. Underlining the PLO's continuity in spite of the radical changes it had recently undergone, 'Arafat reminded the summit that some Arab states had still not fulfilled their commitments to the organization since 1964. He also insisted that Arab states allow the PLO to establish bases and recruitment offices on their soil, stressing that he was neither begging them to allow him freedom of action nor agreeing on their right to regulate it. Restrictions on its anti-Israeli operations from areas bordering Israel should be lifted. He also called on the Arab states to establish formal diplomatic relations with the PLO, since it was representing ninety-seven percent of the PR movement.

The Arab leaders, in marked contrast to their inability to reach agreement on the Egyptian military plan, were united on the Palestinian cause. Indeed, they outbid each other in stating fervent support for the PLO. Boumedienne urged that the PLO be regarded as the exclusive spokesman for the Palestinians, and Numairi stated that the world must recognize the legitimacy of the PR movement. One idea was to convene a special conference at which the Arab leaders would declare their adoption of the PLO's proposal of a Democratic Palestinian State open to members of all faiths.[41]

The Arab rulers went out of their way to praise the PR, reflecting their need for a substitute for the lost spirit of Pan-Arab nationalism. The PLO embodied an authentic version of the Arab national ethos of popular struggle in defiance of foreigners, at a time of morale crisis at the ruling elites' level. Yet the PR was also a threat to Arab regimes due to its social and political revolutionary attributes. That the PLO was urged to form a Palestinian government-in-exile—apparently by Tunisia and Algeria, with Nasir's tacit backing— might attest to Arab regimes' wish to institutionalize the PLO's political status as the nucleus of a Palestinian state, which would obligate the PR to define its aims in terms acceptable to the world community. A major reason for the summit's bolstering the PLO was the USSR's change of attitude toward it. Soviet-PLO relations were evidently on the agenda in Egyptian Vice-President Anwar al-Sadat's visit to Moscow shortly before the summit meeting, following which a PLO delegation was invited to visit Moscow.[42]

'Arafat's request to allow intensified military and political activity by the PR was generally supported, especially by radical states where Palestinian activity had been tightly controlled or nonexistent. Arab leaders agreed to channel the "steadfastness funds" to the inhabitants of the occupied territories via the PLO, overriding King Husain's opposition. Husain's warning that henceforth the PLO would be responsible for the salaries of former Jordanian government officials in the West Bank, hitherto paid by Jordan, remained unheeded. Practically, the king showed no intention of implementing his threat as it would further weaken his own position in the West Bank. Nasir's unflagging support for the PLO at the summit seemed to have indicated cooled relations with Husain. Given growing tension and armed skirmishes in Jordan between Jordanian troops and the PR, Nasir's firm support for the PLO bore serious implications for Jordan's domestic politics.

The growing Palestinian military presence in Jordan and Lebanon and attacks therefrom on Israel resulted in painful Israeli retaliatory raids aimed at forcing these governments to prohibit the use of their territories for guerrilla activities. The collision between the revolution and the state was inevitable, as the PR endeavored to create its autonomous bases of power in Jordan and Lebanon while those states attempted to impose their authority on the PR. By mid-1969, the PR was on the brink of an all-out confrontation with the sovereign governments of Jordan and Lebanon.

In Lebanon, the PR's armed activity generated a prolonged political crisis—one of the most critical in the country's history as an independent state. Israeli retaliations in the border area triggered intra-Lebanese tensions along factional and political lines. The eight-month crisis came to a head in early November, when a series of armed clashes occurred between the Maronite militia, accompanied by regular Lebanese army units, and Palestinian fighters. Syria hovered over all these developments, pressuring Lebanon's government to desist from attacking the Palestinians and deepening the cleavage between Maronites and Sunni Muslims regarding the PR's military presence on Lebanese soil. The crisis was eventually resolved through the Cairo Agreement, signed under Nasir's auspices near the end of November by PLO's new chairman Yasir 'Arafat and Lebanese army commander-in-chief General Bustani. The agreement formally recognized the Palestinians' right to maintain political and military presence on Lebanese soil, though within specified areas, and their right to operate against Israel from Lebanon's territory, subject to coordination with the Lebanese army. The Palestinian refugee camps in Lebanon in effect won recognition as autonomous enclaves.[43]

The Hashemite conflict with the PR was much more profound given the PLO's growing claim to represent the Palestinian people, thus undermining the very legitimacy of the Hashemite regime, whose domain—even without the West Bank—was inhabited by a large number—if not a majority—of Palestinians. They were also at loggerheads concerning a political settlement that might return Hashemite sovereignty to the West Bank, while the PR sought liberation by force, which would assert its claim for this territory. From the PR's viewpoint, Jordan was the ideal "Hanoi": inhabited by a large Palestinian population, the longest Arab border with Israel, and relatively easy access to the Occupied Territories. Yet with the failure to move the battle into the West Bank and Gaza, the PR entrenched in Jordan's territory, primarily in refugee camps as its main bases of power. Despite growing tension and sporadic violent clashes involving the government army, the king's hands were tied by virtue of the large Palestinian population, his alignment with Nasir, and support of Syria and Iraq for the PR, coupled with the presence of an Iraqi division deployed on Jordanian soil. Under this Arab umbrella, a dual rule developed in Jordan in which the PR practically established a "state within a state," which, by February 1970, the regime was virtually forced to acknowledge. But what turned the PR-Jordan showdown inevitable was the provocative and extravagant challenge of the Hashemite sovereignty by the PR, especially the Marxist PFLP led by George Habash. The PFLP maintained that "the road to Palestine passed through Amman," defining the liberation of Jordan from the Hashemite regime as a prerequisite to the liberation of Palestine. Its revolutionary attitude and innovative operations implicated other factions, including Fatah, which were compelled to follow suit or lose prestige.[44]

In June 1970, armed clashes broke out between Jordan's army and the PR, in the most serious crisis the Hashemite authority had ever faced. The crisis was mediated by an inter-Arab committee established by the Tripoli conference, which led to an agreement that reasserted the PR's freedom of action and supported Jordan's immune sovereignty. However, as in the case of earlier agreements, institutional and ideological divisions, and competition among Palestinian factions, turned this agreement into a virtual dead letter. The June crisis apparently brought King Husain to a decision to eliminate the Palestinian threat to his regime, the timing of which was expedited by the eruption of an inter-Arab dispute over the American initiative.

The showdown was patently sparked by further provocations to Jordan's sovereignty by the PR. In late August, an urgent PNC meeting in Amman tacitly declared Jordan as a Jordanian-Palestinian state, following which the PLO's Central Committee called for the overthrow of the Hashemite regime. The situation escalated with the PFLP's four airline hijackings on September 6–9, of which three were forced to land in Jordan, where the hijackers threatened to blow up the airplanes and their occupants unless Israel released Palestinian prisoners. The PFLP operation was apparently meant to trigger a confrontation with Jordan's regime, thus forcing friendly Arab regimes to intervene on behalf of the Palestinians. The hijackings, which met with reserved and uneasy Arab reactions, left King Husain little choice but to turn to arms. Hence, in the final analysis, whether or not Husain misinterpreted Nasir's stand as a "green light" to use massive force against the PR, by late August–early September the PR itself had created a crisis that forced the king to launch his offensive with or without Nasir's approval. His visit to Cairo, however, was instrumental in creating the impression of collusion with Nasir against the PR.[45]

The offensive against Palestinian strongholds, most of them situated in the refugee camps in Amman, alarmed the Arab regimes irrespective of their political systems or ideologies. Engulfed by a wave of sympathy for the Palestinians, they fiercely denounced King Husain. Expectedly, the universal outcry against Jordan served to restore some semblance of unity in the fragmented inter-Arab alignment. Acting at the behest of Tunisia's PM, Nasir convened an urgent summit meeting in Cairo on September 21 with the participation of seven other heads of state (Syria, Sudan, Saudi Arabia, Kuwait, Libya, Lebanon, and PDRY) and Tunisia's PM. Iraq and Algeria boycotted the meeting.[46]

The meeting was held two days after the Jordan crisis had assumed international dimensions. The Syrians had invaded Jordan with armored division strength and captured the area of Irbid in the north. However, due to a schism between the leaders of Syria's army and ruling party about the military intervention, the armored force had received no air defense, exposing it to Jordanian air attacks that had forced the Syrian column to retreat. Involved in the crisis by the United States, Israel was requested to provide an air shield to Jordan against the Syrian invasion, and massed troops in the Jordan Rift Valley, threatening possible intervention by the Iraqi force in Mafraq. The United States warned Moscow to refrain from intervening in the crisis and requested the Soviets to tame their Syrian client. Units of the American Sixth Fleet were ordered to the eastern Mediterranean. The Iraqi force stationed at Mafraq maintained neutrality—despite Iraq's pledge to defend the Palestinian guerrillas—reportedly as the result of coordination between Asad and Saddam Husain, the strong man in Baghdad.[47]

On the military front, Husain's forces overran the Palestinian positions in Amman, while on the political front the king engaged in delaying tactics, seeking to complete the military job before mounting Arab pressure forced him to stop. He sent his newly appointed PM—a Palestinian—General Da'ud, to Cairo's summit, where he defected under intense pressure. As the situation of the PR worsened, so did Husain's own political situation: Kuwait and Libya announced the suspension of financial aid to Jordan (stipulated in the Khartoum summit resolutions); Libya broke diplomatic relations; and Tunisia recalled its ambassador from Amman. The Cairo summit called on Jordan's monarch to halt the slaughter of Palestinians, and sent Numairi to Amman to arrange for a cease-fire, which came into effect on September 24. Three days later, Husain arrived in Cairo, following growing pressures by Arab heads of state who were hoping to work out a new agreement with the king.[48]

Husain and 'Arafat finally signed an agreement, initialled by the representatives of the eight states attending the summit meeting. A committee headed by the Tunisian PM was appointed to oversee the agreement's implementation and to impose collective Arab sanctions on whichever side violated it. Although the accord did not reflect the Jordanian Army's military advantage on the ground, Husain was induced by Nasir to accept it and to avoid his isolation in the Arab world. The Cairo Agreement showed that although Nasir's power and prestige had been seriously eroded since the 1967 war, he was still the primary leader in the inter-Arab arena. It was also his final achievement: on September 28, a day after signing the accord, he died.[49]

Nasir's death notwithstanding, in October, Jordan and the PLO signed three memoranda dealing with the PR's presence in Jordan, but also including important political provisions. Thus, in the October 13 accord, Jordan acknowledged that "Only the Palestinian people, represented by the Palestinian revolution, has the right to determine its own future."[50] In practice, however, the king continued his thrust to eliminate the PR's presence in Jordan, taking advantage of the confusion and lack of a leading power in the inter-Arab arena following Nasir's demise. The September crisis turned Hashemite Jordan anathema to Syria, Egypt, Libya, and Iraq. Yet Iraq's decision in March 1971 to pull its forces out of Jordan, and the heating up of the domestic power struggle in Damascus, removed the last constraints on King Husain regarding further blows against the PR. In July 1971, the Jordanian army conducted a comprehensive mopping-up operation, restoring Hashemite authority over the country as a whole, with the PR's decimated forces, weapons, and headquarters transferred to Syria and Lebanon.

The new Jordanian offensive prompted attempts by Qadhafi to summon an urgent Arab summit meeting, with only partial success. Except for Qadhafi and ʿArafat, only five heads of state attended, from Syria, Egypt, Yemen, and PDRY. ʿArafat and Libya demanded that the Arab states break off relations with Jordan and that it be expelled from the AL. Yet the meeting contented itself with a call to settle the Jordan crisis and implement the Cairo agreement, in addition to extending further financial, military, and moral assistance to the PR. The demand that sanctions be imposed on Jordan was rejected. The Tripoli meeting effectively did little more than express verbal support for the PR, as none of its resolutions—including those on financial and military support— were binding.[51]

That the meeting produced such indecisive results pointed to the participants' recognition of their limited ability to reverse the process, and their disagreement on priorities of collective action. In retrospect, the new rulers of Egypt and Syria might even have felt relieved at the blow to the PR, especially in view of their efforts to stabilize their shaky domestic positions. On Qadhafi's part, the meeting was an indication of his aspiration to assume a central role in regional Arab politics through patronizing the Palestinian cause as a means to consolidating his domestic and inter-Arab position.

8

THE ROAD TO THE OCTOBER WAR

With Nasir's death, and the simultaneous end of the War of Attrition and the September crisis in Jordan, the Middle East entered a new era in both inter-Arab relations and Arab strategy in the conflict with Israel. The symbolic conjunction of Nasir's demise and the crackdown on the PR in Jordan was accompanied, two months later, by another blow to the revolution in the Arab world when Hafiz al-Asad seized power in Syria, ending long army-party strife. The ascendancy of new regimes in two central Arab states paved the way for a new inter-Arab alignment away from Nasir's overshadowing image, boosting the strategy of phases in the conflict with Israel, which he had endorsed but only halfheartedly followed.

The elimination of the PR's presence in Jordan, the withdrawal of the Iraqi expeditionary force from that country, and most of all, Jordan's determination to prevent the use of its territory for further military activity against Israel all but inflicted a death blow on the EC. The Egypt-Jordan coalition came to its end and was replaced by Egyptian resentment toward the Jordanian monarch. Despite the blow to its presence in Jordan, however, the PR gained growing international attention due to its intensified armed struggle against Israel and international terrorism, and the rising influence of Arab oil in world politics. Indeed, Arab governments were bound to accelerate their efforts on behalf of the PLO's international recognition to compensate for their military inaction along Israel's borders and Egypt's enhanced diplomatic efforts in the conflict with Israel.

The early 1970s witnessed a diminished range of collective Arab policy-making through institutionalized inter-Arab forums. Neither the AL's forums nor a full-fledged summit—which failed to convene in the four years before the October war—was an essential framework for political or military cooperation. Instead, new bilateral alignments were to underpin the emergence of an Arab war coalition. By and large, it reflected continuity rather than the change in Egypt's (diminishing) role as a supreme power in regional Arab politics since 1967. Nasir's death heralded the start of a transitory period in which newly emerged regimes turned to revising previous ideological and strategic concepts against the backdrop of strict constraints, a changing regional balance of power, and a new global atmosphere. Nasir's painful failure at the Rabat summit indicated the futility of convening this forum unless it had been sufficiently prepared to produce the results intended by the leading actors.

During and after the PLO's expulsion from Jordan, attempts were made by Tunisia, Egypt, and Libya to convene a summit conference to discuss Jordan's abuse of the Cairo and Amman agreements. King Husain, too, seized on this tactic, urging that a summit be convened to consider overall Arab strategy in the conflict with Israel. Such a meeting would divert attention from his problems with the PR and reassert Jordan's indispensable role in any political settlement with Israel, especially in the light of Sadat's initiative of February 1971 for an Israeli-Egyptian interim agreement in Sinai. The king was also anxious to throw cold water on Sadat's recently mooted idea to establish a Palestinian government-in-exile, which could boost international recognition of the PLO and undermine Jordan's claim for the West Bank.

Sadat's Futile Diplomacy

The main reason for the wait-and-see attitude in the Arab world—a stance most Arab leaders found convenient—was Sadat's ambiguous strategy in the conflict with Israel. The *de facto* prolongation of the Egypt-Israel cease-fire, combined with Sadat's assertion that 1971 would be "the year of decision," led to some bewilderment among Arab leaders: Was Egypt bent on breaking the cease-fire or on launching a new political initiative? Sadat's lingering over a decision on a war initiative was a result of two major factors, both of which underlined his independent diplomacy. First, his futile diplomatic efforts and contacts with Washington, which revealed the low priority the United States had been giving to peacemaking in the Middle East due to perceived Israeli military eminence and the unbridgeable gap between Arab and Israeli positions. Second, his uneasy relations with the Soviet Union over the supply of offensive weaponry and the very idea of turning those arms against Israel.[1] Finally, it was Sadat's frustrated diplomacy that led him to the inevitable decision to go to war—despite Soviet procrastination and reluctance on arms supplies—as a last resort, to catalyze a diplomatic settlement to the conflict.

Sadat succeeded Nasir by virtue of being the vice president, but it was not until May 1971 that he assumed full authority as Egypt's president, following the removal of his Nasirist rivals from the state's centers of power—the presidency, the ruling party, and the armed forces. Sadat's effort to free himself from Nasir's Pan-Arab legacy was symbolically marked by changing the state's name from the anachronistic UAR to the Arab Republic of Egypt, indicating a shift toward a state-centric approach. Domestically, he was to foster alignment with the urban bourgeoisie and the new middle class, as well as the Muslim Brotherhood, for whom Pan-Arabism was anathema. Internationally, Sadat adopted Nasir's independent diplomatic course. Shortly after his ascendancy, Sadat asserted to Washington his interest in advancing the diplomatic efforts, and in November he agreed to extend the cease-fire for another three months. Sadat's efforts thereafter to resume the diplomatic efforts under American auspices reflected his awareness of the absence of a realistic military option for retrieving Sinai due to Israel's military eminence.[2] Sadat's diplomatic effort, however, suffered from extremely narrow margins due to his serious domestic constraints—Nasir's overshadowing image; a longstanding economic austerity; almost-full military mobilization since 1967 and yet inaction, resulting in rapidly dwindling credibility, as expressed by student riots at the end of 1971.

In January 1971, Israeli and Egyptian ideas concerning an interim settlement, focusing on partial Israeli withdrawal from the canal, were discussed with the U.S. government. On February 4, amidst pressure from the military to resume the war of attrition, Sadat announced the cease-fire's prolongation by another month, during which a partial withdrawal of Israeli forces from the canal—to the El 'Arish-Ras Muhammad line, as specified later—would be realized and work toward reopening the Suez Canal for navigation begun. Sadat explained that this would be the first step in a comprehensive implementation of all the provisions of Resolution 242 according to an agreed upon timetable. Five days later, Israel's PM Golda Meir publicly responded in favor of Sadat's approach. Nonetheless, the Egyptian initiative never left the ground. On February 7, Jarring, launching his last mediation effort, submitted to Israel and Egypt an *aide-memoire* suggesting full Israeli withdrawal to the international border, security arrangements, and Egyptian acceptance of peace with Israel. The Jarring proposals, which ignored Sadat's initiative, effectively confirmed Egypt's interpretation of Resolution 242. No wonder Israel responded in the negative while Cairo welcomed the new proposals—although not without additional conditions regarding withdrawal from the Gaza Strip and settlement of the Palestinian refugee problem.[3]

In the absence of U.S. presidential willingness to exert pressure on Israel the gap between the two parties remained unbridgeable. Israel conceived the interim settlement as an indefinite cease-fire, securing its free passage in the canal in return for partial withdrawal of its forces and demilitarization of the evacuated territory. Apart from demanding direct negotiations with the Arabs, Israel refused to return to the pre-June 1967 border even in return for peace with Egypt, adhering to Resolution 242's formula of the right of all states in the region to "secure and recognized borders." In contrast, Egypt was prepared to end the state of war with Israel—the practical meaning of the term "peace" in Sadat's rhetoric—and to allow Israel free navigation in the canal in return for full implementation of Resolution 242. Sadat objected to a separate settlement, insisting—in accordance with Moscow's position—that any interim agreement should be part of a comprehensive one based on full Israeli withdrawal to the pre-1967 borders and solution of the Palestinian problem. Any interim settlement, including a military disengagement, was to be temporary and linked to a comprehensive settlement. In March, Sadat announced his refusal to prolong the cease-fire, declaring 1971 as "the year of decision," either for war or peace. Practically, the cease-fire was preserved and diplomatic efforts continued.[4]

By June 1971, the interim agreement diplomacy came to its futile end. Further talks between FM Riyad and SoS Rogers in September of that year proved no more fruitful. The end of the Vietnam war led to increasing Arab pressure on the U.S. president to undertake active involvement in Middle East peacemaking. In April 1972, Sadat started communicating with the White House through secret intelligence and Saudi channels. Reportedly, Sadat assumed that the United States had the ability to pressure Israel to accept a political settlement that Egypt would approve.[5] Yet a breakthrough in Washington's Middle East diplomacy—even after Sadat's "bombshell" of expelling Soviet combat personnel and military advisers in July 1972—proved still unrealistic. Further contacts with Washington, including two secret meetings (February and May 1973) between Sadat's and Nixon's national security advisers, Hafiz Isma'il and Kissinger, made it clear to Cairo that Washington perceived the gap between Egypt and Israel as too wide for the United States to bridge. Washington was willing to play an active role in the peacemaking process if Egypt moved further toward Israel's position. Meanwhile, Kissinger advised the Egyptians to refrain from a military move that could bring the Arabs another defeat. The first meeting confirmed that a military initiative was inevitable. On April 5, Sadat established a war cabinet under his presidency, in which a specific decision on war was made, though it was by no means irreversible as the second Kissinger-Isma'il meeting showed.[6]

With the failure of the efforts to reach an interim settlement in early 1971, international peacemaking diplomacy effectively came to a standstill. This was a reflection of a *de facto* cease-fire along the Suez Canal and the Jordan River, as well as of the growing intimacy in the relations between Washington and Jerusalem, which resulted in unprecedented levels of military aid to Israel. Israel and the United States seemed to share the conviction that regional stability could be secured by Israel's military edge over any Arab coalition, and that Sadat had no real military option.[7]

Egypt's military capability indeed fell short of securing such an option or balancing Israel's power, representing Cairo's rocky relations with Moscow, whose growing interest in a detente with the United States dictated an avoidance of confrontation in the Middle East. Moscow did seek to consolidate its relations with Egypt's new regime, especially in view of its departure from Nasir's domestic and foreign policies and its development of a dialogue with Washington. The Soviet-Egyptian Treaty of Friendship and Cooperation, signed in May 1971, was the result of Sadat's initiative following the failure of the American mediation efforts. Yet while the Treaty was bound to deepen American and Israeli reservations as to an interim agreement, it failed to meet Egypt's expectations for adequate arms supplies. Moscow's practice of procrastination and delay in supplying Egypt the requested offensive weaponry according to a specified timetable became a source of bitterness among the highest Egyptian political and military echelons.[8]

Egypt's frustration at Moscow's Middle East policy was aggravated by the May 1972 Nixon-Brezhnev summit in Moscow, which indicated that the USSR had given up its Middle East clients in return for detente with its American counterpart. With diplomatic peacemaking efforts stalemated, Sadat had every reason to be concerned lest the detente between the two superpowers freeze the Middle East situation indefinitely in a "no war–no peace" mode. It would also explain the Soviet reluctance to supply Egypt the advanced weaponry it had requested and to support a limited military action to trigger a diplomatic process. Against this backdrop Sadat ordered, on July 8, the expulsion of some eight thousand Soviet combat personnel and military advisers from Egypt. The decision had been advocated—aside from Saudi Arabia—by the high military command and was discussed with the Kremlin in April during Sadat's visit. Its main significance, however, lay in removing an obstacle to an independent Egyptian decision to go to war. Sadat allegedly meant to indicate to Washington that he was willing to rid himself of Soviet influence and thus deserved more active U.S. diplomatic support in the peacemaking effort. The decision indeed led to an immediate invitation from Kissinger to open a secret dialogue on a Middle East settlement, which bore no fruit.[9]

Despite the ensuing freeze in Egypt-Soviet relations, in November 1972 Sadat instructed the new war minister, Ahmad Isma'il 'Ali, to begin military preparations for war with the existing means at Egypt's disposal. The new appointment and decision to prepare for war was necessary to stabilize the domestic arena and bring the Egyptian General Staff into line with the President's concept of a limited war aimed at securing a foothold on the east bank of the canal. In his directions to the military, Sadat emphasized—with some exaggeration—that what was needed for breaking the political stalemate was the "canal crossing and occupation of ten centimeters" of Sinai.[10]

The growing Soviet-Egyptian tension, which culminated in the blow inflicted by Sadat on Soviet prestige in July 1972, prompted Moscow's effort to reinforce its relations with other Arab clients. In April, the Soviet Union concluded a Treaty of Friendship with Iraq, followed by substantial arms supplies. In July, Moscow concluded with Syria a $700 million arms deal, following which the number of Soviet military advisers in that country soared dramatically. This set in motion a continued process of warmer Syrian-Soviet relations, even without a formal treaty between them. Moreover, in March 1973, a new arms deal, unprecedented in its financial volume, was reached between Egypt and the USSR, the cost of which was to be covered mostly by the Arab oil states. Although the main part of this deal would not be implemented until the October war, its very adoption—enabling the return of 1500–2000 Soviet military advisers to Egypt—and an early supply of ground-to-ground SCUD missiles, enhanced Egyptian confidence in its own military capability. Hence, the USSR did play a central role in Arab preparations for war, which, by April–May 1973, gathered a discernible momentum. Indeed, despite Moscow's adherence to diplomatic resolution of the conflict, and interest in detente with the United States, the supply of advanced weapons to Arab clients was necessary to preserve its influence in the area, especially in the face of Egypt's determination to go to war. In the case of Syria, this could be justified by the repeated manifestations of Israel's air force's superiority in clashes with Syria triggered by Israel's retaliations to PR operations.[11]

Jordan, the PLO, and the Occupied Territories

In September 1970, King Husain managed to save his throne, but the price—which he might have eventually paid anyway—was a deep erosion of his claim to represent the cause of the occupied West Bank. Held responsible for massacring the Palestinians and preventing them from resuming activity on Jordanian soil, King Husain was resented and isolated by his Arab counterparts as well as by many Palestinians in the occupied territories. It was in this context, and due to Israel's decision to hold municipal elections in the West Bank, that the king moved to limit his losses by announcing, in March 1972, the United Arab Kingdom plan. The plan proposed the establishment of a federation between Jordan and Palestine, namely, the two banks of River Jordan, which were to assume autonomous executive and legislative authorities, leaving open the possibility of including Gaza in the kingdom as well.

By offering ostensibly equal status to an autonomous Palestinian unit in a joint federation, the king meant to reassert his claim for the West Bank/Gaza Strip and recover his eroded prestige. Apart from the significance of Jerusalem for the Hashemite regime, highlighting its continued involvement in the conflict with Israel was essential as a source of legitimacy and ensurance of continued Arab financial aid. However, the outrageous reactions the king's plan faced, including Cairo's decision to sever diplomatic relations with Amman, pointed to the plan's perceived anachronism in the Arab world. Yet King Husain, once released from the PR burden and his obligation toward Nasir, and encouraged by American military and economic aid, exercised more independence in his regional policymaking. The unprecedented stability and economic progress that marked the period after September 1970 enabled the Hashemite regime to rebuild Jordan's political and socio-economic bases, and reinforce its own authority and stature as the source of power and political legitimacy in Jordan.[12]

The erosion of the Hashemite Kingdom's claim for the West Bank came to be reflected by the rising status of the PLO as the representative of the Palestinian people, a trend accounted for mainly by Sadat. Motivated by a necessity to enhance his political legitimacy—especially against the backdrop of prolonged military inaction against Israel—and to preserve his alliance with Syria, Sadat demonstrated the utmost support for the PLO's claim to be the exclusive representative of the Palestinian people. Moreover, Sadat sought to bring the PLO into line with "state-like" thinking and win its mainstream's support for his own strategy of phases in the conflict with Israel. Sadat thus took further Nasir's concept of Palestinian nationalism and the link between people and a specific territory by emphasizing the PLO's status as the sole representative of the Palestinian people; suggesting that the PLO establish a Palestinian government-in-exile; and calling on the PR and the PLO to accept—as a first stage—the establishment of a Palestinian state in the West Bank and Gaza Strip, an idea that had been raised by Palestinian figures in the West Bank since 1967. Sadat made an effort to promote international recognition of the Palestinian national claim for sovereignty over the West Bank and Gaza Strip. Though the PLO did not accept these ideas, they unmistakably undermined King Husain's claim for the West Bank. Hence, at Hafiz Isma'il's talks with Kissinger, the former raised the possibility that King Husain might be the Arab party for a settlement on the West Bank even though he might not ultimately govern it. In 1973, Egypt officially adopted Bourguiba's call for the establishment of a Palestinian state based on the 1947 UN partition resolution, capitalizing on the international legitimacy of the idea and tacitly accepting a "reduced" Israeli state.[13]

Sadat's thrust to secure international recognition of the Palestinian national dimension in the conflict with Israel coalesced with the growing echoes of PR military operations. The 1970–71 Palestinian trauma in Jordan resulted in the adoption of a radical political attitude by the PLO's mainstream against the Hashemite regime. This was combined with the resorting by Fatah—operating under the title "Black September"—to international terrorism against Jordanian, Israeli, and Western targets, along with other Palestinian groups. Palestinian international terrorism had a strong publicity effect through the world media, which forcefully raised the Palestine cause onto the world agenda. Palestinian guerrilla activity continued sporadically to use Syria's territory, but it was Lebanon that became its mainstay. Having gone through the Jordanian experience, the PR turned to entrench itself in Lebanon by cultivating close cooperation with Lebanese opposition movements, particularly the Muslim militias. In the absence of war between Israel and the Arab states, the PR's activities both along Israel's northern borders and abroad—triggering massive Israeli retaliations against Palestinian bases in Lebanon and Syria and clashes with the latter's armies—was the main expression of hostilities in the conflict in the years 1971–73. Israel's raid on the PR's headquarters in Beirut, in April 1973, generated another Lebanese-Palestinian crisis following the Lebanese army's attempt to restrict the military activities of the PR. This effort, however, was undercut by Syrian intervention on the PR's behalf.[14]

Emergence of the 1973 War Coalition

Contrary to the paucity of collective Arab activity before the October war, far-reaching changes were occurring on the bilateral level, without which neither the war nor its political aftermath would have been possible. Egypt assumed the central role in forging a new pattern of inter-Arab alignments by serving as the axis for a trilateral coalition with Syria and Saudi Arabia. Although Nasir's disappearance from the scene in itself had a positive effect on Cairo's relations with Damascus and Riyad, of even more importance to the ensuing tripartite coalition was Asad's final seizure of power in Damascus and his pragmatic approach to inter-Arab relations.

Most important, however, in shaping the new inter-Arab alignment was Sadat's concept of inter-Arab relations. Once his position as president had been secured, Sadat focused his regional policy on achieving a concrete and practical goal, namely, consolidation of Egypt's relations with its necessary partners in a war coalition, should such war become inevitable. Sadat showed considerable skepticism about the Arab states' willingness to share with Egypt the burden of war with Israel without entangling him in undesired commitments and bickering. He represented a new concept of inter-Arab relations that perceived cooperation—including reception of material aid—with any Arab partner conditional on mutual respect for each other's sovereignty and independent decisions.

Sadat and Asad differed in their political philosophies and type of leadership. Yet they shared a fresh political approach in inter-Arab politics, which can be best defined by their departure from compulsive Pan-Arabism in favor of pragmatic cooperation. The main difference between the two figures hinged on the strategy in the conflict with Israel that was to surface in the aftermath of the October war. Sadat was a master tactician to whom strategy served mainly as a source of legitimacy, a proclamation of intentions under which practical policymaking was to be shaped according to opportunities and constraints rather than being rigidly limited by ideological principles. Sadat's strategic goal in the conflict with Israel—a comprehensive settlement based on Resolution 242, and the establishment of a Palestinian state in the West Bank and Gaza Strip—was to be adhered to but without allowing it to preclude interim settlements, even if they meant political concessions to Israel. Indeed, even before the 1973 war, Sadat unmistakably spelled out his willingness to end the state of war with Israel in return for its withdrawal to its pre-1967 war borders. In contrast, Asad represented the concept of continued struggle against Israel until its final elimination, though without precluding the use of diplomacy as long as it was not to compromise the strategic goal. Thus, his tactics were rigidly linked to the strategic aim, stemming from an overall perception of the struggle against Israel as a "zero sum" conflict, which determined its resolution primarily by military means.[15]

Induced by Syrian military inferiority in the face of Israel, Asad was determined to forge a coalition with Egypt and other Arab states to avoid isolation and perhaps to prevent a potential separate Egyptian-Israeli settlement. Since the paramount goal was the struggle with Israel, military coordination among the confrontation states was a *sine qua non* irrespective of ideological and political differences. Asad's inter-Arab policy was indicated by his joining the federation of Egypt, Sudan, and Libya under the Tripoli Charter only two weeks after the coup that brought him to power. The Charter paved the way for the foundation, in April 1971, of the Federation of Arab Republics (FAR), comprising Libya, Egypt, and Syria, shortly after Sudan announced that it intended to cease activity in the earlier framework. The FAR stipulated full political, military, and economic union, representing Egypt's needs for regional support in the post-1967 years. For Syria, however, given its geographic separation, the union's main purpose was to prevent Syrian isolation, and to serve as a source of regional Arab legitimacy, and political backing. Yet the FAR proved totally ineffective, one reason being the subsequent falling-out between Sadat and Qadhafi.[16]

Egypt's quest for a partner in tangible inter-Arab military cooperation was thus limited to Syria, with whom high-ranking military contacts had been maintained since early 1971. Indeed, Syria's opposition to settling the conflict with Israel on the basis of Resolution 242 did not prevent a rapid rapprochement between the two new leaders. Syria also refrained from criticizing Egypt's diplomatic efforts based on Resolution 242. Asad's assent to Egypt's proposal for a military initiative was preceded, however, by an apparent moderation of the Syrian position on a political settlement. In March 1972, while emphasizing the need for combined military and political action, Asad stated that Resolution 242 would be acceptable if it was understood as a framework for total Israeli withdrawal to the 1967 lines and the restoration of the Palestinian people's rights. Whatever the two countries' divergent views on a political settlement, Asad could hardly turn down the opportunity for a joint military initiative with Egypt, which would serve his regime's domestic needs and achieve just what Damascus had been advocating for years.[17]

Despite intensified Egyptian preparations for war and coordination efforts with Syria, it was only in April 1973—following the failure of diplomatic efforts with the United States—that Sadat and Asad, in their secret meeting at Burj al-'Arab in Egypt, agreed on a common platform and timetable for launching a coordinated attack on Israel. But even at the initial stage of political coordination differences of interest surfaced. Egypt's military situation dictated a limited war goal, namely, crossing the canal and occupying a secure bridgehead along the east bank to a depth of between ten and twelve km. Syria insisted that Egypt commit itself to take over the strategic Gidi and Mitla passes—thirty km deeper into Sinai—which, if realized, would remove a strategic obstacle on Egypt's way to liberating Sinai as a whole. To ensure Syria's participation in the war, Sadat ostensibly accepted Asad's condition and instructed his military aides to prepare a plan for reaching the passes and redefine the war goal accordingly. Practically, however, it was only a facade meant to satisfy the Syrians. Recognizing that the idea of reaching the passes was militarily theoretical, the Egyptian GHQ's revised plan—later revealed by CoS Shazli as sheer deception—remained in fact unchanged in its limited goals.[18]

The offensive was to be launched in surprise, following a deception plan based on the Egyptian armed forces' repeated crossing maneuvers, from one of which an attack was to be developed, held between May and October. In May, such a maneuver caused an Israeli military alert, but only in late August was the final date for the offensive—codenamed "Badr"—confirmed in a meeting between Sadat and Asad in Damascus shortly after a conference of their GHQs had been held in Alexandria to finalize the joint military plan.[19]

The Egyptian-Syrian rapprochement coincided with a basic change in Egypt-Saudi relations. Egypt's declining standing in the Arab world, resulting from its defeat in 1967 and growing economic dependence on the Arab oil states, was already much in evidence at the Rabat summit, when Saudi Arabia and Kuwait spurned Cairo's appeals for increased aid. Nasir's death and Sadat's ascendancy paved the way for Riyad and Cairo to establish a different pattern of relations firmly based on mutual interests and respect for sovereignty. An impoverished, enfeebled Egypt, without Nasir and his ambition for regional hegemony, no longer threatened Faisal. The Saudi monarch would gain leverage over Egypt directly—through generous financial aid—and indirectly, by lobbying for American support of Sadat's political claims in the conflict with Israel.

A paramount objective of Faisal was to distance Egypt from both Qadhafi's radicalism and Soviet influence. Faisal deplored Egypt's total reliance on the USSR, although the Saudis could discern that Sadat was far less committed to Moscow than his predecessor and that his affinity for them was grounded in practical military needs: given the proper inducements, they were told, Cairo would terminate its alliance with Moscow. For his part, Sadat was amenable to opening a new chapter in relations with Faisal, based on equality between their countries and recognition of Riyad's leading position in the Arabian Peninsula. Improved relations between the two regimes was both spurred and reinforced by personal understanding and secret contacts between the two leaders. Ever since his ascendancy, Sadat, a devout Muslim, had been battling against Nasir's ideological and institutional legacy, which was anathema to the Saudi monarch. Faisal was instrumental in bringing about an understanding between Sadat and the Muslim Brotherhood, whose renewed activity was expected to enhance Sadat's domestic stature. Indeed, following the Soviets' expulsion, Sadat's relations with the Saudis and other Gulf monarchies were tightened, leading to the latter's growing financial aid for Egypt's arms procurement from the Soviets as well as from Britain. Altogether, Arab financial aid to Egypt for military purposes, primarily from Kuwait, Qatar, and Abu Dhabi, reached $1250 million of which $700 million was paid directly to Moscow in Egypt's arms deal of March 1973, most of which was fulfilled during the war.[20]

The early 1970s witnessed a dramatic rise in the role and influence of Arab oil producers in the world's energy market and politics. The change was a result of rapidly surging demand throughout the world for oil that could be supplied almost exclusively from Middle East sources. It was particularly the case in the United States where a decline in oil production and reserves, compounded by a monetary crisis, intensified its dependency on Middle East—mostly Arab—oil. Against this favorable backdrop, a revolutionary change occurred in the old pattern of relations between Middle East oil-producing countries and the concessionaire companies. The former consolidated their national control over their oil resources and, while jacking up oil prices, succeeded in securing for themselves a growing share of the revenues.[21]

Initially pushed by radical Libya and Algeria, the Arab oil producers' block, led by Saudi Arabia, played a pivotal role in this trend, which was accompanied by intensified threats to cease oil supply to the Western world due to its pro-Israel stance in the Middle East conflict. Particularly Qadhafi, and from late 1972 King Faisal as well, were active in pressuring Black African states to sever diplomatic relations with Israel. Under these circumstances, the Saudis were ready to play their part in cooperating with Egypt's war plans. By the end of August 1973, Faisal informed Sadat that he would be willing to use oil as a weapon in the campaign against Israel provided a war was of sufficient duration for the West to experience the full impact of the oil shortage.[22]

Following Sadat's decision to prepare for war, the Egyptian GHQ, in conjunction with the new ALSG Mahmud Riyad, embarked on a systematic effort to seek the active participation of Arab forces in the anticipated battle. In meetings of the ADC held since December 1971, pledges for unprecedented contributions of combat units had been underwritten by the Arab states, though most of them were to be implemented only after war had begun, while others were never implemented. By and large, these pledges were obtained through bilateral meetings with Arab heads of state—conducted by Riyad and Egypt's CoS Shazli. They totalled fourteen squadrons, one armored division, and some armored and infantry brigades. The ADC meeting in December 1972 concluded, *inter alia,* to establish an Arab organization for arms production.[23]

Sadat and Asad sought to induce King Husain to take part in the war, or at least to undertake to defend his territory against a possible Israeli attempt to outflank the Syrians. Despite Sadat's and Asad's acrimonious relations with King Husain and his repeated refusal to use his land for waging war against Israel, on September 10, the three leaders held a mini-summit meeting in Cairo at King Husain's proposal. Asad and Sadat might have sought to mend their fences with the king and oblige him to take an active part in the war, while for Husain it was an opportunity to gain Syria and Egypt's renewed recognition. It is doubted, however, that Asad and Sadat would have realistically expected the king to be ready for war less than a month before its defined D-Day, or that he had been fully informed about its details and timetable. Egypt's and Syria's reluctance to share fully their military plans with the king was vindicated by his reported secret visit to Israel on September 25, in which he warned PM Golda Meir about the war that Syria and Egypt had been planning, though without specifying its date.[24]

The priority Sadat gave to building a war coalition and his insistence on refraining from joining inter-Arab disputes over marginal issues was manifested in his sour relations with Qadhafi. Sadat was interested in Libya's financial and material aid but showed little patience for Qadhafi's pressures to realize unity with Egypt while encroaching on Egypt's sovereign decisions on foreign policy. Qadhafi's drive to be involved in the Palestine issue and, as of early 1972, to establish unity with Egypt, represented his own security needs in the face of both domestic and external threats. Qadhafi sought to establish Egyptian economic dependence on Libya and was uncomfortable about Sadat's rapproachement with Asad and Faisal because it seemed to diminish his own standing vis-à-vis Egypt. As a revolutionary, Qadhafi rejected Resolution 242 and as a devout Muslim, who considered communism heretical, he missed no chance to discredit the Soviets and their arms, though it did not prevent him from underwriting a large part of Egypt's purchases from them.[25] Sadat's strained relations with Qadhafi explain why the latter was not informed of the secret war plan until the last minute, despite his considerable material contribution to Egypt's war effort in the form of weapons, oil deliveries, and financial aid. Sadat's troubled relations with Qadhafi culminated in a crisis during the 1973 war and set the tone for their mutual hostility during the rest of Sadat's presidency.[26]

Arab efforts to consolidate the Third World's support against Israel before the October war culminated in the ONAS conference convened in Algiers on September 5. With seventy-eight countries taking part, the Arab leaders unanimously called for concrete political measures against Israel, in what was to become the main form of Arab political warfare in the conflict with Israel after October 1973. The resolutions adopted at the conference included support for the Arab confrontation states and readiness to assist them with all means in liberating their lands. The conference constituted a major Arab success, reflecting the growing influence of Arab oil and the concomitant fear of many African countries that they would lose access to Arab energy sources unless they acted to isolate Israel and express solidarity with the Arab cause. The conference also called for ending U.S. military and other aid to Israel, and recognized the PLO as the sole legitimate representative of the Palestinian people. However, the Arabs' key achievement lay in engineering resolutions encouraging Black African states to cut diplomatic relations with Israel. Indeed, twenty-two African states did so either during or immediately after the war (eight states had severed relations before the war) when further prodded by Sadat following the crossing of the Suez Canal by Israeli forces, as an act of solidarity with an African sister-state made a victim of aggression.[27]

Uniting for War

The outbreak of war in the Middle East on October 6 (the Jewish Day of Atonement) was a strategic surprise to Israel, whose military establishment had adhered to its estimation that Egypt was not prepared for war and hence did not intend to wage it. The war also took most of the Arab leaders by surprise. Nonetheless, the Egyptian and Syrian offensives' initial success and the relative length of the hostilities generated immense enthusiasm and solidarity in the Arab world, demonstrating the compelling force of enmity toward Israel. The immediate result was an outpouring of military, economic, and political assistance to the embattled Arab states on a scale not previously seen.

Nine Arab states (Iraq, Algeria, Jordan, Libya, Morocco, Tunisia, Kuwait, Sudan, and Saudi Arabia) dispatched forces and weaponry to the front—albeit token in a few cases. Saudi Arabia and Kuwait, as well as Morocco, failed to meet their pledges to send Lightning and F-5 squadrons, respectively, but did send land forces. Other Arab states lived up to their promises and in some cases even exceeded them. On the whole, the total magnitude of Arab expeditionary forces was significant: ten squadrons, one armored and one mechanized division, five armored and two infantry brigades, and two infantry battalions.[28]

Regardless of its enmity to Damascus, Iraq sent the largest expeditionary force—two armored/mechanized divisions and four squadrons to the Syrian front and another squadron to the Egyptian front. King Husain withstood heavy external and domestic pressure to open a third front, on the grounds of fear that retaliatory Israeli air strikes would decimate his forces. Yielding to the pressures, he sent two armored brigades to the Syrian front after confiding his decision to Israel. Morocco also sent an armored brigade to bolster the Syrians. Although inter-Arab military coordination on the battlefield proved faulty, the Iraqi and Jordanian expeditionary forces, which sustained heavy losses in the battles of October 12 and 13 respectively, played a crucial role in helping contain Israel's counterattack and preventing it from making even deeper inroads into Syrian territory.[29]

On the Egyptian front, the main contribution of Libya's, Algeria's, and Iraq's expeditionary squadrons was in providing air assistance to ground operations. Additional Arab forces operating on the Egyptian front included a Libyan armored brigade and a Kuwaiti infantry battalion that had already been deployed in Egypt before the war, and an Algerian armored brigade that arrived on October 17, though neither of these units took an active part in the war. After the cease-fire went into effect, a Sudanese infantry brigade arrived in the front.

For the first time in the annals of the Arab-Israeli conflict the oil weapon was used effectively, even though no cohesive or comprehensive boycott plan had existed before the war started. Sadat, anxious to avoid Nasir's mistakes, did not ask any Arab state to make a prior commitment to wield the oil weapon, believing they would follow the Saudi lead once the war began. Still, it was not until October 10 that Sadat approached the Saudis with a request to use the oil weapon, as a countermeasure to the American's air-lifted support for Israel. On October 16, Arab oil ministers convened in Kuwait and proclaimed an embargo on petroleum shipments to the United States and Holland. Tagged on to the embargo was an ultimatum: it would be rescinded only after Israel withdrew from all Arab territories occupied in 1967 and the rights of the Palestinians were guaranteed. To pressure other countries, it was decided to cut their oil supplies by five percent per month until the Arabs' terms were met. Beyond economic calculations, the oil producers' decisions were made to demonstrate their own contribution to the war effort and to ensure their immunity in the face of Arab radicalism.[30] Algeria, Saudi Arabia, the UAE, and Qatar supported the war effort financially as well. The former offered Moscow $200 million to underwrite emergency military aid for both Egypt and Syria, while the Gulf monarchies gave Egypt the same amount as a grant.[31]

But even while the fighting still raged, it was apparent that Arab unity was far from solid. The initial spirit of Arab solidarity and euphoria faded shortly after Israel had retrieved the military initiative (and more so because of Sadat's war diplomacy), giving way to mutual recriminations and bitter inter-Arab differences over both the operative and the strategic goals of the war and its desired course. Qadhafi publicly assailed Sadat's conception of a limited war and called for total war. Husain remained adamant on keeping his territory out of the war, overriding appeals by Sadat to permit PR's raids from Jordan against Israel, as well as Soviet encouragement to enter the war under their air umbrella. Saudi Arabia and Kuwait, the chief repositories of foreign currency reserves, were also the chief wielders of the oil weapon—others used it sparingly, if at all. Thus, Libya and Iraq, their radical postures notwithstanding, did not join the boycott, on grounds of disagreement with Sadat's war diplomacy. Their calculations were partly economic—a chance to increase their revenues, as Iraq stepped up its oil output in this period—and partly political: to show their displeasure at Saudi hegemony in this domain.[32]

Most significantly, ruptures in the united Arab front appeared between Syria and Egypt, the two main protagonists and partners. The Syrians, who had scored impressive achievements in the Golan Hights during the first two days of the war, allegedly asked the Soviets to arrange a cease-fire which was objected by Cairo. By October 9, the Syrians had been turned back to the Purple Line amidst fierce Israeli air raids against in-depth strategic targets, while the Egyptian forces in Sinai continued to dig in, showing no intention of advancing their offensive further to the east as had been agreed beforehand. The Egyptian pause was perceived in Damascus as a blunt breach of Sadat's commitment to advance his forces' offensive to the Sinai passes. The Syrian demand that Egypt launch an immediate charge toward the passes grew in rage and became unavoidable for Sadat following Israel's offensive on October 10–11, which brought its armored forces within gun range of Damascus' suburbs. However, Sadat's orders to his GHQ to wage the requested offensive faced strong objection from the Egyptian field commanders and, when eventually executed on October 14, it ended with disastrous results for the Egyptian armored forces. The Egyptian offensive—later presented as a political decision undertaken to help the beleaguered Syrians—paved the way for the Israeli counter attack and the canal crossing into Egypt's territory on October 16.[33]

Above all, it was the timing and conditions of the cease-fire, and the independent manner that marked its acceptance by Egypt, that caused the discord between Cairo and Damascus. Almost from the beginning of the war, Kissinger, now SoS, maintained direct communications with Egypt in an attempt to obtain a cease-fire and return to the pre-October 5 lines. Egypt responded by demanding an Israeli pledge of full withdrawal to the pre-1967 boundary within a specified time limit. In return, Egypt repeated its willingness to end the state of belligerency as soon as the withdrawal was completed, to be followed by a peace conference. Though neither the United States nor Israel would accept such conditions, the tone of the Egyptian message, pledging to refrain from expanding the fighting into Israel and threatening Western interests, was interpreted by Kissinger as inviting continued dialogue.[34]

The October war was marked by unprecedented American and Soviet involvement with their respective clients as well as between them in managing the crisis and preventing repercussions on their own relations. This took the form of efforts to bring about a cease-fire, and, on October 9–10, a Soviet air and sea lift of arms to Syria and Egypt, followed by an American air lift to Israel, which prolonged the fighting and allowed Israel to turn the military situation in its favor. Despite the Powers' crisis-management efforts, however, a point of declaring nuclear alert by the United States was reached when, on October 24, the Soviets threatened to intervene militarily to prevent Israel—which had renewed its offensive toward Suez in spite of the cease-fire ordered by the UNSC two days earlier—from fully surrounding, and perhaps destroying, Egypt's Third Army in the Suez southern sector.[35]

Egypt's conditions for a cease-fire, fully supported by Moscow, remained intact until October 19, when the Israeli forces' growing penetration west of the canal forced Sadat to accept a cease-fire in place. Sadat notified Asad on October 19 of his intention to accept a cease-fire on the existing lines. The Syrians, however, felt deceived by their war ally, accusing Egypt of acting unilaterally. By so doing, Damascus claimed, Egypt forced Syria to break off hostilities before having retrieved any of the territory Israel had captured in 1967. The Syrian dilemma was further aggravated by Iraq's rejection of the cease-fire ordered by UNSC Resolution 338 as of October 22, which, in addition to reaffirming the need to implement Resolution 242, also called for immediate negotiations between the parties concerned to reach peace settlement "under appropriate auspices." Baghdad threatened—and, when Syria accepted the cease-fire, lived up to its threat—to remove its troops from Syria in the name of "the rights of the Palestinian Arab people" and "serious military and security matters."[36]

Interim Summary

The 1967 war compelled the Arab states to undergo a process of adaptation to the new strategic reality on both collective action toward Israel and inter-Arab relations. By and large, the changes were a reflection of Egypt's new constraints and choices. Its vacillation and dilemmas kept the whole Arab system in limbo, just as its decisiveness and action drew in other Arab states behind its lead. Egypt's diminished regional power and prestige after 1967 notwithstanding, the course of regional politics in the period until 1973 still underlined its centrality to shape the parameters of new inter-Arab relations and alter other Arabs' attitudes in the conflict with Israel.

The defeat and loss of national land sustained by the regimes identified with militant Pan-Arabism and social revolution enabled the oil-rich conservative regimes to acquire further legitimacy and regional influence. The growing flow of oil revenues to the Arab producers gathered momentum in the early 1970s, though its full impact on regional politics was to appear in the wake of the October war. That Egypt and Syria acknowledged Saudi Arabia as a partner in the Arab wartime coalition attested to its enhanced international standing as OPEC's leading power, in addition to its ability to foot the bill for the anti-Israel military and political campaign. Economic calculations were apparently prevalent in the Saudi decision to apply an oil embargo during the war, which boosted Riyad's prestige in the world as a whole.

The altered pattern of inter-Arab relations was increasingly shaped by the confrontation states' financial needs and the ability of the Gulf monarchies to provide the required aid. The result was to enhance the concept of *raison d'état* in the Arab world. Moreover, the Arab states had been forced into an ongoing effort of mobilization and war to retrieve their lost national territories, specifying state identity and the link between people and their homeland. This effort, which entailed internal as well as external struggle, helped to promote state legitimacy and the entrenchment in power of the ruling elite. Hence, the expulsion of the PR from Jordan was not only another blow to the revolution in the Arab world, but also a point of departure for rebuilding the Jordanian state around its Hashemite regime.

Between 1967 and 1973, the attitude of the confrontation states toward Israel had undergone an essential change, from a conflict over existence before 1967 to tacit acceptance of Israel within its 1967 borders on the basis of Resolution 242. For the first time since 1948, Israel possessed territorial assests that could be exchanged for peace with its Arab neighbors. Unlike Nasir's ambivalence to diplomacy, Sadat manifested a bold tendency toward diplomatic settlement with Israel through American involvement. Yet the Arabs' military defeat and Israeli military edge generated a psychological gap between the two sides that proved unbridgeable by diplomacy. Ironically, Sadat's willingness to end the state of war with Israel in return for the 1967 borders underpinned the decision to wage the October 1973 war as a starter for a negotiated settlement.

The rise of the PLO as an actor in Arab regional politics indicated above all a striving for independent national standing and liberation from Arab collective patronage, which in fact was used to legitimate inaction. In contrast to the Khartoum resolutions, the post-1967 PLO struggled to impose its own priorities over the Arab states regarding the recovery of their occupied territories. The PR's collision with the Hashemite and other regimes represented an effort to shift the Palestine issue from its abstract inter-Arab concept to a territorially based national issue represented by its own people.

The defeat and military inaction forced the Arab regimes to prop up their legitimacy by rhetorically competing in their support for the PR. Each of these states, however, sought to prevent PR operations from its own territory and did its utmost to throw the burden of "hosting" the PR—namely, facing Israeli retaliations and harboring "a state within a state"—on others. Jordan, and ultimately Lebanon, the weakest of the confrontation states, finally paid the price. In the process, Arab support, the PR guerrilla warfare, and Israel's retaliations all helped to catapult the Palestinian issue to the forefront of the international agenda and promote the PLO's status as an authentic national representative of the Palestinian people.

IV

THE POLITICS OF THE PEACE PROCESS

"The enthusiastic slogans of the [Pan-]Arab idea . . . cause more disagreement than consent. . . . We should not lose the opportunity for cooperation. . . . We have to realize that the road to unity might be long . . . rejecting cooperation in the name of a noble cause would bring nothing but a deepened division."

—Sadat's "October [1973] Document"

"[T]he issue is not recovering a piece of land, but the way this land is recovered. . . . It is preferable for us that our land remains occupied than recovering it at the expense of our national dignity . . ."

—Asad to Sadat at their last meeting, Damascus, November 16–17, 1977, on the eve of Sadat's visit to Jerusalem (quoted in Karim Bakraduni, *Al-Salam al-Mafqud,* Beirut, 1984).

"Do we not see that some of our rulers . . . give to their individual states a priority equal to, or even higher than, that which they give the Zionist problem, thus allowing themselves to be distracted from remedying the greater, more inclusive danger by attaching undue importance to the lesser, temporary danger?"

—Constantine K. Zurayk, *The Meaning of the Disaster,* Khayat's College Book Co., Beirut, 1956, p. 15.

9

THE DIVISIVE PEACE DIPLOMACY

Opportunities and Constraints

Anwar al-Sadat's diplomatic maneuvering kept the inter-Arab system off balance in the two years following the Yom Kippur War. Egypt's policy fluctuated as it attempted to pursue its own interests via separate interim agreements in growing disregard of Syria, Jordan, and the Palestinians. Yet this policy had to be restricted to prevent damage to Egypt's pivotal status in the Arab world or risk a cutback in the Arab economic aid that helped Sadat to stabilize his domestic arena.

Sadat was obviously motivated by Egypt's domestic pressures, which had been nurtured by years of economic depression and a cessation of infrastructure development for as long as preparations for war had taken precedence. But his actual conduct and decision-making in the peacemaking process reflected a combination of his personal powers of persuasion and his elevated prestige in Egypt and the Arab world as a result of the war. What enabled Sadat to conduct his policy was a host of objectively favorable conditions that distinguished him from his Arab partners and provided him with wider margins of political maneuverability internationally as well as domestically. First, even though the war ended with almost a military disaster for Egypt, Sadat, unlike Asad, managed to score a political victory due to the Egyptian forces' success in holding on to most of the eastern bank of the Suez Canal. Second, Sadat was ready for a strategic shift from the Soviet orbit to the United States which he perceived to be the key to the recovery of Sinai. Sadat's pragmatism and interest in a settlement that would serve Egypt's national interest enabled him to accept Kissinger's "step by step" peacemaking strategy and separate interim agreements. Third, the geostrategic depth provided by the sizable and scarcely inhabited Sinai to both Egypt and Israel offered better opportunities than other occupied Arab lands for the American peace strategy. Fourth, Egypt's regional weight and leadership, coupled with a centralized decision-making process embodied by the president and an apolitical military establishment, gave Sadat room to implement his own perception of the peace process despite his rivals' criticism.

Asad had to cope with an entirely different reality. The peace process was far less crucial for Syria, either economically or strategically. Asad shared neither Sadat's diplomatic experience with the United States nor his authoritative presidential decision-making ability. Representing the 'Alawi minority and the Ba'th ideology, Asad's regime was inherently challenged by radical opponents at home as well as by his hostile radical neighbor Iraq. Syria's politicized military elite and its strong commitment to radical Pan-Arab ideology made any settlement with Israel extremely complicated, slow, and conditional on agreeing in advance on the final objectives. Syria's long-cultivated self-image as the standardbearer of Arab nationalism and carrier of the banner of uncompromising struggle against Israel had the paradoxical effect of fanning Syria's own fears of isolation in the Arab world in the face of the Israeli military threat. Unlike Sadat with his reliance on diplomacy and his tactical approach, Asad rigidly adhered to the strategic goal, insisting that Israel would give up territory only under military pressure produced by a unified Arab front. Similarly to Sadat, however, he perceived peace with Israel as a state of non-belligerency, in return for Israel's full withdrawal to the pre-June 1967 borders and "restoration of the Palestinian national rights."[1]

Israel's peacemaking policy and its essential understanding with the United States on its strategic goals intensified inter-Arab differences. Jerusalem gave priority to a settlement with Egypt, which would divide the Arab front and diminish considerably the threat of another Arab offensive even if no further progress in the peace process were to be made. In contrast to Sinai, the limited size and strategic significance of the Golan Heights, the religious and national attachment to the West Bank, and the proximity of both to Israel's populated areas rendered these territories difficult objects for compromise and interim agreements. Israel's intimate contacts and willingness to negotiate separately with Jordan regarding the future of the West Bank added further weight to Syria's and the PLO's anxiety lest they be left behind in the inequitable inter-Arab race to retrieve their occupied territories from Israel. To prevent such a scenario, Syria led the strategy of a collective approach in the diplomatic process aimed at preserving "Arab solidarity," which would guarantee a comprehensive settlement.[2]

Notwithstanding the discrepancies between each Arab party's opportunities and constraints in the diplomatic process with Israel, inter-Arab relations in the post-1973 era were also shaped by the powerful impact of Arab oil at both regional and international levels. Whereas opportunities for individual territorial gains from Israel tended to divide the Arab states, the latter's policies had also been motivated by expectations for direct financial aid from the conservative oil producers, as well as for a coherent use of Arab oil power internationally in support of the Arab cause. Sponsored by a center group of conservative regimes, Arab oil served at this stage as a cementing force for joint Arab action by those directly involved in the diplomatic process with Israel. Ultimately, Arab oil power proved a secondary consideration in determining the decision-making processes by the Arab actors involved in the peace process. Asad assumed the lead of ensuring simultaneous progress in recovering occupied Arab territories. This meant mainly blocking Sadat's independent diplomatic thrust, which caused stress and growing polarization in the Arab regional system. The claim for Pan-Arab conformity was to be reasserted and selfishly exploited by Syria, the PLO, and other Arab radical actors in the name of Palestine, the Arab nation's most honorable common cause.

The postwar Arab strategy in the conflict with Israel was formalized in two summit meetings held at Algiers and Rabat, in November 1973 and October 1974 respectively. Whereas the Algiers summit had legitimized the use of diplomacy in the pursuit of the Arab goals, the main task of the Rabat summit was to work out the guidelines for the Arab parties in the diplomatic process. During this period the Arab system demonstrated an unprecedented ability to iron out differences and work together under the direction of a core coalition comprised of Egypt, Syria, Saudi Arabia, and Algeria. The key element in this coalition was no doubt the Cairo-Riyad alliance, which was difficult to challenge by other combinations of inter-Arab alignment. Underpinning this alliance was Sadat's and Faisal's agreement on fostering close cooperation with the United States to take advantage of its growing influence on Israel and willingness to act as an "honest broker" in the Arab-Israeli conflict; the need to enlist Western European support for Arab political goals while keeping the USSR at arm's length; and the need for the PLO's institutionalization and a modification of its political attitude, to ensure it a place at the negotiating table.[3]

Diplomacy Legitimated: A Strategy of Phases

On October 16, Sadat publicly announced his concept of postwar peacemaking diplomacy by referring to an international peace conference that would include the states involved as well as the PLO. Yet the circumstances under which the war ended—with Israeli forces positioned west of the Suez Canal and encircling Egypt's Third Army and the city of Suez—called for an urgent and separate solution, even at the cost of souring relations with Syria. Thus, the Kissinger-Sadat meeting in Cairo on November 6 resulted in a substantive understanding on resuming diplomatic relations between Egypt and the United States, the "step by step" peacemaking strategy, and convening a peace conference in Geneva in accordance with Resolution 338. The desperate situation of the Third Army obliged Sadat to accept a POW exchange and to open direct military talks with Israel on a separation of forces in the Suez Canal sector.

To ensure Arab support for these moves, Egypt—with active Saudi backing—began lobbying for a summit conference that would legitimate Arab participation in the peace conference. An integral part of Sadat's concept was Arab adherence to Palestinian national rights and the promotion of the PLO's status as the representative of the Palestinian people at the expense of Jordan, which was meant to legitimate the Arab states' new strategy toward Israel. The summit was also to support steps that would ensure regional and international backing for the Arab diplomatic struggle with Israel, primarily the use of Arab oil wealth to step up cooperation with African countries.[4]

To this end, Egypt had to mend fences with Syria, overcome Libyan and Iraqi opposition to any settlement with Israel, and resolve the PLO-Jordan controversy over representation of the Palestinians in the diplomatic process. In part, these problems were solved even before the summit was held, as both Libya and Iraq announced that they would absent themselves from the meeting. Despite their uneasy relations, Sadat and Asad met in Cairo before proceeding to Algiers and came to a provisional agreement that Syria would support Sadat's line in return for Egypt's pledge to work for a political settlement in the Golan as a parallel to a Sinai settlement. Sadat had no desire to open the question of participation at Geneva to general discussion at the Algiers summit, preferring to let the confrontation states, together with Saudi Arabia and Algeria, decide the matter. Still, the vagueness of the resolution passed on this subject—"political action complements and is a continuation of the military battle"—might have indicated underlying differences on procedural as well as substantive issues relating to the Geneva Conference. Syria, despite its acceptance of Resolution 338, continued to harbor reservations concerning the very concept of a political settlement with Israel. Asad's main concern was to commit Sadat to common progress on all Arab fronts and to prevent Egypt from negotiating a separate settlement with Israel. Asad thus urged a maximalist interpretation of Resolutions 242 and 338, to include the restoration of the Palestinians' rights and the participation of the PLO in the peace conference.[5]

The summit approved a substantial change in Arab strategy, referring to "the interim goal (*al-hadaf al-marhali*) of the Arab nation," which was defined as "the complete liberation of all the Arab lands occupied in June 1967," including "Arab Jerusalem," and "commitment to the restoration of the national rights of the Palestinian people in accordance with the PLO's decision." The adoption of a strategy of phases created new guidelines for handling the conflict with Israel reinforced by collective Arab legitimacy for diplomatic action. The resolution ostensibly implied that the Arabs had not relinquished their long-term goal of liquidating Israel as a whole. Yet the very absence of the three "Nays" of Khartoum provided the Arab actors concerned with maneuverability in the diplomatic process that had never been available before.

Without direct reference to the international peace conference, the final communique expressed the Arabs' "readiness to participate in reaching a just peace" on the basis of two "firm and fundamental" conditions: Israeli withdrawal from all occupied Arab territories including Jerusalem, and "the recovery by the Palestinian people of its established national rights." In effect, the Algiers resolutions accorded the confrontation states freedom to decide to take part in a peace conference on condition that they unswervingly adhere to the goals of the interim phase. Arab participation in a peace conference could not be construed as constituting tacit recognition of Israel but only recognition of borders, based on Resolution 242, implying that the Arabs were willing to end the state of war with Israel. Significantly, no long-term goals beyond the interim phase had been addressed by the summit.[6]

The adoption of a phased struggle against Israel was indeed a realization of Bourguiba's concept, which he had flaunted defiantly to Nasir in 1965, turning the Algiers summit into a personal triumph for him. The Tunisian president was the PLO's most ardent supporter at the conference, calling for the organization to be reaffirmed as the sole legitimate representative of the Palestinian people and urging the PLO to establish a government-in-exile that would speak for the Palestinians in the international arena.

Although the Algiers summit was marked by a bitter PLO-Jordan dispute over representation of the Palestinians, overall it was characterized by a broad consensus vis-à-vis the subsequent Arab strategy in the conflict with Israel. Arab solidarity in the struggle with Israel was given practical expression to a degree previously unknown, drawing considerable encouragement from the successful use of the oil weapon. Yet, although it was decided that military and economic aid to the confrontation states would continue, no specific quotas were set and nothing was concluded about stepping up aid to Egypt and Syria beyond its pre-war level. Four men were perceived as the emblems of the Arab world's new-found military, economic, and diplomatic clout: Sadat and Asad represented the confrontation states, Faisal led the way in wielding the oil weapon, and Boumedienne, a leading revolutionary figure, was credited with the wide support of the ONAS for the Arab cause and with the atmosphere of solidarity at the summit held under his chairmanship. The four emerged as the Arab core coalition, whose significance was expressed by the summit's ability to redefine a core issue such as the Arab strategy in the conflict with Israel.[7]

The absence of Iraq and Libya from the summit, due to their unbending opposition to any political settlement with Israel, heralded the emergence of an Arab "Rejection Front" encompassing as well extremist Palestinian factions (notably the PFLP). The Rejection Front hoped and expected that Syria would also affiliate itself with their stand, particularly in view of Damascus' refusal to attend the Geneva Conference. Asad, however, could hardly afford such a stand. His alliance with Egypt and Saudi Arabia was his only hope of obtaining a decent disengagement-of-forces agreement on the Golan Heights despite the unfavorable outcome of the war on his front.

Sadat's Serpentine Diplomacy

At Algiers, Sadat and Asad managed to coordinate their positions, but soon afterward the wartime coalition sustained repeated blows due to Sadat's independent diplomacy which, once again, manifested the priority he gave to Egypt's interests over Syrian and Palestinian needs. Sadat failed to stand up to his commitment to Asad at their December 10 meeting that military disengagement on Egyptian and Syrian fronts would be simultaneously concluded before the Geneva Conference was convened. Under Kissinger's urging, Sadat agreed to participate in Geneva before a disengagement agreement was achieved, and even without Asad. Furthermore, contrary to Syria's position, Sadat agreed to drop any mention of the Palestinians from the text of the invitation to the conference and to refrain from raising the issue during the meeting. His consent to dividing the forum into bilateral subgroups was another indication of his separatist tendency. It was against this backdrop that Syria opted to abstain from the Geneva conference that opened on December 21, if not to deter Cairo from participation, at least as a manifestation of Damascus' independence and a protest against Sadat's separate peace diplomacy.[8]

The Geneva Conference marked a historical turning point in the Arab-Israeli conflict, highlighted by the precedent of Egypt's and Jordan's willingness to convene officially with Israel in the same room. The need of the Arab participants to ensure domestic and all-Arab legitimacy was fully expressed in their presentations, which had an intransigent tone. Therefore, Kissinger increased his efforts to reach an Israeli-Egyptian agreement on disengagement of forces despite protests from Syria, Libya, Iraq, the PLO, and even Jordan, against Sadat's separate policy, which was said to be shattering Arab unity. In a last, desperate ploy, Asad insisted that no accord be signed until an agreement was also worked out for the Golan Heights, but Sadat went ahead and signed the disengagement agreement with Israel on January 18, 1974, in disregard of its implications for Syria's national security. The separate agreement evoked an angry Arab response. Syria accused Sadat of betraying the common Arab cause. Libya demanded the return of the 25 Mirage aircraft it had lent Egypt for the war, ceased oil deliveries, and cancelled its commitment to supply financial aid, made in Khartoum. Algeria announced the recall of its expeditionary force from the Suez front, saying it was no longer needed.[9]

To enhance its own bargaining position vis-à-vis the United States, the Arab world, and Israel, Syria started border artillery clashes along its cease-fire line with Israel. Cairo, in the meantime, having attained its initial goal and wishing to contain the renewed hostilities on the Syrian front, moved to soothe the feathers it had ruffled in the Arab world and to work together with Syria to secure a parallel accord on the Golan front. After all, Sadat realized that an

Israeli-Syrian agreement was a precondition for progress toward an additional Sinai settlement.

A new complication—firm U.S. pressure on Algeria, Saudi Arabia, and Egypt to terminate the oil embargo as a condition for American mediation between Syria and Israel—led Sadat to summon a four-state mini-summit in Algiers on February 12–13, 1974. At the meeting, Asad was urged by his counterparts to adhere to disengagement and to start by giving Kissinger a list of Israeli POWs. In return, the meeting issued a joint communique that effectively linked the lifting of the embargo to progress in the negotiations for an Israeli-Syrian disengagement of forces. Further American pressure led the meeting of Arab oil ministers in Vienna on March 18 to finally resolve to end the embargo on oil deliveries to the United States, leaving the embargo on Holland intact. The decision to end the embargo before any Israeli-Syrian agreement had been reached was a blunt manifestation of Syria's weakness vis-à-vis the close Sadat-Faisal alliance. Following this achievement for U.S. policy, Kissinger resumed his shuttle diplomacy and after more than a month of tough exchanges an Israeli-Syrian disengagement-of-forces agreement was signed on May 31, 1974, in Geneva under the official umbrella of the international peace conference.[10]

Sadat's remarkable success in tilting the Arab alignment in his favor was primarily due to the close alliance with King Faisal and other conservative regimes. It also represented the isolation of rejectionist Iraq and Libya and especially the antagonism provoked in the Maghreb by the fiasco of Qadhafi's abortive agreement to merge with Tunisia, signed in January 1974. Having done his duty by Syria with respect to a disengagement-of-forces agreement, Sadat, in accord with Kissinger, sought to conclude a similar settlement on the Israel-Jordan front that would preserve the diplomatic momentum and pave the road for an agreement on a deeper Israeli withdrawal from Sinai. Obviously, the PLO was precluded as a partner to such an agreement, although Sadat did his part to help enhance its international recognition, including mediating toward a PLO-American dialogue, assisted by Morocco. Israel and the United States, however, perceived Jordan as the only Arab partner concerned with the West Bank and vetoed any PLO participation in the diplomatic process.[11]

Sadat was encouraged to incorporate King Husain in his diplomatic efforts when the United States accepted the king's request to engineer an agreement with Israel similar to those concluded with Egypt and Syria. Sadat's Jordanian option had been shaped by his search for partners in "step by step" diplomacy and awareness of the inadmissibility of the PLO. But it soon proved unrealistic from a regional Arab viewpoint, resulting in final formalization of the PLO's exclusive status as the representative of the Palestinian people. Underlying Sadat's failure was the eroded legitimacy of the Hashemite regime in the Arab world following Husain's war against the PR in Jordan and his failure to wage war against Israel on his own front in 1973. Furthermore, because the Jordanian front had remained inactive during the war, an Israeli-Jordanian agreement would perforce take on a political character. It was the most sensitive Arab-Israeli front, since it was directly bound up with the Palestinians' national claims and constituted the heart of Biblical Land of Israel (*eretz Israel*), which had become the core of the Israeli nationalists' political platform.

In late 1973, Kissinger had discussed in Amman and Jerusalem the possibility of an interim settlement on the West Bank. Yet despite tacit cooperation in some respects between Israel and Jordan, the prospects for an accord were paradoxically slim. To maximize Arab acceptance of an agreement with Israel, King Husain had to wait until Egypt and Syria reached military agreements on their own fronts, and then to ensure a tangible territorial achievement that would enable him to sustain an agreement with Israel against Arab criticism. Israel, however, was unwilling to discuss territorial concessions—primarily for domestic reasons—suggesting a "functional settlement," namely, a Jordanian authority over the population, but without sovereignty, in parts of the West Bank. Thus, when Kissinger renewed his diplomatic efforts in June–July 1974 in an attempt to stimulate a possible interim agreement along the Jordan River, the gap between the parties was unbridgeable. Husain could not lag behind Egypt and Syria and sign an accord that would not include Israeli withdrawal. The king called for an agreement with Israel based on a mutual withdrawal to an average distance of 6–8 kilometers from the Jordan River, with joint supervision of its bridges. To his Arab rivals, Husain reiterated that only Jordan could restore the West Bank to Arab hands, following which the Palestinians could choose whatever political framework they wished. Israel's government rejected these ideas, arguing that in the absence of war with Jordan in 1973, it was prepared to discuss only a final peace settlement.[12]

On July 16–18, amid American efforts to convince Israel to accept Jordan's proposal, Husain and Sadat held talks in Alexandria on what appeared to be a coordinated venture with Washington. Husain's goal was to obtain Sadat's blessing for an interim agreement with Israel, namely, acknowledging his right to represent the West Bank issue regardless of the PLO's status. On July 18, Sadat and Husain issued a joint declaration in which Egypt clearly deviated from the Algiers resolutions—that had recognized the PLO as "the sole representative of the Palestinian people"—boosting Jordan at the expense of the PLO: "The PLO is the legitimate representative of the Palestinians, with the exception of those living in the Hashemite Kingdom of Jordan." The deliberate ambiguity as to whether "the Hashemite Kingdom of Jordan" also encompassed the West Bank left the way open for Husain to assume responsibility for that territory and take an active role in negotiations toward a political settlement.[13]

The Alexandria declaration incensed most AL members and none more than the PLO, which called for an urgent summit meeting to combat the Egyptian-Jordanian move. The declaration was also denounced by Syria, Algeria, Libya, and Iraq. Unofficial support for the PLO came from Lebanon, Kuwait, and even Saudi Arabia, as well as from the PLO's adherents in the West Bank itself. The power of Arab consensus was fully demonstrated in Sadat's incremental retreat from his declaration with Husain as the only way to reduce his losses. Within less than a week, Sadat gave his declaration with Husain a pro-Palestinian interpretation, explaining that the West Bank had been "entrusted to Jordan" only until its inhabitants were given the opportunity to decide their own future. Yet this interpretation could not appease the PLO, which ruled out any representational role for Jordan in the West Bank, even a temporary one. Sadat continued to backtrack from the declaration in an August 7 communique ending a visit to Cairo by King Faisal in which the two leaders reaffirmed their commitment to the Algiers summit resolutions.[14]

Yet even without the Arab outcry, the chances for an Israeli-Jordanian settlement were slim indeed, given the unbridgeable gap between the two parties' positions as indicated during Israel's PM Rabin's visit to Washington in September 1974. Meanwhile, the PLO had scored unprecedented international recognition following the PNC's twelfth session, held in Cairo that June, which redefined the Palestinian national goal along the lines of the Algiers summit's strategy of phases, implying a willingness to accept, as a first phase, any part of Palestine. These developments, combined with the torrent of criticism following the Alexandria declaration, led Sadat to cast his lot with the PLO once more. On September 21, he met in Cairo with Asad and 'Arafat and they issued a joint statement redefining the PLO's status as "the sole legitimate representative of the Palestinian people," the formula later to be enshrined in the Rabat summit. The statement also condemned "any attempt to conclude separate political agreements, since the problem is an indivisible wholeness."[15]

The Cairo statement notwithstanding, Damascus' concern about Egypt's inclination toward separate diplomacy in the conflict with Israel was increasingly shaping Syria's inter-Arab policy, the harbingers of which appeared even before the Rabat summit. At his October 1974 meeting with Kissinger in Damascus, Asad advocated an early convening of the Geneva Conference at which the Arabs be represented by a joint delegation including PLO representatives. Asad objected to further partial settlements, insisting on a comprehensive and final settlement based on full implementation of Resolution 242 and the end of the state of war with Israel. Aware of his limited opportunities for another partial settlement with Israel, Asad was determined to use the summit to reach an agreement on Arab rejection of separate pacts with Israel, which would tie Sadat's hands and ensure joint Arab progress in the peacemaking with Israel. Syria urged full coordination among the confrontation actors—in the form of an Egyptian-Syrian-Jordanian-PLO joint command—to secure the Arabs' interests and reinforce Arab military strength. A shift in Damascus' official tone toward the U.S. peacemaking efforts—following a period of Syrian optimism and warm relations with the United States—was also discerned when FM Khaddam cautioned his colleagues at the pre-summit deliberations against reliance on Washington as a peacemaker. Egyptian FM Fahmi took strong exception to Khaddam's presentation, insisting that Cairo retain the freedom to maneuver because of its objectively better opportunity to recover more of Sinai from Israel.[16]

The Rabat summit was opened on October 26 with the absence of Qadhafi of Libya and Bakr of Iraq, underlining their isolation and irrelevance regarding the peace process. By contrast, the OAU's president was once again present at the ceremonial opening session, indicating the importance accorded by the summit to Arab-African cooperation as a vehicle for mobilizing international political support for the Arab cause. The summit reflected an underlying concern that Arab bargaining power vis-à-vis the United States had been fading. The deliberations expressed deep concern over Washington's massive arms supplies to Israel, and disappointment at Kissinger's proposals for a second round of interim agreements. Leading the attacks on U.S. arms supplies to Israel since the October war, ALSG Riyad argued that this policy was only making Israel more intransigent and was thus defeating its own peace goals. At the same time, commentaries in the Arabic press expressed fears of a United States–backed sudden Israeli military move in retaliation for the October 1973 Arab offensive. The Arab media maintained its trust in the oil weapon as a major source of influence in the international arena and one that needed to be exploited to wrest more territory from Israel, underlying a general desire to proceed along the path of diplomacy.[17]

The United States now loomed larger in Arab eyes, as it was perceived to hold the key to further diplomatic progress. In the second week of October, Kissinger visited Cairo, Amman, Damascus, Riyad, and Jerusalem to assess possible progress in the peace process under U.S. auspices and to discuss with the Saudis the severe repercussions rising oil prices were having on the world economy. Reportedly, Kissinger presented some ideas—apparently discussed and rejected during the summit—according to which Egypt, Jordan, and Syria would pledge to end the state of belligerency with Israel in return for substantial Israeli territorial concessions in Sinai, portions of the West Bank, and a narrow strip on the Golan Heights. Kissinger's ideas worried those who—like Syria and the USSR—opposed his "step-by-step" approach. They were not reassured by Cairo's clarifications, issued through its media, that Egypt would not countenance any separate or partial settlement that required political concessions to Israel.[18]

The Rabat summit's resolutions seemed to indicate that the Arab world had resolved its internal problems and agreed on a strategy for the political struggle with Israel in line with Syrian attitudes. Apart from the historical resolution declaring the PLO as the sole legitimate representative of the Palestinian people, the summit's most important resolution spelled out its strong objection to any partial political settlement, reiterating the "pan-national (*qawmiyya*) and indivisible nature of the problem." The wording of this principle, with its implicit evocation of a comprehensive settlement, was tantamount to a rejection of Kissinger's "step-by-step" philosophy in Middle East peacemaking. Other resolutions underlined the need for utmost coordination among Arab states—referring, *inter alia,* to financial aid to the confrontation states and the PLO—and a concentrated effort to bring about the total political and economic isolation of Israel.[19]

But almost immediately the conciliatory atmosphere gave way to fierce inter-Arab bickering, which sidetracked the Arabs and reduced the pressure on Israel to surrender more of the occupied territories. The foundations of the accord reached at Rabat were endangered because Sadat—with American encouragement—was determined to pursue Egypt's own interests first in disregard of his Arab partners' anxieties and needs, escalating his conflict with Syria over the peacemaking strategy. The Syrians' bitter lesson was that if anyone's hands were tied it was their own, and that Sadat's peacemaking diplomacy not only was diminishing Syria's chances to recover its land, but threatened its national security. Hence, they moved to effect a balance-of-power strategy toward Egypt through alignment with Jordan and the PLO under their own aegis in an effort to isolate Egypt and prevent its defection from the Arab collective.

In early November, Kissinger commenced a new diplomatic mission that took him to Israel, Egypt, Syria, Jordan, and Saudi Arabia, to explore the feasibility of new partial settlements. Discordant notes were soon heard, however, and the prospects of reconvening the Geneva Conference dwindled, not least because of Israel's absolute rejection of the role assigned to the PLO by the Rabat resolutions. The deadlocked road to Geneva highlighted the feasibility of the Israeli-Egypt separate track, which was soon to be taken. Following another round of shuttle diplomacy by Kissinger in February 1975, Cairo entered negotiations on a second partial settlement in Sinai—ostensibly in the context of parallel accords on the three fronts—clarifying that no contradiction existed between "first movement" on the Egyptian front and the official stance against separate settlements.[20]

Both Syria and the PLO strongly criticized Egypt's stance, adhering instead to a unified Arab diplomacy. Sadat used the breakdown of the talks on March 22, 1975, to reinvigorate his position as the leading figure in the Arab world. To drive the point home, he made a series of visits to Arab capitals, capped by a joint meeting in Riyad on April 22 with Syrian President Asad and the newly crowned Saudi monarch, Khalid, who had assumed the throne after Faisal's assassination a month before. The three leaders agreed to abide by the principle of a comprehensive settlement, emphasizing the need to preserve the Arab joint front in the political and military struggle against Israel. However, neither at the tripartite meeting nor at the Arab FMs semi-annual meeting held in Cairo at the same time, could Egypt and Syria reach agreement on the PLO's role in the Geneva Conference.[21]

Egypt anticipated that negotiations with Israel would resume in the summer, in the wake of Washington's publicly announced "reassessment" of its policy toward Israel, which included a delay in arms shipments. A Sadat-Ford meeting at Salzburg on June 1, 1975, and the reopening of the Suez Canal four days later paved the way for renewing talks on a second Sinai interim accord, which was signed on September 4. The agreement represented a breakthrough in Israel-Egypt relations because it included essential political elements. The agreement was to remain in force until superseded by a new one; the signatories undertook not to use force to resolve their differences; and non-military cargoes destined for or coming from Israel were permitted through the Suez Canal. Israel agreed to a further pullback in Sinai—to the east of the Mitla and Gidi passes—and to handing over the Abu Rudais oil fields. The agreement entailed secret U.S. guarantees on generous financial and military aid to Israel and a pledge not to recognize or negotiate with the PLO until it recognized Israel's right to exist, accepted Resolutions 242 and 338, and renounced terrorism.[22]

The signing of the Sinai II accord sparked a crisis between Egypt on the one hand, and Syria and the PLO, on the other. The new agreement fulfilled Asad's worst fears that Sadat's diplomacy would destroy Arab solidarity and isolate Syria. By abandoning the Arab fighting camp, it was charged, Egypt had made any Arab threat of war against Israel an empty gesture. Syria and the PLO came under attack from the Rejection Front for purportedly taking a "capitulationist" stance themselves. The situation was aggravated by the unauthorized publication, in mid-September, of the secret Israeli-American annexes to the Sinai II accord, which included, *inter alia,* President Ford's letter stating that in any future talks on the Golan the United States would take into account Israel's position that it should not return to the 1967 borders.[23]

Syria responded to these developments by launching a political initiative to isolate Egypt in the Arab world and force it to retract the agreement until a parallel one could be achieved on the Golan front. The Syrian-led coalition included Jordan, with which Syria had established in August an accord for a joint supreme political and military command, Kuwait, Algeria, and the PLO. Even the Saudis voiced objections to Sinai II. The PLO accused Egypt of betraying the Arab and Palestinian cause in return for "a handful of sand from Sinai." Sadat was also criticized for rejecting a proposal, produced by the OAU summit conference in Kampala (August 1975), for Israel's expulsion from the UN, all of which resulted in Egypt's retaliating by shutting down the PLO's radio station in Cairo and restricting PLO activity in the country.[24]

Egypt's new settlement with Israel was achieved against the background of growing economic depression and public grumbling at the low level of effective—as opposed to promised—Arab financial aid to Egypt. In January 1975, food shortages and rising prices of basic commodities triggered the eruption of riots in Cairo, leading to Saudi emergency aid. At Kissinger's prodding during his shuttles in Summer 1975, the Gulf oil states extended further aid to Egypt as a contribution to the promotion of stability and the peacemaking process in the Middle East. Following the signing of the Sinai II accord, Egypt received long-term loans, mostly from Saudi Arabia and Kuwait, of $1.2 billion, in addition to $650 million granted by Washington. Yet the Syria-Egypt disagreement and general Arab discontent with Egypt's independent peace diplomacy threatened the flow of substantial aid to Egypt, leading to its gradual decrease in the following years. By signing the Sinai II accord—and by abrogating the Soviet-Egyptian Treaty of Friendship and Cooperation six months later—Sadat was signalling that his reorientation toward a strategic alliance with the United States instead of the USSR was all but irrevocable. This shift was fraught with implications for Egypt's policy vis-à-vis Israel.[25]

The Issue of Palestinian Representation

The ensuing peace conference and the possibility of negotiations on the future of the West Bank and Gaza Strip rendered the question of the PLO's standing and Palestinian representation a central inter-Arab dilemma on the morrow of the 1973 war. In principle, Sadat wished to have the PLO play an official role in the process, yet this could wreck the diplomatic process before it had even begun, due to Israel's and America's unequivocal rejection of the PLO.

The PLO was determined to replace the Hashemite regime as the rightful representative of the Palestinian occupied territories, and to acquire the status of an equal partner in the peace process. Before the war the U.S. government had rejected the PLO's secret approaches aimed at obtaining American recognition in return for the PLO's acceptance of Israel, a Palestinian takeover in Jordan, and the dismissal of the Hashemite regime. The war triggered a heated public debate within the PR over the policy the PLO should adopt in view of the prospective changes in the Arab strategy in the conflict with Israel. Obviously, the PLO was able neither to resist the Arab core coalition nor to afford standing aloof, leaving the diplomatic arena to its Hashemite enemy. Hence, the PLO's leadership was adamant in preventing Jordan's playing a role in the peacemaking process and insisted on exclusive representation of the Palestinians by the PLO. The PLO's final decision to adopt a pragmatic strategy, accepting the establishment of a mini-state in Palestine as a first phase in their national struggle, represented the impact of the main Arab proponents of this strategy—in addition to strong Soviet influence—on the Palestinian mainstream, led by Fatah.[26]

Jordan's failure to enter the war, coupled with the heavy regional and international emphasis on the Palestinian issue, combined to weaken Husain's standing in the Arab world and to render immaterial his claim to represent the West Bank in possible negotiations with Israel. In a round of visits to Saudi Arabia and other Gulf states prior to the Algiers summit to drum up support for his position, Husain had been given a cold shoulder. In view of the strong Arab support for the PLO, Husain decided not to attend the summit in person, dispatching instead Bahjat al-Talhuni, the chief court chamberlain. In an attempt to save its position, Jordan offered a compromise based on recognition of the Palestinian people's right to determine its fate in a referendum—to be held under international supervision—but only after Jordan had completed its role in the liberation of the West Bank and Jerusalem, implying that the West Bank Palestinians had the right to speak for themselves regardless of the PLO. As far as Jordan was concerned, the PLO could discuss the issue of refugees only following Israel's withdrawal from the occupied territory.[27]

The Algiers summit finally resolved that the PLO was the sole representative of the Palestinian people. The one compromise Jordan managed to extract was that the decision on who should be invited to the Geneva Conference would rest with the UNSC. The adoption of the PLO's position by the Algiers summit—with Jordan the lone dissenter—demonstrated the fundamental change wrought by the war in the Arab world's priorities. Ostensibly, this decision gave the PLO veto power over any decision by the Arab states regarding the conflict with Israel.[28] In practice, though, the Arab states had no intention to allow the PLO to dictate the course of their policies, particularly after a war in which they had scored unprecedented military and political achievements. Thus, underlying the rhetoric was the Arab states' need to legitimize a political settlement with Israel, which seemed to be on the horizon. Furthermore, by casting responsibility for everything relating to the Palestinian issue on the PLO, the Arab states took another step toward disengaging themselves from responsibility for the Palestinian issue and enhancing their own freedom of action regarding bilateral settlements with Israel.

The Algiers summit resolutions and Egypt-Israel disengagement-of-forces agreement convinced the PLO's mainstream that a redefinition of its position in the conflict with Israel was necessary to ensure wide international recognition and participation in the Middle East peace conference. By February 1974, the ensuing shift in the PLO's policy had already become apparent when major Palestinian groups—Fatah, the Syrian-backed Sa'iqa, and the Marxist PDFLP—adopted a "phased strategy," toward accomplishing the ultimate Palestinian goal. Syria's disengagement-of-forces agreement with Israel removed the last obstacle on the PLO's way to reformulating its policy and couching it in language befitting a potential partner in the Middle East diplomatic process. In June, the PNC twelfth session resolutions simultaneously implied PLO approval of a political settlement at some future date and redefined its interim national objective in a more practical tone. Without conceding the strategic goal of an independent Palestinian state in all of Mandatory Palestine, the PLO stated that it would, as an interim stage, establish a "national, independent and fighting authority on any part of Palestinian land to be liberated."[29]

The new PLO position attracted wide interest in the West and set the stage for an intensified, more reasoned Arab diplomatic and propaganda campaign against Israel. In August, the USSR came out in favor of the PLO's right to participate at the Geneva Conference on an equal footing. The Soviets followed this up by backing an Arab initiative that led to the UNGA's official recognition of the organization as a national liberation movement (October 14); henceforth PLO delegates would be able to take part in UNGA deliberations with observer status. The road was thus paved for 'Arafat's UNGA address of November 13, in which he presented an inconclusive message of combined peace and armed threat, reiterating the earlier PLO goal of a Palestinian democratic non-sectarian state. Meanwhile, on October 18, Egypt and the USSR issued a joint statement emphasizing that the establishment of a Palestinian state was essential to achieving Middle East peace and reiterating the necessity for the PLO's equal participation in the Geneva Conference. Indeed, the Arab summit convened in Rabat on October 28 could hardly have ignored these developments when it came to discuss the Jordan-PLO dispute. Still, the tripartite Cairo declaration on the PLO's status did not quell the controversy over this issue, nor by concurring in the statement did Sadat intend to signal that he was denying King Husain's role in the peace process.[30]

Indeed, the main challenge facing the Rabat summit was to bridge the breach between Jordan and the PLO, which threatened to undermine the common Arab front in the peace process and was therefore a matter of special concern to Egypt. At the pre-summit FMs deliberations, the gap between the disputed parties had proved unbridgeable. The Hashemite regime refused to give away its status in the West Bank, drawing on the argument that since Israel and the United States vetoed the PLO, only Jordan could retrieve the occupied territory. The PLO, on its part, set the tone by adopting an offensive approach against Jordan's claims over the West Bank, threatening to walk away if the Arab delegates failed to meet the organization's requests. Drawing on the resolutions of the twelfth PNC meeting, the PLO called on the Arab states to recognize the PLO's authority over all Palestinians everywhere and over all Palestinian lands that might be liberated; to block any attempt at bypassing the Palestinian problem through separate Jordanian-Israeli talks; to provide support for establishing a Palestinian national entity free of outside interference and for applying Palestinian national rights in any liberated part of Palestine.[31]

The deadlocked debate at the ministerial level meant that the issue could only be decided by the heads of state, although with the exception of Jordan, the PLO had secured the unanimous support of the Arab delegates. Indeed, so towering were the PLO's prestige and support that it emerged unscathed even after the Moroccan authorities uncovered a plot to assassinate King Husain on his arrival in Rabat, concocted by personnel from the operational arm of Fatah, the PLO's main faction headed by 'Arafat.[32] The contest between Jordan and the PLO during the summit dominated the proceedings, with intense lobbying by both sides. King Husain's presence, despite the unfavorable conditions for Jordan, indicated the fatefulness of this battle for him. Members of the Jordanian parliament residing in the West Bank sent to the conference—apparently at Amman's behest—a joint memorandum emphasizing the unity of both banks of the Jordan River. Not to be outdone, 'Arafat circulated a document signed by 180 West Bank public figures, trade union leaders, and representatives of voluntary organizations, affirming the PLO as the sole legitimate representative of the Palestinian people.[33]

The PLO delegates also pointed to the organization's growing international standing, as indicated by the UN invitation to 'Arafat to address the GA. To underline its equal footing with the Arab states, the PLO intimated that it was about to establish a government-in-exile, perhaps even before the forthcoming UN debate on the Palestinian question. King Husain led off with a long, apologetic address explaining Jordan's limited participation in the October War and dwelling on his country's historic responsibility for the destiny of the West Bank. He elaborated on his theme that a solution of the Palestinian issue involved two separate and distinct phases that dictated PLO-Jordan coordination rather than exclusive authority: liberating the occupied territories, and solving the Palestinian problem. Jordan's right to liberate the land did not conflict with the PLO's demand for the return of the territories, Husain maintained, and would not impinge on the Palestinians' right to choose their own form of government in an internationally supervised plebiscite. The king issued an implied warning: if the conference entrusted any single element with exclusive responsibility for both liberating the land and deciding its future, all the Arab states would have to assume responsibility for the consequences. Husain's warning fell, however, on deaf ears, just as had Kissinger's earlier warning that bestowing on the PLO an exclusive responsibility for the West Bank would put an end to the U.S. efforts to achieve a political settlement.[34]

The impasse on the PLO-Jordan controversy threatened to block any progress on other topics. A conciliation committee that included the contenders, King Husain and 'Arafat, was formed to resolve the controversy, resulting in full adoption of the FMs' recommendations. The committee's debate reflected awareness of the diplomatic impasse that a pro-PLO decision would generate in the peace process and discussed, in vain, alternative options that would preserve Jordan's role. Yet the Arab main protagonists were captives of their own particular interests and fears of their rivals' aims, ending up with the broadest common denominator: support for the PLO's claim. The summit also adopted the PLO's fresh tactical goal, undertaking to support the establishment of an "independent [Palestinian] national authority" on any land liberated from Israel. Egypt, Syria, and Jordan were specifically called upon to regulate their relations with the PLO on the basis of this resolution.[35]

Husain's reservations about the wording notwithstanding, he had no choice but to accept the conference's verdict. Commentaries to the effect that the king had decided to wash his hands of the entire Palestinian issue proved baseless. Husain's stance was purely pragmatic, dictated by the Arab world's unbending support for the PLO and his attendant fear of isolation and loss of the vital material support of Saudi Arabia if he adopted an adversary position. Arab heads of state were well aware of the practical difficulties of getting the PLO to the negotiating table, not the least of which were the inhibitions of the Palestinians themselves and Israel's unequivocal refusal to meet its archenemy anywhere but on the battlefield. Thus, the summit call for consultations among the confrontation elements seemingly reflected a consciousness of Jordan's indispensable role in the political process and gave Husain a back door to maintain a foothold in future negotiations on the West Bank.[36]

Although Husain officially accepted the summit verdict on the PLO's status, in practice he pressed his Arab colleagues to reconsider the wisdom of the resolution, pointing to its impracticability and the adverse effect it was bound to have, above all, on the Palestinians' own interests. At the PLO's unequivocal appeal, delivered to Husain by King Hasan, not to alter the existing legal status of the Palestinians in the West Bank or Jordan, the King responded favorably, stating on October 30 that Jordan would continue to provide material support and administrative services for the inhabitants of the West Bank, until new arrangements were made. Furthermore, ignoring any boundaries between Jordan and Palestine the king stated that "Jordan will continue to be the homeland of any Palestinian who wishes to be a citizen, without prejudice to his original rights in Palestine. Those Palestinians who choose a Palestinian identity will continue to enjoy all the rights granted to other Arab citizens of Jordan."[37]

Husain indeed maintained a facade of acquiescence in the summit resolutions, going as far as pledging his support for the PLO. Yet despite official statements about a "historic reconciliation" and possible meeting between the two rivals in the near future, Husain's and 'Arafat's relations remained inimical. Husain did not conceal his bitterness over the Rabat resolutions while pledging to carry them out to the letter. Within a few weeks, West Bank inhabitants were excluded from government and parliament. The PLO for its part continued to make provocative declarations and raise old demands, such as the reinstatement of the Cairo and Amman agreements (1970 and 1971, respectively) providing for an armed Palestinian presence in Jordan.[38]

Overall, the Rabat resolutions did not impinge on Husain's position vis-à-vis the Geneva Conference, since the PLO remained anathema to both Israel and the United States. Nor could Jordan be ignored from the military point of view, as Syria and Egypt were well aware. Their own orientation toward the PLO reflected considerations such as the need to obtain legitimacy for their political settlements, to promote inter-Arab consensus, and to accelerate the political struggle against Israel that sought to isolate and weaken the Jewish state.[39] The Rabat resolutions on the PLO's status placed in doubt the very future of the political process, in view of the abyss of hostility between Israel and the PLO. This result was precisely what Syria had sought in order to tie Egypt's hands. Egypt, for its part, was well aware of this dilemma but saw no way to bypass it as long as Arab solidarity coincided with its own economic and strategic interests. Cairo therefore worked to bring about a reconciliation between Jordan and the PLO, and pressed the latter's leaders to adopt a more flexible attitude. The Egyptian press was the main vehicle for these overtures by Egyptian authorities to the PLO to take a responsible and realistic approach in the political process, urging abandonment of the idea of a democratic state in the whole territory of Palestine and support for the principle of a partitioned Palestine.[40]

The Arab Oil: Power and Diplomacy

The immediate worldwide impact of the Arab oil weapon notwithstanding, Arab governments were soon forced to face the limits of its use under unfavorable military circumstances that called for urgent American mediation. From the outset, Kissinger asserted to the Arab rulers that his mediation effort was linked to lifting the oil embargo and returning to normal production. Arabs, on the other hand, deemed the embargo necessary so that the U.S. government could justify its pressure on Israel. The oil producers doubled and quadrupled their revenues during the first three months of the embargo and were in no hurry to make concessions. The disunity demonstrated by the Western oil consumers toward the embargo—the EEC declaration of November 6, 1973, calling for an Israeli withdrawal from the territories occupied in 1967—confirmed its perceived potential.[41]

The Arab attitude toward the use of the oil weapon remained firm as long as no progress was achieved on Israeli withdrawal from Egyptian territory. At the same time, Arab oil producers never lost sight of economic considerations. This was clearly demonstrated in the Algiers summit resolution to continue the use of the oil weapon until Israel retreated to the 1967 borders and the rights of the Palestinians were restored. All consumer states were to be categorized in terms of their stands on the conflict in order to determine the quantity (if any) of petroleum they merited. Yet the summit also decided that the cutback in oil production would continue provided the losses sustained by producers did not exceed one-quarter of their 1972 revenues, which effectively meant an end to reduction of oil production.[42]

The oil producers' interest in making profits, and the erosion of the embargo's practical effects, rendered its formal end dependent on a political decision by the leading confrontation states. Political conditions for ending the embargo ripened once the Israeli-Egyptian agreement on disengagement of forces was signed, and the United States made any further brokering between Israel and the Arabs strictly conditional on lifting the embargo. Thus, despite Syria's reluctance, the embargo came to its official and unconditional end on March 18, after being virtually approved by Egypt, Saudi Arabia, and Algeria.

The aftermath of the 1973 war witnessed a major thrust at taking advantage of the oil weapon's impact in enlisting international support for the Arab cause in the conflict with Israel. The powerful effect of Arab oil on world opinion was clearly reflected in a boosted Arab self-confidence, and the feeling that a new era had begun in Arab history. The Algiers and Rabat summits missed no opportunity to demonstrate solidarity with Black Africa and induce additional Third World nations to sever relations with Israel, thereby magnifying its isolation in the international arena. These summits resolved to convene an Arab-African summit and to establish Arab financial institutions for economic and technical aid to Black African states in response to African requests for assistance to compensate for the spiraling oil prices. However, the aid proffered was far from the sums required by the poor African states, and several of them soon expressed regret at having severed diplomatic relations with Israel.[43]

Collective Arab action and goals in the international arena remained unchanged through the mid-1970s regardless of inter-Arab disputes over tactical matters. The time was marked by extensive political warfare against Israel, supervised by the AL, which employed economic and diplomatic pressure and generous financial allocations for propaganda campaigns, with the Palestinian issue as its spearhead. Given the zero-sum nature of the conflict between the PLO and Israel, enhancement of the former's international legitimacy and recognition seemed strictly at Israel's expense. Thus, 'Arafat's address to the

UNGA at its November 1974 debate on the Palestinian issue, in the presence of Lebanon's president chairing the session and with all the Arab FMs present, was to be the peak of the Arabs' political offensive against Israel.[44]

The Arab message to the international community mingled threats of another war and economic punitive measures with readiness for peace, conditional on U.S. willingness to force Israel to implement the UN resolutions. The vulnerability of the EEC members to an oil shortage turned them into an ideal target for Arab blackmail ultimately aimed at effecting Washington. In March 1974, the ALC responded favorably to a request from the EEC for opening a dialogue on technical, economic, and financial cooperation, to be capped by an Arab-European conference later in the year. The European initiative, made under the pressure of the oil embargo, was a sequel to the pro-Arab declaration issued by the EEC FMs on November 6, 1973.

The Rabat summit approved proceeding with the "Euro-Arab dialogue," but Arab efforts to use this channel to bring about more active involvement by the EEC in the Middle East conflict remained fruitless. Apart from the gulf between the Arabs' interest in exploiting the dialogue for political purposes and the Europeans' pursuit of economic goals, the Arab failure was a result of two main factors. First, the United States succeeded, with Egypt and Jordan's tacit support, in shunting aside the EEC from the peacemaking efforts in the region, just as it did the Soviet Union, giving Washington the power of a sole broker. Secondly, Arab oil-producing states insisted on managing their national economic resources on an economic and bilateral basis and were reluctant to put their economic power at the disposal of the confrontation states.[45]

The conjunction of war with a drastic rise in oil prices nourished the expectations of the Arab confrontation states for a new era of inter-Arab economic cooperation marked by significant financial aid from the oil producers. The gap between the givers and recipients—especially Egypt—however, remained unabridged and even aggravated. Egypt strove to establish a comprehensive "Arab Marshall Plan" that would provide it with constant massive financial support and resolve the huge deficit in its balance of payments. The Gulf monarchies preferred to direct most of their financial aid to joint investments and specific projects in Egypt that would ensure their control over these resources. Hence, in 1974 alone, commitments for financial aid to Egypt reached $2.5 billion, most of which had been assigned to long-term projects of development. That same year, Saudi Arabia granted Egypt $400 million in response to Sadat's personal requests during visits to Riyad.[46]

The Algiers summit did not discuss collective financial aid to the confrontation states, though the Gulf oil-producers were willing to finance arms procurement for Egypt on a bilateral basis. Leading up to the Rabat summit, grumbling over the low level of Arab support for the confrontation states grew bitter, accompanied by sporadic calls for resuming the embargo. At the summit, Syria proposed that the oil countries allocate the stupendous sum of $13.5 billion toward improving the military capability of the confrontation states and the PLO. The conference approved an annual amount of $1.369 billion, in accordance with pledges of the oil states, which demonstrated that they were more willing to increase aid than to wield the oil weapon. The resolution evoked the recipients' bitterness regarding the total amount of aid that had been actually set by the summit ($2.35 billion), but it was the oil producers who set the tone, adhering to the lower figures. Most of the financial burden fell on the Gulf monarchies, while radical Algeria and Libya failed to join the collective commitment to the confrontation states. Nothing was said about the duration of this aid, which was to become a bone of contention between donors and recipients, since the oil states interpreted the summit decision as a one-year aid (for 1975), to the chagrin of the confrontation states. Nor was the use of the oil weapon discussed at the Rabat summit, although Arab oil ministers did consider how to respond to "threats" from oil consumers, namely, the industrial states' idea of forming a united front of oil consumers as a counterweight to OPEC. Indeed, the Arabs found that the oil weapon turned to be a double-edged sword.[47]

10

THE LEBANESE CIVIL WAR: BROKERS AND PAWNS

The Syria-Egypt rift following Sinai II paralyzed the core coalition's potential to advance the peace process with Israel on both regional and international levels. The polarization of inter-Arab politics nourished the eruption of the Lebanese civil war, which turned that country into a battleground of conflicting ambitions, fears, and frustrated hopes. Soon the Lebanon crisis became an antidote to the euphoric mood that had prevailed in the Arab world following the 1973 war and employment of the oil weapon.

Lebanon's civil war was organized violence sponsored by strong social and political revolutionary forces, indigenous and foreign, against an anachronistic, corrupt, and inefficacious political order. In the absence of an effective political center, Lebanon's institutions disintegrated along communal and ideological lines, giving rise to old domestic enmities and external revisionist aspirations. Above all, it was the PR's entanglement in the Lebanese crisis that made it integral to inter-Arab politics and the Arab-Israeli conflict.

Asad's Quest for Regional Hegemony

Asad's failure to prevent Egypt's separate peace diplomacy under Kissinger's supervision apparently led the Syrian ruler to forge a new regional strategy. The obvious lesson drawn from Sadat's independent peace diplomacy was that Damascus could not count on Egypt as a reliable ally in the Arab-Israeli conflict. Hence, Syria should adopt a strategy of self-reliance, based on the consolidation of its own standing as a leading regional power. Syria's regional leadership would enhance its international bargaining position and force Egypt into line with Damascus in the peace process, or at least offset Egypt's loss in the ongoing confrontation with Israel.

This strategy was a new phenomenon in regional Arab politics. Since the UAR's dissolution Syria had been isolated and—a few short respites excepted—nearly always on the defensive and fending off Egyptian efforts to discredit its regime. Under Asad, Syria's inter-Arab policy had moved toward pragmatism and coopeartion with other Arab states, but without a concomitant moderation in its hard-line posture on Arab nationalism, making Sadat's peace-making concept all the more threatening to Damascus' ruling elite.

Syria's geostrategic situation provided Asad with only narrow margins for maneuvering. The bitter relationship with Iraq following the 1973 war sustained further drift as the latter, expecting troubles in its relations with Syria, began construction of a new major pipeline to the Mediterranean through Turkish territory. In April 1975, the Syria-Iraq ideological and political hostility flared up over dividing the Euphrates waters, with the massing of military forces on their border. The crisis was a result of the activation of the new Syrian Tabaqa Dam, which according to Iraqi claims deprived it of its share as a riparian state. While the crisis abated during the summer due to Saudi-Egyptian mediation under the AL's aegis, and both countries pulled back their troops, the hostility between the two regimes remained unchanged.[1]

Given the strategic rivalry with Ba'thi Iraq, the only realistic alternative lay in Syria's immediate sphere of influence, namely, Jordan, Lebanon, and the Palestinians, corresponding to the historic notion of "Greater Syria." Beginning in 1974, Syrian and Palestinian Ba'thist leaders suggested publicly the need for unity among the four components of Greater Syria under the leadership of Damascus. Thus, speaking on March 8, 1974, the anniversary of the Ba'th Party's ascension to power, Asad declared: "Palestine is not only part of the Arab homeland, it is the principal area of Southern Syria. . . . Palestine will remain a liberated part of the Arab homeland and of our Arab Syrian country."[2]

Asad attempted to thaw the icy relations between Jordan and the PLO, but to no avail. He then moved to hitch each of them separately to his own cart. Starting with the PLO, in a speech on March 8, 1975, Asad proposed the creation of a joint Syrian-PLO political and military command. While the PLO leaders responded favorably on a verbal level, they could hardly ignore the coercive nature of Asad's proposal, which took advantage of the massive deployment of Palestinian headquarters and military bases on Syrian soil. Having just achieved unprecedented prestige at Rabat, the PLO was not about to grant Syria the prerogative to steer Palestinian policy according to its own needs. The PLO's insistence on retaining its political independence was one of the factors souring its relations with Syria during the Lebanese civil war.[3]

Parallel to his unification overtures to the PLO, Asad moved to put an end to a long-standing Syrian enmity and subversion toward Jordan. The failed effort to bring the PLO and Jordan to some sort of coordination in the context of the diplomatic process following the Rabat summit enhanced Syria's position as a broker between two essential partners in the peace process. In April 1975, Husain visited Damascus to discuss possible military cooperation and consequently accepted Asad's suggestion to reform the EC along the lines of the pre-1970 command. The rapprochement led to a radical shift in the defensive deployment of the Jordanian army from the Syrian to the Israeli front.

Visiting Amman in June 1975—the first such visit in the annals of relations between the two states—Asad proposed a political union with Jordan, and this was followed by mutual visits of military and civilian delegations to step up cooperation at various levels.[4]

Jordan had its own motives for seeking a rapprochement with Syria, in view of its damaged inter-Arab position following the Rabat summit resolution on the PLO's status. Demonstrating acquiescence to the Rabat resolutions, King Husain followed up by implementing constitutional amendments excluding West Bank residents from service in Jordan's cabinet and parliament. Overall, however, no significant change was discernible in Jordan's policy toward the West Bank; most notably, Amman continued to pump "steadfastness" (sumud) funds to its supporters there. Husain's actions were meant to show the Palestinians and the Arab world as a whole that, as matters stood, Jordan's role in the West Bank was indispensable, and that if Jordan ceased to fulfill that role, the PLO would be incapable of filling the ensuing vacuum. Whatever the PLO might have thought of this, the Arab states accepted the king's position and applauded his efforts.[5]

For Jordan, Syria was the ideal partner to save it from isolation. Both states could only lose from a separate Israeli-Egyptian agreement, although ultimately their guiding motive was their own strategic needs. As far as Damascus was concerned, Jordan—with a long border with Israel and a well-trained army—was the perfect instrument to reinforce Syria's own strategic posture vis-à-vis Israel, including the protection of its southern flank against a thrust through northern Jordan. In Amman's eyes, Syria was the only country capable of restraining the PLO politically and militarily. Syria's quest for a military ally was a golden opportunity for Jordan to restore its impaired legitimacy in the Arab world. To drive the point home, Jordan widely publicized plans to reorganize, streamline, and modernize its armed forces.[6]

Yet despite slogans such as "one homeland," "one country," and "one army," voiced in both Amman and Damascus, Jordan was essentially reluctant to commit itself to anything liable to prejudice its sovereignty or political freedom of action regarding the future of the West Bank. Amman in fact viewed the reconciliation with Damascus as tactical in nature, and when the circumstances engendering it changed, so did the tactics.[7]

Lebanon: Civil War and Foreign Intervention

Lebanon was the third link in the chain of Syria's efforts to establish its influence along the front stretching from Ras al-Naqura, the border post on the Israeli-Lebanese border on the Mediterranean, to the port of Aqaba, the outlet to the Red Sea in the south. In 1972, Asad's regime had made an ambiguous claim to Lebanon as an indivisible part of historic Syria. In January 1975, the

Syrian president paid an official visit to Beirut, the first such in eighteen years, to consolidate their "special relations," concluding a secret agreement on military cooperation. Given Damascus' historical thrust to patronize Lebanon and its frequent meddling in the political affairs of its small, weak neighbor to the west, the Lebanese civil war turned into a testing ground for Syria's exercise of regional power politics. Yet despite the decline of external Egyptian influence on Lebanese domestic politics, Syria could hardly intervene in this country without entangling itself with Arab rivals such as Egypt, Iraq, and Libya, as well as with Saudi Arabia. None of these states would fail to exploit the Palestinian involvement in the crisis to promote its own regional interests through new inter-Arab alignments and tradeoffs.[8]

The civil war was touched off by an incident at ʿAin al-Rummana, in Beirut, on April 13, 1975, between Christian Phalangists and Palestinian *fidaʾiyyun* from the PFLP-GC, led by Ahmad Jibril. The rapid spread of violence reflected a deep-seated tension between the Maronite and Muslim militias, exacerbated by the PR's presence in Lebanon and its response to Kissinger's diplomatic efforts on Sinai. Indeed, the Lebanese civil war was marked by growing collaboration between Israel and the Maronite militias, which might have been behind the latter's decision to escalate the war against the PR. Since its inception, Lebanon's old parochial conflicts had gradually taken on a clear political and ideological character, resulting in the emergence of two rival loose coalitions: the conservatives, largely from the Christian Maronite community, striving to preserve the traditional political-social-economic system in which they were the dominant factor; and the leftist groups, comprised mainly of Muslims and led by the Druze leader Kamal Junblat, which sought radical constitutional, political, and social changes.[9]

The political tension in Lebanon intensified due to the growing PR guerrilla attacks against Israel which demonstrated the PLO's frustration at its exclusion by Israel from the diplomatic process. Intensive Israeli retaliations against south Lebanon, which led to a massive migration of Shiʿi villagers to the north, combined with the PLO's increasing involvement in domestic Lebanese politics, expedited the long-delayed showdown. Since the end of the 1960s, the Lebanese army's Christian command and Maronite militias had demonstrated consistent opposition to the PR's presence in Lebanon, pushing the latter to foster alliances with the leftist-Muslim Lebanese militias. For the PR, Lebanon's political weakness and massive population of Palestinian refugees offered the only substitute for the lost Jordanian base that was independent of Syrian patronage and coercion. Securing the support of indigenous Lebanese Muslim groups was an essential lesson drawn from the PR's defeat in Jordan in 1970–71. The alliance with the Lebanese left provided legitimacy for the PR's military presence and activity against Israel, whereas the Lebanese left perceived the PR as a moral asset and potential source of armed support.[10]

During the second half of 1975, armed clashes between Christian and Muslim-leftist militias in Beirut developed into a countrywide civil war, which triggered growing external intervention. Lebanon became an Arab microcosm, reflecting other inter-state rivalries and tensions elsewhere. Iraq and Libya rushed to proffer political and military support to their radical leftist Lebanese and Palestinian allies in the Rejection Front who fought together against the Maronite militias. Syria's involvement in the crisis—though laden with contradictions—was most significant, indicating Damascus' traditional patronage, special interests, and stakes in Lebanon. Syria could not lag behind Iraq and Libya in supplying military materials to the leftist coalition, thus undermining the existing political system. At the same time, Syria endeavored to prevent a total collapse of the Maronite side by assuming a mediation role between the parties, aiming to preserve Lebanon's political order on both domestic and regional levels.

January 1976 was a turning point in the intensifying Lebanese civil war in view of the Maronite militias' new policy of expelling Muslims and Palestinians from the predominantly Christian northern and eastern quarters of Beirut, in an obvious attempt to create a purely Christian contiguity to Mount Lebanon. In January, this policy resulted in the devastation of two Palestinian refugee camps, while two others came under siege. For the PLO, it indicated that the battle had turned into an all-out war of survival. It was at this stage that Fatah, the largest Palestinian organization, which had hitherto taken a passive stance in the fighting, joined the anti-Maronite camp and at once assumed a leading role, owing to its military prowess and political significance. The PLO's reasons for its direct involvement in the Lebanese civil war notwithstanding, by joining the leftist coalition in the offensive against the Maronites' heartland, the PLO became a full partner in the civil war, which tarnished its image as a national liberation movement and exposed it to inter-Arab conflicting pressures.[11]

The intensive fighting prompted indirect Syrian military involvement, with the dispatching of two battalions of the PLA into Lebanon. This force, its Palestinian personnel notwithstanding, was to all intents and purposes an integral part of the Syrian Army. The move itself—though explained in terms of Syria's commitment to defend the PR—was meant to exert political and military pressure on the parties concerned to seek a settlement. At Syria's instigation, a "Constitutional Document"—designed to introduce a moderate change in the political system—had been signed by President Franjiyya and announced on February 14. The document, however, fell far short of the demands presented by the Lebanese left, headed by the Druze leader Kamal Junblat, who responded with outright rejection.[12]

An agreement was also worked out between the Lebanese government and the PLO to circumscribe the activity of the PR in Lebanon to accord with those rules set by previous bilateral agreements (the 1969 Cairo and 1973 Malkart accords). Pressing its mediating role, Syria undertook publicly to be guarantor of the new agreements, which now became the linchpin of Syrian policy in Lebanon. But Damascus proved incapable of imposing its will on either the Lebanese leftist coalition or the PLO, which combined to resist the Constitutional Document. The failure of Syria's conciliation efforts led to the renewal of fighting and the dispatch of additional PLA and Syrian Army units into Lebanon. In March–April, tension between Syria and the leftist-Palestinian front mounted dramatically as the latter's forces engaged in an offensive against the Maronites' stronghold in Mount Lebanon. The growing dispute with Syria led the latter to exert pressures on the Palestinians and the Lebanese left by a sea and land blockade and a propaganda campaign.

Although a minority of Lebanese Muslim and Palestinian groups backed Syria, the majority of the leftist-Palestinian coalition viewed further Syrian intervention with alarm, believing it was designed to bring them under Damascus' heel. On the inter-Arab level, pressures on Damascus to ease its policy toward the leftist-Palestinian coalition grew heavier on the part of the Saudi regime and rejectionist Libya and Iraq, threatening Syria's exclusive role in Lebanon by "Arabization" of the crisis. The Syrians were equally concerned about French and American intentions to interfere with the crisis in favor of the Maronites. Above all, by late May the Maronite militias' defeat seemed only a matter of time, perceived with horror by Damascus due to its detrimental repercussions on both the domestic and regional orders. Syria was especially concerned lest Lebanon be partitioned into an independent Palestinian-Lebanese radical authority and a small Maronite "state" with strong links to Israel and the West. Such a division could prompt an Israeli takeover of southern Lebanon, thus placing Israel's army in a better strategic position to threaten the Syrian capital.[13]

After a year of failed mediating efforts, faced with the possible fall of Lebanon to the PLO and Lebanese Muslim left coalition supported by Libya and Iraq, and fearing Israeli intervention, Asad finally resorted to military means. The Syrian military intervention in Lebanon on June 1, 1976—which opened with a blitz assault on Palestinian and leftist strongholds—was said to be at President Franjiyya's request. Whether or not the Syrians had meant, or expected, to fight, their offensive was repulsed and failed, resulting in their long and agonizing entanglement in the Lebanese political swamp. Moreover, the confrontation with the PR triggered strong criticism against Asad's regime by both Arab rivals—Egypt, Iraq, and Libya—and domestic Sunni Muslim opposition, seriously eroding its legitimacy.[14]

The Syrian invasion of Lebanon was preceded by a tacit understanding with Israel, mediated by the United States, on a "red line" delineating their respective spheres of military presence on Lebanese soil. The "red line" understanding was to enhance Asad's regional position and to pave his way back to the peace process. It entailed Asad's renewed commitment to take part in the peace process under American supervision with the aim of reaching an agreement with Israel on ending the state of war in return for its withdrawal to the pre-June 1967 borders.[15]

Among Syria's critics, Egypt was especially outspoken, warning that Israel was liable to take advantage of the Lebanon war by occupying parts of the country. In fact, the PLO's involvement in the Lebanon civil war provided Sadat with an opportunity to resume Egypt's leading role in the inter-Arab arena by undertaking the role of the PLO's patron. The PLO, for its part, sought a reconciliation with Egypt that would counterbalance the Damascus-Amman coalition threatening its political gains. By mid-June, 'Arafat had met with Sadat in Cairo for the first time in nearly a year, requesting the latter's support for the PR in the conflict with Christian militias and Syria. Egypt had provided the PLO with limited military assistance and, in January 1976, let it transfer to Lebanon the PLA's Egypt-based 'Ain-Jalut brigade (a battalion in strength).[16]

In April, Cairo and the PLO urged that an Arab summit meeting be covened to discuss the deteriorating situation in Lebanon. More crucial for the PLO was Egypt's effort, together with Iraq, to convince Saudi Arabia and other oil producers to press Syria to desist from its intervention in Lebanon and refer the crisis to AL mediation. These efforts began to bear fruit only after the failure of Syria's June 1 offensive and the subsequent stalemate in Lebanon, which lasted through the summer.[17]

The Syria-PLO confrontation led to a new inter-Arab alignment. The pro-Syrian coalition that had emerged following the Sinai II accord disintegrated and—with the exception of Jordan, which continued to side with Damascus in hopes of weakening the PLO—the entire Arab world was arrayed against Syria. Syria's military forces in Lebanon collided head-on with factions allied with Iraq, resulting in the latter's pressures on Syria and drawing Baghdad—despite its rejectionist position toward Sinai II—and Cairo together. In June, Iraq massed forces on the border with Syria, sent several hundred troops to beef up the Lebanese left, and propagated its demand to station large forces on the Golan Heights, highlighting Syria's military idleness on the front with Israel.[18] Syria could find no satisfaction in the Soviet stance, either. The Soviets publicly criticized Damascus and demanded that Syrian military activity against the Palestinians and the left—Moscow's "natural allies"—be halted and that Syrian troops withdraw from Lebanon. As a gesture to the Palestinians, Moscow gave them some aid, chiefly food and medicine.[19]

Until mid-1976, Syria was able to ward off all Arab efforts to intervene in the Lebanon crisis. Together with Libya and the PLO, Syria boycotted the ALC meeting of October 1975. Damascus also rejected Egypt's offer to dispatch "Arab security forces" to Lebanon to restore order, arguing that these troops should be designated for the war against Israel. But as Arab and domestic criticism mounted following the invasion of Lebanon, Damascus was willing to cooperate with the AL to dilute criticism and gain time until it could subdue the Palestinians and the leftist coalition in Lebanon. Thus, Syria agreed, at an emergency ALC meeting on June 8, 1976, to a cease-fire and the dispatch of "Arab Security Forces" (ASF) to Lebanon. Damascus also expressed willingness to cooperate with Libyan PM Jallud, who was working to advance Qadhafi's initiative for renewed understanding among Syria, the PLO, and the Lebanese left. In mid-July, Jallud's efforts ended in failure, provoking Libyan denunciations of Syria.[20]

The creation of the ASF—the first of its kind since the 1961 Kuwait crisis—reflected the significance Egypt and Saudi Arabia placed on the containment of the crisis and restoration of the coalition with Syria. Moreover, Syria was effectively assigned the role of repressing the revolutionary forces in Lebanon, including the PR itself. Hence, the ASF was subordinated to the Beirut government and was to serve in addition to the Syrian forces in Lebanon. This implicit acknowledgement of the legitimacy of the Syrian presence in Lebanon was hammered home when—to the chagrin of Iraq, the PLO, and the Lebanese left—Syria obtained majority support among Arab states for its own troops to serve in the ASF. In late June 1976, 2,500 troops from Syria, Saudi Arabia, Sudan, and Libya arrived in Beirut under an Egyptian commander, but it soon became apparent that this force was too small to impose order on Lebanon's chaos.[21]

Syria also declared willingness to resume its dialogue with Egypt, paving the road to the June 23 meeting of the PMs of Egypt, Syria, and Saudi Arabia, and the FM of Kuwait, in Riyad. Their joint communique endorsed the ALC's resolutions creating the ASF, and supporting Lebanese unity and sovereignty. In addition, it called on all parties to facilitate the ASF and declared readiness to help arrange reconciliation talks for the Lebanon crisis based on the AL resolutions. The communique indicated the common interest of both Syria and Egypt in reconciliation, declaring—for propaganda purposes—their agreement to renew military cooperation as the principal basis for joint Arab action to implement the Rabat resolutions. Practically, Egypt and Syria agreed to refrain from mutual propaganda attacks and to reactivate the liaison offices between the two states at ambassadorial level. Syria was not called on to remove its forces from Lebanon, and even secured backing for its own demand that the PLO execute the spirit and letter of the Cairo and Malkart agreements. Similarly, the communique's silence on Egypt's signing Sinai II was construed as tacit approval on Syria's part.[22]

Syria's support of the joint communique turned out to be a calculated step in its efforts to gain time for the implementation of its goals in Lebanon. Yet the communique also reflected Asad's narrow margins for maneuvering in the inter-Arab arena and his strategic choice to rejoin the pragmatic coalition of Saudi Arabia and Egypt, rather than to collaborate with Iraq's and Libya's Rejection Front. Given the priority Damascus attached to the Lebanese issue and Syria's hostile relations with Iraq, the price being demanded by the Iraqi-led bloc was intolerable for Damascus: diminished Syrian involvement in Lebanon, which would boost the Palestinians and the left. Iraq and its Lebanese and Palestinian allies also rejected the political process based on Resolutions 242 and 338—a stance that underpinned the failure of the Jallud mission. Thus, while Syria demonstrated its willingness to cooperate with Egypt and Saudi Arabia, it took an intransigent line toward Iraq, vetoing its participation in the ASF or in any mediation efforts in Lebanon.

Following another meeting of Arab FMs (July 12) and intensified Arab pressure to resolve the conflict, Syria and the PLO reached a cease-fire agreement, confirming Syria's insistence that the PR's activity in Lebanon be strictly limited to the provisions of the 1969 Cairo Agreement. Jallud, typically, excoriated the cease-fire, describing it as tantamount to the "liquidation of the PLO." However, the agreement was not implemented, as it fell far short of both sides' expectations and needs. Syria in particular could not accept the status quo; it needed to gain the upper hand to improve its inter-Arab bargaining position. Ultimately, the Syrians' delaying tactics vis-a-vis the Arab world achieved their goal: by the time the summit meeting convened, on October 25, Syria had gained a decisive military advantage over the Palestinian-leftist coalition through two brief offensives in late September and mid-October.[23]

Crisis Management and Restoration of the Pragmatic Coalition

As of late August, Egypt assumed the leading role in advocating the convening of a limited summit conference on the Lebanese crisis, with the participation of Syria, Saudi Arabia, Kuwait, Lebanon, and the PLO. Egypt's suggestion intended to avoid not only criticism for Sinai II, but also the difficulties that an expanded conference would face in working out a practical solution to the Lebanon dilemma. Iraq, Libya, and Algeria fiercely resisted the idea of a limited summit that would exclude them from Arab collective decision making. Furthermore, Iraq insisted that the summit call for the withdrawal of all Syrian forces from Lebanon; Libya demanded that the agenda include its own relations with Egypt, which was allegedly massing troops on their border.

Egypt's initiative represented a growing effort to exploit Syria's entanglement in Lebanon to restore its own leading position in the Arab arena and pressure Damascus to realign with Sadat's diplomacy in the peace process. Egypt maintained that the resolution of the Lebanese crisis must include the withdrawal of all foreign forces from Lebanon, an undertaking by all Arab states not to intervene in Lebanese internal affairs, implementation of the Cairo

Agreement and its annexes, and agreement on a timetable to implement these measures.[24]

Egypt's intensive consultations with the Arab parties directly involved in the Lebanon crisis resulted in a recommendation adopted by Arab FMs meeting in Cairo on September 4, that a summit meeting be held in the third week of October to discuss both Lebanon and Arab solidarity. The limited attendance at the FMs' meeting—only eight of twenty AL member states—underscored the decisive weight of a coordinated action by Egypt and the Gulf oil states. A peace plan for Lebanon was discussed at the meeting, entailing a cease-fire, implementation of the Cairo Agreement, and economic normalization, and requiring significant enlargement of the ASF. The Lebanese Christians insisted that the summit focus on the PR's presence on Lebanese soil while the PLO demanded a total Syrian withdrawal from Lebanon.[25]

Egypt, joined by Saudi Arabia, continued to seek a limited summit, assuming that a prolonged impasse in Lebanon would diminish Syria's ability to sustain its pressure to end the crisis. The underlying premise was that Damascus sought an honorable way out of Lebanon and that the badly weakened Palestinians would moderate their stand under the prodding of Cairo and Riyad. In essence, Sadat anticipated that the exhaustion of Syria and the PLO in the fighting would let him renew the peacemaking efforts and reach a political settlement with Israel. Meanwhile, Cairo continued to use the Palestine issue as a lever to restore its leading role in the Arab world. On September 5, the ALC approved Egypt's request to grant the PLO full AL membership as the representative of Palestine.[26]

While preparations for a full summit meeting were underway, on October 1, Egyptian FM Fahmi announced his government's intention to convene a mini-summit in Riyad, to include Egypt, Kuwait, Syria, Lebanon, and the PLO. He left no doubt as to Egypt's eagerness to resume the Geneva Conference with PLO participation, declaring that in return for Israeli withdrawal to the 1967 lines, the Arab states would agree to end the state of war with Israel. Egypt was indeed bent on advancing the political process by shifting the political focus from the inter-Arab to the international sphere, anticipating that peacemaking efforts would be resumed under U.S. auspices following the November 1976 presidential elections.[27]

Syria continued to play for time, rejecting Egypt's idea of a mini-summit and offering, instead, a meeting with the same participants save the PLO and Lebanon. On October 12, while the AL-mediated negotiations at the Lebanese resort town of Shtura were still under way, the Syrians unleashed a new military offensive against the Palestinian and Lebanese left forces on the outskirts of Beirut and Sidon. The Shtura talks were suspended and Fahmi denounced the Syrian move as a provocation. Syria unequivocally rejected the

Arab protests, asserting that it intended to preserve its military presence in Lebanon and underscoring the AL's impotence. In mid-October, once the Syrian military offensive had secured its main objectives, Damascus signalled its willingness to accept the Saudi invitation to attend a mini-summit in Riayd, just as the Arab FMs were convening in Cairo to finalize the full Arab summit's agenda.[28]

The mini-summit meeting in Riyad was attended by King Khalid, the Kuwaiti Emir, Presidents Sadat, Sarkis, and Asad, and 'Arafat. The two-day meeting of the main parties concerned in Lebanon and the core Arab actors produced an overall agreement, ostensibly responding to the demands of both Lebanon and the PLO. The peace plan for Lebanon entailed a cease-fire and the creation of a Syrian-dominated "Arab Deterrence Force" (ADF) of 30,000 troops, to be subordinated to the president of Lebanon. The ADF would fulfill its mission in two stages. In the first stage, it would supervise the end of hostilities, dismantle barriers and armed positions, collect the combatants' heavy arms, open roads, and reactivate services and institutions in the country according to a detailed timetable. In the second stage, it would oversee the implementation of the 1969 Cairo Agreement which regulated PR-Lebanese relations. A committee (Egypt, Syria, Kuwait, and Saudi Arabia) was set up to supervise the implementation of the Cairo Agreement within ninety days.[29]

The mini-summit's main result lay in the renewal of understanding between Asad and Sadat. The meeting also highlighted the decisive weight of the Egyptian-Saudi-Syrian coalition in the Arab world, in marked contrast to the weakness of the rejectionist states—Iraq, Algeria, and Libya—which responded with ineffectual protests and the dispatch of minister-level delegates to the Cairo summit. On the face of it, the absence of leaders from the radical states, and the Riyad agreement on terminating the Lebanon crisis, supported by the Egyptian-Saudi-Syrian bloc, held out the prospect of a speedy, smooth followthrough at the summit. However, discord over the composition of the inter-Arab force soon surfaced.

The agreement reached in Riyad served as a basis for a detailed draft proposal submitted to the full summit in Cairo for the creation, arming, and funding of the ADF. Yet despite PLO appeals, most Arab states were far from eager to take part in a predominantly Syrian force merely to call attention to its all-Arab character. Thus, Egypt said it would supply the ADF with arms but would not send troops, and the Saudis had no desire to commit more forces to Lebanon beyond the battalion that was part of the ASF. Iraq rejected the entire concept of an inter-Arab force in Lebanon and continued to insist on the immediate pullout of all Syrian forces. The final draft proposal spoke of a force of no more than 10,000 Syrian troops, together with troops from Sudan, Saudi Arabia, North Yemen, and the UAE, at an estimated annual cost of about $180 million. Based on the Riyad conclusions, the FMs also discussed financial aid to restart Lebanon's economy and Arab solidarity. However, the need to rehabilitate the Lebanese economy was quickly shunted to the sidelines.[30]

Iraq's opposition to the "illegitimate" presence of 20,000 Syrian troops on Lebanese soil and 'Arafat's suggestion that no single state account for more than thirty percent of the force were to no avail. The summit decided to give Lebanon's President Sarkis the final word on the makeup of the force. Effectively, this meant that the entire Syrian contingent would remain in Lebanon and constitute the bulk of the ADF, beefed up by the ASF and additional troops of infantry battalion strength. This outcome was a major achievement for Syria, since it implied general Arab affirmation of its military presence in Lebanon, and ensured that these forces would be only nominally subordinated to the Lebanese president.[31]

The summit also decided to set up a fund to underwrite the ADF, the bulk of which was comprised of Syrian forces. The AL was empowered to renew the mandate of the ADF every six months at the Lebanese president's request. While this seemed to present an opening for the countries contributing to the fund to pressure Syria by threatening to withhold the money, in practice this was a very limited avenue of pressure since a relatively small amount was involved and since Syria intended to maintain its military presence in Lebanon anyway. Nevertheless, the Arab states were bent on creating supervisory machinery that would at least enable them to claim success in restraining Damascus.

The meeting failed to specify the sources of financing for the ADF, but unofficially it was indicated that Saudi Arabia, Kuwait, the UAE, and Qatar would jointly account for sixty-five percent of the financing, with the remainder to be contributed by the other Arab states. Ultimately, the entire burden was borne by Saudi Arabia and the Gulf states. Though only Iraq opposed the resolution—which it denounced as perpetuating the Syrian presence in Lebanon—Algeria and Libya too announced that they intended to ignore it and take no part in its implementation. In contrast to financing the ADF, the summit's resolution to extend financial aid to Lebanon remained a dead letter until the Tunis summit meeting in 1979.[32]

The final communique also indicated the oil producers' readiness to resume the Rabat aid to the confrontation states, which had been suspended after one year's payment. During 1976, pressure on the Gulf oil states to resume the Rabat aid mounted, wielded particularly by Egypt, in view of its soaring external debt. In March, Sadat was obliged to succumb to the donors' humiliating condition of putting Egypt's monetary affairs under foreign supervision, to prevent a situation he defined as "economic disaster."[33]

The Egyptian-Saudi-Syrian coalition effectively ignored the topic of Arab solidarity—meaning conflicts unrelated to Lebanon—and contented itself with a reference to the Arab Solidarity Charter adopted at Casablanca in 1965. In fact, this item was of concern only to the rejectionist states, who were on the defensive at the conference: Iraq in its dispute with Syria over Lebanon; Algeria due to the Western Sahara conflict; and Libya amid escalating mutual subversion and military tension on the border with Egypt.[34]

Egypt's performance at the summit underlined the significance of militancy toward Israel as an instrument for mobilizing Arab legitimacy, even though the summit's agenda revolved around the Lebanon crisis. Cairo was the main driving force behind the proposal to have the summit meeting discuss Israel's actions in southern Lebanon, which it castigated as interference in Lebanon's internal affairs in an effort to control the country's south. Egypt's militancy toward Israel also served Cairo in its tense relations with Jordan, reflecting the latter's alignment with Syria and its perceived interest in weakening the PLO to enhance its own political stature. Prior to the summit conference, both Jordan and Egypt were engaged in a competition over which country could raise the issue of Israel's activities—mainly expropriation of land—in the occupied West Bank at the UNSC. At the summit, however, Sadat and Husain were able to iron out their differences, a development the Egyptian leader desired in order to enlist Husain's support for his projected moves in the peace process.[35]

The Cairo summit resulted in a package deal in which Egypt and Syria made ostensible concessions with a view to advance their individual interests. Syria agreed to take part in the diplomatic process under Sadat's leadership, but gained freedom of action in Lebanon; Egypt accepted Syria's hegemony in Lebanon at the expense of the PLO's interest, and, in return, its political approach in the conflict with Israel was sanctioned and the dispute over the Sinai interim agreement was resolved.[36]

The summit's implicit affirmation of the Riyad resolutions on Lebanon pointed up the weakness of the radical states, which had been bypassed in the efforts to resolve the Lebanon crisis. The major role played by Saudi Arabia and Kuwait in bringing about a reconciliation between Sadat and Asad attested to their influence and ability to serve as highly efficacious mediators, thanks to their oil resources and cash reserves. At the same time, one must ask whether the Saudis' success in mediating between Sadat and Asad was not too late in coming, and whether the situation would have been allowed to deteriorate so badly had the kingdom still been ruled by the authoritative Faisal rather than by King Khalid and Crown Prince Fahd.[37]

Despite the radical states' poor performance, the summit did see the further consolidation of a potentially powerful radical bloc, consisting of Iraq, Algeria, Libya, and PDRY. This group actually tried to prevent the holding of the summit once it became clear that the meeting would do no more than rubber-stamp the Riyad resolutions. For the present, these countries were united in their desire to see Syria out of Lebanon and in their support for the PLO and the leftist coalition in Lebanon. This realigned Rejection Front would subsequently seek to block renewed efforts to advance the peacemaking process with Israel.

Moves to refocus the Arab world's attention on that process now encountered a problem in the form of the PLO's tarnished prestige, which was diminished by the setbacks it had sustained in Lebanon. Since the diplomatic strategy vis-à-vis Israel was to be based on the principle of a comprehensive settlement, including resolution of the Palestinian problem, the weakening of the PLO adversely affected the entire Arab posture. Sadat therefore called for greater support for the PLO in order to reinvigorate its international standing. Indeed, while the core coalition states endeavored to enhance the Palestinian issue and the PLO's political status, they were equally concerned with suppressing its revolutionary tendencies. Tunisia's Bourguiba thought the time was propitious to reissue his call to the Arabs to accept the 1947 UN resolution on the partition of Palestine.[38]

Overall, the Cairo resolutions reaffirmed the Rabat and Algiers resolutions on the Palestinians' exclusive representation by the PLO, the Arab states' undertaking not to interfere in the PLO's internal affairs, and the organization's right "to establish its independent state on its own soil." It was now the PLO's turn to make its preparations, with a view to the resumption of the peace efforts in the Middle East, and to that end the thirteenth PNC session was scheduled to convene in March 1977.[39]

11

THE BURDEN OF ARAB CONSENSUS: EGYPT-ISRAEL PEACE ACCORD AND ARAB RESPONSE

The Arab Core Coalition in Action

The Cairo summit resulted in the resumption of the Egypt-Saudi Arabia-Syria coalition, which accounted for a period of outstanding inter-Arab coordination on the diplomatic effort toward Israel. The decisive weight of this coalition was demonstrated by the passive support that accrued to it from most Arab regimes save the Rejection Front—Iraq, Libya, Algeria, and PDRY—which had remained divided and paralyzed. The concept of a comprehensive settlement of the conflict with Israel that was adopted by the core coalition for its diplomacy was compatible with that of the new American administration in Washington, generating positive international reverberations.

The comprehensive peace concept called for full Israeli withdrawal from all Arab territories occupied in June 1967, establishment of a Palestinian state, and termination of the state of war with Israel. These goals were to be achieved within the framework of the Geneva Conference, with the PLO's participation. A vigorous diplomatic and propaganda effort aimed at enlisting Western support for this approach—and, concomitantly, at isolating Israel—had been undertaken by Egypt, Saudi Arabia, and Syria. The Arabs' diplomatic campaign took the Palestinian question as its spearhead. The new U.S. administration under President Carter seemed especially receptive, signalling that the Middle East would be a high priority on its foreign policy agenda and that it would strive for a comprehensive settlement rather than further partial agreements. For the first time in the annals of the conflict an American president spoke about the Palestinians' right to their own homeland.[1]

The positive atmosphere prevailing in the Arab arena was indicated by a series of bilateral and trilateral summits that reinforced the image of unity Arabs wished to project in the international arena. In December 1976 and February 1977, Sadat and Asad met, demonstrating mutual understanding and cooperation through measures such as the formation of a joint political and military leadership. In January 1977, Sadat hosted King Husain for an official visit and for the first time obtained from the Jordanian monarch assent to a joint communique that not only endorsed the establishment of an "independent political entity for the Palestinians" but spoke of an actual "Palestinian state" with which Jordan would wish "to establish the closest relations." While Jordan later reverted to its traditional formula of "a political entity for the Palestinians," the meeting, nevertheless, helped to warm up its relations with Egypt.[2]

Another link in the chain of preparations for Geneva was a Husain-'Arafat meeting during the March 1977 Afro-Arab summit conference in Cairo. The encounter was apparently brought about by Saudi-Egyptian efforts in search of a formula that would facilitate Palestinian representation at Geneva through a joint Jordanian-Palestinian delegation. At the same time, Sadat and Asad made a clear gesture to deter rejectionist Qadhafi. Meeting at Khartoum in February 1977, they declared the establishment of a joint leadership of Egypt, Syria, and Sudan. The accord was a followup to the defense treaty that Numairi and Sadat had signed in July 1976, a move that reflected Numairi's concern over Qadhafi's persistent agitation against his regime.[3]

Saudi Arabia used its economic clout to enhance inter-Arab accord and prevent political radicalism. Riyad used its aid to pressure Syria to take a softer line toward the Palestinian groups in Lebanon and to induce the PLO to keep its distance from the USSR. The Saudis also demonstrated their instrumentality in propagating the Arab attitude in the peace process in the United States. In May, Sadat and Asad met with King Khalid in Riyad on the eve of Crown Prince Fahd's meeting with President Carter in Washington. The talks were part of a coordinated effort to forge a joint stand on the comprehensive settlement following separate meetings with Carter by Sadat, Asad, and Husain.[4]

The tripartite Arab meeting was yet another sign of Saudi Arabia's immense international prestige and its influence in the Arab world, due to its global oil clout. Furthermore, in January, Riyad and the other Gulf monarchies agreed to resume the Rabat financial aid to the confrontation states in 1977–1978. This ended the bitter disagreement that had flared up in 1976 between donors—who had refused to prolong the aid beyond 1975—and recipients, who argued that it was initially meant to be multi-annual. However, disagreement over the scope of the aid persisted. When the recipients continued to carp about the size of the aid, the donors retorted by demanding a review of the ways the vast sums already given had been spent.[5]

Indeed, Arab financial aid to the confrontation states, particularly to Egypt, remained a thin trickle, which fell far from their immense needs. The Gulf donors remained reluctant to provide Egypt with more than measured or emergency assistance, which would prevent a serious danger to Sadat's regime but maintain the latter's dependency on their aid. Hence, the severe food riots that erupted in Egypt in January 1977—later identified as an impetus for Sadat's peace initiative in November 1977—led the Gulf oil states to pledge a

$1.474 billion long-term loan to alleviate Egypt's urgent balance-of-payments burden. Saudi Arabia and Kuwait also rescheduled Egypt's debt and maintained their $2 billion deposits in Egyptian banks.[6]

Cutting the Gordian Knot: Sadat's Road To Jerusalem

The conclusion of a series of individual meetings between the heads of Egypt, Jordan, Saudi Arabia and Syria and President Carter in May revealed the gap dividing Washington from the Arab collective position regarding both procedure and the desired final result of the peace process. Apart from Washington's objection to the PLO's participation at Geneva, the U.S. president's clear stance was that the Arabs must offer a full peace and not just the termination of the state of war with Israel. These meetings were accompanied by hints in the Arab press that economic pressure would be applied against the West if no progress were forthcoming toward a comprehensive settlement.[7] When, in May, the right-wing Likud Party in Israel—with its ideological commitment to preserving the whole Land of Israel, including the West Bank and Gaza—ascended to power, the chances for convening the Geneva Conference on the basis of the comprehensive peace concept seemed to have suffered a severe blow.

Attempts to take advantage of what seemed to be a dead end in Egyptian-sponsored diplomacy and to undercut the pragmatic coalition were made by Arab peripheral states, striving to shift the course of collective Arab policy to their own benefit in the name of the Palestine conflict. In June, Qadhafi called for a summit conference to be convened in Tripoli to discuss the Palestine problem and other issues of collective Arab concern. North Yemen also urged that a summit meeting be held to consider Arab strategy in the conflict with Israel in view of the change in the Israeli government. North Yemen's ulterior motive was to place the issue of Israeli activity in the Red Sea at the agenda's top and get Arab financial aid and political warfare against Israel extended to that region. And behind the anti-Israeli terminology was the growing concern at the Soviet encroachment in Ethiopia since the end of 1976 and its repercussions on Arab security in the Red Sea.[8]

Egypt and Saudi Arabia resented the idea of convening a summit conference before the results were known of the initial contacts between the new Israeli government and the U.S. administration. Thus, Egypt exploited its control of the AL to block Qadhafi's proposal despite his heavy lobbying. The cold water thrown on the Libyan initiative reflected the balance of power between the radical and pragmatic coalitions but also deteriorating Egypt-Libya relations. Libya's agitation in Sudan and Egypt turned the latter all the more adamant in favor of scuttling the mooted Tripoli summit and preventing Qadhafi from enjoying the prestige that accrued to the host of a summit meeting. Egypt accused Libya of consistently sabotaging Arab unity precisely when the Arabs were at a crossroads between war and peace. The growing hostility between the two regimes mounted following Egypt's military buildup in the Western Desert at the expense of the Sinai front, culminating in the July 1977 border clashes between their armed forces.[9]

King Husain too attempted to exploit the new situation to consolidate a favorable formula for Palestinian representation that would ensure his prominent role at Geneva. His lobbying for a mini-summit of the confrontation states, however, failed to win support of the core coalition despite his visits to Cairo, Damascus, and Riyad in July.[10] Signs of a crack in the Arab core coalition surfaced in the summer due to growing doubts that the Geneva Conference would soon reconvene, exacerbating Syria's concern over Egypt's commitment to the collective Arab line. In August, Syria joined the calls to convene an Arab summit conference, hoping to renew Egypt's commitment to the principle of a comprehensive settlement of the Arab-Israeli conflict. Given the unbending opposition of both Israel and the United States to PLO participation in a peace conference, Syria appeared anxious to act as a patron of Palestinian rights, by insisting that at Geneva there would be a single Arab delegation that would include the PLO.[11]

Damascus' position was clearly intended to contain the danger of another separate Egyptian settlement with Israel. At the least, a summit at this juncture could turn into an instrument for obtaining increased aid from the oil producers plus military and political backing for Syria's mission in Lebanon. The deadlocked road to Geneva, and Syria's position, intensified Arab pressures for a summit meeting to forestall a protracted impasse. On September 4, the ALC semi-annual meeting in Cairo resolved that an extraordinary FMs meeting would be held in Tunis on November 12 to prepare for a summit conference.

During the summer, intensive diplomatic efforts were made to resolve the problem of Palestinian representation at Geneva, but to no avail. The PLO wished to attend any conference to which it would be formally invited on an equal footing, but equally resented Resolution 242 as it stood. But President Carter's hands were tied by Kissinger's commitments to Israel following Sinai II. The focus of U.S. diplomatic moves in the Middle East during that period was to persuade the PLO—through Egypt, Syria, and Saudi Arabia—to accept the resolution, even with reservations, since its wording had not mentioned the Palestinians and their national rights. In return, the Carter administration was ready to open an official dialogue with the PLO, although without ensuring the PLO's participation at Geneva.[12]

The PLO had apparantly accepted the American proposals but Syria would not allow an independent United States–PLO dialogue, which could only weaken Damascus' position in the peace process. Syria insisted on having assurances of Israel's total withdrawal from the territories occupied in 1967 as a prerequisite for its participation in the Geneva Conference. Egypt regarded that demand as impractical, urging separate representation by each country— as well as by the Palestinians—at Geneva. Sadat, however, found himself stymied on the issue of PLO participation. He could not convince the PLO either to establish a government-in-exile or to appoint a representative with no clear PLO affiliation to the peace conference.[13]

The perceived threat to Israel that was encapsulated in the comprehensive settlement concept drove PM Begin to seek direct diplomatic channels to Egypt, which had itself been impatiently seeking to remove the obstacles from the road to Geneva. In mid-September, a secret meeting had been held in Morocco between Israeli FM Moshe Dayan and Sadat's emissary, Hasan al-Tuhami. The significance of the meeting was in its very existence rather than its contents or impact on later developments. Dayan apparently made no commitment for full Israeli withdrawal from Sinai, as was commonly argued; thus, this cannot be used to explain Sadat's decision to go to Jerusalem.[14]

The two partners' search for an alternative to Geneva was expedited by the joint United States–Soviet declaration on the Middle East, issued October 1, calling for the early reconvening of the Geneva Conference to negotiate "a fundamental solution to all aspects of the Middle East problem in its entirety." The joint declaration heightened Sadat's discomfort and triggered United States–Israeli tension. Sadat perceived the USSR's participation in the regional diplomatic process as a harmful step that would limit Egypt's freedom of action and stiffen the PLO's and Syria's positions. To Israel, the United States–Soviet declaration implied a recipe for an imposed settlement. Under Israel's pressure the rules for Geneva were reshaped, turning the peace conference into a ceremonial opening after which the parties were to conduct bilateral negotiations.[15]

In late October and early November—as Sadat was secretly weaving his plan to visit Jerusalem, as a dramatic gesture to break the deadlock—parallel Arab efforts sought to convince him of the need for an Arab summit conference, obviously seeking to commit him to a collective Arab policy. The Saudis also joined the thrust, urging him thus at talks in Riyad on October 31. If Sadat had already made up his mind to visit Jerusalem, he disclosed nothing about it to his hosts. On November 9, in the course of a speech to the Egyptian People's Assembly, with ʿArafat present as a guest of honor, Sadat declared that he would even go to the Knesset in Jerusalem to discuss a settlement with Israel "if this could save the life of one Egyptian soldier." The statement drew attention in the Arab world only when PM Begin responded with a public invitation to Sadat to visit Jerusalem. On November 12, Arab FMs met in Tunis to set the agenda for a summit conference on the peace process and the PLO's participation in Geneva. Syria, concerned about Sadat's intention to make a separate peace with Israel, pressed for an immediate summit to block the renewal of the Geneva Conference, scheduled for December. Due to Egypt's opposition, however, the FMs decided that the summit would convene on February 15, 1978.[16]

Sadat's decision to go to Jerusalem was not made heedless of its repercussions among his Arab counterparts. The visit he paid beforehand to Damascus indicated his wish to obtain—though not at all costs—a wide Arab sanctioning for this historic initiative by ensuring the prior approval of a key confrontation state and a leading member of the Arab radical camp. Asad was appalled by Sadat's plan but failed to convince his guest to cancel it, which brought him—as he later revealed—to consider arresting Sadat in Damascus to prevent the disastrous visit. Sadat was undaunted either by Asad's unequivocal opposition or by the Saudi's displeasure expressed on the eve of the visit, and stuck to his original plan to go to Jerusalem and hold direct talks with Israeli PM Begin.[17] It was the third, and by far the most shattering instance since the 1973 war in which Sadat had broken with his commitments to other Arab states and bypassed the principle of joint Arab action in the peace process out of purely Egyptian considerations. Sadat's decision to visit Jerusalem was a blow to President Carter's efforts to work out a framework for comprehensive Arab-Israeli peace with Soviet participation. It indicated the independent nature of decision making by a "client" state on matters of its own national security in defiance of the Superpowers' common policy.

Sadat's speech to the Israeli Knesset on November 20 reflected political realism as well as his commitment to a comprehensive Arab-Israeli settlement. The Arab willingness to reach peace with Israel, he said, stemmed from their awareness that this was the only way to avoid a disaster that might otherwise befall both sides and the world as a whole. Although he failed to mention the PLO, Sadat insisted on Israel's full withdrawal to the 1967 borders and a just solution of the Palestinian problem.[18]

Arab Responses to the Israel-Egypt Peace Negotiations

The reactions of individual Arab states to the visit were not uniform, reflecting three different approaches. Support for Sadat's move was voiced by Morocco, Sudan, Somalia, Oman, and Tunisia; Syria, Iraq, Libya, Algeria, PDRY, and the PLO accused him of betraying the Arab and Palestinian cause and sought to close ranks against Sadat's diplomacy. A third, cautiously reserved approach, was represented by the conservative regimes—Saudi Arabia, the Gulf emirates, and Jordan—which would take no reprisal measures until the outcome of Sadat's visit to Jerusalem became clearer. Indeed, while the radical states characterized the visit as an insult to Arab national dignity, the key question shaping the conservative regimes' position toward Sadat's initiative was his adherence to a comprehensive settlement.[19]

Syria was the party most directly affected by Sadat's policy. For the first time in the conflict's history, it stood effectively alone facing the Israeli threat. In addition, Syria was compelled to keep large forces in Lebanon, where the situation was at an impasse and subject to sabotage, political subversion, and verbal attacks from Iraq. To extricate itself, Syria turned to enlisting Arab and international support for its stand. On the day of Sadat's speech to the Knesset, Asad appealed to the Iraqi leaders for help as the only real option to realign the balance of power between Israel and the eastern front states. Baghdad, however, remained hostile and refused to heed Asad's appeal as long as the latter did not renounce Resolution 242 and withdraw from Lebanon. A year was to pass before Damascus-Baghdad relations showed signs of improvement despite Syria's goodwill gestures toward Iraq. Equally unavailing were mediation efforts by Libya, Algeria, and the PLO. Damascus also took its case to Moscow, arguing that to maintain its strategic balance with Israel in the new circumstances required advanced weapons in large quantities and perhaps even Soviet strategic support in the event of a military clash with Israel.[20]

Syria could find little comfort within its own sphere of influence. Only from the PLO did it get full and active backing. President Sarkis, who held office thanks to Syrian bayonets, nevertheless did not identify with Damascus, advocating instead a collective Arab action. King Husain, while unwilling to associate himself with Sadat's policy, would not commit himself against it, instead following the Saudis' fence-sitting lead and waiting for an official all-Arab position to come from a summit meeting. Even if the king seriously considered an alignment with Sadat—as a counterweight to the Rabat resolutions and to enhance his prospects of regaining the West Bank—his regime's fundamental weakness and the lack of Arab support for his claims denied him that choice. The potential threat posed by Syria, Iraq, the PLO, and the Palestinian population in Jordan itself, outweighed any wish Husain might have had to join Sadat's diplomacy. The king may also have wondered how far he could trust Sadat, given the latter's failure to inform him of his plan during their meeting in Cairo only two days before Sadat's November 9 speech to the People's Assembly.

For the PLO, Sadat's move was devastating, undermining its recent achievements on both regional and international levels. Not only had Sadat called into question the PLO's standing as the Palestinians' exclusive representative by naming King Husain as the preferred partner in peace negotiations, he had even backtracked from the formula of an independent Palestinian state, raising the concept of Palestinian self-determination as part of a peace settlement with Israel. Further, the split between Syria and Egypt greatly limited the PLO's political freedom to maneuver, forcing unreserved alignment with Damascus and denying access to Cairo. Denied the opportunity for political action, the PR undertook to undermine the Israel-Egypt peace process by military means. In March 1978, Israel launched a major operation against Palestinian guerrillas in south Lebanon (Operation "Litani") after a Fatah squad hijacked a bus in the heart of Israel, killing thirty-two Israelis. But not even this Israeli takeover of southern Lebanon for more than a month and pressures from within his own government, induced Sadat to change his policy.[21]

Saudi Arabia's and the Gulf emirates' main concern about Sadat's move was that it might affect their national security by deepening inter-Arab divisions and cementing an alliance of radical states, which would boost Soviet encroachment in the area. Yet Riyad continued to view Egypt as a key ally whose regional weight contributed to the Gulf monarchies' security in the face of strong and envious neighbors. Hence, they sought to control the damage brought about by the conflict between Sadat and his rivals. Riyad held that as long as Egypt's return to common Arab action was possible, no measures should be taken against Sadat's regime. Indeed, the Syrians played on these fears by warning that the inevitable result of Sadat's move would be a heightened Soviet presence in Syria. Although this argument could not reverse the conservative regimes' tacit support for Sadat, it did induce them to continue their financial aid to Syria to forestall a further tightening of its relations with the USSR.[22]

Sadat's shocking visit to Jerusalem led to the resumption of the efforts to convene an Arab summit, whose failure proved that the gap was unbridgeable. Libya renewed its call for a meeting in Tripoli—without Egyptian participation. The Saudis—backed by Kuwait, Jordan, and Morocco—pressed for Egypt to be invited in order to bring it back into the "Arab fold." Only Syria, Iraq, Algeria, PDRY, and the PLO attended the Tripoli meeting on December 5, and decided to freeze their ties with Egypt's government, boycott Egyptian institutions holding contacts with Israel or AL meetings held in Egypt, consider moving the AL's headquarters from Cairo, and review Egypt's membership. The summit also urged giving Syria the aid it needed to offset the results of Sadat's visit to Jerusalem. Finally, Syria, Libya, Algeria, and PDRY resolved to form a mutual defense pact.[23]

The Tripoli joint communique did not close the door on political settlements or renounce the Geneva Conference and Resolutions 242 and 338. Iraq's demands to this effect were opposed by both Syria and the PLO. Damascus also rejected a Libyan proposal for an economic and diplomatic boycott of Egypt, arguing that the point was to isolate Sadat, not to harm the Egyptian people. Libya and Algeria accepted Syria's position, since their goal was to coopt it into the "Steadfastness and Resistance Front" (*jabhat al-sumud wal-tasaddy*) (SRF) established at the Tripoli conference. Since there was no unequivocal rejection of political settlements, Iraq refused to sign the joint statement and later harshly criticized Syria's policy, blaming Damascus for Sadat's

peace move. Sadat himself lost no time in reacting, demonstrating both determination and his contempt for his Arab adversaries. On the very day the
resolutions were published, Egypt announced that it was severing diplomatic
relations with Syria, Libya, Algeria, the PLO, and PDRY. Their ambassadors
were given twenty-four hours to leave Cairo.

The SRF was the first formal Arab coalition organized against Sadat.
Before the Baghdad summit—which would adopt most of the Tripoli resolutions for sanctions against Egypt—the heads of the SRF states met twice more.
Yet the SRF showed neither internal coherence nor the ability to affect the
Israel-Egypt peace process, due to Iraq's hostility to Syria and refusal to
cooperate with the SRF on the basis of the Tripoli resolutions. Without Iraq, the
SRF was unable to impose its attitude on the fence-sitting Arab regimes that
had no objection to settlement with Israel in principle. Syria and the PLO were
bent on a comprehensive Middle East settlement, whereas Iraq, Libya, and
Algeria—sharing no common borders with Israel—adhered to their ultramili-
tant rejection of any settlement with the Jewish state. Libya professed readiness
to acquiesce in Syria's position to ensure the formation of a broad-based radical
anti-Egyptian front and preempt erosion in Syria's position toward Sadat's
peacemaking policy. Algeria joined the front largely in order to ensure political
and military support from Libya in the intensifying Western Sahara conflict
with Morocco. Yet despite Libya's outpouring of radical rhetoric and its repeated pledges to give economic and military aid to Syria or any other confrontation state wishing to fight Israel, Tripoli did absolutely nothing in this regard
throughout 1978.[24]

Until the signing of the Camp David accords in September 1978, Arab
action by both the radical and conservative regimes toward Sadat's peacemaking diplomacy continued to proceed along the lines that emerged right after his
Jerusalem visit. In that period, the common conviction in the Arab world was
that Sadat's initiative would fail and that he would soon be forced to re-identify
with the collective Arab stand.[25] Indeed, shortly after Sadat's visit to Jerusalem
the Egypt-Israel diplomatic channel went awry as a result of essential
differences, giving way to a growing sense of frustration and the loss of a
historical moment. Despite his independent move, Sadat strove to maximize
the legitimacy of his peacemaking policy among the Arabs and thus adhered to
the principles of a comprehensive settlement and rejected any concession of
Arab land. He sought to reach an agreed formula with Israel on a framework
for comprehensive settlement that would serve as a basis for negotiations
between Israel and other Arab states, and free his hands to implement Egypt's
part with or without their participation. Given the problems entailing the PLO
participation, Sadat was willing to include Jordan—together with Palestinian
representatives—in the negotiations over the West Bank. But Sadat's diplomatic role as the Arab world's forerunner was inherently shaky due to the limited

Arab support that accrued to him. This was attested by the fiasco of the preparatory conference in Cairo in mid-December, to which all the parties concerned, including the PLO, had been invited but which only Israel attended.

Israel was obliged to respond to the challenge posed by Sadat's bold initiative by presenting its own proposals for peace, revealing the conceptual gap between the two parties. Israel sought to reach a separate settlement with Egypt that would remove the threat of an Arab war coalition against it and preserve its grip on the rest of the occupied Arab territories, mainly the West Bank and Gaza. Thus, apart from willingness to withdraw from most of Sinai and most of the Golan Heights, Israel put forward a plan for Palestinian autonomy in the West Bank and Gaza Strip, leaving the issue of sovereignty over these areas undecided. The autonomy idea represented an essential shift in Israel's concept concerning the future of the Palestinian occupied territories. The "Jordanian option" advocated by the Labor Party in search of a territorial compromise was replaced by autonomy for the Palestinian population in the occupied terrritories, which was to ensure continued Israeli control over these areas. Furthermore, it was to retain Israel's right to claim sovereignty over these territories if such a claim arose on the part of Jordan or the Palestinians. The Egypt-Israel joint move reduced the chances of pursuing a comprehensive settlement, leaving the American president with little choice but to support the new bilateral thrust. Furthermore, the deadlock with which the Isma'iliyya summit between Begin and Sadat on December 25 ended reiterated the need for active American involvement.[26]

The obstacles confronting the Israeli-Egyptian negotiations encouraged efforts by Saudi Arabia, Morocco, Jordan, and Sudan to reconcile Egypt and Syria. Pressure on Egypt to revoke its peace policy was stepped up every time its talks with Israel seemed to have reached a deadlock. But Iraq's objections to the assumptions underlying this effort and Sadat's refusal to be restricted by Arab collective obligations, as advocated by Syria, demonstrated the limits of a joint Arab action in the face of the dispute among leading Arab states. Israel's incursion into southern Lebanon in March provided a convenient pretext for the ALSG to convene a meeting of Arab FMs in Cairo. In the absence of the members of the SRF, Saudi Arabia, Yemen, Jordan, and Lebanon advocated a summit conference with Egyptian participation. A committee chaired by Sudanese President Numairi was formed to prepare the ground for a summit.[27]

Between April and June, Numairi visited fifteen Arab states trying to reconcile Egypt, the SRF, and Iraq, without success. The initiative had apparently won Sadat's blessing, though he made his participation in a summit conditional on the Arab states' acceptance of his peacemaking diplomacy. While reaffirming his commitment to the principle of a comprehensive settlement, in practice Sadat spurned the reconciliation efforts, assessing that Syria would accept no less than official acknowledgement that his peace initiative had failed. The breach between Sadat and Asad proved unbridgeable despite

Saudi mediation efforts at the highest level in August, when the Israeli-Egyptian peace diplomacy seemed to have run aground.[28]

The Camp David summit of Carter, Sadat, and Begin in September was an unprecedented instance of diplomatic mediation, in which the American president applied his personal weight to rescue the Israeli-Egyptian peace talks. Apart from President Carter's personal attachement to the issue of peacemaking in the Middle East, the presidential effort must be seen against the backdrop of the rapid deterioration of the Iranian Shah's domestic position, the ascendancy of a communist regime in Afghanistan, and the growing Soviet encroachment in the Horn of Africa.

The Camp David accords signed on September 17, sent new shock waves throughout the Arab world, which had confidently expected the tri-lateral summit to fail. By signing the accords, Sadat crossed the Rubicon even from the viewpoint of those countries that had given him tacit support, hoping he would insist on the principle of a comprehensive settlement. Instead, he signed what amounted to a separate peace treaty with Israel, which would secure full Israeli withdrawal from Sinai and a normalized relationship, along with a framework of principles for peace in the Middle East including an agreement on establishing an interim, autonomous regime for the Palestinians in the West Bank and Gaza Strip, though without any ironclad guarantee of Israeli withdrawal from those territories. The Camp David accords gave Israel a decisive role in the West Bank and Gaza during the transitory period: supervising the Palestinian self-governing authority; retaining the right to maintain its military presence there, with no clear commitment to freeze the settlements. Moreover, Egypt acquiesced in the Israeli and American concept of peace as full normalization, including diplomatic, economic, and cultural relations. Sadat's concessions and deviation from the principle of a comprehensive settlement triggered heavy criticism of the accords, even from his own FM Kamel, who, at the end of the summit, resigned his office.[29]

Camp David forced the conservative Arab regimes to take a stand. King Husain, whom Sadat and Carter expected to join the autonomy framework accord, remained uncommitted and backtracked just before the accords were signed. Syria had to admit that it could no longer rely soley on the doubtful support of Libya, Algeria, and PDRY, and that there was no substitute for an effective Arab front—necessarily including Iraq—to fill the military gap caused by Egypt's defection from the confrontation front. But Asad admitted that even if Syria and Iraq entered into full union, the Arab states could no longer expect a military solution to the conflict following Egypt's defection.[30]

Iraq Takes the Lead

On October 1, 1978, Iraq called for a summit conference to be convened in Baghdad, without Egypt, to draft a practical plan of action in the wake of

Camp David. Accompanied by overtures to Syria for bilateral cooperation, Baghdad's move was successfully timed to draw the maximum response from a shocked and confused Arab world. Isolated and on the defensive since the 1973 war, Baghdad now saw a chance to replace Egypt as the leading Arab power by shaping the Arab world's response to the Camp David accords.

Iraq's claim to leadership was underscored by its economic and military prowess, which were particularly significant for Syria in view of Egypt's defection from the Arab-Israeli confrontation arena. As part of its proposal, Baghdad urged the immediate dispatch of military forces to Syria to bolster that country's steadfastness in the face of the Israeli threat, urging the establishment of a $9 billion fund to help the confrontation states in the next decade. Of this, $5 billion would be earmarked as a grant to Egypt, conditional on its abrogation of the Camp David accords.

The Iraqi invitation drew a furious response from Egypt and placed Saudi Arabia and the Gulf emirates on the horns of a dilemma. Riyad tried to mobilize Arab support for getting Sadat invited to the summit while remaining uncommitted to the Iraqi invitation. ALSG Riyad protested against Iraq's violation of the AL charter in not inviting Egypt to attend, and proposed to hold the summit in Riyad to ensure Arab consensus. But the rapidly joined Syrian-Iraqi rapprochement confronted the Arab world with the *fait accompli* of a new regional center of gravity, leaving little room for vacillation or haggling over terms of participation.[31]

Syria's vulnerability after Camp David was manifested in its rush to accept the Iraqi initiative. Within a few days, Syrian official radio adopted a new tone toward Iraq, terming it a "sister state." The rapprochement culminated in a meeting between Asad and Bakr in Baghdad on October 24–26, resulting in the signing of the "Charter of Joint National Action," touted as a historic turning point toward Arab unity, and not as a mere tactical move in response to the Camp David accords. The Charter led to agreements on reopening the common border, which had been closed for nearly two years, as well as on the resumption of bilateral trade.

Under the charter's terms, a joint political committee was created—headed by the two presidents—along with several special committees to tighten Iraqi-Syrian cooperation, including the preparation of a draft defense treaty toward "full military unification." Yet these decisions, which lacked concrete definition of schedule and structure, could hardly hide Syrian reservations, especially among leading Syrian military figures, concerning unity of the two armies and Ba'th parties. Syria was in urgent need of strategic backing, which could be provided by Iraq, but not at the expense of its sovereignty.

As it turned out, the Iraq-Syria rapprochement was instrumental in enforcing Arab sanctions against Egypt, but made no progress in realizing the bilateral unity schemes in the political or the military spheres. In early 1979,

Iraq and Syria stepped up efforts to further their unification plan. The two presidents met in Damascus, and in February they worked together to resolve the Yemen armed dispute. That same month, Iraq agreed to renew its oil exports to the Mediterranean via Syria and the supply of crude oil for Syria's own consumption, letting Damascus earn royalties of $250 million that year. The Iraqi *quid pro quo* would be a more forceful push toward full unity, which Syria tacitly rejected, avoiding any practical steps toward realization of this goal.[32]

A Plan for Sanctions Against Egypt

Iraqi strategy toward the summit was to take a pragmatic line to unite the Arab states around a plan based on the broadest achievable consensus. In this manner, Baghdad hoped to further its rapprochement with Damascus, while also allaying Saudi fears that the summit would adopt extreme anti-Egyptian resolutions. The Saudi press gave expression to these concerns, stressing that the Baghdad summit must reject fanaticism and heal the rifts in the Arab world lest they become even more acute. Furthermore, it called on the summit to show understanding for the coexistence of both individual and Pan-Arab interests. Pursuing its objectives, Riyad agreed with the Gulf emirates that the Baghdad summit should not isolate Egypt or impose sanctions on it in order to keep open avenues to Sadat.[33]

However, the gap between the radicals—Iraq, Syria, Libya, Algeria, the PLO, and PDRY—and the monarchical regimes, headed by Saudi Arabia, Kuwait, and Morocco, regarding the Arab collective response to Sadat's signing of the Camp David accords was not easy to bridge. On the eve of the pre-summit FMs' meeting, which opened on October 30, the Iraqi press published the official text of the Egyptian-sponsored AL resolution from April 1950, adopted following talks between King Abdallah of Jordan and Israeli officials. The resolution unequivocally prohibited the signing of a separate agreement with Israel and specified that any state violating this ban would remove itself from the AL. The other Arab states were to break relations, close their common borders, and terminate all direct and indirect economic ties with the offending country.

The preparatory FMs' meeting faced disagreement between two viewpoints. The radicals' working paper called for applying diplomatic and economic sanctions against Egypt and the removal of the AL headquarters from Cairo. It also addressed the issue of financial aid for the confrontation states. Kuwait, representing the other monarchies, Sudan, and Tunisia submitted their own working paper, suggesting that despite Sadat's separate accord with Israel, Egypt still remained an important part of the Arab nation. An artificial distinction was drawn between the Egyptian people, which must not be economically punished, and the government, against which sanctions should be directed. In any event, no measures should be taken against Egypt before it signed a full peace treaty with Israel. Only then, it proposed, would a special Arab forum be convened to consider the principles that should guide the AL member states in the new circumstances. The Saudi and Sudanese representatives insisted that the conference resolutions must underscore the Arabs' quest for peace. Given these differences, the issue of Arab response to the Camp David accords was referred to the summit itself to decide.[34]

The summit conference opened on November 2 with the attendance of all the Arab states except Egypt and Oman, although only ten heads of state attended the meeting, attesting to its divisive agenda. President Bakr set the summit's tone, declaring, "We do not wish to isolate Egypt, which is in the heart of all Arabs." ALSG Riyad—reversing his former stand against a summit without Egypt—urged the attendees to reject the Camp David accords because they failed to guarantee the rights of the Palestinian people, calling on them to make an effort to bring his country back to the Arab line.[35]

The summit deliberations, however, were marked by a recurrence of the FMs' heated differences. The radicals demanded that the AL's punitive clauses be fully invoked against Egypt, while the Gulf monarchies, Jordan, Morocco, Tunisia, and Sudan, urged moderation and the employment of every possible means that might forestall a total break with Egypt. Iraq, which as the host country saw to the conference's success, made an effort to work out a compromise in behind-the-scenes discussions with Saudi Arabia, Kuwait, and Syria. In an effort to reconcile the two camps, it was agreed to accept ALSG Riyad's suggestion to send a goodwill mission to Cairo in a last attempt to persuade Sadat to abrogate the Camp David accords. Headed by Lebanese PM Salim al-Huss, the delegation bore a message from Iraqi President Bakr intimating the availability of a $5 billion grant from the Arab states so that Egypt could "pursue its national struggle," if Sadat revoked his signature to the Camp David agreement. Sadat, however, refused even to receive the delegation, declaring that the mission was an insult to Egypt.[36]

Sadat's blunt response notwithstanding, the summit's communique was remarkably restrained, imposing no sanctions on Egypt. But it was only a temporary achievement for the conservative bloc, as it had been agreed that the signing of a full-fledged Egyptian-Israeli peace treaty would bring in its wake the application of sanctions. Marked by visible Arab nationalist terminology, the communique reiterated that the Palestinian issue was the core of "the Arab-Zionist conflict," and that the struggle for retrieving the Palestinian people's national rights was an all-Arab commitment. Hence, any separate settlement of this conflict was absolutely prohibited. Along with assailing the Camp David accords as detrimental to the Palestinian cause and calling on Cairo to annul its agreement with Israel, the communique reaffirmed the previous Arab summit resolutions concerning the PLO's status and the Arab commitment to support its national struggle.

At Saudi Arabia's insistence, the summit approved a resolution stating that the Arab nation (*umma*) adhered to a "just peace" based on total Israeli withdrawal from the territories occupied in 1967 and the restoration of Palestinian national rights. It was the first time that peace was defined as the ultimate Arab goal in the conflict with Israel. That it was approved also by Iraq and Libya, the leading rejectionist states, lent the resolution even more significance, though it went unnoticed. Two main decisions were made in response to Egypt's separate agreement with Israel:[37]

1. A fund totalling $3.5 billion per year would be established to support the confrontation with Israel. Of this amount, $1,85 billion was earmarked for Syria, $1.25 billion for Jordan, $250 million for the PLO, and $150 million for the Palestinian dwellers in the West Bank and Gaza, to bolster their steadfastness. The aid would be provided for a ten-year period in three installments annually.

    The PLO claimed exclusive authority to distribute funds allocated for the West Bank and Gaza, colliding with Jordan's essential role in these territories. Though the summit affirmed in principle the PLO's claim, it nevertheless only partly did so in practice, giving the PLO $50 million for distribution in the occupied territories. The remaining $100 million was to be distributed jointly by the PLO and Jordan.[38]

2. Sanctions would be imposed on Egypt if it signed a formal peace treaty with Israel. Arab foreign and economic ministers would then convene in Baghdad to decide on the actual sanctions. Apart from the measures stipulated in the AL's resolution of 1950, additional possibilities were reported by in the Arab press, apparently aimed at deterring Egypt from signing a peace treaty with Israel, such as: termination of economic aid; transfer of the seat of the Organization of Arab (military) Industry (OAI) from Cairo; deportation of Egyptian labor migrants from the Arab oil countries and restriction on their transfer of remittances.[39]

Regional Threats and the New Arab Alignment

The Baghdad summit resulted in Arab consensus underpinned by a new alignment in which Iraq now established itself as the holder of the regional balance, following Egypt's exclusion. The new alignment represented uneasy circumstances in which the three leading actors, Iraq, Syria, and Saudi Arabia, were impelled by divergent needs and expectations. Iraq, striving to extricate itself from its traditional isolation in the Arab world and become the pivot of the new Arab alignment, sought rapprochement with Syria and the PLO. Iraq resumed its recognition of the PLO after six years of subversion against 'Arafat's Fatah, which had come to a head in Summer 1978 in a series of assassinations of moderate Palestinian figures.

Syria sought to translate the new Arab solidarity into immediate strategic and financial means to offset the loss of Egypt in the confrontation with Israel. Equally urgent for Damascus was to impose its hard-line attitude in the peace process upon the conservative regimes led by Saudi Arabia, in order to forestall any other Arab state's following in Sadat's diplomatic footsteps. For these purposes, Damascus put aside its longstanding bitter rivalry with Baghdad to the point of declaring unity between them. An immediate result was that Syria became the major beneficiary of the Arab aid fund.

The Baghdad summit started a steady rapprochement between Jordan and the PLO. Their bitter enmity notwithstanding, they were forced to cooperate in distributing the Baghdad funds allocated to the Palestinians in the occupied territories, establishing the Joint Jordanian-Palestinian Committee to administer this venture. Their relations began shifting in mid-September during the SRF summit in Damascus, when Qadhafi and 'Arafat joined in an unprepared visit to Jordan and a meeting with King Husain and his PM, aiming to keep Husain from joining the Camp David autonomy plan. The Hashemite-PLO joint venture on the West Bank and Gaza Strip, which would culminate in a political dialogue in the mid-1980s, was a clear shift from their hitherto zero-sum game to a mixed-motives pattern of relations. Apart from its economic benefit, the new arrangement affirmed Amman's standing in the territories and afforded the PLO a convenient access to its constituency, to ensure their unflagging obedience to its exclusive leadership. Cooperation with Jordan also enabled the PLO to monitor Amman's policy on the Camp David autonomy plan.[40]

The Iraqi-Syrian alliance established a dominant radical power center, which Riyad found uncongenial but could hardly disregard in view of Sadat's drive for full implementation of the Camp David accords. The Saudis, moreover, had been alarmed by growing Soviet encroachment through revolutionary Ethiopia in the Horn of Africa; assassination of Yemen's president, with PDRY being strongly implicated; and the advent of a Marxist regime in Aden. On the other Saudi flank, the shaky grip on power of the Shah of Iran in the face of growing domestic unrest had already been evident when the Baghdad summit was held, and his fall seemed to be only a matter of time.

Fearful of being drawn into the vortex of radical change in the Gulf region, the Saudis were willing to pay an exorbitant price to maintain Arab solidarity—their last anchor—even if this meant intensifying Sadat's isolation. Given the growing regional instability and concern over Shi'i unrest in the Gulf area, Saudi Arabia and the Gulf emirates sought to close ranks with Baghdad, which had been previously held to be a potential threat to their national security. Riyad's reaction was typical of its cautious foreign policy, shaped by its extremely vulnerable security and enormous oil wealth.[41]

In January 1979 Saudi Arabia and the Gulf emirates were thrown into consternation at the Shah's departure from Iran under growing popular pressure. Given his alliance with the United States and hegemonic posture in the Gulf, the Shah's regime had been regarded as the main bulwark against Iraqi revisionist aspirations and heightened Soviet encroachment in the region. The Shah's fall and the ascendancy of an Islamic revolutionary power in February further eroded possible support for Sadat in the Middle East, reinforcing the blackmailing power of the radical states led by Iraq and Syria. Yet Iraq itself, which thanks to its military prowess now became chief pretender to the crown of hegemony in the Persian Gulf, was urgently seeking Arab backing in the face of a growing threat to its domestic stability emanating from the Iranian Shi'i revolution and its inevitable implications on its own Shi'i majority.[42]

Coincidentally, the unremitting tension between the two Yemens in February 1979 erupted into a month-long armed dispute. Given the PDRY's strong affiliation with the Soviet Union, and the presence of 1,500 Russian and Cuban military advisers on PDRY soil, Saudi Arabia sided completely with North Yemen. Riyad also took advantage of the serious crisis in its immediate neighborhood to recall the Saudi battalion serving with the ADF in Lebanon. At the AL's initiative a cease-fire agreement was reached in the Yemen conflict at the beginning of March. However, continued hostilities led the Americans to dispatch a naval task force to the region as a gesture of support for Saudi Arabia.[43]

The Iraqi-Syrian alliance shunted Libya to a fringe position in the regional Arab system, undercutting its role in the anti-Egyptian front. As a result, Libya retracted its commitments to the aid fund as well as to the replacement of Syrian jet fighters lost in battles with Israel over Lebanon. Finding himself isolated, with the SRF emptied of any substance, Qadhafi took a dim view of Iraqi-Syrian rapprochement. Typically, Qadhafi embarked on propagating the renewal of Palestinian guerrilla war against Israel, presenting himself as the only Arab ruler committed to the conflict with Israel. In December 1978, during 'Arafat's visit in Tripoli, Qadhafi took the opportunity to lash out at Syria and Jordan over their policy of inaction against Israel, promising generous financial and military aid to the PLO, as well as to Jordan and Syria if they supported such activity. Six months later, at Qadhafi's invitation, leaders of the PR held an "emergency summit" meeting in Tripoli, at which they were reportedly offered military support for their guerrilla war against Israel in southern Lebanon. Qadhafi's principal efforts, however, were focused on the North African arena in quest for regional posture as a revolutionary champion. His activity included subversion against Morocco, Tunisia, and Sudan; tightened relations with Ethiopia; and widened occupation of northern Chad and interference in its civil war. In March 1979, a Libyan expeditionary force was defeated in Uganda while trying to rescue Idi Amin's regime.[44]

Peace Negotiations in the Shadow of Arab Sanctions

The Baghdad summit resolution to delay any punitive measures against Egypt until it signed a final peace treaty with Israel reflected, mainly on the conservatives' part, a wishful expectation for failure of the Israeli-Egyptian peace talks and fear lest an early imposition of sanctions on Egypt would lead to a final breakup of relations with Egypt. Sadat, however, remained unmoved. He assailed the summit resolutions and denounced the Arab states, not sparing Saudi Arabia or Kuwait, warning that sanctions against Egypt would be detrimental to the Arab world. Sadat, evidently feeling that the Saudis in particular had let him down, escalated his verbal attacks against them. Egyptian pressure induced King Hasan II and President Numairi to publicly declare their backing for Sadat and his policies after the Baghdad summit. But the Saudi affiliation with the summit resolutions and Riyad's mounting criticism of Sadat's peace moves placed the proponents of the Egyptian leader's policy in a quandary. Moroccan support for Sadat soon began to waver, leaving only Sudan, Oman, and Somalia—all of them beneficiaries of Egyptian military and strategic aid—as openly backing Egypt, despite the relentless tongue lashing they endured from the media in the radical states.[45]

Despite his scornful attacks against his Arab critics, however, Sadat could hardly overlook their impact. Moreover, Cairo and Washington still courted King Husain to bring him into the peace talks on Palestinian autonomy, regardless of the slim chances in this respect. Thus, when the talks on an Israeli-Egyptian peace treaty opened in Washington in mid-October, the Egyptian stand had become perceptibly harder, with a view toward the Baghdad summit, demonstrating Cairo's abiding commitment to the principle of a comprehensive solution of the Arab-Israeli conflict. Pursuing this line, Egypt sought to demonstrate immediate results regarding the Palestinian issue by insisting on various Israeli "gestures," notably the redeployment of Israeli forces in the occupied territories, abolition of the military government, release of prisoners, and permitting a symbolic Egyptian presence—a "liaison office"—in Gaza, as a step toward the implementation of the autonomy plan in that area first. However, Cairo's paramount demand in this connection was for juridically binding linkage between the implementation of the autonomy agreement and the onset of normalization between the two countries—a position that Israel rejected out of hand.[46]

Another obstacle stemmed from a prospective conflict between the Egypt-Israel treaty and Egypt's treaties with Arab states that obliged Egypt to join them in case of war with Israel. Israel insisted that its peace treaty with

Egypt take precedence over all defense pacts to which Egypt was a signatory in order to preclude Egyptian intervention in the event of war between Israel and another Arab country. Egypt, however, rejected this condition, which would be tantamount to annulling its commitment to the AL under the ACSP of 1950. The impact of the Baghdad summit on Sadat's directives to his delegation in Washington was discernible. Egypt publicly asserted its requests regarding Israeli gestures in the Gaza Strip, a linkage between the autonomy and the bilateral peace treaty, and its faithfulness to the military undertakings it had assumed toward the other Arab states under the terms of the ACSP.[47]

With the talks stalled, largely over these issues, the peace negotiations dragged on well into 1979, and it was once again thanks to President Carter's personal intervention and visits to Egypt and Israel in March that a peace treaty was concluded and signed in the White House on March 26. Obviously, the lengthy deadlock reflected Sadat's dilemma of reconciling Egypt's interests and prerogatives as a sovereign state with its commitments to, and deeply rooted ties with, the Arab world. The prolonged negotiations probably worked to Sadat's disadvantage, as he lost a major prop with the Shah's fall and the takeover of Iran by the Islamic revolution in February. Moreover, although Israel undertook to begin discussing the projected autonomy regime immediately after the establishment of diplomatic relations between Jerusalem and Cairo, the linkage between the peace treaty and the autonomy plan was loose, confirming the worst fears of Sadat's critics, who had assailed the separate character of the Camp David accords.[48]

The Arab Sanctions Against Egypt

On March 27, the foreign and economic ministers of fifteen Arab states and a PLO delegation led by ʿArafat convened in Baghdad to discuss the collective Arab response to the Israel-Egypt peace treaty signed the day before in Washington. Sudan, Soamlia, and Oman boycotted the meeting. The separate character of Egypt's agreement with Israel notwithstanding—obliging the application of sanctions against Egypt—the deliberations were marked by a deep schism between the conservative and radical regimes over the appropriate response. Even though the Iraqi hosts sought to play an intermediary role, they revealed a clear inclination toward the radicals. Indeed, Baghdad's tone was set in a joint statement issued on the eve of the conference by the PLO and Iraq's ruling Baʿth Party, calling on the Arab states to attack American interests as well as Sadat's supporters in the Arab world.[49]

With concrete resolutions against Egypt in the offing, the debate heated up between the radicals, led by the PLO, Syria, and Libya, who urged a decisive reaction, and the conservatives, headed by Saudi Arabia, who still sought to prevent an irrevocable rift with Egypt. The main debate revolved

around the PLO's sweeping demand to immediately sever all political, economic, and military relations with Cairo and impose a total boycott on Egypt.
'Arafat also urged an economic boycott against the United States and the
withdrawal of Arab deposits from American banks. These proposals brought to
the surface the essential collision between the principle of state sovereignty
and the obligatory interpretation of Arab solidarity. Contrary to the compulsive
approach advocated by the radicals, the Saudis insisted on mere implementation of the Baghdad resolutions, maintaining that the severance of diplomatic
relations between one Arab state and another rested within the exclusive purview of each state. The Gulf states argued that the Egypt-Israel peace treaty
was Egypt's prerogative as a sovereign state, in which other states had no say.
Yet even the Saudis had to admitt that the Palestinian part of the treaty was a
different matter, because of its all-Arab nature.[50]

Saudi Arabia's adamant opposition to the PLO's demands touched off a
vituperative debate, accompanied by a demonstrative walkout of the session by
the PLO's, Syria's, and Libya's representatives, which generated a crisis atmosphere and led to a suspension of the meeting for one day. The suspension of
talks unleashed vehement threats on the part of the PLO's and Syria's delegates
of sabotage and terrorist attacks against American installations in the region
and Sadat's Arab supporters if a total boycott were not imposed on Egypt and
the United States. Syrian FM Khaddam asserted that the strategic balance,
which had been adversely affected by Egypt's withdrawal from the military
front with Israel, must be restored. Otherwise, he threatened, Damascus would
enter into a defense pact with the Soviet Union.[51]

Jordan's King Husain and Iraqi Vice-President Saddam Husain engaged
in vigorous efforts to patch things up. The resumed deliberations unexpectedly
concluded on the following day with the announcement of comprehensive
political and economic warfare against Egypt. This included an immediate
recall of all Arab ambassadors from Cairo and the severing of all diplomatic
relations with Egypt within one month; suspension of Egypt's membership in
the AL, whose headquarters would be transferred to Tunis; and condemnation
of the United States for bringing about the peace accord. The UN would be
urged to remove from Cairo its regional office for international affairs, and an
effort would be made to have Egypt's membership suspended in the OAU, the
Islamic Conference Organization (ICO), and ONAS. In addition, there would
be an immediate halt of Arab aid to Egypt's government and institutions as
well as a boycott of Egyptian companies, institutions, and individuals maintaining ties with Israel. These were said to be the minimum measures for
dealing with the peace treaty, although each country was at liberty to augment
them. The actions were defined as provisional, to be abolished once their
grounds were no longer valid.[52]

Agreement on these resolutions ostensibly entailed concessions by both camps. The radicals dropped their demand for sanctions against the United States and accepted the Saudis' request that the clause on severing relations with Egypt take the form of a recommendation only, though King Khalid declared that Saudi Arabia would break relations with Egypt on the day the Israeli flag was hoisted in Cairo. The conservative regimes, for their part, agreed to apply a total economic boycott against Egypt. On balance, however, the resolutions pointed to the radicals' success in riding roughshod over the weak, threatened conservative states. Since diplomatic relations between the SRF states and Egypt had been severed as of December 1977, it remained only to force the rest of the Arab states to follow suit.

Jordan and Saudi Arabia made no secret of their bitterness at Washington's role in sponsoring a separate Israeli-Egyptian peace treaty, one that seriously jeopardized their national security because of the radical backlash in the region. Especially for King Husain, whose interest in the West Bank had been entirely ignored by the parties to the peace treaty, adopting a firm stand against Egypt—although not before concluding a new trade agreement with her—may have been intended to prevent any misinterpretation of his position that might lead to undesirable domestic or regional repercussions. It is noteworthy that Jordan was the first Arab state to announce severance of its relations with Egypt.[53]

The radical-conservative schism was also visible in the formers' pressure on the Gulf monarchies to implement the sanctions against Egypt unconditionally and without delay. Iraq was the driving force in implementing the punitive measures against Egypt, bringing pressure to bear for the severance of relations on both conservative Arab states and on international bodies such as OPEC, the OAU, the ONAS, and UN agencies with regional offices in Egypt, such as the WHO and the ILO. Iraq even offered to underwrite the latter's move, to the tune of $1 million. The upshot was that by the end of April 1979, a month after the signing of the peace treaty, all Arab states had cut diplomatic relations with Egypt, with the exceptions of Sudan (which recalled its ambassador when the Israeli embassy in Cairo was opened in May 1979), Somalia, and Oman, which represented Egyptian interests in the Arab states, and vice-versa. In practice, however, the severance of diplomatic relations with Egypt was not absolute, as most Arab states—with the exception of the SRF—continued to maintain consular missions in Cairo.[54]

Sadat, bitterly disappointed at Riyad's decision to break relations, accused the Saudis not only of yielding to the rejectionist states, but also of inducing Morocco and others to do likewise in return for generous financial aid. Sadat lashed out at the oil states over the paltry aid they had extended to Egypt, triggering an angry reaction and the publication by the Gulf monarchies' newspapers of data about their aid to Egypt since 1973, which totalled $13 billion. The Saudis tried to mitigate their action by declaring that the boycott was directed against the Egyptian government, not against the Egyptian people, private firms, or institutions that did not enter into commercial or other ties with Israel.[55]

Pursuing this principle, Saudi Arabia and the Gulf emirates halted all direct financial aid to Egypt for civil or military purposes. This included termination of the Gulf Organization for the Development of Egypt (GODE), a financial instrument established in 1976 by Saudi Arabia, Kuwait, and Qatar to provide Egypt with financial aid of $220 million annually for five years. Also dissolved was the AOI, set up in 1975 by Egypt, Saudi Arabia, the UAE, and Qatar to promote the development of Egypt's military industry. By 1979, it employed 15,000 workers—though only one new plant had been established in Egypt within the AOI framework—and facilitated the transfer of Western military technologies to Egypt as well as procurement of weapons from Western sources. Riyad also withdrew its pledge to underwrite Egypt's purchase of fifty American F-5E fighter aircraft, a deal worth $525 million.[56]

Overall, however, the Arab states, and the oil producers in particular, were highly selective in implementing sanctions against Egypt in the business, trade, and banking sectors, ensuring that their own economic interests would not suffer even when Egyptian governmental bodies were involved. For example, they did not boycott Egypt's national airline, taking advantage of a loophole in the Baghdad resolutions which enabled them to follow the Kuwaiti precedent regarding the Arab boycott on foreign airlines flying to Israel: namely, to boycott individual flights landing at or departing from Israel, but not the airline as such. Nor did these countries cease using the Suez Canal or the Suez-Mediterranean oil pipeline. Militarily, Sudan, Somalia, Oman, and Morocco continued to benefit from Egyptian military aid.[57]

In the economic sphere, then, the Baghdad resolutions were for the most part implemented, but the practical effects were felt largely in terms of trade and the flow of aid funds, while in banking, tourism, and migration of Egyptian workers to other Arab countries the effects were no more than temporary. Indeed, even though by the end of 1979 official Arab economic aid to Egypt had all but dried up, the impact was limited, since the proportion of Arab aid in the overall amount of foreign economic assistance received by Egypt had been declining steadily since 1975. Thus, for example, the $750 million Arab aid for civil purposes that Egypt received in 1978 constituted just one-third of the total foreign capital entering the country that year.

Moreover, Egypt increased considerably its foreign-currency revenues in 1977–1978, which was reflected in a sharp drop in the Arab aid/GNP ratio. In 1973, the total Arab aid to Egypt was 5.9 percent of its GNP, growing to a peak of 26.3 percent in 1975 and dropping back to the level of 5.3 percent of the GNP in 1978. The main sources of foreign currency were remittances from

Egyptian labor migrants in Arab oil states—including Iraq and Libya—totalling $1.7 billion in 1978 and increasing steadily in the following years, along with revenues from the Suez Canal, petroleum sales, and tourism. Also unaffected were Saudi and Kuwaiti deposits in Egyptian banks totalling $2 billion, and another $150 million in private Arab financial investments—half the total of such investments in Egypt. This sector, too, was to grow in the coming years. The remaining sting was largely removed from the Arabs' economic sanctions when, a week after the meeting in Baghdad, the U.S. government proposed a three-year aid program for Egypt worth $1.8 billion annually.[58]

In the political sphere, the anti-Egyptian policy scored only limited success, with the exception of the transfer of AL headquarters. By the end of June, Egypt had been officially expelled from the AL and its affiliated inter-Arab institutions, and the AL's offices had moved to Tunis. Rejecting the Baghdad resolutions, Egypt refused to cooperate in the removal of the AL's headquarters, freezing AL funds and refusing to release its official papers. The international arena proved equally disappointing for Sadat's opponents who failed to expel Egypt from the OAU or the ONAS. The most that Syria, Iraq, and Libya could gain was a condemnation of the Israeli-Egyptian peace treaty by the ONAS FMs, meeting in Havana in September 1979, and a suspension of Egypt's membership in the ICO. Farther afield, Arab pressure worked against Egypt indirectly, causing Western European countries and Japan to show caution when considering Cairo's requests for financial aid.[59]

Interim Summary

The legitimization of a diplomatic settlement of the Arab-Israeli conflict in the wake of the 1973 war represented a common conviction that the oil weapon had shifted the balance of power in the Arabs' favor. In terms of regional dynamics, it was the decisive weight of the Egypt-Saudi Arabia-Syria core coalition that accounted for this major shift in the history of the Arab-Israeli conflict. Representing the main portion of Arab military and economic resources and backed by Syria's and Algeria's Arab nationalist reputations, this coalition was able to enlist consensual support for a redefinition of Arab basic assumptions and strategic goals in the conflict with Israel toward *de facto* acceptance of Israel's existence. The role of the Arab summit as an overall interpretative authority regarding Arab core values was evident in the creation of a "strategy of phases" in the conflict, defining as an "interim" goal the implementation of Resolution 242.

Financial aid from oil-rich monarchies cemented the Egyptian-Syrian-Saudi coalition and lubricated the wheels of Arab consensus toward the peace process. Yet it could not compensate for fundamental disparities between Syria's and Egypt's capabilities, political and ideological persuasions, and the opportunities and constraints that the peace process entailed for each of them. These discrepancies, intensified by Kissinger's "step by step" peace diplomacy and Israel's strategic priorities, caused intermittent crises over principles and procedures to be followed by the Arabs in the peace process.

The peace process pointed to the narrow-based common Arab action in the conflict with Israel, underlining the dividing interests between the states concerned. It obliged each of them to define its own national interests and regional policy, thus encouraging departure from common Arab commitments and taboos in the conflict with Israel. Now that what was at stake was the possibility of retrieving national territory, versus the danger of being abandoned by Egypt's separate diplomacy, the tension between particularism and conformity in inter-Arab relations became all the more crucial.

Egypt's self-image as the Arab world's center of gravity underlay Sadat's bold independent diplomacy in the peace process while still ahdering to a loose concept of a comprehensive settlement. Given its oportunities, Egypt's strategic choice was inevitable, but it proved impracticable for Syria and Jordan, given their limits of power and domestic political constraints.

Despite the unifying effect of inter-Arab financial aid, the oil boom envigorated state individualism and weakened Pan-Arab solidarity. Oil wealth proved to be the state-owned asset that separated those who possessed it from those who could only aspire to benefit from it indirectly. The embezzled use of oil wealth by its owners according to their own priorities while they rationed its flow to the confrontation states generated bitter frustration among the poor countries, primarily Egypt.

Asad's failure to tie Sadat's hands in the peace process through summit resolutions forbidding separate settlements indicated the weakness of this institution in imposing boundaries on a core Arab actor. Asad thus tried to acquire a veto power over other Arab partners to the peace process, by tightening his grip on the PLO and Lebanon and aligning with Jordan. But Syria's improved regional standing and success regarding the Rabat resolution on the PLO's status backfired, in that it left Sadat little choice but to return to his separate diplomacy or accept an impasse. Syria's quest for sub-regional hegemony also proved overambitious. Its military invasion of Lebanon and direct clash with the PR cost Damascus much of the moral capital it had acquired in the Arab world following Sinai II and intensified domestic opposition to the regime.

In the dispute over the peace process, both Egypt and Syria seized on the Palestinian issue as a source of legitimacy for their policies. The result was an enhanced formal commitment to the PLO and its political goals, accompanied by international diplomatic efforts on its behalf. This dynamic, however, turned detrimental to the concept of a comprehensive peace due to the PLO's illegitimacy from an Israeli and American viewpoint. The PLO's enhanced prestige intensified Syria's efforts to subordinate it to its own policy and settle the Lebanese crisis, culminating in a new military collision between state and revolution.

Sadat's visit to Jerusalem was a culmination of the Egyptian break with the paralyzing ideal of Arab consensus rather than with the Arab world, least of all the Gulf monarchies. The Camp David accords provided Iraq an opportunity to replace Egypt's leadership by closing ranks with Syria and creating a new core coalition, which denied the Gulf monarchies' freedom of action toward Egypt and exposed their inherent geopolitical vulnerability despite their wealth and international influence. Abetted by the Iranian revolution and Soviet encroachment, the result was a shift by these monarchies, led by Saudi Arabia, toward their immediate sub-regional interest in the Gulf, in which they sought cooperation with Iraq.

V

THE DECADE OF FRAGMENTATION AND DISARRAY

"Regrettably, each of the Arab rulers acts separately, away from the spirit of partnership. To reach a unity of rank the Arab nation must agree on a certain aim. Today there is neither [a joint] aim nor interest. . . . We are in a state of anarchy, mistrust, and almost hopelessness. . . . If we want to gather, we have to return to the commitments of religion and history."

—Fahd al-Ahmad al-Sabbah to *Akhbar al-Yawm,* November 12, 1983.

"The Arab world without Egypt is an incomplete world."

—King Husain, *MENA,* January 30, 1982.

"The snow of [Mount] Hermon is more compassionate to us than some of the Arab regimes."
—Yasir 'Arafat, quoted in editorial, *Filastin al-Thawra,* January 5, 1985.

THE ARAB WORLD IN THE 1980S: AN OVERVIEW

The Israel-Egypt peace treaty and the Islamic revolution in Iran accounted for a radical structural change of the Arab states system for almost a decade. Egypt's expulsion from the AL left the Arab states system in a state of unprecedented disarray, reflecting Egypt's irreplaceable pivotal role in regional Arab politics. The Iraqi-Syrian coalition, which seemed to have formed a new center of gravity in the Arab world, providing for a new Arab-Israeli balance of power, was short-lived. Less than two years after the Baghdad summit, Iraq touched off a war with Iran and, in the name of Arab interests in the Gulf, split the Arab world and isolated Syria on the Israeli front.

With the eruption of the Iraq-Iran war, the Arab regional system shifted from a single core concern, namely, the Arab-Israeli conflict, to a bi-focal conflict system, which boosted inter-state competition over increasingly eroded Arab resources and priorities. But the major implication of Iraq's move was to shut the door on the Arab military option against Israel until a basic change could be effected in inter-Arab relations and peace restored in the Gulf. With the eruption of the Iraq-Iran war, relations between Baghdad and Damascus deteriorated to overt hostility and a struggle for regional primacy, relegating the conflict with Israel secondary on the Arab agenda.

Syria's strategic weakness in the face of Israel's threat and its fear of political marginalization motivated its uncompromising search for security, resulting in a formal treaty with the Soviet Union, active alliance with revolutionary Iran against Iraq, and a forceful effort to bring the PLO under its control. The alliance with Iran against Iraq enhanced Syria's position vis-à-vis its Arab counterparts and provided Iran an access to the conflict with Israel through the Shi'is in southern Lebanon. Damascus aimed at forcing the Iraqi regime to put an end to the war with Iran and shift collective Arab efforts back to the conflict with Israel. With the prolonged war, however, this policy resulted in Syria's isolation in the Arab world, and seriously intensified inter-Arab divisions and regional threats to domestic stability. Moreover, joined by Qadhafi's Libya in support of Iran, Syria's regional policy gave rise to a renewed ideological struggle for Arab legitimacy that resembled inter-state Arab conflicts two decades earlier.

The Gulf monarchies, especially Kuwait and Saudi Arabia, whose national security was deeply threatened by Iran's Shi'i revolution and the Soviet invasion of Afghanistan, reluctantly aligned with Iraq as their front defense line, providing it with financial and moral support. The gravity of these threats underlay the establishment of a separate sub-regional cooperation council of the Gulf monarchies. The Iraq-Iran war turned into a focal regional issue determining inter-Arab alignment according to proximity to, and level of threat posed by Iran's Islamic revolution. The war also affected Arab and international efforts to resume the Arab-Israeli peace process, which had remained stalemated due to Syria's veto power.

Whereas the Iraq-Iran war shifted common Arab interest and resources away from the conflict with Israel, the Iraq-Syria conflict seriously undercut Arab collective capability and efficacy. The Iraq-Iran war not only nullified the military option against Israel and swallowed huge Arab financial resources, it also exposed Syria to Israeli threat of war. Arab collective paralysis was clearly demonstrated by Israel's 1982 invasion of Lebanon, which involved an attack on Syrian forces, a long siege of Beirut, and the expulsion of the Palestinian establishment. True, in 1979–1982 the Arab states held four consecutive annual summit meetings, an unusual practice even at times of lesser divisions in the Arab world. Underlying these summits was the aggravated problem of national security faced by the leading Arab actors, hence their mutual need to trade off financial and political backing, which also preserved the facade of inter-Arab consensus against Egypt's peace with Israel. In fact, these summits underlined the centrality of Egypt whose expulsion from the AL nullified the prospects for the emergence of a hegemonic core coalition capable of regulating regional order and forging effective collective action on any major issue confronting the Arab world.

The plunge in oil prices and shrinking revenues diminished Arab power internationally and underlay substantial social and political changes in the region, affecting oil producers, labor migrants, and recipients of direct financial aid. The Iranian revolution and the outbreak of war with Iraq had skyrocketed oil prices, which reached unprecedented levels of nearly $40 per barrel. But prices began declining in 1982, crashing sometimes below $10 per barrel in 1986, and stabilizing by 1987 at around $18, where they stayed until the end of the 1980s. In 1988, Saudi Arabia, for the first time in twenty years, resorted to borrowing money after a four-year recession. Reportedly, the official amount Kuwait was giving away in foreign aid had fallen from more than $11 billion a year in 1981 to less than $1 billion in 1986.[1]

The Iranian revolution constituted a political and ideological challenge to all Sunni ruling elites because Khomeini claimed to be the standard bearer, not of Shi'i sectarianism or Iranian nationalism, but of universal Islamic order. Coupled with its geostrategic eminence in the Gulf, Iran's efforts to export the revolution into its Arab neighbors in the name of Islam often blurred the boundaries between religion and chauvinist Iranian nationalism. Above all, the revolution in Iran fuelled domestic concerns in the Gulf and elsewhere in the Arab world due to growing Islamic piety and devotion in Arab-Muslim so-cieties and manifestations of political Islamic radicalism. The Islamic wave derived its force from the growing social and economic depression in Arab societies that was occasioned by the inability of the ruling elites to meet the economic, social, and political needs of a rapidly growing and urbanizing population, and exacerbated by uneven economic growth that widened the gaps between rich and poor. Aggravated by the falling oil prices, this socio-economic predicament deepened the crisis of legitimacy in Arab states, inten-sifying coercion and authoritarianism.[2]

The complex of social and political problems—domestic and regional— striking the Arab world clearly showed the limits of the Arab states system and brought into question its essential premises and efficacy. The bankruptcy of the Arab nationalist-socialist discourse was underlined by the growing weight of the Islamic discourse, which reflected the shifting agenda from supra-national to domestic, socio-economic issues concerning each state. The frustrating state of Arab affairs as of the late 1970s generated a new phase of ideological crisis, epitomizing the intellectual debate on the very existence and meaning of Pan-Arab nationalism. In addition to laments at the state of disintegration in Arab solidarity as a source of weakness in the conflict with Israel, Arab intellectuals pondered the lost opportunity of the "oil decade" and the corruption of power and waste of material resources that led to a growing dependency on the Western capitalist economies.[3]

12

The Iraq-Syria Conflict and the Gulf War

The Collapse of the Anti-Sadat Front

By the end of 1979, the Arab world's punitive policy toward Egypt had run its course, and with it the Arab world's alignment behind the Syria-Iraq axis. The following year witnessed the total collapse of the anti-Sadat coalition as old disputes returned to center stage. Meanwhile, Sadat stood up to his critics and stuck to his undertakings according to the peace treaty regarding the normalization of relations with Israel along with the latter's ongoing withdrawal from Sinai. The sputtering out of Baghdad's drive to impose sanctions was clear when no new measures were decided on at the ALC's semi-annual meeting, held in June 1979 in Tunis.

Domestic and regional changes soon brought to the surface old disputes between Iraq and Syria, the key Arab powers in the anti-Sadat alignment. By June, the Iraq-Syria rapprochement stalemated as disagreement over the crucial issue of constitutional and party unification came to the fore. In early July, President Bakr was forced to resign and was succeeded by Saddam Husain, who appeared to have resented the unity scheme with Syria. The ascendancy of Saddam Husain was accompanied by the ruthless elimination of his rivals in the Iraqi political leadership, on grounds of fostering a plot against the "party and revolution" with Syrian collaboration. Baghdad rejected Damascus' protests and claims of innocence, and relations continued to sour despite mediation efforts by King Husain and 'Arafat, and Asad's declared wish to visit Baghdad and set matters straight. By the end of August, relations between the two Ba'th regimes had been frozen, though both regimes refrained from propaganda attacks until Spring 1980, to avert further deterioration.[4]

The Iraqi-Syrian rapprochement turned out to be a temporary convergence of different aims between old enemies whose disputes over regional hegemony, water resources, oil pipelines, and Pan-Arab legitimacy had remained unresolved. As had often been the case in inter-Arab politics, the reconciliation between the two Ba'thi regimes in October 1978 was as sudden and frantic as their reversion to overt hostility. The shift to an open conflict coincided with a growing deterioration of domestic security in both Iraq and Syria during 1979. Mutual propaganda warfare and political subversion and sabotage through opposition groups became typical manifestations of the Iraq-Syria conflict, especially after the Iran-Iraq war erupted in September 1980.

Saddam Husain's seizure of power came at a time of growing unrest in Iraq's Shi'i community, which constituted more than half the country's population, accompanied by anti-regime violence, widely believed to be encouraged by the revolutionary Shi'a in Iran. The outward thrust of Iran's Islamic revolution seemed to threaten the very existence of the Iraqi regime, especially given its relatively narrow domestic Sunni-Arab base. Tension between Iran and Iraq increased dramatically as a result of Baghdad's violent repression of the Shi'i opposition organization *al-Da'wa al-Islamiyya,* which led both governments to break diplomatic relations and to accelerate their support for each other's opposition groups. In addition to the Shi'i threat, the Iraqi regime was increasingly faced during 1979 with renewed subversion by Kurdish opposition groups inspired and supported by Syria.[5]

Asad's regime was also confronted with domestic enemies, spearheaded by the Muslim Brotherhood movement, which, in the first half of 1979, intensified its terrorist attacks on the Ba'th regime, particularly its party and military 'Alawi figures. Manifestly, the growing regional threats to Asad's regime following the collapse of his rapprochement with Iraq served as an incentive to Syrian opposition groups. In 1980, Islamic terrorist activity turned into a countrywide, almost daily phenomenon, especially in the northern cities of Aleppo and Hamah, strongholds of Sunni conservatism and political opposition to Damascus. The regime's response, which assumed no less violent form against its opponents, also affected relations with Jordan. The latter was accused by Damascus of providing training and other support to the Muslim Brothers. The internal unrest, compounded by Syria's problems in Lebanon, raised doubts about the regime's viability for the first time since Asad's assumption of power in 1970.[6]

The grave domestic and external challenges to both Iraq's and Syria's regimes dictated a common interest in preventing further mutual frictions and an effort to preserve the facade of Arab unity during the Tunis summit conference held in November 1979. Baghdad was obviously concerned with maintaining its leading regional position to ensure wide Arab support in the face of the Islamic revolution in Iran. As for Damascus, it could not afford to jeopardize the significant financial aid it received from the oil states, including Iraq, nor ignore its need for Iraq to offset Israel's strategic threat.

A general interest in preserving an atmosphere of Arab accord was evident at the summit meeting that opened in Tunis on November 20, 1979, despite divisions over Lebanon, the boycott of Egypt, the Sahara conflict, and the Iranian revolution. To minimize controversies and ensure a collective Arab action, it was agreed that the summit would address only Lebanon's demand to put an end to the PR armed presence along the Israeli border, clearly indicating the exhaustion of the sanctions against Egypt. It also attested to Iraq's limitations as a pivotal actor in the Arab states system concerning the conflict with Israel. With Syria recognized as the major confrontation state, any Iraqi involvement—financial or military—in the conflict with Israel had to be subordinated to, or partly channeled through Damascus. Syria, for its part, sought to ensure additional Arab military and financial support and preserve the militant nature of the anti-Sadat front. Backed by the PLO and Libya, Syria suggested that the oil weapon be used against the West, a new version of the JAC be created, and the AL Charter be amended, making majority resolutions binding on member states.[7]

Although Baghdad had traditionally advocated the use of the oil weapon, it now undertook to compromise between the advocates of sanctions against the United States and the oil monarchies, which rejected the very idea of using their oil as a political weapon. Now that Arab sanctions against Egypt had been applied, the best Baghdad could come up with in trying to preserve its leading position was the nebulous notion that inter-Arab cooperation and military prowess should be enhanced by the vast use of economic means. With oil prices soaring, Baghdad urged the shaping of a "comprehensive strategy" concerning the use of the immense Arab economic and political power as leverage to shore up the opponents of the Israeli-Egyptian peace treaty, and to pressure those states that "practice an anti-Arab policy." The formulation of such strategy, however, was deferred to the next summit conference, scheduled for November 1980. Thus, the original idea was boiled down to the usual means of resolving this dispute: buying off the confrontation states by offering them financial aid in return for dropping their demand to use oil as a political weapon.

Just how real was Washington's concern at the summit's possible results in this regard was evident in the visit paid by H. Eilts, former U.S. ambassador to Cairo, prior to the summit, to Riyad and other Arab capitals, to shore up Saudi resistance to the idea of anti-American sanctions. The summit's final resolution contented itself with condemnation of the U.S. role in facilitating the Israel-Egypt peace treaty, threatening that this policy could prove detrimental to American interests in the Arab world.[8]

Inter-Arab Polarization in the Shadow of the Cold War

The Iraq-Syria Rift

The Tunis summit had no impact on the conflict with Israel, indicating the fizzling out of the punitive policy against Egypt and the deterioration of Syria-Iraq relations, which left little common ground for substantive joint Arab action. Within a few months, Syrian-Iraqi restrain came to an end, giving way to a new inter-Arab alignment marked by a bitter split between two rival coalitions, led by Iraq and Syria. The shift resulted from intensified domestic and regional threats to both Iraqi and Syrian Ba'thi regimes, aggravated by the Soviet invasion of Afghanistan, and reaching their peak with the outbreak of the Iraq-Iran war. In the process, weak Arab actors, primarily Jordan and the Gulf oil monarchies, were obliged to take a clear position that would best serve their national security under the new circumstances. Qadhafi, on the other hand, took advantage of the Iraqi-Syrian falling out to improve his relations with Syria and extricate himself from his marginal position in the Arab arena.

The Soviet invasion of Afghanistan on December 27, 1979, profoundly shook the inter-Arab system. Given the Soviet encroachment in the Horn of Africa and PDRY, this new venture added another threat to regional stability, especially to the security of the Gulf countries. This event, coming on the heels of Iran's revolution, prompted these countries to cooperate against the radical menace in both its Islamic and Soviet shapes. The cooling of Soviet-Iraqi relations even before the invasion of Afghanistan, and the impact of the Shi'i revolution on Iraqi domestic politics, left Baghdad no choice but to join with the Arab states' all but universal condemnation—the exceptions were Syria and the PDRY—of the Soviet invasion.[9]

The Soviet invasion of Afghanistan brought home dramatically the danger to Western interests in the Middle East, spurring Washington to obtain military installations and increase the supply of advanced arms to friendly states. Oman and Somalia, facing imminent Soviet-backed threats, permitted U.S. military facilities; Egypt agreed to provide some access. Both U.S. and Soviet moves renewed tension between radicals and conservatives in the Arab world, and inspired a growing Iraqi-Saudi alignment vis-à-vis hostile Syria and Libya. Syria's reluctance to condemn the Soviet invasion showed the growing gap separating it from the Arab mainstream and obliged it to turn to the SRF, revived in the wake of the superpowers' intensifying rivalry.

Qadhafi was the driving force behind the reemergence of the SRF, taking advantage of the Syro-Iraqi rift. The SRF's fourth summit meeting, held in April 1980 at Tripoli, Libya, reflected the radical bloc's split with Iraq, Jordan, and the Gulf monarchies. The SRF lifted the banner of intransigent Arab nationalism, which, under Asad's and Qadhafi's aegis, was to be imposed on the Arab world. It rejected a peaceful solution to the Arab-Israeli conflict; emphasized the "Palestinian armed struggle" and urged Jordan to let the PR fight from its territory; called for a joint command under a Syrian general; and sought Soviet military aid to achieve "strategic parity" with Israel. Dangling military and other material inducements, Qadhafi moved to exploit Syria's isolation and to enhance his own position. On September 1, 1980, in a speech marking the anniversary of his coup, Qadhafi proposed a Libyan-Syrian merger, to which Asad stated his unequivocal consent.[10]

Asad's alignment with Qadhafi—anathema to the West and most Arab states—clearly indicated the low point his domestic and regional position had reached. Facing growing domestic threats to his own regime, Qadhafi stepped up region-wide subversive activity against neighboring regimes such as Sudan, Egypt, Tunisia, and the sub-Sahara states, primarily Chad. Qadhafi assumed the role of the anti-West standard bearer. His vitriolic attacks on the PLO for its international efforts to renew the peace process, as well as on Saudi Arabia for purchasing American intelligence-gathering AWACS planes, led to crises in Libya's relations with the PLO and Riyad.[11]

Tension mounted also between Amman and Damascus, ending four years of political and economic rapprochement. The tension came from Jordan's alleged support for the Muslim Brotherhood opposition to the Asad regime, and was exacerbated as a result of Jordan's rapid rapprochement and economic cooperation with Iraq beginning in 1979. Limited Jordanian-Iraqi cooperation in developing transit facilities to Iraq through the port of ʿAqaba had begun in 1975. Following the Islamic revolution in Iran, however, Iraq increased substantially its financial support for developing transportation and construction projects, as well as its trade relations with Jordan. In the spring of 1980, Saddam Husain and the Hashemite king signed an agreement on military cooperation that would ensure for Iraq a secure access to Jordan's port of ʿAqaba.[12]

King Husain's primary motive for cooperation with Iraq was economic. The alliance with Iraq was essential for ensuring the financial aid allocated by the Baghdad summit to Jordan as well as to the Palestinians in the occupied territories. Indeed, Jordan and the PLO managed to deepen their cooperation through the joint committee despite their competition over these territories, Amman's refusal to allow political activity by the PLO in Jordan, and strong opposition by the PLO radical groups to collaborating with King Husain.[13]

The Iraq-Syria rift reached its peak following the former's all-out war against Iran, which opened on September 22, 1980. From its very start Asad deplored the war against Iran as the wrong war against the wrong enemy, launched on behalf of "American imperialism." Qadhafi too denounced Iraq in support of Asad's primary concern with the Israeli enemy and called for an immediate end to the war against Iran. Concern lest the war might end with a quick Iraqi victory, as many expected during its first few weeks, drove Asad to a growing search for allies to safeguard his regime and Syria's national interest against either Israeli or Iraqi threats. On October 8, 1980, in Moscow, Asad signed a Treaty of Friendship and Cooperation with the USSR, something he had long been reluctant to do. Furthermore, apparently with Moscow's approval, an arms airlift from Syria and Libya began carrying Soviet weapons to Iran. Baghdad retorted by accusing both Syria and Libya of stabbing Iraq and the Arab cause, for whose sake Iraq was fighting, in the back.

Asad's collaboration with Tehran also represented the latter's religious link with Lebanon's Shi'i community and interest in it as a springboard for war with Israel. In mid-1979, Syria had allowed the movement of Iranian volunteers through its territory to Lebanon, where they became involved in military training within the Shi'i community. Asad's rapprochement with Iran might have been motivated by his quest for Islamic legitimacy for his 'Alawi community—perceived as heretical by traditional Sunni Islam. The Iranian connection would also strengthen Asad's position in Lebanon by allying with the large Shi'i community that constituted a majority in the southeastern parts of the country, hence its significance for Syria's security.[14]

The outbreak of the Iraq-Iran war at the former's initiative reflected a mixture of preemptive motives and territorial claims. Given the Iraqi Shi'i majority and secessionist Kurdish aspirations, the war aimed at removing the threat based by a potential Shi'i revolution to the regime's security and Iraq's territorial integrity. The revolutionary chaos in Iran might have tempted Baghdad to seize the opportunity to settle, once and for all, old territorial disputes that would secure strategic waterways to the Gulf for Iraq and perhaps replace Iran as a central power in this area. Thus, the war was also aimed at ridding Baghdad of the 1975 Algiers Treaty it had signed with the Shah—under the pressures of the Iranian-backed Kurdish rebellion and the Soviet curtailment of arms shipments to Iraq—accepting equal division of sovereignty over the Shatt al-'Arab, Iraq's sole waterway to the Gulf.[15]

The Iraq-Iran war turned into an acid test of regional and inter-Arab alignment, revolving around the Iraqi-Syrian cleavage, and marked by the primacy of interest over ideology. This was clearly shown by the alliance of secular-nationalist Syria and the Islamic revolution of Iran, supported by Libya and other radical members of the SRF to whom the Palestine issue was a primary means to obtain Arab legitimacy and extricate themselves from marginality. Iraq, on the other hand, allied with conservative Jordan and Saudi Arabia. As the war began, Jordan became an alternate route to the closed Shatt al-'Arab waterway for the transit of Iraqi civilian and military goods via 'Aqaba. Jordan's collaboration with Iraq, coupled with King Husain's reported efforts to resume the peace process over the West Bank, deepened Damascus' already hostile relations with Amman over the issue of supporting the Syrian Muslim Brothers. Syria's grievances and growing animosity toward the Iraq-Jordan axis were to culminate in the crisis Damascus initiated over the summit conference opened at Amman on November 25, 1980.[16]

A Turn to Coercion: Syria and the Amman Summit

The Amman summit was designed to work out a long-term strategy of inter-Arab economic cooperation—as an alternative to the use of the oil weapon—in accordance with the idea raised by Iraq in Tunis. Preparations for the summit were marked, from their outset in the summer, by division between the two rival blocs, represented by Syria and Iraq. Syria, the PLO, and other SRF members sought to make the Palestine issue the hub of the discussions, insisting that Arab strategy and inter-Arab relations must reflect the fact that the Palestinian problem constituted the fulcrum of Arab interests. This group repeated its demands that the oil weapon be used, that cooperation with the USSR be cultivated, and that Arab states freeze all ties with countries that renewed relations with Israel or recognized Jerusalem as its capital.[17]

Although economic cooperation was to be the focal issue on the summit agenda, the outbreak of the Iraq-Iran war exacerbated Syria's concerns that the scheduled meeting in Amman might be harmful to its national interests. Syria feared that the summit might be used to mobilize all-Arab support for Iraq in the Gulf war at the expense of its own needs in confronting Israel, as well as for Jordan's goals in joining the peace process with Israel. Indeed, Baghdad adopted the argument that it was protecting Arab interests in the Shatt al-'Arab waterway and the Gulf against Iranian aggression. As for King Husain, it remains unclear whether he made any real effort to obtain the summit's support for his goals. In any event, shortly before the summit was to convene, Syria began lobbying to change the summit's venue, and when this failed it called for indefinite postponement of the meeting. To press its demand, Damascus unleashed a propaganda campaign against the Hashemite regime that aimed to delegitimize it as host of the coming summit, because of its aid to Iraq in the Gulf fighting, its attempts to undermine the Arab consensus regarding the PLO's political status, and its complicity in terrorism against the Damascus regime. Above all, Amman was accused of seeking an all-Arab sanction for a political settlement with Israel, which Damascus described as even more calamitous than Sadat's peace policy.[18]

For Jordan, the summit's postponement or change of venue would severely harm King Husain's prestige. Jordan's insistence that the summit take place as scheduled gained broad support from conservative Arab governments, including Saudi Arabia, even though it risked a rupture with Damascus. This support might have expressed the oil monarchies' rage at Syria's alliance with Iran and alignment with Libya. Syria's attendance at the summit remained uncertain until the last hour despite its success in shaping a militant agenda for the summit at the preparatory FMs' meetings that included a bar on negotiating a separate settlement with Israel without the approval of a special Arab summit and the rejection of Resolution 242 as a basis for negotiating a settlement with Israel. Syria, however, remained unmoved in its claim that the summit should be postponed and, faced with the striking number of AL members in favor of holding the summit as scheduled, announced its boycott of the meeting.[19]

Syria's decision to boycott the summit was accompanied by a propaganda campaign against Jordan, closure of their common border, and massing two mechanized divisions at Dar'a, the staging ground for their September

1970 strike into Jordan. Jordan took precautions, but did not move up its own troops, to prevent exacerbation of the situation. Parallel to its military threat, Damascus lobbied for the support of its SRF allies, indicating that the boycott decision had been taken by Syria alone and a concerted diplomatic offensive would be needed to win them over. Lebanon's President, a Syrian client, vacillated over whether or not to attend the summit despite the negative Syrian position. A meeting in Beirut with Syria's CoS Shihabi evidently convinced Sarkis that he could not take an independent line and had to join the boycotters.[20]

The PLO found itself in a quandary. While it could not risk running afoul of Damascus, it feared that following the Syrian line would cost it the support of other Arab states. The situation was compounded by the summit's venue and the possibility that Husain would ask for the summit's approval to enter negotiations on a settlement of the Palestinian problem. 'Arafat's intensive efforts to lobby for postponement, while trying to mediate between Asad and Saddam Husain, were a reflection of the PLO's uneasy situation, which ended up with a decision to join Syria's boycott. The PLO's decision served as a pretext for Algeria's President Shadhli Bin Jadid, explaining his decision to boycott the summit as an act of solidarity with the PLO. Since the purpose of Arab summits was to deal with the Palestinian problem, he later explained, the Algerian people could not be convinced to take part in a summit without the attendance of the Palestinians themselves.[21]

The Syrian move, unprecedented in the annals of Arab summits, was a test of its ability to force its will on the rest of the Arab states by virtue of its being the principal confrontation state and leader of the SRF. A successful summit in Amman posed a palpable threat to Damascus: if it enshrined the Saudi-Iraqi-Jordanian axis as the Arab world's core coalition, thereby assuring the triumph of U.S. policy in the area, Syria would be forced to take a back seat in regional affairs. Despite the tension along Jordan's border with Syria, fifteen Arab states were represented at the summit that opened on November 25. All the Gulf countries, including Iraq and Saudi Arabia, were represented by heads of state, underscoring their concern for the Gulf region's security. However, Syria's boycott and military threat had an unmistakable impact on the summit's deliberations and decisions, which were marked by a conciliatory approach toward Damascus and the PLO. Kuwait and Saudi Arabia set the tone, manifesting willingness to dissipate the tension by sending an arbitration commission to Damascus.[22]

The Iran-Iraq war was tackled with prudence by the summit, obviously to prevent further alienation of Syria. Yet whereas the rulers of Baghdad and Jordan called for unequivocal support of Iraq's "Arab war" in the Gulf, the summit contented itself with a cautiously phrased resolution supporting "Iraq's legitimate right to its land and its waters, in accordance with the international agreements signed between the two countries." Even this reserved support, however, came in the context of the Arab nation's need for total mobilization of resources in its fateful "struggle with the Zionist enemy." Informally, the Arab states concerned with Gulf security agreed to maintain the region's neutrality in the face of superpower rivalry. The defensive capability of the Gulf states was to be enhanced, with Jordan and Iraq offering to assist by providing training and dispatching military experts.[23]

The facade of conciliation toward Syria could hardly conceal the rage of Jordan and Iraq at Damascus' stand and its differences with the Gulf monarchies. Contrary to the final communique's mild support for Iraq in the Gulf war, King Husain's concluding address reflected more truly the rupture between the Iraq-Jordan coalition and Syria. He lashed out at Syria for trying to take over the PLO and accused the boycotting countries of "stabbing Iraq in the back" by effectively siding with Iran. To the press, the king vented his wrath on Syria for the first time since the crisis began, warning Damascus not to repeat the mistake committed by the previous regime in September 1970, when Jordanian forces had routed Syrian armor that crossed the border into Jordan. Practically, however, despite reports that Iraq and the Gulf monarchies had secretly reassessed their financial aid to Syria, no official decision was made to this effect, either in regard to the maintenance of the ADF in Lebanon or to the confrontation with Israel. Only Iraq, which had until then fulfilled all its obligations for aiding Syria in accordance with the Baghdad summit, ceased its financial support due to its burdensome war with Iran.[24]

The summit expressed unreserved support for the PLO, despite King Husain's notable disregard of the PLO in his opening speech as the meeting's host. The summit not only reconfirmed the PLO's standing as the sole legitimate representative of the Palestinian people and its right to establish an independent state on its national soil. The summit unequivocally confirmed the PLO's exclusive right to handle all matters concerning the Palestinian people, calling for the preservation of its independence and implicitly blaming Syria for forcing the PLO to boycott the summit. Obviously, the summit's strong support for the PLO was not only meant to refute any impression that the summit would empower King Husain to represent the Palestinian issue. The summit also responded to President-elect Ronald Reagan's disregard of the PLO's role in a future Middle East settlement, deploring his use of the term "terrorist organization" to describe the PLO.[25]

Regarding the radicals' demand to employ the oil weapon against the West, Iraq, acting in close accord with the conservative oil producers, suggested that petrodollars be earmarked for accelerated Arab economic development. In the summer, Iraq had put forward a plan for decade-long economic development in the Arab world, including the establishment of a multi-billion Arab fund to finance it. The joint Saudi-Iraqi backing for this position left the radical Arabs with no option but to go along. Pursuant to previous summit resolutions, the AL's economic bodies drafted three documents aimed at tightening cooperation and reducing economic gaps in the Arab world, including a strategy of economic cooperation until the year 2000; a charter for a Pan-Arab economy; and a standardized agreement for investment of Arab capital in Arab states. These plans reflected sound economic reasoning, and were later adopted by the summit meeting. Yet they were to become another monument to the unattainability of inter-Arab economic complementarity.[26]

The ten-year development plan sustained a severe blow. Iraq originally cited a figure of $15 billion, or $1.5 billion per year, for this purpose. In view of the war with Iran, however, the development fund's capital was finally set at only one-third of that amount, half a billion dollars per year. The fund would make available to Arab states low-interest loans (one percent) for development projects. The plan's tacit purpose was evidently to forestall separate requests from aid recipients, or demands for the use of the oil weapon. To enhance the economic character of the Amman conference—later labelled "the first economic summit"—a symposium on regional Arab economic development and integration was held at the same time in the Jordanian capital, in which scholars, journalists, and officials of Arab and non-Arab institutions took part.[27]

Within two weeks after the summit Syria withdrew its forces from the Jordanian border, thanks to a high-ranking Saudi mediation effort that ironed out differences personally with Asad. Damascus, however, refused to acknowledge the summit's resolutions, despite the conciliatory efforts of the AL's committee headed by SG Qulaibi with Saudi and Algerian participation. Asad rejected the economic resolutions adopted by the summit and, following the pullback, stepped up his propaganda warfare against Jordan, portraying it as an illegitimate entity, a creation of imperialism ruled by an "alien and imported" regime, and called openly for its overthrow and replacement by a "national government."[28] Syria's resort to military threat against Jordan and its forceful control of the PLO and Lebanon offered incontrovertible proof as to its destructive potential. Syria-Jordan relations deteriorated further as the former's isolation in the Arab arena deepened and its domestic difficulties grew. It involved mutual subversion and Syrian-backed terrorist attacks against Jordan, leading both countries to recall their ambassadors and step up their propaganda campaigns.[29]

Notwithstanding the Jordan-Syria tension, the Amman summit was above all a showdown between Iraq and Syria. The irreconcilable positions of Jordan, Iraq, and Syria meant that the struggle against Israel and the Camp David accords could not be a first priority at the summit. Consequently, the delegates turned to long-term strategic and economic plans as a means of glossing over the Arab world's fragmentation. However, Syria's rejection of these plans—combined with the impasse regarding the Gulf war—robbed the plans of concrete significance. The sphere in which the Arab world could demonstrate some combative spirit in the context of the struggle against Israel was through expressing support for the PLO and the Palestinians of the West Bank and Gaza Strip, and reaffirmation of previous summit resolutions regarding the peace process that met Syria's interests.

As for King Husain, even though the summit produced in poor results pertaining to his role in the peace process, he benefitted in other ways. The unprecedented gathering of Arab heads of states in Amman was a landmark in the Arab recognition of Jordan's sovereignty, as well as of King Husain's prestige. In view of the blow King Husain had suffered at the 1974 Rabat summit, which had effectively denied his right to represent the West Bank, the Amman meeting underlined Jordan's central role in the Gulf-based Arab coalition together with Iraq, Saudi Arabia, and Kuwait. Thus, paradoxically, the crisis with Syria served King Husain, who could display leadership and control of the situation to boost his regime's credibility and value as a potential ally, hence also its national security.

The support evinced by the oil monarchies for the Iraqi-Jordanian axis provided renewed evidence of their deep-seated fear of Iran's Islamic revolution, as well as intensified Soviet encroachment in the region. Thus, a common strategic interest overrode fundamental differences between the Gulf monarchies and radical Iraq. This, however, did not impinge on the Saudis' traditional eagerness to mediate between Arab states through sophisticated manipulation of financial leverage to advance their own interests. Riyad and the Gulf emirates were anxious to prevent inter-Arab polarization—especially the sort marked by ideological conflict—which would threaten their highly vulnerable regimes and the flow of their vital oil exports.

Inter-Arab Relations and the Cold War

The growing tension and competition in the Middle East between the two superpowers following the Soviet invasion of Afganistan, injected a new dimension of contention to inter-Arab conflicts. Efforts by the newly inaugurated Reagan administration to build strategic cooperation with Middle Eastern states, primarily Egypt, Saudi Arabia, and Israel, fuelled regional conflicts from the Western Sahara to the Gulf, marking them with strong linkage to West-East rivalry.[30]

Washington's policy gained considerable momentum in U.S.-Egypt joint military maneuvers, Washington's approval of the sale of AWACS aircraft to Saudi Arabia, renewal of arms supplies to Morocco, and U.S. readiness to sign a strategic memorandum with Israel. Although the concrete significance of such a memorandum was unclear, the Syrian regime accepted it as a full-fledged strategic pact, which Syria soon matched by stepping up strategic cooperation with its Soviet ally. In July 1981, Soviet forces conducted a landing exercise on the Syrian coast during joint maneuvers with the Syrians—the first such exercise ever held between the USSR and an Arab state.[31]

While the Soviet maneuvers were evidently intended as a reply to U.S. activity in the region, their timing might have been decided by the growing Israel-Syria military tension concerning the Syrian-emplaced anti-aircraft missiles in Lebanon's valley (*biqa'*). Moscow also agreed to resume arms supplies to Iraq following Israel's bombing of the former's nuclear reactor (see below); Soviet arms supplies to Iraq were suspended on the outbreak of the Iraq-Iran war, despite the Soviet-Iraqi Treaty of Friendship.[32]

The deep inter-Arab divisions underlined the vulnerable authority and sovereignty of those regimes identified with the newly established strategic cooperation with the United States when faced with condemnation by anti-Western regimes such as those of Iran, Syria, and Libya. Touching on a sensitive chord of deeply rooted resentment to the West among Arab peoples, American policy in the Middle East was described by radical Arabs as an attempt to infiltrate military forces into the region under the guise of cooperation with, and defending Arab states, and blamed the United States for the rifts in the Arab world. The attacks against strategic collaboration with the United States were instrumental in blackmailing financial and declarative support from the oil-rich Gulf states, contrary to their best national interests.

The third summit of the ICO, held in late January 1981 at Ta'if, strongly reflected these tendencies in the region's politics. The very nature and venue of the congress made it incumbent on the hosts to demonstrate Islamic unity. However, the meeting represented mainly an effort to prevent discussion of contentious subjects and satisfy the radical states—Iran included—by anti-Israeli and anti-American declarations. The avoidance of inter-Arab or inter-Muslim affairs by the summit was particularly salient in view of Syria's isolation at the meeting due to the absence of Libya and Iran, which boycotted the meeting. Thus, unity of rhetoric was manifested by expressing support for the PLO, rejection of the Camp David accords, and denunciation of Israel, primarily for its policy in Jerusalem and its threat to Islamic interests in the holy city. The congress also reiterated the call issued by the Saudi crown prince in August 1980 for a Holy War (*jihad*) against Israel. The United States was vehemently denounced and threatened with economic sanctions, while the Soviet Union, by contrast, was only rapped over the knuckles for its invasion of Afghanistan.[33]

Inter-Arab polarization was fueled by Qadhafi's intrigues and subversive activities in the sub-Sahara states, especially Chad, as well as in Sudan, Egypt, and Somalia. Qadhafi's regional policy aggravated U.S.-Libya relations, culminating in the expulsion of the Libyan diplomatic mission from Washington in April. In August 1981, U.S. war planes had downed two Libyan airforce fighters over the Gulf of Sirte in what seemed to be a deliberate American action to teach Qadhafi a lesson. The Soviets, while restraining their public reaction toward the United States, used the incident in their efforts to persuade Gulf states against allowing a U.S. military presence on their soil. Qadhafi used the incident to garner extensive Arab support, with even the Gulf states condemning the United States. Seeking worldwide recognition as the leader of the world liberation movement, on the thirteenth anniversary of his revolution Qadhafi held in Tripoli an international conference of national liberation and radical movements from eighty-six countries to demonstrate solidarity with his regime.[34]

Washington's quest for reinforced strategic relations with Middle Eastern countries topped the agenda of the SRF's fifth summit meeting, convened at Benghazi a month after the air clash on the Gulf of Sirte. The meeting, initially held to show solidarity with Libya in its clash with the United States, called for eliminating every form of U.S. military presence in the Arab homeland and taking steps against Arab states collaborating with Sadat. The meeting also called for measures against Sadat following his mass arrests of opponents earlier that month and expulsion of the Soviet ambassador and 1500 Russian experts employed in civilian industry, allegedly for instigating unrest in Egypt. Echoing Syria's strategic disadvantage in confronting Israel, the conference also resolved to seek a framework of relations with Moscow paralleling the U.S.-Israel relationship in order to attain "strategic parity" with Israel.[35]

The division and infirmity of the Arab world were demonstrated in the strategic freedom of action it provided for Israel toward its Arab neighbors. On June 6, amid the missile crisis with Syria, Israel bombed the almost-completed Iraqi nuclear reactor near Baghdad. The operation stunned the Arab world and generated wide international condemnation. Washington reacted by suspending the supply of four F-16 aircraft to Israel. Yet the Arab world responded cautiously, contenting itself with condemning Israel and appealing to the UN for sanctions against her, perhaps guided by the moderate Soviet reaction.[36]

The Arab States and the Iran-Iraq War

Although Iraq was the Arab state most immediately affected by the Iranian revolution, the Gulf monarchies in general came under its threat due to their geographic proximity and the high percentage of Shi'is among their populations. Shi'is constituted a majority in Bahrain and Qatar, a significant percentage of the UAE and Kuwaiti citizen population, and a substantial part of Saudi Arabia's oil-rich north-east province. The social revolutionary appeal of the new Iranian regime had especially strong echoes among the socially and economically depressed Shi'i Arab and Iranian groups in the Gulf Arab states. No less threatening to the Gulf Arab states where the Iranian-based activities of

subversion and propaganda aimed at delegitimation of their monarchical systems as unIslamic institutions.

As of late 1979, a growing social and political unrest was witnessed
among the traditionally disenfranchised Shi'i population of Saudi Arabia,
which threatened to stifle the oil industry in al-Hassa province. On November
20, a radical Islamic group seized control of the Ka'ba Mosque in Mecca, the
holiest shrine of Islam. Kuwait witnessed growing agitation by Shi'i radical
opposition groups which culminated in the December 1983 series of bombings
against American targets in Kuwait City, perpetrated by an Islamic radical
group. In Bahrain, traditionally claimed to be an Iranian sovereign territory, a
coup attempt undertaken by Shi'i grass-roots groups in December 1981, amidst
Iran's military offensive, was put down before it could make any headway.[37]

Apart from initiating domestic social policy aimed at defusing the Shi'i
communities' grievances and unrest, the Gulf monarchies responded to the
growing regional and domestic threats by founding, in May 1981, the GCC,
comprising Saudi Arabia, Kuwait, Qatar, Bahrain, the UAE, and Oman. The
GCC, a new phenomenon in regional Arab politics, was the result of Saudi
Arabia's persistent efforts following the onset of the Gulf War to consolidate
cooperation among the Gulf monarchies. The GCC was an uneasy alliance of
rulers whose main bond was their fear of Iran and Iraq. Revolutionary Iraq was
left out, though it took part in the preliminary talks on the GCC, to prevent the
group's identification as an anti-Iranian bloc. Threatened by Iran's Islamic
revolution, Soviet encroachment on the region's periphery, and growing social
and political Islamic radicalism at home, the GCC aimed primarily at assuring
close cooperation among its member states on regional security, such as establishing a joint military command, as well as on foreign and economic policies.
In January 1982, the GCC member states' DMs decided to allocate $30.6
billion in 1982 for defense, about 25 percent of their expected oil revenues.
Although the advent of the GCC was received with general understanding, it
also raised some criticism in Arab public discourse for its exclusive nature as
an oil-rich bloc, and concern lest it separate itself from future regional Arab
plans of economic cooperation.[38]

By the end of September 1981, the Iranians had broken the siege of
Abadan, and from November to the end of May 1982, they embarked on an
offensive strategy, regaining most of their lost territories in the southern and
central fronts. On May 23, Saddam Husain, fearing an Iranian invasion of
Iraq's territory, invoked the ACSP of 1950, to obtain military aid from the
League's members, but to no avail. The Iraqi military setbacks had a discernible impact on the regime's security, escalating sabotage and terrorism by the
Shi'i *al-Da'wa* movement and calling into question the loyalty of the Shi'i
community at large. Thus, twenty months after Saddam Husain had opened the

war, expecting a swift victory, his decision turned out to be a horrendous miscalculation which could be disastrous for the Iraqi Ba'th regime, with far-reaching repercussions on the Gulf monarchies as well.

Whether or not Saudi Arabia and Kuwait had secretly backed Saddam Husain's decision to wage the war, their response to its shifting balance in Iran's favor was nothing but a reflection of their depth of concern about their own national security. For the Gulf Arab monarchies, the combined threats of militant Shi'ism and military offensive that Iran posed to their internal stability reinforced their disposition to further consolidate their relations and to support Iraq even more overtly. Iraq was bent on playing on the Gulf states' fear of the Iranian threat to their internal stability and vital economic interests, in order to bolster its demand for full political and material support from the Arab world in its war with Iran.[39]

In late 1981, Saudi Arabia signed a series of domestic security cooperation agreements with Bahrain, the UAE, Qatar, Oman, and Morocco, culminating in an agreement with Iraq to mark their common border, long a contentious issue. With Riyad's signature went an unequivocal declaration of support for Baghdad by the Saudi interior minister, Amir Na'if, asserting that Iraq's war with Iran was in defense of not only its own sovereignty and territory but the entire Arab nation. At the end of December, Bahrain—following a Shi'i coup attempt—and Yemen expelled Iranian representatives, prompting Iraq to urge that all Arab governments follow suit. The GCC members, however, refrained from adopting an explicit stance of collective support for Iraq, though they did offer it generous financial aid to help underwrite the war. Instead, they contented themselves with urging Iran to respond favorably to the international mediation moves afoot in order to bring about a peaceful conclusion, one that "safeguards the legitimate rights of the disputing parties."[40]

The Gulf states' growing concern in the face of the Iranian threat had the effect of thrusting Syria into an even more markedly isolated position in the inter-Arab arena. In addition to its overt support of Iran, Syria was accused of torpedoing the Fahd Plan and causing the collapse of the November 1981 Fez summit (see below). Thus, the Israeli Knesset approval of the Golan Law of December 14, applying the Israeli law in the occupied Golan Heights, handed Damascus a cause with which to rebuff the sharp criticism of its policy and urge Arab solidarity with its confrontation role against Israel. Damascus could draw hope for such change in view of Washington's excoriation of the Israeli decision and suspension of the strategic memorandum of understanding that it had signed with Israel just three weeks earlier. Asad's round of visits a week later to Saudi Arabia and the Gulf emirates resulted in a renewal of diplomatic relations between Saudi Arabia and Libya and in a Syrian-Kuwaiti mediation initiative aimed at ending the Gulf war. However, both Iran and Iraq rejected the Syrian mediation effort. The Iraqi government again castigated the Asad regime for supporting Iran, accusing it of indirect collusion with Israel, which was also supplying arms to Iran.[41]

Despite Asad's and Khaddam's consecutive visits to the Gulf monarchies in late 1981 and early 1982 respectively, Syria failed to obtain the former's approval for using the oil weapon against the United States in retaliation for its veto of a UN resolution on sanctions against Israel. Syria also failed to obtain further financial aid from the Gulf monarchies, despite warnings that in the absence of additional funds Syria would have to tighten its strategic cooperation with the USSR as a counterweight to the U.S.-Israel accord. Obviously, the indifference evinced by most Arab regimes toward the Golan Law reflected Syria's isolation and growing domestic troubles, but also their displeasure at Syria's role in the Fez summit debacle, its alignment with Iran, and its hostile relations with Jordan. Meeting in February 1982, the Arab FMs refrained from committing themselves to costly action, resolving only to "reassess" Arab political and economic relations with countries that supported Israel and to work for Israel's expulsion from the UN.[42]

Meanwhile, tension between Jordan and Syria intensified, with the two regimes exchanging mutual accusations of responsibility for sabotage and other subversive activities. Jordan accused the Syrian regime of causing several explosions in Amman, and expelled the Syrian military attache, while Syria pointed to the infiltration of a Jordanian force into its territory and an attack against a border patrol. Overall, the Muslim Brotherhood's increasing violent activity against Asad's regime within Syria spurred Damascus to intensify its denunciations of Hashemite support for this activity. Syrian-Jordanian relations were further set back following King Husain's televised appeal to Jordanian youth on January 28, urging them to volunteer for the war against Iran in the name of defense of the Arab homeland. Husain's call, reflecting Iran's penetration into Iraqi territory, provoked fierce assaults from both Syria and Libya, which were, in turn, accused of betraying the Arab cause in the Gulf and of having "commercialized the Palestinian problem."[43]

The Muslim Brotherhood uprising in Hamah during February was indeed the most serious domestic test to Asad's regime since its ascendancy, forcing it to rush substantial military forces to Hamah to crush the uprising before it could spread outward. The uprising and its repression were a horrible testimony to the real domestic threats to Asad's regime and their implications on its antagonistic regional policy. Above all, the Hamah showdown attested to the regime's willingness to defend itself even at the cost of thousands of civilian lives and the destruction of large sections of the city.[44]

The growing internal tension in Syria intensified the regime's hostility toward regional enemies, primarily Iraq, which had been under escalated Iranian offensive. Both Damascus and Baghdad stepped up propaganda attacks, and violent subversion against each other through the use of opposition elements. At the height of the Hamah events, Damascus launched a furious diatribe against Saddam Husain, charging that "the butcher of Baghdad" was responsible for the Hamah events and questioning his Pan-Arab national motivation.[45]

The Gulf war had far-reaching economic implications on the Arab world as a whole, which were all the more burdensome due to Syria's strategic alignment with Iran. In mid-March 1982, Syria and Iran signed agreements on economic cooperation and trade worth $2 billion a year. Consequently, three weeks later Syria closed its border with Iraq and halted the flow of Iraqi oil through Syrian territory to Mediterranean terminals—a devastating blow to Iraq's economy and a further economic burden on the Gulf Arab states. This action, it later emerged, was performed in exchange for Iran's agreement to supply Syria 8.7 million tons of crude oil a year for ten years at a reduced price. Syria's move deprived Iraq of more than a quarter of its oil revenues (an annual shortfall of $4–5 billion); Baghdad was now reduced to a single oil pipeline through Turkey and compelled to build another, through Saudi territory, at a staggering cost. Concurrently, the Iranians on March 22 launched a new offensive, inflicting another defeat on Iraq and capturing the remaining Iranian territory that Iraq had seized. In their offensive, the Iranians evidently used large quantities of Soviet arms, supplied by Syria with Moscow's knowledge and tacit assent. As a result, the Iraq-Syria propaganda war became even more heated, and tension flared up along their border. The closure of the Iraqi pipeline not only showed Syria's determination to bring down Saddam Husain's regime. It strengthened Damascus' bargaining position vis-à-vis the Arab sphere as well as with Iran. Asad's formal alliance with Iran might have been a response to Egypt's growing collaboration with Iraq (in March, Egypt agreed to sell Iraq $ 1.5 billion worth of self-made ammunition and used Soviet-made weapons) and the prospect which was being mooted, of Egypt's return to the Arab fold once Israel completed its withdrawal from Sinai, slated for April 25, 1982.[46]

The Gulf war's cumulative effect on the oil monarchies, combined with the sharp plunge of revenues, led to substantial reduction of financial aid to the confrontation states and the PLO. Iraq's worsening military situation and economic straits concerned primarily Kuwait and Saudi Arabia, leading to repeated efforts on their part to conciliate Syria and Iraq. The Saudis, however, who were afraid of alienating Syria, given its potential role in helping either to end the war or to threaten the Gulf states' security, continued to give Damascus most of the aid pledged at the 1978 Baghdad summit. In fact, the Saudis preferred to go on paying off both Iraq and Syria rather than try to punish the latter. Although reports that they intended to halt aid to Syria proved unfounded, the Syrians let it be known that such a step would not go by unheeded.[47]

Between 1981 and 1986, Iraq received more than $40 billion from Saudi Arabia and Kuwait, mostly in grants. By the end of 1986, its external debt had mounted to $55 billion, half of which was to be paid to Saudi Arabia and Kuwait. It is noteworthy that the scope of aid to Iraq exceeded by far the total financial aid ever given to all the states confronting Israel. The massive support for Iraq reflected the donors' recognition that it was shielding them from the spread of Iran's Islamic revolution, as well as direct Iraqi threats. Indeed, the combination of extreme vulnerability to domestic and foreign threats and an abundance of oil wealth brought the use of financial resources by the GCC states as a means of national security to the limits of absurd. Equally absurd were the normal relations the Gulf Arab states continued to maintain with Iran (even Iraq officially severed its diplomatic relations with Iran only in late Summer 1987), while, at the same time, their relations with Egypt remained severed.[48]

The GCC monarchies were in a dilemma regarding the Gulf war. Particularly Kuwait and Saudi Arabia, while seeking to minimize their political and material commitments to Iraq and vulnerability to Iran, could not overlook Iran's military and religious threat to their own national security. At the same time, some of the GCC member states, primarily Oman and the UAE, maintained friendly relations with Iran, while others also insisted on keeping the road open to conciliation with Tehran. Thus, despite frantic reactions to Iran's military successes and dire warnings in their media of the consequences should Iran harm them, the GCC members were constantly reluctant to join a firm collective anti-Iranian resolution, as repeatedly urged by Iraq. In the wake of Iran's recapture of Khoramshahr, an emergency meeting of the GCC FMs (May 31, 1982) issued only a lukewarm call for a united Arab stand in order to end the war.[49]

As for Iraq, confronted with Iran's military pressure on the battlefield, from late 1981 on, it made repeated efforts to obtain a collective resolution committing the Arab world to stand by Iraq according to the AL Charter and the ACSP, but to no avail. Iraq requested that the Arab world put the Iraq-Iran war on an equal footing with the Arab-Israeli conflict, which would entail Arab political and material backing for Iraq. Whether such a declarative commitment would have fundamentally altered Arab states' policies regarding the Gulf war is doubtful. However, given its desperate war for survival, Iraq could not overlook any possibility of attaining moral gains that might be transformed into material payoffs. Indeed, the sweeping nature of such an Arab commitment to Iraq made it rather impractical, especially in view of other armed conflicts between Arab and non-Arab states.[50]

Israel's invasion of Lebanon provided Iraq with an opportunity to enlist Arab support without losing face. On June 20, Saddam Husain declared his intention to unilaterally withdraw all his forces from Iranian soil (ostensibly in order to help rebuff Israel's invasion) if the Arab states aligned themselves unreservedly with him in accordance with the AL Charter. The Iraqi announcement was a recognition of military reality more than any signal of willingness for concessions. At any rate, the Gulf states did not do anymore for Baghdad, and this response remained unchanged despite a new Iranian offensive in the south, launched July 14 toward Basra, within Iraqi territory. The Gulf states' stand was reinforced when the Iranian offensive bogged down and the battlefield situation remained deadlocked.[51]

The Iraqi effort scored only a minor success at the Fez summit held in the aftermath of the Lebanon war. Under pressure from the heads of the Gulf states, Jordan, and Morocco, Syria accepted a resolution by which it undertook "to defend all the Arab lands and to view any act of aggression against any Arab region anywhere as tantamount to aggression against all the Arab countries." Despite Baghdad's entreaties, the Arab leaders were unwilling to anchor this undertaking in the AL Charter and the ACSP. Indeed, they might well have wished to leave it vague. Yet for the first time Iraq secured general Arab verbal support, encompassing also the SRF states represented at the meeting.[52]

The decision, however, turned out to have made no effect on Syria. Neither Syria's assent to the resolution, nor the meeting held during the conference between the Iraqi and Syrian presidents made any change whatsoever in Syria's hostile position. Reports on a possible reconciliation were at once denied by both countries. Syria's clarification of its position toward the Iraq-Iran war was particularly sharp, in order to allay Iranian apprehensions, stating that Syria continued to oppose Saddam Husain and to desire his downfall. In reporting the conference, the Syrian media totally ignored the resolution dealing with the Gulf war.[53]

Another Iraqi attempt to win an unequivocal and useful support resolution was made at the Casablanca summit in August 1985, but in vain. While it took a strong tone in reaffirming the commitment made at Fez in support of Iraq, the summit did not go beyond warning Iran that continued refusal to end the war might lead Arab governments to reconsider relations with it. The summit opted to confine its action toward Iran to diplomacy through an Arab committee of FMs, established in March 1984 at Iraq's request to exert pressure on Iran to end the war. Yet even this resolution was militantly attacked by Syria, Libya, and Iran, whose FMs, gathering in Damascus, condemned the "Saddam-Husain-Mubarak-'Arafat axis," underlining Iran's deepening involvement in regional Arab politics.[54]

The Gulf War as a Focal Arab Issue

In 1986 the Iraq-Iran war, stalemated on the front lines, began spilling over into the Gulf, posing a direct danger to the Arab monarchies' security and drawing in the United States. Egypt's centrality in the Arab world gained further acknowledgment but remained resisted by Syria. Arab conciliatory efforts, undertaken by Saudi Arabia in accordance with the Casablanca summit resolutions, brought on rapprochement between Syria and Jordan, but failed to bridge the gap between Syria and Iraq.

Asad's positive response to Arab mediation efforts with Jordan reflected a convergence of mutual interests and severe economic constraints. Syria was willing to resume diplomatic relations with Jordan despite continued contention on the Gulf war and Amman's renewed diplomatic relations with Egypt in 1984, in order to deepen the PLO's isolation and attain more control of the renewed American peace efforts. On the economic front, the annual Arab aid had fallen by one-third, while Syria was suffering from lack of basic commodities, high inflation, and a decline of foreign currency reserves resulting from high defense expenditures plus a $14 billion external debt, mostly to the Soviet Union. In his April 1987 visit to Moscow, Asad came to learn from the new Soviet leader Mikhail Gorbachev that Moscow would not continue to support Syria's concept of "strategic parity," suggesting instead a coordinated effort to advance a settlement of the conflict with Israel.[55]

The alliance with Iran became a liability for Syria, as Iran held Arab Iraqi land and threatened the Gulf monarchies. The Shi'i siege of Palestinian refugee camps in Lebanon, perceived to be backed by Damascus, further eroded Syria's Arab legitimacy. Iran's support for its radical Shi'i client Hizballah posed a challenge to Syria's dominance in Lebanon and occasionally soured relations with Damascus. By late 1985, Iran-Syria relations had deteriorated over financial differences, resulting in the cessation of Iranian oil shipments to Syria.[56] Syria's moderated militancy might also have been influenced by the bombing raid in April 1986 against Qadhafi's military headquarters and residence for sponsoring terrorism against American targets and subverting U.S. allies in the region. Syria, itself a major terrorist sponsor, drew a lesson from the Arab states' reluctance to do anything to help Qadhafi beyond denouncing the American attack.

Inter-Arab mediating efforts after March 1986 focused on improving Syria-Iraq relations in order to undercut the Iranian menace and bring an end to the Gulf war. Led by the Jordanian and Saudi monarchs, they labored for more than a year to organize a summit meeting between Asad and Saddam Husain, but to no avail. Syria wanted full Iraqi commitment to its own priority—the conflict with Israel—but had little to offer in return, since it could not persuade Iran to end the war. Iraq insisted that Syria should take a neutral position in the Gulf war and establish normal relations with it before any further steps were taken. Normalization was indeed a common interest of both sides in terms of opening their common border and, particularly, renewing the flow of Iraqi oil to the Mediterranean via Syria's territory. Even this, however, became less crucial to Iraq's economy in view of the alternative oil transportation systems via Turkey and Saudi Arabia that had been developed during the war. In fact, Damascus seemed interested in using the prospect of conciliation with Iraq as a lever to gain Iranian concessions, a strategy that led to an Iranian agreement, in Summer 1986, to renew oil shipments to Syria for six months just as a meeting of Iraq's and Syria's FMs seemed imminent.[57]

Meanwhile, in the stalemated Iraq-Iran war, largely fought on Iraq's territory since early 1983, Baghdad escalated the conflict in order to force Iran to accept Arab and international mediation efforts. As of Spring 1984, Iraq embarked on missile attacks on Iranian cities; the use of chemical weapons; and air attacks on Iran's main oil terminal and means of transport, as well as on tankers and other ships carrying its cargo. Iran responded by widening the tankers' war and escalating direct military threats to Kuwait's oil industry. Iranian missile attacks and subversion against Kuwait in the early months of 1987, led the latter to request U.S. reflagging for its oil tankers, which, together with reinforcement of Western fleets in the Gulf, meant an internationalization of the war. Once again in its short history, Kuwait's vulnerability and skepticism about Arab support left it no choice but to appeal for Western protection. In July, the United States and other Western states sponsored UNSC Resolution 598, urging an immediate cease-fire between Iraq and Iran.

The presence of Western warships in the Gulf exacerbated the tension between the Arab camps aligned with Iraq and Iran, provoking a highly-charged anti-Western sentiment. Saudi Arabia, Kuwait, and Iraq favored the warships as necessary to bring pressure to bear on Iran to end the war. In contrast, the radical states perceived any American military presence in the area as "imperialism" and a menace to their regimes, preferring instead an international force under UN auspices and incorporating the Soviet Union as well. The "ideological" rift was further aggravated by the U.S. decision to give Iraq $1 billion in food aid in 1988, while banning the import of Iranian oil. Iran's direct threat to Kuwait prompted a new Saudi-Jordanian mediating effort between Syria and Iraq, which was also undertaken by the Soviets. In April, Asad and Saddam Husain met twice at their common border. In their talks, the rival Ba'thi leaders took the same inflexible stances as before, although the summits did result in a temporary mitigation of their mutual hostility through cessation of media propaganda, an exchange of prisoners, and a mutual halting of subversion.[58]

The acuteness of the Gulf war as a regional issue gathered momentum in Summer 1987, which saw the Iranian-provoked bloodbath in Mecca on July 31, during the annual pilgrimage (*hajj*); escalated subversive and terrorist activities by extreme Shi'i groups in the Gulf monarchies; the UNSG's efforts to promote implementation of SC Resolution 598 and the possible application of sanctions against Iran should it refuse to heed it. Under these circumstances, the long-delayed Arab collective action was resumed when the AL FMs' meeting in Tunis, on September 20, called for convening an emergency summit in Amman on November 8, to discuss the Gulf war.[59]

Convening an Arab summit, however, depended primarily on Syria, which had expressed constant objection to any summit devoted to discussing the Gulf war, threatening to boycott the meeting unless it focused upon the Arab-Israeli conflict. Further, Syria and Libya vigorously opposed imposing any sanctions on Iran, maintaining that the war's termination required, first and foremost, the withdrawal of foreign fleets from the Gulf. The Saudis once again found themselves in the position of mediators between Syria and Iraq, willing to meet Syria's demand by including in the agenda the Arab-Israeli conflict and Lebanon's situation. Iraq, however, opposed such a move, fearing that it would diminish the significance of the Gulf war as the summit's central issue. Baghdad insisted upon the need to reach "practical and effective" resolutions on support for Iraq and the imposition of sanctions on Iran if it continued refusing to implement Security Council Resolution 598. The Iraq-Syria controversy was resolved and Saddam Husain's participation confirmed only when the summit actually convened, following vigorous mediation efforts by the Saudi and Jordanian monarchs.[60]

The Iranian missile attack on Kuwait in October and the imminent summit lent new urgency for readmitting Egypt to the AL, further eroding Syria's opposition on that matter. Egyptian leaders were quick to voice full solidarity with Kuwait, maintaining that "the defense of the Gulf is an integral part of Arab national security." These declarations were accompanied by diplomatic contacts with Kuwait and by press statements regarding military aid to Kuwait in exchange for economic aid to Egypt. Some Arab governments announced their intention to resume diplomatic relations with Egypt due to the escalation of the Gulf war and the important role Egypt could play in strengthening Arab defenses there.[61]

The upcoming summit stimulated vigorous inter-Arab efforts, particularly on King Husain's part, for conciliation among rivals—however superficial and temporary—to ensure the maximum presence of heads of state at the summit. Particularly salient was the resumption of diplomatic relations in September between Libya, on the one hand, and Jordan (which had renewed diplomatic relations with Egypt in 1984) and Iraq, on the other. This attested to Libya's declining position in the region due to a series of setbacks: the plunge of oil prices, the American air raid in the previous year, a severe blow to its military involvement in Chad, and loss of its influence on the Sudanese regime to Egypt. In view of the summit's intention to discuss Egypt's return to the Arab fold, however, Qadhafi absented himself from the meeting, as he had done since 1969.[62]

Despite efforts at conciliation, inter-Arab disputes remained unresolved both in the Maghreb—revolving around the Sahara conflict—and in the core Palestinian conflict system. Jordan-PLO relations had been abrogated in the wake of the Amman Accord's breakdown (see below, Ch. 14). Palestinian refugee camps in Beirut and Sidon were still besieged by the Syrian-backed Shi'i Amal movement, despite 'Arafat's efforts with Damascus and the Algerian-mediated PLO-Amal agreement of February 1987 on ending the siege. Relations between the presidents of Syria and Lebanon had been broken off two years previously, due to the latter's objection to the Lebanese inter-communal conciliation agreement signed in Damascus in December of 1985, under Syrian auspices.[63]

The proliferation and severity of the inter-Arab conflicts again was reflected by the urgent call in Arab media, primarily in the Gulf states, Egypt, Jordan, and the PLO, to Arab leaders to cooperate, portraying the imminent summit as the "last chance" to extricate the Arab nation from its division and weakness. Especially strong was the Palesinians' quest to restore their problem to the top of the Arab agenda. The imminent meeting between President Reagan and Chairman Gorbachev in December in Washington was also taken up, to emphasize the need for unity and pragmatic decisions at the Amman summit.[64]

The controversy over the summit's agenda and fear of its premature breakdown led to an unprecedented decision to forgo the prior convening of the FMs to set the agenda and left this task to the heads of state. This facilitated the radical leaders' decision to participate without being committed to a specific agenda dictated by their rivals. This, however, was bound to result in compromises and half-tone resolutions on the Gulf war as well as on other issues on the agenda in order to demonstrate unity and prevent the summit's collapse. The uncertain fate of the summit underlay King Fahd's decision to abstain from attending the conference, sending Crown Prince 'Abdallah in his place. His decision was attributed to vigorous Syrian opposition to imposing diplomatic sanctions on Iran and differences among the GCC states themselves on such a motion.[65]

For the first time in the annals of Arab summit conferences, the Arab-Israeli conflict was not the focal issue of the Amman meeting, despite Syria's prior warnings that it would not allow a "marginal" issue such as the Iran-Iraq war to dominate the summit. The Iran-Iraq war and the situation in the Gulf topped the summit agenda, as would be noted in its concluding statement. The Iranian challenge to the summit, expressed by the firing of two ground-to-ground missiles at Baghdad during its opening ceremony, underscored the urgency of this issue. Indeed, most of the four-day conference was dedicated to vigorous efforts by King Husain, heads of the GCC states, and Algeria's president Bin Jadid to persuade Asad to come to terms with his sworn enemy Saddam Husain and accept a collective resolution condemning Iran and calling for sanctions against it.

Saddam Husain's demand for a resolution expressing unequivocal support for Iraq and promoting efforts to terminate the war was undercut by both the Gulf states' indecisive stance and the radicals' objections. The concluding statement and the secret resolutions on the Gulf war were a tolerable compromise for Syria, Algeria, and certainly for the UAE and Oman, whose close relations with Iran precluded their backing a harsh decision. Thus, the call for applying UN sanctions against Iran for failing to implement Resolution 598, reflected an effort on part of the GCC states to avoid a clash with Iran, delegating that duty to others. The concluding statement condemned Iran only moderately, referring to its occupation of Iraqi territory and procrastination in accepting Resolution 598. The conference also confirmed its solidarity with and support for Iraq and Kuwait in confronting the Iranian regime's aggression and protecting their territory and waters. More unequivocal was the denunciation to the "criminal acts perpetrated by the Iranians . . . in Mecca."[66]

This was the first time since the war had broken out that Syria had been a party to any resolution that both condemned Iran for occupying Iraqi territory and explicitly supported Iraq. Furthermore, the secret resolutions stipulated that the Arab states would "reassess" their economic relations with any country supplying arms to Iran, should it continue its offensive against the Gulf states. Obviously, the resolution did not require cutting diplomatic relations with Iran, and—in light of the secret nature of arms supplies—had limited real value on restraining Syria. As to the presence of Western fleets in the Gulf, Syria gave its consent to the measures taken by Kuwait—requesting U.S. protection for its oil tankers—as a self-defense necessity against Iranian attacks. To avoid resentful Iranian response to Asad's concessions at the summit, however, the Syrian media omitted any mention of the condemnation of Iran, claiming that Asad had blocked a united anti-Iran position. Damascus also sought to deny the very fact of a conciliatory meeting between Asad and Saddam Husain during the summit.[67]

Syria's cooperation on decisions condemning Iran, as well as regarding the situation in the Gulf and renewal of diplomatic relations with Egypt, was apparently obtained in return for the Gulf monarchies' promises to provide Syria with additional financial aid. Syria was reportedly promised $2–2.5 billion, part of which it would receive immediately. Most of the aid, however, would be delivered in installments contingent on Syria's implementing the resolutions. The Iraqi-Syrian conciliation, reportedly achieved between Asad and Saddam Husain, turned to be reluctant, temporary, and fragile. Thus, political relations remained unchanged, although the two regimes ceased their mutual propaganda attacks and renewed telephone communication.[68]

Because of the urgency and prominence of the Gulf war at the summit, Syria insisted that the concluding documents of the summit express collective Arab commitment toward the Palestine conflict and define such commitment in terms of strengthening Arab capabilities for the confrontation. The summit put forward two separate documents: a vaguely-phrased communique, and secret resolutions, ostensibly more concrete, which were meant to appease Syria. Thus, the secret resolutions pointed to the need to consolidate the entire Arab potential in order to achieve strategic balance with Israel, reasserting a comprehensive settlement of the conflict. Regarding the Palestinian issue, the final communique reiterated that the Palestinian problem was "the core and essence" of the conflict with Israel, and that there would be no peace without the restoration of all the occupied Arab territories, including Jerusalem. The secret resolutions used stronger phrases that could be interpreted as referring to the pre-1967 Palestine: "the struggle for restoration of the plundered Arab rights in Palestine and the return of occupied Arab lands is a Pan-Arab [*qawmi*] responsibility." These resolutions also called for the attainment of material and moral support for the Palestinian people's struggle against Israel.

The Amman summit marked the end of a ten-year period of collective financial aid to the confrontation states and the Palestinians, established at the 1978 Baghdad summit. Since then, Saudi Arabia had been the only state that had stood up to its full financial commitments to Syria, Jordan, the PLO, and the Palestinians in the occupied territories, which were to have received a total of $3.5 billion a year from the oil-producing countries, including Iraq. Effectively, Libya and Algeria had avoided fulfilment of their share. Starting in 1981, Iraq itself had become a recipient of Arab aid, while most GCC states, including Kuwait, had reduced significantly the amounts of aid they offered. In light of falling oil prices, increasing domestic and regional security needs, and the enormous volume of support to Iraq, the GCC states had defined themselves as "confrontation states," legitimizing the hoarding of their own resources and limiting aid to other Arab countries.[69]

The Amman summit, the first in five years to include all AL members, represented a collective effort to end inter-Arab differences and the continued erosion of Arab strategic capabilities due to the exclusion of Egypt, the Syria-Iraq rift, and the exhausting Iraq-Iran war. In practice, however, the summit's main result was the legitimacy given to restoration of diplomatic relations with Egypt. The ideal picture of reconciled inter-Arab relations was no more than a temporary facade that concealed further fragmentation and departure from the Palestinian issue. The summit indicated the growing weight of the oil-rich Gulf states in shaping the Arab strategic priorities due to their financial resources and direct stake in the war. Thus, the summit legitimized the primacy of investing Arab economic and military inputs in the war against Iran. This was reflected in the use of terminology borrowed from the vocabulary of the conflict with Israel: the Gulf countries were portrayed as "Gulf confrontation states;" the Arab effort against the Iranian threat was termed "defense of legitimate Arab rights"; and the Gulf war constituted a "threat to the entire Arab nation." In contrast, the Amman summit highlighted the weakened position of the radical states, particularly Syria, due to its ideological and political isolation and economic predicament. These two factors forced Damascus to demonstrate solidarity with Iraq, to join the condemnation of Iran, and to acquiesce in a resolution that paved the way for most of the Arab states to resume diplomatic relations with Egypt.

13

CROSSROADS OF THE LEBANON WAR

Israel's invasion of Lebanon and its declared aim of eliminating the Palestinian semi-autonomous territorial base in that country put to test the Arab state's commitment to the PLO as a political structure as well as to the region's order and stability. The Arab states system's disarray and strategic weakness was salient in its response to Israel's military offensive and long siege of Beirut, which ranged between compliance and tacit collaboration with the latter's goal to expel the armed PLO personnel and headquarters from Lebanon. Indeed, nowhere else was the Arab states system's impact so evident as when it practically eliminated the PR's autonomous foothold in Lebanon. Underpinning this compliance was the strong adherence to the principles of national sovereignty and territorial integrity shared by all Arab states and supported by a wide Lebanese consensus. The destruction of the Palestinian armed presence in Lebanon, and Israel's lingering withdrawal from Lebanon, expedited radical socio-political changes in this country on the way to reshaping of its political system.

The Lebanon war taught both Israel and the PLO a lesson of political realism concerning the limits of military power. Israel's partial achievements in the war generated new problems, primarily the rise of militant Shi'i resistance in south Lebanon, which proved to be far more effective than the PR. The PLO proved its political vitality despite the military blow it sustained. Moreover, the war exacerbated the acuteness of the Palestinian problem as an international issue. To the PLO, the war embodied the conditional nature of Arab support for its cause and the threats to its independence from jealous regimes such as Syria's. The PLO's loss of their autonomous base in Lebanon and the rise of international awareness to the Palestinian cause reaffirmed all the more the growing significance of political flexibility and diplomacy as a means for survival and tangible gains in the Arab-Israeli relations.

The Southern Lebanon Imbroglio

In 1977, Lebanon's hopes for national conciliation following the Riyad and Cairo summits had steadily faded out, giving way to renewed tension and violence on both domestic and regional fronts. The main obstacle derived from the PLO's refusal to fully implement the provisions of 1969 Cairo Agreement, primarily in southern Lebanon. Syria's efforts to restrict Palestinian armed presence outside of the refugee camps scored only partial success. 'Arafat managed to procrastinate, and ultimately ignore, his commitment to full execution of the Cairo Agreement by the PR through typical manipulation of inter-Arab differences over its practical interpretation.

Differences indeed prevailed within the quadripartite supervisory committee assigned to implement the Riyad and Cairo summits' resolutions. Ever since his election to the presidency, Elias Sarkis had insisted on strict application of the Cairo Agreement and restoration of Lebanon's sovereignty in the south, through redeployment of newly restored Lebanese army units, as a prerequisite for Lebanese national reconciliation. In contrast, Egypt, Saudi Arabia, and Kuwait, eager to avoid a clash with the PLO and resume peace diplomacy, effectively supported the latter's claim for maintaining the status quo in view of Israel's military threat to the PR presence in southern Lebanon. Indeed, the no-man's-land character of that area helped the PLO avoid the summit's resolutions regarding its position in Lebanon, while its proximity to the Israeli border diminished Syria's ability to gain effective control of the PR in the area.[1]

With Sadat's visit to Jerusalem in November 1977 and the consequent inter-Arab repercussions, the diplomatic impasse of the Lebanese crisis gave way to renewed inter-factional and Lebanese-PLO disputes. Sadat's bold peace initiative all but extinguished Syria's willingness to get entangled in pressuring the PLO to limit its armed presence and activity on Lebanese soil. Representing the core of the conflict with Israel, the PLO was an indispensable ally in Damascus' endeavors to consolidate an Arab nationalist front against Egypt. The Lebanese conundrum was further complicated by the growing Israeli political and military involvement in Lebanon—in support for the Christian militias in the north since the civil war and more evidently along its southern border. Even before Operation Litani Israel had incrementally applied its patronage over this zone, based on civil and armed collaboration by the local Maronite population, and led by Lebanese army officers. Thus, what had begun as humanitarian support for southern Lebanese Christians effectively dragged Israel into active military alliance with this population against Palestinian encroachment.

The Israel-Egypt peace process exacerbated the tension between Syria and Israel, indirectly affecting their Palestinian and Lebanese clients. Israel deepened its involvement in southern Lebanon to go along with its growing secret military and intelligence cooperation with the Lebanese Maronite factions in the north, while Syria and the PLO closed ranks on the latter's deployment in the south. Given the impotence of the Sarkis government, this schism paved the road to renewal of the civil war and increasingly violent clashes in Beirut between the Syrian army and the Maronite militias, led by the Phalange Party (*hizb al-kata'ib*). The heavy bombardments of Christian neighborhoods by the Syrian army, shortly after the Camp David accords had been signed, established the formula that would ultimately drag Israel into the Lebanese fray.[2]

Although the Lebanese question remained on the collective Arab agenda, it scored no tangible progress. The Baghdad summit reaffirmed the Riyad and Cairo resolutions, expressing support for Lebanon's efforts to apply its sovereignty on its territory as a whole, including the south. In Summer 1979, the issue of south Lebanon came to the fore, following intensive armed clashes between Palestinian guerrillas and the Israeli-backed Christian militia in this area. Local Shi'i inhabitants, caught in the middle, suffered mounting casualties and property damage, and were increasingly driven to migrate to the north, aggravating the Lebanese economic depression. Renewed efforts by the Beirut government to send army units to the south were stymied by the Palestinians and Israelis alike. Toward the Tunis summit conference, Lebanese President Sarkis lobbied the Arab world to place the situation in Lebanon—especially in the south—high on the agenda as an integral part of the conflict with Israel.

The Lebanese issue was the most divisive item on the summit agenda. The Sarkis government submitted a plan that demanded specific measures to secure the restoration of Lebanon's sovereignty in the south. These measures included stationing Lebanese army units there and severely restricting the activity of the Palestinian groups: they would pull back to north of the Litani River and desist from issuing communiques from Lebanese territory following actions against Israel. The paper also gave an itemized account of the damage inflicted on the country by the fighting, and an estimate of the financial aid needed for rebuilding. Yet under the current inter-Arab circumstances, the Lebanese plan had no chance to be accepted, especially by the PLO or Syria.[3]

Before the summit had convened, the PLO had already expressed opposition to Lebanon's demands that the PR curtail its activity on Lebanese territory. Syria also took a dim view of Sarkis's intention to raise the Lebanon issue at the summit meeting, which could give Iraq a pretext to suggest a general review of the Syrian role in Lebanon. Yet Syria could not reject either the summit itself, which would jeopardize the Arab financial aid, or handling the issue of south Lebanon in the context of the conflict with Israel. Arab governments were largely unwilling to impinge on the PLO's status in Lebanon, particularly in the south, thereby effectively backing the PLO's adamant opposition to any restriction on its activity on Lebanese soil. In line with

Syria's logic, however, most Arab governments could not deny the urgency of
the Lebanon problem in the context of the conflict with Israel. Thus, they were
finally impelled to discuss possible aid to the inhabitants of the south.[4]

Indeed, Lebanon was bound to pay the price for this constellation of
inter-Arab interests because it constituted the weakest party in the dispute.
Besides provoking the embarrassing demand to allow guerrilla activity to be
launched from Jordan and Syria, any attempt to dislodge the PLO from its
entrenched positions in Lebanon could incite the wrath of the PR against
conservative oil producers. Especially for Damascus, to openly undercut the
PLO would be self-defeating when the Palestinian issue was the spearhead of
its struggle against the Israel-Egypt peace process. This was clearly expressed
at the Arab FMs' meeting to prepare the summit, when a majority of the
participants supported the Syrian proposals, gliding over basic differences with
ambiguous, self-contradictory rhetoric.[5]

While sounding the alarm against Israeli intervention in southern
Lebanon, Syria contorted itself in trying to satisfy everyone, calling at the same
time for restoration of Lebanese military and civilian sovereignty over the
south and reiterating the PR's right "to wage its struggle on all the Arab fronts."
In effect, Syria sought to establish coordination between the PLO and the
Lebanese government based on previous inter-Arab resolutions that had reaffirmed both Syria's military presence in Lebanon and Palestinian military
activity on Lebanese soil. Notwithstanding strong Lebanese objection, the
Syrian formulation was generally accepted by the FMs and was referred to the
summit for approval.

The Lebanon issue triggered a heated argument and mutual recriminations between President Sarkis and the PLO's 'Arafat. Sarkis stated that the
Lebanon problem could not be resolved as long as the PR remained on
Lebanese soil. Lebanon, he said, had neither the desire nor the ability to serve
as the Arab world's prime battleground, while also being the only country to
pay the price of the Palestinian problem. He urged the conference to restrict the
activity of the PR and call for their withdrawal from Lebanon. Yet these
grievances fell on deaf ears. Sarkis came under heavy pressure—primarily
from Asad—to accept an agreement with 'Arafat based on the Syrian proposals. Sarkis was urged to withdraw his objection to the PR's continued
presence in southern Lebanon; implicitly, this was understood to be a proviso
for the allocation of economic aid to Lebanon. The agreed formula resembled
an attempt to square the circle, urging coordination between Lebanon and the
PLO and declaring that Lebanese forces could deploy throughout Lebanon,
while the PR would remain in the UNIFIL-controlled areas in the south. 'Arafat
undertook to suspend temporarily Palestinian military activity from southern
Lebanon, although the clause stating that the Palestinians could operate against
Israel on all fronts remained intact. The final resolution represented the Arab

leaders' desire to avoid appearing to impinge on Lebanon's sovereignty while effectively sacrificing it in deference to the PLO. The Lebanese President had to swallow the bitter pill of having his requests rejected, hoping that the summit would compensate him with substantial financial aid.[6]

Sarkis having agreed to withdraw his objection, it was resolved to grant Lebanon reconstruction aid totalling $2 billion for a five-year period beginning in 1980. The annual sum of $400 million was far lower than Lebanon's original request; moreover, the resolution stipulated that only half the funds were to be earmarked for rehabilitation, with the remainder to go toward bolstering the country's "steadfastness." Only Saudi Arabia, Iraq, Qatar, Kuwait, and the UAE undertook to provide their share of the aid to Lebanon. Algeria informed Lebanon that it was precluded from contributing due to economic difficulties, and Libya refused to pay anything at all.[7]

The summit resolutions were not designed to solve the problem of south Lebanon but to maintain the status quo and induce the Beirut government to live with it. Although it had been the main item on the agenda, the southern Lebanon issue was obscured in the conference's final communique and resolutions. Not only did the summit sidestep almost all of Beirut's requests, but the entire issue was put under the category of the "Arab-Zionist conflict." The official statement was a vivid example of legitimizing collective inaction by indulging in long-winded, highly rhetorical phraseology in the context of the conflict with Israel: the Palestinian question was the essence of "the fateful Arab struggle to preserve its civilization" against "the Zionist menace that threatens the whole Arab nation." The summit lauded the role of the PR, reaffirmed resolutions of previous summits expressing the all-Arab commitment to the recovery of Palestinian national rights and the prohibition of separate solutions to the Arab-Israeli conflict. Yet beyond the summit's rhetorical support for the PLO, the latter was strongly criticized in the Gulf media for its involvement in internal Lebanese affairs and objection to sovereign Lebanese demands based on a wide national consensus.[8]

Syria's dominant role in shaping the summit's resolutions on southern Lebanon also determined the follow-up efforts to promote coordination between Lebanon and the PLO. The implementation of this decision was left to a committee—chaired by Lebanon's PM and comprised of Syria, the PLO, and the ALSG—which held intensive contacts with the Lebanese and PR factions involved in the civil war. It was obvious that without active Syrian involvement in support of Beirut's insistence on deploying its forces in the UNIFIL zone any effort of the follow-up committee would be in vain. Yet the Syrian member acted merely as an observer. The PLO professed itself ready to take a neutral stand and let the Lebanese Army deploy in the south, while effectively stepping up its armed activity and buildup of troops in that area. Israel, for its part, added fuel to the fire through further military involvement and efforts to prevent the deployment of Lebanese troops in south Lebanon. The growing migration of Shiʻi population to the north and armed clashes between the Lebanese Forces (LF)—the united Christian militias led by Bashir Jumayyil—and the Palestinians in Beirut, increased the likelihood of a major flareup.[9]

The Arab states' inability to take action to ease Lebanon's internal predicament was also manifested at the ICO conference held in Taʼif in January 1981. Sarkis, the only Christian head of state at the meeting, blamed the PLO for Israeli attacks on Lebanon and urged the participants to free his country from bearing the brunt of the Arab-Israeli conflict. Sarkis's pleas to the Islamic leaders to influence Syria and the PLO elicited only verbal responses: reassuring Lebanon's sovereignty and territorial integrity; calling on the AL to work out a comprehensive strategy toward Israel, and on the PLO to abide by its agreements with Lebanon. It was another demonstration of Arab-Muslim unity around a declarative anti-Israeli posture, concealing fierce inter-Arab disagreements and collective weakness.[10]

Prelude to War

Israel's invasion of Lebanon in June 1982 was born of the increasing political chaos in Lebanon as a whole and in its southern part in particular. Israel was pulled into the Lebanese web by its Christian proteges, but also pushed by its own political motives. Begin's right-wing government, having begun its second term as of July 1981, with Ariel Sharon as DM, was increasingly tempted to seize the opportunity presented by a perceived political and military freedom to maneuver on both regional and international levels in order to realize strategic goals on the northern front.

In early April 1981, heavy fighting broke out between the LF and Syrian army units, initially in Beirut and then in the predominantly Christian town of Zahlah in the Biqaʻ which came under Syrian siege, gradually pulling Israel into the fray. Israel's escalated intervention in Lebanon was apparently affected both by the LF's cries for help in the face of what had been exaggeratedly described as "genocide" and by its need to prove the credibility of its commitment to protect the Christians in Lebanon. Israel's decision was also influenced to no small degree by its apprehension of a Syrian takeover of the Biqaʻ and the peaks overlooking the port of Juniya, which had become the Maronites' lifeline to the outer world. For its part, Damascus saw the significance of the Biqaʻ and Zahlah as a possible breakthrough point for Israel in an armored attack on Syria.[11]

On April 28, Israel downed two Syrian helicopters near Zahlah, which provoked Syria to move anti-aircraft missiles into the Biqaʻ, announcing its determination to defend its strategic interests in Lebanon. The Syrian action clearly brought to an end the 1976 tacit understanding between the two governments on Syria's military presence in Lebanon. Israel held the Syrian step to be a violation of that understanding, which threatened its air force's freedom to maneuver in Lebanon, demanding the immediate removal of the missiles and threatening their destruction. The mounting tension over the missiles became a matter of concern for the two superpowers, both of which moved to calm their clients. The United States in particular was active in the efforts to defuse the tension. In fact, even before the Zahlah crisis, the growing potential for an Israeli-Syrian military flareup over Lebanon, coupled with President Sarkis's urgent appeals, had stimulated active diplomatic involvement by the new American administration in the Lebanese crisis. At the beginning of May, President Reagan dispatched a special envoy, Under-SoS Philip Habib, to the region as a mediator, using the crisis to demonstrate again Washington's exclusive ability to restrain Israel and show the Arabs its value as a power broker. Although Israel had planned to attack the missiles just before Habib's mission, and despite Begin's initial insistence on their removal, he eventually gave Habib his consent for a diplomatic resolution of the crisis.[12]

The missile crisis and the siege of Zahlah drew verbal expressions of support for Syria from Saudi Arabia and Kuwait, which pledged to place all their resources at Syria's disposal. Iraq, although bogged down in the war with Iran, declared its readiness to come to Syria's aid in the event of an Israeli attack. Jordan and Egypt, however, condemned Syria's attacks on Zahlah and called for withdrawal of its forces from Lebanon. Seeking to extract Egypt from its position of isolation in the Arab world, Sadat accused Asad of trying to drag the entire Middle East into war. He also reiterated his proposal that the PLO establish a Palestinian government-in-exile and meet with Israel at the retrieved town of al-'Arish in northern Sinai. On May 22, a special meeting of the Arab FMs in Tunis expressed full support for Syria and the PLO, ignoring Lebanon's appeal to end the war and assure its independence. Nevertheless, it was reportedly Habib's diplomatic endeavors and Saudi Arabia's mediating role—through the Arab follow-up committee for Lebanon—that paved the road to a solution of the Zahlah crisis and the removal of the Syrian siege on June 30.[13]

The escalating tension between Israel and Syria over Lebanon highlighted the growing linkage of Syrian and Lebanese national security, hence, Damascus' determination to veto the LF's collaboration with Israel. Backed by Saudi Arabia and the Sarkis government, Syria made its lifting the siege of Zahlah conditional on receiving Bashir Jumayyil's written commitment to cease all contacts with Israel. Moreover, Syria was anxious to secure its continued presence in Lebanon, particularly in view of the hostility evinced by Bashir Jumayyil who, in November 1981, called for the withdrawal of all Syrian troops from Lebanon. In June, the Sarkis government—with Shafiq al-Wazzan as PM—presented a similar demand to the Arab follow-up committee, within a comprehensive program for the resolution of the Lebanon crisis that would also include full implementation of the Cairo Agreement and cutting off contacts with Israel. It was against this backdrop that Syria initiated intensive contacts with Beirut, aimed at reaching an agreement on special bilateral relations to its own advantage, with a view toward the Lebanese presidential elections scheduled for September 1982. Syria allegedly sought to shape the results of the elections, evincing readiness to support the extension of Sarkis's term of office and play an active role in a national reconciliation encompassing all the rival communities in Lebanon.[14]

Amid Habib's deadlocked efforts to resolve the missile crisis, in mid-July international attention was shifted to a new military eruption in southern Lebanon. Massive Israeli air and sea strikes against Palestinian targets in this area as well as in Beirut were answered by Palestinian barrages of artillery shells and rockets on northern Israeli towns and villages. Yet Israeli attacks—notably the bombing of PLO headquarters in Beirut on July 17—not only failed to induce the PLO to cease its fire, but sparked mounting criticism from the U.S. White House and Congress. The suspension of arms shipments to Israel, initially applied following the air raid against the Iraqi reactor, was extended, and Habib was sent again to the region, this time to mediate between the PLO and Israel. Habib's efforts, which led to a tacit cease-fire agreement on July 24, constituted a milestone in the PLO's struggle for international recognition. Evidently, Habib's contacts with the PLO were conducted via Syrian, Lebanese, and Saudi intermediaries. However, the episode reaffirmed the anomaly of Washington's rejection of direct contacts with the PLO despite its crucial role in the Middle East conflict. No less disturbing for Jerusalem was the practical result of Habib's mediation, namely, a tacit cease-fire agreement between Israel and the PLO, another step toward the latter's international recognition.[15]

Despite the April–July crises in Lebanon, the Fez summit conference held in November continued to demonstrate inaction on this issue, contenting itself with declarative support against the "Israeli aggression." As in the past, the actual measures to be taken had been entrusted to a small committee—a proven method for shelving an issue through foot-dragging. Moreover, the statement of general Arab support for deploying Lebanon's army in the country's south had been so worded as to permit divergent interpretations. The upshot was that in the wake of Israel's Golan Law Syria wanted to use this committee on Lebanese affairs to formulate joint Arab strategy toward Lebanon and the Golan Heights as one front.[16]

Meanwhile, Israel was preparing for a comprehensive military attack on Lebanon in close collaboration with the LF. As of Summer 1981, Israel's core decision-making group on security and foreign affairs was comprised of militant figures, especially DM Sharon, FM Shamir, and CoS Eitan, who were determined both to eliminate the Palestinian military infrastructure in Lebanon and to drive the Syrians out of the country. Beyond the immediate goals of destroying the Palestinian military presence in southern Lebanon and the Syrian missiles in the Biqaʻ, Israel was reportedly aiming to implement a grand strategy, identified with DM Sharon, the main components of which were:

1. Elimination of the PLO as a military and political power, which would facilitate the implementation of Israel's autonomy plan in the occupied territories and the possible replacement of the Hashemite regime by a Palestinian government.
2. Creating a strong Lebanese government led by Bashir Jumayyil, that would ally itself with Israel and secure withdrawal of the Syrian forces from Lebanon.

Accordingly, the Israeli operation aimed to reach the area controlled by the LF and attack the Syrian forces, assuming that the U.S. stand was essentially supportive. The intensive military and political cooperation between Israel and the LF, including their shared operational plans, were no secret to the PLO and Syria. Based on intelligence—apparently leaked from Christian sources—as well as on press reports, as of Winter 1982 leading Syrian and Palestinian figures were warning of Israel's imminent invasion of Lebanon, with various estimates about its scope and goals.[17]

Although the July 1981 cease-fire sustained for nine months, it was doomed to fail because Israel demanded that it encompass all operations by the Palestinian groups while the radical Palestinian groups, primarily the PFLP and DFLP, resented any cease-fire across the international border. The internal Palestinian debate was aggravated by the ongoing unrest in the West Bank and Gaza Strip following Israel's repression measures against the local Palestinian leadership organized in the "Committee of National Guidance," including deportation and dismissal of Arab mayors. From the radicals' viewpoint, the cease-fire in southern Lebanon ran contrary to the PLO's commitment to assist the Palestinians in the occupied territories. Thus, a major explosion was only a matter of time, with leading figures on both sides looking for a pretext to extricate themselves from an undesirable cease-fire. In April and May, Israeli air force planes raided Palestinian bases in Lebanon in retaliation for hostilities in the "security zone," the later of which were answered by rocket barrages against Israel's northern towns by the DFLP. In mid-May, PM Begin declared the cease-fire in Lebanon null and void amid press reports of an Israeli military buildup on the border with Lebanon. Finally, the attempt on the life of Israel's ambassador in London by the Iraqi-backed Palestinian group led by Abu Nidal gave Israel the pretext to invade Lebanon on June 6, 1982.

The Arab States and Israel's Lebanon War

Israel's declared goal upon launching the "Peace for Galilee" operation was to destroy the armed Palestinian infrastructure in a forty-kilometer-deep zone in southern Lebanon, while avoiding a collision with the Syrian army in the Biqaʿ. Soon after its beginning, however, the Israeli offensive assumed unexpected political and military dimensions. On June 8, Israeli forces engaged in air and ground battles with the Syrians, provoking American pressure for a cease-fire, which was concluded on June 11. Concerning the Palestinians, however, Israel's military decisionmakers disregarded the cease-fire. By June 14, the first Israeli units linked up with the LF, beginning a ten-week siege of West Beirut aimed at destroying the armed Palestinian existence in the city. Israel's Lebanon war turned into a three-year-long bitter "war by choice" that shattered its society's consensus on national security and initiated war as a last resort, tarnishing the IDF's prestigious image. What was initially meant to be an amplified repetition of Operation Litani, effectively entangled Israel in a long and costly war motivated by DM Sharon's greater design.[18]

The inveterate weakness and splits in the inter-Arab alignment were starkly revealed during the Lebanon war, and especially during the Israeli siege of Beirut, lifted only when the armed Palestinians evacuated the city. The sense of despair marking the Arab world in this period recalled the aftermath of the June 1967 defeat. The Syrian regime came under fierce criticism from the PLO and rival Arab states, especially Egypt, Jordan, and Iraq, each of whom tried to seize the opportunity to help itself. Initially, Syria was condemned for standing aside and letting Israel hammer the Palestinians during the first three days of the war, and later for accepting a cease-fire after its forces were attacked by Israel. Even Syria's ally Libya joined the chorus.

The war revealed the inherent mistrust between the PLO and Syria, which grew bitter and led to mutual recriminations during the siege of Beirut. Syria accused ʿArafat of conducting diplomatic efforts aimed at reaching a separate peace settlement with Israel through American and Western European mediation, and collaboration with the Islamic (Sunni) opposition in Syria and northern Lebanon. The war presented the SRF as an empty vessel, labelled by a leading PLO figure "the talk front" for its inaction during the war. Although two of its members, Syria and the PLO, were directly involved in the war and consistently requested the Front's military support, Libya and Algeria remained unmoved. Although Damascus reciprocated by criticizing Arab indifference to the war, the Israeli invasion of Lebanon threw into bold relief Syria's isolation in the inter-Arab arena. The criticism of Syria was not merely an outlet for anger at that regime for "destroying Arab solidarity," in the words of Jordanian PM Badran. It was mainly geared to justify Arab governments' inaction on behalf of Syria and the Palestinians, by blaming Asad for the events.[19]

The outbreak of hostilities, and President Sarkis's call for convening an urgent summit meeting, triggered intensive inter-Arab contacts but drew no immediate response in Arab capitals. The Arab FMs convened only on June 27, at the demand of the PLO, whose leaders and most of whose armed forces had come under siege in Beirut by Israel and its Lebanese allies. Israeli forces put heavy pressure on the armed Palestinians and Syrian army units trapped in the city, while negotiating with them through U.S. mediator Habib to obtain their surrender and removal from Lebanon. The Sarkis government effectively endorsed Israel's demand, insisting that the armed Palestinians withdraw from Beirut and out of Lebanon.

That the Arab states were hardly interested in a summit conference was shown in the fact that only nine of them were represented at the June 27 assembly of their FMs. Given the divided viewpoints of the participating states, the only decision taken was to establish a six-member committee composed of the FMs of Saudi Arabia, Kuwait, Syria, Lebanon, Algeria, and a PLO representative. The committee was appointed to hold contacts with the superpowers to expedite implementation of the UNSC resolutions on a cease-fire and withdrawal of Israeli forces from Lebanon. In practice, the committee, chaired by the Saudi FM, served henceforth as an inter-Arab "umbrella" for Saudi diplomacy conducted by King Fahd himself from his summer resort at Ta'if.[20]

Beginning in late June, Ta'if was visited by King Husain, Bashir Jumayyil—empowered by President Sarkis as his candidate for presidency—and Asad, following which the Saudis could submit to Habib the Arab response to Israel's ultimatum demanding the evacuation of the PLO's leadership and armed forces from Beirut. The U.S. mediating role in the crisis was conspicuous both in the Middle East and Washington. Before Israeli forces had begun the siege of Beirut, Washington had made clear its viewpoint regarding a settlement of the crisis, based on the total withdrawal of all foreign forces—Palestinian, Syrian, and Israeli—from Lebanon, the establishment of a strong central government in Beirut, and a guarantee of quiet on Israel's northern border. In July, Washington began advocating the deployment of a multinational force in Beirut to supervise the evacuation of the armed Palestinians from the city.

Although this formula was in line with PM Begin's position, its accomplishment was imbued with major obstacles. Israeli decisionmakers envisioned a peace treaty with a friendly Lebanese government led by Bashir Jumayyil, while throughout the war the latter was anxious to play down his relations with Israel. Thus, Jumayyil refused to take part in the military pressure on the besieged Palestinians so as to secure his election to Lebanon's presidency and prevent Arab alienation toward his future government, just as he would be reluctant to commit himself to a formal peace treaty with Israel. Jerusalem and Jumayyil were also divided on the Palestinians' future in Lebanon. Israeli PM Begin maintained that the Palestinians should be pastoralized and finally settled and naturalized in Lebanon. Like Sharon, Jumayyil insisted that any resolution of the Lebanon crisis must include the removal of all the Palestinian refugees from the country, and not simply the PLO's military and political apparati from Beirut.[21]

Israel's lengthy siege of West Beirut, with its attendant aerial bombings and blocking of essential goods from reaching the civilian population—combined with Arab divisions and political impotence, Moscow's inaction, and Washington's support for the departure of armed Palestinians and Syrians from Beirut—all explain the growing inclination of Arab governments, including Syria, to collaborate with Washington's diplomatic effort to resolve the crisis. Indeed, once it became clear that the main price was to be paid by the PLO, Syria sought to secure its own interests through advanced dialogue with Washington. Chances for such dialogue seemed to improve as the image of absolute U.S. support for Israel's moves in Lebanon came somewhat unstuck following the resignation of SoS Alexander Haig on June 25, and the growing American criticism of Israel's violations of the cease-fire and heavy attacks on civilian neighborhoods in Beirut.[22]

As to the PLO leadership, it came under heavy pressures from Sarkis's government and Lebanese Muslim leaders to accept the Israeli demand in order to prevent massive destruction of West Beirut. Under this pressure, which Syria and other Arab governments tacitly joined, the PLO leaders were convinced that their departure from Beirut was inevitable. Nonetheless, the PLO conducted tenacious negotiations through French, Lebanese, and Saudi diplomatic channels with the United States, to secure maximum gains in two main respects:

1. Salvaging its military stronghold in Lebanon by redeploying its armed forces in the refugee camps. The PLO also insisted that the evacuation of Beirut assume the form of disengagement-of-forces, to be implemented under international auspices.
2. Securing a political *quid pro quo* in the form of direct diplomatic contacts with the United States and an American commitment to work in earnest for a solution to the Palestinian problem.[23]

Egypt backed the PLO demands in an attempt to blur the fact that its own peace treaty with Israel in fact underlay the Arab world's impotence in the face of the Israeli offensive in Lebanon. Egypt was caught between its commitment to the peace treaty with Israel and its basic interest in rebuilding bridges to the

Arab world. Egypt, in line with its traditional practice, seized on the Palestinian issue to reassert its commitment to the Arab core cause, preempt Arab criticism of its adherence to the peace treaty with Israel, and expand its contacts in the Arab world, notably with the PLO, Jordan, and Saudi Arabia. In addition to calling for an Arab summit, President Mubarak and other leaders met with senior PLO representatives in Cairo to brief them on Egypt's contacts with the United States, Western European countries, and Israel on the situation in Lebanon. The Egyptians sought to secure wide publicity for this activity, especially their pressure on the United States to stop Israel's bombing of West Beirut and ensure the withdrawal of Israeli forces from the city. Egypt itself provided food and medical aid to the PLO, but refused to supply arms.

On July 20, Egypt and France joined in submitting a draft resolution to the UNSC that called for an immediate cease-fire throughout Lebanon and a disengagement of forces in the Beirut area under the auspices of a UN observer force. Egypt's and France's motion sought to use the Lebanon crisis to advance an overall solution to the Palestinian issue based on simultaneous Israel-PLO mutual recognition. Egypt stated that the PLO was ready to conduct negotiations with the United States on mutual recognition with Israel, insisting that the Palestinians' departure from Beirut must be linked to clear political undertakings for a solution of the Palestinian problem.

The French-Egyptian initiative faced conflicting inter-Arab interests, which facilitated a U.S. veto. Denying the PLO's independence, the Syrians rejected linkage between the evacuation of Beirut by the armed Palestinians and a peace process, maintaining that the balance of power favored Israel. Indeed, Syria would not support a resolution bound to weaken its grip on the PLO and restore Egypt's legitimacy in the Arab arena. Syria, for its part, insisted on Israeli withdrawal from Lebanon, arguing that its own military presence in Lebanon was sanctioned by the legal Lebanese government as well as by the Arab heads of state. Syria, Iraq, and Algeria were mentioned by American officials as candidates for absorbing the Palestinians evacuated from Beirut. But it was Damascus that set the tone in this regard, turning the evacuation of the Palestinians into a bargaining chip toward Riyad and Washington. Thus, after an initial rejection of the American proposals, Syria gave its assent to evacuation of the armed Palestinian forces from Beirut to Arab states, sending a message of interest in improved relations with the United States. This paved the road to President Reagan's and SoS Shultz's meeting with the Saudi and Syrian FMs at the White House on July 20.[24]

On July 28, the AL's six-member committee reached "full agreement" on the need for the PLO to announce the removal of its military forces from Beirut and spell out the guarantees it required in this respect. The committee also demanded that Israeli forces withdraw, the siege of Beirut be lifted, and international observers be sent to ensure the well-being of the population. This statement, issued with the assent of the PLO, was the first public evidence of the latter's readiness to evacuate its personnel from Beirut without first obtaining a clear political *quid pro quo*.[25]

Nevertheless, Syria and the PLO, evidently encouraged by the growing criticism of the Israeli government—both domestically and in Western countries—over the protracted siege of West Beirut, continued to play for time by obstructing moves toward evacuation. They were forced to moderate their stance when, at the beginning of August, Israel stepped up military pressure by inching forward into the besieged area and intensifying its air raids on the city, which reached their zenith on August 12, resulting in a final consent of the PLO to leave Beirut. Syria's moderation stemmed from fear of an Israeli assault into West Beirut and resumption of military confrontation in the Bika'.

Although Syria officially expressed readiness to absorb some of the Palestinian fighters, in practice it referred only to those factions under its direct control. Syria, however, was willing to receive also senior commanders and PLO staff bodies—provided the PLO formally requested it to do so. Syria evidently sought to take advantage of the hard-pressed positions of 'Arafat and his cohorts to force them to approach Syria as their patron and protector. That Syria continued to set the tone where Lebanon was concerned was underscored when, following its lead, Jordan, Iraq, the two Yemens, Tunisia, and Sudan also declared their readiness to admit some of the Palestinian forces.[26]

On August 19, formal approval was obtained from the PLO, Lebanon, and Israel for evacuating the armed Palestinians and Syrian forces from Beirut. The agreement provided for the arrival of an international peace force, composed of American, French, and Italian troops, to oversee the pullout and the dispatch of the armed Palestinians into various Arab states. In the course of the evacuation—which was completed at the end of August—8,000 Palestinians left by sea while 6,000 Syrian troops and members of PLA brigades went east on the Beirut-Damascus highway to an area under Syrian control. 'Arafat himself travelled to Greece, where he was welcomed by PM Papandreou. 'Arafat made Greece his first stop to show his displeasure with Arab governments' inaction, though officially it was explained that 'Arafat wished to thank the Greek government for its help in the evacuation process.[27]

Israel had indeed succeeded in destroying the Palestinian military infrastructure throughout the Lebanese territory it had captured, but Sharon's unhidden agenda of eliminating the PLO politically and wiping out the Palestinian problem by military force had obviously turned out to be self-defeating. The fact that the PLO's leadership had held out during the ten-week Israeli siege of West Beirut, together with the diplomatic activity conducted in Arab capitals, Jerusalem, and Washington in order to secure PLO withdrawal from Beirut, highlighted the Palestinian problem. The war manifested the United States' isolation in the international arena on the Lebanon issue and the drastic decline in Israel's standing in international public opinion. Typically, a resolution was adopted by the UNGA on August 19, following a four-day emergency session, that called for the establishment of a Palestinian state and sanctions against Israel. Formulated by the PLO and Syria, this resolution was passed by an overwhelming majority, with only Israel and the United States casting negative votes.

Even more crucial for Israel was the damage that the long and brutal war caused to its relations with Washington. What had begun with American understanding of Israel's motivation and tacit political cooperation, ended with growing mistrust and disagreement, which peaked when President Reagan's peace initiative was announced on September 1. Although as early as August 8, Washington had been reportedly engaged in a "comprehensive reassessment" of its Middle East policy, the new plan was a surprise to Jerusalem. The Reagan plan stipulated the establishment of Palestinian self-rule in the West Bank and Gaza in association with Jordan. Reagan explained that the Lebanon war had brought home the need for a just solution to the Palestinian problem and had underlined Israel's inability to achieve security through military superiority. He stressed that while the United States did not support the establishment of an independent Palestinian state in the West Bank and Gaza Strip, neither did it advocate Israeli annexation of, or permanent rule over these territories. Basing himself on the Camp David accords, Reagan proposed a five-year transition period during which the inhabitants of the territories would obtain full autonomy and Israel would desist from establishing new settlements. Reagan reaffirmed Washington's adherence to the principle of "land for peace," and asserted that Israel must implement Resolution 242 and withdraw on all fronts, with border adjustments to be determined in negotiations with the neighboring Arab states. Under the Reagan Plan, Jerusalem would remain undivided, its final status to be determined in negotiations. Although the American plan was based on the Camp David accords, it also represented some retreat from them, mainly in terms of linking the West Bank and Gaza to Jordan, and in tacitly obliging Israel to withdraw from most of these territories. The American initiative was apparently a gesture to the Arab regimes in return for their diplomatic efforts and mediation with the PLO, taking advantage of the PLO's weakness and Israel's low prestige to enhance the U.S. posture in the Arab world.[28]

The agreement on evacuation of the Palestinian military forces from Beirut instigated a Saudi call for convening an Arab summit conference at Fez, to discuss the results and ramifications of the war. In fact, the Saudis meant to seize on the diplomatic momentum created by the war to advance the Arab cause in the conflict with Israel based on the disputed Fahd peace plan. Yet the summit was marked by heightened tension between Damascus and Beirut, following the latter's outspoken demand that foreign intervention in Lebanon be terminated, citing Syria, the PLO, and Israel in one breath. The Lebanese delegation to the summit boldly demanded the cessation of Palestinian military activity in and from Lebanon, and the termination of the ADF mandate. The Lebanese position was one result of Bashir Jumayyil's election as President of Lebanon on August 23, amidst active Israeli assistance and despite opposite Syrian pressures and intimidation efforts.[29]

Syria insisted that it was operating in Lebanon by virtue of an all-Arab decision and that Israel's invasion of Lebanon, aimed at forcing that country to sign a peace treaty, posed a threat to the entire Arab nation. Syria described Jumayyil's election as "the appointment of a Lebanese president by Israel," and objected to a presidential election in Lebanon under the shadow of the occupation. In view of Israel's growing influence on the Lebanese government, Syria sought to focus the summit on the crisis in Lebanon, hoping to consolidate a Pan-Arab front against Jumayyil's alleged intention to sign a peace treaty with Israel. A complicating factor where Syria was concerned was the expiry of the AL mandate for its forces in Lebanon on July 27. Although Damascus stated that it would maintain its presence in Lebanon as long as Israeli forces were there, Syria required Arab reaffirmation of its military presence. Tension was also apparent between Asad and 'Arafat from the outset, when Asad was the only head of state to absent himself from the festive welcoming ceremony for 'Arafat. 'Arafat's disregard of Syria in his plenum speech—and the disparity between their stands on the Reagan Plan—was taken as an indication of the deepening crisis in Syrian-PLO relations.[30]

Lebanon's demands occupied most of the summit's deliberations and threatened its success. However, a Lebanon led by Israeli-backed Bashir Jumayyil and lacking the means to pressure other Arab states was incapable of gaining collective support for its demands. Only after Lebanon threatened to walk out of the conference was a partial compromise attained between Beirut and Damascus, although the dispute over the ongoing armed Palestinian presence in Lebanon remained unsettled. The summit resolutions failed to mention the Lebanese demand for the PLO's expulsion from Lebanon, though neither was the PLO able to obtain sufficient support for its request to have the 1969 Cairo Agreement revivified or have Lebanon guarantee the safety of its Palestinian inhabitants.[31]

It was precisely because they had sat idly by during the war and the siege of Beirut and now sought to exploit the existing situation to advance a solution to the Palestinian problem, that the Arab governments could not afford a confrontation with the PLO such as would inevitably result from supporting the Lebanese stand. As for Syria, the conference "took note" of Beirut's insistence that the ADF mandate be terminated, but left the implementation, ostensibly, to bilateral Syrian-Lebanese negotiations. In practice, not only did the summit grant Syria general Arab backing to decide on this issue, it also created linkage between ending Syria's presence in Lebanon and an Israeli withdrawal from that country.

The upshot was that Lebanon again paid the price for the weakness, division and indifference that characterized the behavior of Arab governments toward Syria and the Palestinians during the war. On the other hand, these same factors accounted also for the conference's disregard of 'Arafat's proposals for a comprehensive Arab military-political-economic strategy in the conflict with Israel based on the ACSP. Similarly, the summit ignored the Lebanese delegation's request for the establishment of an Arab fund to underwrite Lebanon's rehabilitation.

The shakiness and internal split of the inter-Arab alignment came strikingly to the fore again only a week after the festive closing of the Fez summit meeting. On September 14, the Lebanese president-elect, Bashir Jumayyil, was assassinated, shattering any remaining hope for a recovery of stability and normal life in Lebanon. In the wake of the assassination, seemingly perpetrated under Syrian aegis, Israeli forces, in another breach of the government's promises, took over West Beirut and allowed units of the Phalange, Jumayyil's party, to enter the Sabra and Shatila Palestinian refugee camps and perpetrate an indiscriminate massacre among their inhabitants. The mass slaughter generated a new furor among Arab public opinion, accompanied by feelings of frustration and grief at Arab weakness and divisions. A few days later, the Arab FMs convened in an emergency session, but proved unable to reach a consensus on what measures to take in reaction. The best they could come up with was a sharp condemnation of Israel and the United States, maintaining that without Washington's backing the situation would not have reached such a pass. Syrian and Libyan calls for sanctions against the United States were rejected.[32]

In Israel, the Sabra and Shatila massacre and its worldwide echoes of outrage provoked a massive wave of criticism and protest against the government's policy in Lebanon, culminating in the establishment of a state committee of inquiry to investigate the responsibility of Israeli political and military echelons for the atrocity. Thus, the wide public acceptance that had marked the beginning of the operation and its limited goals gradually faded, giving way to growing discontent with the war's political agenda. The siege of Beirut and the Sabra and Shatila massacre intensified a public debate, unprecedented in Israel's history, about the necessity and morality of war. The deviation from a traditionally defense-rooted concept of war and the obscurity of the political decision-making process, heralded the first serious rupture in the Israeli consensus on the issue of national security.[33]

Syria's Veto Power

The end of the battle for Beirut and the Reagan peace plan combined to confront Asad's regime with a serious challenge, which threatened to ignore Syria's national security needs and diminish its regional posture. The war proved Israel's military edge, especially in the air, revealing Syria's strategic isolation in the Arab world. The deployment of Israeli forces in both the Golan Heights and southern Biqa' valley put Syria in a dangerous position, with its core area stretching from Damascus to Homs in the jaws of a potential Israeli pincer operation. Israel's strategic goals in Lebanon—namely, a peace agreement with that government, ensuring the ousting of PLO and Syrian forces—seemed to be within reach and to enjoy U.S. backing.

Focusing on the Palestinian problem, Reagan's peace initiative not only threatened to disclaim Syria's leading role in this Arab core issue. It was a vehement reminder of Washington's disregard of Syria's national interest and cause in the conflict with Israel, despite Syria's early efforts to cooperate with the United States in order to win its support for Israel's withdrawal from Lebanon. This disregard accounted for Syria's destructive policy in Lebanon and the peace process in the next three years, reflecting, in effect, an outcry for acknowledgement. The assassination of Bashir Jumayyil had been the first step in a series of Syrian actions in Lebanon which turned into a battleground for undoing Israel's achievements in Lebanon and the American peace plan.[34]

Damascus perceived the Reagan initiative, the presence of U.S. forces in Lebanon, and Israel's goals as parts of a strategy aimed at imposing on it their conditions of peace in accordance with the Camp David accords. Syria thus embarked on a preventive policy, defined by Arab critics as "veto power," in the name of Arab national security. Syria's determination to impose its own needs and priorities on other Arab actors, by violent means if needed, proved destructive to collective Arab action. This was manifested by the prolonged postponement of the next regular summit by its prospective Saudi hosts and the incomplete gathering at the August 1985 Casablanca summit, which was boycotted by Syria and other SRF member states.[35]

That Syria managed to employ its veto power—particularly regarding the Lebanese arena—was due to a convergence of political determination as well as geopolitical conditions: no other central Arab power was able to balance Syria; and the alliance with Iran gave it more influence over the Gulf Arab monarchies, whose national security had been under imminent threat of the Shi'i revolution. In addition, Syria assumed a unique role as the only actively fighting state in the Arab-Israeli conflict and as the leader of the radical bloc, weak and divided as it was. Its military presence in Lebanon facilitated Damascus' masterful manipulation of inter-factional relations in Lebanon, exploiting the changing balance of power between them following the expulsion of the PR to shape a sound base of influence in that country. Thus, within two years, Syria managed to regain the initiative in Lebanon, force Israel's withdrawal, and restore itself as the dominant power in the country. Lebanon was indeed too crucial for Syria's national security to let any other external force gain the upper hand there or to permit the country's security and foreign relations to be considered an "internal affair." The domestic Islamic fundamentalist challenge to Asad made a strong regional policy all the more necessary.[36]

Yet Syria's violent policies also manifested its limitations and sometimes created counterproductive effects, particularly with regard to the PLO. Syria's undertaking to be the Arab standard-bearer in the confrontation with Israel by virtue of being "the most Arab among the Arab states," and despite its weak economy and military inferiority, exacted a high economic and political price. Damascus reasserted the ideas of "popular war" in Lebanon and the need to attain "strategic parity" with Israel, which would have enabled Damascus to defy United States–sponsored peacemaking efforts and deter another Israeli attack. Aware of its isolation in the Arab world—with Iraq still bogged down in war with Iran and Egypt adhering to its peace agreement with Israel—Syria argued that the strategic balance would be achieved through "Soviet active backing." Henceforth, achieving "strategic parity" with Israel became the pillar of Asad's domestic and regional policies, a concept attesting to Syria's isolation, and yet to its persistent thrust to play a leading role in the Palestine conflict. To legitimize its devastating economic price, the strategic parity was given a comprehensive—economic, social, and political—interpretation.[37]

The aftermath of the Lebanon war witnessed a rapid growth of Syria's armed forces and arsenal, leading to a slowdown of its economic growth. While the Israeli and American threats to Syria served to legitimize the heavy burden of rapid military buildup on its poor economy at home, Syria presented her efforts as a collective Arab interest. This claim was used to obtain financial aid, justify action against other Arab actors, and promote Damascus' self-defined image as the ultimate barrier against "capitulationist" settlements.[38]

Another challenge to Syria was the onset of a PLO-Jordan political dialogue in response to the new U.S. peace initiative, which deepened the animosity between Syria and the PLO, now labelled by Palestinians as a "bleeding open wound." The dialogue was aimed at producing a formula for joint political action that would bridge the gap between U.S. and Arab positions regarding the appropriate representation of the West Bank and Gaza. The PLO-Jordan dialogue collided with Syria's unhidden wish to gain control of the PLO and subordinate the Palestinian cause—viewed as an essential concern of national security—to its own policy. Syria argued that a PLO-Jordan accord would marginalize its role, and claimed priority for the Lebanon cause—namely, Israel's withdrawal—over the Palestine issue before any renewal of the peacemaking diplomacy. Syria perceived the Lebanese arena as the most immediate threat to its national security, a view that it tried to use to overcome its isolation in the Arab world. With the exodus from Beirut, however, the PLO's leadership paradoxically acquired more freedom to maneuver and was more determined than ever before to preserve its independent decisionmaking, even if this would lead to a collision with Syria.[39]

Syria thus sought to regain its hegemony in Lebanon and tighten its control of the PLO in order to enhance its national security. This obviously obliged Syria to reduce Israeli influence in Lebanon and undercut the threat to its own security. To realize these goals Syria was willing to use any means or measures, combining political intrigues, terrorism and assassination, guerilla warfare, and even the use of its regular forces. The Syrian policy took largely the form of an indirect strategy, using Lebanese and Palestinian proxies in order to minimize the risk of direct clash with Israel or the United States. Avoiding direct responsibility for striking at Palestinian or other Arab targets also limited potential domestic political fallout. Syria's veto policy in Lebanon was thus aimed at containment of the Maronite-based Lebanese government and the PLO, and at forcing Western intervention forces and Israel to withdraw from Lebanon.

Mastering the Lebanese Swamp

Syria's most immediate concern in the aftermath of the war was to prevent Israeli strategic gains in Lebanon by using inter-factional rivalries to weaken Israel's Maronite allies. Syria persisted in its rejection of the United States–mediated Israel-Lebanon peace negotiations and, in particular, their drawing a parallel between the Israeli and Syrian military presence, as implied in the widely accepted call by Western and Arab governments for all foreign forces to withdraw. Damascus repeatedly distinguished between its legitimate military presence in Lebanon, sanctioned by Arab and Lebanese stances, and Israel's "invading forces," aiming at subjugating this country to U.S. domination.[40]

Syria's hostility to President Amin Jumayyil—elected to replace his brother—and his government failed to attract the immediate support of non-Christian militias except the Druze, whose deeply-rooted dispute with the Phalange made them Damascus' leading ally in Lebanon. The largest Muslim militia—the Shi'i Amal movement—however, initially supported Jumayyil, expecting he would adopt a policy of national reconciliation and social reforms.[41] Indeed, the Lebanese militias' position toward the government—as well as on the U.S. and Israeli presence—was ultimately determined by inter-communal considerations. Thus, as Jumayyil became increasingly identified as the LF's factional leader rather than as a national figure, the non-Christian militias rallied against the government as a full-fledged party in the inter-communal strife.

Syrian military support to Druze militia against the LF weakened the government's position and posed a serious dilemma to Israel. Though aligned with the Christian forces, Israel sought to avoid involvement in internal Lebanese feuds, especially in view of growing domestic discontent with the government's policy in Lebanon. It was, however, the May 17, 1983, Israel-

Lebanon peace agreement that helped Syria mobilize other political forces against Lebanon's government. The agreement gave Israel extensive concessions, including a free hand in most of Lebanon's air space and on the ground in the south, seriously restricting Lebanon's sovereignty. Most disturbing, however, was an annexed secret letter from Israel to the U.S. government, conditioning its own phased, partial withdrawal from Lebanon on a simultaneous pull-out of the Syrian and remaining Palestinian forces.[42]

In July 1983, opposition to Amin Jumayyil and the peace agreement with Israel was institutionalized by the establishment of a Syrian-backed "National Salvation Front" (NSF), bringing together the Shiʻi Amal and Druze militias against the LF and Christian army units. Under these circumstances, Israel evacuated the Shuf area in September 1983 and withdrew south of the Awwali river, indicating its acquiescence in the hopelessness of the peace agreement with Lebanon. Despite the presence of the multinational force and U.S. efforts to rebuild the disintegrated Lebanese army, the Jumayyil administration could not implement the accord. The LF's weakness in the face of the Druze offensive made Israel even less willing to support them.[43]

Amal's turn against the Maronite-dominated government arose from the LF's preference for the Sunni Muslims as allies, and the cleansing efforts of Shiʻi residents from the slums of west and south Beirut. Above all, it was determined by the growing weight of political radicalism among Shiʻis, escalating inter-communal competition and power struggle within the movement. In 1983–84, Amal gradually accelerated guerrilla warfare against Israel in south Lebanon, amidst constant pressure of activist Shiʻi elements whose religious fervor in fighting the foreigners acquired growing prestige and legitimacy in Lebanese and intra-Shiʻa politics. Shiʻi Islamic radicalization had represented, since the early 1970s, a general trend of social and political awakening and protest among members of this community, led by religious scholars who had acquired their education in Iran's Shiʻi religious centers. Rooted in long-lived socio-economic and political deprivation, this process had been intensified by Israeli retaliations against Palestinian bases in south Lebanon, since the late-1960s, which drove tens of thousands of Shiʻis northward into the impoverished suburbs of Beirut. The prolonged hostilities in the south, and the government's inability to provide the residents with security, proved to be an enormous rallying force and impetus for creating a militia for self-defense, especially against the Palestinian guerrillas who were seen as the source of the Shiʻi troubles. Already in the three years before Israel's invasion, Shiʻi militia had become involved in armed clashes with Palestinians in south Lebanon and Beirut.

Amal movement was ultimately launched due to the effect of Iran's revolution and material aid, Syrian support, and popular resistance activity against Israel's presence in southern Lebanon. During the 1982 war, about

1,500 Iranians of the Revolutionary Guards (*pasdaran*) arrived in the Biqa' and worked with dissidents from Amal to start what would become the Party of God (*hizballah*). Whereas Amal perceived itself as a communal interest group to improve the conditions of the Shi'is in Lebanon within the existing political order, Hizballah sought a revolutionary solution by establishing an Islamic state along Iranian lines and armed struggle against Israel, the United States, and the Lebanese government. Hizballah's militancy pressed Amal to work more actively with Syria against the Lebanese government. Though sponsored by Iran, Hizballah turned out to be also an effective ally for Syria by committing mass-killing suicide car bomb attacks against the U.S. embassy in Beirut, the multinational force, and Israeli bases, leaving altogether more than four hundred dead, mostly Americans.[44]

Syria's unmistakable role behind the atrocities against the multinational force led, in December 1983, to American air attacks and naval bombardment against Syrian bases in Lebanon. The attack came shortly after the United States and Israel revitalized their dormant strategic accord, arousing criticism on the part of the United States' Arab allies for further weakening their ability to defy Syria. Yet Washington had no interest in a deeper involvement in internal Lebanese strife. The collapse of Beirut's government forces and the fading of any hope that Jumayyil might establish a stable regime led the United States and the other participants in the multinational peace force to withdraw from Beirut in February 1984.

With Israeli and international withdrawal from Beirut and its environs, Jumayyil tried to save at least his own position by shifting allies. At the end of February 1984, he went to Damascus, demonstrating his acceptance of Syria's hegemony. An immediate expression of the new Syria-Lebanon relations was the replacement of PM Shafiq al-Wazzan with the well-known Syrian-oriented Rashid Karami. On March 5, 1984, the Lebanese government abrogated the agreement with Israel and in July the Israeli liaison office in Beirut was closed. Damascus portrayed the treaty's annulment and the Western forces' withdrawal as its own victory against the world's greatest power.[45]

Syria dealt with Israel's presence in southern Lebanon by supporting Amal, Hizballah, and Palestinian leftist groups waging anti-Israeli guerrilla warfare. In 1984, Israel was bogged down in a hopeless war of attrition with an increasingly hostile Shi'i population in an area with ideal topography for guerilla warfare. By mid-January 1985, the official toll of Israeli casualties in Lebanon since June 1982 was 609 and the annual cost of continued occupation was $240 million, exacerbating domestic criticism of the government's Lebanon policy and adding to the growing disenchantment at the economic stalemate and hyperinflation. In January 1985, Israel's newly established national coalition government decided to withdraw unilaterally from Lebanon except for a strip along the border defined as a "security zone." The decision came in the wake of futile Israel-Lebanon military talks, held in the Lebanese border town of Naqura under UN auspices, in an effort to reach an accord on Israeli withdrawal and security arrangements in the south. The failure was occasioned by the lack of authority of the Lebanese delegates to accept anything less than full Israeli withdrawal with no security guarantees, while being subjected to Syrian and radical Shiʻi pressures.[46]

Thus, within less than three years, Syria had reversed a military defeat in Lebanon into a political victory. Asad had little reason to feel sorry about the PLO's evacuation, while U.S. and Israeli troops had also left, and Lebanese Christian leaders bowed to Damascus, which managed to forge an alliance with its Druze and Shiʻi clients. All these gains had not cost Syria a single substantive concession. Ironically, Israel's war, designated to eradicate Palestinian armed presence from Lebanon, triggered the rapid development of an even more efficacious enemy, embodied by Hizballah. In hindsight, the destruction Israel inflicted on the PR in Lebanon paved the road for restoration of indigenous Lebanese domination in most of Lebanon's territory, sanctioned by Syria. Even though southern Lebanon would remain a battlefield long after Israel had withdrawn to a "security zone," the replacement of the PR by the Shiʻi militias in fighting Israel indicated an essential shift of motivation and intentions. While the PR's armed struggle against Israel was a strategic goal, the Shiʻi militias sought to drive Israel completely out of Lebanon, using this struggle as a springboard for gaining access to power and resource allocation within the Lebanese political system.

The Syria-PLO Confrontation

Following the evacuation from Beirut, Syria's growing antagonism toward ʻArafat for his flirtation with King Husain intensified criticism within Fatah over their leader's political and military decisions during and after the Lebanon war. Damascus seemed to realize a long-awaited opportunity to get rid of the "treacherous" ʻArafat as the PLO's leader and replace him with a more obedient figure. In May 1983, the split within Fatah became a matter of fact when its bases in the Biqaʻ under Syrian control attacked ʻArafat's loyalists. The rebellion's timing was apparently set to take advantage of ʻArafat's initial failure to come to terms with Jordan and the United States in April, which was viewed as a blow to his prestige and further evidence of his weakening position. That same month, the Syrian regime launched a series of assassination and sabotage actions against PLO political figures and Jordanian diplomats, implemented by the then-Syrian-backed Abu-Nidal terrorist group. The first victim of this campaign was ʻArafat's aide, and an outspoken advocate of peace negotiations with Israel, ʻIsam Sirtawi.[47]

ʻArafat's attempts to improve his relations with Asad were vehemently rebuffed, and his June visit to Damascus which ended with an expulsion,

turned into a humiliating failure. Damascus' hostile attitude also ignored conciliation efforts by the Soviet Union and Arab and nonaligned governments.
These efforts and others in the following years reflected a sustained belief
among Fatah leaders that despite the bitter conflict, Syria had remained their
indispensable ally and guarantor of their strongholds in Lebanon.[48]

The Syria-PLO relations turned into an all-out confrontation following
'Arafat's return to northern Lebanon in October 1983, trying to reassert his
presence in Tripoli. Entrenched with loyalist forces in the Nahr al-Barid and
Badawi refugee camps near the city, and supported by Tripoli's radical Sunni
Muslim movement, 'Arafat virtually forced the Syrians to either fight or compromise with him. 'Arafat's only hope was to hold on fighting long enough to
muster the Arab world's support and force Damascus to come to terms with
him as the legitimate leader of the PLO. Militarily defeated, abandoned by the
Arab states, his dialogue with the Hashemite king at an impasse, and his own
personal leadership in jeopardy, 'Arafat resorted to using his last semi-
independent base in Lebanon as a means of political survival. Indeed, nothing
could attest better to 'Arafat's desperate situation than his military position—
besieged by Syrian and Palestinian enemies and confined to a small enclave
with his back to the sea.[49]

The Syrian response to the challenge posed by 'Arafat revealed the
unbridgeable gap between these former allies. During November and into
December, Syrian-based Palestinian forces backed by Syrian regular units
besieged and bombarded 'Arafat's stronghold in the camps, which ultimately
imposed on the PLO leader a second exodus from Lebanon. The Arab response
to 'Arafat's calls for support remained confined to protests and renunciations of
the Syrian regime issued mainly by Iraq, as well as to Saudi and Lebanese
mediation efforts, which paved the road to 'Arafat's evacuation of Tripoli.
While most Arab governments had remained indifferent to 'Arafat's predicament, they all harshly criticized the newly-agreed-upon strategic agreement
signed at the end of November between Israel's PM and President Reagan.[50]

Yet Syria's victory backfired, forcing the PLO leader to renew his traditional alignment with Egypt. 'Arafat's decision to leave Tripoli directly to
attend a meeting with Mubarak in Cairo—his first visit there since Sadat's trip
to Jerusalem—came as a shocking surprise to his closest colleagues in Fatah.
Though 'Arafat had maintained contacts with Mubarak since the siege of
Beirut, his visit at once tacitly legitimized Egypt's peace agreement with Israel,
broke the Arab summit boycott, and violated Fatah's principle of "collective
leadership." So harsh was the criticism levelled at 'Arafat's visit to Cairo, that
he went on to North Yemen rather than return to Tunis immediately and face a
bitter debate with his lieutenants.[51]

Syria's hostilities left 'Arafat with little choice but to cross the Rubicon
and seek alliance with the pragmatist Arab states that would preserve his

personal leadership and political independence. Hence, he resumed the political dialogue with King Husain, concluding, in February 1985, an agreement that enabled him to move toward close alignment with Amman. If the second exodus from Lebanon had any impact on 'Arafat's position, it was likely to have strengthened his position as the leader and symbol of Palestinian nationalism. The bulk of Fatah's leadership remained united and 'Arafat's legitimacy among Palestinians proved strong enough to sustain the split with Damascus and its Fatah rebels. The latter failed to gain much support among Palestinians, except among those units under Syrian control.[52]

The Battle of the Camps

The 'Arafat-Husain accord of February 1985 triggered another violent Syrian attempt to impose its own rules and agenda on the PLO by encouraging Amal militiamen and Shi'i units of Lebanon's army to assault and besiege Palestinian refugee camps in Beirut and Sidon. Amal's assault in May 1985 came amidst continued efforts by 'Arafat to reinforce his armed presence in Lebanon by shipping men and weapons to the refugee camps, thanks to tacit agreement with the Maronites. Indeed, while negotiating with Jordan and indulging in a diplomatic effort, 'Arafat continued his thrust to reinforce his position in Lebanon, threatening Syria's efforts to stabilize the Lebanese arena. 'Arafat's success in bringing about an urgent meeting of the ALC to handle the new Palestinian agony in Lebanon attested to Syria's isolation in the Arab arena.[53]

Faced with wide Arab discontent at its policy toward the Palestinians in Lebanon, Syria, although initially dismissing the fighting in the camps as an "internal Lebanese affair," reluctantly attended the gathering to prevent hostile resolutions. The Arab states' supportive response to the PLO's request reflected the latter's enhanced stature in the region's politics due to its agreement with King Husain. It was also due to the unity of all Palestinian factions in fighting against Amal regardless of ideological cleavages and despite the rejection of the Amman Accord by the radical groups, rallied in the Palestinian National Salvation Front (PNSF).

The ALC meeting (June 8–9), however, once again demonstrated the weakness of collective mediating mechanisms in inter-Arab politics. The ALC urged an immediate cease-fire and an end to the siege, authorizing the ALSG to ensure the implementation of these resolutions, with an ALC followup meeting to be held within two weeks. The ALC also expressed its implicit support for the PLO's armed presence in Lebanon by urging the latter's government to cooperate with the PLO on related matters. 'Arafat's relative success in the meeting notwithstanding, the fighting went on, manifesting Syria's ability to disregard the ALC decisions. Effectively, the main result of the meeting was setting the dynamics for convening an emergency summit conference following 'Arafat's call and the Moroccan monarch's official initiative in this respect.[54]

The Syrian pressure on the PLO also included oppressive measures against Palestinians in Syria itself, such as massive arrests, restriction of the movement of leading radical figures, and violent quelling of protest demonstrations. That Syria held the key to resolving the crisis was shown in the negotiations conducted between Amal and the PNSF under Vice-President Khaddam's supervision, resulting in the June 17 Damascus Agreement on a cease-fire. The PLO denounced the agreement as an attempt to delegitimize the 'Arafat-led PLO and abrogate the Cairo agreement. Yet the agreement neither lifted the siege nor ended violent clashes between 'Arafat's loyalists and Amal. A tacit agreement with President Amin Jumayyil in 1986 provided the PLO's armed troops access to Lebanon via the Maronite port of Juniya, leading to Amal's repeated failures in the battle of the camps despite the use of Syrian-supplied tanks. The siege of the Palestinian refugee camps in Beirut and Tyre had remained in force—despite Algeria's mediation and the PLO-Amal agreement of February 1987 on ending the fighting and siege—until early 1988, when it was lifted as a gesture to the Palestinian uprising in the occupied territories.[55]

By the mid-1980s, Syria tightened its grip over the Shi'i and Druze communities. However, relations with the Maronite militia and President Jumayyil reached a crisis due to the latter's objection to the inter-communal conciliation agreement signed in Damascus in December 1985, under Syrian auspices. The rupture between Asad and Jumayyil was evident at the Amman summit held in November 1987, which hardly noted Lebanon's severe economic and political crisis. That the Lebanon issue was discussed at the summit at all was mainly due to Iraq's and the PLO's effort to embarrass Asad by exploiting his failure to settle the inter-communal conflict in Lebanon. Thus, Syria's rivals called for withdrawal of all foreign forces from Lebanon and the resolution of its internal conflicts without outside intervention or compromise of its independence.[56]

In practice, the summit opted to ignore Jumayyil's call for urgent economic aid to Lebanon and his warning that otherwise its destructive forces might spread to other Arab countries. The concluding statement made no reference to the Lebanese economic crisis or Arab aid, confining itself to expressing support for Lebanon's independence and its territorial integrity. The tragic dimension of the Lebanese problem was underlined by Jumayyil's questioned legitimacy at home and the indifference shown by his Arab colleagues at the summit. As he noted, Lebanon was the weakest link in the Arab system, thus, its problems of survival commanded the least attention of all the issues on the summit's agenda.[57]

14

IN SEARCH OF ANOTHER PEACE PROCESS

The collective sanctions adopted against Egypt for signing a separate peace treaty with Israel by no means indicated that the Arabs abandoned the diplomatic option in the conflict with Israel. Nor did it mean that Egypt acquiesced in its ouster from the Arab fold. Egypt's Arab policy during the 1980s was marked by a continuous effort to reestablish its central position in the Arab world by paving the road for other Arab actors to participate in a renewed peace process. The exhaustion of punitive measures against Egypt and the stalemated Israeli-Egyptian autonomy talks—suspended by Sadat in August 1980—seemed to encourage Arab efforts to seek an alternative diplomatic framework to the Camp David ACCORDS. King Husain, who had never acquiesced in the 1974 Rabat summit resolution which recognized the PLO's status as the exclusive representative of the Palestinians, was frequently reported to be involved in efforts to enhance his diplomatic option regarding the West Bank, primarily through Washington's assistance.[1]

King Husain's efforts were also provoked by the PLO's vigorous diplomatic activity and growing posture in the international arena. Indeed, for the PLO's mainstream, led by 'Arafat, the deepening schism between Baghdad and Damascus, on the one hand, and the growing Saudi-Iraqi alignment in the face of Iran's Islamic revolution on the other, gave an opening for greater freedom to maneuver in the international arena. Thus, contacts intensified between PLO leaders, Western European officials, and ranking figures in the Socialist International as well as with Israeli peace activists—thanks to Austrian Chancellor Bruno Kreisky—despite Syrian and Libyan criticism. 'Arafat might have held out hopes for an EEC plan to supersede Camp David and enable the PLO to participate officially in renewed negotiations.[2]

King Husain's interest in renewing his involvement in the peace process, however, could hardly gain support among his Arab counterparts, whose overt divisions and lack of collective action turned their support for the PLO and the cause of Palestine into an ever more valuable resource of political legitimacy. Thus, predictions that the November 1980 Amman summit would give King Husain a mandate to represent the Palestinians proved unfounded. Not only did the PLO's standing remain unimpaired—despite its absence from the summit due to Syrian pressure—the summit reconfirmed the PLO status and urged that its independence be preserved.

The Fahd Plan and Arab Response

The July 1981 PLO-Israel military confrontation in southern Lebanon and American mediation led to a renewed interest in the PLO's political standing. It dovetailed with the new American administration's effort to resume peacemaking efforts in the Middle East based on a new formula within the Camp David framework. Among Western European and American political circles the feeling grew that the deadlocked autonomy talks required a change in framework and participants. President Sadat, capitalizing on recent developments in south Lebanon, joined the efforts and on August 5, in a visit to Washington, urged President Reagan to open a dialogue with the PLO. Sadat praised the Saudis for bringing a cease-fire to south Lebanon and expressed his hope that this would lead to a mutual and simultanuous recognition between Israel and the PLO.[3]

Two days later, Saudi Crown Prince Fahd presented his eight "guiding principles" for a comprehensive settlement of the Arab-Israeli conflict. The Fahd Plan's main principles stipulated full Israeli withdrawal from all the territories occupied in June 1967, including East Jerusalem, and removal of all the Israeli settlements from these areas; establishment of a Palestinian state with East Jerusalem as its capital; affirmation of the right of all the states in the region to live in peace; and ensuring the Palestinian people's rights, with compensation for those refugees not interested in returning to their homeland.[4]

The Saudi plan was meant to provide an alternative framework to the Camp David accords, which would gain Arab and international legitimacy through adoption by an Arab summit conference and the UN, respectively. The initiative was timely in view of Syria's isolation in the Arab world and Iraq's entanglement in the war with Iran. Riyad's underlying motives in presenting a collective Arab peace plan were consistent both with its key position in the region's politics due to its wealth, and with its extreme vulnerability to domestic and regional threats. The initiative was in line with the Saudi doctrine of national security—based on regional stability and tacit alliance with the United States—and Saudi interest in reducing contradictions between their Arab obligations and links with Washington. The Camp David accords clashed with Riyad's needs: Egypt-Israel peace had polarized inter-Arab relations and intensified political radicalism, obliging the Saudis to stand against the United States–sponsored treaty in deference to Arab solidarity. The perils of this situation, aggravated by the Iraq-Iran war and the Soviet invasion of Afghanistan, were reflected in the radicals' blackmailing pressures, urging the use of Arab oil as a political weapon in the conflict with Israel; closer Syrian-Soviet relations; and radical Islamic subversion in the Gulf monarchies, inspired by Khomeini's Iran.

The advent of the Reagan administration paved the way for closer relations between the two countries, after two years of distant and somewhat cool relationships caused by the Israel-Egypt peace treaty. To promote strategic cooperation, Washington was ready to sell the Saudis unprecedented amounts and types of arms, in addition to five early-warning intelligence-gathering AWACS aircraft. Riyad's major aim, however, was to persuade the administration that a comprehensive resolution of the Arab-Israeli conflict based on recognition of the PLO was a necessary basis for strategic cooperation between Washington and Arab states.[5]

The Fahd Plan initially caused little stir in the West, perhaps because of the uncertain Arab response and the perceived prospects for renewal of the autonomy talks in view of the Begin-Sadat meeting in Alexandria on August 26. However, Sadat's assassination on October 6, a day after Saudi FM Sa'ud al-Faisal presented the eight-point plan to the UNGA, aiming to attain its confirmation, made the Fahd Plan a matter of interest at the highest levels in Washington. Reagan himself praised it as offering recognition of Israel's right of existence as a nation. The Fahd Plan also won the unreserved support of the EEC's Council of Ministers—it had much in common with the "Venice Declaration" of June 1981—whose chairman, British Foreign Secretary Lord Carrington, visited Riyad to discuss it with the Saudi rulers.[6]

As in Summer 1977, a key element of the plan was Riyad's intention to have Washington lift its self-imposed restrictions on contacts with the PLO, in order to initiate a United States–PLO dialogue. The Saudis made a concerted effort to obtain support from 'Arafat, who, as in 1977, was in quandary. The top collective leadership of Fatah may have been ready to accept the Saudi plan with minor modifications in order to help shift Washington's attitude toward the PLO.[7] 'Arafat, however, could not overlook the prospective opposition of militant Palestinian groups and hardliners even within Fatah. It is not unlikely that in his Riyad visit in November, 'Arafat pledged support, or may have misled the Saudis into thinking that he supported their plan. Yet until the summit conference met at Fez that same month, 'Arafat stuck to an ambivalent, fence-sitting posture, which would spare him Syrian and Libyan rage as well as opposition within the Palestinian community.[8]

The Fahd Plan was received with diverse reactions in the Arab world despite the diplomatic campaign waged by the Saudis to garner support for their initiative. They lobbied the Gulf states and other pragmatic regimes, such as Jordan, Tunisia, Morocco, Somalia, Sudan, and North Yemen, although their main target was Syria, the key state in the context of the Palestine conflict. The Gulf states did back the plan, although with evident caution. A GCC summit meeting held in Riyad in November took no decision on the Saudi plan but requested that it be included on the Arab summit agenda.[9] Expectedly, the SRF members denounced the plan in scathing terms, with Qadhafi trying to keep it off the summit agenda. The SRF was particularly hostile to the seventh point, affirming the right of all countries of the region to live in peace, which was tantamount to a recognition of Israel. The short-lived resumption of the Israeli-Egyptian autonomy talks in Cairo on November 13, 1981, may have contributed to the radical states' unbending resistance to the Saudi plan. A few days later, the FMs of the SRF, along with a PLO representative, issued from Damascus a statement asserting that Arab solidarity was grounded in the conflict with Israel and its ally the United States, and that the military option was still valid. Apprehensive that the SRF members, with Syria in the lead, would boycott the summit, the Saudis expressed willingness to introduce changes in their peace plan at the summit and emphasized their adherence to the Baghdad and Tunis summit resolutions. Yet despite the Saudi efforts Asad remained vigorously hostile to the plan, arguing that its very presentation at the summit meeting could split the Arab world.[10]

The Saudi peace plan dominated the preparatory meetings of the FMs, and eventually led the summit to a deadlock and suspension at its opening session. Heated disagreement marked the FMs' deliberations over the Saudi plan, mirroring the existence of two divergent world views, which recalled the dispute sparked by Bourguiba's proposals in 1965. Most of the Arab states represented—Jordan, the Gulf emirates, Morocco, Tunisia, Somalia, Djibouti, and North Yemen—took a positive attitude toward the Fahd Plan. They maintained that the time had come for a common Arab peace strategy to supersede Camp David, which had reached an impasse. Such a strategy would ensure a solution of the Palestinian problem and enable Egypt to return to the Arab fold. The Saudi FM, who was the chief spokesman for this group, said that the seventh point—referring to peace with Israel "though without recognizing it"—was not intended to alter the current situation: Israel would remain an adversary with which the Arabs maintained no relations of any kind. The Arab states had nothing to lose, since Palestinian rights were already plundered. Given that East and West were united when it came to guaranteeing Israel's existence, the only possible strategy was based on stages. As long as the present situation persisted and as long as the Arabs were unable to implement the military option, they must cater to the West's frame of mind and propose a plan consistent with the Western concept that a Middle East settlement be grounded in the principle of mutuality. The goal must be to obtain a UNSC approval for the Fahd Plan to replace Resolution 242. The Saudi FM succinctly concluded that the summit had the alternative of accepting the plan or acknowledging that it was abandoning activity on behalf of the Arab cause in the conflict with Israel.

In contrast, the SRF states, supported by Iraq and the PLO, held that to countenance a continuation of Sadat's path was out of the question, and that Egypt's peace treaty with Israel ruled out a dialogue with Cairo. A comprehensive settlement of the Arab-Israeli conflict was feasible only if the Arabs dealt with it from a position of strength or—in Syria's terminology—if "strategic parity" with Israel was attained. FM Khaddam, who was the SRF's chief spokesman, launched a bitter attack against those Arab states that, he said, were allowing the Americans to consolidate their military presence in the region and undercut the Arabs' bargaining power. He insisted that the conflict with Israel must be accorded top priority at the summit meeting. However, Khaddam argued, it would be a tactical mistake to put forward a plan that would be construed as the Arabs' maximum demand, since this would mean forgoing in advance the Arabs' strategic goals in the conflict with Israel. Syria could not accept Israel's existence within the 1967 borders, as this would recognize Israeli control over four-fifths of Palestine.

Hoisting the Palestinian flag, Khaddam argued that only the PLO could determine Palestinian rights. However, Khaddam made it clear that the PLO authority in this regard was nominal as far as Damascus was concerned: if the PLO adopted a stand conflicting with "the Arab national position," Syria would fight it. Khaddam in fact signalled to the PLO leadership that they must reject the Saudi plan in accordance with Syria's considerations or collide head-on with Syria. Addressing himself to the idea that support for the plan would be tactically useful because it would expose Israel's true face for all to see, Khaddam said that even if this were so, it would be a small achievement compared with the concession of principle entailed by adopting the Saudi plan. The Fahd Plan would certainly divide the Arab world, Khaddam warned his audience, but would be far less likely to drive a wedge between the United States and Israel.[11]

The heated debate on this issue induced none of the parties to alter their stands. Representatives of the SRF states reiterated their outright rejection of the Fahd Plan unless substantive changes were introduced, primarily abolition of the seventh point. The Saudis remained unmoved: they would brook no changes in the plan, and most definitely would not retract its seventh point. They also rejected Iraq's proposal to discuss the plan at a forthcoming summit meeting, and Libya's demand that the subject be struck from the agenda. Finally, it was agreed to refer the Saudi plan to the summit meeting and leave it to the Arab heads of state to decide.

Despite their overtly firm position the Saudis made a considerable effort to prevent a rift and salvage the summit meeting by offering to formulate a new "Arab peace plan." It would be based on the Fahd Plan, but objections could be raised and new ideas introduced in it at the summit. This proposal was the subject of correspondence between the Saudi and Syrian heads of states right up to the convening of the summit meeting, but to no avail. Syria would not retract its demand for the abolition of the seventh point, while the Saudis insisted that it remain, aware that without it the entire plan would be perceived as worthless by the United States and Western Europe. Just before the summit's opening, all the PLO guerrilla groups—with the exception of Fatah—issued a joint statement rejecting the Fahd Plan, exposing 'Arafat's indecisive position on it.[12]

The Arab states' ineptitude in dealing with a contentious matter such as the Fahd Plan was evidenced in the opening of the summit on November 25 at Fez, without the presidents of Syria, Libya, Algeria, Iraq, Mauritania, Tunisia, and Sudan. Only Asad's absence was directly related to the Saudi plan and its inclusion in the agenda. Still, the absence of seven heads of state—from Syria and Iraq especially—seriously undermined the summit's credentials and called into question the validity of its resolutions. 'Arafat's attendance, the exception among the SRF leaders, was yet another indication of the growing gulf between Damascus and its Palestinian proteges.

The opening session demonstrated the radicals' veto power, unified by their objection to the Saudi plan. The dilemma faced by the host, King Hasan II, was how to adjourn the summit in order to avoid a clash with the radicals, but without losing face. As host, King Hasan was determined to ensure the meeting's success, or at least its respectful conclusion, even if this were only a facade. To this end, he paid lip service to the eight-point plan, asserting that it had become the property of the entire summit conference, and as such could not be written off. However, since the opposition could not be disregarded either, Hasan proposed to suspend the conference, but while still leaving it open, as he put it, in order to allow continued inter-Arab consultations on an agreed formulation that would enable the summit plenum to be reconvened.

Emir Fahd provided Hasan with a way out of the impasse by stating that Saudi Arabia was ready to entertain proposals for changes in its peace plan, but in view of the Arab objection to the plan, he urged that it be dropped altogether from the agenda to prevent division of the conference. Assenting to this approach while also expressing support for the plan, King Husain noted that the Saudi plan had been favorably received in the West, putting Israel on the defensive in its international public relations. Shelving the plan, he argued, would be an Arab setback in the international arena, handing Israel new ammunition to back up its allegation that the Arabs did not want peace. 'Arafat, asked for his opinion of the Fahd Plan, was plainly in a quandary. Failing to sidestep the issue by suggesting that it was time for prayer, 'Arafat admitted that he had accepted the plan with certain reservations but now urged that it be dropped from the agenda. The PLO chairman, however, commented that Israel would be the only winner if the plan were torpedoed by the Arabs themselves.

Hasan's motion to suspend the meeting gained majority backing. To preclude the impression of failure and division, it was agreed to issue a communique stating that the first session had been devoted to the Lebanon issue—following an emotional appeal by President Sarkis "to the conscience of all the Arab leaders to come to Lebanon's aid"—and that the relevant working paper had been approved. The communique issued by Hasan did not mention the Saudi plan or the deliberations surrounding it. King Hasan's statement notwithstanding, the deep inter-Arab division surrounding the Saudi plan made it plain that no prospect existed for its acceptance, and that restoration of Arab solidarity entailed shelving the entire plan, at least temporarily. Reflecting this division was the early publication by the Lebanese press of the complete minutes of the FMs' debates as well as of the summit's single session.[13]

The summit fiasco notwishstanding, the Saudi initiative constituted a milestone in the evolving attitude of the Arab world toward the conflict with Israel. Essentially, the Fahd Plan contained no ideological innovations and made no practical contribution to the prescription for a settlement of the Arab-Israeli conflict, basically corresponding to Resolution 242 in terms of territorial and political factors. Even in the controversial Article 7, the Saudis did not exceed the letter and spirit of Resolution 242—indeed, nowhere was Israel's name mentioned. Yet the Fahd Plan was the first peace initiative espoused by a leading Arab state since Sadat's visit to Jerusalem. Indeed, as the Syrian FM tacitly suggested, it was one thing to accept Resolution 242 as a basis for settlement, and an entirely different step for the Arabs to submit it as their own proposal, practically offering Israel an opportunity to negotiate further Arab concessions. Regardless of the Saudis' selfish motives, their persistence in defending the plan was noteworthy, as was their eagerness to obtain an all-Arab approval for the plan, despite anticipated confrontation with the radical Arab states. In this context, inter-Arab discussions at Fez, Riyad, and Damascus were a bitter disappointment for the Saudis.

Possibly the combination of the Iran-Iraq war and the problems faced by Syria at home and in Lebanon may have given the Saudis hope that opposition to their plan would be meager. However, the Ba'th regimes in Syria and Iraq overcame their enmity to reject the Fahd Plan on the principle that recognizing Israel's existence was unacceptable. The external and domestic difficulties of both countries may have led them to stiffen further their resistance. The fiasco of the Saudi plan showed that in the absence of Egypt neither economic clout nor influence in the West, nor even the support of a majority of Arab states, was sufficient to gain backing for a definitive political line on the Arab-Israeli conflict without the assent of the predominant confrontation state, namely, Syria.

The PLO, whose assent was indispensable to any Arab consensus regarding a solution to the Palestinian question, demonstrated once again that it was prone to political paralysis and incapable of reaching a decision at times of severe inter-Arab division. The PLO's overwhelming dependence on Syria since the latter's massive invasion of Lebanon in 1976 greatly limited the organization's ability to maneuver politically without jeopardizing its precarious unity. Given the formal all-Arab consensus that only the PLO had the right to speak for the West Bank and Gaza, and the Syrian leverage over the PLO, any peacemaking initiative was bound to depend largely on the assent of Damascus. Syria viewed the PLO as a political asset buttressing its own regional posture and acting as a buffer against any diplomatic peace efforts that failed to jibe with Damascus' approach and demands regarding a peaceful settlement with Israel.

Nevertheless, the Fahd Plan, by the very fact of its being placed before the Arab world for consideration at the highest political level, demonstrated that for the majority of Arab states formal acceptance, or even a peace agreement with Israel, was in principle no longer anathema. Even though the Fahd Plan made willingness to acquiesce in the existence of a sovereign Jewish state in the Middle East contingent upon demands unacceptable to Israel, it could not diminish the significance of the Saudi plan as another step forward in the Arabs' ever-growing pragmatism toward Israel since 1967.

The Making of the Fez Plan

The Saudi peace plan returned to center stage in the wake of Beirut's siege and President Reagan's peace initiative of September 1, 1982. The Arab governments were compelled to take a stand on President Reagan's peace plan, which reinforced the existing tendency to place the Palestinian question at the center of the ensuing Arab summit at Fez. In contrast to the Israeli government, which dismissed the Reagan Plan outright, the majority of Arab governments accepted it as a basically positive move that reflected a shift of U.S. policy in the Arabs' favor, even if some of the plan's essential elements were untenable. It was expressly because of the falling-out between Washington and Jerusalem—and to preserve the momentum of the U.S. preoccupation with the Palestinian question—that the Arab governments espousing a political solution felt obliged to counter it with a positive alternative plan of their own. In doing so they sought to take advantage of the negative echoes triggered by Israel's Lebanon war in world opinion. Most blatant in support for the Reagan Plan—although a non-participant in the summit—was Egypt, where the press called on Arab governments to adopt the plan as a "lifebelt" and a brake against Israel's annexation of the West Bank and Gaza Strip.[14]

Notwithstanding bitter inter-Arab disputes and a morale crisis at the results of the war, the summit was marked by a sense of urgent need to reach consensus. Thus, although two days of the FMs deliberations failed to produce an agreed agenda for the summit conference, it was decided to submit for the perusal of the heads of state all the topics under discussion since the 1981 Fez summit, notably the Fahd Plan. This once again underlined the exclusive authority of the Arab heads of state in making decisions on foreign policy, and the technocratic status of their FMs. Before the summit began, the leading participants had reached understanding on the agenda in a series of bilateral contacts conducted by the Saudi leaders and King Hasan II with the rulers of Amman, Baghdad, and Damascus.

The Saudis in particular were engaged in vigorous diplomatic activity to obtain the support of the Syrian president for the Fahd Plan and to ensure his attendance, while King Husain lobbied the Iraqi president in the same vein. The final agenda was composed of four principal subjects: the Arab-Israeli conflict; the Israeli invasion of Lebanon; the Gulf war; and the Somali-Ethiopian war. The strict procedures applied in this summit also reflected the joint efforts by Saudi Arabia and Morocco to assure success. Discussions were held secretly, reporters were barred from Fez, the number of participants was limited to no more than three per delegation, and restrictions were placed on releasing information to the press.[15]

The summit session opened with the attendance of the presidents of Syria and Iraq, the Jordanian and Saudi monarchs, and the rulers of the Gulf emirates, which dramatized the difference between this conference and its precursor in November 1981. 'Arafat was greeted upon arrival in Fez by the monarchs and presidents with an impressive display of solidarity, a ceremony from which President Asad absented himself. All Arab states were represented at the summit, excepting only Egypt, which had not been invited, and Libya, which boycotted it. Algeria, Mauritania, Tunisia, and Lebanon were represented by a lesser figure than the head of state, evidently to show their displeasure at the summit, none of which directly related to the Saudi plan. King Hasan's opening remarks dwelt on the grave circumstances in which the Arab states found themselves, terming the meeting "the final opportunity" of the Arab nation to extricate itself from the political, military, and morale nadir in which it was mired.[16]

Both Asad and 'Arafat expressed their expectations for generous Arab financial aid aimed at enhancing their ability to handle the burdens of the conflict with Israel. Asad reiterated his credo regarding the necessity of an Arab strategy, which he said was dictated by "the historic confrontation with the Zionist enemy." Therefore, he asserted, it was essential to attain strategic parity with Israel, irrespective of whether the Arab world was bent on war or peace. 'Arafat, who avoided explicit criticism of the Arab states for their inaction during the siege of Beirut, called on them to end their disputes and rifts, and to act jointly in order to repulse the Israeli threat. In this context, he reiterated his request for material and moral assistance for Palestinians living under the Israeli occupation.

'Arafat also refrained from criticizing the Reagan Plan, though he used it as a reason to reaffirm Arab support for the PLO's status and Palestinian political rights. Obviously, 'Arafat could not accept the American initiative because it had only proposed Palestinian autonomy under Jordanian auspices. Thus, he insisted that the Arab peace plan on the conflict with Israel express a clear commitment to the PLO as the Palestinians' exclusive representative as well as to supporting its goal of establishing an independent Palestinian state.[17]

The Arab-Israeli conflict was discussed by a committee consisted of the heads of Saudi Arabia, Syria, Jordan, Lebanon, the PLO, Morocco, and Tunisia. It dealt with King Fahd's "eight-point plan," Bourguiba's 1965 proposals to adopt the UN 1947 partition resolution, and with the Reagan Plan. The resolution adopted on this issue was actually a revised version of the Fahd Plan, reflecting an effort to bridge the gulf between the stands of Riyad and Damascus, which had caused the collapse of the previous summit. The Saudis, prodded by Syria and the PLO, made significant concessions on Fahd's original plan:

1. The controversial Article 7 was amended to read, "The Security Council will provide guarantees for peace among all the states of the region, including the independent Palestinian state." According the UN a central role in implementing a settlement of the conflict dovetailed with Syrian policy, which opposed direct negotiations or granting any form of recognition to Israel. Moreover, the article implicitly affirmed the integration into the Middle East peace process of the USSR and Western Europe, a development that would deprive the United States of a monopoly in this regard.

2. In the new wording, the PLO was explicitly cited in the plan as playing a central role in realizing the Palestinian national goals, whereas the original version of the Fahd Plan had referred to the PLO only in an explanatory annex. Moreover, the wording of the resolution gave maximum, if vague, expression to the bulk of the Palestinians' territorial and political demands. Thus, besides the right for self-determination, mention was also made of "the inalienable national rights," which could be interpreted either as relating to the right of the Palestinian refugees to return to their homes in Israel or as ruling out any compromise of Palestinian territory.

3. Mention of the Bourguiba plan in the preamble to the new Arab plan confused the Arab intention with respect to the borders to which Israel must withdraw. Indeed, at least two articles spoke explicitly of an Israeli pullback to the June 1967 borders—King Hasan stated explicitly that the West Bank and Gaza Strip were "the future Palestinian homeland." Under the Bourguiba plan, however, Israel would be called on to withdraw to the

partition boundaries as stipulated in the UN's November 1947 resolution.[18]

Once these changes had been inserted, Asad found no difficulty in lending the plan his support, the more so as the preamble also lauded the "steadfastness" of the Syrian forces in the Lebanon war. For Damascus, this was a major contribution toward offsetting the harsh criticism levelled at it during the war by other Arab states. Although the final format continued to bear the imprint of the original Fahd Plan, which Syria had opposed so vehemently, the revisions voided it of its manifestations of moderation. Thus, the Syrian press could assert that Damascus alone had prevented the conference from sliding into defeatism. Asad's readiness for concessions was demonstrated in the absence of condemnation of the Reagan Plan in the summit's resolutions, though his press presented it as worse than the Camp David accords. The Syrian delegation also dropped its demand that the resolutions take note of the Arab governments' intentions to mobilize all their resources in the confrontation with Israel.[19]

The upshot was that despite its isolation in the inter-Arab arena and its questionable military role during the war in Lebanon, Syria remained indispensable in any attempt to secure an all-Arab consensus for a positive plan of action on the Arab-Israeli conflict. Syria's top priority was formulating the collective Arab position on a settlement of the conflict with Israel. To this end, it was willing to accept, in response to repeated Iraqi demands and pressures of the Gulf monarchies, a vague Arab commitment to defend the latter's land against foreign aggression. Syria also managed to bar any discussion of Egypt's return to the Arab fold, which had been suggested by Sudan and seconded by Iraq and Jordan, but without gaining any support from Saudi Arabia. Indeed, without Egypt, the conservative states led by Riyad found that the attainment of an Arab consensus where the conflict was concerned entailed lining up behind Syria.[20]

The summit decided to dispatch a delegation to Washington and the other capitals of the UNSC's permanent members to promote the Arab peace plan and to clarify U.S. policy in light of the Reagan Plan. Indeed, in stark contrast to Israel's outright rejection of the plan, the Arabs were bent on persuading Washington to alter its ideas in the direction of the Arab plan by evincing a positive approach and flexibility. The delegation was to consist of representatives from the states participating in formulating the Arab peace plan, including the PLO. The co-option of a PLO delegate to the committee was meant to bypass Washington's prerequisites for conducting a dialogue with the organization.

That Arab consensus was reached on the Saudi plan despite the participants' acrimonious divisions and rivalries attested to a temporary convergence of needs and constraints rather than to agreement on a new joint strategy. The apparent unity was somewhat illusory, as would be attested to by Syria's confrontation with the PLO six months later. Notwithstanding their over-whelming weight at the meeting, the pragmatic states espousing a moderate socio-political approach and Western orientation had to accept far-reaching compromises to satisfy Syria and the PLO and ensure a consensus.

As it turned out, however, the new Arab strategy, designed to drive a wedge between Israel and the U.S. administration, was not even remotely consistent with the principles enunciated by Reagan, leading Washington to reject the Fez Plan. The United States was particularly troubled by the vague-ness of the clause concerning recognition of Israel and by the pivotal role assigned to the PLO in a settlement. Israel, for its part, dismissed the Arab plan and called for direct, immediate negotiations. Indeed, despite its strict ter-ritorial demands the Fez Plan aimed at best to terminate the state of war with Israel, thereby falling short of the precedents set by the Israel-Egypt peace treaty regarding full recognition and normalization of relations in return for an Israeli withdrawal to the June 1967 lines.[21]

Still, the Fez Plan constituted a historical precedent in the Arab collec-tive attitude in the conflict with Israel. For the first time, an Arab summit conference resolution on the conflict with Israel not only avoided the use of war terminology, or intransigent rhetoric, it was also non-transitional, depart-ing from the strategy of phases. The final statement refrained from using the traditional phrase of "the Arab-Zionist conflict," or its equivalent term, "the Palestine problem," which ignored the existence of Israel. Instead, the summit used the pragmatic term, "the Arab-Israeli conflict," ambiguously indicating acquiescence in Israel's legitimate existence. Indeed, the Arab peace plan was aimed mainly at the U.S. administration, reflecting growing awareness of Israel's strategic preponderance in its conflict with the Arabs. More than any other single factor, it was the shortfall in oil prices—combined with the bur-dening economy of the Gulf war—that diminished the Arabs' bargaining position in the international arena and eroded the oil monarchies' willingness to place their national resources at the service of the confrontation actors.

The PLO-Jordan Dialogue

The Jordan-PLO political dialogue was an effort by veteran rivals to address their particular urgent needs, despite residues of mutual hostility and mistrust, in view of the political conditions created by the Lebanon war and Reagan's September 1 peace initiative. The course and substance of the PLO-Jordan dialogue was in the context of Reagan's peace initiative, which envi-sioned Jordan as Israel's negotiating partner over the West Bank and Gaza Strip. However, the renewed all-Arab recognition by the Fez summit of the

PLO's status and endorsement of the establishment of a PLO-run Palestinian state left both contenders at an impasse.

Political contacts between Jordan and the PLO were by no means a new phenomenon. Since late 1978, both sides had conducted a limited collaboration in distributing Arab financial aid to the occupied territories, institutionalized in the Joint Jordanian-Palestinian Committee.[22] A meeting between Jordan's FM and ʿArafat, held in Athens on September 3, 1982, paved the road to King Husain's call for a Jordanian-Palestinian dialogue to work out a formula for "unification between the two peoples" and to discuss the nature of relations between Jordan and the Palestinian entity. ʿArafat's acceptance of Husain's initiative marked a new phase in their political collaboration.[23]

King Husain's recognition of the PLO as the Palestinians' sole legitimate representative notwithstanding, his call was a ploy to take advantage of the PLO's enfeeblement and Washington's support for a Jordanian-Palestinian federation under the Hashemite crown, upheld by the king since 1972. The proposed dialogue was to reflect Jordan's primacy in any new relationship with the PLO and interest in transforming the latter into an acceptable interlocutor to the United States, which would need ʿArafat's acceptance of Resolution 242.[24]

The Lebanon war enhanced worldwide consciousness of the gravity of the Palestinian problem and the need to further support ʿArafat. Yet it also deprived the PLO of its semi-independent territorial base in Lebanon and forced it to disperse its forces among a number of Arab countries. Moreover, the weak response of the Arab states and the Soviet Union to the Israeli invasion and siege of Beirut, their acceptance of Israel's demand for the evacuation of armed Palestinians from the Lebanese capital, and the intensifying crisis in Syria-PLO relations, all combined to define the PLO's political situation as rather gloomy. With the benefit of hindsight, however, the blow inflicted by Israel and Syria on the PLO's military posture and autonomous territorial base in Lebanon also forced the PLO to reassess its political strategies and priorities, resulting in greater freedom of political maneuvering on both Palestinian and inter-Arab levels. An astute Palestinian commentator went as far as to welcome the exodus from Lebanon and the end of the "Fakahani Republic," which had entangled the PLO in unnecessary battles, exhausted its power, and distracted the movement from its original political agenda.[25]

For ʿArafat, the dialogue was a matter of political survival. It provided an opportunity to escape from Syrian tutelage and to balance its influence through closer relations with the pragmatic camp—Egypt, Jordan, Morocco, and Saudi Arabia—which had been seeking to resume the peace process under U.S. auspices. The dialogue was also an opportunity to pave the road to American acknowledgment of the PLO if the Reagan initiative was to make any headway. Indeed, throughout the dialogue with Jordan ʿArafat would repeatedly insist that in view of Arab weakness and disarray, his diplomacy meant to generate a basis for political action—namely, a dialogue with the United States and American recognition of the Palestinian right for self-determination—not a political solution. The dialogue with Jordan was also expected to enable the return of PLO political and military headquarters to Amman to solidify the PLO's influence in the occupied territories as well as among the substantial Palestinian community in Jordan.[26]

The PLO feared Jordan's restoring its claims and influence on the West Bank but its own weakness made collaboration with Amman a compelling necessity. Similarly, Jordan needed cooperation with the PLO as it lacked Arab legitimacy or political backing among Palestinians to represent their cause. The PLO and Jordan were also impelled to work together by Israel's vigorous settlement movement in the West Bank which threatened both of them, not least with the specter of large-scale Palestinian emigration from that territory to Jordan. Such specter was conceived as a realistic possibility deliberately intended to undermine the Hashemite regime's stability and substantiate the idea that "Jordan is Palestine"—in the Arabic terminology, the "alternative home-land" (*al-watan al-badil*)—prevalent among the ruling Israeli right-wing Likud party.[27]

In addition to their own constraints, 'Arafat and Husain had to reckon with the objections to their diplomatic cooperation sounded by Syria and radical Palestinian groups. Syria, in particular, sought to prevent independent PLO diplomacy, which would diminish its own bargaining position in the peace process. The sixteenth PNC session, held in Algiers in February 1983, approved the establishment of a special relationship with Jordan, the future form of which would be a confederal union between two independent states. Yet the PNC retained its objection to UN resolution 242, implicitly rejecting the Reagan initiative for ignoring the PLO.[28]

The PLO-Jordan talks involved intensive diplomatic activity, in which other Arab governments as well as the Powers played a role. The Saudi and Moroccan monarchs preferred a collective Arab framework, rather than a bilateral PLO-Jordanian one, for advancing the peace process. Yet both monarchs opted to encourage the PLO-Jordan dialogue on the basis of Reagan's initiative and mediated between the PLO and the U.S. administration in an attempt to obtain assurances for the Palestinians' demands. Syria and the Soviet Union maintained pressures on both Jordan and the PLO not to adopt the American initiative, with Damascus warning that disobedience would cause withdrawal of its recognition of the PLO.[29]

On April 3, 'Arafat and King Husain initialled a draft agreement on "establishing a confederal connection between Jordan and Palestine that will maintain the separate national identities of both peoples." The two sides agreed to conduct joint political activity that would lead to peace talks aimed at

"Israel's withdrawal from the Palestinian and Arab occupied territories," based on the Fez summit and UN resolutions recognizing the Palestinian national rights, as well as on the Reagan initiative. The draft agreement, however, failed to gain support of Fatah's leadership and the PLO's Executive Committee. PLO leaders offered amendments, mainly the omission of the Reagan initiative, which Husain rejected. Instead, Jordan announced the failure of the efforts to come to an agreement, blaming the PLO and reiterating its commitment not to represent the Palestinians or hold separate negotiations on their cause. Jordan reaffirmed the inadequacy of the Fez summit's resolutions as a basis for a renewed peace diplomacy.[30]

The dialogue's breakdown was the first in a series of setbacks for the PLO that culminated in 'Arafat's expulsion from Tripoli in late 1983, which seemed to mark the organization's political demise. Faced with Syrian efforts to subjugate the PLO, 'Arafat's visit to Egypt directly when leaving Tripoli was a vigorous message of persistence at maintaining the PLO's independence by alignment with Syria's Arab adversaries while pursuing the diplomatic option under American auspices. To advance such a policy and recover the PLO's political posture, however, 'Arafat had to put the PR in order by convening the PNC, to ensure a solid basis of support for his leadership and prospective policy.

The internal Palestinian discourse on convening the PNC revealed serious disagreement between Fatah and the radical leftist and Syrian-based PLO factions that hinged on relations with Jordan, prospects of peace diplomacy, and the conference's venue. The advent of a Labor-led government in Israel in August 1984—headed by Shimon Peres, a strong advocate of the "Jordanian Option"—and the expectation for enhanced American efforts to revive the peace process following the presidential elections, all gathered to inject new life into the region's diplomacy. In September, Jordan resumed its diplomatic relations with Egypt, a measure that overtly violated the Baghdad summit's boycott against that country and gained a strong ally for the peacemaking diplomacy with Israel.

In November, King Husain offered to host the seventeenth session of the PNC in Amman, breaking a Palestinian deadlock on this matter and deepening the rupture within the PLO between 'Arafat and the leftist factions that opposed any dialogue with the Hashemite regime. The ensuing PNC session in Amman led Syria to intensify its subversion and anti-Hashemite terrorism, whose victims included Jordanian diplomats and newspaper editors, the 'Aliya Jordanian Airline, and the dismissed Mayor of Hebron, Fahd Qawasmi. Nonetheless, the PNC was convened in Amman despite Syrian and Libyan pressures on Palestinian delegates to refrain from attending the meeting, and a boycott by the PFLP and DFLP. The event boosted 'Arafat's prestige among Palestinians in Jordan and the occupied territories, and in his critics' absence, broadened his freedom of action. Thus, the PNC emphasized independent Palestinian decision-making, approved rapprochement with Egypt, and accepted the king's call for a joint political action with Jordan.[31]

In February 1985, 'Arafat and King Husain signed an accord that evaded the problem of the PLO's rejection of Resolution 242 by adopting a formula of "land for peace as mentioned in the UN resolutions, including the Security Council resolutions." The agreement called for peace talks under the auspices of an international conference, sponsored by the UNSC's five permanent members, and invited all parties to the conflict, including the PLO, within a joint Jordanian-Palestinian delegation. The signatories sought both American acceptance of the international conference as an umbrella for a comprehensive peace, and recognition of the PLO's status as an equal participant.[32]

The agreement indicated a departure from the Fez Plan at three points: a) confining the peace effort to the Palestinian sector only rather than pursuing a comprehensive settlement as stated by the Fez Plan; b) stipulating that Palestinian independence was to materialize within the framework of a confederation with Jordan rather than in an independent Palestinian state; c) providing no reservations regarding Arab commitment to peace and to the instruments of its implementation, while the Fez Plan sought to receive the territories from the UN, naming the UNSC as the peace guarantor.

The Amman Accord represented another step in King Husain's retreat from his original claim to the West Bank and adaptation to more equal relations with a Palestinian entity in this territory, albeit under Hashemite leadership. Still, the accord could hardly conceal essential differences between the signatories on two main issues: the PLO would not accept less than an independent Palestinian state (as a prerequisite for establishing confederal relations with Jordan), or agree to direct negotiations and full peace with Israel. The PLO-Amman accord was fiercely attacked by the radical Syrian-backed PNSF, though reservations at the accord's wording were also expressed by the PLO's Executive Committee and Fatah senior members. Palestinian criticism focused especially on the provisions of confederation and the joint delegation to the peace negotiations, which was said to collide with the principle of Palestinian independent decision-making and the establishment of an independent state. 'Arafat's critics also pointed to the absence of reference to the Palestinians' right for self-determination and the rejection of Resolution 242 encapsulated in the phrase "land for peace," as well as of direct negotiations with Israel. Thus, while the PLO ratified the accord, it insisted on two amendments reflecting the Palestinian reservations, which were resentfully accepted by Jordan.[33]

Deadlocked Diplomacy

In July 1985, Morocco, impelled by the siege of the Palestinian refugee camps in Lebanon, offered to host an emergency summit meeting, and seemed to have mustered wide Arab support for the PLO. Aside from the prestige accruing to a summit host, King Hasan was apparently motivated by expectations for external financial reward—to help his accumulating economic difficulties—for taking the lead in resuming Arab peace efforts based on the Fez Plan. Syria rejected the proposal and once again convinced its radical counterparts and Lebanese client to go along with its "sense of Pan-Arab national responsibility" and its opposition to legitimizing "capitulationist" political moves or letting Egypt return to the Arab fold.[34]

Given Egypt's exclusion and Iraq's low profile because of its war with Iran, the Saudi acceptance of King Hasan's invitation for an Arab summit was crucial in determining its very convening. However, the agenda proposed by Morocco—including a discussion of the Amman Accord and its compatibility with the Fez Plan—remained contested and the preparatory meeting of the Arab FMs failed to reach an agreement. The provocative agenda presented by Libya as a precondition for Qadhafi's attending the summit—conducting a trial of Iraq's and Jordan's rulers for their relations with Egypt; Arab unity, and the "liberation of Palestine"—underlined the unbridgeable gap between the pragmatist regimes and the SRF.[35] In view of the possibility of the summit's approving the Amman Accord, Syria, along with its partners in the SRF—Libya, Algeria, and PDRY—and Lebanon, boycotted the summit conference. Moreover, of the sixteen AL members that attended the summit, only ten were represented by heads of state, with the rest indicating their ambivalence, or political constraints about the Amman Accord. Particularly salient were the absences of King Fahd and Saddam Husain.

The summit deliberations, which hinged on the Palestinian cause—the siege of the camps and the Amman Accord—revealed differences even between Jordan and the PLO. King Husain presented the agreement as an operative plan based on the Fez Plan and as one "excelled by clarity and realism," which might lead to "a just and comprehensive peace to all the region's peoples and the world." Dramatizing his appeal to the summit, the king warned that failure to give full backing to the Amman Accord would thrust the Arab world into a position of "paralysis and silence." The PLO-Jordan agreement was "the last opportunity" to secure a breakthrough of the deadlocked peace process, the king said and, if it failed, "may Allah save Palestine and its people." In contrast to King Husain's request, disagreement within the PLO was bluntly demonstrated in a memorandum presented to the summit by Faruq al-Qaddumi, in charge of PLO's foreign affairs and a leading hardliner of 'Arafat's Fatah, suggesting that the discussion on the Amman Accord be transferred to the ordinary summit due in Riyad.[36]

The radicals' absence ostensibly provided an opportunity to adopt resolutions that accorded with the interests of Jordan, the PLO, and the Gulf states. However, the delegates could not ignore the Amman Accord's implications on the collective Arab strategy in the conflict with Israel, particularly on Syria. Their caution was obviously shown in the summit's resolution expressing general and non-committal "full appreciation" of 'Arafat's and King Husain's explanations that their agreement would implement the Fez Plan. Further, in its concluding statement the summit reiterated the Arab collective adherence to the Fez summit resolutions and principles, thus indirectly rejecting any role for Jordan in the peace process. Another important resolution expressed support for an international peace conference, under UN auspices with "participation of the Soviet Union, the United States, other permanent members of the Security Council, the PLO and other parties concerned." Although this resolution coincided with the Amman Accord, the emphasis on Soviet participation was apparently meant to reassure Syria that the process would not be dominated by the United States.[37]

'Arafat was the summit's real winner, since it reaffirmed the PLO's political status and Arab collective support for establishing an independent Palestinian state. The summit also reiterated the PLO's right to exercise full independence in its policymaking without external interference—a slap at Syrian attempts to impose control on the organization—and confirmed its special status in Lebanon by calling on both sides to implement the agreements between them through cooperation. As for Syria, it demonstrated again its ability to prevent collective Arab moves that it deemed contrary to its own interests. Yet Syria's excessive use of force and its threat to veto unfavorable Arab policies were shown to have limits by the summit's very convening and its unequivocal support of the PLO. Moreover, for the first time in its annals, an Arab summit renounced terrorism—excluding Palestinian armed struggle from this category—in unequivocal language in its concluding announcement, aiming unmistakably at Syria and Libya for sponsoring terrorism against Jordanian and Palestinian targets.

In the final analysis, the summit hardly helped to advance the Amman Accord, as requested by King Husain and 'Arafat. In fact, it underlined once again the necessity for Syria's full participation in the peace process. In this context, the call for convening an international peace conference represented an antidote to the Camp David separate peace, suggesting a framework that even Syria could accept under certain conditions. In retrospect, this modality was to gather momentum in the following years despite the stalemated peace diplomacy, thanks to the Amman Accord and the efforts of the Moroccan and Saudi monarchs, as well as of Israel's Labor party, to advance this idea by winning Washington's support.

The Amman Accord had indeed become the basis for diplomatic contacts between Jordan, the PLO, and the United States aimed at obtaining Washington's support for the Jordanian-Palestinian formula of political action. The diplomatic endeavor hinged on the PLO's participation and standing in the proposed international conference. Jordan and the PLO sought to bring about a meeting between their joint delegation and U.S. officials. Following that meeting the PLO would announce its acceptance of Resolutions 242 and 338, which would be reciprocated by official U.S. recognition of the PLO and the Palestinian right of self-determination, followed by normalization of relations between them.[38]

By mid-1985, however, the United States and the PLO were moving in a vicious circle. At Israel's request, Washington insisted that the Palestinian members in the joint delegation be independent and refrain from identifying themselves with the PLO, a request the latter utterly rejected as an encroachment on its exclusive national authority. To the contrary, the PLO insisted that its participation in the international conference be on an equal and independent footing, albeit in a joint delegation with Jordan. The PLO insisted on being recognized as the only authority appointing the Palestinian delegates and supervising their activity.[39]

The PLO was willing to accept resolutions 242 and 338 only in exchange for American recognition of the Palestinian people's right for self-determination. The PLO justifiably argued that such recognition was necessary given the lack of any reference in these resolutions to the Palestinians or to their national rights. Washington, however, adhered to its basic prerequisites for opening a dialogue with the PLO: an unequivocal recognition of Resolutions 242 and 338; renunciation of terrorism; and acceptance of direct negotiations with Israel. In January 1986, during King Husain's visit to Washington, the Reagan administration informed him that it was willing to invite the PLO to an international conference if it would accept these three conditions.[40]

Washington's conditions deepened the cleavage between the PLO and Jordan. The PLO opposed the American-Israeli principle of direct negotiations, perceiving the international conference as a way of imposing a settlement on Israel without committing the Palestinians to parallel concessions. Further, Husain's hope for flexibility on the PLO's part concerning Resolution 242 was frustrated when the PLO firmly rejected the new American proposal. The PLO submitted its own proposals in order to rescue the negotiations with Washington, which included one new element, namely, the PLO's willingness to negotiate, in an international conference, a peace settlement for the Palestinian problem with the Israeli government.[41]

The ensuing deadlock caused by the PLO's position raised the tension between the two Arab parties, leading the king to announce, on February 20, the suspension of the Amman Accord until the PLO changed its political position. The manipulative nature of the king's step was evident in his speech, which he directed primarily at the Palestinians in the occupied territories. The king blamed the PLO's ineptitude in tackling responsibly their urgent problem and appealed for their help in moderating its position. Husain focused on the threat to the demographic and political status quo on both sides of the Jordan River posed by Israel's settlement policy in the occupied territories, which would inevitably lead to the expulsion of its Palestinian inhabitants. He reiterated the need to protect the Jordanian entity and the Palestinian existence in the West Bank and Gaza by the latter's perseverance and, in the long run, through a comprehensive settlement based on the necessary connection of Jordan and the PLO. These premises and goals were soon to be translated into a $1,015 million five-year program for social and economic development in the occupied territories, to promote their perseverance in the face of Israel's policy of creeping annexation. The unilateral program, announced by Husain in November, entirely ignored the PLO and even avoided using the word "Palestine" or "Palestinians" in reference to the territories or their population, referring to them instead as "Jordanians" or "Arabs."[42]

King Husain's new policy won Israel's tacit support as it seemed to weaken the PLO's position in the occupied territories, in addition to the closure of PLO military headquarters in Jordan. Politically, Amman's plan was intended to be based on the existing Jordanian administrative system in the West Bank, local businessmen and loyalist notables, as well as the Islamic Waqf establishment. Still, the plan's weakest point was lack of funding. Given the kingdom's scant financial resources, prospects for the plan's implementation depended on the Gulf oil states' aid, which never came to be.[43]

The suspension of the Amman agreement coincided with rapprochement between Amman and Damascus following six years of hostility. Syria's interest in this rapproachement was apparently to deepen the PLO's isolation and diminish the prospect for renewal of the peace process exclusively over the Palestinian issue. The PLO made an effort to avoid burning its bridges with Amman, reiterating its adherence to the agreement with King Husain. With the king's development program, however, a growing abyss of suspicion yawned between Jordan and the PLO. Despite the king's repeated assurances that he would not act as a surrogate for either the Palestinians or the PLO, the latter interpreted the program as a vehement effort to enhance Jordan's influence in the occupied territories at its own expense.[44]

The return of PLO-Jordan relations to a "zero-sum" mode not only paved the way for a new Israeli-Jordanian rapprochement but also led ʿArafat to patch up his relations with radical Palestinian factions, especially the PFLP and DFLP, which had opposed rapprochement with Jordan. Relations with these groups improved through military cooperation during Amal's siege of the refugee camps in Lebanon. In April 1987, on the eve of the eighteenth PNC session, an agreement was reached between Fatah and these movements to nullify the Amman Accord, following which the radicals resumed their active participation in the PNC and other PLO institutions. ʿArafat thus sacrificed the meager chance for progress in the peacemaking efforts for the sake of internal Palestinian unity.[45]

The PLO reunion also involved renewed criticism of Egypt's peace agreement with Israel and accounted for a shift toward reconciliation with Syria. Egypt retaliated by closing the PLO's offices in Cairo and Alexandria, and ordered the Palestinian 'Ain Jalut Brigade to leave Egypt. The radicals' comeback indeed seemed to moderate Fatah figures to be a low ebb in the PLO's political posture and a retreat from the post-Lebanon achievements, as the PLO's leadership had become hostage to a radical minority.[46]

The diplomatic deadlock generated a sense of frustration among moderate Arab governments regarding the American administration's undetermined policy on the peace process. Washington's approach to the peace process reflected its own reluctance to involve the USSR in the mediation process, as well as its acquiescence to the Israeli government's objection to the concept of an international conference. In Israel, the Labor-Likud political parity within the national coalition government underpinned the division regarding an international conference, epitomizing the paralysis that marked the political system. Peres, the Labor Party leader, endorsed the idea and endeavored to promote it against the objection of his Likud counterpart Shamir, who portrayed it as a "trap" designed to impose territorial concessions on Israel. Yet even Peres accepted such a conference only as an "umbrella" for direct Israeli-Arab negotiations, restricting the role of non-regional powers to observers and precluding any PLO representation there.[47]

The political stalemate was demonstrated by Peres's futile efforts to mobilize sufficient Arab, American, and Israeli support for his concept of an international conference even following the Amman Accord's breakdown. Peres represented a fresh Israeli approach to peacemaking with the Arabs, as opposed to the rigidity of his Likud partners in the national coalition government and some of his own party's colleagues. His relentless efforts to break the stalemate in the peace process were directed at achieving a settlement with Jordan in cooperation with Palestinians in the West Bank and Gaza. Peres's diplomatic endeavor was noteworthy, albeit fruitless, in developing avenues for dialogue with moderate Arab leaders. Particularly salient in this regard was his official visit and meeting with President Mubarak in September 1986, which indicated the renewal of Israeli-Egyptian dialogue at the highest level after four years of cold distance. This was made possible by Israel's consent to resolve the Taba dispute by referring it to an international arbitration.

Another highlight of Peres's peace diplomacy was his dramatic visit to Morocco and meeting with King Hasan in July 1986, culminating a decade of secret contacts and mutual interests between the two countries. The significance of the public visit was especially conspicuous in view of King Hasan's position as a Chairman of the Arab summit and President of the ICO. The visit's occurrence, and the generally restrained Arab reactions to it, indicated the sea change in the Arab attitude toward peace with Israel since Sadat's historic visit to Jerusalem. Only Syria and Libya, along with Iran, responded in an aggressive manner, severing diplomatic relations and waging fierce propaganda campaigns against the Moroccan monarch, which underlined their isolated stand in the Arab arena on the Gulf war as well. Qadhafi's reaction to the visit brought to an end the two-year-old anomalous Morocco-Libya treaty of union.[48]

In April 1987, as FM in Shamir's government, Peres reached an agreement with King Husain in London on attending an international conference that would function as an umbrella for direct negotiations between Israel and a Jordanian-Palestinian delegation. No approval or participation of the PLO in the conference was mentioned nor did Jordan demand Israel's full withdrawal from the occupied territories as a prerequisite. The agreement, however, encountered the strong opposition of PM Shamir—even though he also met secretly with King Husain shortly afterward.[49]

The mid-1980s witnessed an intensified ideological tension within Israeli society regarding the future of the West Bank and Gaza. The public debate was a reflection of the Likud-Labor divisions and paralysis within the national coalition government over the resumption of the peace process. In addition, the demographic threat posed by the existence of 1.5 million Palestinians in the occupied territories—apart from Israel's 700,000 Arab citizens—turned into a major issue in Israel's public discourse. This was indicated *inter alia* by the appearance of extreme right-wing groups publicly adhering to the idea of "transfer"—a euphemistic term for expulsion—of Palestinians from the territories under Israel's control.[50]

In the West Bank and Gaza, a disquiet and tense atmosphere gathered momentum, expressed in a rise of spontaneous violent activities against Israeli civilians and military. The Palestinian society in the occupied territories was in the process of taking a growing role in national affairs at a time of political and military eclipse of the PLO. Militancy among Palestinians was fuelled all the more by the Israeli government's renewed efforts at settlement- and infrastructure-building in the West Bank, and growing economic difficulties among Palestinian residents. Indeed, the more the Arab world seemed divided and unable to threaten Israel's national security, the more vulnerable its domestic front seemed to its socio-political core.

The Jordan-PLO rift and Israel's diplomatic overtures toward King Husain underlined the perils of the imminent summit in Amman for the PLO. Thus, the PLO sought to ensure the summit's confirmation of its status as a full-fledged partner in an international Middle East peace conference according to the resolutions of the 1982 Fez and 1985 Casablanca summits. Anticipating difficulties with Husain and Asad on this issue, 'Arafat made vigorous diplomatic efforts to secure Arab and international support. In October, a PLO delegation visited Damascus in an effort to coordinate policy with Syria on the international peace conference, the release of thousands of Palestinian political prisoners in Syria, and lifting the Shi'i siege of Palestinian refugee camps in Lebanon. 'Arafat also visited the Soviet Union, for the first time in five years, and met with Gorbachev, resulting in official Soviet support for the PLO as a full-fledged partner in an international conference.[51]

'Arafat's diplomacy was inspired by a new American diplomatic initiative in October, following SoS Schulz's visit to the Middle East and Moscow. The American proposal advocated direct negotiations between Israel and the Arab states under the auspices, and following a formal opening of an international conference co-sponsored by the United States and the Soviet Union, with no other extra-regional participants. The proposal was reported to have gained Israel's reluctant approval but to have been rejected by King Husain who insisted on a full, active international conference. With the failure of this initiative, the chances for any imminent progress faded. Given the forthcoming elections in Israel and the U.S. presidential elections of 1988, it was believed that resumption of the peace process would be postponed until 1989.[52]

The Arab summit convened in Amman in November 1987 witnessed an unprecedented shared attempt by Asad and King Husain to undermine the PLO's status as "the sole legitimate representative of the Palestinian people," a formula that, since its adoption at the Rabat conference of 1974, had become a basic tenet of collective Arab politics. Reflecting their rapprochement, and taking advantage of the PLO's predicament, Asad and Husain objected to including the PLO as an independent element in an international peace conference. Asad insisted on its absorption into a joint Arab delegation, whereas Husain insisted that the PLO accept a joint Jordanian-Palestinian delegation to the international conference. Asad further voiced his opposition—tacitly shared by the Hashemite king—to establishing an independent Palestinian state, maintaining that the PLO would have to be satisfied with "administrative independence" (*istiqlal idari*).[53]

The Syrian caveat was defied this time by Iraq, with Saudi and Kuwaiti backing. It enabled Saddam Husain not only to identify himself with the Palestinian cause but also to attack Syria for attempting to divide the PLO ranks. The Iraqi president made an unsuccessful bid to conciliate between 'Arafat and Husain, who at his opening speech ignored the PLO. As the summit's host, the king deprived the PLO leader of the honor to which he was entitled as the head of a member state of the AL. It was no coincidence that the English text of the concluding statement, disseminated by the conference's organizers, omitted the translation of the Arabic clause defining the PLO as "the sole legitimate representative of the Palestinian people."[54]

Husain's and 'Arafat's bitter relations was echoed in the competition between their followers in the West Bank during the summit, with each side producing petitions to demonstrate its wider base of public support. Husain's proponents called for a Jordanian-Palestinian confederation based on the Hashemite principle of "unity of the two banks," thereby ignoring the role of the PLO in peace negotiations. In contrast, PLO supporters espoused incorporation of the PLO as a full-fledged partner in an international conference. Although Arab financial aid channelled to the West Bank and Gaza through the Joint Jordan-PLO Committee still served as an incentive for cooperation, the bitter political rivalry between Husain and 'Arafat seemed incurable.[55]

The concluding statement partly reflected the Syria-Jordan collaboration in undermining the PLO status. The summit approved the PLO's status according to the 1974 Rabat resolution and reiterated support for a UN-sponsored international Middle East peace conference, in which the PLO would participate on an equal footing. However, both the concluding statement and the secret resolutions failed to mention the goal of an independent Palestinian state, with the exception of an indirect reference that mentioned the Fez resolutions. This implied a retreat in Arab support for the PLO's political objectives for the first time since the 1976 Cairo summit. This outcome reflected the summit's low priority regarding the Palestinian issue, to which the Palestinian political community responded with overt rage and frustration.[56]

Whether or not the Amman summit had any direct impact on the outbreak of the uprising (*intifada*) in the West Bank and Gaza Strip in December 1987, it certainly provided a vivid demonstration of the PLO's political dwindling. The intifada was to reassert the centrality of the Palestinian problem in the region's politics, wiping out King Husain's achievement in diminishing the PLO's position as a partner in the peacemaking process. Indeed, the assumption that the Palestinian problem could wait or be relegated to the bottom of the Arab system's agenda was disproved by the unprecedented wave of violence, which became the focus of world interest and a matter of immediate concern to the Arab governments.

Egypt's Return to the "Arab Fold"

The ascendancy of Husni Mubarak following Sadat's assassination on October 6, 1981, gave rise to wishful expectations for Egypt's return to the Arab fold. This was apparent especially among conservative Arab regimes whose sanctions against Egypt had been dictated by external pressures rather than by self-interest or ideological persuasion. Yet despite a growing convergence of interests and practical cooperation between those conservative regimes—in addition to Iraq—and Egypt, the latter's full return to the Arab fold was to be delayed till 1989, mainly due to Syria's veto power.

Underlying the expectations for Egypt's return to play an active role in the Arab arena was the assumption that Israel's final evacuation of Sinai by April 1982 would enable Egypt to free itself from the Camp David framework for peace. Egypt would then be able to tip the scales decisively in favor of the Saudi-led pragmatic camp whose efforts to resume the Arab-Israeli peace process had sustained a blow in the Fez summit of November 1981.[57] These expectations were also nourished by President Mubarak's avowed goal of restoring Egypt's relations with other Arab states. Once elected as president, Mubarak, while insisting on his commitment to the peace treaty with Israel and interest in preserving Egypt's cooperation with the United States, sent a clear message of reconciliation to the Arab states by halting propaganda attacks against those that had severed relations with Egypt.[58]

Representing continuity, rather than change, of Sadat's foreign policy, Mubarak viewed the peace treaty with Israel as a strategic interest of Egypt, a backtracking on which would cause not only a return to war but also the loss of U.S. economic and diplomatic support. Without Sadat's baggage, Mubarak was in a better position to reconcile with Egypt's Arab rivals, albeit not at the expense of Egypt's peace with Israel, maintaining that the Arab states needed Egypt as much as or more than the other way around. Reconciliation with the Arab states thus depended on them, and would entail the resumption of diplomatic relations with Egypt, acknowledgement of its Arab leadership, and return of the AL headquarters to Cairo.

The circumstances that brought Mubarak to power served as a constant reminder of Egypt's grave economic situation and its dangerous repercussions on domestic politics, which were agitated by growing opposition that consisted of primarily Islamic fundamentalist factions. Mubarak thus strove to strike a "balance" in Egypt's relations with Israel and the Arab world following the completion of the withdrawal from Sinai. Henceforth, he kept relations with Israel on a low burner and avoided paying a visit to Israel, pending development of the peace process, in which Egypt endeavored to assume the lead as a vehicle for rebuilding its regional Arab reputation. Like Nasir and Sadat before him, Mubarak regarded Egypt's international reputation and regional leadership as directly interrelated, determining Egypt's ability to secure continuous foreign aid. Like them, he saw keeping the Palestinian question high on the public agenda—utilizing occurrences of unrest and violence between Israel and the Palestinians—as a spearhead in his efforts to extricate Egypt from its imposed isolation and restore its regional leadership.[59]

Egypt's absence as a political and military linchpin in the region was soon brought forcefully home by such growing menaces as Iran's threat to Iraq and the Gulf states; Libya's subversion against Sudan; and the Ethiopian threat to Somalia. Yet with the exception of Iraq, which was forced by the exigencies of the war to purchase large quantities of ammunition and military equipment from Egypt, the Arab states' relations with Egypt remained practically unchanged. The deference of the conservative block, led by Saudi Arabia, to the radical regimes effectively precluded any substantial change in the boycott policy against Egypt unless it had been sanctioned by a collective Arab decision. The ambivalent attitude of the monarchical states, Tunisia, and Yemen to Egypt's return to the Arab fold was expressed by terming it "inevitable" and "essential," while acknowledging their inability to affect a change in this regard. While they perceived Egypt's peace with Israel as an "unforgivable mistake," it had also become the lesser evil, since to abandon it would lead to war and complicate even further the Arab world's situation.[60]

Israel's final withdrawal from Sinai as scheduled aggravated the inter-Arab division concerning relations with Egypt. Sudan, Oman, Somalia, and Morocco lobbied intensively for convening an Arab summit that would sanction the restoration of Arab relations with Egypt. King Husain joined these efforts and, indicating Iraq's tacit approval, congratulated Egypt and welcomed its return to the Arab fold. The repercussions of Egypt's absence from regional Arab politics were underlined by the fiasco of the Fahd Plan at Fez in November 1981. The Saudi suggestion that attempts to attain an Arab consensus— i.e., concerning the Fahd Plan—be abandoned in favor of uniting the majority around an agreed plan of action triggered a furious Syrian reaction to the attempt to exclude it from the Arab game. The Saudi attitude, drawing on Mubarak's support for the plan, was welcomed by Cairo as a transparent blaming of Syria for the Arab world's inability to act in unison and, hence, tacitly justifying cooperation with Egypt. Understandably, Syria and Libya spared no effort to prevent legitimation of Egypt's peace with Israel, resorting to threats and intimidation against the conservative regimes. The efforts to rehabilitate Egypt's position in the Arab world revivified the SRF, adding another dimension to its attacks on the strategic ties between Egypt, Oman, Somalia, Sudan, and Morocco and the United States.[61]

The Israeli incursion into Lebanon lent added urgency to Egypt's rapprochement with the Arab world. Yet even an event as momentous as Israel's invasion of Lebanon proved insufficient for bridging the abyss dividing Egypt from the Arab collective. Cairo used the war as a lever to promote its relations with the Arab states by demonstrating its commitment to the Palestinian and Lebanese cause, and by playing up its central role in the enfeebled, divided inter-Arab system. Yet neither Cairo's vigorous diplomatic efforts to put a halt to the Israeli bombings of West Beirut and bring about an Israeli withdrawal from the city, nor the recall of its ambassador from Tel Aviv following the massacre in the Sabra and Shatila refugee camps, nor even the fact that his return was made contingent on Israel's withdrawal from Lebanese territory, led Arab governments to effect any official change in their attitudes toward Cairo.

The cumulative effect of Egypt's political action on behalf of the Palestinian and the Lebanese cause during the summer months, its military aid to Iraq, the freeze of the autonomy negotiations, and the voiding of the normalization accords with Israel of all content, all forged a more convenient atmosphere for rapprochement with Egypt, especially on the part of Iraq, Jordan, and the PLO. The war indeed legitimized open political overtures to Egypt by individual Arab regimes, mainly the conservatives and Iraq. These included visits of high ranking Arab officials to Cairo and invitations of Mubarak to Riyad—to attend King Khalid's funeral—and Baghdad, to take part in the ONAS conference.[62]

The Lebanon war highlighted the need to reassess Egypt's expulsion from the AL by demonstrating the linkage between the Arab world's split and Israel's threat to impose its own peace conditions in the region by force. Nevertheless, at the Fez summit convened in September 1982, Syria prevailed in refusing to accept a Sudanese proposal to discuss Egypt's return to the Arab fold. A parallel lobbying effort by President Mubarak to secure Egypt an invitation to the summit also failed. Syria was able to impose its position thanks largely to the unwillingness of the GCC member states, led by Saudi Arabia, to support the Sudanese proposal. King Fahd, who led the effort on behalf of his peace plan, was unwilling to risk its approval and the meeting as a whole by alienating Syria. Iraq, too, stuck to its condemnation of the Camp David accords, and refused to pay the political price of renewing diplomatic relations with Egypt. Certainly, the deep rift in the inter-Arab arena virtually ruled out the possibility of a collective decision advocating the restoration of official relations with Cairo.[63]

Although Egypt's return to the Arab fold was still blocked, there were some indications of its incremental readmission, albeit mostly without resumption of diplomatic relations. A modest indication of such evolution was manifested by the Fez summit, which expressed no condemnation of Egypt's peace treaty with Israel or of Arab states' maintaining diplomatic relations with Cairo. In January 1984, President Mubarak was invited to the ICO's summit meeting held in Casablanca after five years' absence from this forum, which had previously denounced the Camp David agreements and rescinded Egypt's membership. Mubarak's participation in the summit signalled a collective break in the boycott against Egypt and a tendency to ignore the principle of consensus dictated by a radical minority led by Iran, Syria, and Libya. In September, Jordan resumed its diplomatic relations with Egypt, underlining the growing weight of a new Arab coalition of Egypt, Jordan, the PLO, with tacit Iraqi participation, which took a pragmatic approach in the Arab-Israeli conflict and sought closer relations with the United States. Iraq's involvement in this coalition reflected its growing economic and military problems emanating from the long war with Iran and the latter's resumed offensives. In addition to increasing its arms purchases from Egypt—including missiles and chemical weapons—Iraq attempted to muster international support for itself through the resumption of diplomatic relations with Washington, which had been severed in 1967.[64]

Iran's winter offensive on Basra in early-1987 and growing tension with the GCC states stressed the need for Egypt's return to play an active role in the Arab arena. President Mubarak's participation in the ICO summit in Kuwait (January 1987) was another step on that road. By contrast, Iran boycotted the summit and escalated its sabotage and violent threats against Kuwait. The growing Iranian threat to Iraq and the Gulf monarchies, culminating in the missile attack on Kuwait in October, lent new urgency for Egypt's return to the Arab fold. The imminent summit in Amman boosted the demand for readmitting Egypt to the AL. Despite Syrian opposition, some Arab governments announced their intention to resume diplomatic relations with Egypt for the important role it could play in strengthening Arab defense in the Gulf war. The significance of Egypt to the Gulf Arab states' security was indicated before the summit when the GCC states resumed their financial aid to Egypt, estimated at $1 billion in 1987. This support continued after the summit to help Egypt repay its external debt.[65]

Despite Saddam Husain's bold demand to let Egypt resume its membership in the AL without prior abrogation of its peace treaty with Israel, Syria's and Libya's vigorous objections precluded any possibility of Arab consensus on the matter. Ultimately, a compromise was reached, deeming renewal of diplomatic relations with Egypt each Arab state's sovereign decision. Although several Arab states (Sudan, Somalia, Oman, and, since 1984, Jordan) had maintained full diplomatic relations with Egypt regardless of the collective Arab sanctions, the new summit resolution was still necessary for others as a source of legitimacy. Within a single week, the six GCC states, along with Iraq, Morocco, and Yemen, announced the resumption of diplomatic relations with Egypt. In spite of Egypt's clarifications that it would not deploy military forces in the defense of the Gulf states, the latter perceived Egypt as a strategic buttress and an "umbrella of defense," especially in view of the foreign fleets' possible withdrawal from the Gulf.[66]

The decision legitimating renewal of diplomatic relations with Egypt was another blow to the concept of coercive Pan-Arab solidarity advocated by radical Arab regimes—particularly those of Asad and Qadhafi—in the name of messianic imperatives. It was the inevitable result of regional constraints and those regimes' plummeting influence in the Arab arena. Still, the need for an explicit resolution on the matter, and its justification in terms of the urgent exigencies of Pan-Arab national security, underscored the weight of Arab national values as a source of legitimacy, even if it appeared to be mere verbiage. Although the renewal of relations with Egypt was justified by the Gulf war, in practice it meant acquiescence in the Israel-Egypt peace treaty. Furthermore, it extended an implicit legitimacy to Israel, despite explanations by high-ranking Arab spokesmen to the contrary.[67]

VI

THE DIALECTIC OF FORCE AND
DIPLOMACY

"National unity is precious in any country: but in Jordan it is more than that . . . .
It is the foundation of our national security and the source of our faith in the
future. . . . Based on that, safeguarding national unity is a sacred objective that
will not be compromised."

—King Husain's speech of disengagement from the West Bank, July 31, 1988,
JPS 18, 1(1988). p. 282.

"The [Arab] disagreements concern not the peace with Israel but the capability of
Arab leaders to obtain internal backing to conduct negotiations with Israel."

—Egypt's PM Kamal Hasan 'Ali to *October,* October 9, 1983.

BETWEEN THE PALESTINIAN AND GULF CRISES

With the end of the Iran-Iraq war in August 1988 and the ongoing Palestinian uprising in the West Bank and Gaza Strip, the focus of regional politics seemed to have shifted back from the Gulf area to the Arab-Israeli conflict. Since the early 1980s, these two poles of Middle East politics had strenuously competed for Arab resources and international attention. With Iraq's invasion of Kuwait in early August 1990, however, after nearly three years of Palestinian uprising had produced an impasse, the pendulum of regional politics moved back to the Gulf region, with unprecedented magnitude and repercussions for the Middle East as a whole. The new Gulf crisis reasserted the centrality of the Arab-Israeli conflict in, and its tight link to, regional politics, paving the way to a concerted international effort toward its peaceful resolution, despite the low ebb of the PLO's political posture and reputation both regionally and internationally.[1]

The Gulf crisis was above all an inter-Arab crisis, about power, political survival, and economic resources. Yet it coincided with the end of the Cold War and growing cooperation between Washington and Moscow, culminating in the latter's consent to the United States–led military action against Iraq. Indeed, what linked the Arab-Israeli conflict to the Gulf war was not Saddam Husain's appeals to fundamentalist and populist sentiments, despite his relative success. Nor was it Saddam's attempt to link the Kuwaiti crisis' resolution to its Arab-Israeli parallels, which could not be ignored. That the conflict with Israel was brought into the Gulf crisis was essentially a byproduct of the ideologically driven difficulties shared by central Arab participants in the international anti-Iraq coalition, and the United States–Soviet willingness to trade off a joint commitment to convene an international peace conference after the crisis for the Arabs' active support. What accounted for the renewed focus on the Palestine problem were the deep inter-Arab and intra-societal divisions about the legitimacy of inviting, and sharing with, a Western power's intervention in an Arab-Arab dispute. The public debate that engulfed the Arab world during the six-month crisis on the American-led international intervention was marked by both pros and cons' tendency to invoke the Palestine problem to legitimize policies, which attested to the inherent magnitude of this issue in the region's Arab-Muslim political culture, especially when that culture found itself in confrontation with Western powers.[2]

The Arab-Israeli and Arab-Arab crises between 1988 and 1990 resulted in four Arab summit conferences, all convened under "emergency" and "extraordinary" circumstances: the Palestinian uprising in the occupied territories; the eruption of a new cycle of civil war in Lebanon involving Syria and Iraq; Israel's perceived threats to "Arab national security," as a result of the influx of Soviet Jews to Israel; and the Iraqi invasion of Kuwait. None of these summits, however, was able to cope effectively with the problems on its agenda. Their main significance and function remained as it had been before, namely, to reassert and legitimize core actors' alignments and interests in their quest for an agreeable regional Arab order. It was in this context that Arab states manifested little enthusiasm to support the Palestinian uprising, which threatened to undermine their fragile domestic order.

15

THE INTIFADA AND NEW REGIONAL ALIGNMENT

The Intifada in a Regional Context

Less than a month after the Amman summit conference had relegated the Palestinian issue to its lowest point in the annals of this forum, a genuine popular uprising (*intifada*) erupted in the Gaza Strip and the West Bank. Seen on television screens around the world, the Intifada took the PLO, Israel, and the Arab world by surprise. The Intifada captured the imagination of the Arab masses in the neighboring countries and returned the Palestinian issue to the forefront of Arab and international concerns, raising the PLO from its low ebb to a new political apex. The uprising's most important message, which became increasingly shared by Israeli society as well as by American decision-makers, was that the long status quo of Israel's occupation of the West Bank and Gaza, as well as the denial of Palestinian national rights, was no longer a viable option. Yet despite the sustained uprising, the parties' cognizance continued to lag behind reality, being captive to long-held perceptions.[3] It was to take a few years of mass violent occurrences and the cataclysmic Gulf war before Israel and the PLO would be forced by their deadlocked strategies to undertake long-delayed compromises.

Theoretically, the Intifada provided the Arab states with an opportunity to further weaken Israel through mobilizing political and financial resources in its support. Such a course would be particularly in line with Syria's interest in shifting the focus of regional Arab politics back to the conflict with Israel, to deflect Arab criticism for its alliance with Iran. Yet the Arab regimes' official responses to the Intifada were slow and indecisive, attesting to the dilemma with which this unprecedented phenomenon of organized civil disobedience confronted them. For Egypt, but particularly for Jordan and Syria with their relatively large Palestinian refugee populations, the Intifada was a source of concern lest it spill over into their own constituencies, or be used by local opposition groups to legitimize agitation and protest. Fully identified with the PLO, the Intifada dealt a blow to Syria's and Jordan's efforts to undermine the PLO's position, hence their efforts to reduce the damage to their images.

On the whole, the Arab ruling elites endeavored to maximize their individual benefits from this occurrence, both domestically and regionally, using the usual pompous rhetoric to blur genuine ends and legitimize their authority. At the same time, Jordan, Egypt, and Syria all sought to stem the tide of anti-government sentiment spurred by the uprising's success, taking coercive steps to prevent agitation and uncontrolled support for the Intifada. Thus, despite initial expressions in the Arab media, hailing the "heroes of the stones," the Intifada's local Unified National Leadership (UNL) repeated calls for convening an Arab summit in its support fell on deaf ears. For Cairo, the Intifada was a golden opportunity to promote its credentials both domestically and in the Arab world by appealing to the United States to renew its peacemaking efforts on the Palestinian issue. Syria and Jordan conducted an intensive media and public relations campaign in support of the uprising, to improve their credibility and balance their strict measures to suppress spontaneous public manifestations of support for the Intifada. In Lebanon, the Amal's three-year siege of Palestinian refugee camps was lifted, apparently by Asad's directive.[4]

Once it became clear that the Intifada was not a one-time explosion of anger and frustration but a sustained and organized conflagration, the American administration decided to resume its Arab-Israeli peacemaking efforts, after a long period of diplomatic stalemate. Yet the vigor and urgency that marked U.S. SoS Schultz's initiative from February 1988 to its failure six months later could hardly compensate for the obsolescence of his plan. Although focused on the Palestinian issue, the new American peace initiative constituted a combination of the Camp David autonomy principles, the Reagan 1982 plan, and the idea of an international conference solicited by most Arab governments and the PLO as the ideal framework for negotiating a comprehensive settlement of the Arab-Israeli conflict. To overcome Israel's objection to the international conference, the American plan adopted the idea of using this forum as an opening, ceremonial framework, with no authority to intervene in the negotiations between the parties concerned. To encourage Arab acceptance of the new initiative, Schultz suggested that negotiations on the final status of the West Bank and Gaza begin within one year instead of the three to five years cited in the original autonomy plan.[5]

The main weakness of the plan, as far as the Arab world was concerned, was its focus on Palestinian self-rule rather than self-determination, which proved a stumbling block even for King Husain. In the course of only a few weeks, however, another major element of the American proposal would become a non-starter, namely, its premise that Israel's partner in the negotiations on the West Bank and Gaza Strip would be a Jordanian-Palestinian delegation that excluded the PLO. By the time Schultz made his first visit to the region after the uprising began, the PLO had already assumed political supervision of the Intifada through the UNL and ordered a total ban on meetings with Schultz.[6]

Under these circumstances, and given the Intifada's unequivocal identification with the PLO, King Husain remained officially reluctant toward the American initiative. In retrospect, it was another imagined opportunity in the king's long, but futile, battle to retrieve the lost Palestinian territory. The "Jordanian option," which had never left the ground, was finally buried by the Intifada. For Jordan to accept the Schultz proposals, even with Palestinian self-determination as their declared goal, would mean running the risk of colliding head-on with the PLO over the lifelong issue of the Palestinians' representation. Caught in an election year, Israel's government was also adamant on refusing the American plan, on grounds of objection to any kind of international conference. It is noteworthy that the Schultz initiative's main principles were to constitute the platform for the Madrid international peace conference held in late October 1991, indicating the changes that the regional parties' stances underwent following the Gulf war.

The continuous Intifada put the Hashemite regime in a quandary. Jordan's proximity to the West Bank and the regular in-out movement of Palestinians across the Jordan River, underscored the state's high permeability to the symbolic impact of the Intifada. Thus, the Hashemite regime resorted to preemptive measures consisting of mass arrests and restrictions on public activity among Palestinians in the refugee camps. While King Husain was obliged to demonstrate full rhetorical support for the Intifada, he implicitly adhered to his claim to represent the Palestinians in the occupied territories. Soon, however, the king's overt effort to champion the Intifada was rebuffed by the UNL's leaflets, which took on an increasingly anti-Jordanian tone. By mid-March, this trend culminated in a call to the Palestinians in Jordan's parliament to resign, interpreted by the Jordanians as a frontal assault on the concept of unity of the two banks. By the time the plenary Arab summit convened in Algiers, Husain had lost the battle to the PLO. What was left for the Hashemite monarch to seek was sharing in some of the Arab financial aid that might be allocated to the Intifada, to help his faltering economy and mend his fences with the PLO as a fallback position.[7]

'Arafat's soaring prestige as a result of the Intifada played an important role in a renewed Syrian effort to bring the PLO under its control. In April 1988, Asad was willing to meet 'Arafat in Damascus—on the occasion of Abu Jihad's funeral—and again during the summit in Algiers, yet without altering the policy he had taken toward the PLO since the aftermath of the Lebanon war. Apparently, 'Arafat's insistence on retaining the PLO's political independence was the stumbling block. That both meetings were fruitless was indicated by a further cycle of Syrian-sponsored artillery barrages on Palestinian refugee camps in Beirut, forcing 'Arafat to turn to Egypt for help. Asad was clearly motivated by his growing isolation in the Arab arena, the PLO's growing prestige, and the prospects for tapping part of the expected financial aid to the Intifada. A close coordination with the PLO would place Syria in a better regional position also in view of the American peace initiative, whose possible result in a separate Israeli-Palestinian agreement would effectively diminish Syria's chances of ever retrieving the Golan.[8]

By the end of January 1988, the Arab FMs, under urgent appeals by the PLO, met in Tunis to discuss financial and political support for the Intifada. But the forum was content with establishing a committee to coordinate Arab political efforts on behalf of the Palestinians, making no specific decisions on financial support. Though the meeting had declared that everything necessary would be provided, no financial assistance was to be offered in the coming months, a fact bitterly criticized by 'Arafat. The meeting was marked by bitter competition, especially between the PLO, Jordan, and Syria, each trying to capitalize on the Intifada to exclusively reap its political and financial rewards. Syria had reportedly proposed a committee that would have an operative control over the uprising and the PLO, but the PLO's reputation was now strong enough to resist it.[9]

As the uprising continued, Arab regimes came under growing domestic pressure to take an active and visible role at the highest level in support of the Palestinian uprising. Given the inhibitions of the confrontation states, the call for an Arab summit on behalf of the Intifada went out first from Morocco and Algeria. The Gulf states, which would be called upon to foot the bill for the Palestinians, were far more reluctant to convene a summit. Jordan, still with an eye on the Schultz initiative, and in no hurry to boost the PLO, was also reticent about attending a summit, though given its large Palestinian population and exposure to the Intifada, Amman could hardly resist it.

Although the summit conference was designated to discuss the Intifada, the familiar inter-Arab pre-summit bargaining, with each party eager to promote its own agenda, was inevitable. Thus, to secure maximum participation, the Iraq-Iran war and the Lebanese crisis were also added to the agenda. Both these issues put Syria in the crossfire and involved its strong opposition. Yet Damascus had to yield in its objection to the inclusion of the Gulf war in the agenda, this time under the Gulf monarchies' pressure, in return for their consent to precluding Egypt's return to the AL. The summit's final resolutions condemned Iran, despite Syria's opposition. In contrast, it turned a cold shoulder to Lebanon's President Jumayyil, who did his utmost to obtain support for his request that all foreign forces withdraw from Lebanon.[10]

The Algiers summit was dubbed "the Intifada summit," to indicate its avowed goals to provide support for the Palestinian uprising. The summit embodied the contribution of the Intifada to the PLO's return to center stage by meeting most of the latter's requirements for political support. 'Arafat's insistence on reconfirmation of previous summits' resolutions on his political and legal status were crucial in view of the bitter memories of the Amman summit, and the continued challenge posed to his leadership by Syria and Jordan. It was all the more crucial in view of the American peace initiative, which focused on King Husain at the PLO's expense. The summit's final statement thus concluded, "to establish an independent Palestinian state on their [the Palestinians] national soil under the leadership of the PLO, their sole legitimate representative." The PLO's participation in the international conference, on an equal footing with other participants, was also recognized.[11]

As expected, King Husain's message to the summit represented an unequivocal withdrawal of his past claims regarding representation of the Palestinians. He clearly meant to be seen as 'Arafat's most ardent supporter, and hoped that his past actions not be misconstrued as a power struggle between Jordan and the PLO. To increase his credibility, the king was now highly critical of the Schultz initiative and the American role in the Arab-Israeli conflict in general. By giving up his claims to represent the Palestinians in the West Bank, which had already been lost, the king managed to refute without difficulty the PLO's claim to represent also the Palestinians in the East Bank.[12]

On the issue of financial aid to the Intifada, 'Arafat managed to gain a vague commitment, which was a far cry from the amount and terms he had requested. The PLO claimed to have obtained a commitment for an immediate boost of $128 million, with an additional $43 million a month promised for the remainder of the year. Yet the specific details of the commitment were not mentioned in the final statement—hence, it was widely interpreted as a rebuff of the PLO. The respective contributors maintained that they had only agreed to negotiate periodically with the PLO the amount to be paid. The PLO was also met by a strong Jordanian objection to Arafat's request to have exclusive authority for channelling the financial aid to the Intifada, thereby cutting Jordan out of the funding loop. The compromise decision stated that support would be channelled through the PLO and "available international channels," apparently referring to the Red Cross or the UNRWA. The Gulf monarchies meant to retain a say in allocating the funds, but no less importantly to refrain from undermining the Schultz initiative, especially at a time when an American military presence in the Gulf was so crucial for their tankers' safety. The compromise would also keep the monarchies' relations with Syria on track, and prevent King Husain's weakening.[13]

The summit's financial commitments to the Intifada became a sticking issue between the PLO and the Gulf monarchies. 'Arafat's and other PLO leaders' repeated complaints that the summit commitments had not been fulfilled failed to change the Gulf oil states' approach to the issue. The growing Palestinian bitterness toward the Gulf monarchies over the limited scope of financial support for the Intifada was to erupt forcefully following the Iraqi invasion of Kuwait and lead to the PLO's support for Baghdad. The vehemence of Arab indifference to the Intifada, interpreted as a "plot," attested to the fears of Arab ruling elites regarding its socio-political implications regionwide.[14]

By reasserting its political support for the PLO under 'Arafat's leadership, the Algiers summit's resolutions reaffirmed the defeat inflicted on the Hashemite regime by the Intifada. With his development plan for the West Bank grounded for lack of financial resources and by the summit decision to channel financial aid through the PLO, the king was left with little room to maneuver. In view of the Intifada's domestic and regional ramifications for Jordan, coupled with the kingdom's economic woes, Husain faced an inevitable decision to cut his losses and protect his sovereignty east of the River Jordan.[15]

On July 31, without previous consultation with the PLO, the king threw down the gauntlet by announcing his decision to sever Jordan's legal and administrative ties with the West Bank. While not officially dissolving the 1950 union of the two banks, King Husain, for the first time in his generation-long struggle with the PLO, effectively renounced his claim of sovereignty over the West Bank, although he undertook to continue Jordan's participation in the peace process. Whether or not the king meant to shock his rivals with his decision, hoping to deter them by the sudden and immense responsibility he had charged them with, will probably remain a matter of conjecture. In theory, nothing would have precluded the king's reversing his announcement had the PLO and the UNL appealed to him to reconsider it. What did make Husain's move irreversible was the PLO's decision to translate it to political gain by declaring the Independent Palestinian State four months later, and the State's consequent worldwide recognition, including by Jordan.[16]

Although Husain's disengagement decision meant to insulate the East Bank from the winds of the Intifada, its main significance in the long run was in the context of state-formation. The disengagement from the West Bank signalled the "Jordanization" of the Hashemite Kingdom and its consolidation as a sovereign nation-state based on real boundaries and political control. The king made it clear that Jordanian Palestinians would be expected to behave as loyal Jordanian citizens, otherwise they would have to seek citizenship elsewhere. Effectively, the Jordanian government stopped paying salaries to most of the 24,000 government employees in the West Bank, and limited the validity of West Bankers' passports to two years. These measures were implemented amidst a media offensive against the PLO and the Palestinians' "dual loyalty," generating an atmosphere of uncertainty and insecurity within the Jordanian-Palestinian society. The Jordanian government also revised the conventional estimate that Palestinians constituted a majority of the population in the East Bank, maintaining that their proportion had shrunk to only one-third.[17]

The PLO-Jordan New Alignment

Though caught offguard, after overcoming its initial rage and skepticism at King Husain's decision, the PLO, under pressure from the Intifada grass-root leadership, faced no choice but to come to terms with Amman over the practical implications of its decision. Husain's retreat from competition over the West Bank paved the way for improvement of his relations with the PLO. In October, Mubarak, ʿArafat, and Husain held a mini-summit in ʿAqaba which helped smooth over PLO-Jordan relations and cleared the road to the declaration of the Palestinian State in November. In January 1989, the embassy of the State of Palestine was opened in Amman, marking a new era in the Jordanian-PLO relations.

Mutual interests and anxieties, as well as existential dependency, came to underpin the new alliance between yesterday's contenders, for whom the new political situation meant opportunities as well as uncertainties. The PLO's new freedom of action on Jordan's soil enabled ʿArafat to enhance his capability for political action in the occupied territories and promote his control of the Intifada. This proved increasingly important in view of the growing power of the Islamic Resistance Movement (*hamas*) in the occupied territories since the beginning of the Intifada, and the challenge it posed to the PLO as the sole Palestinian national authority. In fact, King Husain and ʿArafat shared a joint threat given the growing power of the Islamic movement in Jordan and its links with its counterpart west of River Jordan.[18]

From a Hashemite viewpoint, the PLO came to serve as an agent in its process of state-formation, smoothing the separation from the West Bank. With PLO support, King Husain's Jordanization policy effectively sent a message to the Palestinians in Jordan, especially to the refugee camps' residents, that they were to consider themselves Jordanian citizens. The PLO also proved instrumental in smoothing King Husain's other domestic hardships, stemming from the deteriorating economy. Thus, during the April 1989 riots in Jordan, undertaken mainly by native-Jordanian state employees, the PLO played a pacifying role among the Palestinians in Jordan, preventing their participation in similar disorder. The transfer of the PLO National Fund's headquarters and financial assets to Amman in August 1989 helped its economy and halted the dangerous deterioration of the Jordanian Dinar, which had severely affected West Bankers and Jordanians alike.[19]

The Jordan-PLO cooperation culminated in the PLO's policy of "noninterference" during Jordan's parliamentary elections in November 1989, the first to be held in the kingdom since 1967. The Jordanian decision to hold elections, though it had been on the agenda for a few years, became crucial in the process of consolidating the Jordanian state in the wake of Husain's disengagement from the West Bank. The PLO's mainstream, for its part, saw fit to keep away from taking any active role in the elections or allying with Palestinian candidates—despite their underrepresentation—in order to reinforce the territorial boundaries between Jordan and the Palestinian state-to-be and prevent confusion regarding the Palestinian representation.[20]

'Arafat's main goal in the aftermath of Husain's disengagement decision, however, was to break the deadlock in his relations with the United States and become fully incorporated in the peace process. This tendency had been encouraged by various gestures and announcements made by Schultz in the course of his initiative, which narrowed the gap between Washington and the PLO. Thus, at the Algiers summit, a document formulated by 'Arafat's adviser, Bassam Abu Sharif, was circulated among the summiteers, indicating a shift in the PLO's policy on essential issues concerning the peace process. It accepted Resolutions 242 and 338 unambiguously, as well as the concept of direct negotiations with Israel within the framework of an international conference. Though the document was classified "personal," it sparked infighting within the PLO ranks, and probably bore much of the responsibility for the deepening disagreement with Asad. Above all, Abu Sharif's document expressed the growing influence of the inside Palestinian leadership on the PLO's decision-makers and then pressure to adopt the idea of a Palestinian independent state in the West Bank and Gaza Strip. It was this enhanced power of the inside leadership that set the stage for the nineteenth PNC session in Algiers in November, which resulted in the declaration of the Independent State of Palestine, based on the UN partition resolution of November 29, 1947. The PNC session adopted a new "political program," yet its resolutions and final statement failed to exhibit the precision and unambiguity required to open the American door to the PLO on the crucial issues of unreserved acceptance of Resolutions 242 and 338 and renouncing terrorism. These prerequisites were finally met by 'Arafat's statement in Geneva in December, leading to Washington's announcement on starting a diplomatic dialogue with the PLO.[21]

The American-PLO dialogue was another political achievement of the Intifada, drawing on the declaration of the Independent State of Palestine which had soon obtained wide international and Arab recognition. Yet the assumption that came to guide the U.S. government's Middle East policy, namely, that there was no way to advance the peace process without the PLO, was unacceptable to Israel. However, even Israel's national coalition government could not entirely ignore the momentous political process generated by the Intifada. While its opposition to acknowledging the PLO and denial of its role in the peace process remained intact, the Labor Party's growing pressure for change forced the right-wing parties in the national coalition government to adopt, in May 1989, a new political initiative.

The Israeli plan called for negotiations with elected Palestinian representatives from the West Bank and Gaza Strip, on the basis of the Camp David autonomy agreement. For the first time in Zionist and state history, Israel defined the Palestinians, rather than Jordan or any Arab neighboring state—though the inclusion of Arab states in the peace talks remained optional—as its main partners for a peaceful settlement. Israel's initiative was apparently meant to preserve the national coalition government and drive a wedge between the PLO, the ultimate representative of the diaspora, and the Palestinians of the West Bank and Gaza Strip. However, the tacit assumption underpinning the Israeli election plan—described by ʿArafat as a "conspiracy"—that the local leadership would be able to negotiate with Israel separate from the PLO, proved baseless. The PLO insisted that elections must be preceded by Israel's withdrawal from the occupied territories, and left no doubt that its authority was still effective among their Palestinian residents. This was reaffirmed by the failure of the Bush administration's effort to hammer out an acceptable procedural formula for electing the Palestinian representatives. The Israeli plan put the PLO in quandary, entangling it in a new cycle of futile diplomacy and embittered relations with the United States and Egypt.[22]

With time passing by without any tangible breakthrough in the peace process, the PLO was quickly losing the diplomatic momentum of the previous year, while confronted with a growing tide of deadlocked opportunities. At the Casablanca summit of May 1989, with Egypt back in the AL and fully behind the PLO, ʿArafat, now assuming the title of President of Palestine, was looking for the summit's backing for his "political program" and for reaffirmation of the Arab financial aid on the parameters of the Algiers summit. The summit confirmed the PLO's new strategy, but declined ʿArafat's request for substantial financial aid beyond the donations made by Saudi Arabia, Iraq, Libya, and the UAE. The summit contented itself with empty rhetoric of support for the Intifada, disregarding ʿArafat's report on the huge financial losses of the Palestinians under Israeli occupation due to the Intifada and his criticism of Arab states for failing to stand up to their financial commitments. At the same time, relations with Syria remained stalemated, epitomized by Damascus' refusal, in contrast with all the other Arab states, to recognize the State of Palestine, explaining that such recognition would signify recognition of the state of Israel.[23]

As of early 1990, the PLO's political achievements and prospects had shrunk dramatically, with growing ruptures in its relations with Egypt and the United States. Since its return to the AL, Egypt was less in need of fostering close relations with the PLO, especially when they ran contrary to its own national interests. Thus, the PLO's failure to condemn the February 4 Palestinian terrorist attack on Israeli tourists near the Egyptian city of Ismaʿiliyya led to unprecedentedly vitriolic attacks on the PLO leaders by the Egyptian media, accusing the PLO of violating Egypt's law and sovereignty. While paying the obligatory verbal support for the Palestinian cause, Cairo portrayed the PLO leaders as inept, corrupted, and unfit to lead the Palestinian uprising. In addition, it suspended all senior-level contacts with the PLO and adopted repressive measures against its activities in Egypt. The PLO did not fail to counterattack, accusing Egypt of "stabbing the Intifada in the back" and urging it to withdraw from the Camp David accords.[24]

In mid-1990, the already deadlocked dialogue with the United States was suspended by the latter when 'Arafat refused to denounce the attack from the sea on Israel's beaches in May—in conjunction with the summit meeting in Baghdad—by the PLF, one of the PLO's member factions. The American decision culminated a mounting tension and mutual recriminations between the PLO and Egypt—which claimed credit for bringing about the United States–PLO dialogue—reflecting their frustrated hopes for a breakthrough in the peace process. On the whole, a growing sense of political and economic impasse came to prevail among the Palestinians in both Jordan and the occupied territories, deriving from the Gulf Arab monarchies' continued disregard of 'Arafat's appeals for increased financial aid on behalf of the Intifada; the fading energy and international echoes of the Intifada toward the end of 1989; economic and psychological exhaustion of the Palestinian inhabitants; growing intra-Palestinian violence at the grassroots level; and dangerous erosion of Fatah's political prominence in the occupied territories due to Hamas's growing popularity among the masses.[25]

The rising tide of Soviet Jewish immigration into Israel as of late 1989 sent new tremors into Israeli-Arab relations. Both Jordan and the PLO perceived it as a serious threat to their common cause. Both sides envisioned massive Israeli settlement of newcomers in the occupied territories, which, apart from changing their Arab character irreversibly, would cause massive emigration to Jordan, which would endanger its political stability and the very existence of the Hashemite regime. As the Arab parties most affected by the Soviet Jewish immigration, they combined efforts in appealing, in early 1990 for an emergency Arab conference to combat this threat. Facing Egyptian reluctance due to Iraq's increasing militancy and threats toward the United States and Israel, both 'Arafat and Husain strove to augment Arab financial aid through mobilizing inter-Arab attention to the Palestinian cause.[26]

At the summit, held in Baghdad in May 1990, 'Arafat complained that only Saudi Arabia had fulfilled its pledges of financial support for the Intifada. He elaborated on the Palestinian losses as a result of the uprising, which he estimated at $2.9 billion and appealed for double of what had been allegedly promised to him in Algiers. The Baghdad summit's resolutions indicated the declining Arab interest in the Intifada and its low priority in their strained budgets' financial obligations. The summit's final statement spoke highly of the Intifada and expressed its solidarity with Jordan, but failed to specify any amount of financial support to either of them. The only specific commitment came from Iraq, which pledged to donate Jordan $50 million, a far cry from the $400 million Jordan had received from the GCC states the year before.[27]

Even before the summit meeting, Iraq and the PLO appeared to have tightened their relationships. With the diplomatic option deadlocked, its financial requests ignored, and its inability to mend fences with Syria a given, the PLO's choices had narrowed to perceiving Saddam Husain as an ally. Iraq was willing to provide limited financial aid, absorbing Fatah armed units in Iraq and doubling the transmission hours of the Iraqi-based Voice of Palestine. But its most important contribution to the PLO was Saddam's playing the drums of confrontation with Israel, which seemed to present the Arab world—the Palestinians in particular—with an irresistible challenge. Thus, even before invading Kuwait, Saddam Husain came to be seen by Palestinians as their hero and the only Arab leader committed to their cause.

The Iraqi invasion of Kuwait marked a watershed in both Jordan's and the PLO's relationships with the Arab world, which further solidified the Jordanian-PLO alignment. Their support of Saddam Husain, albeit more explicit in the case of the PLO, was mainly a reflection of domestic political constraints. The rising tide of sentiment hostile to the United States and Israel, especially among Palestinians, and Jordan's renewed parliamentary life, which boosted the activity of the Muslim Brotherhood Movement and other opposition groups, effectively limited the king's freedom to maneuver in his foreign policy.

Egypt's Return to the Arab League

The speed that marked most Arab governments' decisions to resume their diplomatic relations with Cairo seemed to indicate that Egypt's readmittance to the AL was imminent. Especially with the Palestinian uprising in progress, Egypt had an opportunity to promote its drive for regional leadership by forging Arab and international support for the Palestinian cause. But inter-Arab alignment on the issue, breaking down along traditional lines, contained a vivid memory of Syria's veto power. Syria remained unchanged in its objection to Egypt's participation in the Algiers summit, despite overt support for it from Jordan, Saudi Arabia, and Kuwait's monarchs. King Husain took the lead in seeing to Egypt's invitation to the summit, looking to Egypt to provide him with more latitude in pursuing a settlement on the West Bank and Gaza. As for Kuwait and Saudi Arabia, Egypt's political and military weight was the only hope for counterbalancing regional threats to their national security. Thus, fearing repeated riots provoked by Iranian fundamentalist pilgrims to Mecca, the Saudi government imposed a quota on the Iranians permitted to attend that year's pilgrimage. Indeed, any political backlash the Saudis had experienced in the past due to their open support for Egypt was now dissipated by the ever-increasing security threats and the size of the pro-Egypt lobby.[28]

Iraq's position was more ambiguous: while Egypt's readmittance to the AL would counter Iraq's arch-rival, Syria, it would also mean a threat to Iraq's own standing in the Arab arena. As the war with Iran seemed to approach its end, Saddam, with an eye to the future, began advocating the Egyptian cause only after Algeria had decided not to invite Egypt. Following the end of the Gulf war, however, assuming that Egypt's return to the AL was only a matter of time, and more a thorn to Asad than to himself, the Iraqi ruler became more active in supporting Egypt on this matter in the run up to the next summit in Casablanca.

The PLO was torn between its vested interest in mending fences with Asad and its need for Egypt's political support to prevent a Syrian takeover, as well as to boost its cause in the peacemaking process. Syria's leverage on the PLO had been demonstrated repeatedly through its control of the Palestinian rejectionist groups, and by the siege of refugee camps in Lebanon by their Shi'i allies. In the final analysis, the PLO opted to take a back seat on the issue. Syria adhered to its veto attitude in this regard as a tradeoff for its willingness to compromise on inclusion of the thorny issue of the Iraq-Iran war in the summit agenda. Syria's insistence on excluding Egypt from the summit stemmed from fear that it would reinvigorate the American-sponsored peace efforts, which threatened to ignore its cause. Thus, Asad, along with Qadhafi, made it clear that he would not attend the summit should Egypt be invited. Qadhafi warned that if Egypt were accepted back into the AL, Libya, together with two or three other Arab states would quit.[29]

The Algerian hosts, eager to mollify their Syrian and Libyan allies, refused even to accede to Egypt's request to send an observer to the opening session of the summit while inviting Iran to do exactly that. The Algiers summit decided to postpone the debate on Egypt until the next summit, handing the militant regimes a temporary victory in blocking its return to the AL. Commenting on this outcome, Damascus praised the successful efforts at the summit to abort Egypt's persistent attempts to resume its role in the AL and in Arab action at a time when "the Zionist enemy's flag flies in the skies of Cairo." Following the summit, Egypt and Algeria swapped bitter barbs through their respective media, and within two weeks, Egypt recalled its chargé d'affaires from Algiers. Within a year, however, Algeria and Egypt were to exchange ambassadors.[30]

Egypt's final return to the AL was a result of the new balance of power in the Arab states' system prompted by the end of Iran-Iraq war, which, in the final analysis, aggravated Syria's regional isolation. Another factor in weakening Syria's position regionally was the fading Cold War and loss of Soviet strategic backing, compelling Asad to restore his relations with the United

States and its regional allies. The new inter-Arab alignment took the form of two new regional blocs, established in February 1989: the Arab Maghreb Union (AMU) of Mauritania, Morocco, Algeria, Tunisia, and Libya; and the Arab Cooperation Council (ACC) comprised of Iraq, Egypt, Jordan, and Yemen. The ACC gave Egypt the springboard it needed to take that final step back into the AL, when its member states vowed to attend the Casablanca summit as a group or not at all.

Though embellished with much rhetoric about Arab unity and economic integration, the new regional councils were another indication of the fading concept of Pan-Arab unity, giving way to geographical, economic-and security-oriented alignments of sovereign states. Still, the haste with which the ACC council had come into being and the salience of politics and rhetoric involved, justifiably called into question its genuine motives and viability. The ACC lacked the logic of the other two Arab regional unions, the GCC and the AMU. At least with these two groupings there existed a commonality of geography, economic interests, perceived security threats, and even shared aspects of identity. Among the ACC members, however, there hardly existed such bonds. Not only were the four countries not all geographically contiguous, they were not even all in the same sub-region. There was a common economic challenge emanating from the EEC's growing integration, but that challenge was shared by the entire region and would have been confronted more effectively by a more rational economic union. About the only common economic thread connecting them was each country's massive external debt.[31]

The ACC did intend to promote economic integration among its members by "easing movement and work of ACC nationals within each others' territory," as well as reaching other economic and trade agreements. The problems of enhancing economic cooperation among the signatories obviously stemmed from the similarities of their economic production and resources in terms of labor forces and consumer industries, which were bound to create competition and economic conflict. The ACC declaration that it was open to other states to join could not disguise two thorny issues: the exclusion of Syria, explained by its severed relations with Iraq and Egypt, and the inclusion of North Yemen, representing Baghdad's intention to create a potential threat to Saudi Arabia. The lack of substantive common incentives among the ACC members attested to its ad-hoc, shallow basis and was to contribute to the ACC's demise in the wake of the Kuwaiti crisis.[32]

The formation of the ACC was motivated principally by short-term political considerations. Iraq looked for strategic benefits by further isolating Syria in her already lonely world and bolstering its own military position vis-à-vis Iran. Above all, it was to provide Iraq with the means to play a leading role in the Arab arena especially in view of its self-defined victory in the war with Iran, and the huge order-of-battle with which it ended the war. Whether

Saddam Husain had already been planning to invade Kuwait when he was establishing the ACC is not clear. However, he obviously attempted to include in its charter a component of military cooperation, which was firmly rejected by Mubarak. For Jordan, the ACC was to balance external threats to its national security posed by Israel, Syria, and Iraq. Yet King Husain had to take great pains to reassure Syria that the ACC was not directed against it. For peripheral and poor Yemen, which had been excluded from the GCC, membership in a club with the two most powerful Arab states provided an enhanced bargaining position toward Saudi Arabia and higher ranking in Arab regional politics.

The end of the Iraq-Iran war in August 1988 intensified the threats to Syria's national security stemming from Iraqi determination to punish Syria for its alliance with Iran. Though it emerged from the war as a "crippling indebted nation," Iraq returned to its dispute with Syria and the Palestine conflict, though only as a side effort which might have been meant to distract Arab attention from its plans in the Gulf. Lebanon was where Syria's complex political presence and troubles provided a fertile ground for an indirect Iraqi involvement. The end of President Amin Jumayyil's term without electing a new president, threw Lebanon into a constitutional crisis, and drew Baghdad into the Lebanese swamp. Baghdad cast her weight behind the Maronite LF and army units led by General Michelle 'Awn, who had established himself as PM—in disregard of the Syrian-backed al-Huss government—and declared a war of liberation to rid Lebanon of Syrian occupation.

The new cycle of civil war in Lebanon, marked by massive Syrian bombardments and Iraqi military support for 'Awn, prompted the AL to set up a Kuwaiti-led committee of FMs to resolve the dispute. But efforts in this regard failed to stop the tide of violence, leading to another emergency summit conference, in Casablanca, to tackle the crisis. The resort to an Arab summit attested to the severity of the crisis and potential dangers for the region as a whole. The Gulf monarchies in particular feared the Lebanon crisis would ignite a direct confrontation between Syria and Iraq, the price of which they would have to pay. Indeed, the heavy fighting in Lebanon achieved dimension unprecedented in the annals of that country's civil war, as Iraq provided 'Awn with sophisticated weapons, including ground-to-ground FROG missiles. Jordan and Egypt cooperated in facilitating shipments of Iraqi weapons through 'Aqaba and the Suez Canal.[33]

Syria, overwhelmed by economic recession and regional isolation, the renewed battles in Lebanon underlined the impasse to which Asad's antagonistic and demanding strategies had led his country. Internationally, Syria was considered by the United States to be a state sponsoring terrorism, while Soviet strategic backing was on the decline. The revitalized Syria-Iraq struggle in Lebanon made the return of Egypt to the AL all the more urgent for the Gulf states amid decreasing Syrian objection. At the same time, Iraq's growing pressure on Kuwait for territorial concessions turned Syria in the eyes of the Gulf monarchies into an important counterbalancing power to Iraq.[34]

Against this backdrop, Asad gave his consent to Egypt's participation in the Casablanca summit in return for the Gulf states' support in blocking Iraq's demand to condemn Syria's role in Lebanon and call for "withdrawal of all foreign forces from Lebanon." The significance of Lebanon for the Syrian regime was attested to by Asad's willingness to soften his position toward the PLO, and to go as far as supporting "Iraq's historical claims on Shatt al-'Arab," which exceeded the official Iraqi position evinced in the negotiations with Iran. Asad's positions in the summit marked the beginning of an incremental departure from "beleaguered isolation" toward an alignment with the Gulf monarchies and Egypt, which culminated in Syria's participation in the international coalition in the Gulf war. Still, Asad insisted on a series of resolutions focusing on the conflict with Israel in which Syria's primary role would be underlined. These resolutions reiterated the commitment to mobilize Arab resources for gaining a "strategic parity" and support the convening of an international conference to reach a comprehensive peace according to the Arab peace plan of Fez. Although there was nothing new in these resolutions, as they had been adopted by previous Arab summits, their reassertion came to highlight Damascus' adherence to its basic ideology and to distinguish its attitude on these issues from the PLO's "political program."[35]

On the whole, the summit made no progress in resolving Lebanon's predicament. The tragedy of Lebanon was demonstrated by its absence from the summit, due to its constitutional crisis and the schism between its Muslim and Christian-Maronite governments. The idea of Arabizing the Lebanon crisis, advocated by Egypt, Jordan, Iraq, the Gulf states, and the PLO, was met with immovable Syrian intransigence, eventually compromising on another committee to be headed by King Fahd. The summit's failure to condemn Syria was indicated by Saddam Husain's decision to return home before the meeting came to its official end. Within a few days, however, his response came in the form of a new arms deal with General 'Awn.[36]

The summit's main significance was Egypt's full readmittance to the AL, which restored the Arab regional system's hierarchical equilibrium as Egypt moved quickly to fill the vacuum it had left behind in 1978. Egypt returned to the AL in grand style, without apologies and under its own terms. Qadhafi's and Asad's presence made Egypt's return all the more significant. Even though Asad spared no criticism of Mubarak for the peace agreement with Israel, Syria had already been on the road to resume diplomatic relations with Egypt (December 1989). The honor accorded President Mubarak of addressing the summit's opening session indicated that the Arab world was looking to Egypt for guidance, and Mubarak's speech made it clear that Egypt was willing to provide that service. Mubarak focused on the Palestinian issue, asserting his intention to play a substantive role in brokering a Palestinian-Israeli peace. Such an accomplishment would be the ultimate vindication of Egypt's foreign policy.[37]

16

THE KUWAIT CRISIS AND THE PEACE PROCESS: TOWARD A NEW MIDDLE EAST ORDER?

The Kuwait Crisis and International Intervention

The origins of Iraq's invasion of Kuwait have been extensively analyzed and debated elsewhere in an attempt to offer a satisfactory explanation for the Iraqi decision-making process. While a comprehensive analysis of Iraq's motivation and considerations is beyond the scope of this study, a brief presentation of the main arguments is in order.

It has been commonly argued that the Iraqi invasion of Kuwait, like the offensive against Iran ten years earlier, was principally defensive, stemming from a deeply rooted sense of domestic and geostrategic insecurity. There is also a wide agreement that in spite of longstanding Iraqi territorial claims over Kuwait, the immediate goals of the invasion were territorial access to the Gulf and its oil resources. Notwithstanding differences about periodization of Saddam Husain's decision-making regarding the invasion, it is recognized that had the Kuwait takeover gone unchecked, it would have enabled Iraq to impose its hegemony over the Gulf area and possibly over the region as a whole. It is another question whether that hegemony was intended to liberate Palestine, unify the Arab world, or both, in a modern version of the ʿAbbasi Empire.[1]

The origins of Iraq's invasion of Kuwait were rooted in the conditions under which the Iraq-Iran war had ended. Albeit portrayed by Iraq as a "victory," the war ended without a clear winner or loser, and even this was due to the increasing Western strategic support for Iraq while applying a tacit strategic blockade against Iran. Khomeini's decision to end the eight-year war with Iraq resulted primarily from economic difficulties, which culminated in early 1988 when Iran was unable to compensate any longer for its inferiority in arms, financial resources, and international backing by continuing to resort to massive manpower and high motivation. But Tehran was by no means willing to come to terms with Baghdad on a settlement of their conflict, even over a mutual exchange of POWs, at a time when Iraq's strategic and domestic predicament made it incumbent on Baghdad to seek a conclusive settlement with Tehran. Indeed, not only had Saddam Husain failed to rid himself of the Islamic revolutionary regime, the war had virtually helped its consolidation and legitimation on the domestic level.[2]

Given Iran's decisive edge in terms of geostrategic preponderance and human and economic resources, the war results were indeed detrimental to Saddam Husain's aspirations for hegemony in the Gulf if not for his own political survival. The staggering external debt with which Iraq ended the war—half of which was to be repaid to Saudi Arabia and Kuwait—coupled with the social, economic, and political pressures of maintaining a huge wartime force—more than one million soldiers—which had remained mobilized, underlined the impasse faced by Saddam Husain. Above all, the Iraqi-initiated war ended without fulfilling its minimum declared military aim, namely, to seize the remaining half of the Shatt al-'Arab waterway along its fluvial frontier with Iran, which had been surrendered in the 1975 treaty with the Shah.

With its only outlet to the Gulf blocked, Iraq was at an intolerable strategic disadvantage, especially since the renewal of hostilities by Iran seemed a real possibility. Hence, despite the huge external debt and continuing fall in oil prices, which threatened Iraq with suffocation, the regime continued to invest financial resources in purchasing military-oriented technologies and developing missiles as well as chemical and biological weapons. Thus, alleviating the financial burden and obtaining a reliable and secure access to the Gulf were Saddam Husain's most urgent needs, which he eventually would seek to satisfy by invading Kuwait. Kuwait was willing to write off the Iraqi debt in return for Baghdad's recognition of its borders, which raised Iraqi claims over territory that Kuwait had allegedly taken over during the war with Iran. By early 1990, with his demands that Kuwait cede to him the Warba and Bubian Islands and give him financial aid going unheeded, Saddam Husain began a series of activities aimed at resolving his most urgent difficulty, that of financial bankruptcy.[3]

In addition to diplomatic pressures on the GCC monarchies, particularly Kuwait, to meet his claims, Saddam launched a mounting confrontational campaign against Israel and the United States aimed at rallying the Arab world behind his leadership and justifying his financial and territorial demands. In February, at the ACC summit in Amman, Saddam urged his colleagues to exert pressure on the Gulf monarchies to provide him with substantial aid beyond forgiving their wartime loans to Iraq. On the same occasion, Saddam called for the United States to leave the Gulf and for the Arabs to liberate Jerusalem. Saddam focused on castigating the United States's total backing of Israel as expressed by Congress' recognition of unified Jerusalem as Israel's capital and assistance for absorbing the wave of Soviet Jewish immigration, which he portrayed as a device to subjugate the Arabs.

Following Western criticism of Iraq's efforts to acquire hi-tech military-oriented devices and of its disrespect of human rights, Saddam escalated his outcry against the United States, accusing it of meaning to perpetuate the Arabs' technological inferiority. He presented Iraq as the Arab world's fore-runner in possessing advanced technology whose developed military capability would deter any external threat and guarantee the Arabs' national security. Having in mind Israel's attack on the Iraqi nuclear reactor in 1981, Saddam revealed on April 2 that Iraq possessed a binary chemical weapon, threatening to retaliate with it and burn "half of Israel" if it dared to attack Iraq. To substantiate his claim for all-Arab leadership, Saddam undertook to assist any Arab state that would seek Iraq's help in retaliation for an attack by Israel.[4]

Saddam's provocative tone coincided with a discernible rise in the Arab states' investments in purchasing and developing unconventional military capabilities, particularly chemical weaponry and medium-range missiles. The potential danger of a proliferation of such capabilities in the Middle East triggered a sense of urgency in Israel and Washington. Nonetheless, Western European countries continued to develop their arms trade deals with Iraq, which was also racing, as revealed after the Gulf war, to possess a nuclear weapon. Yet in spite of Saddam's provocative tone and escalating attacks on the United States, Washington misread his behavior and adhered to an appeas-ing approach that reflected a continuation of the American support for Iraq during its war with Iran. The American failure to send Saddam Husain an unequivocal message during the period prior to the invasion, and Saddam's misinterpretation of the Soviet Union's decline, might have accounted for Iraq's miscalculation of Washington Middle East policy.[5]

Saddam Husain revived the flamboyant and symbolically loaded style of Arab political speech that had predominated on the eve of the 1967 war. He portrayed the world surrounding the Arabs as threatening and merciless, where the Soviet Union was no longer able to provide them with strategic backing as before. Thus, he urged his audience to prepare for a fateful struggle against Israel and the United States in defense of "Arab national security" under his own leadership. Saddam's claim for all-Arab leadership was based on Iraq's advanced technological capability, said to be the only answer to Israel's nu-clear threat. Saddam's aggressive and brutal rhetoric echoed strongly in the Arab world. His defiance of the United States and threats to strike Israel with unconventional weapons captured the imagination of the masses as well as the shapers of public opinion.[6]

Saddam Husain's prestige indeed soared as he came to be seen—and self-portrayed—as a mythological hero-savior, the heir of Nasir, or even Salah al-Din. What fascinated the Arab audience, apart from threatening Israel and the United States, was Saddam's offer of strong and daring leadership, corre-sponding to deeply-rooted longings for power and dignity (*'izza wa-karama*) in Arab political culture. The demonization of Israel and its threat to the whole region turned all the more fateful the role of Iraq's political and technological leadership in defending Arab collective survival, honor, Islamic values, and legitimate national aspirations for a place in the sun. Saddam revived the myth of Israel's expansionist dream of reigning from the Nile to the Euphrates, tying it to the wave of Soviet immigration to Israel and generating a strong followup from 'Arafat and the Arab media. The war against Israel and its American ally was defined in religious and historic terms. It was a struggle of civilizations, Islamic holy war (*jihad*) against the new Crusaders, aimed at liberating Palestine and Jerusalem. The war against Israel was presented as an "imperative," which would inevitably lead to Israel's destruction. An important element in Saddam's populist rhetoric were his contemptuous, inflammatory attacks against the rich oil monarchs, whom he portrayed as a group of corrupt, inept, and insensitive rulers, claiming a new and equitable division of the Arab wealth.[7]

Whether Saddam's aggressive declarations were meant to cover up his real intentions about Kuwait, or to exert pressure on the GCC monarchs to meet his financial requests, the electrified atmosphere of imminent war that he created in the region failed to bear fruit. It apparently paved his way to host the next Arab summit conference in Baghdad. Yet the summit underlined, if anything, the hollowness of Saddam's claim for Arab leadership and produced a refusal by the Gulf monarchies to meet his requests for financial aid, presented by King Husain. Syria—and Lebanon—boycotted the summit, challenging Iraq's president, which, given the history of enmity between the two Ba'thi regimes, needed no explanation.[8]

No less a setback for Saddam were the contrasting concepts that he and President Mubarak represented at the summit regarding regional and international issues. Saddam's aggressive and angry approach was squarely countered by Mubarak's realistic pragmatism, which heralded the renewal of Iraqi-Egyptian competition for Arab regional leadership. In fact, even before the summit Mubarak was clearly heading toward resuming Egypt's central role in the Arab arena by restoring his relations with Asad and Qadhafi. On March 24, a mini-summit of Egypt's, Syria's, Libya's, and Sudan's heads of state was held in Tubruk, following a rapprochement in Egypt-Libyan relations. The gathering discussed the ideologically loaded issue of "Arab national security" and the need for a joint Arab strategy to cope with Israel's threats. Its significance, however, rested in the growing understanding between Mubarak and Asad at the expense of Saddam Husain. Clearly, Syria's acquiescence in Egypt's peace with Israel and its incremental move toward the Cairo-Saudi axis, made the alignment with Asad a higher priority for Mubarak than alignment with the ACC, where Saddam Husain played a central role.[9]

Saddam's speech at the Baghdad Arab summit epitomized his efforts to subordinate the oil-rich monarchies to Iraq's needs by bold intimidation and militant rhetoric about Israel's threats to "Arab national security." Saddam demanded total mobilization of all Arab material resources behind his firm lead, threatening that there would be no tolerance for the faint-hearted and the cowards. The same spirit marked Saddam's response to Washington's and Moscow's message to the summit to support the peace process and refrain from militant resolutions. He called upon the Arab world to exploit the collapse of the "nightmare" of a paralyzing bi-polar global balance of power by establishing their own "regional balance of deterrence." Saddam reasserted that Iraq would retaliate with mass destructive weapons against any Israeli attack on Iraq or other Arab countries. Demonstrating the effort to turn the Arab world's attention to Israel, Saddam revealed his contacts with Iran's President for the sake of peace between them.[10]

King Husain and 'Arafat joined Saddam's warnings regarding the threats to "Arab national security," repeating their urgent need for financial aid. King Husain focused on the Soviet Jewish immigration to Israel, pointing to Jordan and Palestine as the first and most vulnerable targets of Israel's expansionist plans. 'Arafat joined Saddam's anti-American attack, accusing Washington of "procrastination, vagueness, and ambiguity," in its peace efforts while Israel was free to implement its expansionist plan "from the Nile to the Euphrates." President Mubarak sounded a different note, asserting the Arab world's need for peace in the region through international legitimacy, which he argued should also resolve the Arabs' concerns regarding Soviet immigration to Israel. He urged his colleagues to recognize the changes of global order and called for cooperation, not confrontation, with the international community, and suggested that the Middle East be made a zone "free of all weapons of mass destruction."[11]

The summit's final communique expressed nothing of the behind-the-scenes tension generated by Saddam's paralyzing claims from the Gulf monarchies. It reaffirmed support for the PLO's "political program," but made no mention of Resolution 242, which implied recognition of Israel. Jordan's needs were to be considered through bilateral contacts, making no specific Arab commitment either on this issue or on the Palestinian uprising. In spite of all the hostile rhetoric, the conference made no reference to the issue of Jewish immigration to Israel within its pre-1967 borders.[12]

Although the summit provided no clue to Iraq's decision to invade Kuwait, it certainly reflected the new inter-Arab alignment, with Iraq and Egypt as the pivotal actors of rival coalitions. In July, following the resumption of diplomatic relations between Iran and Kuwait, Saddam Husain shifted his target from Israel to Kuwait, accusing it of stealing billions of dollars worth of Iraqi oil from Rumaila field near their common border. Iraq also accused Kuwait and the UAE of causing Iraq a $14 billion loss by cheating on their OPEC oil export quotas, thus driving the prices down. Saddam's claims prompted Arab diplomatic efforts to defuse the tension, involving Mubarak and ʿArafat, in which—according to Mubarak's version—the Iraqi ruler gave his word not to use force against Kuwait, which was reported to Arab and Western governments. Saddam himself later argued that he had undertaken to refrain from using force against Kuwait prior to a summit meeting with its Amir, sending a clear message of threat. At Saudi and Kuwaiti requests, an emergency OPEC meeting was convened in Geneva on July 26 for arbitration in the dispute. Kuwait agreed to reduce its oil exports but the meeting declined to meet Iraq's demands to raise oil prices. On August 1, while Iraqi troops were already massing on the Kuwaiti border, another Iraqi-Kuwaiti effort to resolve the crisis was made at a meeting in Jidda. Its breakdown after a few hours removed the last barrier from Saddam's road to the invasion of Kuwait.[13]

If Saddam had assumed that the GCC states would not challenge his aggression, he committed a gross mistake. Given their military weakness, the Gulf monarchies turned immediately to mobilizing external support to force Iraq to withdraw from Kuwait. However, the emergency meeting of Arab FMs in Cairo on August 3 failed to confirm an appeal for foreign intervention, or even to accept Kuwait's demand to create an Arab force to counter Iraq. Indeed, the precarious nature of the Arab states system was strongly demonstrated in that meeting of the Arab FMs who seemed to hardly grasp the gravity of the Iraqi invasion. Although a majority of fourteen votes, with five abstentions, condemned Iraq and called for its immediate withdrawal from Kuwait, the abstaining representatives refused to name the aggressor in the resolution, on the grounds that that would hamper future mediation efforts.[14]

King Husain's mission to Baghdad on August 4—in coordination with Mubarak—failed to convince Saddam Husain to withdraw from Kuwait, despite reports to this effect. Indeed, Iraq's further actions in Kuwait during the first few days after the invasion by no means indicated that the conquest was meant to be temporary. In any event, the almost immediate American-Soviet joint condemnation of the invasion and the U.S. pressure on its Saudi allies to confirm the deployment of American troops on their soil, seem to narrow the chances of Arab mediation. The GCC rulers, with no real force available to stop the Iraqi army from storming Saudi Arabia's territory or attacking their oil fields, were least of all willing to put their trust in an "Arab solution." They showed little hesitation in backing the Saudi appeal for American troops to protect them, even without a collective Arab sanction. Not only were the GCC monarchies traditionally allied with the United States as the ultimate assurance of their security in the face of strong, greedy Arab neighbors; they explained that their appeal for international intervention was in line with their commitments as members of the AL and the UN and that, as sovereign states, they had absolute freedom to choose the means they might deem fit to preserve their security, sovereignty, and national soil. Indeed, the public discourse aroused by the Kuwait crisis across the Arab world was noticeable in reiterating those principles of state sovereignty and the immunity of national territories and boundaries anchored in international law. Aggression and the acquisition of territories by force were strongly denounced, referring also to Israeli and Iranian irredentist aspirations.[15]

The hopelessness of finding an "Arab solution" for the crisis was confirmed by Saddam Husain's announcement on August 8, of the formal annexation of Kuwait to Iraq, on grounds that it had always been part of the Iraqi "mother state." Meanwhile, an international military and economic blockade was imposed on Iraq, and that same day the first American forces arrived in Saudi Arabia to defend it from Iraqi attack, operating till the end of the war under titular Saudi command. Thus, by the time the emergency Arab summit convened in Cairo, on August 10, Saddam had effectively been left no room for conciliation. Moreover, inter-Arab debate shifted dramatically from a discussion of Iraq's act of aggression to an ideological debate on the admissibility of foreign military intervention in an Arab-Arab dispute.[16]

The summit meeting in Cairo on August 10 was marked by the bold determination of the Arab majority coalition—led by Egypt, Saudi Arabia, and Syria—to adopt the resolutions needed for legitimating Arab and international action against Iraq. The proponents of an "Arab solution," including the PLO, Jordan, Yemen, Libya, Algeria, and Sudan, were not a coherent group and constituted a minority. Mubarak stressed the necessity for Arab participation in the international military action in the Gulf, to ensure that it would remain within the boundaries set by the Arabs and commit no harm to their collective interest. The efforts made by Iraq and its supporters—mainly the PLO, Sudan, Libya, and Jordan—to distract the deliberations from the occupation of Kuwait and lead the summit toward an "Arab solution," were vehemently blocked by the Egypt-led coalition, which refused even to present them to a vote. The idea of an "Arab solution" was perceived as a ploy to gain time that would allow Iraq to complete its annexation of Kuwait and establish its hegemony in the Gulf. In the annals of Arab summits, an "Arab solution" usually referred to the familiar pattern of mediation and conciliation—often a euphemistic code name for procrastination and inaction—"within the framework of the one Arab family." Finally, the summit endorsed the Arab FMs' and the UNSC's resolutions, condemning the Iraqi attack on and annexation of Kuwait. The summit also supported the GCC's "right of legitimate defense" and the steps taken to implement it, and agreed to dispatch Arab forces to support the Gulf states in defense of their territory, against "any Arab aggression." Following the summit, Egypt, Syria, and Morocco sent troops to Saudi Arabia.[17]

The summit resolutions were endorsed by a majority vote of twelve states against the votes of Iraq, the PLO, and Libya. Yemen and Algeria abstained, while Jordan, Sudan, and Mauritania expressed reservations, and

Tunisia was absent. The four-hour-long summit and its resolutions, adopted by majority vote and not unanimously, set a precedent for this forum, but also generated bitter criticism by the adherents of an "Arab solution" to the crisis. Unlike those critics of the summit's procedures, its proponents perceived the results, especially the majority vote, as a virtual normalization of this Arab forum. Yet the significance of the summit resolutions was essential rather than procedural. By rejecting the idea of an "Arab solution," referring to international norms and rules and actively following them, the summit made a step toward internalizing those norms and further incorporating Arab states into the world order. Another result was the resignation of ALSG Qulaibi, facilitating the final return of the AL's headquarters to Cairo.[18]

The positions adopted by 'Arafat, King Husain, and Yemen's president at the summit—reasserted in a mini-summit in Baghdad with Iraq's president on December 4—brought on them harsh retaliation by Egypt and the GCC states, which was to last long after the Gulf war ended. King Husain's continued mediation efforts on both regional and international levels, interpreted as defending Saddam Husain, led to Saudi sanctions against Jordan, including the closure of their common border, expulsion of Jordanian diplomats, and an end to all financial aid and oil shipments. King Husain responded by reassuming the title "Sharif," snubbing the Saudis by his Hashemite family's historical rights in Hijaz, usurped by the House of Sa'ud. Although Mubarak himself tried, in November and December, to convince Saddam to withdraw from Kuwait, Egyptian media strongly denounced 'Arafat's thankless behavior, leading to a crisis in PLO-Egypt relations: cessation of diplomatic contact and closure of the Voice of Palestine radio broadcasting from Cairo.[19]

Saudi Arabia and the GCC states poured their wrath on 'Arafat and the PLO, calling the first a "thug" and the latter a "terrorist organization," and absolving themselves of their financial commitments to the PLO and the occupied territories. In addition, Saudi Arabia expelled all PLO diplomats and, along with other Gulf states, stopped all financial remittances from Palestinian employees to the PLO, resulting in an overall loss of some $400 million to the Palestinians as a whole. Yet the harshest retaliation was an expulsion of close to one million Yemeni and Palestinian labor migrants, mostly from Saudi Arabia and Kuwait, during the crisis months prior to and after the war. The expulsions might have been in retaliation for Yemen's and the PLO's blunt support for Iraq, but the Gulf monarchies might also have used the opportunity provided by the war to get rid of a domestic source of tension and potential threat to their national sovereignty.[20]

The ideological debate triggered by the foreign military intervention in the Gulf revealed a deep sense of crisis at the failure of the core concept of collective Arab security and solidarity. Indeed, not only did the appeal for foreign intervention against an Arab member-state attest to the shorthandedness of the Arab collective, it was, ironically, sanctioned by *the* forum that had still been perceived as a symbol of Arab unity. The imminent confrontation between Western forces—joined by Arab troops—and the Iraqi army, unprecedented in postcolonial Arab history, destroyed a major taboo in the region's political culture.

The Kuwait crisis demonstrated the magnitude of Arab-Islamic symbolism and sentiment and their important role in Middle East politics, particularly in the context of public and oppositional protest. The scope and duration of the military buildup on Saudi soil during the six-month crisis provided the Iraqi propaganda machine a credible context for denouncing the deployment of Western forces on Saudi soil and challenging the legitimacy of Arab collaborating regimes. Appealing to Arab-Islamic sentiments, Saddam Husain denounced the arrival of the international forces as "American neocolonialism" and a desecration of Islam's holiest shrines in Mecca and Madina, calling for *jihad* by all Muslims to "purify the Holy Land from the robbers." Particularly appealing to Arab public opinion was Saddam's statement of August 12, linking the Iraqi withdrawal from Kuwait with Israeli withdrawal from the territories it had occupied in 1967. The strong echo this statement had in the Arab world heralded an intensified Iraqi effort to attract the Arab masses' support by belligerent rhetoric against Israel. Yet the more support he enlisted in the Arab world the less he was willing to compromise his prestige for the sake of preventing a collision with the American-led coalition. The Iraqi effort to entangle Israel in the crisis culminated in launching SCUD missiles attacks on Israel during the war for the purpose of provoking Israeli retaliation against Iraq, which would oblige the other Arab regimes to withdraw from the American-led coalition.[21]

Saddam Husain's Islamic rhetoric made it all the more necessary for the Saudi rulers to legitimize their policy by Islamic rhetoric as well, namely, by issuing *fatwas* justifying the deployment of foreign forces on Saudi soil and the use of force against the Iraqis by declaring a *jihad*. Yet although Saddam Husain's nationalist and Islamic messages had a discernible echo among Muslims across the Arab world, the Islamic institutionalized response proved restrained due to the dependence of many of the Islamic groups on Saudi financial aid. Another element in Saddam's campaign was his confrontational message toward the greedy and corrupted wealthy oil rulers. Saddam's social message, interpreted as aiming at a new distribution of Arab national wealth, touched a sensitive nerve among the have-nots in the Arab world. But while this message strongly appealed to Palestinians—impoverished and frustrated by three years of fruitless uprising—and Yemenites, it did not score much success in other poor societies like Egypt.[22]

The occupation of Kuwait was by and large unacceptable to the Arab ruling elites, mainly on pragmatic grounds. Yet many of those who opposed

Saddam's military move were even more adamant in resisting the presence of foreign military forces, perceived as a new Crusade. The inadequacy of an "Arab solution" of the crisis notwithstanding, public protest and anti-Western sentiment, led by Islamic and nationalist opposition groups, forced shaky regimes to take a fence-sitting position or even sympathize with Iraq. This was apparently the case with Algeria, Tunisia, Yemen, and Jordan. In the case of Jordan, King Husain's position represented deference to strong domestic support for Saddam Husain especially among Palestinians, on top of potential Iraqi threats, rather than any ideological reservation at the international intervention. Indeed, it was the masses to whom Saddam Husain addressed his Islamic and Arab nationalist messages, in an effort to amplify intrinsic psychological inhibitions and agitate public sentiments against ruling elites, reflecting a normative gap between state and society.

The inter-Arab alignment in the Kuwait crisis was primarily a reflection of long-lived cleavages as well as recently established grievances and interests. Arab states' alignment in the crisis was essentially marked by realpolitik, combining calculation of regional, international, and domestic affairs: the external threat to one's national security; ability to contain domestic pressures; and the prospective strategic and material benefits one's policy might produce. Clearly, those governments that decided to take an active role in the international coalition had been motivated by political and economic interests and expectations for tangible rewards, no matter how they explained their policies. Egypt's participation in the anti-Iraq coalition was reciprocated by writing off $14 billion of its external debt—$7 billion by the GCC states, and the other 7 billions by the United States. Syria's role in the Gulf crisis represented, apart from its longstanding enmity to the Baghdad regime, the changing policy toward Egypt and the United States since the beginning of 1990. Still, by joining the anti-Iraq coalition Damascus was allowed to reap immediate benefits in the form of tacit support by the Western alliance in getting rid of General 'Awn, whose access to an Iraqi arms supply had been cut off by the total embargo imposed on Iraq in the wake of its aggression. This paved the way to the "Agreement of Fraternity and Cooperation" signed between Syria and Lebanon in May 1991, which effectively turned Lebanon into a Syrian protectorate. 'Awn's departure enabled Syria to dismantle the armed militias and implement constitutional reforms based on the Ta'if Lebanese national conciliation accord of October 1989. Beyond expectations for an improvement of Syria's image in Washington and Western Europe, Asad could reasonably hope for financial reward—after the war Syria received $2 billion from the Saudis—and for ridding himself of his arch-rival Saddam Husain. By contrast, for those who opted to support Iraq, particularly the PLO, Yemen, and Jordan, there was—on top of domestic risks—little or no benefit expected from opposing Saddam Husain. Indeed, with the exception of Syria, the crisis showed the continuity of foreign policies pending domestic constraints, which may explain Syria's reservations about its troops operating under foreign command.[23]

The six-month-long crisis was marked by a confused political language that indicated the limited usefulness of ideological rhetoric—perhaps its obsolescence—in inter-Arab disputes. The abusive, cynical, and self-interest-driven nature of that rhetoric was employed equally by political opposites, religious or secular, militant or moderate, even more than in the "Arab cold war" of the late 1950s and early 1960s. Saddam Husain personified this trend, with his call for *jihad* which stood in flagrant contrast to his life-long secular conduct and record of cracking down on Islamic movements. Iraq's invasion of Kuwait was condemned as "foreign aggression," while the Western coalition came to serve the goal of "legitimate defense of Arab territory." No less confusing was Syria's objection to Saddam's attempt to link the Gulf crisis to the Arab-Israeli conflict, or its argument that its forces had gone to Saudi Arabia to protect the holy places.

The ideological debate during the Gulf crisis reaffirmed the permeability of state boundaries and the vulnerability of national sovereignty in the Islamic-Arab region, especially under circumstances of confrontation with non-Muslims. Yet normative inhibitions seem to have also played a role in setting boundaries for Arab states' regional policies. The GCC rulers no doubt wished the war to end with Saddam Husain's removal from power. Yet from the outset, Arab participation in the anti-Iraqi coalition was precarious, confined to the liberation of Kuwait, which might have ultimately impeded the possibility of a large-scale land operation into Iraq's territory to depose Saddam Husain. Turkey and Iran obviously shared this inhibition, objecting to a possible dismantling of Iraq and the establishment of a Kurdish state in the northern part of the country, fearing that such a state would provoke irredentist aspirations among their own Kurdish minorities. Despite the impact of defiant Islamic rhetoric on Arab-Islamic societies, the crisis also manifested the limits of cross-national symbolism and sentiments in the face of state power and the latter's ability to contain Islamic opposition movements. Also salient was the tendency among Islamic groups to express accommodation and compromise in their political behavior according to their particular domestic conditions and practical considerations.[24]

On the whole, the crisis underlined the primacy of state sovereignty over supra-national ideologies, which also shaped Iran's neutrality in the crisis. Yet although Arab states' alignment was determined by realistic considerations, it tended to assume an ideological nature as a source of legitimacy, underlining the role of Arab-Islamic rhetoric in regional and domestic politics. Thus, even though the Kuwaiti crisis was by its origins and essence a clear case of inter-Arab power politics, the conflict with Israel had been forcefully brought to center stage, even before the United States became involved, by virtue of its qualitative significance in the region's politics. That Saddam Husain chose to focus on the Palestine theme to inflame Islamic-Arab sentiments against those regimes collaborating with the United States, unmistakably attested to the perceived centrality of this issue in the region's political culture. Indeed, a collaboration of Arabs with an international force—without Israel—against an Arab state had been difficult enough to justify, let alone when Israel itself was on one side in the hostilities. In retrospect, Saddam Husain's strategy may seem an anachronistic attempt to employ Nasir's Pan-Arab populist rhetoric against regional and Western enemies. But it was this constrained Arab participation in the international coalition that substantiated the claim for vigorous American involvement in resuming the Arab-Israeli peace process in the wake of the war.

The New Peace Process: Madrid, Oslo, and Beyond

The Gulf war, the breakup of the Soviet Union, and the end of the Cold War reshaped the Middle East strategic and political scene. The end of the Gulf war, however, left unresolved the two interlocked questions of regional Arab security and stability and the Arab-Israeli conflict, which the war had strongly emphasized. Particularly for the GCC monarchies, national security meant new region-based checks and rules to prevent another aggression against them by envious neighbors. Even before the war was over, GCC spokesmen expressed the need for a "new Arab order, based on legality, mutual respect, noninterference in internal affairs, and the primary role of the economy to create mutual interests."[25]

While these principles were no different from what the AL's Charter or the ACSP stood for, what the GCC governments were looking for was obviously an effective, long-term regional security arrangement. On March 6, following a series of talks between the Arab war coalition members, they issued in Damascus a joint declaration on regional security principles. The Damascus Declaration affirmed its adherence to the principles of international legitimacy, particularly those relating to respecting states' sovereignty, noninterference in domestic affairs, and settling conflicts through peaceful means. Practically, it was agreed that Egypt and Syria would provide the nucleus of an Arab peacekeeping force in the Gulf, apparently in return for financial aid. The agreement gained American support, to include joint exercises of the United States's and these Arab states' forces. The Damascus Declaration, however, failed to implement its operational part of creating an Arab peacemaking force, an Arab economic grouping, and an Arab high court. Yet it proved instrumental in prompting the renewed postwar American efforts to convene an international peace conference on the Arab-Israeli conflict. The Gulf war and the Damascus Declaration underlined the Arab states' growing incorporation into the global system and its rules, though without abandoning the concept of "regional Arab order."[26]

As the only remaining superpower, the American administration was more determined than ever before to establish a peaceful and stable Middle East in conjunction with the envisioned "new world order." The Gulf war resulted in enhancing U.S. leverage on its allies, such as Israel and the Gulf monarchies, as well as on non-participants in the anti-Iraq coalition, primarily Jordan and the PLO. Hence, the end of the Gulf war witnessed a vigorous effort by the Bush administration to advance the resumption of the peace process in the Middle East. Still, no less than eight months and seven shuttle visits by SoS James Baker to the Middle East, and a Soviet-American agreement, were needed to forge the Madrid framework based on Resolutions 242 and 338 and Israel's initiative of May 1989.

The historical significance of the Madrid peace conference, opened on October 30, 1991, stemmed from the scope of Arab participation and the procedural framework, which in fact had to do with substance. In addition to all Arab states neighboring Israel, other Arab states were represented in the conference, primarily the GCC states and Morocco. For the first time since 1947, a Palestinian delegation was present at an international peace conference on the Middle East, though within a Jordanian-Palestinian delegation. Even more important was Israel's willingness to deal with the Palestinian delegation as an equal party and, later, on a bilateral and separate level. The Arabs accepted the principle of direct and bilateral negotiations with Israel without foreign interference, and the goal of reaching a contractual agreement of peace. This track was to be reinforced by a multilateral track of negotiations on key regional problems, serving as a confidence-building measure toward normalized relations among the Middle East nations.

That the United States was able to convene the Madrid peace conference on such terms, apart from its enhanced international prestige and determination, had to do primarily with the new reality in the Middle East in the wake of the Gulf war. The end of the Cold War diminished Israel's bargaining position as a strategic asset to the United States in the face of Soviet threats. At the same time, the Gulf war exposed Israel's vulnerability to strategic weapons possessed by Arab states. Israel's request for a $10 billion loan guarantee to enable absorption of the massive wave of Jewish immigrants from the former Soviet Union gave the U.S. government some leverage on Jerusalem. However, Israel's right-wing government, headed by Itzhak Shamir, was ideologically committed to settling the entire Eretz Israel, and rejected the "land for peace" principle.[27]

Egypt, still the only Arab state at peace with Israel, was particularly active in supporting the U.S. diplomatic effort that eventually led to the Madrid peace conference. For Egypt, any advancement of an Arab-Israeli settlement would reinforce its legitimacy and leadership in the Arab world, and perhaps reward it economically by the United States. Along with Saudi Arabia, Egypt was particularly instrumental in convincing Asad and 'Arafat to accept the Madrid framework, including the principle of bilateral talks with Israel. It is noteworthy that the Arab states system assumed no role in approving the Madrid formula. Egypt objected to the PLO's attempts to convene an Arab summit before the Madrid conference to secure support for its position, insisting, instead, on consultations at the level of FMs of the Arab parties concerned.[28]

The Gulf war brought Saudi Arabia to a closer relationship with the United States than it had enjoyed before, leading the kingdom to vigorously follow its particular interests in cultivating this relationship. The Saudis played a central role in persuading Syria to accept the Madrid framework and attend the conference. They also made a salient effort to appear as strongly involved in, and willing to cooperate with, the Madrid peace process. In mid-July, the Saudis announced that they were willing to lift the Arab boycott on Israel in return for Israel's consent to stop all new settlement activity in the occupied territories. Such a gesture, offered without linking it to the issue of East Jerusalem and its Muslim shrines, was an obvious shift from established Arab and Islamic attitudes and a clear message of assurance to the United States and Israel about the peace process. The Saudis continued to provide support for the negotiations in Washington through their ambassador to the United States, Emir Bandar Bin Sultan, and were apparently helpful, along with Egypt, in convincing the PLO to accept Israel's "Gaza-Jericho first" scheme.[29]

The destructive political and economic repercussions of the Gulf war for the Palestinians provoked a wave of internal criticism of 'Arafat's war policy and suggestions for reducing his authority under the title "democratization of the PLO." The mass expulsion of the bulk of the Palestinians from Kuwait after the war, the termination of financial aid from the Gulf states, and Israel's policy of enforcing long closures on the West Bank and Gaza Strip—all created a sense of despair among Palestinians both in the occupied territories and the PLO's headquarters in Tunis. At the same time, Syria continued to exert pressure on the PLO to close ranks with its Palestinian client factions. Above all, the PLO feared losing ground in the occupied territories to its main political rival, Hamas. While the PLO was compelled to reduce essential social and political activities, Hamas had been in a constant mode of expansion, gathering popular support and challenging the PLO's exclusive national authority.[30]

Denied its bargaining power and under constant pressure, both from its adherents among the "inside" Palestinian leadership as well as from Egypt and Saudi Arabia, the PLO had no choice but to accept Israel's demands regarding Palestinian participation at Madrid: no representation of the Palestinians by a separate delegation; no participation by PLO, Jerusalemites, or expelled figures. In addition, the negotiations were to deal with Palestinian self-government only. Even more discouraging for the PLO was Israel's refusal to freeze the settlements in the occupied territories before Madrid. On the United States's part, even after the PLO approved the Madrid framework, Washington still remained adamant against renewing the dialogue with the organization. The U.S. Government confined itself to contacts with the local Palestinian leadership in the West Bank and Gaza, which had been effectively guided and controlled by the PLO. Nontheless, the latter had to remain on guard to prevent possible alliances between the local leadership and Jordan. Thus, accepting the Madrid framework by the PLO represented a realistic decision which contented itself with appointing the Palestinian delegation, while temporarily shelving the principles of self-determination, a Palestinian state, and East Jerusalem.[31]

Despite its position during the Gulf crisis, the Jordanian regime showed clear interest in joining the American effort to convene an international peace conference, which had been King Husain's goal since the mid-1980s. The shift in the king's foreign policy was heralded by the new government established in June, without participation of Islamic representatives. Jordan's interest in the American motion was motivated by practical reasons, both economic and political. Aside from the continued Saudi sanctions, the poor Jordanian economy was overburdened by mass immigration of hundreds of thousands— mostly Palestinians—from the Gulf states. What seemed a shift in the king's policy effectively represented the regime's traditional alliance with the West and its persistent effort since 1967 to advance a diplomatic settlement of the conflict with Israel. With no other alternative in sight, and given the built-in interest in the Palestinian territories, the Hashemite regime could not but join the American diplomatic thrust.[32]

Syria adhered to its concept of a comprehensive settlement conditional on an early Israeli commitment for full withdrawal from the Golan Heights— without holding bilateral negotiations with Israel—to be followed by negotiations on Palestinian autonomy. Even when the Syrians eventually accepted the principle of bilateral talks with Israel, they remained adamant on nonparticipation in the multilateral talks as long as Israel had not committed itself to full withdrawal from the occupied Golan. Moreover, Damascus continued to provide a safe base for those Palestinian groups, leftists as well as Islamists, rejecting the peace process and challenging ʿArafat's legitimacy. Syria's ambivalence was obviously meant to manipulate its weak Arab partners and recover its veto power over the peace process.

From the outset, Syria attempted to acquire control over Jordan, the PLO, and Lebanon in the ensuing Madrid conference by summoning their representatives to Damascus, ostensibly to forge a collective Arab position. Yet at the same time Asad signalled his willingness to sign a separate agreement with Israel, stating that "even if one of the parties sign a separate or bilateral agreement [with Israel], it should not be called a separate peace." Apart from

Lebanon, however, Syria failed to create a collective decision-making forum under its supervision, revealing a discernible erosion of its veto power within the boundaries of "Greater Syria." Thus, contrary to Syria's rigid tone at the opening session of the Madrid conference, the messages of the Palestinian and Jordanian delegates were conciliatory and conscious of Israel's security needs. Jordan's and the PLO's willingness to take part in the multilateral talks despite the Syrian and Lebanese boycott, attested to the obsolescence of the concept of collective Arab action in the Madrid peace process.[33]

Even more salient was the absence from the Madrid peace process of an ideological debate or collective Arab forums to hammer out coordinated strategy toward Israel. The process was marked by mutual suspicion between each of the Arab participants and everyone else, revealing each party's thrust to advance its own interests independently of other Arab partners, and despite criticism of other partners of the lack of inter-Arab coordination. Thus, the Israel-Jordan joint agenda agreement of October 1992 triggered Syrian and Palestinian criticism. Syria's unofficial position was that it would adhere to its nationalist principles and "responsible" position even if it remained alone in the process of negotiations. Yet when, in late December, Israel deported more than four hundred Hamas activists to Lebanon, the Syrians were reluctant to link the renewal of the Washington talks with the return of the deportees, as demanded by the PLO. Syria's criticism of the separate PLO-Israel DOP and the Jordan-Israel peace accord presented them as documents dictated by Israel due to its military advantage, calling for following Damascus' perseverant stand. Syria tacitly pointed to its concept of "strategic parity" as a prerequisite for a decent agreement that would recover the Golan on its own terms rather than those of Israel.[34]

As long as the Shamir government had been in power, no progress had been achieved either with Syria or with the Palestinians, though Israel was willing to conduct separate talks with the Palestinian delegates. As a matter of fact, Israel was dealing indirectly with the PLO, which remained the source of authority and legitimacy for the Palestinian delegation. The June 1992 elections in Israel, which the Labor Party won narrowly, brought a discernible change in Israel's position toward Syria when PM Rabin agreed to apply the principle of "land for peace" on the Golan, thus intensifying mutual suspicion among the Arab partners.

Still, the gaps between the two sides regarding the depth of Israel's withdrawal from the Golan and Syria's concept of peace remained the main stumbling block. Faced with unexpected public objections to a major withdrawal from the Golan, including within the Labor Party, and unconvinced that Asad had truly undergone a strategic change—that is, committment to fully normal peace relations with Israel—PM Rabin opted to focus on reaching security measures first, before any discussion over the depth of withdrawal was to take place. Intensive mediation efforts by U.S. President Clinton and SoS Christopher helped to advance the negotiations to the level of direct meetings between Israel's and Syria's ambassadors and, in the Spring of 1995, even their CoS's, but with no tangible progress.[35]

Before the elections, Rabin had promised a deal with the Palestinians on autonomy within six months to a year. Yet time went by and the talks led to nowhere, with Rabin blaming it on the PLO, effectively admitting that there was no alternative to the PLO as a partner to agreement with Israel, though he still believed that nothing could come out of direct contacts with it. The prolonged impasse at the official Israeli-Palestinian talks, combined with increasing armed operations by Hamas, were behind the secret talks that started in early 1993 between Israeli scholars—with unofficial approval of Deputy FM Beilin—and PLO officials in Oslo, under Norwegian auspices. Threatened by a government coalition crisis due to the prolonged stalemate and without a better alternative, Rabin gave his consent to turning the Oslo secret channel into full-fledged official negotiations between Israel and the PLO. That the PLO preferred secret and direct negotiations without U.S. involvement attested to its attempt to bypass the Palestinian official delegation composed of West Bank and Gaza figures. These negotiations led to the historical mutual recognition between Israel and the PLO and the Document of Principles (DOP), signed on September 13 on the White House lawn with a handshake between Rabin and 'Arafat. The DOP shaped the principles of a prospective process of establishing a five-year interim Palestinian self-governing authority, first in the Gaza Strip and the Jordan Valley's town of Jericho, to be expanded later to other parts of the West Bank, and the election of a Palestinian council. The PLO undertook to omit from the Palestinian National Charter all statements denying Israel's legitimacy or calling for war against it. The permanent status of the self-governed territory, borders, Jerusalem, the Palestinian refugees, and the Israeli settlements, were left open without being prejudged by the interim arrangements. The implementation of the first stage of the DOP in May 1994 set in motion a state-building process led by 'Arafat's PLO, with financial support from Western donors and Japan.[36]

The Israel-PLO accord came under strong Syrian criticism. While not officially condemning it, the Syrians criticized the PLO for recognizing Israel, for making a separate agreement and far-reaching concessions. While Syria continued to support the peace process, it summoned its Palestinian clients in Damascus for a conference that condemned 'Arafat's agreement with Israel and formed a unified front to fight against it. On the whole, however, its low-key response—abstaining from using force against Palestinian targets in Lebanon—reflected the loss of its veto power over the Israeli-Palestinian peace process.[37]

The Israel-PLO DOP obviously prompted King Husain to seek his own settlement with Israel. That same month, Israel and Jordan agreed on a framework for a peace accord. But the king still hesitated to take his own course and finalize the long-awaited peace agreement with Israel in order to allow time for Syria to pursue its own negotiations, apparently in concern about its reaction. Yet the deadlocked Israeli-Syrian negotiations, growing economic constraints, the implications entailed by the Israeli-Palestinian process for Jordan's national security, and American encouragement to take a bolder stance, independent of the pace set by Syria, all paved the road for an Israeli-Jordanian peace agreement signed on October 26, 1994. Syria responded by questioning the legitimacy of the agreement, mainly because of the territorial concessions made by Jordan in the form of leasing a small area cultivated by Israeli farmers in Wadi Araba to Israel, which King Husain dismissed with unprecedented vehemence, advising the Syrians to mind their own business. It is noteworthy that Mubarak absented himself from the ceremony of signing the agreement, demonstrating his discontent at its substance and lack of Egyptian involvement in its conclusion.[38]

Syria's antagonism notwithstanding, the Olso agreement had a far-reaching impact on Israel's position in the Arab world, especially among the Gulf monarchies and Maghreb states. On September 30, 1994, the GCC member states decided to abolish the indirect boycott on Israel, and Morocco, Mauritania, Oman, and Tunisia established low-level diplomatic relations with Israel, without heed for Syria's protests. Particularly significant was King Fahd's address to the 1994 pilgrims, praising the Israel-PLO Cairo agreement of May 1994 on establishing the PA in Gaza and Jericho as "the beginning of a new phase of coexistence." The king also called for cooperation between Islam and the rest of the world regardless of religious differences and further incorporation of Islam in the international system. The Middle East Economic Summit that convened in Casablanca (October 1994) and Amman (October 1995) under the auspices of the American and Russian Presidents, with participants from most Arab countries and Israel, indicated, despite its pitfalls, the beginning of a new era in Middle East history.[39]

The impact of the Oslo agreement on Middle East politics confirmed the significance of the Palestinian issue as the heart of the Arab-Israeli conflict, regardless of its ever-declining weight in shaping Arab states' behavior. Yet it also revealed the vast gaps of interest and attitude regarding Israel between the Arab states on the periphery, to whom the Palestine cause had been mainly a moral commitment, and those directly entangled in the Palestine conflict, to whom it still entailed real political stakes—by Israel's very existence as a neighbor—on both regional and domestic levels. This difference underlay the Mubarak-Asad-Fahd summit in Alexandria in late December 1994, following a visit by PM Rabin to Oman. This summit indicated Syria's effort to promote its control over the pace and substance of the Arab-Israeli peace process in the name of Arab solidarity, thus pressuring Israel into further concessions on the Golan. Even though the summit resulted in no practical measures, it was a signal to the Gulf states to slow down their plans for economic cooperation and normalized relations with Israel.[40]

The post–Gulf war period and the Madrid peace process witnessed a new cycle of Arab self-searching debate underpinned by a deep sense of ideological crisis (*azma*) and despair at the disastrous inter-Arab fragmentation and hostility revealed during the Gulf crisis and their meaning for the future regional system. A major theme in the intellectual debate was inevitably the essence of Pan-Arab nationalism, but even more, the implications of a new world order on the Arab states system. The debate pointed to the necessity for social and political reforms in Arab states as a key condition for economic development and regional cooperation. The urgent need for a new social and political order was underlined by the growing threat of radical Islamic groups to domestic security and stability in Egypt and Algeria, and the dependency of most Arab states on food imports, and hence, on foreign aid, leading to inflated national debt. The search for collective Arab dignity through social and political change almost generated a consensus that in view of the bankruptcy of Arab regimes, democracy represented the only possible escape from the continued Arab national impasse. Since the Arab masses genuinely and unquestionably adhered to Pan-Arab nationalism, it was argued, the implementation of democracy could start the rejuvenation of Arab nationalism. Yet democracy was apparently yearned for less as a liberal, humanistic philosophy of equitable social and political order than as a "panacean" solution to the Arab world's political division and weakness, particularly evident in the conflict with Israel.[41]

The Arab intellectual debate gathered momentum in view of the emerging triangle comprised of Israel, the Palestinians, and Jordan, and the new discourse on the "Middle East Market," epitomized by the economic summits held in Casablanca and Amman. The main stream in the debate reveals a strong quest for revival of the *Arab* regional system based on cooperation and mutual interests of security and economic development. Hence, this stream fiercely criticizes the idea of a Middle East Market—or "Mideasternism" (*sharqawsatiyya*)—as an alternative regional concept aimed at legitimizing Israel's involvement in Middle East economic and political life. The spokesmen of the conservative line lamented the eagerness of Arab regimes to establish economic and diplomatic relations with Israel in disregard of crucial unresolved Arab-Israeli issues, and warned that the Middle East Market would enhance Israel's aspiration for regional hegemony and marginalize the AL role. Indeed, the salience of the the Middle East economic summits has been particularly apparent in the absence of Arab summit conferences between 1990 and 1996. Contrary to the "new Middle East" vision of relations based on purely economic and strategic interests rather than Arab allegiance, which may include Turkey, Iran, and Israel, the nationalist approach regards such possiblity with concern lest it besiege the Arab states.[42]

The "new Middle East" debate represents a mixture of old and new fears of Israeli regional hegemony due to its powerful economy and access to external resources, advanced technology, and nuclear capability, its tacit alliance with the United States and links with the Jewish diaspora. Yet the extensive debate over the "new Middle East" and Israel's role must be seen in the context of intra-Arab politics involving ideology, Arab socio-economic discrepancies, and claims for radical reforms, as well as of inter-state struggle for prestige and resources. Hence, opposition groups tend to highlight the danger to Arab and Islamic identity in the region that the peace process with Israel entails, effectively attacking ruling elites for their foreign policy. At the official level, Israel's growing acceptance in the Arab world serves as an incentive for those Arab states interested in weakening the burden of collective Arab instruments and commitments and fully exercising their sovereignty. This trend threatens Egypt's inherent need to assume regional leadership, which may explain its efforts to slow down diplomatic normalization between Israel and other Arab states. Moreover, as of spring 1994, Egypt renewed its effort to reduce Israel's strategic posture, demanding that Israel join the NPT and utilizing the AL to enlist collective Arab pressure to make the Middle East free of mass-destruction weapons. Egypt's regional policy went still further, and—to Washington's discontent—challenged America's preferential approach to Israel's strategic capabilities.[43]

CONCLUSION

The history of regional Arab politics reveals a steady growth of the state in terms of its ability to insulate itself from rallying issues of symbolic Arab concerns and conduct its autonomous policies. At the same time, there has been a decline in the moral and political effect of centripetal forces, deriving from common supra-state identity and culture, on regional politics. This trend has been demonstrated even in the case of the states immediately concerned with, and most affected by, the Palestine conflict, the most powerful centripetal symbol in Arab-Muslim societies. Yet carving out fully independent and sovereign nation-states from a larger Arab body of territory and society, said to be one nation, is a historical process. The prevalence of supra-state symbols and beliefs in Arab-Muslim societies is bound to remain a potential source of regional tension and instability.

The Arab state obtained further effective autonomy primarily thanks to domestic processes of state-building; cumulation of capabilities; development of state administration, penetration, and monopolizing coercive means; socialization of distinctive allegiance; and the like. This process, however, took place in close interplay with the regional Arab states system, acting through its institutions as an all-Arab authority to lend credence to the regional status quo and legitimize departure from traditional attitudes on questions of Arab normative significance. Regional Arab politics may seem like recurrent cycles of shifting manipulation, coercion, and alignments of individual actors in a perpetual effort to increase one's own capabilities at the expense of other actors and the collective as a whole. A historical perspective, however, shows that inter-Arab relations developed along lines of regional order/disorder in conjunction with social changes and the conflict with Israel.

The AL's foundation indicated a "Westphalian order," which collapsed during the 1950s with the advent of revolutionary regimes in Syria, Egypt, and Iraq. Henceforth, almost all Arab regimes became entangled in prolonged and extensive disputes against each other which threatened to draw the confrontation states into an undesirable war with Israel. Although a temporary return to the Westphalian order had been affected before 1967, it was only in the wake of the war that the pendulum began to swing back momentously to a system of mutually recognized sovereign states.

The shift from collectivity to state sovereignty necessitated a parallel process of "normalization" of the conflict with Israel, diminishing its symbolic significance and its extensive use in claiming conformity, particularly by active actors in the conflict. Thus, the new regional order developed along with a reshaping of collective Arab strategies for joint action in the Palestine conflict. Historically, these changes were led by Egypt, from whom the conflict had claimed the highest toll and which, thanks to its strategic weight and national capabilities, was able to sustain collective Arab sanctions.

The pivotal role of the Palestine conflict in the Arab states system and Egypt's primacy in both spheres, converged in interaction that set in motion a process of changing relations between Pan-Arab nationalism and state particularism. The decline of compulsive Arab conformity was by and large a reflection of Egypt's regional policy, shaped by its capabilities and constraints. Just as Egypt's high level of stateness and capabilities underlay the Pan-Arab challenge to other Arab states' legitimacy, so were they instrumental in reshaping the Arab states system along norms of mutual respect for sovereignty and territorial integrity.

From the outset, blurred boundaries between nation and state obstructed the process of state formation. Yet although in theory Pan-Arabism and statehood were mutually exclusive, they in effect coalesced in tense interaction, generating vague, and often confusing, political language and institutions. This ambiguity nourished state-society conflicts and attracted political competition on both domestic and regional levels, often articulated in revolutionary suprastate concepts that threatened the state's very legitimacy. Hence, regional Arab politics represented a constant tension between the status-quo order—based on sovereign states—and claims for its revision, often serving an egoistic quest for recognition and power.

In this turbulent socio-political environment, the Palestine conflict became the most powerful rallying issue in regional Arab politics, even before Israel's foundation in 1948. Due to its symbolic significance for Arab-Muslim societies and political implications on the neighboring Arab states, the Palestine conflict attracted the growing involvement of Arab politics both in the context of state-society conflict and inter-Arab competition for regional leadership. The issue became especially useful for the revolutionary regimes throughout the 1950s and 1960s in their laborious quest for legitimacy, conducted primarily through ideological campaign. As such, the Palestine conflict aggravated regional comptetition and instability. Mainly after 1967, however, the conflict with Israel also accounted for growing interdependence between Arab states and clearer definition of their distinctive interests and constraints, introducing elements of order into the region's politics.

The outcry for Arab conformity, interlocked with militancy toward Israel, was a useful instrument for legitimizing authority and, ultimately, for state-formation, due to its powerful attraction among the masses. At the same time, an extensive use of supra-state symbolism in Arab politics claimed its toll, interrupting the process of state-formation and regional order. That supra-state values were played up by Arab regimes was often an indication of a government's desperate need to enhance its prestige or combat domestic and regional threats to its authority and state sovereignty. Exacerbating this pattern of behavior were the elasticity and arbitrary interpretation of Arab nationalist core issues, as well as the inconsistency between the image and the practical role of all-Arab institutions. Yet inter-Arab competitions also helped define boundaries and particular interests of the Arab states, as did their collaboration and routinized relations.

Nasir's approach to the conflict with Israel epitomized this contradiction. Until 1967, the concept of total Arab war against Israel, determined by Pan-Arabism, collided with international norms and Israel's widely recognized existence. Apart from cost/benefit military calculations, a military action against Israel was commonly perceived to be a collective venture for which Arab governments were to unify capabilities and command, running the risk of external Arab interference and eroded state sovereignty. Moreover, taking up the Palestine cause was a vehicle for the articulation of grievances by envious Arab neighbors and populist movements, and a potent force against incumbent regimes. Hence, Nasir's decision in 1964 to champion the issue of Palestine and his subsequent preparation for war against Israel was intended mainly to tame Syria's militancy and postpone such war indefinitely.

The losses sustained by the Arabs, particularly Egypt, in the 1967 war and after, combined with inter-Arab fragmentation and inherent strategic constraints, compelled the Arab regimes to adapt to reality and redefine their political goals. No less importantly, growing state machinery, political stability, and control of power provided Arab ruling elites with increased ability to defy external Arab threats and contain, coopt, or repress domestic Pan-Arab movements and non-state actors, challenging their authority and the very concept of independent and sovereign Arab states.

Growing control of the domestic political arena by the state resulted in a declining impact of supra-state symbols on Arab societal behavior, as demonstrated in Arab responses to Israel's invasion of Lebanon, the Intifada, and the Gulf war. In fact, state-building turned these symbols into a burden on most ruling elites, making inevitable their departure from Pan-Arab rhetoric and commitments. The process entailed an ongoing inter-Arab political dialogue, conducted by intellectuals and politicians, media campaigns, and power struggles over values and beliefs, vision, reality, norms and rules of political behavior. It was this half-century of "routinization" of inter-state relations, coupled with bitter lessons of military failures and broken dreams, that shaped the boundaries of state sovereignty, enhancing autonomous foreign policy *vis-à-vis* the conflict with Israel.

The close interplay between the Arab-Israeli conflict and regional Arab politics necessitated a parallel change in both these respects. In late 1963, Nasir was forced to seek a balance between his revolutionary claim for regional hegemony and his need for inter-Arab stable order, based on mutual respect of independence and sovereignty. To secure this balance, it was crucial to control the Palestine conflict through mechanisms of collective Arab action. Yet a retreat from proclaimed revolutionary Pan-Arabism and a move to secure an all-Arab consensus over the indefinite delay of war against Israel needed an institutional procedure for legitimizing the redefinition of collective Arab goals. It was in this context that the Arab summit conference, representing the highest collective authority of the Arab nation (*umma*), came into being. A mediating institution between *raison d'état* and *raison de la nation,* the summit conference provided formal legitimacy to deviation from established common Arab norms, reformulation of collective strategies in the conflict with Israel, and regulation of inter-Arab relations.

It was the 1967 war, however, that set in motion a sustainable process of return to the Westphalian concept of a regional Arab states system. The Arab debacle left Nasir with no alternative but to seek normalization of the traditionally disputed inter-state Arab system so as to secure its material support and adherence to his endorsement of Resolution 242. Beginning in the early 1970s, with Nasir's passing away, the expulsion of the PR from Jordan, and the defeat of the neo-Ba'th revolutionaries in Syria, inter-Arab political discourse incrementally shifted from one marked by coercion and militant ideologies to one marked by realism and pragmatism. Above all, the loss of national territories to Israel in 1967 obliged the Arab states concerned to enter into give-and-take with Israel, turning an ethno-religious total conflict over Israel's legitimacy into a "normal" one, over national territory and boundaries. In view of these trends, Arab summit conferences became a crucial mechanism for facilitating the change.

From their inception in 1964, Arab summit conferences were ostensibly meant to organize the Arab world for the inevitable war against Israel. Indeed, the Palestine conflict topped the agenda of almost all the sessions of this institution. In a critical perspective, however, these summits were concerned primarily with maintaining stability and order in the Palestine conflict system, through cooptation of Pan-Arab militancy, providing conflict-management offices to inter-Arab disputes and financial tradeoffs to enhance regional security. By granting high priority to inter-Arab balance and agreed conformity in handling the conflict with Israel, Arab summits effectively diminished the prospects of a total Arab war against Israel. No wonder that Sadat wove his plans for the October 1973 war in disregard of the AL's military instruments. But following the war, Arab summits were brought back as a useful mechanism for legitimating the diplomatic process in the conflict with Israel. Even the 1978 Baghdad summit, whose main thrust was to defy the Camp David accords, was more interested in reshaping the Arab states system without Egypt than in pursuing the next war with Israel. Indeed, this was essentially Qadhafi's argument against Arab summits and the explanation for his personal absence from most of them.

Arab summit conferences were by no means equally concerned with the issues or grievances of all Arab states. "Arab national security," a code-name for compulsive Pan-Arab conformity, hardly applied to Arab peripheral states in the Maghreb or the Horn of Africa. In fact, Arab summits were controlled and manipulated by core actors whose capabilities and involvement in the Palestine conflict accorded them a leading stature in the regional system as a whole. With few exceptions, mainly in the 1980s, Arab summit conferences convened to confirm an agenda that had already been agreed upon by allied core states.

The inception of the PLO in 1964, sanctioned by the early Arab summit conferences, was in line with the latters' purpose to prevent untimely Arab-Israeli war and preserve Nasir's prestige. By defining the PLO as a political entity, Nasir sought to preempt Palestinian activist tendencies and subordinate them to *raison d'état.* In hindsight, it was the first step in the Palestinians' long struggle to assume exclusive responsibility for their national cause. The crystallization of the PLO's status as a recognized national leadership gathered momentum following the 1967 war. The priority that Arab states gave to the recovery of their occupied territories and the shift toward a diplomatic settlement with Israel made it incumbent on the core Arab states to encourage the PLO's institutionalization and promote its regional and international status as a legitimate representative of the Palestinian people. Transferring nominal responsibility for the Palestinian cause to the PLO met the latter's own demand, but was also aimed at containing arch-nationalist criticism and legitimizing Arab states' diplomatic efforts to recover their own territories.

The growing differences between Egypt and Syria in the aftermath of the 1973 war attested to the linkage between national constraints, ideological outcry for Pan-Arab conformity, and regional politics. Syria represented, as of the mid-1960s, the second pivotal actor in the Palestine conflict system at the expense of Iraq. A historical cradle of "pan" ideological movements, Syria enjoyed neither Egypt's traditional stateness nor its human and geostrategic resources, which would allow it to trade off flexible foreign policy for material gains. Under Asad, Syria shifted from its previous revolutionary policy to pragmatic inter-Arab cooperation. Yet Syria was soon to learn from the post-1973 peace process that it was not strong enough to balance Egypt's agenda in the peace process. Syria, however, could veto undesirable developments—by coercive means, if needed—even at the price of isolation.

As in the case of Nasir, Asad, under growing external and domestic threats to his regime, abandoned this cooperative approach in the early 1980s, replacing it with "strategic parity," which indicated a thrust for greater capabilities and self-reliance in the face of Israel. The new concept legitimized a domestic and regional policy of coercion, intimidation, and subversion, aimed at imposing Syria's will on its weak neighbors, Jordan, Lebanon, the Palestinians, and, to a lesser extent, the Gulf monarchies. Asad followed Nasir's example of championing compulsive Pan-Arab conformity as a means to enhance Syria's capabilities and national security. At the same time, he adopted a pragmatic regional policy by allying with revolutionary Iran against Arab Iraq and taking violent actions against Arafat's PLO after 1982.

In addition to Egypt and Syria, a new political center emerged in the late 1960s, represented by the oil-producing Gulf monarchies led by Saudi Arabia. Identified with traditionalism, individualism, and excessive wealth, these states suffered from extreme vulnerability in their national security, hence their inevitable dependence on tacit alliance with Western powers to rebuff external threats, mainly from envious Arab neighbors. It was this vulnerability and need for national security that motivated the Gulf monarchies' vast use of financial aid to the Arab collective effort in the conflict with Israel as a source of legitimacy and a means to defy radicalism and regional instability. At the same time, however, this financial flow enhanced the confrontation states' capabilities and authority. The cumulation of imaginary oil revenues by this block in the post–1973 war era, coupled with growing international and regional influence, gave rise to a new social and economic sub-system marked by pragmatic, businesslike norms in handling Arab regional relations.

The rest of the Arab states moved back and forth among these leading centers in search of a beneficial alignment that would enhance their resources and security. The patterns of inter-Arab alignments changed over the period under discussion representing the level of regional order. Between the late 1950s, and 1967, the dynamics of inter-Arab relations was shaped primarily by domestic threats and regime changes and less by external threats. It was, however, tightly linked with inter-state competitions for regional hegemony, with propaganda and subversion as their main instruments. As a result, Arab coalitions assumed unstable and short-lived forms, turning a collective action in the conflict with Israel into an abstract objective, postponed to an indefinite future. The post-1967 inter-Arab alignments assumed a more pragmatic character, representing the growing military and economic needs of the confrontation states in the accelerated conflict with Israel. The 1967 war forced the Arab confrontation states to adopt, for the first time since 1948, a workable strategy *vis-à-vis* Israel, which imposed inter-Arab cooperation between previous adversaries.

The post-1967 process of adaptation and reappraisal led to a conflict between state and revolution, which culminated in the PR-Hashemite showdown of 1970. A similar effort to contain this non-state actor marked the PLO-Syria collision in Lebanon in 1976 while Israel's Lebanon war was intended to eliminate the PR. The defeat of the PR by the state attested to the latter's growing authority, jealousy for its sovereignty, and persistent quest for regional security and order. *A priori,* the PLO perceived any strategy shaped by the Arab states as self-serving and bound to accommodate Israel. Yet the PR's lost battle for a revolutionary all-Arab strategy toward Israel reasserted its quest for exercising exclusive authority over the Palestinian community as a whole. In fact, the PLO adopted mechanisms of institution building and state-formation, although without territorial sovereignty.

The pragmatic trend in inter-Arab relations culminated in the 1973 war coalition of Saudi Arabia, Egypt, and Syria, representing the main sources of Arab political power. This coalition remained the pillar of common Arab action—albeit with intermittent crises—until Sadat's visit to Jerusalem. The Arab decision to embark on an indirect peace process reflected a sense of success in the war but even more so, confidence in the oil weapon's impact on the West and its ability to complement the pressure needed to force Israel to meet the Arab demands. Yet the Arab gains in the war proved insufficient, and the oil weapon too short-lived and illusory, resulting in stress and disintegration of the wartime coalition.

The peace process was a major catalyst in the departure from Pan-Arab national conformity. In addition to the division between "rejectionist" and "pragmatist" states, ruptures surfaced among those supporting the peace process over national priorities, explained by commitment to Palestine and Arab nationalism. Under Sadat, Egypt led a gradual departure from Pan-Arab conformity and the quest for an independent policy toward Israel. The combination of the peace process—with its opportunities for Egypt and constraints on others—and the frustrated expectations over Arab oil power turned Arab consensus into a staggering price for Sadat. Egypt's separate peace treaty with Israel, though unintentionally, sent a clear message that Pan-Arab conformity had become a liability rather than an asset.

Egypt's partial and separate settlements with Israel collided with Syria's and the PLO's insistence on a strategy of comprehensive settlement that would prevent Egypt's defection and the consequent weakening of their own bargaining position *vis-à-vis* Israel. Egypt was able to sustain the price of peace with Israel and expulsion from the AL, whereas the rest of the Arab states remained divided over the legitimacy of that peace model for another ten years. Making peace with Israel always involved the risk of colliding head-on with symbols and myths deeply rooted within Arab societies, hence the reluctant, apologetic approach of Arab leaders to this option. It was doubly more difficult to make progress given the Arab group dynamics and gaps of attitude and constraints among its members. Indeed, if any single cause turned inter-Arab relations into a "zero-sum game," it was the competition for territorial gains from Israel and the prospect of a separate Arab-Israeli settlement.

Inter-Arab division was aggravated by the frustrating inter-Arab dialogue over more equitable sharing of the growing oil wealth with its Arab producers, driving Sadat to assume further independence in the peace process. The widening gap between rich and poor Arab states further emptied Pan-Arab solidarity of its altruistic contents. Nonetheless, Arab financial aid served as a major instrument in advancing regional stability and security, before and after the Egypt-Israel peace treaty. Indeed, the post–1973 war peace process accounted for a radical shift in Arab political atmosphere, from the symbolically loaded Nasirist era to the ever-growing legitimacy of a state's independence in quest of its own best interests.

Egypt's peace treaty with Israel denied the Arabs' option of war against Israel and left the Arab regional system in disarray, without a stable center of gravity. Iraq's failure to fill the gap, due to its deadly rivalry with Syria and entaglement in war with revolutionary Iran, attested to its strategic inadequacy as the new pivotal Arab state. Thus, regional Arab politics in the 1980s were increasingly marked by geographic fragmentation, threats from non-Arab actors, and economic constraints, shunting the conflict with Israel to an ever-lower priority on the Arab collective agenda.

It was, however, the Shi'i revolution and Iraq-Iran war that dealt the death blow to any active eastern front against Israel. It aggravated the Iraq-Syria antagonism and shifted the oil-rich Gulf states' main concern to the Gulf. The state of inter-Arab fragmentation and weakening collective interest was clearly manifested in the absence of a rallying theme at Arab summits in the 1980s. Moreover, they witnessed a gradual abandonment of the traditional search for consensus and a facade of unity, which had hitherto paralyzed effective Arab common action.

The Iraqi invasion of Kuwait was ostensibly an extreme version of Nasir's revolutionary outcry for Pan-Arab conformity under his leadership. Above all, it exposed the institutional inadequacy of the Arab regional system as a guarantor of its members' sovereignty and territorial integrity. Indeed, no previous inter-Arab dispute inflicted so serious a blow to the concept of "Arab national security." The intensive use of this ambiguous, emotionally loaded term in the 1980s attested to the deepening inter-Arab fragmentation and growing outcry for rallying around one's individual needs in the name of Arab solidarity, in disregard of the same claims by other states.

The Kuwait crisis also inflicted a serious blow to the presence of Arab labor migrants in oil-rich Arab states, primarily in the Gulf area, which, as of the late 1970s, had been the most salient expression of inter-Arab economic integration. Whatever caused the mass expulsion of Palestinians and Yemenites from the Gulf monarchies, the Gulf crisis provided the latter an opportunity to exempt themselves from foreign and potentially destabilizing elements and enhance their fragile national security.

The growing departure from Pan-Arab commitments for the sake of narrow state-based interests was salient in the Arab responses to the Intifada.

The official declarative support for the Palestinian uprising could hardly conceal the elites' concern at its possible spillover into their own constituencies. With the growing influence of radical Islam in Arab societies, the 1989 food riots in Jordan and Algeria came as a shuddering reminder of the impact of socio-economic constraints on domestic stability. Hence, despite its longevity, regional and international gains, Arab financial support remained limited, nourishing Palestinian support for Saddam Husain's invasion of Kuwait.

The Intifada culminated the shifting center of gravity of Palestinian politics from the Arab arena into the occupied territories, evinced ever since the PLO's expulsion from Lebanon. This trend represented the PLO's shrinking prestige in regional Arab politics due to growing disenchantment with its entanglement in internal Arab affairs and ineffective strategies, epitomized in the Arab rulers' tacit cooperation with Israel in expelling the PLO's forces from Lebanon. At the same time, socio-political and economic processes intensified political activism and institution-building among Palestinians in the West Bank and Gaza Strip, leading to a growing focus of Palestinian political strategies on the occupied territories. Historically, it was the process of state-formation that kept the PLO under constant pressure of Arab ruling elites to accept subordination to their particular national interests or run the risk of detrimental collision with the state. In the process, which culminated in the Gulf war, the PLO was limited to its national constituency in the occupied territories as the only basis for independent survival. In the final analysis, it was this low ebb in the PLO's regional posture, in addition to Hamas' growing threat to its political position, that paved the road to the separate PLO-Israel Oslo accord, which might yet lead to a Palestinian state.

The Intifada accounted for ending the PLO-Hashemite rivalry over the West Bank, whose historical duration and severity were second only to the Arab-Israeli conflict. The Hashemite-Palestinian dispute was the inter-Arab dimension of the struggle for historic Palestine, of which Israel constituted the third party. The triangular conflict epitomized the unfinished shaping of the post-Ottoman Fertile Crescent on the basis of modern states, a tenacious remnant of conflicting revisionist claims that had their roots in the emergence of Jordan and Israel on both sides of the Jordan River, sharing a strategic interest in defying Palestinian nationalist aspirations for statehood. Thus, King Husain's disengagement from the West Bank and the PLO's declaration of an independent Palestinian state were complementary steps toward consolidation of the Jordanian state, just as they were a prerequisite for the Israeli-Palestinian 1993 accord.

This study shows that the Arab states system carried little practical substance other than in the Palestine conflict. Collective Arab decision-making proved unequivocally concerned with this conflict mainly due to its menace to regional stability and appeal to Arab and Islamic sentiments. Hence, Iraq's repeated efforts to obtain an Arab summit's recognition of the war with Iran as a collective Arab thrust were futile, even though in terms of strategic threats, human and financial losses, this war's cost exceeded by far all the Arab-Israeli wars put together. The declining commitment of Arab states to the Palestine conflict was, for the most part, shaped by regional, rather than global, processes. Still, the end of the Cold War was crucial in paving the road to the Madrid peace process, which sanctioned the principle of bilateral talks between Israel and each of the Arab parties, including a Palestinian delegation. This procedure restricted the possibility of cross-Arab interference in each other's negotiations. Unlike the post-1973 peace process, the Madrid negotiations were marked by meager involvement of the AL or the summit conference and a near-absence of any inter-Arab political struggle. In fact, the Palestine conflict returned to its original dimension, involving the immediate neighboring Arab states and the PLO, with minimum mutual intervention—even on Syria's part—in each other's affairs.

The triumph of the state in Middle East politics is salient given the defeat of non-state actors and supra-state ideological movements. The state has also been accepted as a viable and necessary socio-political concept by radical Islamic movements. Unlike Pan-Arabism, these movements are in no ideological contradiction with the individual state, confining their political and social goals within, rather than out, of its borders.

The changing stature of the state in regional Arab politics, culminating in the growing Arab recognition of Israel in the post-Oslo accord, allows one to maintain that the "classic" Arab-Israeli conflict is over. This statement underestimates neither the obstacles entailing a final Israeli-Palestinian settlement, nor the unresolved conflict between Israel and other Arab states, nor future comptetion over regional leadership. Nonetheless, the growing strategic constraints overburdening the Arab states as well as their divergent interests and policies toward Israel may well ensure the continued routinization of Israel's relations with its Arab neighbors and the continued use of diplomatic means in conflict resolution. Moreover, increasing acceptance of Israel by Arab states leads to a new regional order and alignments based on strategic and economic considerations rather than ethno-national or religious identity. While the vision of a prosperous Middle East market is bound to face serious political and economic constraints, the new regional system represents a clear shift from the Pan-Arab regional system, giving way to the state as an independent actor in regional and international politics.

APPENDIX A: BASIC DATA ON MIDDLE EAST COUNTRIES

State	Area in 1,000 Sq. Km.	Population in Millions 1990	% Annual Population Growth 1985–90	Main Natural Resources	GDP $ (1989) Total in Millions	GDP $ (1989) Per Capita	External Debt in $ millions
Algeria	2,381	24.96	2.72	Oil, Natural Gas, Iron	53,116	2,170	26,067
Bahrain	0.691	0.52	3.67	Oil	3,090	6360	5,897
Djibouti	23.2	0.41	2.88		333	1070	180
Egypt	997.7	52.43	2.39	Oil, Cotton, Farm Products	32,501	630	48,799
Iran	1,648	54.61	2.74	Oil, Natural Gas	97,600	1,800	20,500
Iraq	438.1	18.92	3.48	Oil, Natural Gas, Dates	35,000	1,940	65,000
Israel	21	4.60	1.66	Potash, Farm Products	44,131	9,750	24,000
Jordan	91.8	4.01	3.25	Potash, Farm Products	5,291	1,730	6,972
Kuwait	17.8	2.04	3.40	Oil, Natural Gas	33,082	16,380	6,882
Lebanon	10	2.70	0.25	Farm Products			2,000
Mauritania	1,030	2.02	2.73		953	490	2,200
Morocco	710.8	25.06	2.58	Phosphates	22,069	900	20,85
Oman	212.4	1.50	3.79	Oil	7,756	5,220	2,974

continued

GDP $ (1989)

State	Area in 1,000 Sq. Km.	Population in Millions 1990	% Annual Population Growth 1985–90	Main Natural Resources	Total in Millions	Per Capita	External Debt in $ millions
Qatar	11.4	0.37	4.16	Oil, Natural Gas	4,077	9,920	1,100
Saudi Arabia	2,150	14.13	3.96	Oil, Natural Gas	89,986	6,230	19,000
Somalia	637.65	7.50	3.26		1,035	170	2,137
Sudan	2.5	25.20	2.88	Cotton, Cereals	13,226	540	12,965
Syria	185.18	12.53	3.61	Oil, Farm Products	12,812	1,100	5,202
Tunisia	163.6	8.18	2.38		10,089	1,260	6,899
UAE	83.6	1.59	3.26	Oil, Natural Gas	28,449	18,430	11,070
Yemen (North)	195	9.20	3.76	Cotton, Coffee	7,203	640	3,324
Yemen (South)	332.9	2.49	3.04	Oil	1,200	495	2,505

Source: World Resources 1992–93, Oxford: Oxford University Press, 1992.

Appendix B: Summit Meetings and Resolutions 1964–1990

Venue & Date	Main Issues and Resolutions	Main Behind-the-scenes Issues
Cairo, January 13–16, 1964	1. Confirmation of the plan for diversion of the River Jordan. 2. Establishing a Joint Arab Command (including financial allocations). 3. Empowering Ahmad al-Shuqairi to conduct consultations on organizing the Palestinians politically.	General inter-Arab conciliation, especially between Egypt and Saudi Arabia over the Yemen war.
Alexandria, September 5–11, 1964	1. To begin implementation of the diversion plan after further preparations (Jordan added to the original plan). 2. Empowering the JAC's CoS to deploy Arab expeditionary forces along Israel's borders. 3. Confirming (post factum) of the PLO's foundation and establishing the PLA.	Conciliation of the Egypt-Saudi conflict over Yemen
Casablanca, September 13–17, 1965	1. To continue the implementation of the diversion plan. 2. Reinforcement of the JAC and continuation of the military preparations according to the plan for the liberation of Palestine. 3. To enlarge the PLA and facilitate the PLO's political activity in Arab states. 4. Clearing the Arab atmosphere.	1. Bridging the gap between Syria and Egypt on the diversion plan of River Jordan. 2. Formulating the Charter of Arab Solidarity.

continued

Venue & Date	Main Issues and Resolutions	Main Behind-the-scenes Issues
Khartoum, August 29-Septmber 1, 1967	1. The recovery of the occupied Arab territories is a common Arab responsibility, hence the need for total mobilization of Arab resources. 2. Renewal of oil production and its use to aid financially the Arab states economically hurt in the war (specific underwritings for financial aid were given by Saudi Arabia, Kuwait and Libya). 3. Unification of the Arab diplomatic efforts to ensure Israel's withdrawal to the pre-June 5 borders, on the basis of the following basic principles: No peace with or recognition of Israel; no negotiations with it and adherence to the Palestinian people's right to its homeland.	1. Nasir-Faisal agreement on Egyptian withdrawal from Yemen. 2. Financial aid from the oil states to Egypt and Jordan.
Rabat, December 21–23, 1969	1. A small additional financial aid to the confrontation states. 2. Extending financial aid to the PLO and the Palestinian residents of the West Bank and Gaza Strip.	Egypt's requirements for substantial Arab aid (rejected by the oil states).
Cairo, September 21–28, 1970 (emergency summit)	Ending the Jordanian-Palestinian confrontation and mediating an agreement between King Husain and 'Arafat.	
Algiers, November 26–28, 1973	1. Formulating an "Arab strategy of phases" in the conflict with Israel. 2. To continue the use of Arab oil as a political weapon in the struggle for retrieving the Arab occupied territories. 3. The PLO recognized as "the sole representative of the Palestinian people." 4. Enhancing Arab economic and technical aid to African countries.	Resolving the Jordan-PLO disagreement over representation of the Palestinians.

continued

Venue & Date	Main Issues and Resolutions	Main Behind-the-scenes Issues
Rabat, October 26–28, 1974	1. Enhancing the Arab military power; extending substantial financial aid to the confrontation states and the PLO. 2. Rejection of separate settlements with Israel; emphasizing the comprehensive nature of the issue. 3. The PLO recognized as "the sole legitimate representative of the Palestinian people." 4. Waging an international campaign to isolate Israel politically and economically.	Removing Jordan's objection to the PLO's new political status.
Cairo, October 25–26, 1976	1. Confirmation of the plan for a peace settlement in Lebanon concluded by the Riyad mini-summit, including the establishment of the "Arab Deterrence Force." 2. Renewal of the Arab financial aid to the confrontation states and the PLO. 3. Extending financial aid to Lebanon for its economic rehabilitation. 4. Reassertion of the Arab commitment to support the PLO's right to establish its "independent state on its national land."	
Baghdad, November 2–5, 1978	1. Applying sanctions on Egypt once it signs a peace treaty with Israel. 2. Establishing an Arab fund for ten-year financial aid to the confrontation states, the PLO and the Palestinians in the West Bank and Gaza Strip. 3. Working out a plan for economic rehabilitation of Lebanon.	1. Efforts of the oil Gulf monarchies to delay the sanctions against Egypt until a full-fledged peace agreement signed with Israel.
Tunis, November 20–22, 1979	1. Continued adherence to the boycott of Egypt and its peace agreement with Israel. 2. Confirmation of a five-year plan of financial aid to Lebanon (total of $2 billion).	Debate on the use of oil as a weapon against the U.S. or to enhance inter-Arab economic cooperation.

continued

Venue & Date	Main Issues and Resolutions	Main Behind-the-scenes Issues
Amman, November 25–27, 1980	1. Reaffirmation of the objection to the Israel-Egypt peace agreement. 2. Confirmation of plans for enhancing inter-Arab cooperation. 3. Reasserting the Arab support for the PLO and its free will. 4. Calling for the resolution of inter-Arab differences. 5. Calling to put an end to the Iraq-Iran war in the name of the common Arab-Islamic struggle against Israel.	
Fez, November 25, 1981	1. Extending financial support to Lebanon. 2. Adjourning the meeting and keeping it "open" (without discussing the "Fahd Plan").	
Fez, September 6–9, 1982	1. Confirming an Arab peace plan (an altered version of the "Fadh Plan"). 2. Denouncing the Israeli aggression against Lebanon and the Palestinians. 3. Expressing appreciation to Iraq's willingness to end the war with Iran and commitment to defend "all Arab lands." 4. Extending support to Somalia in its war with Ethiopia.	
Casablanca, August 7–9, 1985	1. Expressing adherence to the Fez peace plan; appreciation to Husain and Arafat's announcements regarding the Amman accord. 2. Supporting an international peace conference under UN auspices, including the PLO. 3. Establishing two Arab conciliation committees on Syria's disputed relations with Iraq and Jordan, and Libya's relations with Iraq and the PLO. 4. Reiterating the PLO's independence and status in Lebanon. 5. Expressing support to Iraq and warning Iran that continued refusal to end the war would affect its relations with Arab states.	1. Adoption of the Amman accord. 2. Renouncing Syria's pressures against the Palestinians in Lebanon (the capms' siege).

continued

Venue & Date	Main Issues and Resolutions	Main Behind-the-scenes Issues
Amman (emergency summit), November 8–11, 1987	1. Condemnation of Iran's occupation of Iraqi territory, calling for UN sanctions against it for failing to end the war. 2. Expressing commitment to reinforce Arab capabilities in the conflict with Israel; strong commitment to restore Palestinian rights. 3. Supporting a UN-sponsored international peace conference with PLO's full participation. 4. Legitimating resumption of Arab diplomatic relations with Egypt.	1. Reconciliation between Asad and Saddam Husain; additional financial aid to Syria. 2. Hashemite-Syrian effort to marginalize the PLO's political status. 3. Hashemite-PLO competition for the West Bankers' support.
Algiers (emergency summit), June 7–9, 1988	1. Extending financial support to the Palestinians in the West Bank and Gaza Strip for their uprising. 2. Reaffirmation of Arab recognition of the PLO's status; support for establishing a Palestinian state under the PLO's leadership. 3. Condemnation of Iran.	1. Egypt's return to the Arab League. 2. Hashemite-PLO competition to control Arab funds in support of the Palestinian uprising.
Casablanca (emergency summit), May 23–26, 1989	1. Egypt's full re-admittance to the AL. 2. Establishing a conciliation committee to resolve the Iraq-Syria dispute in Lebanon. 3. Supporting Iraq's rights on Shatt al-'Arab.	1. Arabization of Lebanon's domestic crisis. 2. Conciliation between Asad and Saddam Husain; between 'Arafat and Asad. 3. PLO's effort to enlist support for its "political program."

continued

Venue & Date	Main Issues and Resolutions	Main Behind-the-scenes Issues
Baghdad (emergency summit), May 28–30, 1990	1. Condemnation of the Soviet Jewish immigration to "Palestine and the other occupied Arab territories" as a threat to "Arab national security," and urging UN intervention to prevent influx and settlement of Jewish migrants in the occupied territories. 2. Denouncing Israeli and American "threats" against Iraq, endorsing the latter's right to protect its national security in the way it deems fit. 3. Endorsing the idea of making the Middle East a zone "free of all weapons of mass destruction," urging free Arab access to modern technologies for legitimate purposes. 4. Calling to guarantee the Palestinian people's national rights; expressing support for the PLO's "political program" and UN-sponsored international peace conference.	1. Iraqi claims for heavy financial aid from the Gulf oil monarchies. 2. PLO and Jordan's appeals for financial support.
Cairo (emergency summit), August 10, 1990	1. Condemnation of Iraq's aggression against Kuwait; urging its immediate evacuation by Iraq; endorsing UNSC resolutions in this respect. 2. Supporting the GCC states' "right of legitimate defense" and steps taken in this regard; agreeing to dispatch Arab forces to support the Gulf states defense "against any external aggression."	1. Attempt to adopt an "Arab solution" to the Kuwait crisis. 2. Iraqi intimidation of Gulf monarchs.

Appendix C: AL Members' Participation and Level of Representation at the Summit Conferences 1964–1990

Member State since	1	2	3	4	5	6	7	8	9	10	11	12	13	14	15	16	17	18	19	20
Algeria 1962	H	H	H	M	H	A	H	H	M	M	M	B	M	M	B	H	H	H	M	H
Bahrain 1971	-	-	-	-	-	-	H	H	H	H	H	H	H	H	H	H	H	H	H	H
Djibouti 1974	-	-	-	-	-	-	-	-	M	M	-	-	-	-	-	-	-	-	H	H
Egypt 1945	H	H	H	H	H	H	H	H	H	-	-	-	-	-	-	-	H	H	H	H
Iraq 1945	H	H	H	H	P	B	B	P	M	H	H	H	P	H	P	H	P	H	H	P
Jordan 1945	H	H	H	H	H	H	H	H	H	H	H	H	H	H	H	H	H	H	H	H
Kuwait 1961	H	H	H	H	H	H	H	H	H	H	H	B	H	H	P	H	H	M	H	H
Lebanon 1945	P	H	H	H	H	H	H	H	H	H	H	H	H	H	P	H	H	M	H	H
Lybia 1952	P	H	P	P	H	H	B	L	M	M	M	B	M	B	B	P	H	-	B	H
Mauritania 1973	-	-	-	-	-	-	H	H	H	H	M	H	M	L	H	A	H	L	H	M
Morocco 1961	H	M	H	P	H	A	H	H	H	M	M	P	M	M	P	H	M	H	M	M
Oman 1971	-	-	-	-	-	-	H	H	H	B	H	H	M	H	H	H	M	H	M	M
PLO 1976	H	H	H	H	H	H	H	H	H	H	H	B	H	H	P	H	H	H	H	H
Qatar 1971	-	-	-	-	-	-	H	H	H	P	P	B	P	H	B	H	H	H	H	*
PDRY 1968	-	-	-	-	-	-	-	H	H	P	H	P	P	H	P	H	H	H	*	*
Saudi Arabia 1945	H	H	H	H	H	H	H	H	H	P	H	H	H	H	B	H	H	H	H	H
Somalia 1974	-	-	-	-	-	-	-	-	H	L	H	P	M	H	P	H	M	M	H	M
Sudan 1956	H	H	H	H	H	H	H	H	H	H	H	B	M	H	B	H	H	H	H	H
Syria 1945	H	H	H	B	M	H	H	H	H	H	H	H	M	H	B	H	H	H	B	H

continued

Member State since	1	2	3	4	5	6	7	8	9	10	11	12	13	14	15	16	17	18	19	20
Tunisia 1957	H	M	B	B	M	P	H	H	M	M	H	P	P	P	P	H	H	H	H	A
UAE 1971	-	-	-	-	-	-	H	H	H	H	H	H	H	H	H	H	H	H	H	H
YAR 1945	H	H	H	H	H	L	H	H	P	P	H	H	H	H	P	H	H	H	H	H

*United with YAR (1989).

1- Cairo, 1964
2- Alexandria, 1964
3- Casablanca, 1965
4- Khartoum, 1967
5- Rabat, 1969
6- Cairo, 1970
7- Algiers, 1973
8- Rabat, 1974
9- Cairo, 1976
10- Baghdad, 1978
11- Tunis, 1979
12- Amman, 1980
13- Fez I, 1981
14- Fez II, 1982
15- Casablanca, 1985
16- Amman, 1987
17- Algiers, 1988
18- Casablanca, 1989
19- Baghdad, 1990
20- Cairo, 1990

Legend: H—Head of State; P—PM or Crown Prince; M—Minister; L—low-ranking official; A—Absence; b—Boycott

NOTES

1. Introduction: Explaining Regional Arab Politics

1. Michael Barnett, "Institutions, Roles, and Disorder," *ISQ* 37(1993): pp. 271–296; Bahgat Korany, "The Dialectics of Inter-Arab Relations 1967–1987," in *The Arab-Israeli Conflict: Two Decades of Change,* Y. Luckacs and A.M. Battah (eds.) (Boulder: Westview Press, 1988), p. 165; Walid Kazziha, "The Impact of Palestine on Arab Politics," in *The Arab State,* Giacomo Luciani (ed.) (Berkeley: University of California Press), 1990, pp. 300–318.

2. I use this term in its historical meaning, that is, since the British Mandate, interchangeably with the term "Arab-Israeli conflict."

3. Lisa Anderson, "The State in the Middle East and North Africa," *Comparative Politics* 20 (1987): pp. 1–18; Robert H. Jackson, *Quasi-States: Sovereignty, International Relations, and the Third World* (Cambridge: Cambridge University Press, 1990), pp. 21–26.

4. I use this term instead of "supra-national" to refrain from confusion with Pan-Arab nationalism.

5. Ernest Gellner, *Nations and Nationalism* (Oxford: Blackwell, 1983), p. 1.

6. Hedley Bull, *The Anarchical Society: A study of Order in World Politics* (London: Macmillan, 1977), pp. 65, 74; Helen Milner, "The Assumption of Anarchy in International Relations Theory: A Critique," *Review of International Studies* 17 (1991): pp. 68–74.

7. Fouad Ajami, *The Arab Predicament: Arab Political Thought and Practice Since 1967* (Cambridge: Cambridge University Press, 1981), pp. 78, 126–127; Joel S. Migdal, *Strong Societies and Weak States: State-Society Relations and State Capabilities in the Third World* (Princeton: Princeton University Press, 1988); Victor Azaria, "Reordering State-Society Relations: Incorporation and Disengagement," in Donald Rothchild and Naomi Chazan (eds.), *The Precarious Balance: State and Society in Africa* (Boulder: Westview Press, 1988), pp. 3–21.

8. Gabriel Ben-Dor, *State and Conflict in the Middle East* (New York: Praeger, 1983), pp. 242–243; Tawfic E. Farah (ed.), *Pan-Arabism and Arab Nationalism: The Continuing Debate* (Boulder: Westview Press, 1987); See also his "Attitudes to the Nation and State in Arab Public Opinion Polls," in *The Politics of Arab Integration,* Giacomo Luciani and Ghassan Salame (eds.) (London: Croom Helm, 1987), pp. 94–108.

9. For a review, see F.A. Gerges, "The Study of Middle East International Relations: a Critique," *British Journal of Middle Eastern Studies* 18, 2(1992): pp. 208–220; Rex Brynen, "The state of the Art in Middle Eastern Studies: A Research Note on Enquiry and the American Empire," *ASQ* 8 (1986): pp. 404–419.

10. P.J. Vatikiotis, *Islam and the State* (London: Croom Helm, 1987), p. 13; Korany, *ibid.,* pp. 164–165; Ben-Dor, *State and conflict,* p. 164; Michael Hudson, *Arab Politics: The Search for Legitimacy* (New Haven: Yale University Press, 1977), p. 54; Paul C. Noble, "The Arab System: Opportunities, Constraints and Pressures," in Bahgat Korany and A.E.H. Dessouki (eds.), *The Foreign Policies of Arab States* (Boulder: Westview Press, 1984), pp. 48–50.

11. Anderson, pp. 1–18; Gabriel Ben-Dor, "Stateness and Ideology in Contemporary Middle Eastern Studies," *JJIR* 9, 3(1987): pp. 10–37; Rex Brynen, "Palestine and the Arab state System: Permeability, State Consolidation and the Intifada," *Canadian Journal of Political Science* 24, 3(1991): pp. 595–621.

12. Charles Tilly, "Reflections on the History of European State-Making," in his (ed.), *The Formation of National States in Europe* (Princeton: Princeton University Press, 1975), pp. 27, 44–45, 70; Bull, pp. 40–52; Jackson, pp. 34–40.

13. Quoted from Barnett, p. 279; Jackson, pp. 13–26; Tilly, p. 46.

14. For a review, see Janice E. Thomson, "State Sovereignty in International Relations: Bridging the Gap between Theory and Empirical Research," *ISQ* 39 (1995): p. 219; Kenneth Waltz, *Theory of International Politics* (Reading, Mass.: Addison-Wesley, 1991), p. 96.

15. Tilly, p. 32; Thomson, p. 221; Barnett, pp. 272, 279.

16. Elizabeth Picard, "Arab Military in Politics: from Revolutionary Plot to Authoritarian State," in Luciani, *The Arab State,* pp. 192–193, 197.

2. The Regional Arab System

1. R. Falk and S. Mendlowvitz (eds.), *Regional Politics and World Order* (San Francisco: W.H. Freeman and Co., 1973); Louis J. Cantori and Steven L. Spiegel, *The International Politics of Regions: A Comparative Approach* (Englewood Cliffs: Prentice-Hall, 1970), p. 4; Werner J. Feld and Gavin Boyd (eds.), *Comparative Regional Systems* (New York: Pergamon Press, 1980); William R. Thompson, "The Regional Subsystem," *ISQ* 17 (1973): pp. 89–117.

2. Iliya Harik and L.J. Cantori, "Domestic Determinants of Foreign Policy and Peace Efforts in the Middle East," *Conflict* 8, 1(1988): pp. 49–51; Barry Buzan, *People, States and Fear: The National Security Problem in International Relations* (Brighton: Wheatsheaf Books, 1983), pp. 18–35; Mohammed Ayoob, "The Security Problematic of the Third World," *World Politics* 43, 2(1991): pp. 259–270, 278–281; Steven David, "Explaining Third World Alignment," *ibid.:* pp. 234–245.

3. Malcolm Kerr, *Regional Arab Politics and the Conflict with Israel* (Santa Monica: Rand Co., 1969), pp. 29–30; Leonard Binder, "The Middle East as a Subordinate International System," *World Politics* 10 (April 1958): pp. 411–415; Cantori and Spiegel, pp. 25–37; Carl L. Brown, *International Politics and the Middle East: Old Rules, Dangerous Games* (Princeton: Princeton University Press, 1984), pp. 4–5, 198–221.

4. William R. Thompson, "Delineating Regional Subsystems: Visit Networks and the Middle Eastern Case," *IJMES* 13 (1981): pp. 214–217; Cantori and Spiegel, pp. 6–7; Feld and Boyd, p. 13.

5. Bernard Lewis, *The Middle East and the West* (New York: Harper Torchbooks, 1964), pp. 9–27; Brown, pp. 7–11; Nikki R. Keddie, "Is There a Middle East?," *IJMES* 4, 3(July 1973): pp. 255–271; J.P. Piscatori and R.K. Ramazani, "The Middle East," in Feld and Boyd, p. 296; Tareq Y. Ismael, *International Relations of the Contemporary Middle East* (Syracuse: Syracuse University Press, 1986), pp. 3–10; Jamil Matar and Ali al-Din Hilal, *Al-Nizam al-Iqlimi al-'Arabi* (Cairo: 1983), pp. 24–32, and Mohamed H. Heikal, "Egyptian Foreign Policy," *Foreign Affairs* 56, 4(July 1978): pp. 719–722, argue that the term Middle East is a Western-based concept created to legitimize Israel's existence in the region.

6. Matar and Hilal, p. 32; K. Boals, "The Concept of Subordinate International System: A Critique," in Falk and Mendlowvitz, p. 409; Wilfred C. Smith, *Islam in Modern History* (New York: Mentor Books, 1957), pp. 24, 97–119; Basheer Meibar, *Political Culture, Foreign Policy and Conflict: The Palestine Area Conflict System* (Westport: Greenwood Press, 1973), pp. 143–153.

7. Ajami, *Arab Predicament,* p. 71; Rashid Khalidi, *Under Siege: P.L.O. Decisionmaking During the 1982 War* (New York: Columbia University Press, 1986), p. 153; Meibar, p. 148; Morroe Berger, *The Arab World Today* (New York: Anchor Books, 1964), p. 306–312.

8. Ben Dor, "Stateness and Ideology," p. 21; Pool Cammack and Tordoff, *Third World Politics* (Baltimore: Johns Hopkins University Press, 1988), p. 37; H.J. Wiara and H.F. Kline, *Latin American Politics and Development* (Boulder: Westview Press, 1985), p. 76.

9. Samir Makdisi, "Economic Interdependence and National Sovereignty," in Luciani and Salame, pp. 111–140; the editors' "Introduction," *ibid.,* pp. 16–30; Matar and Hilal, pp. 173–181. In 1987, inter-Arab trade was roughly 7 percent of the total Arab trade, compared to more than 50 percent among the industrialized countries of their total trade (*The Middle East* [February 1989], p. 24). Latin American intra-regional trade increased roughly to 16 percent in the 1970s (Luciano Toamssini, "The Disintegration of the Integration Process: Toward New Forms of Regional Cooperation," in *Regional Integration: The Latin American Experience,* Altaf Gauhar [ed.] [Boulder: Westview Press, 1985], p. 223).

10. E. Shils, *Center and Periphery, Essays in Macrosociology* (Chicago: The University of Chicago Press, 1975), pp. 34–38.

11. Walid Khalidi, "Thinking the Unthinkable: A Sovereign Palestinian State," *Foreign Affairs* 58, 4 (1978): p. 69; Mohamed H. Heikal, "Egyptian Foreign Policy," p. 714.

12. Hudson, *Arab Politics,* pp. 5–7, 20; James A. Bill and Robert Springborg, *Politics in the Middle East,* Third Edition (Glenview and London: Scott, Foresman, Little, Brown, 1990), pp. 31–32; Alan Richards and John Waterbury, *A Political Economy of the Middle East* (Boulder: Westview Press, 1990), pp. 300–301.

13. Halim Barakat, "Ideological Determinants of Arab Development," *Arab Resources: The Transformation of A Society,* Ibrahim Ibrahim (ed.) (Washington, D.C.: Croom Helm, 1983), p. 183.

14. Raymond Aron, *Politics and History* (New Brunswick: Transactions Books, 1984), p. 245. For a typology of Arab ideologies and regimes see, Bill and Springborg, pp. 65–84; Richards and Waterbury, pp. 302–322; Ajami, *Arab Predicament,* p. 52.

15. P. Noble, "The Arab System," in Korany and Dessouki, p. 48. See for example Farouq Qaddumi's reference to inter-Arab conflicts as a "family row," in an interview to *QNA* (October 29, 1987), *FBIS/DR* (October 30, 1987).

16. On the AL's foundation, see Ch. 3. For the principles of the Westphalian system and its dynamics, see Lynn Miller, *Global Order: Values and Power in International Politics,* 2nd Edition (Boulder: Westview Press, 1990), pp. 20–29.

17. Yehoshua Porath, *In Search of Arab Unity, 1930–1945* (London: Frank Cass, 1986), pp. 257–267; Amado Sesay *et al., The OAU after Twenty Years* (Boulder: Westview, 1984), pp. 1–6; Robert W. Macdonald, *The League of Arab States: A Study in the Dynamics of Regional Organization* (Princeton: Princeton University Press, 1965), p. 44; Lynn H. Miller, "The Prospects for Order through Regional Security," in Falk and Mendlowvitz, p. 58; Naomi Chazan *et al., Politics and Society in Contemporary Africa* (London: Macmillan, 1988), pp. 347–348.

18. Noble, "The Arab System," Korany and Dessouki, p. 48; Mohamed H. Heikal, *Kharif al-Ghadab* (Beirut: Sharikat al-Matbuʿaat, 1985), p. 148.

19. Mohammed Ayoob, "Unravelling the Concept: 'National Security' in the Third World," in *The Many facets of National Security in the Arab World,* B. Korany, R. Brynen and P. Noble (eds.) (New York: St. Martin's Press, 1993), pp. 36–50; M.E. Yapp, *The Near East Since the First World War,* Vol. II (London: Longman, 1991), p. 438; Cyrus Bina, "A Prelude to Internationalization of the Post-War Economy," *Journal of Economic Democracy* 2, 2(1992): pp. 1–5.

20. Roger Owen, *State, Power and Politics in the Making of the Modern Middle East* (London and New York: Routledge, 1992), Ch. 2–3; Fouad Ajami, "The End of Pan-Arabism," *Foreign Affairs* 57, (1978–79): p. 364; Ben-Dor, *State and Conflict,* pp. 134–138; Nazih Ayubi, "Arab Bureaucracies: Expanding Size, Changing Role," in Luciani, pp. 129–149; James H. Lebovic, "The Middle East: The Region as a System," *International Interactions* 12, 3 (1986): pp. 267–289.

21. Amazia Barʿam, "Mesopotamian Identity in Baʿthi Iraq," *MEJ* 19, 4(1983): pp. 426–455; Emmanuel Sivan, "The Arab Nation-State: In Search of a Usable Past," *Middle East Review* 19, 3(Spring 1987): pp. 21–30; Hassan A. Turabi, "Islam as a Pan-national Movement," *RSA Journal* (August/ September 1992): pp. 608–619; "Al-Sahwa al-Islamiyya wal-Dawla al-Qutriyya fi al-Watan al-ʿArabi," in *Al-Sahwa al-Islamiyya, Ru'ya Naqdiyya Min al-Dakhil* (Beirut: al-Nashir lil-Tibaʿa wal-Nashr, 1990), pp. 86–108.

22. Tilly, p. 32; J.P. Nettle, "The State as a Conceptual Variable," *World Politics* 20, (July 1968): pp. 559–592; Ben-Dor, "Stateness and Ideology," pp. 18–21.

23. Hourani, *A History of the Arab Peoples* (Cambridge: Harvard University Press, 1991), p. 310; Noble, "The Arab State," Korany and Dessouki, pp. 55–56; Anderson, p. 5.

24. William I. Zartman, "Military Elements in Regional Unrest," in *Soviet-American Rivalry in the Middle East,* J.C. Hurewitz (ed.) (New York: U.S. Cultural Center, 1969), p. 75; Matar and Hilal, p. 31; Manfred Halpern, *The Politics of Social Change in the Middle East and North Africa* (Princeton: Princeton University Press, 1963), pp. xiv–xv; Piscatori and Ramazani, in Feld and Boyd, p. 275.

25. Wajih Kawtharani, "Thalathat Azmina fi Mashruʿ al-Nahda al-ʿArabiyya wal-Islamiyya," *al-Mustaqbal al-ʿArabi* 120 (February 1989): pp. 4–25.

26. Michael Brecher, "The Middle East Subordinate System and Its Impact on Israel's Foreign Policy," *ISQ* 13, (1969): pp. 120–129; Noble, "The Arab System," in Korany and Dessouki, p. 49; Binder, "The Middle East as a Subordinate International System," pp. 420–421; Yair Evron, *The Middle East: Nations, Superpowers, and Wars* (London: Elek Books, 1973), pp. 192–200; Ismael, pp. 3–13.

28. Ali E.H. Dessouki, "The New Arab Political Order," in M. Kerr and E.S. Yassin (eds.), *Rich and Poor States in the Middle East* (Boulder: Westview Press, 1982), p. 322; Hudson, *Arab Politics*, p. 54.

29. William R. Thompson, "Center-Periphery Interaction Patterns: The Case of Arab Visits, 1946–1975," *International Organization* 35, 2(Spring 1981): p. 373; also his "Delineating Regional Subsystems," pp. 214–217, 226.

30. Mark Tessler, "Center and Periphery Within Regional International Systems: The Case of the Arab World," *JJIR* 11, 3(September 1989): p. 88.

31. Lebovic, p. 273; Jamil Matar in "Mustaqbal al-Nizam al-Iqlimi al-'Arabi," (Discussion), *Al-Mustaqbal al-'Arabi,* 163 (September 1992): p. 63.

32. Quoted from: North Yemeni FM al-Iriani to *al-Siyasa* (Kuwait), July 11, 1988, and J.C. Hurewitz, "Arab Regional Politics and the Dispute with Israel: Changing Focuses after Sadat's Visit to Jerusalem," in Robert O. Freedman (ed.), *World Politics and the Arab-Israeli Conflict* (New York: Pergamon Press, 1979), pp. 127–128; Ahmad al-Shuqairi, *Hiwar wa-Asrar Ma'a al-Muluk wal-Ru'asa'* (Beirut: Dar al-'Awda, n.d.), p. 86, maintained that Arab heads of state speak in "two tongues, two languages, and two dialects."

33. 'Abd al-Hamid al-Muwafi, *Misr fi Jami'at al-Duwal al-'Arabiyya* (Cairo: al-Hay'a al-Misriyya al-'Aamma lil-Kitab, 1983), pp. 187–188, 208; Malcolm Kerr, *The Arab cold War: Gamal 'Abd al-Nasir and his Rivals* (Oxford: Oxford University Press, 1971), pp. 28–30.

34. 'Arafat's interview, *Fikr,* no. 6(June 1985): pp. 29–32; Abu-Iyad's interview, *al-Tadamun,* September 14, 1985; Sabri Jiryis, "'Ishrun Sana Min al-Kifah al-Musallah: Nahwa Nizam Filastini Jadid," *Shu'un Filastiniyya* 142–143 (January–February 1985): pp. 14–21; Ajami, *Arab Predicament,* p. 37; Ben-Dor, *State and Conflict,* pp. 199–205.

35. Thomas Schelling, *Strategy of Conflict* (Cambridge, Mass.: Harvard University Press, 1960), pp. 4–5.

36. Stephen M. Walt, *The Origins of Alliances* (Ithaca: Cornell University Press, 1987), pp. 50–146. Walt concluded (pp. 148–153) that the primary motive for alliances in the Middle East in the years 1955–1979 was balancing an external threat. For a domestic-oriented approach and critique of Walt's conclusions, see David, pp. 233–256.

37. King Fahd on the establishment of the GCC in May 1981, *al-Riyad,* May 25, 1985; Richard B. Parker, "Appointment in Oujda," *Foreign Affairs* 63, 5(1985): p. 1095.

38. Yair Evron and Yaacov Bar Simantov, "Coalitions in the Arab World," *JJIR* 1, 2(Winter 1975): pp.77–79.

39. Yehoshafat Harkabi, *Arab Strategies and Israel's Response* (New York: Free Press, 1979), pp. 17–25; Walt, pp. 144–146.

40. Ghassan Salame, "Inter-Arab Politics: The Return to Geography," in *The Middle East: Ten Years After Camp David,* William B. Quandt (ed.) (Washington D.C.: The Brookings Institution, 1988), pp. 319–341.

41. Matar and Hilal, p. 113; Kerr, *Regional Arab Politics,* p. 11; Fouad Ajami,

"Geopolitical Illusions," in Steven L. Spiegel (ed.), *The Middle East and the Western Alliance* (London: Allen & Unwin, 1982), pp. 155–158.

42. Hasan Abu Talib, "Mu'tamarat al-Qimma wa-Tahaddiyat al-'Amal al-Mushtarak," *al-Siyasa al-Dawliyya* 80, (April 1985): pp. 9–13; Kerr, *Arab Cold War,* p. 14.

43. Ajami, *Arab Predicament,* p.128. On Nasir's fluctuating inter-Arab policy, see Anouar Abdel-Malek, *Egypt: Military Society, the Army Regime, the Left and Social Change Under Nasser* (New York: Vintage Books, 1968), pp. 125–129, 157–166; Raymond A. Hinnebusch, *Egyptian Politics Under Sadat* (Cambridge: Cambridge University Press, 1985), pp. 21–29; John Waterbury, *The Egypt of Nasser and Sadat: The Political Economy of Two Regimes* (Princeton: Princeton University Press, 1983), pp. 94–100; Kerr, *Arab Cold War,* pp. 28–30.

44. Muwafi, p. 202; Abdel Malek, pp. 256, 260.

45. Hassan Nafaa, "Arab Nationalism: A Response to Ajami's Thesis on the 'End of Pan-Arabism,'" *JAA* 2, 2(1983): p. 181–182.

46. "Idjma'," *The Encyclopedia of Islam,* Vol. III (Leiden and London: E. J. Brill, 1971), pp. 1023–1025; G.E. Von Grunebaum, "The Problem: Unity in Diversity," in his (ed.) *Unity and Variety in Muslim Civilization* (Chicago: Chicago University Press, 1956), p. 31.

47. Colin Legum (ed.), *Middle East Contemporary Survey,* Vol. 6 (1981–82) (New York: Holms and Meier Publishers, 1984), pp. 227–279; Itamar Rabinovich and Haim Shaked (eds), *Middle East Contemporary Survey,* Vol. 10 (1986) (Boulder: Westview, 1988), pp. 101–102.

48. Robert D. Putnam, "The Lessons of Western Summitry," in Samuel P. Huntington and Joseph S. Nye (eds.), *Global Dilemmas* (The Center for International Affairs, Harvard University, and University Press of America, 1985), p. 19; Abu Talib, p. 23.

49. Adeed Dawisha, "Arab Regimes, Legitimacy and Foreign Policy," in *The Arab State,* Giacomo Luciani (ed.) (Berkeley: University of California Press, 1990), pp. 284–299; Interview of the Moroccan ex-PM Ahmad Bin Sawda, *al-Siyasa,* August 24, 1985.

50. Roger W. Cobb and Charles Elder, *International Community: A Regional and Global Study* (New York: Holt, Rienhardt & Winston, 1970), pp. 134–136; Makdisi, pp. 112–113.

51. Elias H. Tuma, *Economic and Political Change in the Middle East* (Palo Alto: Pacific Books, 1984), pp. 34–51.

52. Hisham Sharabi, "The Poor Rich Arabs," in Ibrahim, *Arab Resources,* pp. 301–303; George T. Abed, "Arab Financial Resources: An Analysis and Critique of Present Deployment Policies," *ibid.,* pp. 43–69; Yusif A. Sayigh, "A New Framework for Complementarity Among the Arab Economies," *ibid.,* pp. 147–166; M. Bani Hani, "Causes of Failure of Previous Arab Attempts to Integrate," in *The Problems of Arab Economic Development and Integration,* Ada Guecioueur (ed.) (Boulder: Westview, 1984), pp. 177–189.

53. George Lenczowski, "Major Piplines in the Middle East: Problems and Prospects," *Middle East Policy* 3, 4(1995): pp. 40–46.

54. Macdonald, p. 204; Saad el-Shazly, *The Crossing of the Suez,* (San Francisco: American Mideast Research, 1980), pp. 195–196; Guecioueur, pp. 196–197.

55. Mohammed Imadi, "Patterns of Arab Economic Aid to Third World Countries," *ASQ* 6, 1–2 (1984): p. 72; Maurice J. Williams, "The Aid Programs of the OPEC Countries, *Foreign Affairs* 54, (October 1975): p. 311; *al-Ra'i al-'Am,* February 25, 1976.

55. Libya paid nothing; Algeria paid its share ($7 million) only in the first year and added $1 million in 1984; Iraq paid its full share ($14.9 million) only in the first year, $11.1 million in the second year, and then ceased its payments (*MECS 1978–79,* p. 295); *al-Fajr* (Jerusalem), December 3, 1985. During the first seven years, only Saudi Arabia fulfilled all its commitments (*al-Nahar* [Jerusalem], November 5, 1987); *al-Jazira,* November 11, 1987.

56. Hazem Beblawi, "The Rentier State in the Arab World," in Luciani, pp. 95–98.

57. UNCTAD, *Financial Solidarity for Development, Review 1983* (New York: United Nation, 1984), pp. 3–6, 13–18. The four leading Arab national development funds' total disbursements in 1973–1981, reached $3.5 billion (UNCTAD, *International Solidarity For Development, Review 1985* New York: United Nations, 1986], p. 6).

58. UNCTAD, *Financial Solidarity for Development, Review 1987* (New York: United Nations, 1988), pp. 4–6, 17.

59. UNCTAD, *Financial Solidarity, 1987,* p. 5; UNCTAD, *Financial solidarity, 1983,* pp. 3–5, 10; Abed, in Ibrahim, *Arab Resources,* p. 65; Gil Feiler, *The History of Economic Relations Between Egypt and the Arab Peninsula Oil States, 1967–1984,* unpublished Ph.D. thesis, Tel Aviv University, 1989, pp. 113–116.

60. Feiler, p. 44; UNCTAD, *Financial Solidarity 1987,* pp. 8, 12, 17; John Law, *Arab Aid, Who Gets it, For What and How* (New York: Chase World Information Corporation, 1978), p. xvi.

61. Kamal Hasan 'Ali, *Muharibun wa-Mufawidun* (Cairo: Markaz al-Ahram, 1986), pp. 74–75; Makram Ahmad in *al-Ahram,* November 16, 1974.

62. Feiler, pp. 97–98; Waterbury, *The Egypt of Nasser and Sadat,* pp. 414–420; Dessouki, in Kerr and Yassin, *Rich and Poor,* pp. 329–335.

63. Richards and Waterbury, p. 379.

64. Roger Owen, "The Political Environment for Development," in Ibrahim, *Arab Resources,* pp. 141, 145; George Sabagh, "Immigrants in the Arab Gulf Countries: 'Sojourners' or 'Settlers'?" in Luciani, pp. 349–372; Sharon S. Russell, "Migration and Political Integration in the Arab World," *ibid.,* pp. 373–393; Beblawi, "The Rentier State," *ibid.,* pp. 84–85.

65. *Ibid.,* pp. 389–392; Ibrahim Saad Eddine Abdallah, "Migration as a Factor Conditioning State Economic Control and Financial Policy Options," in Luciani and Salame, pp. 141–158.

66. Matar and Hilal, p. 122; Interviews with Kuwaiti scholars, *al-Qabas,* October 20, 22, 1982.

67. Especially after accepting UNSC Resolution 242 (see below), Sadat to *al-Ahram,* July 3, 1975.

68. Ben-Dor, *State and Conflict,* pp. 186–201.

69. Ajami, *Arab Predicament,* p. 126; Tuma, pp. 35–47; Dessouki, "The New Arab Political Order," in Kerr and Yassin, pp. 319–347; Hisham Sharabi, "Arab Policy and the Prospects for Peace," *American-Arab Affairs* (Summer 1982): p. 108; 'Adel Husain, "Al-Mal al-Nifti 'A'iq lil-Tawhid wal-Takamul," *al-Mustaqbal al-'Arabi* (January 1979), pp. 16–31.

70. A.M. Al-Mashat, "Arab National Security In the 1980s. Threats and Strategies," *International Interactions* 12, 3(1986): pp. 245–265; Salame, "Inter-Arab Politics," pp. 319–353.

71. For a conservative Arab perception of this notion, see Mahmud Riyad, *Mudhakkirat, 1948–1978,* Pt. II (Beirut: al-Mu'assasa al-'Arabiyya lil-Dirasat Wal-Nashr, 1987), pp. 256–259. See also Mashat, pp. 261–264.

72. Walid Kazziha, *Palestine in the Arab Dilemma* (London: Croom Helm, 1979), p. 17; Kerr, *Arab Cold War,* p. 114; Faisal Hawrani, "Mu'tamarat al-Qimma al-'Arabiyya wal-Mawqif min Isra'il, 1964–1966," *Shu'un Filastiniyya* 150–151 (September-October 1985): p. 91.

73. Ahmad al-Shuqairi, *'Ala Tariq al-Hazima Ma'a al-Muluk wal-Ru'asa'* (Beirut: Dar al-'Awda, 1972), p. 124. I have heard this term frequently from Palestinians. See also Kazziha, *Palestine,* pp. 15–19.

74. Ahmad al-Shuqairi, "Dhikrayat 'an Mu'tamar al-Qimma fil-Khartoum," *Shu'un Filastiniyya* 4 (September 1971): pp. 91–92; Text of final announcement of the 18th PNC, April 26, 1987, in Algiers, distinguishing between Egypt's people and regime, *JPS* 16, 4(Summer 1987): pp. 201–204; 'Arafat to *al-Watan al-'Arabi,* November, 30, 1984.

75. Eric Rouleau, "The Future of the PLO," *Foreign Affairs* 62, 1, (Fall 1983): p. 145.

76. *Filastin al-Thawra* (editorial), January 5, 1985; Jiryis, pp. 16–21; Fouad Mughrabi, "The Palestinians After Lebanon," *ASQ* 5, 3(Summer 1983): p. 211; Yezid Sayigh, "Fatah: The First Twenty Years," *JPS* 13, 4 (Summer 1984): p. 115.

77. Jiryis, *ibid.,* pp. 19–41, and also his "Hiwar Min Naw' Akhar Hawl "al-Hiwar" wal-Wahda al-Wataniyya," *Shu'un Filastiniyya* 170–171 (May–June 1987): pp. 21–29.

78. Herbert C. Kelman, "The Palestinization of the Arab-Israeli Conflict," *The Jerusalem Quarterly* 46 (Spring 1988): pp. 3–15.

3. The Emergence of a Regional Conflict System

1. Clifford Geertz, *The Interpretation of Cultures* (New York: Basic Books, 1973), p. 221; Ernest Dawn, "The Formation of Pan-Arab Ideology," *IJMES* 20, 1(1988): pp. 67–91, 83; Sylvia Haim, *Arab Nationalism, An Anthology* (Berkeley and Los Angeles: University of California Press, 1976), pp. 6–9, 30–31; Cecil Hourani, "In Search of a Valid Myth," *Middle East Forum* 47, (1971): p. 41.

2. Aziz al-Azmeh, *Islams and Modernities* (London: Verso, 1993), pp. 64–65; Dawn, pp. 69–70; Haim, pp. 12–15, 20–23.

3. Reeva Simon, *Iraq Between the Two World Wars* (New York: Columbia University Press, 1986), pp. 75–114; Dawn, pp. 80–82; Haim, pp. 49–51. Albert

Hourani, *Arabic Thought in the Liberal Age* (New York: Oxford University Press, 1962), p. 292.

4. Elie Kedourie, "Religion and Nationalism in the Arab World," in his *Islam in the Modern World* (London: Mansel, 1980), pp. 54–55; Bassam Tibi, *Arab Nationalism: A Critical Enquiry* (New York: St. Martin's Press, 1971), pp. 90–91; Lewis, *The Middle East*, pp. 59–60, 82–83; Azmeh, pp. 66–70; Smith, pp. 80–83, 98–100, 105–107.

5. Dawn, pp. 80–83; Berger, pp. 304–312.

6. Tibi, p. 173; Cecil Hourani, "The Arab League in Perspective," *MEJ* 1 (April 1947). p. 41; Sati' al-Husri, *Mudhakkirati fil-'Iraq*, Part II, 1927–1941 (Beirut: Dar al-Tali'a lil-Tiba'a wal-Nashr, 1968), pp. 463–464.

7. Husri, *ibid.*; Haim, p. 39; Lewis, *The Middle East*, pp. 93–94.

8. Geertz, pp. 234–254; Albert Hourani, "Independence and the Imperial Legacy," *Middle East Forum* XLII, 1(Winter 1966): pp. 5–27.

9. Yehoshua Porath, "'Abdallah's Greater Syria Programme," *Middle Eastern Studies* 20, 2(April 1984): pp. 172–189; "Nuri Al-Sa'id's Arab Unity Programme," *ibid.* 4(October 1984): pp. 76–98; Daniel Pipes, *Greater Syria, The History of an Ambition* (New York: Oxford University Press, 1990), pp. 40–96.

10. Ahmed M. Gomaa, *The Foundation of the League of Arab States* (London: Gomaa, 1977), pp. 8–14; Porath, *In Search*, pp. 148–158.

11. Meir Zamir, *The Formation of Modern Lebanon* (Ithaca: Cornell University Press, 1985), pp. 38–96.

12. Albert H. Hourani, *Syria and Lebanon* (Oxford: Oxford University Press, 1946), pp. 263–266; Patrick Seale, *The Struggle for Syria* (Oxford: Oxford University Press, 1965), pp. 94–95; Reuven Avi-Ran, *The Syrian Involvement in Lebanon Since 1975* (Boulder: Westview, 1991), pp. 3–5.

13. Haim, pp. 45–51; Israel Gershoni, *The Emergence of Pan-Arabism in Egypt* (Tel Aviv: Tel-Aviv University, 1981), pp. 29–43, 72–83; Porath, *In Search*, pp. 149–159; Adeed Dawisha, *Egypt in the Arab World* (New York: John Wiley, 1976), pp. 4–5.

14. James Jancowski, "The Government of Egypt and the Palestine Question 1936–1939," *MES* 17, 4(October 1981): pp. 427–449; Israel Gershoni, "Muslim Brothers and the Arab Revolt in Palestine, 1936–39," *MES* 22, 3(July 1986): pp. 367–397; Haim, *ibid.;* Porath, *In Search*, pp. 149–159; Abdel-Malek, p. 251.

15. Avraham Sela, *The Question of Palestine in the Inter-Arab System, 1945–1948*, Unpublished Ph.D. thesis, Hebrew University of Jerusalem, 1986, Ch. 2; Barry Rubin, *The Arab States and the Palestine Conflict* (Syracuse: Syracuse University Press, 1981), pp. 23–184.

16. Avraham Sela, "The 1929 Wailing Wall Riots as a Watershed in the Palestine Conflict," *The Muslim World* LXXXIV, 1–2, (January–April 1994): pp. 60–94; Porath, *In Search*, p. 162; Dawn, p. 69.

17. Kedourie, *Islam*, pp. 56–57, 78.

18. Husri, pp. 473–475; Anis Sayigh, *Filastin wal-Qawmiyya al-'Arabiyya* (Beirut: Munazzmat al-Tahrir al-Filastiniyya, 1966), pp. 5–9; Kedourie, *Islam*, p. 79.

19. Quoted, respectively, in Ernst B. Haas, *The Uniting of Europe* (Stanford: Stanford University Press, 1958), p.16; and Macdonald, p. vi. Text of Charter (Pact), Macdonald, pp. 319–326; Porath, *In Search*, pp. 257–267; Bruce Maddy-Weitzman,

The Crystallization of the Arab States System 1945–1954 (Syracuse: Syracuse University Press, 1993), pp. 7–23; T.R. Little, "The Arab League: A Reassessment," *MEJ* 10, 2(Spring 1956): p. 140.

20. Sayyid Nawfal, *Al-'Amal al-'Arabi al-Mushtarak, Madih wa-Mustaqbalih* (Cairo: 1968), p. 82.

21. Seale, *The Struggle for Syria,* pp. 8–9.

22. Wm. Roger Louis, *The British Empire in the Middle East, 1945–1951* (Oxford: Oxford University Press, 1984), p. 137; Sela, *The Question of Palestine,* pp. 91–93; Little, p. 142.

23. Maddy-Weitzman, *Crystallization,* pp. 33–35.

24. Sela, *The Question of Palestine,* p. 22; Louis, pp. 134–143; Muwafi, p. 150.

25. Ajami, *Arab Predicament,* p. 162; Nafaa, p. 192; Abdallah Laroui, *The Crisis of the Arab Intellectual* (Berkeley: University of California Press, 1976), p. 171.

26. Mary C. Wilson, *King Abdullah, Britain and the Making of Jordan* (Cambridge: Cambridge University Press, 1987), pp. 190–198.

27. Seale, *The Struggle for Syria,* pp.90–91; Little, p. 143; Muwafi, pp.151–152.

28. Muwafi, pp. 152–157; Hussein A. Hassouna, *The League of Arab States and Regional Disputes* (New York: Oceana Publ., 1975), p. 13; Pact's text; Macdonald, pp. 327–333.

29. Nadav Safran, *From War to War, The Arab-Israeli Confrontation 1948–1967* (New York: Pegasus, 1969), pp. 100–106; Michael Oren, *The Origins of the Second Arab-Israeli War* (London: Frank Cass, 1992), pp. 109–125.

30. Leonard Binder, *The Ideological Revolution of the Middle East* (New York: John Wiley, 1964), pp. 198–229. Shimon Shamir, *Yeridat Hanasirism, 1965–1970* (Tel-Aviv: Mif'alim Universita'iyim, 1978), pp. 1–38.

31. Louis, pp. 244–253, 331–344; Riyad, *Mudhakkirat,* Pt II, pp. 50–61; Mohamed H. Heikal, *Cutting the Lion's Tail: Suez through Egyptian Eyes* (New York: Arbor House, 1987), pp. 52–59; Brown, pp. 162–167.

32. Patrick Seale, *The Struggle for Syria, A Study of Post-War Arab Politics 1945–1958* (London: Oxford University Press, 1965), pp. 186–237; Amnon Cohen, *Political Parties in the West Bank Under the Jordanian Regime 1948–1967* (Ithaca: Cornell University Press, 1980), pp. 97–98; Dawisha, *Egypt,* pp. 13–14; Mohamed H. Heikal, *Al-'Uqad al-Nafsiyya allati Tahkum al-Sharq al-Awsat* (Cairo: al-Sharika al-'Arabiyya lil-Tab' Wal-Nashr, 1958), pp. 21–61, 103–116.

33. Brown, *ibid.;* Dawisha, *Egypt,* p. 13; Safran, *From War to War,* pp. 106–111.

34. *Al-Hayat,* November 11–16, 1956; Michael B. Oren, "A Winter of Discontent: Britain's Crisis in Jordan, December 1955-March 1956," *IJMES* 22(1990): pp. 171–184.

35. Mohamed H. Heikal, *Sanawat al-Ghalayan* (Cairo: Markaz al-Ahram, 1988), pp. 275–276; Hourani, "In Search," p. 40.

36. Seale, *The Struggle,* pp. 308–326; Kerr, *Arab Cold War,* pp. 7–16, and *Regional Arab Politics,* pp. 19–20; Heikal, *Sanawat,* pp. 271–281; Dawisha, *Egypt,* pp. 29–31.

37. Kerr, *Arab Cold War,* pp. 16–18; Uriel Dann, *Iraq Under Qassem: A Political History, 1958–1963* (New York: Praeger, 1969), pp. 156–163, 187–191; Dawisha, *Egypt,* pp. 25–28; Heikal, *Sanawat,* pp. 540–542.

38. Kerr, *Arab Cold War,* pp. 28–30; Dawisha, *Egypt,* pp. 34–35; *Al-Ahram,* February 23, December 22, 1962; *al-Mithaq al-Watani* (Cairo: Dar al-Tahrir, 1964).

39. William J. Burns, *Economic Aid and American Policy toward Egypt, 1955–1981* (Albany: SUNY Press, 1985), p. 126.

40. Muhammad Hafiz Isma'il, *Amn Misr al-Qawmi fi 'Asr al-Tahaddiyat* (Cairo: Markaz al-Ahram, 1987), p. 97; Muhammad Fawzi, *Harb al-Thalath Sanawat, 1967–1970,* (Cairo: Dar al-Mustaqbal al-'Arabi, 1986), pp. 22–26; Heikal, *Sanawat,* pp. 626–628; Mohamed H. Heikal, *Al-Infijar 1967* (Cairo: Markaz al-Ahram, 1990), pp. 63, 222.

41. Kerr, *Arab Cold War,* pp. 29–41; M. Capil, "Political Survey 1962 Arab Middle East," *Middle Eastern Affairs* 14, 2 (February 1963): pp. 34–46; Bill and Springborg, p. 38.

42. Riyad, *Mudhakkirat,* Pt. II, pp. 212–214; Kerr, *Arab Cold War,* pp. 48–75; Dawisha, *Egypt,* pp. 41–42.

43. Kerr, *Arab Cold War,* pp. 85–88, 92–93.

44. Capil, p. 45. By late 1963 Egypt had 20,000–40,000 troops in Yemen (Dawisha, *Egypt,* p. 39); Kerr, *Arab Cold War,* p. 96; Muwafi, pp. 232–238; Shuqairi, *Min al-Qimma ila al-Hazima Ma'a al-Muluk Wal-Ru'asa'* (Beirut: Dar al-'Awda, 1971), pp. 32, 49; Hassouna, pp. 212–214.

45. Muwafi, pp. 188–190, 210–223, 226–228; Kerr, *Arab Cold War,* pp. 39–41; Dann, pp. 349–353; Shuqairi, *Hiwar wa-Asrar,* pp. 120–121.

46. Yehoshafat Harkabi, *Arab Attitude to Israel* (Jerusalem: Israel Universities Press, 1971), pp. 1–49; *Arab Strategies,* pp. 3–16; Kerr, *Regional Arab Politics,* pp. 33–40. Fawzi, *Harb,* p. 49.

47. Itamar Rabinovich, *The Road not Taken: Early Arab-Israeli Negotiations* (New York: Oxford University Press, 1991), p. 35–47; Maddy-Weitzman, *Crystallization,* pp. 127–141.

48. Rabinovich, *The Road,* pp. 3–64; Oren, *The Origins,* pp. 95–128; Avi Shlaim, *The Politics of Partition: King Abdullah, the Zionists and Palestine 1921–1951* (New York: Columbia University Press, 1990), pp. 355–389; Rubin, *The Arab States,* pp. 205–215.

49. Kerr, *Regional Arab Politics,* p. 33–40; Rabinovich, *The Road,* pp. 17–24.

50. Labib Shuqair (ed.), *Hadith al-Batal al-Za'im Jamal 'Abd al-Nasir Ila al-Umma* (Cairo: Dar al-Tahrir, 1965), Vol. 4, pp. 314, 338; *Al-Ahram,* February 23, 1964; Heikal, *Al-Infijar,* p. 208. Harkabi, *Arab Strategy,* pp. 8–12.

51. Moshe Shemesh, *The Palestinian Entity 1959–1974, Arab Politics and the PLO* (London: Frank Cass, 1988), pp. 3–8.

52. Yehoshafat Harkabi, *Palestinians and Israel* (Jerusalem: Keter, 1974), p. 35; Burns, p. 122.

53. Muhammad K. al-Azhari, "Al-'Alaqat al-Urduniyya-al-Filastiniyya: Qira'a Watha'iqiyya," *Shu'un Filastiniyya* 193, (April 1989): p. 48; Shuqairi, *Min al-Qimma ila al-Hazima* pp. 58–60; Shemesh, pp. 5–7, 11–34.

54. Harkabi, *ibid.,* pp. 24–37; Baruch Kimmerling and Joel S. Migdal, *Palestinians: The Making of a People* (New York: The Free Press, 1993), pp. 188–220.

4. For the Sake of Palestine: "Unity of Action"

1. Omar Z. Ghobashi, *The Development of the Jordan River* (New York: Arab Information Center, 1961), p. 34; *al-Hayat*, June 14, 1961.

2. Ahmad 'Abd al-Karim, *Tahwil Majra Nahr al-Urdun*, Kutub Qawimyya, [1959], n.p., pp. 29–33. S. N. Saliba, *The Jordan River Dispute*, The Hague, Martinus Nijhoff, 1968, p. 75; Kathryn B. Doherty, *Jordan Waters Conflict*, Carnegie Endowment for International Peace, no. 553 (New York: 1965), pp. 33, 47–56.

3. Burns, pp. 140–141; Fred J. Khouri, "Friction and Conflict on the Israel-Syria Front," *MEJ* 17, 1–2(Winter–Spring 1963): pp. 14–34; Yaacov Bar-Siman-Tov, *Linkage Politics in the Middle East* (Boulder: Westview, 1983), pp. 106–108, 130–131.

4. Oded Remba, "The Middle East in 1962—An Economic Survey: I," *Middle Eastern Affairs* 5 (May 1963): p. 103. Burns, p. 145. Yael Vered, *Hafikha Umilhama Beteiman* (Tel Aviv: 'Am 'Oved, 1967), p. 169; Heikal, *Sanawat*, pp. 729–730; Fawzi, *Harb*, p. 49.

5. *Ruz al-Yusuf*, December 16, 1963. 'Abd al-Karim, p. 31; Leila S. Kadi, *Arab Summit Conferences and the Palestine Problem, 1936–1950, 1964–1966* (Beirut: PLO, 1966), pp. 91–93; *'Al Hamishmar*, January 19, 1963.

6. *Al-Ahram*, December 24, 1963; May 2, 1964; Heikal, *Sanawat*, p. 730.

7. *Al-Ahram*, January 15, 1964.

8. Kerr, *Arab Cold War*, p. 98; Heikal, *Sanawat*, p.731.

9. Kadi, pp. 96–100; *Ruz al-Yusuf*, January 20, 1964; *al-Ahram*, January 19, 1964; Shuqairi, *Min al-Qimma*, pp. 37–50.

10. Riyad, *Mudhakkirat*, Pt. II, pp. 69, 231; Hani Ahmad Faris, "Nahr al-Urdun," in *Filastiniyyat*, Anis Sayigh (ed.) (Beirut: PLO, 1968), pp. 226–230; Yoram Nimrod, *Mei Meriva: Hamahaloket 'Al Mei Hayarden* (Giv'at Haviva, Merkaz Lelimudim 'Arviyim, 1966), pp. 92–94; Kadi, pp. 109–111.

11. *Al-Ahram*, September 12, 1964; *al-Jumhuriyya*, October 24, 1964; Kadi, p. 109; Heikal, *Sanawat*, p. 767.

12. Text of final communique, *al-Ahram*, January 18, 1964.

13. Kadi, p. 101; *al-Ahram*, January 19, 1964; Riyad, *Mudhakkirat*, Pt. II, p. 230; Shuqairi, *'Ala Tariq al-Hazima*, p. 144; *al-Ahram*, January 19, 1964.

14. Quoted in Fawzi, *Harb*, p. 48; *al-Ahram*, July 2, 1964; Heikal, *Sanawat*, p. 763; Kerr, *Arab Cold War*, p. 116.

15. Heikal, *Sanawat*, p. 767; *al-Ahram*, September 7, 9, 1964.

16. Shuqairi, *'Ala Tariq al-Hazima*, p. 144; Riyad, *Mudhakkirat*, Pt. II, p. 236–237; *al-Hayat*, September 11, 1964.

17. *al-Ahram*, January 19, 1964; Kadi, pp. 123–124; Shuqairi, *'Ala Tariq al-Hazima*, p. 7.

18. Shemesh, pp. 1, 5, 19–28.

19. Shemesh, pp. 33–34; Shuqairi, *Min al-Qimma*, pp. 57–60.

20. Shemesh, pp. 34–35; *al-Ahram*, January 18, 1964.

21. *Ruz al-Yusuf*, January 20, 1964; Kadi, p. 99. Shuqairi, *'Ala Tariq al-Hazima*, pp. 5–8, 50.

22. Shuqairi, *Min al-Qimma*, pp. 46–47, 61–62; Shemesh, p. 41; King Husain in *Anba' al-Urdun*, April 14, 1964.

23. *Al-Ahram,* January 18, 1964; Kadi, pp. 101, 228.

24. Shuqiari, *Min al-Qimma,* pp. 61–63.

25. Shuqairi, *Min al-Qimma,* pp. 63–69; Shemesh, pp. 44–45.

26. *al-Ba'th* (Syria), September 7, 1964; Shuqairi, *Min al-Qimma,* pp. 72–76, 81–84.

27. *Al-Hayat,* September 4, 1964; Shemesh, pp. 47–53.

28. Helena Cobban, *The Palestinian Liberation Organization* (Cambridge: Cambridge University Press, 1983), pp. 95–106; Kadi, pp. 104–105; Shemesh, p. 53.

29. Shuqairi, *Min al-Qimma,* pp. 127–143; Kadi, p. 136; Heikal, *Sanawat,* p. 764; *al-Jihad,* September 5, 1964.

30. A demilitarized zone southeast of Lake Tiberias, overtaken by Syria in late 1949.

31. Riyad, *Mudhakkirat,* Pt. II, pp. 238–239; Shuqairi, *Min al-Qimma,* p. 141; *al-Ahram,* September 11, 1964.

32. Shuqairi, *Min al-Qimma,* pp. 149–150; Hawrani, "Mu'tamarat al-Qimma," p. 74; Text of final communique, *al-Nahar,* September 12, 1964.

33. *Damascus Radio,* May 29, 1964; *al-Usbu' al-'Arabi,* July 13, 1964; Kerr, *Arab Cold War,* pp. 101–102.

34. Heikal, *Sanawat,* p. 732, 765; Muwafi, p. 228; Adeed I. Dawisha, "Intervention in the Yemen: Analysis of Egyptian Perceptions and Policies," *MEJ* 29, (Winter 1975): p. 55; Ali Abdel Rahman Rahmi, *The Egyptian Policy in the Arab World: Intervention in Yemen 1962–1967 Case Study* (Washington, D.C.: University Press of America, 1983), pp. 189, 196.

35. *Al-Ahram,* September 4, 1964; Kadi, p. 129; Shuqairi, *Min al-Qimma,* pp. 122–124.

36. *Al-Ahram,* September 10, 1964; Kerr, *Arab Cold War,* p. 107; Rahmi, pp. 200–201.

37. Cobban, *The PLO,* p. 30; *al-Ahram,* January 18, 1964; Heikal, *Sanawat,* pp. 732, 764; Kerr, *Arab Cold War,* pp. 100–102.

38. Kadi, p. 115; Hassouna, p. 234.

39. *Al-Ahram,* August 21, 28, and September 4, 1964; Heikal, *Sanawat,* pp. 758–762.

40. *Al-Ahram,* July 2 and September 6, 1964; Nasir in *The Observer,* July 6, 1964.

41. Heikal, *Sanawat,* pp. 732–733; Kerr, *Arab Cold War,* p. 100. For the internal Israeli debate, see: Yitzhak Rabin, *Pinkas Sherut* (Tel-Aviv: Ma'ariv, 1979), pp. 121–129; *Ha'aretz, Ma'ariv,* March–April, 1965.

42. Muwafi, p. 228; Heikal, *Sanawat,* p. 732. See Chapter 5.

5. Collapse of Summitry and the Road to War

1. Heikal, *Sanawat,* p. 768.

2. Kerr, *Arab Cold War,* pp. 106–107; Shuqairi, *'Ala Tariq,* pp. 10–21, 45–53; Kadi, pp. 141–142.

3. Riyad, *Mudhakkirat,* Pt. II, pp. 243–244; Heikal, *al-Infijar,* p. 20.

4. Heikal, *Sanawat,* pp. 205–206; *al-Ba'th* (Syria), June 4, 1965, July 2, 1965; *al-Ahram,* May 2, 1965; Kadi, pp. 143–144; Shuqairi, *'Ala Tariq,* pp. 73–74; *al-Hayat,* January 22, 1965.

5. Burns, pp. 150–155; Riyad, *Mudhakkirat,* p. 41–43; Heikal, *Sanawat,* pp. 733–757, 774–775; *al-Infijar,* pp. 158–160, 164–166, 175; Safran, *From War to War,* pp. 167–169.

6. *Al-Ahram*'s editorial, April 18, 1965; Nasir's speech to the PNC in Gaza, *ibid.,* June 1, 1965; Shuqairi, *'Ala Tariq,* pp. 42–43.

7. Shuqairi, *Min al-Qimma,* pp. 152–154; Husain's letter to Nasir, October 1965, Heikal, *al-Infijar,* pp. 351–353.

8. Salah Khalaf, *My Home My Land, A Narrative of the Palestinian Struggle* (New York: Times Books, 1981), pp. 44–49; Shuqairi, *Min al-Qimma,* pp. 156–157; Shemesh, pp. 40–42, 48–50; Cobban, pp. 29–30, 34–35.

9. Majid Khadduri, *Al-Ittijahat al-Siyasiya fil-'Alam al-'Arabi* (Beirut: al-Dar al-Muttahida lil-Nashr, 1972), p. 218; Yehoshafat Harkabi, *Fatah Baastrategia Ha'arvit* (Tel-Aviv: Ma'arakhot, 1969), pp. 27–47; Cobban, pp. 22–33. Ehud Yaari, *Strike Terror: The Story of Fatah* (New York: Sabra Books, 1970), pp. 49–55.

10. Yaari, *Strike Terror,* pp. 56–79; Mu'assasat al-Dirasat al-Filastiniyya, *Al-Watha'iq al-Filastiniyya wal-'Arabiyya li-'Am 1965* (Beirut: 1966), p. 353.

11. Shuqairi, *Min al-Qimma,* pp. 171–188, 229–231, 251–256.

12. Safran, *From War to War,* pp. 154–156, 167–169. Heikal, *al-Infijar,* pp. 137–142.

13. *al-Ahram,* March 10, 11, 15, 1965; Kadi, p. 149; Shuqairi, *Min al-Qimma,* pp. 27–34.

14. *Al-'Amal* (Tunisia), April 23, 1965, *Al-Watha'iq al-Filastiniyya wal-'Arabiyya li-'Am 1965,* pp. 78–82. On Bourguiba's ideas, see Cecil Hourani, *An Unfinished Odyssey, Lebanon and Beyond* (London: Weidenfelt & Nicolson, 1984), pp. 83–89.

15. *Al-'Amal* (Tunisia), April 30, 1965, in *Al-Watha'iq al-Filastiniyya al-'Arabiyya li-'Am 1965,* pp. 185–188; Nasir's attacks on Bourguiba, *al-Ahram,* May 2, 1965, *ibid.,* pp. 193–200; *al-Hurriyya,* July 1, 1965, *ibid.,* 338; Shuqairi, *Min al-Qimma,* pp. 201–204.

16. Shuqairi, *Min al-Qimma,* pp. 204–211; *al-Nahar,* April 30, 1965.

17. *Al-Wathai'q al-Filastiniyya wal-'Arabiyya li-'Am 1965,* pp. 484–491. Tunisia rescinded its boycott of the AL after 1967.

18. *Al-Watha'q al-'Arabiyya, 1965* (Beirut: al-Jami'a al-Amirkiyya, n.d.), p. 611. Hawrani, p. 88.

19. Isma'il, p. 116; Heikal, *al-Infijar,* pp. 185–188; Kerr, *Arab Cold War,* pp. 108–112; Vered, pp. 229–236; Text of the agreement, W. Khalidi and Y. Ibish (eds.), *Arab Political Documents 1965* (Beirut: The American University of Beirut, n.d.), pp. 309–310; Rahmi, p. 224.

20. *Al-Ahram,* September 11, 1965; Heikal, *al-Infijar,* p. 207.

21. Shuqairi, *'Ala Tariq,* pp. 78–81; Kadi, pp. 176–177.

22. Shuqairi, *'Ala Tariq,* p. 81; Heikal, *al-Infijar,* pp. 213–217.

23. Kadi, p. 180; Riyad, *Mudhakkirat,* Pt. II, p. 249; Muhammad Ahmad Mahjub, *Al-Dimuqratiyya fil-Mizan* (Beirut: Dar al-Nahar lil-Nashr, 1973), p. 113; Kerr, *Arab Cold War,* p. 124, doubted that Nasir was behind the coup.

24. Text of the Charter and summit's final communique, *al-Ahram,* September 18, 1965; Mahjub, pp. 112–113; Shuqairi, *'Ala Tariq,* p. 83.

25. Nasir argued that the summit allocated 200 million Egyptian pounds for military ends, *al-Ahram,* November 19, 1965.

26. A. Ben Tzur (ed.), *Mifleget Haba'th Hasurit Veisrael* (Giv'at Haviva: Merkaz Lelimudim 'Arviyim, 1968), pp. 5–8; Sami al-Jundi, *Al-Ba'th* (Beirut: 1969), pp. 164–166.

27. Shuqairi, *'Ala Tariq,* pp. 98–106.

28. *Al-Ahram,* September 18, 1965.

29. Daniel Dishon (ed.), *Middle East Record,* Vol. 3, 1967 (Jerusalem: 1971), pp. 107–110; Kerr, *Arab Cold War,* pp. 106–128; Mahjub, pp. 112–113; Shuqairi, *'Ala Tariq,* p. 147.

30. Kerr, *Arab Cold War,* p. 108; Vered, p. 209.

31. Heikal, *Al-Infijar,* pp. 232–237; Rahmi, pp. 224–227; Kerr, *Arab Cold War,* p. 109

32. Dawisha, "Intervention in the Yemen," pp. 57–58; Heikal, *al-Infijar,* p. 239; Mahjub, p. 113, argues that Faisal's initiative was assigned to him by the Casablanca summit.

33. *Al-Ahram,* February 23, 1966; March 13, 23, 1966; Shuqairi, *'Ala Tariq,* pp. 125–141.

34. *Al-Ahram,* June 6, 1966; April 27, May 3, 15, 1967; The conspiracy argument is elaborated by Heikal: *al-Infijar,* pp. 239–246, 420–423; and *Sphinx and Commissar: The Rise and Fall of Soviet Influence in the Middle East* (London: Collins, 1978), pp. 166–168. Burns, p. 168; Dawisha, *Egypt,* pp. 46–47.

35. Itamar Rabinovich, *Syria Under the Ba'th 1963–1966, The Army-Party Symbiosis* (Tel Aviv: Israel Universities Press, 1972), pp. 204–208; Bar-Siman-Tov, *Linkage,* pp. 151–157; Kerr, *Arab Cold War,* pp. 117–122.

36. By March 1967, Arab funding for Jordan had reached £24.5 million, Kerr, *Arab Cold War,* pp. 114–116; Heikal, *al-Infijar,* pp. 351–353, 430–431; Safran, *From War to War,* p. 284; Shuqairi, *'Ala Tariq,* pp. 110–122, 165–209.

37. *Al-Ahram,* July 23, 1966; *al-Ba'th* (Syria), April 4, October 24, 1966; Kerr, *Arab Cold War,* p. 112.

38. *Cairo Radio,* October 25, December 23, 1966; February 22, 1967; *al-Ahram,* December 24, 1966; Kerr, *Arab Cold War,* pp. 114–117.

39. On the eve of the June war, the Arab states' debt to the summits' projects was about 42–53 percent (£54–70): Shuqairi, *'Ala Tariq,* p. 152; *al-Ahram,* January 27, 1966; *al-Akhbar,* February 10, 1967; *MER 1967,* p. 134.

40. Heikal, *al-Infijar,* pp. 423–425; *al-Ahram,* March 16, 1966; *Cairo Radio,* February 5, and May 15, 1967; *MER, 1967,* p. 160; Kerr, *Arab Cold War,* pp. 125–126; R.B. Parker, "The June 1967 War: Some Mysteries Explained," *MEJ* 46 (1992): p. 177.

41. *Al-Ahram,* December 8, 11, 1966; *al-Watha'iq al-'Arabiyya, 1966* (Beirut: al-Jami'a al-Amirkiyya, n.d.), pp. 868, 923–924; *al-Watha'iq al-'Arabiyya, 1967* (Beirut: al-Jami'a al-Amirkiyya, 1968), pp. 13–16; Shuqairi, *'Ala Tariq,* pp. 259–272.

42. *Al-Ahram,* March 15, 1967; Heikal, *al-Infijar,* p. 425; Shuqairi, *'Ala Tariq,* pp. 274–276, 284–293.

43. Walter Laqueur, *The Road to War* (London: Pelican, 1968), p. 62; Heikal, *Sphinx*, pp. 161–163; Heikal, *al-Infijar*, pp. 362–368; Kerr, *Arab Cold War*, p. 122; Shuqairi, *al-Hazima al-Kubra* (Beirut: Dar al-'Awda, 1973), Pt. II, pp. 33–37, 49–61.

44. Heikal, *al-Infijar*, p. 407. Syria's annual royalties from the pipeline were $28 million, while Iraq's were some $250 million: Kerr, *Arab Cold War*, p. 125; Bar-Siman-Tov, *Linkage*, p. 155.

45. On the evolution of the May–June crisis, Safran, *From War to War*, pp. 274–302; Laqueur, pp. 85–100; Kerr, *Arab Cold War*, pp. 127–128; *MER 1967*, pp. 183–204.

46. Fawzi, *Harb*, p. 71. Nasir claimed that it was confirmed by Egyptian intelligence, Safran, *From War to War*, p. 274.

47. 'Abd al-Latif al-Baghdadi, *Mudhakkirat* (Cairo: al-Maktab al-Misri al-Hadith, 1977), p. 274; Fawzi, *harb*, pp. 93–94, 113–114, 124–126; Heikal, *al-Infijar*, pp. 659, 573–574, 829.

48. Shlomo Ahronson with Oded Brosh, *The Politics and Strategy of Nuclear Weapons in the Middle East* (Albany: SUNY Press, 1992), p. 325 (note); Oded Brosh, *Tfisot Shel Hameimad Hagar'ini Besikhsukhim Ezoriyim Rav Tzdadiyim Ve'emdot Be'i-nyanan*, Ph. D. thesis, The Hebrew University, Jeursalem, 1990, p. 117; A. Levite and E. landau, *Be'enei Ha'arvim, Dimmuya Hagar'ini Shel Israel* (Tel Aviv: Papirus, 1994), pp. 41–42.

49. Ahronson, pp. 95–97; Levite and Landau, pp. 39–41; Heikal, *Sphinx*, p. 151.

50. Avner Cohen, "Cairo, Dimona, and the June 1967 War," *MEJ* 50, 2(Spring 1996): p. 199.

51. Moshe Dayan, *Avnei Derekh* (Jerusalem: 'Idanim, 1976), pp. 418–420, 482; Safran, *From War to War*, p. 292; Heikal, *al-Infijar*, pp. 448–518.

52. Baghdadi, pp. 167–219; Anwar el-Sadat: *In Search of Identity, An Autobiography* (New York: Harper and Row, 1977), pp. 164–172; Fawzi, *Harb*, pp. 21, 32–85; Heikal, *al-Infijar*, pp. 573–574, 818–819.

53. Fawzi, *Harb*, pp. 72–73.

54. *Al-Ahram*, May 23, 1967; *al-Wathaiq al-'Arabiyya 1967*, pp. 334, 336, 338–339.

55. *Al-Ahram*, May 30, June 5, 1967; Heikal, *al-Infijar*, pp. 653–661; Shuqairi, *Al-Hazima*, Pt. I, pp. 192–220.

56. Benjamin Shwadran, *Middle East Oil Issues and Problems* (Cambridge: Schenkman, 1977), pp. 7–8. Farouk A. Sankari, "The Character and Impact of Arab Oil Embargoes," in N. A. Sherbini and M. A. Tessler (eds.), *Arab Oil* (New York: Praeger, 1976), pp. 268–269. Shuqairi, *al-Hazima*, Pt. 2, pp. 144–152.

6. A Turning Point in Khartoum

1. *Al-Ahram*, June 10, 1967. On the Arab self-searching, see Yehoshafat Harkabi (ed.), *Lekah Ha'arvim Mitvusatam* (Tel Aviv: 'Am 'Oved, 1969), pp. 7–68; Ajami, *Arab Predicament*, pp. 24–75.

2. E. Sheffer, "The Egptian Economy Between the Two Wars," in I. Rabinovich and H. Shaked (eds.), *From June to October: The Middle East Between 1967 and 1973* (New Brunswick: Transaction Inc., 1978), pp.140–142.

3. *Davar,* June 2, 5, 19, 1987; Dayan, *Avnei Derekh,* pp. 491, 512; Rabin, p. 227; Abba Eban, *Pirkei Hayim* (Tel-Aviv: 1978), p. 430; *MER, 1967,* p. 274; *al-Ba'th* (Syria), August 31, 1967; Mahjub, p. 146; *The Egyptian Gazette,* June 25, 1967; *The Financial Times,* June 15, 1967.

4. *Al-Ahram,* June 10, 1967; Harkabi, *Arab Strategies,* pp. 17–25; Fawzi, *Harb,* pp. 188–190.

5. Harkabi, *Arab Attitude,* pp. 12, 68–69; Daniel Dishon, "Inter-Arab Relations," in Rabinovich and Shaked *From June to October,* p. 159; Mahmud Riyad, *Mudhakkirat 1948–1978* (Beirut: al-Mu'assasa al-'Arabiyya lil-Dirasat wal-Nashr, 1985), pp. 106–108.

6. Harkabi, *Arab Strategies,* p. 22; Fawzi, *Harb,* p. 188.

7. Quoted by Fawzi, *Harb,* p. 199, 193–196; Dawisha, *Egypt,* p. 51.

8. Kerr, *Arab Cold War,* p. 138; Eberhad Kienle, *Ba'th v. Ba'th: The Conflict between Syria and Iraq 1968–1989* (London: Tauris & Co Ltd, 1990), pp. 35–38.

9. Heikal's editorials, *al-Ahram,* June 30, July 21 and 28, and August 18, 1967; 'Ali Sabri in *al-Jumhuriyya,* August 20, 1967.

10. *Al-Ahram,* June 12, July 24, 1967; *al-Jumhuriyya* (Egypt), June 19, 1967; *Times,* July 4, 1967, quoted Egypt's Deputy PM Qaisuni that Egypt had received by then $100 million. Feiler, pp. 51–55, concluded that the total Kuwaiti aid to Egypt from late 1963 to June 1967 reached $252 million in loans, constituting one-third of Egypt's commercial deficit in these years.

11. *MER, 1967,* pp. 135–136.

12. *Amman Radio,* June 18, 1967.

13. Riyad, *Mudhakkirat,* pp. 109–122, 130–131; Mahjub, pp. 131–133. Despite its militancy, Algeria contributed 40 Mig 17 air-fighters to Egypt (Fawzi, *Harb,* p. 186).

14. *Al-Ahram,* July 24, 1967; Shuqairi, *al-Hazima,* Pt. II, pp. 79–82; Saudi complaints about the oil embargo: *al-Bilad,* July 2, 1967, *'Ukkaz,* July 4, 1967, and *Mecca Radio,* July 11, 1967.

15. Shuqairi, *Al-Hazima,* Pt. II, pp. 115–132; Mahjub, pp. 137–138; *MER, 1967,* p. 262; *al-Hawadith,* August 4, 1967.

16. Shuqairi, "Dhikrayat 'An Mu'tamar al-Qimma fi al-Khartoum," *Shu'un Filastiniyya,* no. 4(September 1970): pp. 92–93; *al-Hazima,* Pt. II, pp. 118–122, 138–140.

17. Shuqairi, *Al-Hazima,* Pt. II, pp. 141–142. Mahjub, pp. 138–139.

18. Shuqairi, *al-Hazima,* Pt. II, pp. 141–160.

19. *Damascus Radio,* September 1, 1967; Shuqairi, *al-Hazima,* Pt. II, pp. 167–168, reveals that Syrian FM Ibrahim Makhus was nonetheless dispatched to Khartoum to hold unofficial talks with the summit participants.

20. Mahjub, pp. 155–166; *al-Nahar,* August 29, 1967; *al-Ahram,* August 28, 1967; *MER, 1967,* pp. 140–141.

21. On the summit deliberations, *MER 1967,* pp. 262–264; Shuqairi, *al-Hazima,* Pt. II, pp. 170–227; Riyad, *Mudhakkirat,* pp. 130–137; Mahjub, pp.141–147.

22. On the talks, *MER 1967,* pp. 39–41.

23. *Al-Hayat,* September 3, 1967; *Voice of Palestine from Cairo,* September 2, 1967; Shuqairi, *al-Hazima,* Pt. II, p. 194.

24. *MER 1967,* pp. 270–271.

25. Shuqairi, "Dhikrayat," pp. 96–97; Mahjub, p. 147. The concluding communique, *al-Jumhuriyya* (Egypt), September 2, 1967.

26. Shemesh, pp. 86–90.

27. Shuqairi, *al-Hazima,* Pt. II, pp. 206–208; *MER 1967,* pp. 264–265.

28. Text of final communique and resolutions, *al-Ahram,* September 2, 1967; Riyad, *Mudhakkirat,* p.131; Shuqairi, *al-Hazima,* Pt. II, p. 208; Mahjub, pp. 141–143. The financial aid totalled $392 million (Kerr, *Arab Cold War,* p. 139).

29. Mohamed H. Heikal, *The Road to Ramadan* (London: Colins, 1975), pp. 267–268; Sadat, *In Search,* p. 188; 'Arif's interview, *SWB,* September 9, 1967; *al-Ahram,* September 8, 1967.

30. *Al-Ahram,* September 5, 1967.

31. *Al-Hayat,* September 3, 1967; Heikal in *The Sunday Times,* September 10, 1967; King Husain in *Amman Radio,* October 2, 1967; Nasir in *al-Ahram,* November 24, 1967; Mahjub, p. 147; *MER 1967,* pp. 264–269, 274; *SWB,* September 3, 5, 8, 1967.

7. The Beleagured Nasir

1. Sayyid Mar'i, *Awraq Siyasiyya* (Cairo: al-Maktab al-Misri al-Hadith, 1979), p. 570; Sadat, *In Search,* p. 195.

2. Moshe Zak, "Israel-Jordanian Negotiations," *Washington Quarterly* 8, 1(Winter 1985): p. 169; Shemesh, p. 130; Dayan, *Avnei Derekh,* p. 542.

3. Daniel Dishon (ed.), *Middle East Record,* Vol. 4, 1968 (Jerusalem: 1973), pp. 135–146; Mahjub, p. 149.

4. Kerr, *Arab Cold War,* pp. 138–139; *MER 1968,* pp. 143–144; Daniel Dishon (ed.), *Middle East Record,* Vol. 5, 1969–1970 (Jerusalem: 1977), p. 519.

5. *Kul Shai',* July 13 and September 2, 1968; *al-Hawadith,* September 13, 1968.

6. Fawzi, *Harb,* pp. 202–205; Shemesh, pp. 99–100; *MER 1968,* pp. 161–164; Kienle, pp. 38–58.

7. Moshe Ma'oz, *Asad, the Sphinx of Damascus* (London: Weidenfeld and Nicolson, 1988), pp. 36–38; Kienle, p. 58; Bar-Siman-Tov, *Linkage,* pp. 164–165.

8. Fawzi, *Harb,* pp. 204, 316–319, 351–353; Saad el Shazly, *The Crossing of the Suez* (San Francisco: American Mideast Research, 1980), p. 13.

9. William B. Quandt, *A Decade of Decisions: American Policy Toward the Arab-Israeli Conflict 1967–1976* (Berkeley: University of California Press, 1977), p. 85.

10. *Al-Ahram,* July 24, 1969.

11. Shuqairi, *'Ala Tariq,* p. 139; *MER 1969–1970,* pp. 529–530.

12. *Al-Ahram,* September 4, 1969; *MER 1969–1970,* pp. 529–532.

13. *MER 1969–1970,* pp. 577–586; Z. Levkovich, "Hapsagot Shel Yerah September," *Skira Hodshit,* no. 8–9 (1969), p. 11.

14. *Al-Nahar,* November 18 and 19, 1969; Fawzi, *Harb,* p. 206.

15. *Al-Ahram,* November 11, 1969; *al-Nahar,* November 11, 1969; *MER 1969–1970,* pp. 535–536.

16. Heikal, *The Road to Ramadan,* pp. 75–76.

17. *MER 1969–1970,* p. 538.

18. *Al-Ahram,* December 5, 12, and 19, 1969.

19. Riyad, *Mudhakkirat,* pp. 220–222; *al-Idha'a wal-Talafisiun,* November 22, 1969; Quandt, *Decade,* pp. 89–92; Fred Khouri, *The Arab-Israeli Dilemma* (Syracuse: Syracuse University Press, 1976), pp. 363–364; *MER 1969–1970,* pp. 30–41.

20. Riyad, *ibid.;* Quandt, *Decade,* p. 91; *al-Hawadith,* January 2, 1970; *al-Nahar,* December 24, 1969.

21. Dov Yinon, "Mitzraim Lifnei Pisgat Rabat Veahareiha," *Skira Hodshit* 1(1970): p. 26; *al-Nahar,* December 23 and 24, 1969; *Reuters,* December 24, 1969; *MER 1969–1970,* p. 540.

22. Marry-Jane Deeb, *Libya's Foreign Policy in North Africa* (Boulder: Westview Press, 1991), p. 59.

23. Riyad, *ibid.,* p. 230; *al-Hawadith,* January 2, 1970; *al-Nahar,* December 24, 1969.

24. *Al-Hawadith, ibid.; al-Nahar, ibid.*

25. *Al-Ahram* and *Akhbar al-Usbu',* December 25, 1969, reported a £40 million increased aid (*MER 1969–1970,* p. 543). By early 1971, Egypt's total debt for its arms deals with the USSR since 1967 reached 4.5 billion Egyptian pounds (Fawzi, *Harb,* pp. 236–238, 345–362); *al-Sayyad,* January 1, 1970.

26. Fawzi, *Harb,* pp. 350–351; Sadat, *In Search,* p. 196.

27. Kerr, *Arab Cold War,* p. 146.

28. Deeb, pp. 59–61; *MER 1969–1970,* pp. 589–592, 543; Fawzi, *Harb,* p. 207.

29. *MER 1969–1970,* pp. 545–546; Shemesh, p. 119; Bar-Siman-Tov, *Linkage,* p. 165.

30. *MER 1969–1970,* pp. 547–552; *al-Ahram,* May 2, 1970. On the Iraqi-Libyan plan, *al-Jumhuriyya* (Baghdad), June 20–26, 1970.

31. Quandt, *Decade,* p. 99.

32. Khalaf, p. 79; Heikal, *The Road,* pp. 93–95; Dayan, *Avnei Derekh,* pp. 520–522; Riyad, *Mudhakkirat,* pp. 295–296; Quandt, *Decade,* p. 102; Fawzi, *Harb,* pp. 209–210; Isma'il, p. 162.

33. Riyad, *Mudhakkirat,* pp. 295–296; *MER 1969–1970,* p. 560; Kerr, *Arab Cold War,* pp. 140–145; Khalaf, pp. 73–81.

34. Riyad, *Mudhakkirat,* p. 294; Khalaf, p. 79; *MER 1969–1970,* pp. 552–560; Kerr, *Arab Cold War,* pp. 146–147.

35. *Al-Hurriyya,* October 2, 1967; *al-Ahram,* January 19, 1968; *Ruz al-Yusuf,* August 26, 1968; *al-Anwar,* May 25, 1969.

36. Quoted from *al-Ahram,* January 1968, *MER 1968,* p. 135.

37. Shemesh, p. 92; Cobban, pp. 39–42.

38. Harkabi, *Palestinians and Israel,* pp. 49–69; Shemesh, pp. 103–108; Cobban, pp. 36–46; Riyad, *Mudhakkirat,* p. 185.

39. *Al-Nahar,* December 21, 1969.

40. *MER 1969–1970,* p. 539.

41. *Al-Musawwar,* December 26, 1969; *al-Nahar,* December 25, 1969. On the concept of a Palestinian Democratic State, see Mohammad Rasheed, *Towards a Democratic State in Palestine* (Beirut: PLO Research Center, 1970); Harkabi, *Palestinians and Israel,* pp. 70–106.

380 Notes*Notes*

---

380 *Notes*

42. Moshe Ma'oz, "The Palestinian Guerrilla Organization and the Soviet Union," in his (ed.) *Palestinian Arab Politics* (Jerusalem: Jerusalem Academic Press, 1975), pp. 97–99; *al-Anba'*, December 18, 1969; and *al-Musawwar*, December 26, 1969.

43. *Al-Nahar*, April 20, 1970.

44. Khalaf, pp. 74–76; Shemesh, pp. 132–138; Kerr, *Arab Cold War*, p.140–143.

45. Shemesh, pp. 140–142; Khalaf, pp. 75–78; *MER 1969–1970*, pp. 792–815, 833–843.

46. On the summit, see Heikal, *The Road*, pp. 98–99; Musa Sabri, *Watha'iq Harb October* (Cairo: al-Maktab al-Misri al-Hadith, 1975), pp. 167–206; Riyad, *Mudhakkirat*, pp. 299–302; Khalaf, pp. 85–91.

47. Henry Kissinger, *White House Years* (Boston: Little Brown and Co., 1979), pp. 606, 623; Cobban, *The PLO*, p. 52; Quandt, *Decade*, pp. 113–119; Khalaf, pp. 180–186. For another explanation of Syria's motivation and defeat, see Patrick Seale, *Asad* (Berkeley: University of California Press, 1988), pp. 158–159.

48. *MER 1969–1970*, pp. 843–862; Khalaf, pp. 81–87.

49. *Al-Ahram*, September 28, 1970.

50. *MER 1969–1970*, pp. 871–875.

51. *Al-Ahram*, August 1, 1971.

8. The Road to the October War

1. Riyad, *Mudhakkirat*, pp. 420–422, 427; Quandt, *Decade*, pp. 128–129; Galia Golan, *Soviet Policies in the Middle East From World War Two to Gorbachev* (New York: Cambridge University Press, 1990), p. 82.

2. Sadat, *In Search*, pp. 221–222; Shazli, pp. 18, 31; Muhammad 'Abd al-Ghani al-Jamasi, *Harb October 1973* (Paris: al-Manshurat al-Sharqiyya, 1990), pp. 214–215; For an opposite argument, see Muhammad Fawzi, *Harb October 'Aam 1973* (Cairo: Dar al-Mustaqbal al-'Arabi, 1986), pp. 48–49; Heikal, *The Road*, pp. 204–205.

3. Mordechai Gazit, *The Peace Process 1969–1973: Efforts and Contacts* (Jerusalem: The Magness Press, 1983), pp. 61–65; Sadat, *In Search*, pp. 219, 279.

4. Isma'il, pp. 173–179; Sadat, *In Search*, pp. 279, 299, 301; Dayan, *Avnei Derekh*, pp. 525–528.

5. Heikal, *The Road*, pp. 116, 140, 152–155; Kissinger, *White House*, pp. 1280–1293; Quandt, *Decade*, pp. 133–143; Shimon Shamir, "Nasser and Sadat," in Rabinovich and Shaked, *From June to October*, pp. 195–196; Riyad, *Mudhakkirat*, pp. 343, 410; Fawzi, *Harb October*, p. 51.

6. Isma'il, pp. 256–281; Sadat in *Al-Ahram*, October 7, 1977; Henry Kissinger, *Years of Upheaval* (Boston: Little, Brown and Company, 1982), pp. 215–216, 225; Quandt, *Decade*, pp. 154–155, 160–162.

7. Quandt, *Decade*, p. 122, 147; Mahmud Riyad, *The Struggle for Peace in the Middle East* (London: Quartet Books, 1981), p. 223; Kissinger, *Years*, p. 206, 221; Gazit, p. 11.

8. Isma'il, p. 180; Heikal, *The Road,* pp. 167–170; Sadat, *In Search,* p. 225; Golan, p. 77; Kissinger, *White House,* p. 1284; Shazli, pp. 127–129, 173–174; Jamasi, pp. 214–215.

9. Isma'il, pp. 206–208, 210–220; Riyad, *The Struggle,* p. 232; Sadat, *In Search,* pp. 228–230; Quandt, *Decade,* pp. 151–152.

10. Sadat, *In Search,* p. 244; Isma'il, p. 233; Fawzi, *Harb October,* pp. 5–6; Shazli, p. 106; Jamasi, pp. 225–226.

11. Robert O. Freedman, "The Soviet Union and Syria: A Case Study of Soviet Policy," in M. Efrat and J. Bercovich, *Superpowers and Client States in the Middle East: The Imbalance of Influence* (London: Routledge, 1991), pp. 145–146; Feiler, p. 63.

12. Husain's plan, *al-Dustur,* March 16, 1972; Quandt, *Decade,* p. 123; Uriel Dann, "The Jordanian Entity in Changing Circumstance," in Rabinovich and Shaked, *From June to October,* pp. 231–244; Shemesh, pp. 224–225.

13. *MENA* from Damascus, April 2, 1971; *MENA,* June 25, 1971; Kissinger, *Years,* pp. 215–216, 219; Muhammad Abu-Shalbaya, *La Salam Bighair Dawla Filastiniyya Hurra* (Jerusalem: Matabi' al-Quds, 1970), Shemesh, pp. 175–176, 195–199; Bourguiba in *al-Akhbar,* September 4, 1973.

14. Christopher Dobson, *Black September, Its Short, Violent History* (London: Macmillan, 1974); Khalaf, pp. 97–120.

15. Ma'oz, *Asad,* pp. 45–47, 86; Shemesh, 187–188; Harkabi, *Arab Strategies,* pp. 41–63.

16. *Al-Thawra* (Syria), November 17, 1970; *MER 1969–1970,* pp. 598–600; Ma'oz, *Asad,* p. 39; Deeb, pp. 72–75.

17. Seale, *Asad,* pp. 190–191; Itamar Rabinovich, "Continuity and Change in the Arab-Israeli Conflict," in Rabinovich and Shaked, *From June to October,* p. 225. On the military coordination, Jamasi, pp. 216–217.

18. Shazly, pp. 37–39; Isma'il, p. 304; Fawzi, *Harb October,* pp. 7, 93; Jamasi, pp. 387–391, denied this allegation.

19. Sadat, *In Search,* p. 242. Shazli, p. 39. Jamasi, pp. 267–268. Shamir, "Nasser and Sadat," in Rabinovich and Shaked, *From June to October,* p. 201.

20. Heikal, *Kharif al-Ghadab,* pp. 124, 163, 269–270; *The Road,* pp. 119–120, 157, 184; Shazli, 147–149; *al-Akhbar,* May 23, 1972; *al-Usbu' al-'Arabi,* September 3, 1973; *al-Ahram,* July 2, 1973; *al-Anwar,* August 24, 1972; 'Adil Husain, *Al-Iqtisad al-Misri, Min al-Istiqlal Ila al-Taba'iyya, 1974–1979* (Cairo: Dar al-Mustaqbal al-'Arabi, 1982), pp. 79–80.

21. Shwadran, *Middle East Oil,* pp. 17–25; and his *Middle East Oil Crises Since 1973* (Boulder: Westview, 1986), pp. 34–40.

22. Heikal, *The Road,* p. 266; Anwar El-Sadat, *Those I Have Known* (New York: Continuum, 1984), p. 69; and his interview, *Ruz al-Yusuf,* February 3, 1975; Arye Oded, *Africa and the Middle East Conflict* (Boulder: Lynne Rienner Publishers, 1987), p. 5.

23. Jamasi, pp. 245–246; Fawzi, *Harb October,* pp. 18–19; *al-Hawadith,* March 29, 1973; Riyad, *The Struggle,* pp. 234–235; Shazli, pp. 195–197, 277.

24. *Al-Ahram,* September 12–13, 1973; Riyad, *Mudhakkirat,* pp. 431–433, 440. On Husain's visit to Israel, see *Yedi'ot Aharonot* and *Ha-Aretz,* September 15, 1993.

25. Sadat, *In Search,* pp. 233; Deeb, pp. 78–81; Heikal, *The Road,* pp. 190–191, 194, 196; Ajami, *Arab Predicament,* pp. 125–126; Ruth First, *Libya: The Elusive Revolution* (New York: Penguin African Library, 1974), pp. 233–235; Shazli, pp. 74–95.

26. Heikal, *The Road,* p. 196, estimated these contributions at $1 billion; Sadat in *Ruz al Yusuf,* January 13, 1975; Deeb, pp. 74–75. Official Egyptian version minimized Libya's assistance to the war effort: Hassan al-Badri, Taha el Magdoub, and Mohammed Dia el Din Zohdi, *The Ramadan War 1973* (Virginia: Dunn Loring, 1978), pp. 15–27; Sadat, *Those,* p. 46.

27. *Al-Ahram,* September 4, 9–10, 1973; Sadat, *In Search,* pp. 239–240; V.T. Levine and T.W. Luke, *The Arab-African Connection, Political and Economic Realities* (Boulder: Westview, 1979), pp. 7, 15–16.

28. Shazli, pp. 277–279; Fawzi, *Harb October,* p. 14.

29. Chaim Herzog, *The War of Atonement* (London: Weidenfeld and Nicolson, 1975), pp. 135–140. Jamasi, p. 378; Dayan, *Avnei Derekh,* p. 542.

30. Shwadran, *Middle East Oil,* p. 72; Uzi B. Arad, "The Short-Term Effectiveness of An Arab Oil Embargo," in H. Shaked and I. Rabinovich (eds.), *The Middle East and the United States, Perceptions and Policies* (New Brunswick: Transaction Books, 1980), pp. 244–245.

31. Ismail Fahmi, *Negotiating for Peace in the Middle East* (London: Croom Helm, 1983), p. 109; Shazli, p. 278; Heikal, *The Road,* pp. 267–270; Mar'i, pp. 727–743; Isma'il, p. 325.

32. Shwadran, *Middle East Oil,* pp. 72–73.

33. Isma'il, p. 315; Heikal, *The Road,* pp. 214–216, 226–227; Sadat, *In Search,* pp. 252–253; Shazli, pp. 245–251; Al-Badri *et al.,* pp. 95–96; Fawzi, *Harb October,* pp. 93–96; Jamasi, p. 385; Seale, *Asad,* pp. 210–211.

34. Kissinger, *Years,* pp. 499–500; Isma'il, p. 317.

35. Golan, pp. 88–94; Kissinger, *Years,* pp. 545–599.

36. Heikal, *The Road,* p. 230; Sadat, *In Search,* pp. 259–265; Riyad, *Mudhakkirat,* pp. 466–468; *Baghdad Radio,* October 29, 1973, *FBIS/DR,* October 30, 1973.

9. The Divisive Peace Diplomacy

1. *NYT,* December 18, 1974; Asad's interview, *Newsweek,* February 25, 1975; Ma'oz, *Asad,* pp. 49, 105–106.

2. Kissinger, *Years,* pp. 779–781, 783–784, 936–937; Seale, *Assad,* pp. 227–249.

3. *Al-Nahar,* October 29, 1974; *NYT,* November 8, 1974.

4. Riyad, *Mudhakkirat,* pp. 464–474; Kissinger, *Years,* pp. 640, 643, 665; *Akhbar al-Yawm,* November 15, 1973.

5. Riyad, *Mudhakkirat,* pp. 464–469, 475–477; Itamar Rabinovich, "Milhemet Yom Hakippurim Vehayehasim Habein'arviyim," *Ma'arakhot* 236 (May 1974): p. 14; *al-Nahar,* November 21, 1973.

6. Text of final resolutions, *al-Nahar,* December 4, 1973; *Arab Political Docu-*

ments 1973, pp. 527–530; Lebanon's FM interview, *Beirut Radio*, December 5, 1973.

7. *L'Orient le Jour*, January 15, 1975.

8. Isma'il, pp. 377–378; Seale, *Asad*, pp. 229–233.

9. *Akhbar al-Yawm* (Egypt), March 3, 1974; *al-Nahar*, April 14, 1974; Seale, *Asad*, pp. 237–238; Daniel Dishon, "The Web of Inter-Arab Relations 1973–1976," *The Jerusalem Quarterly* 1, 2, (Winter 1977): pp. 45–59.

10. Riyad, *Mudhakkirat*, pp. 500–501; Fahmi, pp. 83–85, 90–91; *al-Ra'i al-'Aam*, March 19, 1974; Kissinger, *Years*, pp. 882, 893–894, 939, 946–951, 1060–1061; Seale, *Asad*, pp. 240–241.

11. Kissinger, *Years*, pp. 1037–1038; Seale, *Asad*, p. 253. On February 25, 1974, the Islamic summit conference at Lahore recognized the PLO as the sole legitimate representative of the Palestinian people, Mu'assasat al-Dirasat al-Filastiniyya, *Al-Watha'iq al-Filastiniyya wal-'Arabiyya li-'Aam 1974* (Beirut; 1976), p. 63.

12. Interview, *Newsweek*, June 17, 1974; Kissinger, *Years*, pp. 847–848; Quandt, *Decade*, pp. 255–258.

13. *Al-Dustur* (Jordan), July 19, 1974; Shemesh, pp. 297–298.

14. *Al-Watha'iq al-Filastiniyya wal-'Arabiyya li-'Aam 1974*, pp. 262–264, 266–267, 277–278; *al-Dustur* (Lebanon), August 5, 1974; *al-Ahram*, July 24 and August 8, 1974; *al-Dustur* (Jordan), July 26, 1974; *al-Dustur* (Lebanon), August 5, 1974; *PNA*, July 24, 1974.

15. *Al-Ahram*, September 22, 1974; Itamar Rabinovich, "Ve'idat Rabat—Reka' Vehashlakhot," *Skira Hodshit*, Tel-Aviv, no. 12, (December 1974): p. 25. On the 12th PNC session, see below.

16. *Al-Nahar*, October 22, 1974; *al-Hawadith*, November 8, 1974; Seale, *Asad*, pp. 250–251; Shemesh, p. 308.

17. *Al-Fajr al-Jadid*, October 24, 1974; *al-Hawadith*, November 8, 1974; *al-Thawra* (Syria), October 23, 1974; *al-Akhbar*, October 20, 1974; *al-Jumhuriyya* (Egypt), October 10, 1974; *al-Ba'th* (Syria), October 7, 17, 1974; *al-Nahar*, October 18, 1974.

18. *Facts on File 1974*, Vol. 34, No. 1771, October 19, 1974; *al-Ahram*, October 12, 15, 1974; *al-Akhbar*, October 12, 1974; *MENA*, and *al-Nahar*, November 3, 1974; Seale, *Asad*, pp. 255–256.

19. *Al-Safir*, November 30, 1977. On the Palestinian representations and inter-Arab financial aid, see below.

20. Sadat's statement, *MENA*, January 24, 1975; *al-Jumhuriyya* (Egypt), January 16, 1975; *MENA*, February 2, 1975.

21. *Al-Akhbar* (Egypt), April 23, 1975; *al-Thawra* (Syria), April 24, 1975. On Syria and the PLO's campaign against Egypt, *al-Anwar*, February 26, 1975; *al-Nahar*, February 25, 1975; Asad's speech, *al-Ba'th* (Syria), February 26 and March 4, 1975; *Filastin al-Thawra*, February 15, 1975; *FoF 1975*, No. 1792, August 8, 1975.

22. *NYT*, September 17–18, 1975; *FoF*, No. 1817, September 6, 1975.

23. *Al-Thawra* (Syria), August 23, 1975, September 8, 14, 1975; Heikal in *al-Anwar*, October 13, 15, 17, 1975. For an Iraqi critique of Syria and the PLO, see, *al-Jumhuriyya* and *al-Thawra* (Iraq), March 3, 1975; Saddam Husain's interview, *al-Dustur* (Lebanon), August 25, 1975; Seale, *Asad*, p. 259.

24. *Al-Thawra* (Syria), September 14, 1975; Heikal in *al-Anwar*, October 13, 15, 17, 1975; *al-Muharrir*, August 3, 1975, quoting *Filastin al-Thawra; al-Akhbar*, (Lebanon), August 23, 1975; *FoF*, No. 1819, September 20, 1975.

25. Fahmi, pp. 172–177. On Arab economic aid to Egypt and Sinai II, see *MEED*, January 3, 1975; *al-Ahram*, January 21, February 15, August 15, 1975; *Financial Times*, August 22, 1975; William B. Quandt, *Saudi Arabia in the 1980s: Foreign Policy, Security, and Oil* (Washington D.C.: The Brookings Institute, 1981), p. 112.

26. Khalaf, pp. 134–137; See also his "Afkar Jadida Amam Marhala Ghamida," *Shu'un Filastiniyya* 29 (January 1974): pp. 5–10; Cobban, pp. 58–62, 155–156.

27. *Reuters*, November 26, 1973; *AP*, November 28, 1973; *al-Nahar*, December 5, 1973; Kissinger, *Years*, pp. 757–758.

28. Kissinger, *Years*, pp. 756–757.

29. *Filastin al-Thawra*, June 12, 1974; Khouri, *Arab-Israeli*, p. 374.

30. *Al-Ahram*, October 16, 23, 24, 1974; *FoF 1974*, Vol. 34, No. 1727, October 26, 1974; *al-Nahar*, October 4, 1974; *JPS* 4, 2 (1975): pp. 191–192.

31. *MENA*, October 17, 1974; *al-Ahram*, October 23, 24, 27; *al-Akhbar*, October 27, 1974; *Reuters*, October 23, 1974; *PNA*, October 25, 1974.

32. *AP*, October 25, 1974; Fahmi, pp. 99–101; *al-Nahar*, October 23, 1974; Khalaf, pp. 144–148; Riyad, *Mudhakkirat*, p. 519; Dobson, pp. 11–21.

33. *Al-Ra'i*, October 23, 1974; *al-Nahar*, October 28, 1974.

34. *Al-Dustur* (Jordan), October 29, 1974; *Cairo Radio*, October 28, 1974; *al-Akhbar*, October 22, 1974.

35. Text of the summit resolutions, *al-Safir*, November 30, 1977; *AP*, October 29, 1974; Shemesh, pp. 310–311.

36. *FoF 1974*, Vol. 34, No. 1773, November 2, 1974; Khalid al-Hasan, *Al-Ittifaq al-Urduni al-Filastini* (Amman: Dar al-Jalil lil-Nashr, 1985), p. 86. For a retrospective critique of the decision, see M.J. Kishk in *al-Hawadith*, March 8, 1985.

37. *Al-Nahar*, October 29, 1974; Husain's interview, *al-Anba'* (Morocco) and *al-Ra'i* (Jordan), October 31, 1974; *al-Dustur* (Jordan), November 5, 1974; al-Hasan, *ibid.*

38. Husain's interview, *NYT*, November 4, 1974; *al-Urdun*, November 10, 1974; *Amman Radio*, November 23, 1974; *al-Ahram* and *al-Nahar*, October 31, 1974; 'Arafat interview, *Times*, November 11, 1974; *Filastin al-Thawra*, November 5, 1974; *al-Diyar*, December 13, 1974.

39. Haitham al-Ayyubi, *al-Usbu' al-'Arabi*, November 4, 1974.

40. *Al-Ahram*, October 31 and November 3 and 7, 1974; *al-Akhbar*, October 27, 1974; *al-Jumhuriyya*, October 30, 1974.

41. Kissinger, *Years*, pp. 879–883; Riyad, *Mudhakkirat*, pp. 479–480, 490.

42. *UPI*, November 28, 1973; *Arab Political Documents 1973*, pp. 530–531; Shwadran, *Middle East Oil* (1986), pp. 59–62; Sankari, "The Character and Impact of Arab Oil Embargoes," in Sherbini and Tessler, pp. 270–275.

43. *Cairo Radio*, October 30, 1974; *al-Hawadith*, June 13, 1975; Levine and Luke, pp. 31–41; Oded, pp. 131–146.

44. *Al-Nahar*, December 1, 4, 1973.

45. Yorgen S.Nielsen (ed.), *International Documents on Palestine 1973* (Beirut:

Institute for Palestine Studies, 1976), pp. 348–349; *Al-Ahram,* October 21, 1974; Matar and Dessouki, pp. 110–111; *al-Ba'th* (Syria), May 4, 1977; *al-Ahram,* December 19–21, 3O, 1976.

46. Sayyid Mar'i, *Likay Nazra'al-Mustaqbal: al-Mashru' al-'Arabi lil-Tanmiya* (Cairo: Dar al-Ma'arif, 1975), pp. 138–154; *al-Jumhuriyya,* June 25, 1975; *Akhbar al-Yawm* (Egypt), August 8, 1974; *MEED,* August 9; August 16; November 13, 22, 29, 1974; *al-Ahram,* November 11, 1974.

47. King Hasan's press conference, *Cairo Radio,* October 30, 1974. Arab financial aid was to be given by Saudi Arabia and Kuwait ($400 million each), UAE ($300 million), Qatar ($150 million), Iraq ($100 million), Oman ($15 million), and Bahrain ($4 million), *al-Safir,* November 30, 1977. See also *MEES,* November 11, 1974; January 24, 1975; *FoF 1974,* Vol. 34, No. 1773, November 2, 1974; Riyad, *Mudhakkirat,* pp. 517–518; *al-Hawadith,* August 21, 1975; *'Akhir Sa'a,* February 11, April 19, 1976.

10. The Lebanese Civil War: Brokers and Pawns

1. Colin Legum (ed.), *Middle East Contemporary Survey,* Vol. 1, 1976–1977 (New York: Holmes & Meier, 1978), p. 161; Saddam Husain interview, *al-Dustur* (Lebanon), August 25, 1975; *FoF 1975,* No. 1801, May 17, 1975.

2. *Al-Thawra* (Syria), March 9, 1974; June 3, 1978; August 18, 1982; *Tishrin,* November 22, 1976; *Trau,* March 31, 1977; Itamar Rabinovich, *The War for Lebanon 1970–1985* (Ithaca: Cornell University Press, 1985), pp. 36–37; Seale, *Asad,* pp. 267–268.

3. *Al-Thawra,* March 9, 1975. Zuhair Muhsin's interview in *al-Hayat,* May 19, 1975; *al-Hawadith,* June 26, 1975; Rabinovich, *Lebanon,* p. 52; Ma'oz, *Asad,* pp. 114, 129.

4. *Al-Ba'th* (Syria), January 5, 1975; *PNA,* January 13, 1975; *al-Siyasa,* February 13, 1975; *Filastin al Thawra,* June 29, 1975; *MECS 1976–1977,* pp. 154–157.

5. *Al-Siyasa,* February 13, 1975; *al-Ahram,* March 2, 1975.

6. *Amman Radio,* May 10, 1975; *al-Ra'i* (Jordan), July 2, 11, 1975; *al-Hawadith,* July 18, 1975.

7. Asad's interview, *Damascus Radio,* August 2, 1975; *al-Ra'i* (Jordan), August 22, 1975; *al-Thawra* (Syria), August 21, 1975.

8. *Al-Yawm,* and *al-Ba'th* (Syria), January 5–6, 1975; Avi-Ran, pp. 5–6, 58.

9. Rabinovich, *Lebanon,* pp. 43–54; Khalaf, pp. 164–165; Seale, *Asad,* pp. 272–273.

10. Walid Khalidi, *Conflict and Violence in Lebanon: Confrontation in the Middle East* (Cambridge: Harvard University Press, 1979), p. 81; Avi-Ran, pp. 34–35.

11. Cobban, *The PLO,* pp. 67–68; Avi-Ran, p. 33; Karim Bakraduni, *Al-Salam al-Mafqud: 'Ahd Ilias Sarkis 1976–1982* (Beirut: 1984), p. 21.

12. Kamal Junblat, *Hadhihi Wasiyyati* (al-Mukhtara: al-Markaz al-Watani, 1987), pp. 130–131.

13. *Al-Hawadith,* March 19, 1976; *al-Safir,* May 21, 1976; *al-Nahar,* May 28,

1976; Junblat, p. 131, 143–145; Bakraduni, pp. 19–21; Khalaf, pp. 180–185. On Libya's role, *al-Qabas*, May 5, 1976.

14. Asad's speech explaining the invasion, *Tishrin* (Syria), July 21, 1976; and his interview, *al-Hawadith*, October 1, 1976; Rabinovich, *Lebanon*, pp. 54–59; *al-Qabas*, July 5, 1976; Syria's intervention received the *post factum* imprimatur of the Lebanese president (Riyad, *Mudhakkirat*, p. 543).

15. Rabin, p. 503; *Times*, September 13, 1976; *The Washington Post*, December 2, 1976; *Time*, January 17, 1977; Avi-Ran, pp. 53–55; Seale, *Asad*, pp. 279–280.

16. *Al-Ahram*, January 14, 1976; *al-Nahar*, January 22, 28, 1976; *al-Hawadith*, February 6, 1976; *al-Ahram*, July 23, 1976.

17. *Al-Ahram*, January 20, February 13, April 21, 1976; Seale, *Asad*, pp. 284–286.

18. *Baghdad Radio*, June 11, 1976; *Ma'ariv*, June 15, 1976; *al-Anwar*, September 20, 1976; *al-Ra'i* (Jordan), October 15, 1976; *al-Nahar*, November 17, 1976.

19. *TASS*, August 26, October 13, 1976; *Le Monde*, July 20, 1976; Asad's interview, *al-Hawadith*, October 1, 1976; Khalaf, p. 200; Seale, *Asad*, pp. 268–269.

20. *Al-Nahar*, June 8, 10, 11, 1976; *al-Safir*, June 10, 1976; *Akhbar al-Yawm*, June 12, 1976; *al-Safir*, June 28, July 15, 16, 1976; *al-Anwar*, June 16, 1976.

21. *Al-Nahar* and *al-safir*, June 14, 1976; *Beirut Radio*, July 2, 1976.

22. *Al-Ahram*, June 25, 1976.

23. *Al-Ahram*, July 29, 1976; *al-Nahar*, July 3, 13, 29, 1976; *Tishrin* (Syria), July 15, 1976; *al-Safir*, July 8, 15, 1976; Avi Ran, pp. 28–37.

24. FM Fahmi in *al-Ahram*, August 30, 1976.

25. *Al-'Amal* (Lebanon), September 11, 1976; *MENA*, September 13, 14, 17, 1976; *al-Ahram*, September 5, 7, 19, 25, 26, 1976; *al-Hawadith*, October 1, 1976; *al-Nahar*, September 4, 6, 1976; *al-Anwar*, September 5, 1976.

26. *Al-Ahram*, September 25, 1976; Fahmi, p. 114.

27. *Al-Nahar*, October 2, 1976; *MECS 1976–1977*, pp. 147–150.

28. *Al-Hawadith*, October 15, 1976; *al-Ba'th* (Syria), October 14, 1976; *al-Anwar* (Lebanon), October 17, 1976; *al-'Amal* (Lebanon), October 16, 1976.

29. *Tishrin* (Syria), and *al-Anwar*, October 19, 1976.

30. Khalaf, p. 197; *al-Thawra* (Iraq), October 22, 1976.

31. *Al-'Amal* (Lebanon), October 24, 1976; *al-Nahar*, *al-Bairaq*, and *al-Ahram*, October 26, 27, 1976; *al-Anwar*, October 26, 27, and November 6, 1976.

32. On financing the ADF, see *al-Thawra* (Syria), October 30, 1976; *al-Ahram*, October 27, 1976. An emergency aid of $5 million was granted by Saudi Arabia to Lebanon (*al-Anwar*, November 29, 1976).

33. *MEED*, March 5, 1976; *al-Ahram*, March 25, 1976.

34. *MECS 1976–1977*, pp. 163–165.

35. *Al-Liwa'*, October 13, 1976.

36. *Tishrin* (Syria), October 24, 1976.

37. Quandt, *Saudi Arabia*, p. 79.

38. *Al-Ahram*, October 26, 1976; *al-'Amal* (Tunisia), October 27, 1976.

39. Text of final communique and resolutions, *al-Ahram*, October 27, 1976. For the thirteenth PNC session, see Cobban, *The PLO*, pp. 81–87.

11. The Burden of Arab Consensus: Egypt-Israel Peace Accord and Arab Response

1. Fahmi, pp. 191–192; Jimmy Carter, *Keeping Faith: Memoirs of a President* (New York: Bantam, 1982), pp. 279–281; Ma'oz, *Asad*, p. 139; Seale, *Asad*, p. 296; *al-Nahar*, February 23, 1977; *Tishrin* (Syria), March 11, 1977.

2. *NYT*, February 5, 1977; Fahmi, p. 112; *MENA*, January 14, 1977; *al-Ra'i* (Jordan), January 16, 1977.

3. *NYT*, February 5, March 1, 9, 1977; Fahmi, pp. 110–112.

4. Carter, *Memoirs*, pp. 282–284, 286–287; *MECS 1976–1977*, pp. 158–160.

5. For a typical polemic on this issue, see *al-Ba'th* (Syria), February 20, 1977, and *al-Anba'* (Kuwait), February 22, 1977.

6. *MEED*, January 21, 1977, p. 19; *al-Sayyad*, April 21, 1977; *MENA*, March 23, 1977; Heikal, *Kharif*, pp. 219–227.

7. *Al-Nahar*, February 23, May 6, 1977; *al-Liwa'*, March 1, 1977.

8. *MECS 1976–1977*, pp. 173–176.

9. *Al-Mustaqbal*, July 30, August 6, 1977; *al-Ahram*, July 20, 1977; *MECS 1976–1977*, pp. 165–169.

10. *MECS 1976–1977*, p. 158.

11. Asad's interview, *NYT*, August 29, 1977.

12. Carter, *Memoirs*, p. 287; Fahmi, pp. 197–198, 213; Seale, *Asad*, p. 297. For a different version, see Cobban, *The PLO*, pp. 88–89.

13. 'Arafat's interview to *al-Watan al-'Arabi*, November 30, 1984; William B. Quandt, *Camp David, Peacemaking and Politics* (Washington D.C.: The Brookings Institution, 1986), pp. 85–95, 100–102; Fahmi, pp. 204, 252.

14. Moshe Dayan, *Breakthrough: A Personal Account of the Egypt-Israel Peace Negotiations* (New York: Alfred A. Knopf, 1981), pp. 43–53; Mohamed I. Kamel, *The Camp David Accords: A Testimony* (London: KPI, 1986), p. 307; Seale, *Asad*, p. 303.

15. Carter, *Memoirs*, p. 294; Fahmi, pp. 235–236; Seale, *Asad*, pp. 300–301.

16. *Al-Nahar*, November 12–13 1977; *al-Anwar*, November 13–14, 1977; Riyad, *Mudhakkirat*, pp. 558–559; Fahmi, pp. 252–273.

17. Bakraduni, pp. 140–141; Colin Legum (ed.), *Middle East Contemporary Survey*, Vol. 2, 1977–1978 (New York: Holmes & Meier, 1979), pp. 732–733, 680–681.

18. Sadat, *In Search*, p. 334, Kamel, 17–18.

19. *MECS 1977–1978*, pp. 213–231; Carter, *Memoirs*, p. 300; Kamel, pp. 132–133; Badraduni, pp. 139–140.

20. Kienle, pp. 131–132; Seale, *Asad*, pp. 310–311.

21. Kamel, pp. 135–137, 233–237, 255–257.

22. *Al-Thawra* (Syria) and *al-Anba'* (Kuwait), September 27, 1978; *Tishrin* (Syria), September 26, 1978; *SANA*, September 23, 1978, *DR*, September 25, 1978.

23. *Al-Fajr al-Jadid*, December 5, 1977; *The Economist*, December 10, 1977.

24. *MECS 1977–1978*, pp. 219–224; Qadhafi's declaration, *JANA*, October 8, 1977; *al-Ba'th* (Syria), September 24, 1978.

25. *MENA*, December 5, 1977; Daniel Dishon, "Sadat's Arab Adversaries," *The Jerusalem Quarterly* 2, 8(Summer 1978), p. 9.

26. *al-Ahram,* November 26–27, 1977; Carter, *Memoirs,* p. 307; Kamel, pp. 53–61; Dayan, *Breakthrough,* pp. 93–100.

27. Quandt, *Camp David,* pp. 150–205; Riyad, *Mudhakkirat,* pp. 566–567; Kamel, pp. 132–133, 140–141.

28. *Al-Akhbar*'s editorial (Egypt), March 21, 1978; Riyad, *Mudhakkirat,* pp. 568–571; On Fahd's efforts, see *QNA,* August 7, 1978; *al-Nahar,* August 29, 1978; Kamel, pp. 255–257.

29. King Husain's interview, *al-Ra'i,* October 11, 1978; *al-Siyasa* (Kuwait), October 10, 1978; Fahmi, pp. 285–299; Kamel, pp. 316, 372–373.

30. 'Ali, pp. 78–81; Kamel, pp. 334–335, 343; *Yediot Aharonot,* October 31, 1978; Carter, *Memoirs,* pp. 373, 404.

31. *INA,* October 1, 1978; *al-Musawwar,* October 20 and 27, 1978; *al-Sharq al-Awsat,* October 25, 1978; *al-Thawra* (Iraq), October 26, 1978; Riyad, *Mudhakkirat,* p. 593.

32. *Damascus Radio,* October 9, 1978; *al-Thawra* (Iraq), October 26, 1978; *al-Hawadith,* January 26, 1979; *al-Kifah al-'Arabi,* February 26, 1979; *al-Thawra* (Syria), December 22, 1978; *al-Ba'th* (Syria), February 1, 1979; Kienle, pp. 134–143; Robert Stephens, "Union in the Fertile Crescent," *MEI,* March 2, 1979.

33. *Al-Riyad,* October 26, 1978; *al-Qabas,* October 27, 1978; Interview, the Saudi FM to *UPI,* October 28, 1978; *al-Thawra* (Iraq), October 30, 1978.

34. *Al-Thawra* (Iraq), October 10, 1978; *al-Nahar,* November 1, 2, 1978; *al-Thawra* (Iraq), November 1, 2, 1978; *al-Dustur* (Jordan), November 2, 1978; *Yediot Aharonot,* November 2, 1978.

35. Riyad was criticized in Egypt (*al-Akhbar* and *al-Ahram,* November 3, 1978). He resigned his office in March 1979 (Riyad, *Mudhakkirat,* p. 608).

36. Proceedings of the summit were published in *al-Kifah al-'Arabi* from April 2 through May 7, 1979; Riyad, *Mudhakkirat,* p. 593–601; *al-Thawra* (Iraq), November 5, 1978; Bakr's statement, *INA,* November 2, 1978; *Tishrin* (Syria), November 5, 1978.

37. Text of the final statement, *al-Thawra* (Iraq), November 6, 1978.

38. Contributors to the fund were to be Saudi Arabia, $1 billion, Kuwait and Libya $550 million each, Iraq $520 million, Algeria $250 million, the UAE $400 million, and Qatar $230 million; Riyad, *Mudhakkirat,* p. 600; *al-Thawra* (Iraq) and *al-Nahar,* November 6, 1978.

39. *Al-Watan al-'Arabi,* November 10, 1978; *al-Nahar al 'Arabi wal-Dawli,* November 13, 1978.

40. *Tripoli Domestic Service,* September 22, *DR,* September 25, 1978; *al-Ra'i* (Jordan), September 18, 1978; *Filastin al-Thawra, al-Watan* (Kuwait), September 23, 1978; Colin Legum (ed.), *Middle East Contemporary Survey,* Vol. 3, 1978–1979 (New York: Holmes & Meier, 1980), pp. 295–296.

41. *NYT,* February 8, 1979.

42. Adeed I. Dawisha, "Iraq and the Arab World: The Gulf War and After," *The World Today,* 37, 5(May 1981), pp. 141–142.

43. *NYT,* March 5–7, 1979; *FoF,* No. 1999, March 9, 1979, and No. 2000, March 16, 1979.

44. *Shu'un Filastiniyya* No. 83, (October 1978), pp. 156–158; *al-Hawadith,* January 26, 1979; *MECS 1978–1979,* p. 698; *FoF,* No. 2005, April 13, 1979.

45. *Al-Ahram*, November 11, 1978; *The Washington Post*, December 9, 1978; *Time*, December 11, 1978; Numairi's interview, *al-Hawadith*, January 26, 1979.

46. 'Ali, pp. 98–100, 107–110, 130, 140; Quandt, *Camp David*, pp. 268–281; Dayan, *Breakthrough*, pp. 207–212, 216–217; Sadat to *al-Ahram*, November 11, 1978.

47. *Al-Ahram*, November 8, 10, 12, 24, 1978; December 3, 1978; Dayan, *Breakthrough*, pp. 235–236.

48. 'Arafat to *al-Nahar al-'Arabi wal-Dawli*, March 19, 1979; *al-Ba'th* (Syria), March 18, 21, 25, 1979; *al-Dustur*, September 23, 1979; Fahmi, p. 295.

49. The meeting's proceedings were published in *al-Kifah al-'Arabi*, June 18 through August 27, 1979; *AP*, March 30, 1979.

50. The PLO's proposals, *International Douments on Palestine, 1979* (Beirut: Institute for Palestine Studies, 1981), pp. 135–136; *Gulf Mirror*, March 24, 1979; Saudi FM's statement, *MENA*, March 30, 1979.

51. *Voice of Palestine from Lebanon*, March 29, 1979; *SNA*, March 28, 1979.

52. *Al-Nahar*, April 1, 1979; The final communique, *INA*, March 31, 1979; Bahrain's FM statement, *MENA*, March 29, 1979.

53. *AP*, March 31, 1979; Editorial, *'Ukkaz*, January 20, 1979; King Husain's interview, *Newsweek*, April 2, 1979; *The Washington Post*, April 15, 1979.

54. *Al-Usbu' al-'Arabi*, September 6, 1979; Ali, p. 286.

55. *Cairo Radio*, May 1, 1979; *al-Riyad*, April 24, May 22, 1979. A Kuwaiti official source portrayed Egypt as a "bottomless barrel" (*al-Qabas*, April 14, 1979). *Al-Nahar al-'Arabi wal-Dawli*, November 10, 1978 argued that the total Arab aid to Egypt since 1967, including deposits and investments, reached $17 billion.

56. *The Washington Post*, April 27, 1979; Victor Lavy, "The Economic Embargo of Egypt by Arab States: Myth and Reality," *MEJ* 38, 3(Fall 1984): pp. 423–424; *al-Ahram al-Iqtisadi*, April 15, 1979, pp. 14–17; 'Ali, pp. 275–277.

57. *The Financial Times*, September 3, 1979; *MECS 1978–1979*, pp. 218–219.

58. Feiler, p. 85; Lavy, p. 421–422, 429–431; *al-Kifah al-'Arabi*, April 16, 1979.

59. *MECS 1978–1979*, pp. 420–423.

12. The Iraq-Syria Conflict and the Gulf War

1. Richards and Waterbury, pp. 61, 67–68, 379, 395; *The Economist*, June 6, 1988, p. 56; May 20, 1989; *The Middle East*, February 1988, p. 26; *al-Nahar Arab Report and Memo*, Vol. 9, no. 23, August 2, 1985, p. 5; David Lamb, "Arab Power on the Wane Despite Oil," *LAT*, July 14, 1985; I. Rabinovich and H. Shaked (eds.), *Middle East Contemporary Survey*, Vol. 10, 1986 (Boulder: Westview Press, 1988), pp. 240–242.

2. Saad Eddin Ibrahim, *The New Arab Social Order* (Boulder: Westview Press, 1982), pp. 167–174; Philip Khoury, "Islamic Revival and the Crisis of the Secular State in the Arab World: An Historical Appraisal," in Ibrahim, pp. 213–237; Issa J. Boullata, *Trends and issues in Contemporary Arab Thought* (Albany: SUNY Press, 1990), pp. 143–150.

3. Mohamed H. Heikal, *Illusions of Triumph, An Arab View of the Gulf War* (London: HarperCollins, 1993), pp. 49–67; Boullata, *ibid.*; Hazem Beblawi, "The Arab

Oil Era (1973–1983)—A Story of Lost Opportunity," *JAA* 5, 1(1986): pp. 15–34; Kerr, "Rich and Poor in the New Arab Order," *JAA* 1, 1(1981): pp. 1–26; Farah, *Pan-Arabism,* especially chapters 5–9; Hasan Hanafi and Muhammad ʿAabid al-Jabiri (eds.), *Hiwar al-Mashriq wal-Maghrib* (Cairo: Madbouli, 1990), pp. 50–57, 109–115, 185–187.

   4. *INA,* June 19, 1979; *al-Raʾi al-ʿAm,* August 11, 1979; *al-Siyasa,* August 11, 1979; Kienle, pp. 148–149, 154. Seale, *Asad,* pp. 354–355.

   5. Hanna Batatu, "Shiʿi Organizations in Iraq: al-Daʿwah al-Islamiyah and al-Mujahidin," in Juan R. I. Cole and Nikki A. Keddie (eds.), *Shiʿism and Social Protest* (New Haven: Yale University Press, 1986), pp. 194–195; Dilip Hiro, *The Longest War, The Iran-Iraq Military Conflict* (New York: Routledge, 1991), pp. 25–31; Kienle, pp. 156–158.

   6. Colin Legume (ed.), *Middle East Contemporary Survey,* Vol. III, 1978–79 (New York: Holms and Meier, 1980), pp. 803–809; Seale, *Asad,* pp. 321–331.

   7. *Al-Nahar,* October 17, 1979; *al-Liwaʾ,* November 22, 1979; *al-Thawra* (Syria), November 16, 1979.

   8. *Al-Nahar,* October 2, 1979; *Tishrin* (Iraq), November 19, 1979; *al-Liwaʾ,* November 22, 1979; *The Financial Times,* November 21, 1979.

   9. Adeed Dawisha, "Iraq: The West's Opportunity," *Foreign Policy,* 41 (Winter 1980–81): p. 138.

   10. *Al-Dustur* (Jordan), July 16, 1979; *JNA,* April 15, 1980; *al-Baʿth* (Syria), September 11, 1980; Colin Legume (ed.), *Middle East Contemporary Survey,* Vol. V, 1980–81, (New York: Holms and Meier, 1982), pp. 283–284; *al-Mustaqbal,* October 18, 1980.

   11. *Time,* February 11, 1980; *The Washington Post,* October 29, 1980, January 8 and 17, April 26, 1981; ʿAli, p. 297; *MENA,* May 15 and June 15, 1980; *JANA,* June 18, 1980; John Cooley, "The Libyan Menace," *Foreign Policy,* 42 (Spring 1981): p. 91; *al-Hawadith,* November 11, 1979; *al-Anwar,* November 8, 1979.

   12. *Al-Qabas,* November 19, 1979: Laurie Brand, "Economics and Shifting Alliances: Jordan's Relations with Syria and Iraq 1975–81," *IJMES,* 26, 3(1994): pp. 404–408.

   13. *Al-Anbaʾ* and *al-Siyasa* (Kuwait), August 14, 1979.

   14. *The Washington Post,* October 8, 1980; *Tishrin* (Syria), December 5, 1979; *al-Ahram,* February 3, 1980; *al-Baʿth* (Syria), April 28, 1980; Khaddam's explanation for the treaty with Moscow, *al-Nahar al-ʿArabi wal-Dawli,* October 13, 1980; Seale, *Asad,* pp. 352, 355–358.

   15. Seale, *Asad,* p. 363; Hiro, pp. 37–39; Christine M. Helms, *Iraq, Eastern Flank of the Arab World* (Washington D.C.: The Brookings Institution, 1984), p. 150, 164–166.

   16. *Al-Sharq al-Awsat* and *al-Jazira,* September 24, 1980; *al-Hawadith,* October 31 and November 7, 1980; *Reuters,* November 13, 1980. On the Jordan-Syria crisis, *Ha-ʾaretz,* November 17, 1980; *MECS 1980–81,* pp. 236–239; *The Financial Times,* November 26, 1980.

   17. *Al-Baʿth* (Syria), July 8, 1980; *al-Nahar,* July 13, 14, 1980; *al-Usbuʿ al-ʿArabi,* July 21, 1980. The Jerusalem issue was played up following the Knesset's law declaring the reunited city Israel's eternal capital.

   18. *Al-Majalla,* October 18, 1980; *INA,* November 21, 1980, *FBIS/DR,* Novem-

ber 24, 1980; *Damascus Radio,* November 24, 1980; *The Financial Times,* November 21 and 23, 1980; *Guardian,* November 24, 1980.

19. *FBIS/DR,* October 30, 1980; *al-Dustur,* November 22, 1980; *Beirut Radio,* November 21, 1980; *al-Ahram,* November 21, 1980; *al-Ra'i* and *The Financial Times,* November 23, 1980.

20. *The Daily Telegraph,* November 24, 1980; *NOW,* December 5, 1980; *MECS 1980–81,* pp. 795–797; Jordan's PM Badran, *al-Dustur,* January 16, 1981; Pakraduni, pp. 230–231.

21. *International Documents on Palestine, 1980* (Beirut: Institute for Palestine Studies, 1983), pp. 314–315; *al-Mustaqbal,* October 20, 1981.

22. *Al-Thawra* (Iraq) and *al-Ra'i,* November 26, 1980; *al-Majalla,* December 13, 1980.

23. *Al-Thawra* (Iraq), November 25, 1980; *al-Dustur,* November 28, 1980; *al-Siyasa,* November 29, 1980.

24. *Al-Dustur* and *al-Ra'i,* November 28, 1980; *al-Siyasa,* November 29, 1980; *al-Nahar,* December 18, 1980, January 24, 1981; King Husain in *al-Watan,* December 18, 1980.

25. Commentaries by *Reuters* and *UPI,* November 25, 1980; *al-Ra'i,* and *Tishrin* (Syria), November 26, 1980; *al-Dustur,* November 28, 1980.

26. Yusif A. Sayigh, "A New Framework for Complementarity among the Arab Economies," in Ibrahim, pp. 147–163.

27. *Al-Watan al-'Arabi* and *al-Dustur,* November 28, 1980; Guecioueur, pp. 177–215.

28. *Al-Majalla,* December 13, 1980; *AP,* December 8, 1980; *Reuters,* December 21, 1980; *The Washington Post,* December 4, 1980; *Damascus Radio,* November 27, 1980; *al-Sharq al-Awsat,* January 2, 1981; *al-Thawra* (Syria), January 9, 23, 1981; Jordan PM's statement, *al-Dustur,* January 16, 1981.

29. *Damascus Radio,* March 25, 1981; *FBIS/DR,* January 25, 1981; *al Ba'th* (Syria), March 10, 1981; *al-Thawra* (Syria), January 23, 1981.

30. SoS Haig to the congressional committees, March 18 and 19, 1981; *FoF,* March 20, 1981; Robert O. Freedman, "Soviet Policy toward the Middle East since Camp David," in his *The Middle East After the Israeli Invasion of Lebanon* (Syracuse: Syracuse University Press, 1986), pp.17–41; *The Middle East,* 86(December 1981), pp. 20–21.

31. *NYT,* March 26, 1981; *Algiers Radio* (in English), March 29, 1981, *FBIS/DR,* March 31, 1981; *IHT,* July 4, 5, 1981.

32. *FoF,* July 10, 1981.

33. *Al-Akhbar* (Jordan), January 22, 1981; B. Maddi-Weitzman, "The Fragmentation of Arab Politics: Inter-Arab Affairs Since the Afganistan Invasion," *Orbis* 25, 2(Summer 1981): pp. 389–407; *The Middle East,* 75 (January, 1981), p. 10; *al-Ra'i al-'Am,* January 29, 1981; *FoF,* February 6, 1981.

34. Freedman, *Ibid.,* p. 33; *The Middle East,* 85 (November 1981), p. 16; *Tripoli Voice of the Arab Homeland,* September 1, 1981; *FBIS/DR,* September 1, 1981.

35. *FoF,* September 25, 1981; *MECS 1980–81,* pp. 244–245; *JNA,* September 19, 1981; *FBIS/DR,* September 1981; Asad's speech, *Damascus Radio,* April 11, 1981, *FBIS/DR,* April 13, 1981.

36. *MECS 1980–81*, pp. 203–204.

37. Helms, pp. 182–183; Hiro, pp. 75–76; R.K. Ramazani, *Revolutionary Iran, Challenge and Response in the Middle East* (Baltimore: The Johns Hopkins University Press, 1986), pp. 39–54, 259.

38. John Christie, "History and Development of the Gulf Cooperation Council: A Brief Overview," in John A. Sandwick (ed.), *The Gulf Cooperation Council* (Boulder: Westview Press, 1987), pp. 7–20; Fuad H. Bsaisu, "Majlis al-Ta'awun al-Khaliji wa-A'faq al-Tawajjuh al-Istratiji al-'Arabi al-Mutawazin," *al-Mustaqbal al-'Arabi*, September 1981, pp. 51–52; *al-Jazira*, February 19, 1981; *al-Nahar al-'Arabi wal-Dawli*, June 1, 1981; *al-Riyad*, May 25, 1985 (Special Supplement).

39. *Al-Thawra* (Iraq), January 6, 1982; Hiro, pp. 55–70; Helms, pp. 172–175.

40. *FoF*, Feb. 5, 1982; Colin Legum et. al. (eds.), *Middle East Contemporary Survey*, Vol. 6, 1981–82 (New York: Holmes and Meier, 1984), pp. 230–231.

41. *Al-Ra'i al-'Aam*, December 13, 1981; *al-Nahar al-'Arabi Wal-Dawli* (Lebanon), January 4, 1982; *NYT*, December 18 and 21, 1981; *al-Jazira*, December 31, 1981; *al-Safir*, January 5, 1982; *al-Dustur* (Britain), February 15, 1982; *al-Thawra* (Iraq), February 16, 1982.

42. *FoF*, January 22, 1982; *al-Sharq al-Awsat*, January 5 and 12, 1982; *Akhbar al-Khalij*, February 2, 1982; Ahmad Iskandar in *Monday Morning*, February 1, 1982; *al-Nahar*, February 14, 1982; *'Ukkaz*, February 14, 1982.

43. *Al-Thawra* (Syria), January 23, 1982; *al-Sharq al-Awsat* January 24, 1982; Interviews, Jordan and Syria's FMs, *al-Majalla*, January 14, 1982; *al-Dustur* (Jordan), February 2, 1982; *Tishrin* (Syria), February 2, 1982; *al-Ba'th* (Syria), January 31 1982; *The Washington Post*, February 1, 1982.

44. *Al-Liwa'* (Jordan), February 17, 1982; *FoF*, February 26, 1982; [The Muslim Brotherhood], *Hamah: Ma'sat al-'Asr allati Faqat Majazir Sabra wa-Shatila* (Cairo: 1984). The number of casualties went up to 30.000; Moshe Ma'oz, "Profile: Hafiz al-Asad of Syria," *Orbis* 31, 2(Summer 1987): p. 215; Thomas L. Friedman, *From Beirut to Jerusalem* (New York: Anchor Books, 1989), pp. 76–87.

45. *Reuters*, February 22, March 7, 1982; *al-Ba'th* (Syria), March 18, 1982; Syrian DM's article, *ibid.*, April 9, 1982.

46. *The Washington Post*, April 9, 1982; *al Ba'th* (Syria) and *al-Nahar*, April 15, 1982; *al-Nahar al-'Arabi Wal-Dawli*, April 19, 1982; *The Financial Times*, April 21, 1982; *NYT*, May 24, 1982. Building the pipelines through Turkey and Saudi Arabia cost $8 billion (Heikal, *Illusions*, p. 94).

47. Until March 1982, the Saudi and Kuwaiti financial aid to Iraq was estimated at $22 billion: *Reuters*, April 18, 19, 21, 1982; *FoF*, No. 2167, May 28, 1982; *MECS 1981–82*, p. 234. The Gulf monarchies' average aid to Syria was $1.1 billion a year (*ibid.*, p. 217); Aharon Levran, "Syria's Military Strength and Capability," *Middle East Review* 19, 3(Spring 1987): p. 10.

48. *Ha'aretz*, July 2, 1987, translated from *Die Zeit* (n.d.); *NYT*, November 8, 1987; Mahmud Riyad in *al-Musawwar*, November 7, 1987.

49. *'Ukkaz*, May 17, 1982; *MECS 1981–82*, pp. 234–235; *Riyad Radio*, May 31, 1982; *Reuters* May 17, 1982.

50. A similar request was made by the Somalis following the entry of Ethiopian forces into their territory during their fighting in July 1982 (*al-Safir*, November 29,

1981); *al-Hawadith*, December 4, 1981; *al-Watan al-'Arabi*, January 27, February 4, 1983.

51. *Baghdad Radio*, June 9 and 10, 1982; *FoF*, No. 2174, July 16, 1982; *MECS 1981–82*, p. 235.

52. *Al-Nahar* and *al-Mustaqbal*, September 11, 1982; *al-Hawadith* and *al-Watan al-'Arabi*, September 17, 1982.

53. Ahmad Iskandar in Tehran, *AP*, September 10, 1982; *al-Ba'th* (Syria), September 9, 1982; *Amman Radio*, September 14, 1982; *al-Anba'* (Morocco), September 13, 1982.

54. *Tishrin* (Syria), August 26, 1985; *al-Thawra* (Syria), August 12, 1985.

55. *Newsweek*, September 21, 1987; Levran, pp. 8–9; *Ha'aretz*, October 27, 1986; May 6, 1987, estimated Syria's expenditures on defense, without arms procurement, at 25 percent of its GNP; *NYT Magazine*, April 1, 1990, p. 44; Helena Cobban, *The Superpowers and the Syrian-Israeli Conflict* (Washington, D.C.: Praeger, 1991), p. 38.

56. Syria's debt to Iran was $1.5 million for five years of oil shipments at reduced price which had not been paid (Kienle, pp. 167–168); *MECS 1986*, pp. 95–100.

57. *MECS 1986*, pp. 98–99.

58. *NYT*, October 4, 10, 28, 1987; *Ha'aretz*, October 18, 1987; *al-Fajr*, November 8, 1987; Kienle, pp. 168–169; I. Rabinovich and H. Shaked (eds.), *Middle East Contemporary Survey*, Vol. XI, 1987 (Boulder: Westview Press, 1989), pp. 121–122.

59. *Al-Ra'i* (Jordan), September 21, 1987.

60. *Al-Jazira*, November 3, 1987; *Jordan Times*, November 11, 1987.

61. *Al-Ittihad*, April 13, and October 24, 1987; *al-Siyasa*, October 27, 1987; *al-Jazira*, October 26, November 2, 1987; *The Sunday Times*, October 25, 1987; *al-Ra'i al-'Am*, November 7, 1987.

62. "Gaddafi Desperate for Friends," *Middle East and Mediterranean Outlook*, 44 (December 1987); *NYT*, October 9, 1987.

63. *Al-Jazira*, November 1, 3, 1987; The siege was lifted as a gesture to the "Palestinian struggle" in the Occupied Territories (*Times*, January 18, 1988).

64. *Al-Sharq al-Awsat*, October 7, 1987; *al-Musawwar*, November 7, 1987; *al-Watan* and *al-Jazira*, November 1, 1987; *Shu'un Filastiniyya*, 176–177 (November-December 1987), p. 115; *al-Quds* and *al-Nahar* (Jerusalem), November 7, 8, 1987;

65. *Al-Ra'i al-'Am*, November 7, 1987; *Shu'un Filastiniyya, op. cit.*, pp. 116–117.

66. Text of the concluding statement, *al-Ra'i*, and *al-Jazira*, November 12, 1987; Excerpts from the secret resolutions, *al-Yawm al-Sabi'*, November 23, 1987; *al-Qabas*, November 25, 1987.

67. *Damascus Radio*, November 11, 1987, *FBIS/DR*, November 13, 1987; *al-Thawra* (Syria), November 14, 1987; *al-Qabas*, December 24, 1987.

68. *Al-Ra'i al-'Am* and *al-Anba'*, November 11, 1987, *FBIS/DR*, November 13, 1987; *al-Quds*, November 12, 1987; *al-Tadamun*, November 21, 1987; *al-Kifah al-'Arabi*, December 14, 1987; James Bruce and Tony Banks, "Middle East: after the Amman Summit," *Janes Defence Weekly*, December 5, 1987, p. 1323.

69. An official Saudi statement, *al-Jazira*, November 3, 4, 1987; *Ha'aretz*, April 7, 1986, May 6, 1987; *al-Quds*, November 5, 1987; King Husain's press conference,

Amman Television, November 11, 1987, *FBIS/DR,* November 13, 1987; *AFP,* November 14, 1987.

13. Crossroads of the Lebanon War

1. Bakraduni, pp. 95–105; Avi-Ran, pp. 74–76.
2. Bakraduni, pp. 155–159, 168, 177–180, 206; Arie Naor, *Memshala Bemilhama* (Tel Aviv: Lahav, 1986), pp. 18–19; *al-Nahar,* October 18, 1978; Avi-Ran, pp. 88–94.
3. Bakraduni, pp. 201–211; *al-Watan al-'Arabi,* November 5, 1979; *al-Anwar,* November 21, 1979.
4. *Al-Nahar* and *al-Bairaq,* November 12, 1979; Bakraduni, p. 210–213.
5. *MENA,* November 18, 1979; Bakraduni, pp. 212–214.
6. *Al-Mustaqbal,* December 1, 1979; *al-Riyad,* December 10, 1979.
7. The burden of aid was to be divided as follows: Saudi Arabia, $114 million (28 percent); Kuwait, $63 million (16 percent); Libya, $63 million (16 percent) Iraq, $60 million (15 percent); UAE, $46 million (12 percent); Algeria, $28 million (7 percent); and Qatar, $26 million (6 percent) (*al-Anwar,* March 27, 1980; *al-Hawadith,* March 21, 1980).
8. *Al-Nahar,* November 24, 1979; *al-Liwa',* November 22, 1979; *al-Anba'* (Kuwait), November 25, 1979.
9. *Al-Nahar,* December 12, 1979, and January 17, 1980; *al-Bairaq,* January 17, 1980; Bakraduni, p. 209, 236; *MECS 1980–81,* p. 673.
10. *Al-Safir,* January 29, 1981; *al-Watan al-'Arabi,* February 6, 1981; *al-Nahar,* March 25, 1981.
11. Ze'ev Schiff and Ehud Ya'ari, *Israel's Lebanon War* (New York: Simon and Schuster, 1984), pp. 32–35; *FoF,* April 10, 17, 1981; Avi-Ran, p. 119.
12. *Al-Ba'th* (Syria), May 22, 1981; Freedman, *ibid.,* pp. 30–31; Schiff and Ya'ari, *Lebanon,* pp. 34–37; Bakraduni, pp. 242–244; Avi-Ran, pp. 122–123.
13. *Al-Ra'i, al-Ahram,* May 7, 1981; *al-Sharq al-Awsat, al-Bilad,* May 13, 1981; *al-Siyasa,* May 24, 1981; *al-Nahar,* June 9, 1981; *MECS 1980–81,* pp. 135, 676–677; *al-Ahram,* May 15, 1981; Bakraduni, p. 244.
14. Jumayyil's call, *AP,* November 29, 1981; al-Wazzan's reaction, *al-Usbu' al-'Arabi,* December 12, 1981; *al-Watan al-'Arabi wal-Dawli,* January 29, 1982; *al-Nahar,* January 21, 24, 1982; *al-Safir,* January 21, 1982; Bakraduni, pp. 233, 236, 245–247.
15. *LAT,* July 5, 1981; editorial, *'Ukkaz,* August 8, 1981; *MECS 1980–81,* pp. 302–305.
16. *Al-Bairaq,* December 21, 25, 1982; *Al-Sharq,* January 14, 1982; Bakraduni, p. 250. On the Fez summit, see below.
17. *Reuters,* March 18, 1982; *al-Khalij,* January 12, 1982; *al-Sharq al-Awsat,* December 29, 1981; *al-Ittihad,* January 26, 1982; *al-Nahar,* March 7, 1982; *al-Ra'i al-'Am,* February 9, 1982; Schiff and Ya'ari, *Lebanon,* p. 31; *NYT,* February 9, 1982; *Time,* February 27, 1982; *The Daily Telegraph,* April 14, 1982; Naor, pp. 25–31; Avi-Ran, p. 124, 148–149; Seale, *Asad,* p.371.

18. Naor, pp. 15–17; Avi-Ran, pp. 151–152; Seale, *Asad*, pp. 380; Aharon Yariv, "Milhemet Breira—Milhemet Beleit Breira," in his (ed.) *Milhemet Breira* (Tel Aviv: Hakibutz Hameuhad, 1985), pp. 9–29.

19. *MECS 1981–1982*, pp. 248–251; Abu Iyad to *Al-Shark al-Awsat*, September 23, 1982; *Amman Radio*, June 14, 1982, by *AP,* June 15, 1982; Avi-Ran, p. 133; Seale, *Asad*, p. 403.

20. Bakraduni, p. 272; *AFP,* June 8, 1982; Reports by *AP; Reuters, QNA,* and *INA,* June 27, 1982.

21. *MECS 1981–1982*, p. 251; Bakraduni, pp. 262–263; Naor, pp. 118, 127–128, 136, 145.

22. On the proceedings of Reagan and Shultz's meeting with the Syrian and Saudi FMs in Washington on July 20, see *al-Safir,* September 10, 1982. See also *al-Majalla,* June 15, 1983; *FoF,* June 11-July 2, 1982; ALGS Qulaibi, in *al-Mustakbal,* September 4, 1982; Alexander M. Haig, *Caveat: Realism, Reagan and Foreign Policy* (New York: Macmillan, 1984), p. 342.

23. Schiff and Ya'ari, *Lebanon,* p. 208; Rashid Khalidi, *Under Siege: PLO Decisionmaking During the 1982 War* (New York: Columbia University Press, 1985), pp. 68–69, 83, 86–87, 114–115, 124, 135–137, 183–184; Bakraduni, pp. 260–261; *NYT,* July 10, 1982; Khalid al-Hasan to *al-Hawadith,* September 3, 1982.

24. *MENA,* June 17, 1982; *al-Siyasa* (Egypt), August 25, 1982; *al-Watan al-'Arabi,* August, 13, 1982; *UNSC Provisional* S/15317, July 28, 1982; Khalidi, *Under Siege,* pp. 151–159; *FoF,* July 16, 1982; *al-Safir,* September 10, 1982.

25. Khalidi, *Under Siege,* pp.94–95; 139–140; *FoF,* August 6, 1982; *AP,* July 29, 1982; .

26. *FoF,* August 13, 1982; Schiff and Ya'ari, *Lebanon,* p. 224; Khalidi, *Under Siege,* p. 151; 'Abdalla al-Ahmar to *al-Thawra* (Syria), August 18, 1982; Khalid al-Hasan to *al-Hawadith,* September 3, 1982; *al-Safir,* September 10, 1982.

27. *FoF,* September 3, 1982; *al-Safir,* September 10, 1982.

28. *NYT,* August 8, 1982; *FoF,* September 3, 1982; Naor, pp. 141, 158–159, 146–147.

29. *Al-Nahar,* August 30 and 31, 1982; commentary, *al-Ba'th* (Syria), August 30, 1982; *FoF,* July 30, 1982; *al-Mustaqbal,* September 4, 11, 18, 1982; For the FM's proceedings, *al-Watan al-'Arabi,* January 27, February 4, 11, 25, 1983;

30. *Al-Nahar,* September 11, 1982; *al-Hawadith* and *al-Watan al-'Arabi,* September 17, 1982; *al-Bayan,* September 7, 1982; *AFP,* September 8, 1982; *MENA,* September 17, 1982.

31. *'Ukkaz,* September 12, 1982; *al-Anba'* (Morocco), September 13, 1982.

32. Schiff and Ya'ari, *Lebanon,* pp. 253–285; *al-Watan* (Kuwait), September 26, 1982; *INA;* September 22, 1982: *SNA,* September 23, 1982; Seale, *Asad,* pp. 392–393.

33. Dan Horowitz, "Israel's War in Lebanon: new Patterns of Strategic Thinking and Civilian-Military Relations," *JSS* 6 (September 1983): pp. 83–102.

34. *Al-Ba'th* (Syria), January 20, 1983; Elie Chalala, "Syrian Policy in Lebanon, 1976–1984: Moderate Goals and Pragmatic Means," *JAA* 4, 1(1985): p. 80; Adeed Dawisha, "The Motives of Syria's Involvement In Lebanon," *MEJ* 38, 2(Spring 1984): pp. 228–236.

35. Abu Iyad's interview, *al-Tadamun,* September 14, 1985; Yezid Sayigh,

"Azmat al-Khalij wa-Ikhfaq al-Nizam Al-Iqlimi al 'Arabi," *al-Mustaqbal al-'Arabi*, July 1991, pp. 8–10; 'Ali, pp. 339–340.

36. Roberto Aliboni, "The Inter-Arab Picture in 1985: A European View," *The International Spectator* 20, 3/4 (July–December 1985): p. 58–59; *al-Ba'th* (Syria), January 20, 1983.

37. Editorials in *al-Ba'th* (Syria), August, 15, 16, November 25, 29, December 1, 1982; PM al-Kazm in, *ibid.*, October 31, 1982; *Tishrin* (Syria), November 3, 6, 9, 1982; Asad's speech, *ibid.*, August 5, 1985; *al-Thawra* (Syria), November 11, 1982; DM Tlas to *Tishrin*, November 16, 1983.

38. Z. Ma'oz, "The Evolution of Syrian Power, 1948–1984," in M. Ma'oz and A. Yaniv (eds.), *Syria Under Assad* (London: Croom Helm, 1986), pp. 78–80; Kais Firro, "The Syrian Economy under the Assad Regime," *ibid.*, p. 63; Ma'oz, *Asad*, pp. 59, 179.

39. *Al-Safir*, January 20, 1983; Rashid Khalidi, "The Assad Regime and the Palestinian Resistance," *ASQ* 6, 4(1984): pp. 259–266; Dawisha, "The Motives of Syria," pp. 228–236; Rouleau, pp. 144–145; Jiryis (1985), pp. 28–29; al-Hasan, p. 94.

40. *Al-Thawra* (Syria), November 6, 1982; *Tishrin* (Syria), November 6, 19, 1982, May 18, 30, 1983; *al-Ba'th* (Syria), November 25, 29, and December 1, 1982; *al-Safir*, May 16, 1983; *al-Shira'*, May 23, 1983.

41. Augustus R. Norton, *Amal and the Shi'a, The Struggle for the Soul of Lebanon* (Austin: University of Texas Press, 1987), p. 94.

42. Colin Legum et. al. (eds.), *Middle East Contemporary Survey*, Vol. 7, 1982–83 (New York: Holmes and Meier, 1985), pp. 690–696; Seale, *Asad*. pp. 408–410.

43. Avi-Ran, pp. 160–164.

44. Avi-Ran, p. 167; Norton, pp. 46–52, 66, 87–106.

45. Avi-Ran, p. 174.

46. *FoF*, January 18, 1985, pp. 17–18; My own experience as a member of Israel's delegation to the Naqura talks.

47. Rouleau, pp. 138–154; Alain Gresh, *The PLO, The Struggle Within* (London: Zed Books, 1985), p. 232; Bruce Hoffman, "The Plight of the Phoenix: The PLO Since Lebanon," *Conflict Quarterly* 5, 2(Spring 1985): pp. 5–17; *LAT*, February 6, 1983, p. 2.

48. Abu-Iyad to *al-Tadamun*, September 14, 1985; the PLO's PNC resolutions, *JPS* 16, 4(Summer 1987): pp. 201–204; Jiryis (1987), p. 266.

49. 'Arafat's interview under siege, *al-Hawadith*, October 14, 1983; *The Guardian*, October 31, 1983.

50. *Al-Thawra* (Iraq), November 30, 1983; Saddam Husain to INA, December 2, 83, *FBIS/DR*, December 5, 1983; *al-Siyasa* (Kuwait), December 1, 1983; *'Ukkaz*, November 18, 1983; *al-Ahram*, December 4, 1983; *al-Dustur* (Jordan), December 1, 1983.

51. 'Arafat to *Ruz al-Yusuf*, December 4, 1983; *MENA*, December 5, 1983, *FBIS/DR*, December 5, 1983; *QNA*, February 6, 1984, *DR*, February 6, 1984; *al-Hadaf*, February 20, 1984; Abu Iyad to *al-Tadamun*, September 14, 1985.

52. A. Susser, "The PLO," in H. Shaked and D. Dishon (eds.), *Middle East Contemporary Survey*, Vol. 8, 1983–84 (Tel Aviv: Tel Aviv University, 1986), p. 197.

53. A. Susser, "The Palestine Liberation Organization," in I. Rabinovich and H. Shaked (eds.), *Middle East Contmporary Survey,* Vol. 9, 1984–85 (Tel Aviv: Tel Aviv University, 1987), p. 219; *al-Watan,* May 21, 1985; *al-Safir,* May 22, 1985.

54. *Al-Nahar; al-Sharq al-Awsat; al-Safir,* June 10, 1985.

55. *Shu'un Filastiniyya,* 150–151 (September–October 1985), pp. 113–118; *al-Jazira,* November 1, 3, 1987; *Times,* January 18, 1988; J. Teitelbaum, "The Palestine Liberation Organization," *MECS 1986,* p. 195.

56. *Al-Jazira,* November 2, 1987, on UN economic survey of Lebanon. For the Amman summit, see below.

57. *Al-Nahar,* November 5–6, 1987; *al-Jazira,* November 12, 1987; *Algiers Radio,* November 12, 1985, *FBIS/DR,* November 13, 1985; *al-Qabas,* November 10, 1987; *Shu'un Filastiniyya, op. cit.,* pp. 120–121; *Beirut Radio,* November 10, 1987, in *FBIS/DR,* November 12, 1987.

14. In Search of Another Peace Process

1. *Al-Ra'i,* November 14 and 23, 1979; *al-Dustur,* November 7, 21, 1979; *al-Ittihad* and *al-Anwar,* November 8, 1979; *NYT,* September 8, 11, 1979; *al-Watan al-'Arabi,* September 20, 1979; *al-Hawadith,* November 11, 1979; President-elect Reagan's statement, *Reuters,* November 13, 1980.

2. 'Arafat's, Kreisky's, and Willy Brandt's joint communique, *Filastin al-Thawra,* July 10, 1979; Uri Avnery, *My Friend the enemy* (London: Zed Books, 1986), pp. 172–183.

3. *MENA,* August 6, 1981, *FBIS/DR,* August 7, 1981; *FoF,* August 7, 14, 1981.

4. *SANA,* August 8, 1981; *al-Nahar,* August 8, 1981; Fahd's interview, *al-Hawadith,* December 4, 1981.

5. *Al-Nahar,* August 8, 1981; Kuwait's FM on the Fahd Plan, *al-Yamama,* August 14, 1981; *al-Ra'i al-'Am,* November 17, 1981.

6. *SPA* from Riyad, October 5, *FBIS/DR,* October 6, 1981; *FoF,* November 6, 1981.

7. *'Ukkaz,* August 11, 1981; 'Arafat's interview, *GNA,* November 17, 1981; *FBIS/DR,* November 17, 1981; *al-Nahar,* October 18, 30, 1981; *al-Safir,* November 9, 1981.

8. 'Arafat's interview, *Beirut,* October 30, 1981; *FoF,* November 6, 1981; "Mubadarat Fahd wal-Hiwarat al-Filastiniyya Bisha'niha," *Shu'un Filastiniyya* 121(December 1981) pp. 186–189; Cobban, *The PLO,* pp. 113–115.

9. *Al-Bayan,* November 12, 1981; *al-Sharq al-Awsat,* November 12–13, 1981.

10. *Ha'aretz,* November 20, 1981; *Voice of Palestine,* November 1981; *FBIS/DR,* November 19, 1981; *al-Thawra* (Syria), November 18, 1981.

11. *Al-Wattan al-'Arabi,* November 27, 1981; *al-Safir,* November 29, 1981; *al-Mustaqbal,* December 5, 1981. The FMs' proceedings, *al-Safir,* November 29–30, 1981; *al-Hawadith,* December 4, 1981.

12. *Ha'aretz,* November 23, 1981; *al-Siyasa,* November 26, 1981.

13. King Hasan's statement, *al-Hawadith,* December 4, 1981. The summit's proceedings, *al-Mustaqbal,* December 5, 1981.

14. *Akhbar al-Yawm,* September 4, 1982; *al-Ahram,* September 6, 1982; *Ruz al-Yusuf,* September 13, 1982; *al-Musawwar,* September 10, 1982; Khalid al-Hasan, in *al-Hawadith,* September 3, 1982; *The Washington Post,* August 28, 1982.

15. *Al-Mustakbal,* September 4, 11, 1982; *Reuter,* September 6, 1982; King Hasan's statement, *Rabat Radio,* September 10, 1982.

16. *Al-'Amal* (Lebanon), August 31, 1982; *Reuter,* August 31, 1982; *INA,* September 6, 1982; *al-Mustakbal,* September 11, 18, 1982; *Monte Carlo Radio,* September 7, 1982 (7 P.M.). On the summit deliberations, see *al-Nahar,* September 11, 1982; *al-Hawadith,* September 17, 1982; *al-Watan al-'Arabi,* September 17, 1982.

17. *Al-Ba'th* (Syria), August 30, 1982; *al-Bayan,* September 7, 1982; *MENA,* September 17, 1982, and *AFP,* September 8, 1982.

18. *Al-Anba'* (Morocco), September 13, 1982.

19. *Tishrin* (Syria), September 12, 1982;. Editorial in *al-Thawra* (Syria), September 16, 1982; *MECS 1981–82,* p. 255.

20. Syria's Minister of Information in Tehran, *AP,* September 10, 1982; *al-Ba'th* (Syria), September 9, 1982; *Amman Radio,* September 14, 1982; King Hasan's comments, *al-Anba'* (Morocco), September 13, 1982.

21. *FoF,* September 10, 1982; *al-Anba'* (Morocco), September 13, 1982.

22. In 1979–84, the committee received $378.3 million from oil-rich Arab states for distribution among Palestinians in the occupied territories. In 1980–85, the committee distributed $430 million. See ch.2, note 55.

23. *Al-Watan* (Kuwait), September 21, 1982; *FoF,* September 17, 1982; *al-Usbu' Al-'Arabi* October 18, 1982; *al-Ra'i,* February 20, 1986

24. Husain's interview, *al-Watan* (Kuwait), September 30, 1982; Aaron D. Miller, "Jordan and the Arab-Israeli Conflict: The Hashemite Predicament," *Orbis* 29, 4 (Winter 1986): pp. 815–816.

25. Jiryis (1985), pp. 19–20. Fakahani is that part of Beirut where the PLO's headquarters were located.

26. *Fikr,* 6 (June 1985): p. 39; *MECS 1982–83,* pp. 296–298; Cobban, *The PLO,* p. 134; *al-Watan al-'Arabi,* April 22, 1983; 'Arafat in *al-Sharq al-Awsat,* March 1, 1985, and *al-Ahram,* February 21, 1985; Abu Iyad in *al-Tadamun,* September 14, 1985; al-Hasan, pp. 81–86, 102–103; Rouleau, pp. 147–151.

27. Al-Hasan, pp. 81–86, 136–139; *South,* January 1983, pp. 9–10; *'Akhir Sa'a,* November 2, 1983; King Husain in *al-Ra'i,* February 20, 1986; July 13, 1986; Jiryis (1985), p. 26.

28. *JPS* 12, 3 (Spring 1983): pp. 251–252.

29. *Al-Watan al-'Arabi,* April 15, 22, 1983; *al-Mawqif al-'Arabi,* May 2, 1983; al-Hasan, p. 93.

30. A draft agreement with 'Arafat's handwritten amendments, *al-Mawqif al-'Arabi,* May 2, 1983; *al-Watan al-'Arabi,* April 15, 1983; *al-Ra'i,* April 11, 1983.

31. 'Arafat to *al-Watan al-'Arabi,* November 30, 1984; Jiryis (1985), p. 41; Seale, *Asad,* p. 465; *Filastin al-Thawra,* December 8, 1984; King Husain's opening speech at the PNC, *FBIS/DR,* November 26, 1984, pp. 13–18.

32. Al-Hasan, pp. 104–115, 158–159; *Shu'un Filastiniyya* 148–149 (July–August 1985), p. 109.

33. Abu-Iyad to *al-Tadamun,* September 14, 1985; *Shu'un Filastiniyya* 144–145

(March–April 1985): pp. 117–124; *ibid.,* 148–149 (July-August 1985): p. 109; *FoF,* March 1, 1985; *al-Hurriyya,* March 3, 1985, p. 35.

34. *Al-Ba'th* (Syria), July 29, 1985; *al-Thawra* (Syria), July 19, August 6, 1985.

35. *Al-Nahar,* July 28, 1985; *Shu'un Filastiniyya* 150–151 (September–October 1985), p.145.

36. *Al-Dustur* (Jordan), August 8, 1985; *al-Nahar,* August 8–9, 1985.

37. *Shu'un Filastiniyya* 150–151 (September–October 1985): pp. 123–125; *al-Watan,* August 11, 1985; *The Economist,* August 10, 1985; *al-Dustur* (Jordan), August 19, 1985; *al-Sharq al-Awsat,* August 22, 1985.

38. King Husain's speech, *al-Ra'i,* February 20, 1986.

39. *Al-Sharq al-Awsat,* May 12, 1985; *al-Safir,* May 31, 1985; Abu Iyad in *Filastin al-Thawra,* September 7, 1985, and *al-Tadamun,* September 14, 1985.

40. *Al-Tadamun,* September 14, 1985; *NYT,* July 15, 1985; King Husain's speech, *al-Ra'i,* February 20, 1986.

41. *Al-Sharq al-Awsat,* August 22, September 1, 1985; Abu Iyad in *Filastin al-Thawra,* September 7, 1985; *Shu'un Filastiniyya* 108–109 (May–June 1986), pp. 82–86.

42. King Husain's speech, *al-Ra'i,* February 20, 1986; *al-Dustur* (Jordan), November 1, 1986; The Hahsemite Kingdom of Jordan, Ministry of Planning, *A Program for Economic and Social Development in the Occupied Territories 1986–1990* (Amman), November 1986.

43. *MECS 1986,* pp. 64–66.

44. *Filastin al-Thawra,* March 15, December 1, 1986.

45. *Filastin al-Thawra,* May 2, 1987; Jordan's official reaction, *Sawt al-Sha'b,* April 22, 1987.

46. Jiryis (1987), pp. 2–16; The 18th PNC resolutions, *JPS* 16, 4(Summer 1987), pp. 201–204; *Jordan Times,* April 29, 1987.

47. Hamied Ansari, "Egypt in Search of A New Role in the Middle East," *American-Arab Affairs* 12 (1985): pp. 46–49; Aliboni, p. 60; King Husain's speech, *al-Ra'i,* February 20, 1986; *Davar,* February 25, 1985; *'Al Hamishmar,* June 10–11, 1985.

48. *MECS 1986,* pp. 66–68, 101–102; King Hasan revealed that at his invitation, PM Rabin had visited Morocco and met with him already in 1976, *Washington Post,* February 7, 1992; Rabin's approval, *Ha'aretz,* February 9, 1992.

49. *MECS 1987,* pp. 78–79; *Ha'aretz,* 7 February, 1993.

50. Amos Elon, "A Letter from Israel," *The New Yorker,* July 27, 1987, pp. 33–34.

51. *Al-Hurriyya,* November 8, 1987; *al-Nahar,* November 2, 1987; *al-Jazira,* October 31, 1987; *al-Bayan,* November 28–29, 1987.

52. *NYT,* October 15, 22; November 7, 1987.

53. 'Arafat in *al-Yawm al-Sabi',* November 23, 1987; *al-Quds,* November 12, 1987; *Shu'un Filastiniyya* 166–167 (November–December 1987): p. 119.

54. *NYT,* November 12, 1987; *al-Fajr* (Jerusalem), November 15, 1987; *al-Hurriyya,* November 15, 1987.

55. *Al-Nahar,* November 8–11, 1987; *al-Fajr, ibid.; al-Yawm al-Sabi',* November 23, 1987; *al-Ahram,* October 27, 1987.

56. *Al-Fajr, ibid.; al-Ahram,* October 27, 1987; *Monte Carlo Radio,* November 12, 1987, in *FBIS/DR,* November 13, 1987.

57. Tunisian PM Mazali in *al-Yawm* (Saudi Arabia), December 24, 1981; *Akhbar al-Yawm* (Egypt), January 30, 1982; *al-Dustur* (Jordan), March 31, 1982; M.H. Heikal estimated that the Israel-Egypt peace treaty had no future after April 1982, *QNA*, March 22, 1982.

58. Mubarak's interview with Walter Cronkite, *MENA*, October 8, *FBIS/DR*, October 10, 1981; Mubarak, by *MENA*, February 9, 1982; ALSG Qulaibi in *al-Khalij*, January 20, 1982.

59. Ali E. H. Dessouki, "Egypt and the Peace Process," *International Journal* 45, 3(1990): pp. 557–558; Shimon Shamir, "Basic Dilemmas of the Mubarak Regime," *Orbis* 30 (1986): pp. 169–188.

60. *Al-Hawadith*, April 16, 1982; Sa'ud al-Faisal's interview, *Lebanese Television*, November 8, 1981; *MECS 1981–82*, pp. 237–238; *al-Dustur* (Jordan), March 31, 1982.

61. King Husain's interview, *al-Ahram*, May 6, 1982; *QNA*, April 26, 1982, May 1, 1982; *Reuters*, May 5, 1982; *Sawt al-'Arab* (Egypt), May 17, 1982; *al-Thawra* (Syria), May 2, 1982; *SNA*, May 10. 1982; *al Ba'th* (Syria), May 19, 1982; *MECS 1981–82*, pp. 227–229, 246.

62. *Al-Nahar*, October 7, 1982; *MECS 1981–82*, p. 239.

63. *Al-Nahda* (Kuwait), July 17, 1982; *al-Nahar al-'Arabi wal-Dawli*, October 4, 1982; *al Mustakbal*, September 4, 1982; *MECS 1981–82*, p. 253; Numairi's interview, *al-Ayyam* (Sudan), August 27, 1982.

64. Liz Thurgood, "Islamic Moderates Welcome Egypt," *MEED* 28, 4, (January 27, 1984): pp. 12–13; Jim Muir, "Why Husain Crossed the Bridge to Cairo," *MEI* 235 (October 12, 1985): pp. 13–15; *MEED*, January 27, 1984, p. 13; Amatzia Baram, "Ideology and Power Politics in Syrian-Iraqi Relations," in Yaniv and Ma'oz, p. 137; Heikal, *Illusions*, pp. 91–93.

65. *Al-siyasa*, January 20–21, October 27, 1987; *al-Ittihad*, April 13, October 24, 1987; *al-Jazira*, October 26, November 2, 1987; *Sunday Times*, October 25, 1987; *al-Kifah al-'Arabi*, December 14, 1987; *The Guardian*, January 9, 1988.

66. Mubarak's statement, *al-Jazira*, December 16, 1987.

67. Jordan FM's comment, *al-Mustaqbal*, November 21, 1987, and Iran's response, *NYT*, November 13, 1987; Abba Eban's comments, *ibid.*, November 17, 1987.

15. The Intifada and New Regional Alignment

1. Ami Ayalon and Haim Shaked (eds.), *Middle East Contemporary Survey*, Vol. XII, 1988 (Boulder: Westview Press, 1990), p. 5; Lamis Andoni, "The PLO at the Crossroads," *JPS* 21, 1(Autumn 1991): p. 54.

2. Bernard Lewis, "Rethinking The Middle East," *Foreign Affairs*, 71, 4(Fall 1992): p. 101; Ann M. Lesch, "Contrasting Reactions to the Persian Gulf Crisis: Egypt, Syria, Jordan and the Palestinians," *MEJ* 45, 1(Winter 1990): pp. 39–48; Heikal, *Illusions*, pp. 16–18, 156.

3. King Husain's lament on the U.S. peace initiative in the Algiers summit, *Amman Domestic Service*, June 8, 1988: in *FBIS/DR*, June 9, 1988; *MECS 1988*, pp. 559–560.

4. *Middle East Report* (May–June 1988), p. 47; Sh. Mishal and R. Aharoni, *Speaking Stones, Communiques from the Intifada Underground* (Syracuse: Syracuse University Press, 1994), pp. 68–69, 73, 78–79, 88–89, 99; *MECS 1988*, p. 139.

5. *MECS 1988*, pp. 16–20.

6. Mishal and Aharoni, pp. 65, 67–69, 78–80; *MECS 1988*, pp. 85–91.

7. Laurie Brand, "The Intifada and the Arab World: Old Players, New Roles," *International Journal* XLV (Summer 1990): pp. 503–504; Gregory Gause, "The Arab World and the Intifada," in Robert O. Freedman (ed.), *The Intifada: Its Impact on Israel, the Arab World, and the Superpowers* (Miami: Florida International University Press, 1991), p. 198; *MECS 1988*, p. 580; *The Economist*, May 14, 1988.

8. Brand, *ibid.*, pp. 517–518; Fred Lawson, "Syria," in Rex Brynen (ed.), *Echoes of the Intifada: Regional Repercussions of the Palestinian-Israeli Conflict* (Boulder: Westview Press, 1991), p. 226; Rashid Khalidi, "The PLO and the Uprising," *Middle East Report* 154, (September–October 1988): pp. 22–23; *The Economist*, April 30, 1988; *The Times*, April 26, 1988.

9. Gause, p. 193; *MECS 1988*, pp. 141–142.

10. *MECS 1988*, pp. 143, 148; *Beirut Voice of Lebanon*, June 8–9, 1988, *FBIS/DR*, June 9, 1988; *KUNA*, June 11, 1988; *ibid.*, June 13, 1988.

11. *Amman Dommestic Service*, June 8, 1988, *FBIS/DR*, June 9, 1988; *MECS 1988*, p. 168.

12. *Amman Domestic Service*, June 8, *FBIS/DR*, June 9, 1988; *al-Ra'i*, June 8, 1988; *MECS 1988*, p. 143.

13. *Al-Ra'i al-'Am*, June 11, 1988; *The Times*, and *NYT*, June 9, 1988; *Algiers Television Service*, June 9, 1988; *FBIS/DR*, June 10, 1988; *al-Qabas*, June 23, 1988; *MECS 1988*, p. 171.

14. *Al-Ahram*, October 19, 1988; *al-Muharrir*, November 25, 1989; *al-Watan*, October 13, 1989; *al-Jumhuriyya* (Iraq), August 28, 1991; *al-Majalla*, April 5, 1989; 'Abd al-Rahman Munif, *Al-Dimuqratiyya Awwalan, al-Dimuqratiyya Da'iman* (Beirut: al-Mu'assasa al-'Arabiyya lil-Dirasat wal-Nashr, 1992), p. 33.

15. Schirin H. Fathi, *Al-'Amil al-Filastini fi al-Intikhabat al-Barlamania al-Urduniyya lil-'Am 1989* (Jerusalem: PASSIA, 1990), pp. 8–11; Gause, p. 200; *MECS 1988*, pp. 589–590.

16. Lamis Andoni, "Jordan," in Brynen, *Echoes of the Intifada*, p. 170; *MECS 1988*, pp. 597–599; *MEI*, August 26, 1988, pp. 19–20.

17. *The Economist*, November 12, 1988; Gause, p. 202; Andoni, pp. 173–176.

18. *Ziad Abu-Amr, Islamic Fundamentalism in the West Bank and Gaza* (Bloomington: Indiana University Press, 1994), pp. 65–73; Matti Steinberg, "The PLO and Palestinian Islamic Fundamentalism," *The Jerusalem Quarterly* 52, (Fall 1989): pp. 43–46.

19. *Al-Quds*, February 2, 9, 1989; Andoni, in Brynen, *Echoes*, pp. 178–181; Gause, p. 204; Brand, "The intifada,", pp. 510–512.

20. Fathi, pp. 21–23; *MECS 1989*, p. 463.

21. *The Economist*, November 19, 1988; *MECS 1988*, pp. 91–94.

22. Elyakim Rubinstein, *Yozmat Hashalom Shel Memshele Israel Mahi?* (State of Israel, Information Center, Jerusalem, 1989); *WAKH*, May 20, 1990, *FBIS/DR*, May 22, 1990.

23. *Al-Anba'* (Kuwait), May 22, 1989; 'Arafat's speech, *Baghdad Voice of the PLO,* May 25, 1989; *FBIS/DR,* May 26, 1989; Brand, "Intifada," p. 517; Gause, p. 207.

24. *Al-Jumhuriyya* (Egypt), February 8, 1990; *al-Akhbar,* February 17, 1990; *al-Ahram,* February 12, 1990; *Sawt al-Bilad,* February 15, 1990.

25. Abu-Amr, pp. 69–75; Ami Ayalon (ed.), *Middle East Contemporary Survey,* Volume XIV, 1990 (Boulder: Westview Press, 1992), pp. 115–116, 120.

26. Mahmud Muharib, "Tahjir al-Yahud Wal-Salam al-Mafqud," *Qadaya* 3(May 1990): pp. 3–18; Interview, 'Adnan Abu-'Awda—King Husain's advisor—*al-Hayat,* February 1 1990.

27. *MECS 1990,* pp.137–142, 235–236.

28. *Tishrin* (Syria), June 5, 1988; *al-Ittihad* (Abu Dhabi), May 31, 1988; *al-Wafd,* June 11, 1988; *FBIS/DR,* June 14, 1988.

29. *Al-Ittihad,* May 31, 1988; *FBIS/DR,* June 1, 1988.

30. *AFP,* June 25, 1988; *RBIS/DR,* June 27, 1988; *MECS, 1988,* p. 144; *Damascus Domestic Service,* June 10, 1988, *FBIS/DR,* June 13, 1988.

31. O. Romadhani, "The Arab Maghreb Union: Toward North African Integration," *Arab-American Affairs* 28 (Spring 1989): pp. 43–45; G. O'Reilly, "The Greater Maghreb Union: Geo-Strategic and Geo-Political Significance," *Middle East Strategic Studies Quarterly* 1, 2(1989): pp. 39–49; O. Al-Hassan, "The Arab Co-Operation Council: Was it Born to Stay?" *ibid.,* pp. 31–38; The AMU failed to score practical progress, *Africa Research Bulletin* 28, 9 (September 1–30, 1991): pp. 10255–6; *The Middle East,* April 1989, p. 34; Mohamed Wahby, "The Arab Cooperation Council and the Arab Political Order," *Arab-American Affairs* 28 (Spring 1989): pp. 60–67.

32. *Arab-American Affairs* 28 (Spring 1989): pp. 116–121; O. Al-Hassan, pp. 32–36; *The Middle East,* April 1989, p. 34; *al-Watan,* April 27, 1989; Heikal, *Illusions,* pp. 116–123.

33. *MEED,* October 28, 1988, p. 2; Ami Ayalon (ed.), *Middle East Contemporary Survey,* Volume XIII, 1989 (Boulder: Westview Press, 1991), p. 122; *The Guardian,* May 22, 1989; *Washington Times,* June 27, 1989; *NYT,* July 5, 1989; Hiro, pp. 250, 266.

34. *MEED,* October 28, 1988, p. 3; *The Economist,* May 20, 1989; *al-'Amal* (Lebanon), June 2, 1989.

35. *Al-Siyasa,* May 28, 1989; *Sabah al-Khair,* June 10, 1989; *The Financial Times,* May 22, 1989; *MEI,* May 26, 1989, p. 9; June 9, 1989, pp. 4–5.

36. *Amman Domestic Service,* May 25, 1989; *FBIS/DR,* May 26, 1989; *The Washington Post,* May 26, 1989; *al-Nahar,* May 27, 1989; *The Financial Times,* May 26, 1989, reported a $100 million arms deal.

37. *MENA,* May 25, 1989; *FBIS/DR,* May 26, 1989; *al-Jumhuriyya* (Egypt), May 28, 1989; *MEI,* May 26, 1989, pp. 9–10

16. The Kuwait Crisis and the Peace Process: Toward a New Middle East Order?

1. Ofra Bengio, (ed.), *Saddam Speaks on the Gulf Crisis* (Tel-Aviv: Tel-Aviv University, 1992), p. 12; E. Karsh and I. Rautsi, "Why Saddam Hussein Invaded

Kuwait," *Survival* (January–February 1991), pp. 18, 29; Ken Matthews, *The Gulf Conflict and International Relations* (London: Routledge, 1993), pp. 39–45; Joseph A. Kechichian, "Iraq and the Arab World," *Conflict* 11: pp. 1–15; Heikal, *Illusions*, pp. 175–181. For a grand-design theory, see Laurie Mylroie, "Why Saddam Husain Invaded Kuwait," *Orbis* (Winter 1993): pp. 123–134.

2. Bengio, p. 12; Hiro, pp. 243–244, 255.

3. The total cost of the Iraq-Iran war was $390 billion (Heikal, *Illusions*, pp. 94, 206–208). Iraq's total debt reached $80 billion, of which 31–34 were indebted to Japan, Western countries, and the Soviet Union (Hiro, pp. 249–253). See also Bengio, pp. 12–13; Barry Rubin, *Cauldron of Turmoil: America in the Middle East* (New York: HBJ, 1992), p. 145; Matthews, pp. 41–42; Kechichian, p. 7.

4. *INA*, April 19 and May 2, 1990, *FBIS/DR*, April 21 and May 4, 1990; *al-Dustur* (Jordan), May 9, 1990; *al-Muharrir* (Paris), May 10, 1990; *The Boston Globe*, May 7, 1990; Mylroie, p. 129; Bengio, pp. 14–16.

5. *Washington Times*, May 22, 1990; *Independent*, March 29, 1990; *Time*, April 30, 1990; *Davar*, February 5, 22, 1990; *Ha'aretz*, April 6, 1990; Rubin, *Cauldron*, p. 156; 188–194; Matthews, pp. 46–48.

6. *Al-Ahram*, March 4, 1990; *al-Nahar*, April 5, 1990; *al-Yawm al-Sabi'*, July 16, 1990; *al-Dustur* (Jordan), May 9, 1990.

7. *Al-Qadisiyya*, April 24, 1990; *al-Jumhuriyya* (Iraq), May 10, 1990; *al-Sharq al-Awsat*, May 18, 1990; *al-Muharrir*, May 8, 1990; *Independent*, April 12, 1990; *The Economist*, May 12, 1990; Walid Khalidi, *The Gulf Crisis: Origins and Consequences* (Washington D.C.: Institute for Palestine Studies, January 1991), pp. x, 23–31; Bengio, pp. 16–21.

8. *Al-Ba'th* (Syria), May 15, 1990; *Damascus Television*, May 21, *FBIS/DR*, May 22, 1990; Heikal, *Illusions*, p. 214. PLO's critique of Syria's position, *al-Yawm al-Sabi'*, July 16, 1990.

9. *Cairo Domestic Service*, May 28, *FBIS/DR*, May 29, 1990. On the mini-summit, see *al-Ahram*, March 24, 1990; *al-Jumhuriyya* (Egypt), March 27, 1990; *al-Sha'b* (Egypt), March 27, 1990.

10. *Baghdad Domestic Service*, May 28, *FBIS/DR*, May 29, 1991.

11. *INA*, May 23, 28–30, 1990; *al-Ufuq*, June 7, 1990. Mubarak's speech was criticized by *al-Sha'b* (Egypt), June 5, 1990.

12. *Baghdad Domestic Service*, May 30, *FBIS/DR*, May 31, 1990.

13. Heikal, *Illusions*, pp. 228–229.

14. *MENA*, August 3, 1990, *FBIS/DR*, August 6, 1990. In favor of the condemnation were Egypt, Algeria, Syria, Morocco, Tunisia, Djibouti, Lebanon, Somalia, and the GCC members. Jordan, Sudan, Mauritania, Yemen, and the PLO abstained. Libya's delegate withdrew from the meeting.

15. Heikal, *Illusions*, pp. 263–280, 318; Mathews, pp. 102–103; *Riyadh Domestic Service*, August 9, 1990, *FBIS/DR*, August 10, 1990; *al-Wafd*, *al-Madina*, August 12, 1990.

16. *MENA*, August 10, 1990, *FBIS/DR*, August 10, 1990; *al-Jumhuriyya* (Egypt), August 11, 1990; Heikal, *Illusions*, pp. 286–290.

17. *MENA*, August 10, 1990, *FBIS/DR*, August 13 1990; *Monte Carlo Radio*,

August 10, 1990, *ibid.*, August 10, 1990; *Ruz al-Yusuf,* August 10, 1990; *al-Jumhuriyya* (Egypt), August 11, 1990; Heikal, *Illusions,* pp. 293–298.

18. Editorial, *al-Ahram,* August 10, 1990; Tunisia's president Bin 'Ali's speech, *Tunis Domestic Service,* August 11, 1990, *FBIS/DR,* August 13, 1990; Khalidi, *The Gulf,* pp. 16–18; M.H. Heikal, "Out with the Americans, In with a New Arab Order," *The Times,* September 12, 1990; *al-Ba'th* (Iraq), August 13, 1990; *Sawt al-Sha'b* (Jordan), August 14, 1990.

19. *Monte Carlo Radio,* September 22, *FBIS/DR,* September 24, 1990; *Jordanian Television,* September 25, *FBIS/DR,* September 28, 1990; *IHT,* October 23, 1990; *al-Jumhuriyya* (Iraq), October 13, 1990; *The Economist Intelligence Unit,* Saudi Arabia, Country Report, 4, 1990, p. 10; *MECS 1990,* pp. 156–157, 265; Heikal, *Illusions,* pp. 319–322, 332, 356, 359–360.

20. *Middle East Monitor,* August 31, 1990, pp. 14–15; *al-Hayat,* August 21, 1990; *IHT,* October 23, 1990.

21. *Baghdad Domestic Service,* August 10, 11, *FBIS/DR,* August 13, 1990; Elie Podeh, "In the Service of Power: The Ideological Struggle in the Arab World During the Gulf Crisis," *Conflict Quarterly* 14 (Fall 1994): pp. 7–20; Heikal, *Illusions,* pp. 313–325, 330.

22. James Piscatori, "Religion and Realpolitik: Islamic Response to the Gulf War," in his (ed.), *Islamic Fundamentalism and the Gulf Crisis* (Chicago: The American Academy of Arts and Sciences, 1991), pp. 9, 18–23. Demonstrations in support of Iraq were held in Egypt, Algeria, Tunisia, Morocco, Jordan, Sudan, and Pakistan, *Ha'aretz,* January 13, 21, 25–26, 28, 1991; *al-Ahram,* February 6, 1991; *al-Watan al-'Arabi,* February 18, 1991; Lesch, pp. 38–41.

23. *Al-Jumhuriyya* (Egypt), October 27, 1990; *al-Hayat,* February 15, 1990; *Jerusalem Post,* February 9, 1990; *Ha'aretz,* May 23, 1991; Robert Satloff, "A Madrid Post-Mortem," *Middle East Insight* 8, 3(1992): p. 6.

24. GCC SG, 'Abdallah Bishara's interview, *La Republica* (Rome), February 24–25, *FBIS/DR,* February 28, 1991; Piscatori, pp. 16–22; *Ha'aretz,* November 18, 1992, February 11, 1993.

25. *La Republica,* February 24–25, 1991, *FBIS/DR,* February 28, 1991.

26. *Damascus Domestic Service,* March 6, 1991, *FBIS/DR,* March 7, 1991; *FoF,* March 1991, p. 166; *al-Musawwar,* October 25, 1991.

27. Nasser Aruri, "The Road to Madrid and Beyond," *MEI,* November 8, 1991, pp. 16–17; Emma Murphy, "After Madrid: Slim Prospects for a Land-for-Peace Deal," *ibid.,* November 22, 1991, pp. 16–17.

28. Max Rodenbeck, "The Role Cairo will Play," *MEI,* October 25, 1991, p. 8.

29. *Economist Intelligence Unit,* Saudi Arabia, Country Report, 3 (1991), pp. 11–12; *ibid.,* 4, p. 10; *ibid.,* 1 (1992), p. 11; *NYT,* September 1, 12, 1993.

30. Muhammad Muslih, "The Shift in Palestinian Thinking," *Current History* (January 1992): pp. 22–27; *Ha'aretz,* August 2, 1992, May 11, 1993.

31. Muslih, *ibid.,* pp. 27–28; Lamis Andoni, "A Leap into Darkness," *MEI,* October 25, 1991, pp. 4–5. Chris Manning, "The Screws tighten in Palestine," *ibid.,* November 22, 1991, p. 17; Satloff, pp. 4–6.

32. King Husain's speech in Parliament, *al-Ra'i,* October 13, 1991; Satloff, p. 7; George Hawatmeh, "Mood of Resignation," *MEI,* October 25, 1991, pp. 6–7.

33. Asad's interviews, *al-Wasat* (London), March 10, 1993, and *Time*, November 30, 1992; *al-Hayat*, February 25, 1993; *al-Quds*, March 3, 1993; *Akhbar al-Usbu'* (Jordan), March 11, 1993; Satloff, pp. 6–7; Gerald Butt, "Asad the Coordinator," *MEI*, October 25, 1991, p. 7.

34. *Damascus Domestic Service*, January 28, *FBIS/DR*, January 28, 1991; *Akhbar al-Usbu'*, March 11, 1991; *Mideast Mirror*, July 12, 1994; *MECS 1992*, pp. 552–553; *Ha'aretz*, March 10, 1993.

35. Asad's and Rabin's interviews, *Time*, November 11, 1992; *al-Wasat*, March 10, 1993; Ambassador Rabinovich in *Ha'aretz*, December 31, 1992;

36. For the Oslo secret talks, see Amos Elon, "The Peacemakers," *The New Yorker*, December 20, 1993, pp. 77–85; *NYT*, September 5, 1993. Text of recognition letters and DOP, *ibid.*, September 10, 1, 1993. Text of the political platform of the PA, *Davar*, May 31, 1994.

37. *Tishrin* (Syria), September 17, 1993; *NYT*, September 12, 16, 1993, July 14, 16, 1994;

38. King Husain's interview, October 25, *FBIS/DR*, October 26, 1994; *FoF*, October 20, 1994, p. 768; *Ha'aretz*, February 19, 1995.

39. King Fahd in *The Saudi Gazette*, May 23, 1994; Iraq's reaction, *Washington Post*, May 28, 1994; *al-Majalla*, February 25, 1995, p. 69; Alfred Hermida, "Opportunity for Israel," *MEI*, November 4, 1994; "Talks but no Deals," *ibid.*, November 18, 1994.

40. Godfrey Jansen, "Ineffective Mini-Summit," *MEI*, January 6, 1995, p. 11; *MEED*, January 13, 1995, p. 19.

41. 'Irfan Nizam al-Din, *Harb al-Khalij wa-Judhur al-Mihna al-'Arabiyya* (London: Dar Al Saqi, 1991); Munif, pp. 5–69; As'ad AbuKhalil, "A New Arab Ideology?: The Rejuvenation of Arab Nationalism," *MEJ* 46, 1 (winter 1992): pp. 22–36.

42. Nasif Y. Hitti, "al-Tahawwulat fil-Nizam al-'Alami wal-Manakh al-Fikri al-Jadid wa-In'ikasih 'Ala al-Nizam al-Iqlimi al-'Arabi," *Al-Mustaqbal al-'Arabi* 165(November 1992): p. 51; "Al-'Arab wal-Tahaddiyat 'al-Sharq Awsatiyya' al-Jadida," (coloquium), *ibid.*, 189(January 1994), especially Ghassan Salama, "Afkar Awwaliyya 'an al-Suq al-Awsatiyya," pp. 67–89; "Mustaqbal al-Nizam al-Iqlimi al-'Arabi" (Colloquium), *ibid.*, 163(September 1992), pp. 59–82; *Mideast Mirror*, June 17, 1994; *al-Sha'b* (Egypt), October 28, 1994; *Ha'aretz*, October 31, November 1, 1995.

43. Fouad Ajami, "The Phantoms of Egypt," *U.S. News and World Report*, April 10, 1995, p. 55; P.R. Kumaraswamy, "Egypt Needles Israel," *The Bulletin of the Atomic Scientists* 51, 2(1995): p. 11; *The Economist Intelligence Unit*, Egypt, Country Report, 2nd Quarter, 1995, pp. 14–15; *Ha'aretz*, February 15, 1995 and February 9, 1996; *Davar*, December 2, 1994 (based on *al-'Alam*).

SELECTED BIBLIOGRAPHY

Books

Ajami, Fouad. *The Arab Predicament, Arab Political Thought and Practice Since 1967.* Cambridge: Cambridge University Press, 1981.

'Ali Kamal Hassan. *Muharibun wa-Mufawidun.* Cairo: Markaz al-Ahram, 1986.

Avi-Ran, Reuven. *The Syrian Involvement in Lebanon Since 1975.* Boulder: Westview Press, 1991.

Baghdadi, 'Abd al-Latif. *Mudhakkirat.* Cairo: al-Maktab al-Misri al-Hadith, 1977.

Baqraduni, Karim. *Al-Salam al-Mafqud: 'Ahd Ilias Sarkis 1976–1982.* Beirut: 1984.

Ben-Dor, Gabriel. *State and Conflict in the Middle East.* New York: Praeger, 1983.

Brynen, Rex (ed.). *Echoes of the Intifada: Regional Repercussions of the Arab-Israeli Conflict.* Boulder: Westview Press, 1991.

Brown, Carl L. *International Politics and the Middle East: Old Rules, Dangerous Game.* Princeton: Princeton University Press, 1984.

Cobban, Helena. *The Palestinian Liberation Organization: People, Power and Politics.* Cambridge: Cambridge University Press, 1983.

Dawisha, I. Adeed. *Egypt in the Arab World: The Elements of Foreign Policy.* New York: John Wiley & Sons, 1976.

Dayan, Moshe. *Avnei Derekh.* Jerusalem: 'Idanim, 1976.

Dayan, Moshe. *Breakthrough: A Personal Account of the Egypt-Israel Peace Negotiations.* New York: A.A. Knopf, 1981.

Fahmi, Ismail. *Negotiating for Peace in the Middle East.* London: Croom Helm, 1983.

Falk, R.A., and S.H. Mendlowvitz (eds.). *Regional Politics and World Order.* San Francisco: W. H. Freeman and Co., 1973.

Farah, Tawfic E. (ed.). *Pan-Arabism and Arab Nationalism: The Continuing Debate.* Boulder: Westview Press, 1987.

Fawzi, Muhammad. *Harb al-Thalath Sanawat, 1967–1970.* Cairo: Dar al-Mustaqbal al-'Arabi, 1986.

Feld, Werner J., and Gavin Boyd (eds.). *Comparative Regional Systems.* New York: Pergamon Press, 1980.

Golan, Galia. *Soviet Policies in the Middle East from World War Two to Gorbachev.* Cambridge: Cambridge University Press, 1990.

Harkabi, Yehoshafat. *Arab Strategies and Israel's Response.* New York: Free Press, 1979.

Harkabi, Yehoshafat. *Palestinians and Israel.* Jerusalem: Keter, 1974.

Hassouna, Hussein A. *The League of Arab States and Regional Disputes.* New York: Oceana Publications, 1975.

Heikal, Mohamed H. *Kharif al-Ghadab, Qissat Bidayat wa-Nihayat 'Asr al-Sadat.* Beirut: Sharikat al-Matbu'at, 1983.

Heikal, Mohamed H. *Sanawat al-Ghalayan.* Cairo: Markaz al-Ahram, 1988.

Heikal, Mohamed H. *Al-Infijar 1967.* Cairo: Markaz al-Ahram, 1990.

Heikal, Mohamed H. *Cutting the Lion's Tail: Suez Through Egyptian Eyes.* New York: Arbor House, 1987.

Heikal, Mohamed H. *The Road to Ramadan.* London: Collins, 1975.

Heikal, Mohamed H. *Sphinx and Commisar; The Rise and Fall of Soviet Influence in the Middle East.* London: Collins, 1978.

Heikal, Mohamed H. *Illusions of Triumph, An Arab View of the Gulf War.* London: HarperCollins, 1993.

Hilal, 'Ali al-Din, and Jamil Matar. *Al-Nizam al-Iqlimi al-Arabi.* Beirut: Markaz Dirasat al-Wahda al-'Arabiyya, 1983.

Hiro, Dilip. *The Longest War; The Iran-Iraq Military Conflict.* London: Paladin Grafton Books, 1989.

Ibrahim, Ibrahim (ed.) *Arab Resources, The Transformation of a Society.* Washington D.C.: Croom Helm, 1983.

Ismael, Tareq Y. *International Relations of the Contemporary Middle East.* Syracuse: Syracuse University Press, 1986.

Isma'il, Muhammad Hafiz. *Amn Misr al-Qawmi fi 'Asr al-Tahaddiyat.* Cairo: Markaz al-Ahram, 1987.

Jamasi, Muhammad 'Abd al-Ghani. *Harb October 1973.* Paris: al-Manshurat al-Sharqiyya, 1990.

Kadi, Leila S. *Arab Summit Conferences and the Palestine Problem, 1936–1950, 1964– 1966.* Beirut: PLO, 1966.

Kamel, Mohamed Ibrahim. *The Camp David Accord: A Testimony.* London: KPI, 1986.

Kerr, Malcolm H. *The Arab Cold War, Gamal 'Abd al-Nasir and his Rivals 1958–1970.* Oxford: Oxford University Press, 1971.

Khalaf, Salah. *My Home, My Land, A Narrative of the Palestinian Struggle.* New York: Times Books, 1981.

Khalidi, Rashid. *Under Siege: PLO Decisionmaking During the 1982 War.* New York: Columbia University Press, 1985.

Kienle, Eberhard. *Ba'th v. Ba'th: The Conflict between Syria and Iraq 1968–1989.* London: I.B. Tauris, 1990.

Kissinger, Henry. *Years of Upheaval.* Boston: Little, Brown and Company, 1982.

Korany, Bahgat, and Ali E. Hillal Dessouki (eds.) *The Foreign Policies of Arab States.* Boulder: Westview Press, 1984.

Luciani, Giacomo, and Ghassan Salame (eds.) *The Politics of Arab Integration.* London: Croom Helm, 1988.

Luciani, Giacomo. *The Arab State.* Berkeley: University of Califronia Press, 1990.

Ma'oz, Moshe. *Asad: The Sphinx of Damascus.* London: Weidenfeld and Nicolson, 1988.

Meibar, Basheer. *Political Culture, Foreign Policy and Conflict: The Palestine Area Conflict System.* Westport: Greenwood Press, 1973.

Muwafi, 'Abd al-Hamid. *Misr fi Jami'at al-Duwal al-'Arabiyya.* Cairo: 1983.

Owen, Roger. *State, Power and Politics in the Making of the Modern Middle East.* London and New York: Routledge, 1992.

Quandt, William B. *Camp David, Peacemaking and Politics.* Washington, D.C.: The Brookings Institution, 1986.

Quandt, William B. *Decade of Decisions: American Policy toward the Arab-Israeli Conflict 1967–1976.* Berkeley: University of California Press, 1977.

Quandt, William B., (ed.) *The Middle East: Ten Years After Camp David.* Washington, D.C.: The Brookings Institution, 1988.

Rabinovich, Itamar. *The War for Lebanon 1970–1985.* Ithaca: Cornell University Press, 1985.

Ramazani, R.K. *Revolutionary Iran: Challenge and Response in the Middle East.* Baltimore: Johns Hopkins University Press, 1986.

Richards, Alan and John Waterbury. *A Political Economy of the Middle East: State, Class, and Economic Development.* Boulder: Westview Press, 1990.

Riyad, Mahmud. *Mudhakkirat Mahmud Riyad 1948–1978.* Beirut: al-Mu'assasa al-'Arabiyya lil-Dirasat wal-Nashr, 1985; Pt II, 1987.

Sabri, Musa. *Watha'iq Harb October.* Cairo: al-Maktab al-Misri al-Hadith, 1975.

Al-Sadat, Anwar. *In Search of Identity: An Autobiography.* New York: Collins, 1978.

Safran, Nadav. *From War to War: The Arab-Israeli Confrontation 1948–1967.* New York: Pegasus, 1969.

Schiff, Ze'ev, and Ehud Ya'ari. *Israel's Lebanon War.* New York: Simon & Schuster, 1984.

Seale, Patrick. *Asad: The Struggle for the Middle East.* Berkeley: University of California Press, 1988.

Shemesh, Moshe. *The Palestinian Entity 1959–1974: Arab Politics and the PLO.* London: Frank Cass, 1988.

Shamir, Shimon. *Yeridat Hanasirim 1965–1970.* Tel-Aviv: University Publishers, 1978.

Shazly, Saad el. *The Crossing of the Suez.* San Francisco: American Mideast Research, 1980.

Al-Shuqairi, Ahmad. *Min al-Qimma ila al-Hazima, Ma'a al-Muluk wal-Ru'asa'.* Beirut: Dar al-'Awda, 1971.

Al-Shuqairi, Ahmad. *'Ala Tariq al-Hazima, Ma'a al-Muluk wal-Ru'asa'.* Beirut: Dar al-'Awda, 1972.

Al-Shuqairi, Ahmad. *Al-Hazima al-Kubra, Ma'a al Muluk wal Ru'asa'.* Beirut: Dar al-'Awda, 1973, Pt. 1–2.

Shwadran, Benjamin. *Middle East Oil, Issues and Problems.* Cambridge: Schenkman, 1977.

Tibi, Bassam. *Arab Nationalism, A Critical Enquiry.* New York: St. Martin's Press, 1971.

Tilly, Charles. *The Formation of National States in Europe.* Princeton: Princeton University Press, 1975.

Vatikiotis, P.J. *Arab and Regional Politics in the Middle East.* London: Croom Helm, 1984.

Vered, Yael. *Hafikha Umilhama Beteiman.* Tel-Aviv: 'Am 'Oved, 1967.

Walt, Stephen M. *The Origins of Alliances.* Ithaca: Cornell University Press, 1987.

Weizman, Ezer. *The Battle for Peace.* Toronto: Bantam Books, 1981.

Articles

Abu, Iyad. "Afkar Jadida Amam Marhala Ghamida." *Shu'un Filastiniyya,* No. 29 (January 1974), pp. 5–10.

Abu, Talib Hasan. "Mu'tamarat al-Qimma wa-Tahaddiyat al-'Amal al-'Arabi al-Mushtarak." *Al-Siyasa al-Dawliyya,* No. 80 (April 1985), pp. 8–23.

Abukhalil, As'ad. "A New Arab Ideology?: The Rejuvenation of Arab Nationalism." *The Middle East Journal,* Vol. 46, 1(Winter 1992), pp. 22–35.

Ajami, Fouad. "Stress in the Arab Triangle." *Foreign Policy,* Vol. 29 (Winter 1977–78), pp. 90–108.

Ajami, Fouad. "The End of Pan-Arabism." *Foreign Affairs,* Vol. 57 (1978–9), pp. 355–373.

Ayoob, Mohammed. "The Security Problematic of the Third World." *World Politics,* Vol. 43, 2(1991), pp. 257–283.

Barnett, Michael. "Institutions, Roles, and Disorder." *International Studies Quarterly,* Vol. 37 (1993), pp. 271–296.

Beblawi, Hazim. "The Arab Oil Era (1973–1983)—A Story of Lost Opportunity." *Journal of Arab Affairs,* Vol. 5, 1(Spring 1986), pp. 15–34.

Binder, Leonard. "The Middle East as a Subordinate International System." *World Politics,* Vol. 10 (1958), pp. 408–429.

Brand, Laurie. "The Intifada and the Arab World: Old Players, New Roles." *International Journal,* Vol. 45 (1990), pp. 501–528.

Butrus, Samir. "Al-Mihna al-'Arabiyya Mundhu 1967: Radd 'Ala Ara' Fouad 'Ajami." *al-Mustaqbal al-'Arabi* (1986), pp. 141–156.

Cantori, Louis J., and Iliya Harik. "Domestic Determinants of Foreign Policy and Peace Efforts in the Middle East." *Conflict,* Vol. 8, 1(1988), pp. 49–68.

Dawisha, I. Adeed. "Intervention in the Yemen: Analysis of Egyptian Perceptions and Policies." *The Middle East Journal,* Vol. 29 (1975), pp. 47–64.

Dawisha, I. Adeed. "Iraq: The West's Opportunity." *Foreign Policy,* Vol. 41 (1980–81), pp. 134–153.

Dawisha, Adeed. "The Motives of Syria's Involvement in Lebanon." *The Middle East Journal,* Vol. 38, 2(1984), pp. 228–236.

Dawn, Ernest. "The Formation of Pan-Arab Ideology." *International Journal of Middle East Studies,* Vol. 20, 1(1988), pp. 67–91.

Dishon, Daniel. "The Web of Inter-Arab Relations 1973–1976." *The Jerusalem Quarterly,* Vol. 1, 2(1977), pp. 45–59.

Dishon, Daniel. "Sadat's Arab Adversaries." *The Jerusalem Quarterly,* Vol. 2, 8(1978), pp. 3–15.

Gerges, Fawaz A. "The Study of Middle East International Relations: A Critique." *British Journal of Middle Eastern Studies,* Vol. 18, 2(1992), pp. 208–220.

Heikal, Mohamed H. "Egyptian Foreign Policy." *Foreign Affairs,* Vol. 56, 4 (1978), pp. 714–727.

Hitti, Nasif Yusuf. "Al-Tahawwulat fil-Nizam al-'Alami wal-Manakh al-Fikri al-Jadid wa-In'ikasih 'Ala al-Nizam al-Iqlimi al-'Arabi." *Al-Mustaqbal al-'Arabi,* no. 165 (November 1992), pp. 29–54.

Hourani, Albert. "Independence and the Imperial Legacy." *Middle East Forum,* Vol. 42, 1(1966), pp. 5–27.

Hourani, Cecil. "In Search of a Valid Myth." *Middle East Forum,* Vol. 47, (1971), pp. 39–43.

Hourani, Faisal. "Mu'tamarat al-Qimma al-'Arabiyya wal-Mawqif Min Isra'il 1964– 1966." *Shu'un Filastiniyya,* No. 150–151 (September–October, 1985) pp. 79–95.

Kerr, Malcolm H. "Rich and Poor in the New Arab Order." *Journal of Arab Affairs,* Vol. 1, 1 (1981), pp.1–26.

Khalidi, Rashid. "The Assad Regime and the Palestinian Resistance." *Arab Studies Quarterly,* Vol. 6, 4(1984), pp. 259–266.

Lavy, Victor. "The Economic Embargo of Egypt by Arab States; Myth and Reality." *The Middle East Journal,* Vol. 38, 3(1984), pp. 419–432.

Lebovic, James H. "The Middle East: The Region as a System." *International Interactions,* Vol. 12, 3(1986), pp. 267–289.

Lesch, Ann Mosely. "Contrasting Reactions to the Persian Gulf Crisis: Egypt, Syria, Jordan and the Palestinians." *The Middle East Journal,* Vol. 45, 1(1991), pp. 30– 50.

Lewis, Bernard. "Rethinking the Middle East." *Foreign Affairs,* Vol. 71 (1992), pp. 99– 119.

Little, T.R. "The Arab League: A Reassessment." *The Middle East Journal,* Vol. 10, 2(1956), pp. 138–150.

Al-Mashat, Abdul-Monem. "Stress and Disintegration in the Arab World." *Journal of Arab Affairs,* Vol. 4, 1(1981), pp. 29–46.

"Mustaqbal al-Nizam al-Iqlimi al-'Arabi." (Discussion) *Al-Mustaqbal al-'Arabi,* no. 163 (September 1992), pp. 59–82.

Thopmson, William R. "The Regional Subsystem." *International Studies Quarterly,* Vol. 17 (1963), pp. 89–117.

Thompson, William. "Center-Periphery Subsystems: The Case of Arab Visits 1946– 1975." *International Organization,* Vol. 35, 2 (1981), pp. 355–373.

Thompson, William. "Delineating Regional Subsystems: Visit Networks and the Middle East Case." *International Journal of Middle Eastern Studies,* Vol. 13, 2(1981), pp. 213–235.

Thomson, Janice E. "State Sovereignty in International Relations: Bridging the Gap Between Theory and Empirical Research." *International Studies Quarterly,* Vol. 39 (1995), pp. 213–233.

Zak, Moshe. "Israel-Jordan Negotiations." *The Washington Quarterly,* Vol. 8, 1(1985), pp. 167–176.

Middle Eastern Newspapers and Periodicals

Egypt	Akhbar al-Yawm; al-Ahram; al-Akhbar; Fikr (Paris); al-Idha'a wal-Talafizion; al-Jumhuriyya; Mayu; al-Musawwar; October; Ruz al-Yusuf; al-Sha'b; al-Siyasa al-Dawliyya; al-Wafd.
Jordan	Akhbar al-Usbu'; al-Akhbar; al-Jihad; al-Dustur; al-Liwa'; al-Ra'i; al-Urdun
Tunisia	Al-'Amal

Lebanon Al-Usbu' al-'Arabi; al-'Amal; al-Anwar; al-Bairak; Beirut; al-Diar; al-Hawadith (Paris); al-Hayat (London); al-Kifah al-'Arabi; Kul-Shai'; Monday Morning; al-Mustaqbal (Paris); al-Nahar; al-Nahar al-'Arabi wal-Dawli; Sabah al-Khair; al-Safir; al-Sayyad; al-Sharq; al-Watan al-'Arabi (Paris).

Syria Al-Ba'th; al-Thawra; Tishrin

Morocco Al-Anba'

Libya Al-Fajr al-Jadid

Kuwait Al-Anba'; al-Qabas; al-Ra'i al-'Am; al-Siyasa; al-Nahda; al-Watan

Saudi Arabia Al-Bilad; al-Jazira; al-Madina; al-Majalla; al-Riyad; al-Sharq al-Awsat (Paris); al-Tadamun; 'Ukkaz; al-Yawm.

Iraq Al-Ba'th; al-Thawra; al-Jumhuriyya; al-Qadisiyya

Algeria Al-Sha'b

PLO/ Filastin al-Thawra; al-Hurriyya; al-Yawm al-Sabi' (Paris); al-Quds, al-
Palestinians Nahar, and al-Fajr (East Jerusalem); Filastin al-Muslima

Israel Ha'aretz; 'Al Hamishmar; Ma'ariv; Yedi'ot Aharonot; Davar

Sudan Al-Ayyam

Bahrain Akhbar al-Khalij; Gulf Mirror

UAE Al-Khalij; al-Ittihad; al-Bayan

INDEX